Two week

The Young Drinkers

A CROSS-NATIONAL STUDY
OF SOCIAL AND CULTURAL INFLUENCES

JOYCE O'CONNOR

The Young Drinkers

A CROSS-NATIONAL STUDY
OF SOCIAL AND CULTURAL INFLUENCES

with a foreword by
D. L. DAVIES

TAVISTOCK PUBLICATIONS

First published in 1978
by Tavistock Publications Limited
11 New Fetter Lane London EC4P 4EE

Typeset by Red Lion Setters, London
and printed in Great Britain
at the University Printing House
Cambridge

© *Joyce O'Connor 1978*

ISBN 0 422 76380 2

Contents

Research team

Director

Joyce O'Connor

Senior Research Assistant

Mary Elliott

Research Assistants

Mary Buckley   Teresa Brannick
Ann Kennedy

Statistical Consultant

Rory Hearne   An Foras Forbartha Teo, Dublin.

Fieldwork Consultants

Bert Thrift   Anna Winston

Secretarial Assistance

Ann Coogan   Maelíosa de Bhaldraithe

Acknowledgements

I am indebted to many individuals whose encouragement and advice made this research possible. To accomplish work of this sort is to contract a series of debts that one can never hope to repay but merely acknowledge. In 1971, I was awarded a research fellowship by the Medical Council on Alcoholism to develop a research programme that would focus on young people. The present study developed from this context. The initiative of the Medical Council on Alcoholism in awarding me a research fellowship and in funding the project is gratefully noted, as is the help of the Medico-Social Research Board and the Irish National Council on Alcoholism. I am indebted to all the members of the Anglo-Irish Project Research Committee; to each and every member of the committee, my sincere thanks and appreciation: Admiral Sir Dick Caldwell (Chairman), Professor Ivor Browne, Dr D.L. Davies, Dr Geoffrey Dean, Mrs Anne Hawker (Secretary), Mr Richard Perceval, Professor Harold Stewart, and Professor Conor K. Ward.

I would like also to remember Brigadier Glynn Hughes, who was a member of the committee, I will never forget his kindness and helpfulness at the early stages of the project. My sincere appreciation to Dr L. Davies who was instrumental both in initiating the study and locating me in the Institute of Psychiatry during the initial stages of the project. He introduced me to colleagues and friends in the Addiction Research Unit, Institute of Psychiatry, London University, and throughout England. My special thanks for his support throughout the study, and for the generous help, encouragement, friendship, and advice he always made available.

This book is based upon a Ph.d. thesis prepared in the Department of Social Science, University College, Dublin. To Professor Conor K. Ward, Department of Social Science, my academic adviser, friend, and colleague, my sincere gratitude for his continued encouragement, for advice at all stages of the project, for the many discussions that raised the type of questions which helped to formulate and clarify my ideas, for reading many of the earlier drafts of the report, and for whose teaching I will always be indebted. The ethos of his Department and its concern for the pursuit of knowledge had an enduring effect upon my work. To my friends and colleagues there, my sincere thanks. To Professor Emeritus, Bishop Kavanagh, Department of Social Science, my thanks for his interest and encouragement in this work.

I would like to mention Professor Michael Shepherd who was most generous giving me a base in his unit in the Institute of Psychiatry which provided me with many facilities and an ethos of constructive criticism and study. Admiral Sir Dick Caldwell and Mrs Ann Hawker always provided support, advice, and shelter for which I am most grateful. To Dr Geoffrey Dean, who, with the Medical Council on Alcoholism, was instrumental in initiating this study, my thanks for his continued support and helpfulness in all matters. Professor H. Stewart visited the research team in the Dublin area, my thanks for his interest and support. To the Irish National Council on Alcoholism and the Alcohol Scientific Research Committee for their continued interest, and to Mr Richard Perceval, my thanks for their support and encouragement.

I would like to express my appreciation to the Staff of the Computer Centre, University College, Dublin, for continuous and unfailing help and advice, to the librarians of University College, Dublin, especially Deirdre O'Connell, who courteously and unfailingly met all my many demands upon them.

I am especially grateful to Mrs Anne Coogan, the secretarial assistant throughout the project, whose cheerfulness, patience, and skill made the preparation of work for the project and the final preparation of this work less arduous.

I would like to express my appreciation to the work of other members of the research team. The interviewing in Dublin and the two areas in London involved a working day which frequently extended from midday to midnight and the commitment of the interviewers laid the foundations for the success of the study. The research workers, Mary Elliott, Ann Kennedy, and later Mary Buckley and Teresa Brannick, who continued to work assiduously throughout the tedious months of coding and preliminary analysis, deserve my special thanks. In relation to the organization of the project in London, my thanks are due to Mr Bert Thrift and Miss Anna Winston. Miss Winston provided an invaluable link as supervisor of our research team in London at the later stage of fieldwork, and her professionalism and expertise was greatly appreciated.

A number of consultants assisted us at different stages of the project leaving an imprint on our work. My greatest debt is to Mr Rory Hearne, Research Officer and Statistician, An Foras Forbaratha, Dublin, Statistical Consultant to the project. He gave of his time, expertise, and energy without question, read many drafts, and also assisted in drafting the more detailed methodological sections. To Dr Joan Brothers, Dr D.L. Davies, Mr Ray Mulvihill, and Dr Martin Plant, who read through the final typescript and made helpful and constructive criticisms, my appreciation and thanks. To John Kilcullen and Sean Fitzpatrick my sincere gratitude for help in checking the very many tables. To Dr Paddy Doran, Department Head, European Studies NIHE, Limerick, for his encouragement to complete this book; to Mrs Doreen O'Dwyer and Mrs Mary Murphy my thanks for secretarial assistance.

I would also like to thank all those people who must remain anonymous in the areas under study. In addition to thanking all those interviewed for their able and willing co-operation I would express my gratitude to those whom we consulted, those who helped us organize the survey, and for all those who were so helpful to individual members of the team in the course of the interviewing. I am particularly indebted to the parish priest and the curates in the Dublin area, who provided the project with a base and support throughout the whole of the fieldwork. I am most grateful to the Council members in the London Areas, who provided us with the expertise and knowledge of the area they had acquired themselves over the years. Their advice was invaluable and helped us achieve the successful completion of the fieldwork.

Finally, I would like to thank very sincerely my father, mother, and brother; they consistently encouraged me in my work, and provided the necessary support throughout. My husband sustained me, and devoted many hours to being listener, sympathizer, devil's advocate, copyreader, and encourager. I dedicate this work to them, and to Aoife O'Connor who made it all seem worthwhile.

Joyce O'Connor
January 1977

Foreword

by D. L. Davies
Medical Director,
the Alcohol Education Centre, London

That some ethnic groups are very vulnerable to misuse of alcohol, whilst others, though not abstinent, are almost immune, is a hard fact in this area of study and has provided a jumping-off point for much research along sociological and anthropological lines.

Too much of this, perhaps, has concerned itself with primitive societies, using relatively crude measures of the human variables involved. By contrast, this book concerns itself with readily accessible and articulate young people, the Irish and English 18-21 year olds, and their parents, whose drinking habits are generally believed to be very different, and brings in a third group, the Anglo-Irish, seen here as a group culturally in transition between the other two.

The design of the enquiry enables many factors operating on drinking, such as ethnicity, sex, parental attitudes and peer involvement, to be measured directly and in relation to each other.

Personal attitudes come under scrutiny as well as extent and pattern of alcohol intake. Rarely, if at all, has such complex material been brought together so elegantly, and analyzed so completely, to allow of conclusions so far-reaching in their implications, both theoretical and practical.

If the effect of ethnicity, as emerges here, is made manifest through parental attitudes as perceived by the young, and by peer involvement, the traditional view that excessive drinking derives from constitutional factors of a metabolic or psychological kind becomes even less tenable than at present. On the practical side, it brings much nearer the likelihood of explaining changes in group consumption by changes in these underlying social and personal factors. It is interesting to set alongside this, current attempts by epidemiologists to construct mathematical models of consumer groups within a country, to explain the relationships known to exist between national and group consumption of alcohol. Thus, from two different directions, research converges on group drinking.

The long-term importance of this is the prospect it holds out of complementing fiscal and other environmental controls on alcohol consumption — always likely to arouse public resentment — by more restrained drinking in line with changed attitudes towards, and an understanding of, alcohol. If such is to be striven for, as a far-seeing public health measure, then the findings of this study become essential knowledge for those who would seek such a goal. Though there is only a beginning in this book, such a reconnaissance in depth of entrenched attitudes and habits becomes of the greatest importance for ensuring the well-being of a society which will wish to have its drink, and not to suffer the hazards of excess.

This is the first European study of its kind, carried out on a big scale, yet measuring very fine differences of attitude, and interaction. The facts are presented against a historical background, which itself makes fascinating reading, not least because of current political and religious differences in a divided world.

Essentially, through the study of a piece of behaviour which has characterized man from his early emergence to that state, it deals with a microcosm of human behaviour in a way which reflects the greatest credit on the techniques of sociological enquiry employed, and the competence of Joyce O'Connor, who has carried out this research.

Introduction

This book is about drinking and young people. It is a topic that creates a great deal of reaction. In the press, on radio and television, the fact that young people drink is constantly referred to as a problem. The implication would seem to be that young people's drinking is linked very closely to deviant patterns of behaviour such as drug abuse, delinquency, illicit sexual relationships, violence, and so on. Very often it is felt that 'something must be done about the situation'. These reactions reflect to a great extent definite and strongly held emotional attitudes towards drinking and the young. Yet despite this concern very little is known about the drinking behaviour of the young and the influences that help in the development of this behaviour. This is especially true in Great Britain and Ireland where little research of this nature has been carried out to date. This book is an attempt to contribute to the knowledge and understanding of this area of social behaviour. At heart, the present study is about the importance and interaction of factors which may influence patterns of drinking behaviour and attitudes among young people. The central foci are (1) parental influences, (2) peer group influences, (3) social and personal influences, and (4) ethnic and cultural influences.

The study is presented in three main parts. The first part comprises four chapters. Chapter 1 reviews some of the major research themes of sociological work concerned with alcohol and young people, and Chapter 2 discusses the methodology of the study. Chapter 3 is concerned with drinking in Irish and English societies viewed from an historical perspective, and the temperance movement in England and Ireland is the subject of Chapter 4.

The second part of the study presents a picture of drinking among the three groups of young people studied. This section which is mainly descriptive consists of three chapters. Chapter 5 describes the introduction to the use of alcohol and the extent and prevalence of present-day drinking among the 18-21 year olds and their parents who were interviewed. The customs and patterns of present-day drinking and a descriptive analysis of the social meaning and function of alcohol among the three groups of young people interviewed is presented in Chapter 6.

The second part of the study is completed in Chapter 7 with a description of the social rules in relation to drinking. These are centred around three themes: (1) social rules for children as reported by parents, (2) social rules defined by young people for their peers drinking, and (3) levels of permissiveness in relation to drinking behaviour. Experience of and exposure to drink-related problems among the young people studied is also included.

The third part of the study, Chapters 8 to 11, is concerned with the importance and relative influence of parents, peers, social and personal, and ethnic and cultural factors in the transmission of drinking behaviour.

Chapter 8 looks at parental influences, and attempts to define the importance and interrelationships of parental influences in the transmission of drinking behaviour. Peer group influence is the subject of Chapter 9, which also brings together some of the findings already described in Chapter 6 and specifies its relative influence on young people's drinking behaviour. Chapter 10 examines social and personal correlates of drinking behaviour. It aims at bringing together some of the descriptive data presented in the second part of the study, to provide a more adequate analysis of factors associated with the drinking behaviour of the young people under study. This chapter centres more on the young people themselves and examines how they define and interpret their social situation.

At this stage the main findings of the use of alcohol among the young people studied, as well as the influences in the transmission of drinking behaviour will have been documented. Chapter 11 presents a general model of the development of drinking among young people. Finally, Chapter 12 summarizes the major findings of the study.

A bibliography and six appendices accompany the main text. Appendix 1 contains the tables referred to in the main text. Tables relating to the detailed analyses in Chapters 8 to 11 are not contained in this book, but are available for examination in the Library of the Medical Council on Alcoholism, 8 Bourdon Street, Davies Street, London W1X 9HY, in O'Connor 1976b, or by writing to the Department of Social Science, University College Dublin, National University of Ireland (O'Connor 1976a). A copy of the two questionnaires and notes to interviewers is given in Appendix 2. A list of scales and indexes used in the study appear in Appendix 3. More detailed information regarding the methodology and statistical procedures is given in Appendices 4 and 5. A brief discussion of the type of drinker index is given in Appendix 6. The bibliography contains those books I found useful in the preparation and writing of this book. Not all have been referred to directly in the text. The bibliography is not proposed as an exhaustive list of the relevant works on the subject of social and cultural influences in general, or of drinking behaviour in particular.

1
Social and cultural factors influencing drinking behaviour

In general, sociological research on drinking behaviour has tended to focus on diverse fragmentary problems such as the examination of drinking patterns and practices and the development of problem drinking and alcoholism among various ethnic, social, cultural, and regional groups, as well as varying age, sex, and socio-economic groups. Studies have tended to develop theories and hypotheses in relation to (1) all cultures or societies, (2) to specific cultures and/or comparisons between specific cultures, (3) institutions such as family and religion, and (4) demographic variables such as age, sex, social status, ethnicity, urban or rural background, and socio-economic status. Throughout, the main concern has been on various influences on drinking behaviour and the incidence of drink-related problems among various groups. This is especially true in the study of young people, where the main concern has been the influences in the transmission of drinking behaviour. Four main influences appear to have caught the imagination of researchers, these are (1) ethnic and cultural, (2) parental, (3) peer group, and (4) social and personal influences.

Ethnic and cultural influences

Ethnic origin has been shown to play a major role in the development of drinking behaviour (Wilkinson 1970; Roebuck and Kessler 1972; Moser 1974; O'Connor 1975). Studies carried out over the years have produced evidence of different patterns of drinking, as well as showing that different manifestations of 'normal' and 'abnormal' drinking occur (MacAndrew and Edgerton 1970). Studies have also shown that various ethnic groups exhibit different rates of alcoholism and drinking pathologies. Among the sub-cultures in American society, Jews (Snyder 1958, 1962), Chinese (Singer 1974), and Italians (Lolli *et al*. 1957) have very low rates of alcoholism. The Italians and Jews are presented as models of people who have low rates of alcoholism in their own countries. Other societies like France (Sadoun, Lolli, and Silverman 1965), Ireland (Walsh and Walsh 1973), Scotland (Dight 1976), England (Shaw 1976; Robinson 1976), Finland (Makela 1971), and the USA (Cahalann and Room 1974) are shown to have high rates of alcoholism. The related attempts to explain these differences theoretically are many and varied. One of the main explanations put forward is the cultural one. Studies using this perspective stress the social meaning and function of alcohol, drinking, and drunkenness. They describe how different patterns of alcohol use have emerged in different societies. The focus of these studies has been on socialization into drinking patterns, the structure of social norms, and the rates of drink problems. This is the approach adopted by the present study.

The society in which we live equips us all with attitudes and norms or rules in relation to patterns of behaviour. Drinking can be seen as a culturally defined pattern of behaviour, a social act, something we all learn in the context of our society or culture. It is possible to classify cultures in relation to their drinking practices and attitudes, while bearing in mind that variations exist within each culture (Heath 1975: 7). Four 'ideal' cultural types of attitudes towards drinking have been suggested by the sociologist David Pittman (1967: 3). The four cultural attitudes are:

1 Abstinent cultures
2 Ambivalent cultures
3 Permissive cultures
4 Over-permissive cultures

(1) An abstinent culture is one where the use of alcohol is prohibited and where alcohol arouses very strong negative feelings. Abstinence from alcohol has been a part of the lifestyle of numerous cultures. In general three broad cultural groupings should be noted: (i) people associated with Islamic traditions, (ii) people associated with the Hindu trandition, and (iii) people associated with the Ascetic Protestant tradition.

Historically the Islamic traditions have been antagonistic towards the person who drinks, in parts of North Africa, the Middle East, and India. That Moslems drink in these areas is a reflection of the cultural diffusion of European patterns and the decay of tradition. Travellers to North Africa will notice that the use of alcohol is not widespread, the number of outlets for the sale of alcohol is still very limited.

In Hindu Indian society both custom and tradition have established a moral standard which is very much against the use of alcohol. The principle of abstinence and prohibition is reflected in the Indian Constitution.

In Western culture, particularly in Northern and Western Europe, and in the USA and Canada, the emergence of temperance movements was initially related to Ascetic Protestantism. The effects of the early and later temperance movements are still in evidence and have had an effect on people's attitudes towards drinking, especially in Northern Europe, Ireland and the USA. Abstinent sub-cultures are in existence today in a number of cultures and religious traditions. Countries concerned are Finland, Sweden, Norway, Ireland as well as Canada and the United States of America. The religious groups concerned are varied, for example, Christian Scientists, Seventh-Day Adventists, some Methodists and Baptists. As a general rule drinking is less widespread among people in environments which proscribe the use of alcohol. However, there is some evidence to suggest that problem drinking as opposed to normal drinking is slightly higher amongst people in a restrictive environment than in a permissive environment. Straus and Bacon (1953) found a relatively high incidence of heavy drinking and intoxication among Mormon students who came from an abstinence background. They concluded that alcoholism was more likely among members of abstinence groups, since their drinking was not controlled by any drinking norms.

(2) In ambivalent cultures, attitudes to the use of alcohol are contradictory in that there are two directly opposed value systems in relation to the use of alcohol, operating in the culture at the same time (Room 1976). Examples of this type of culture are Scotland (Dight 1976), Ireland (O'Connor 1975), and the USA (Pittman 1967). Researchers (Whitehead and Harvey 1974) suggest that, when in any group or society customs, values, sanctions and attitudes with respect to drinking are well established and agreed upon by all, and when these are consistent with the rest of the culture, the rate of alcoholism will be low. In a society in which drinking norms are well supported, the drinker is under social pressure to conform to the standards that are expected of him. Examples of this type are found among the Jewish people in the United States and the Italians. If, on the other hand, the culture does not have a well integrated system of controls, the individual is left in a situation of ambivalence which may be conducive to alcoholism.

(3) A permissive culture is defined as one where attitudes to the use of alcohol tend to be favourable, but there are strong and consistent social sanctions against intoxication or drunkenness or other forms of deviant drinking. Examples of this type of culture are found in Spain, Italy, Portugal, and among some Jewish religious groups.

(4) An over-permissive culture is one where the attitudes towards drinking are favourable but are also favourable to other forms of deviant

behaviour while drinking. An example of this type of culture is France.

To the outsider, Italy and France have many things in common, especially the use of wine. However, statistics show that Italy's rate of alcoholism is much lower than that of France, although the research on Italy is now being seriously challenged. Researchers (Lolli *et al.* 1957; Sadoun, Lolli, and Silverman 1965) have shown: (1) that more wine is taken in Italy than in France, and that the pattern of drinking is different in the two cultures. (2) The quantities of wine consumed with meals in France and in Italy are about the same but the use of wine between meals is greater in France than in Italy. Other types of alcoholic drinks such as cider, beer, spirits, are used more frequently in France than in Italy and these other types of alcohol are more likely to be consumed on an empty stomach in France. (3) The introduction to the use of alcohol appears to be viewed differently in the two countries. The French seem to hold rigid attitudes, either strongly in favour of or against childhood use, while Italian parents see the use of alcohol as an integral and normal part of a child's development. (4) In France there appears to be a widespread social acceptance of intoxication as fashionable, humorous or at least tolerable; excessive drinking is in some way associated with virility. Among Italians intoxication is consistently regarded as a personal and family disgrace.

The apparently wider acceptance by the French compared to the Italians of a relatively large daily consumption of alcohol is seen to be important. Given this greater acceptance of heavy daily intake, a Frenchman with psychic difficulties may be more likely to become an alcoholic than an Italian with comparable psychic difficulties.

In general, research has shown that for groups that use alcohol to a significant degree, the lowest incidence of alcoholism is associated with certain habits and attitudes:

1 The children are exposed to alcohol early in life, within a strong family or religious group. Whatever the beverage, it is served in a very diluted form and in small quantities, with consequent low blood-alcohol levels.
2 The beverages commonly, although not invariably used by the groups are those containing relatively large amounts of non-alcoholic components, which also give low blood-alcohol levels.
3 The beverage is considered mainly as a food and usually consumed with meals, again with consequent low blood-alcohol levels.
4 Parents present a constant example of moderate drinking.
5 No moral importance is attached to drinking.
6 Drinking is not viewed as a proof of adulthood or virility.
7 Abstinence is socially acceptable.
8 Excessive drinking or intoxication is not socially acceptable. It is

not considered stylish, comical or tolerable.

9 Finally, and perhaps most important, there is wide and usually complete agreement among members of the group on what might be called the ground rules of drinking.

In looking at the use of alcohol in a culture it is necessary to have both an appreciation of the socio-cultural climate in which drinking takes place, i.e. knowledge and understanding of the social meaning, norms, and functions of alcohol in the society, as well as a knowledge of the complications associated with the level of consumption of alcohol on both a societal and individual level.

To look at ethnic influences it was decided to take two ethnic groups, Irish and English, known to have different rates of drinking problems. This assertion is based partly on empirical indicators and partly on the images of both groups as particular types of drinkers. The stereotype of the Irishman is a humorous and boisterous drunk, and the Irishman appears to have this image both at home and abroad. The stereotype image of the Englishman on the other hand is one of a moderate type of drinker, yet epidemiological studies have shown that the English do in fact have a problem with regard to drinking. The selection of these ethnic groups was dictated in part by their close proximity to one another. The fact that there was a large number of Irish people in England made the possible selection of these groups very attractive, as it was possible to look at people of Irish origin living in another cultural setting. An additional, third group was required to assist in the assessment of the relative importance of ethnic and cultural, parental, peer, and social and personal influences. This group is referred to throughout the study as the Anglo-Irish. It consists of 18-21 year olds born in England and socialized in an English cultural environment by Irish parents who were born and reared in the Republic of Ireland.

The next section looks at the images and theories surrounding the use of alcohol for the Irish in Ireland, the Irish in England, and the English in England.

Theories and images

There is an inherent imbalance in the presentation of these images and theories. Relatively little information is available on the Irish in England or the English in England, compared with the colourful images surrounding the Irishman at home in Ireland and his love for 'the drink'. The Irish have a reputation for a particularly strong thirst, for their carefree manner in quenching it, and a strong disregard for the consequences of heavy indulgence in the 'demon drink'. The concept of the 'drunken

Irish', with a shillelagh in one hand and a glass of Guinness in the other, is played up not only on radio, television, and in popular literature, but also by researchers who have helped to reinforce this image even as far back as 1946 (Bales 1946: 480). The best known and most often quoted research on the Irish and drinking is that of Robert Bales (1962).

Several studies have used Bales' interpretation of Irish drinking patterns. His research was concerned with cultural differences in the rates of alcoholism. As part of this work he compared Irish and Jewish drinking practices and attitudes, and suggested that the explanation for the extreme differences in Jewish-American and Irish-American rates of alcoholism were the social norms which centred around the act of drinking itself. Bales saw drinking in Ireland as being integrated into the social and economic structure and accepted as a form of behaviour. The Irish drank for utilitarian and convivial reasons, but it was this utilitarian attitude to drinking that led to alcoholism and accounted for the high rate of alcoholism among the Irish. Bales' work was based on documentary material from the sixteenth century to the late nineteenth century, and on Arensberg and Kimball's (1940) work on the Irish family which was carried out in County Clare at the beginning of the 1930s. While Bales' analysis of Irish drinking practices and attitudes was an adequate description of drinking practices from the mid-sixteenth to the mid-nineteenth century, some of his basic assumptions were faulty and his sources incomplete. To base an analysis of present-day Irish drinking on his work is misleading.

First of all, he made no reference to the Irish temperance movement, which had a strong impact on Irish attitudes and drinking practices, especially from the middle of the nineteenth to the middle of the twentieth century. Present-day studies also show that its influence still prevails (O'Connor 1974, 1975). Second, he assumed uniformity of norms and behaviour among the Irish population and took normative statements as descriptions of actual behaviour. Third, his view of Irish family life was based exclusively on the work of Arensberg and Kimball. Their work has contributed significantly to the image of the mother-dominated Irish family and has been used by Bales and other researchers who place emphasis on family-structure-personality explanations for the high rate of alcoholism among the Irish. However, recent research carried out by Hannan and Katsiaonni (1977) challenges this view of Irish family life. Fourth, the emphasis of Bales' work was qualitative in that he never examined the Irish people living in Ireland. His sample of Irish-Americans were never defined so that we do not know of what generation they were, whether first, second, or third generation American. The sample consisted of eighty institutionalized alcoholics of Irish origin in an American hospital.

Little effort then or indeed in later studies was devoted to the task of establishing quantifiable measures of alcohol consumption or measuring actual drinking patterns of the Irish in Ireland. Implicit in Bales' work was the assumption that what he found was peculiar to the Irish situation. However, English customs, usages, and attitudes were very similar to Irish drinking patterns around the same period with which Bales' work dealt (Fitzpatrick 1971c; O'Connor 1974). By using Bales' view of the Irish, other researchers have assumed that Irish society was and still is characterized by (1) absence of change, (2) universal concensus, (3) social harmony, (4) all social processes contributing to the design of the whole, and (5) isolation (Dahrendorf 1958: 115). Finally, there is an implicit assumption in his and other works that these practices and attitudes persist from one generation to the next. This has never been tested.

Although it has been constantly maintained that the Irish drink excessively, explanations of the phenomenon differ. The Irish are seen to have an ambivalent culture and this ambivalence was considered the cause of heavy drinking and alcoholism. Theories centred on family-structure-personality explanations are based on Arensberg and Kimball's work, and are also linked with social organization explanations. Field's (1962) cultural study of drunkenness in primitive societies concluded that social organization determined drinking behaviour, and as he saw it, it was the loose social organization and family structure that gave rise to heavy drinking among the Irish.

The Irish use of alcohol to sublimate sexual tension is a theme in many literary as well as scientific works. As one researcher comments:

> '...one comes away from reading the empirical literature convinced that the Irish are guilt ridden, sexually repressed, superstitious, unhappy, frustrated, maladjusted and given frequently to alcoholism in search of emotional release.'   (Greeley 1971: 42)

These sexual and emotional problems were considered by Arensberg and Kimball to be engendered in part by the demographic and social facts that so few Irish married and even among those who did, marriage came late.

Irish society during the mid-nineteenth century was mainly agricultural. In the family there was a well-defined role system. Only one son inherited the farm and thus had to wait to marry until the father turned over the property to him. Those who remained behind rarely married unless they were fortunate enough to earn a living in a nearby town. In a society where the marriage rate was low, and the emphasis on sexual purity laid down by the Catholic Church was rigid, the formation of a bachelor group could be considered a natural response to both family and religious pressures. And Arensberg and Kimball (1940), McNabb (1964), Stivers (1971), and Brody (1973) suggest that this bachelor group was a strong drinking group. The activities of the bachelor group included attending athletic events, storytelling, gambling, and hard drinking. McNabb points out that this situation is changing and the males are seeking leisure activities outside the immediate area in which they live.

Stivers' work, based on documentary material, suggested that the drinking problem among the Irish was a result of the collapse of traditional Irish culture under the impact of the famine in the middle of the nineteenth century. Heavy drinking became a means of establishing and sustaining one's status in the bachelor group.

Despite this general agreement that the Irish drink a lot and get into trouble frequently as a result, some commentators question whether Irish drinking in Ireland involves a high level of alcoholism or not (Walsh and Walsh 1973; Lynn and Hampson 1970; O'Connor 1975). Most studies carried out in Ireland have tended to be problem-centred — the basic question being '... how many alcoholics are there in this country?'. Research has centred mainly on hospital admissions for alcoholism, alcoholism and cirrhosis of the liver, drunkenness, alcohol consumption, and deaths from alcoholism (Walsh and Walsh 1973; O'Hare and Walsh 1972; Duffy and Dean 1971; Perceval 1955; Kearney, Lawler and Walsh 1969).

There is a need to look at normal drinking behaviour in Ireland, so as to give some indication of what drinking patterns obtain. While this study does not look at all of Irish society it gives us some understanding of the complex nature of the general drinking habits.

The Irish in England

The image of the Irish has travelled abroad and gathered momentum on its journey. The Irish in England are seen to be prone to very heavy drinking. This image has a basis in fact in that a number of studies have shown that the Irish are more likely to experience problems with drink than either the English themselves or other ethnic groups living in England (Edwards *et al.* 1972a and b; Cook 1975). A number of studies in criminology have also shown that the Irish commit consistently high numbers of drinking offences. As Bottoms (1967: 359) pointed out '...the two stereotype images of the Irish delinquent in England are that he was a single man and he was very prone to heavy drinking'. During the period 1950-60, McClintock and Avinson's (1968) work showed that the Irish maintained their traditional pre-eminence in fights in pubs. While the statistical association between heavy drinking and Irish crime in England has been shown, Russell's view that '... all (whom I met) were unanimous that drink lies at the root of the great bulk of Irish crime in England today' (Russell 1964: 138) is perhaps oversimplified. Cook's (1975) work on vagrant alcoholics showed, that while the majority of vagrant alcoholics in London were Irish and Scottish, more examination needs to be given to how and why they turn up in such large numbers. No study of normal drinking, the social meaning and function of drinking, and the customs and norms of present-day drinking has been carried out on a group of Irish people who emigrated to England, married, and settled down, and whose children were socialized in English society.

English drinking

The Englishman is traditionally portrayed in literature and the media as being a moderate type of drinker, who drinks a pint a night in his local, and one or two before lunch on a Sunday. Despite this image, epidemiological studies (Shaw 1976) have shown that the English have a problem with regard to drinking with an apparent increase of problem drinking among the young (Offences of Drunkenness 1974, 1976; Hawker 1977).

This study hopes to contribute to the understanding of normal drinking behaviour in England.

Parental influences

Before discussing parental influences a brief overview of research on general factors of young people's drinking is given.

General perspective

The 'typical' young person in our society eventually learns to drink. It is a socially and culturally defined pattern of behaviour, a behaviour that research has shown will increase with age. As research in the USA and Europe (Maddox 1964a and b; Fitzpatrick 1970a and b; Demone and Wechsler 1976) has shown:

1 The average age at which students had their first drink was between fourteen to fifteen years, although tasting of alcohol may have occurred before this age. Some recent studies in America show that between the ages of eleven and thirteen years, 63 per cent of boys and 53 per cent of girls had tried alcohol (Smart 1976).
2 For those who had not taken a drink at this age the probability of their use increased with age. As Bruun and Hauge (1963) found

'... At the age of 18 it is unusual for a boy not to have consumed alcohol.'

3 Location of the first drink was usually in the home with parents.

4 Beer was the usual drink taken.

5 The legalization regarding age of drinking appeared to have little relation to drinking practices.

6 In some of the studies the results showed that one in four young people who took a drink claimed to have been 'high' on at least one occasion in the month prior to interview. One in ten reported that they had been drunk in that month. Recent studies in America found that one in seven seventeen year olds were getting drunk once a week (Hawker 1977).

7 The reasons for starting to drink centered around three themes (i) celebrating a holiday or special occasion, (ii) offered drink by their families, (iii) curiosity about drinking.

8 Among the reasons given for present drinking were, joining in with the rest of the crowd, or ideas of personal enjoyment such as 'to be gay'. These results also suggest that the drinking behaviour of the adolescent or young person is best seen as an expression of anticipatory adulthood rather than an act of rebellion.

Parental influences

While research to date has not been entirely clear-cut and consistent, there is little doubt that, as in other areas, parents have a strong influence on the development of drinking behaviour, and the formation of social rules in relation to the use of alcohol (Maddox 1964b; Stacey and Davies 1970; O'Connor 1976d; Zucker 1976). Research in the United States and Europe has suggested that the most accurate basis for predicting what an adolescent will think and do with alcohol is to know what his parents thoughts and actions are in this respect. The studies seem to suggest that if both parents take a drink, the probability is high that their children will also drink. It is known that problem drinkers and young alcoholics are more likely to have parents who themselves experience difficulties with alcohol, and are more likely to come from homes in which there has been some kind of family disruption. The first drinking experience usually takes place within the family. Davies and Stacey (1972), in a study carried out in Glasgow, showed that the majority of boys and girls reported that parents were the people who first introduced them to alcohol.

In some countries, notably Italy, children drink diluted wines at meal times. It is contended that learning to drink moderately at meal time within the family setting provides children with a model of responsible drinking. Recent research by Jahoda (1972) and colleagues showed that children begin to learn about alcohol early in life, even before primary school. The study suggested that children's views develop out of an interplay of factors such as parents' behaviour and attitudes, the official school view, as well as the growing influence of peers and other social factors such as the mass media. Davies and Stacey found that heavy drinkers tended to have parents who were more disciplinarian and more disapproving, than those of the moderate drinkers. Also heavier drinking seemed to be associated with increasingly hostile attitudes towards the older generation, as well as other authority figures. Research has shown that as the child grows older, drinking tends to take place out of the home away from adult supervision (Davies and Stacey 1972). Despite the vast quantities of research little is known about how parental behaviour and attitudes influence the new drinking situation. Few studies relate parental drinking behaviour, attitudes, and involvement or interest in their children's activities to the development of drinking practices and attitudes of young people.

In general, studies use measures that are too crude for these questions. For example, parents are classified as 'drinkers' or 'abstainers', or as having 'favourable' or 'unfavourable' attitudes to drinking. However, a great many different types of drinking behaviour are possible within the general category of 'drinker'. The effects of different parental drinking patterns on the development of the drinking practices of their children needs to be investigated. Likewise, a great many things are subsumed under the general heading of favourable or unfavourable attitudes. Little is known of parental attitudes towards their children drinking in different situations, to the amount of alcohol they consume, and how and what they drink. Furthermore, the effects of these attitudes on children's drinking behaviour and the development of children's attitudes to other people drinking is not known. When parental characteristics are specified, two things tend to happen. First, it is the children's description of either both parents as one unit, or of the fathers' attributes, that are taken as a satisfactory description of the unit. Seldom have parents' practices and attitudes been ascertained from parents themselves, or have both parents' attitudes been obtained and analysed. Recent research in political socialization, which looks at the role of the family in the way behaviour is learned, has concentrated on the simultaneous study of parents and their children. These studies indicate that it is necessary to differentiate the contributions of fathers and mothers in order to understand more fully the socialization process within the family circle (Jennings and Niemi 1974).

A review of the literature also suggests that it is not only to parental practices and attitudes that the drinking practices and attitudes of young people are closely related. However, since drinking can be seen to be a learned pattern of behaviour, it is necessary to look at the possibility that drinking behaviour is influenced by parents before appealing to other explanations. Thus, parental influence is a central concern of this study. Specifically, an attempt is made to define the importance and interrelationships of parental influences with the other influences examined in the transmission of drinking behaviour. The parental influences investigated are (1) general family relationships, (2) parental drinking behaviour as defined by a type of drinker index, and (3) parents' social rules for their children's drinking.

Peer group influences

As some commentators see it, the perennial sociological problem of the young person is that he must live in three worlds and solve the 'problem' of integrating the family world, the peer world, and the non-family adult world (Bossard and Boll 1960). Both popular and professional literature reflect continuing concern with what has been called 'the problem of generations' (Mannheim 1952). The literature abounds with studies suggesting either the presence or absence of generational differences (Simmons 1971; Thomas 1974; Kasschan, Ransford, and Bengtson 1974; Bengtson, Furlong, and Laufer 1974).

Despite evidence of the overall influence of parents and the apparent similarity of values among children, the image of youth as a group in conflict with adult society exists. This image has arisen in part out of literature that suggests that there is a basic discontinuity between the generations, which leads to the development of a youth culture (Mead 1947, 1970; Parsons 1954; Eisenstadt 1963). Coleman declared in 1961 that 'adolescents today are cut off, probably more than ever before, from adult society' (Coleman 1961: 9). A more extreme view of youth's position is that of Roszak (1969: 42) who spoke of youth as 'radically disaffiliated from the mainstream assumptions of our society'. However, recent work has stressed that the influence varied with the situation and the issue (Larson 1972; Thomas 1974; Heyneman 1976). The most active research controversy has centred on the interrelated pressures from peers and parents (Brittain 1963; Epperson 1964; Campbell and McSweeney 1970; Jensen 1972; Elder 1972; Manning and Truzzi 1972; Gottlieb 1972; Reich 1972; Curtis 1974; Smith 1976).

Studies in relation to other drug use (Young 1971; Young and Brooke-Crutchley 1972: 11; Plant 1975), tobacco (Wiener 1970), and delinquency (Cloward and Ohlin 1960; Sutherland and Cressey 1970; Young, Taylor, and Walton 1973; Matza, 1969; Matza 1961; Cohen 1955, 1972), indicate the importance of peer group influence.

In relation to drinking behaviour, friends, like parents, are important figures in the determination of whether, how, and when, behaviour becomes integrated into the lifestyle of a young person. From the early teens onwards, more drinking takes place outside the home. The importance of friends' influence grows parallel with this shift in location. Davies and Stacey (1972) found that peer group pressure, and the need for peer group standing or esteem appeared to be very strong influences upon adolescent drinking. However, little is known of the type of influences that operate in this new setting. Research has shown that the nature of the peer group to a considerable extent patterns the type of drinking that takes place. Drinking that is an integral part of social activities and general sociability is important in establishing controlled drinking practices. Peers' influence is not to be equated with coercion (Fitzpatrick 1972). The use of alcohol, viewed as an expression of adolescent rebellion does not appear to be supported by the evidence (Maddox 1964a and b; Fitzpatrick 1970b; Johnston 1973; Smart 1976). Drinking that centres around delinquent activity or just drinking for drinking's sake has not been shown to be conducive to the development of a 'normal' drinking pattern (Stacey and Davies 1970). While drinking among young people has been shown to take place mainly in a peer group context it has not been established whether it is the context or the frequency of drinking in such a context that is of importance. The influence of social rules defined for peers, and the levels of permissiveness while drinking with peers, needs to be explored.

Research on youth has tended to focus on high-school and college students (Maddox 1964a and b; Moos, Moos, and Kulik 1976). Research on youth in general and in the area of drinking behaviour has had little to do with those not engaged in the higher education system. Emphasis in many of the studies referred to above has been on male rather than female groups. Studies have tended to ignore young people, both male and female, as they enter adulthood and assume adult-type roles, like working and earning their own money, while still remaining in the sphere of influence of the home and their parents. Little is known of the effect of community or ethnic characteristics on the degree and content of parental and peer influences. In relation to the parent-peer controversy it is important to look at the interplay of parental, peer, and cultural influences on young peoples' drinking behaviour. This is the concern of the present study.

Social and personal factors

The relationship between drinking behaviour and social and personal factors has long been the concern of those interested in the development of drinking behaviour. Sociologists have looked at drinking behaviour in relation to two concepts which have proved helpful in other connections. One of these is alienation which is usually used to identify feelings of estrangement or detachment from self, others, or society in general (Holmes 1976; Fischer 1976). The concept of alienation has tended to be used in two ways in the study of alcoholism (Kinsey and Phillips 1968: 892): (1) as a condition existing prior to alcoholism, where the individual chooses alcoholism as a form of adaptation; (2) as a condition which develops along with alcoholism, related in some way to the 'loss of control' phenomenon. Kinsey and Phillips qualify the last use by suggesting that the condition develops at a particular stage of alcoholism. The other concept is anomie. According to some sociologists a society which lacks clear-cut norms or rules to govern men's aspirations and moral conduct is characterized by anomie. Durkheim (1951, 1965) used it to describe an imperfect relationship between man and the social context in which he lived, caused by rapid social change, leaving a vacuum in which a state of normlessness or lack of rules exists.

The research of Jessor and his associates (1969) has established connections between extreme drinking and peaks of 'anomie', in the sense of a disassociation between cultural goals and means (Merton 1964), and in terms of a simple breakdown in normative consensus. Excessive drinkers have been found to exhibit signs of anomie and alienation. Connor's (1962) and Park's (1962) work has shown evidence of alcoholics and incipient alcoholics structuring their social roles in accordance with the role requirements of an impersonal complex society. Skid Row can be viewed as embracing varieties of the retreatist mode of adaptation to the anomie of modern society. While men on Skid Row are largely alienated from the mainstream of social life, the Skid Row constitutes a sub-cultural system, binding men in a complex network of social relationships with distinctive norms and values (Jackson and Connor 1953; Rubington 1958; Archard 1973, 1975; Cook 1975). Jackson and Connor (1953) showed that the small drinking groups on Skid Row sustained mutual survival and provided emotional support in a way that did not force the alcoholic to recognize that he was dependent on the group.

In studies on youth the focus has been on alienation as a personality variable and its association with drinking (Smart 1970). Researchers like Blane, Hill, and Brown (1968) found feelings of alienation in general, of normlessness and powerlessness in particular, together with favourable attitudes towards the irresponsible use of alcohol among high-school students. However, rather than concentrating on alienation as a psychological variable leading to excessive drinking, research should enquire more broadly into how it contributes directly, and in conjunction with other influences, to the development of drinking behaviour among young people.

Sociological investigations of drinking in complex societies have focused on diverse fragmentary problems such as drinking patterns related to sex groups (Maddox 1964b; Bacon and Jones 1968; Stacey and Davies 1970; Davies and Stacey 1972), income (Mulford 1964; Davies and Stacey 1972), occupation (Cahalann, Cisin, and Crossley 1969; O'Connor 1976a and b; Plant 1977) and education (Cahalann, Cisin, and Crossley 1969; O'Connor 1976a and b). As has been shown, many studies have reported differences in the drinking behaviour of various ethnic sub-groups. Besides the family, the other social institution most frequently seen as playing an important part in the development of drinking behaviour, is religion. Consistent findings have been reported concerning the use of alcohol by major religious sub-groups. Most of this research comes from the USA and has been concerned with religious group differences in drinking behaviour. Jews are presented as having the highest percentage of drinkers of any major religious groups. The 'liberal' Protestant and Catholic groups have consistently higher percentages of drinkers compared with Methodist, Baptist, Mormon, or Fundamentalist traditions. Research has indicated that groups with high percentages of drinkers have tended to have a greater proportion of heavy drinkers. The exception to this finding are the Jews, although some researchers question this fact. They suggest that the tendency to aggregate Jewish men and women together clouds the fact that while few Jewish women may be heavy type drinkers, many Jewish men are (Cahalann *et al.* 1969: 56). However, there appears to be a general consensus that rates of alcoholism are lower among the Jews than among other groups (Robinson 1976). The theoretical explanations for this have centred around the solidarity of the Jewish group (Snyder 1962) and suggest an in-group out-group hypothesis. The effectiveness of the Jewish group's control over its members suggests that drinking is also controlled by the group. If the in-group relationships were weakened and out-group contacts were increased, heavy type drinking among the Jews would increase. The attitude of Jews towards drinking are seen to help them drink in a controlled manner (Bales 1946; Glad 1947-48). Drinking customs and group norms are mainly concerned with the avoidance of excessive drinking, while normal drinking is well integrated into their overall lifestyle. Other researchers have suggested that Jews drink for instrumental rather than for personal or 'affective' reasons, and this is considered to give rise to normal type drinking. However there has been a tendency for Jews to be considered as a homogeneous group, and further research needs to look at differences among Orthodox, Conservative, and Reform Jews.

Researchers have put forward three main theoretical positions as to why there appears to be a relationship between abstinence and certain religious groupings. Skolnick (1958) and others (Knupfer and Lurie 1961; Knupfer 1963; Knupfer and Room 1967; Preston 1969) have suggested a relationship between abstinence teachings and intemperance among those members who drink. In these cases attitudes towards drinking stress the harmful aspects of drinking, normal use being prohibited. Since extreme drinking is the norm, there is no such thing as moderation. Some researchers use the concept of the Protestant ethic (Thorner 1953) to explain why some religious groups drink more than other groups, while other researchers use it to explain why some religious groups are less likely to drink to excess (Cahalann, Cisin, and Crossley 1969: 155). It has been suggested that people from groups which proscribe drinking tend to have different motives for heavy drinking than do those from more permissive groups (Knupfer 1963).

In comparison with the amount of theoretical work on Jewish and Protestant drinking and alcoholism, Catholic drinking patterns have received little theoretical treatment. The empirical work shows that Catholic drinkers seem more likely to experience problems with alcohol, to be heavy type drinkers, as well as more likely to have a high rate of alcoholism.

Most of the research carried out has focused on drinking patterns among religious groups either as incidental information in a large survey or specifically collected for this purpose. In many cases, race, ethnicity, age, sex, social class, area of residence, and other social and cultural factors have not been held constant. Most work has tended to neglect the idea of religion as a value-orientating, motivating force and meaning system, which also has an effect on other areas of the social life of the individual.

The work of Jessor, Collins, and Jessor (1972) on the general area of socialization of problem behaviour looks at the shift for young people from abstainer to drinker status. One of the factors they looked at was religiosity measured in terms of involvement with religion, and the personal importance of religious practices, as well as religious behaviour. Their work showed that the level of religiosity in conjunction with other social and psychological variables, had a bearing on becoming a drinker. The present study adopts a similar approach and looks at the fact of church membership and attendance at religious services, as well as the importance of religious beliefs in the lives of the young. The analysis is such that the relative influence of religiosity along with parental, peer, social, personal, and ethnic and cultural influences can be ascertained.

The approach of the study suggests that a comprehensive understanding of alcohol use requires knowledge of how it is learned, the context of its use, the amount drank, the social meaning and function of alcohol, as well as the consequences of its use. What it hopes to illustrate is the complex interplay of cultural, ethnic, parental, and peer group influences all of which contribute to the development of a young person's drinking behaviour.

2
Methodology

In 1971 I was awarded a research fellowship by the Medical Council on Alcoholism to develop a research programme that would have young people as its focus. The present study developed from this context. It is a sociological study designed to explore and examine empirically the importance and interaction of factors which may influence patterns of drinking behaviour and attitudes among young people. To do this a field study was undertaken using the techniques and methods commonly employed in work of this nature, notably intensive interviewing. The four areas introduced in the previous chapter, form the essence of the study:

1 Ethnic and cultural influences
2 Parental influences
3 Peer influences
4 Social and personal influences

To study the relative influences discussed above the research design provided for a detailed description of drinking behaviour and attitudes and a comparative study of (1) parents and children and (2) young people differing in country of origin and parental ethnic background. Three groups of young people — aged 18-21 years, were chosen to be studied. This age group is of particular relevance in understanding the emergence of patterns of drinking, because it is at this age, the transition stage, that the roles of childhood are replaced by those of adulthood. The precise definition of this transitional stage is neither possible nor relevant. In the process of becoming an adult, appropriate roles and skills are learned that are defined by the culture as being part of adulthood. As the

Table 1   Socio-economic characteristics of respondents: mothers and fathers (Q.8a, Q.10a, Q.7, Q.6a, Q.5)

	*Occupation**	*Irish*	*Anglo-Irish*	*English*
F	Professional	0.3	0.7	6.6
M	Occupation	0.0	0.0	0.0
F	Managerial	19.9	14.0	28.7
M			2.8	9.2
F	Non-	12.3	11.2	7.3
M	Manual	2.0	8.5	7.8
F	Skilled	29.9	23.1	32.6
M		0.3	0.0	1.4
F	Unskilled	25.9	44.0	17.9
M	Semi-skilled	3.7	6.2	4.6
F	Housewife/	11.6	6.0	7.9
M	Unemployed	93.2	82.4	77.0
F		301	134	178
M		354	176	217

*Hall-Jones Classification

	Net income per week	*Irish*	*Anglo-Irish*	*English*
F	£30+	19.6	32.1	33.1
M		0.0	1.1	0.0
F	£25-	23.3	23.1	23.6
M	£30	0.6	1.1	0.5
F	£20-	22.6	22.4	16.3
M	£25	0.8	2.3	4.1
F	£16-	8.6	11.2	6.7
M	£20	1.7	5.7	7.4
F	£10-	4.7	2.2	1.7
M	£16	5.1	20.5	26.7
F	−£10	5.0	3.0	1.1
M		6.5	33.0	26.3
F	Do not	11.3	5.2	15.7
M	know/	2.3	2.8	6.0
	refused to answer			
F	Does not	5.0	0.7	1.7
M	work	83.1	33.5	29.0
F		301	134	178
M		354	176	217

	Marital status	*Irish*	*Anglo-Irish*	*English*
F	Married, living	96.0	97.8	97.8
M	with spouse	87.6	92.6	93.1
F	Widowed	3.7	2.2	1.7
M		10.5	6.3	4.6
F	Married, not	0.3	0.0	2.3
M	living with spouse	2.0	1.2	0.6
F		301	134	178
M		354	176	217

	Size of family	Irish	Anglo-Irish	English
F	2-3	2.0	8.2	23.0
M		2.3	8.0	13.8
F	4-5	17.9	53.0	47.8
M		18.1	49.4	57.1
F	6	15.0	15.7	11.2
F	7	16.9	9.7	7.3
M		15.5	11.4	6.0
F	8	9.0	5.2	5.6
M		9.9	8.0	4.6
F	9	12.6	3.7	0.6
M		11.3	4.5	1.8
F	10	7.6	2.2	1.7
M		9.0	2.8	1.8
F	11	5.3	0.0	0.0
M		5.8	0.6	0.5
F	12	12.6	2.2	2.2
M		13.0	1.7	2.8
F	Other	1.0	0.0	0.6
M	answer	0.8	0.0	0.0
		301	134	178
		354	176	217

	Place of birth	Irish	Anglo-Irish	English
F	Urban	88.6	40.1	93.2
M		85.4	42.6	96.4
F	Town	1.6	11.9	
M		4.8	10.8	
F	Rural	9.6	42.5	2.3
M		9.9	46.6	1.1
F	Infor-			5.6
M	mation			1.4
	incomplete			
F		301	134	178
M		354	176	217

	Length of residence	Irish	Anglo-Irish	English
F	25+	44.2	32.1	52.8
M		41.5	26.7	49.3
F	21-25	18.3	31.3	7.3
M		16.9	22.2	8.3
F	17-20	19.9	19.4	12.4
M		24.0	23.9	17.1
F	11-16	7.6	5.2	7.9
M		7.1	7.4	6.9
F	6-11	5.6	5.2	6.5
M		4.5	6.3	6.7
F	0-6	4.3	6.7	12.4
M		5.9	13.1	11.1
F	Information		0.6	0.6
M	incomplete			0.9
F		301	134	178
M		354	176	217

Table 2   Socio-economic characteristics of the 18-21 year-old respondents (Q.10ab, Q.14, Q.9a, Q.5, Q.76a). In each block the top line is the figure for male respondents

*Occupation**

		Irish	Anglo-Irish	Eng-lish
M	Professional	0.0	1.1	2.5
F	Occupation	0.0	0.0	0.0
M	Managerial	0.0	3.2	1.7
F		0.0	0.0	1.0
M	Non-	27.4	23.6	29.5
F	Manual	55.0	80.2	76.8
M	Skilled	35.3	36.6	43.6
F		3.7	1.2	5.1
M	Unskilled/	18.9	10.8	8.4
F	Semi-skilled	29.9	0.0	3.0
M	Unemployed	18.4	24.7	14.3
F		11.4	18.9	14.1
M		190	93	119
F		187	86	99

*Hall-Jones Classification

Age of respondents

		Irish	Anglo-Irish	Eng-lish
M	18	27.4	32.3	21.0
F		23.5	32.6	33.3
M	19	29.5	26.9	30.3
F		26.7	40.7	28.3
M	20	24.7	23.7	26.1
F		28.3	17.4	24.2
M	21	18.4	17.2	22.7
F		21.4	9.3	14.1
M		190	93	119
F		187	86	99

Educational level reached

		Irish	Anglo-Irish	Eng-lish
M	Primary	18.9	0.0	0.8
F		32.4	0.0	0.0
M	Secondary	63.7	76.2	81.5
F		63.1	85.0	99.0
M	3rd level	17.4	23.7	17.6
F		2.1	15.1	5.0
Never sat an exam				
Information		0.0	0.0	0.0
incomplete		0.5	0.0	0.0
M		190	93	119
F		187	86	99

Net income per week		Irish	Anglo-Irish	English
M	£30+	4.7	9.7	6.7
F		0.0	0.0	1.0
M	£25-	4.2	7.5	13.4
F	£30	0.0	2.3	2.0
M	£20-	8.9	20.4	23.5
F	£25	1.1	12.8	5.0
M	£16-	20.0	25.8	27.7
F	£20	14.4	27.9	39.4
M	£10-	35.3	21.3	16.0
F	£16	60.4	37.2	38.4
M	to £10	13.7	7.5	5.0
F		11.8	8.1	8.1
M	Refused to	3.1	3.6	1.6
F	answer	1.1	0.0	1.0
M	Does not	10.0	4.3	5.9
F	work	11.2	10.5	4.0
M		190	93	119
F		187	86	99

Religion		Irish	Anglo-Irish	English
M	Roman	91.5	93.5	7.6
F	Catholic	99.0	97.6	3.0
M	C of I, C of E,	1.1	0.0	55.5
F	Anglican	0.0	0.0	70.7
M	Baptist,	0.0	0.0	3.5
F	Methodist, Presbyterian	0.0	0.0	12.2
M	Salvation Army,	2.1	0.0	1.6
F	Congregationalist, Jehovah's Witness, Christian	0.5	0.0	3.0
M	Not a member of	4.3	6.5	32.1
F	any religious group	0.0	1.2	11.0
M	No answer	1.1	0.0	0.0
F		0.5	1.2	0.0
M		190	93	119
F		187	86	99

Length of residence		Irish	Anglo-Irish	English
M	21+	10.5	8.6	12.5
F		12.3	0.0	8.1
M	16-21	67.4	58.1	57.1
F		56.7	61.6	55.6
M	11-16	15.3	9.7	15.1
F		17.6	15.1	12.1
M	6-11	3.7	10.8	5.9
F		5.3	17.4	11.1
M	0-6	2.6	12.9	9.2
F		7.5	5.8	13.1
M	Infor-	0.5	0.0	0.0
F	mation incomplete	0.5	0.0	0.0
M		190	93	119
F		187	86	99

Number of children in family of origin**		Irish	Anglo-Irish	English
M	Only	3.7	6.5	15.1
F	child	0.0	10.2	8.1
M	2-3	15.2	43.1	52.1
F		16.2	61.7	66.7
M	4-5	26.8	29.1	22.7
F		34.1	14.0	12.1
M	6-7	25.3	15.0	5.1
F		19.3	10.5	7.0
M	8+	28.9	6.5	5.0
F		29.9	3.5	6.0
M	Information	0.0	0.0	0.0
F	incomplete	0.5	0.0	0.0
M		190	93	119
F		187	86	99

**Respondents included

individual comes to understand what it means to be an adult in general terms, he learns the attitudes and patterns of behaviour in relation to the use or non-use of alcohol that are defined by the culture as being appropriate. Eighteen years of age is also authorized by the legal system as the age that is defined as appropriate for young people to drink (WHO 1952: 19).

The two ethnic groups chosen were the Irish and English, groups known to have different rates of drinking problems (Fitzpatrick 1971c). A third group of Anglo-Irish — a group of Irish origin living in another cultural environment — was selected to assist in the assessment of the relative.importance of the various influences studied.

The young drinkers: how they were chosen

The following criteria were used in the selection of subjects for study:

> *Irish group*: Households in a selected area in Dublin containing 18-21 year olds born and reared in the Republic of Ireland, who were living at home at least four nights a week, for five months a year, whose parents were born and reared in the Republic of Ireland.
>
> *Anglo-Irish group*: Households in a selected area in London containing 18-21 year olds born and reared in England, who were living at home at least four nights a week, for five months a year, whose parents were born and reared in the Republic of Ireland.
>
> *English group*: Households in a selected area in London containing 18-21 year olds born and reared in England, living at home at least four nights a week, for five months a year, whose parents were born and reared in England.

The process of choosing the areas where the study was to take place, and of locating young people and their parents who would fulfill our selection criteria, was complicated and time consuming. While this was true for all groups, the Anglo-Irish young people and their parents were particularly difficult to locate.

Location of study

A difficulty in most studies of this nature is to find areas that are truly comparable. The research as designed required an area of study that would be (1) urban, and having comparable socio-economic characteristics, and (2) a settled homogeneous area, indentifiable as such to the residents and to the outsider (see *Tables 1* and *2*).

London was chosen as the area of study in England, and Dublin was chosen in Ireland. The choice of London was dictated by the availability and location of the 'Anglo-Irish' group, as indicated by documentary research (Markham 1971; Fitzpatrick 1971b).

There were differences both in and between groups in many of the socio-economic characteristics. To ensure that the differences that arose in drinking behaviour, were not due to differences in socio-economic characteristics, analysis was undertaken to check whether these differences had in fact an effect, both in and between groups.

Sampling procedure

Empirical data was obtained through interviews with samples of Irish, Anglo-Irish, and English 18-21 year olds of both sexes and their parents. Altogether 774 18-21 year olds, 613 fathers, and 747 mothers were interviewed. Among them there were 545 family units consisting of a father and a mother, and a son or a daughter. Parents and children were interviewed separately. *Table 3* gives the breakdown of people interviewed by ethnic origin and sex.

Table 3   Number of people interviewed by ethnic origin and sex

Ethnic origin	Fathers	Mothers	Males	Females
Irish	301	354	190	187
Anglo-Irish	134	176	93	86
English	178	217	119	99

A random sample of households in the chosen area in Dublin was taken. (See Appendix 4 for details of sampling procedure in all three areas, and O'Connor 1976b.) The sample was selected using the criteria listed above. Two hundred males and their parents and 200 females and their parents were selected. This number was decided upon because it was felt that it would both allow for detailed analysis and be acceptable within the financial constraints placed on the study. In the London areas, total coverage was aimed at.

In the case of there being more than one 18-21 year old applicable in any one household, the 18-21 year old whose next birthday was nearest to the date of interview was chosen. This ensured randomness of selection where such a situation arose.

Planning and pilot study

Table 4 presents the sequence of the various stages in the planning and analysis of the data. The research design was completed by July 1971,

Table 4   Distribution of time and planning sequence of the project

---

PLANNING AND ORGANIZATION

February 1971 – July 1971

Research proposal
Review of literature

August 1971 – December 1971

Planning of study, fieldwork organization
Recruiting of senior staff; interviewers in Dublin
Drawing up interview schedules

January 1972 – February 1972

Piloting of interview schedules in Dublin and London
Analysis and redrafting of schedules
Re-piloting of schedules in Dublin and London
Selection of area of study in Dublin – Piloting for area of study in London

FIELDWORK

Dublin	*London*
March 1972 – May 1972	April 1972
Training of interviewers in Dublin Fieldwork in Dublin	Selection of areas in London and selection and training of interviewers in London
	May 1972 – September 1972
	Fieldwork in Anglo-Irish and English areas

CODING

July 1972 – November 1972

ANALYSIS

December 1972 – May 1973

Preliminary computer analysis

June 1973 – September 1973

Preliminary tables

October 1973 – December 1973

Data reduction process

January 1974 – May 1974

Detailed analysis; construction
of indexes and scales

June 1974 – October 1974

Complex analysis
Compiling summary report

December 1975

Final report

---

and the planning and administration of the study was undertaken between September and December 1971, with the selection of staff in both Dublin and London taking place in that period. At the same time the preliminary drafting of the interview schedule was undertaken, and certain sections of the questionnaire were tested. These pre-runs were carried out on three groups of people: (1) first year university students in Dublin, (2) nursing and general staff in a psychiatric hospital, and (3) a mixed group of young people in London. Between December 1971 and February 1972, the researcher drew up a number of separate and increasingly refined interview schedules. Refinements were made after an analysis of the test runs. By the beginning of 1972 an interview schedule for both parents and 18-21 year olds had been developed. These schedules were then piloted extensively in both Dublin and London by the researcher and senior staff and were then analyzed and refined. The time span per interview during piloting ran up to fifty minutes for each parent, for the 18-21 year-old questionnaire it was between two and four hours. The final schedule was tested for a time span of thirty minutes per parent and just over one hour ten minutes per 18-21 year old.

The pilot study was regarded as an integral part of the research design, a dress rehearsal for the main study, and was essential in the context of this study in order to evaluate the adequacy of the research methods used in all three areas. This pre-testing or pilot study was conducted in areas similar to, but outside the three chosen areas of study.

Selection of interviewers

When one calls to mind the number of things an interviewer must and must not do, the perfect interviewer appears to be an ideal type person. Survey experts have their own views on the relative importance of various characteristics but little systematic evidence has been published on this particular topic (O'Connor 1973b; Pernanen 1974). For the present project the following five points dictated whether an interviewer was selected as part of the research team:

1 Sex of interviewer
2 Age
3 Drinker status and attitudes to drinking, drunkenness, and alcoholism
4 Nationality of parents and place of birth of interviewers
5 General interviewing ability

1. *Sex of interviewer*   General studies have indicated the importance of sex where interviewer bias is concerned. Kirsch, Newcomb, and Cisin (1965: 20), after an experiment on the use of methodology in surveys on

drinking practices, proposed the use of 'only men interviewers who are non-abstainers'. Their study concluded that men are more likely than women to get answers indicating a much higher level of drinking. However Cosper (1969) shows that these sex differences are not as clearcut and consistent as Kirsch, Newcomb, and Cisin's study suggests. He concludes, rather, that it is the initial selection of the interviewers themselves, regardless of sex, which might be of more importance than subsequent training, if interview bias is to be controlled.

After careful consideration of the facts and taking into account the realities of the situation it was decided to select female interviewers who had a degree or experience in the social sciences.

2. *Age*   All interviewers were thirty years of age or under. This was felt to be a good procedure.

3. *Drinker status and attitudes to drinking, drunkenness, and alcoholism*
Studies carried out by Mulford and Miller (1963) found that interviewers who took a drink got reports of higher rates of drinking than did interviewers who were abstainers. As it was felt that it was more desirable to guard against errors of underestimation than errors of overestimation, interviewers who took a drink were employed. This decision also took into account the experience of previous research I had undertaken in Ireland.

All those who were selected were deemed to have 'favourable' and moderate attitudes to drinking, and were neither problem drinkers nor abstainers. All interviewers were selected by the researcher and an interviewing board. The decision on the interviewers' attitudes towards drinking was made after answers were given to questions eliciting their attitudes on various aspects of drinking behaviour.

4. *Nationality of parents and place of birth of interviewers*   In the Dublin area, all the interviewers were Irish, born in the Republic with parents born in the Republic. In the London area, part of the team were English born, with parents born in England, and part were from Dublin. Here the Irish and English interviewers formed a mixed team and were allotted interviews on a random basis.

5. *General interviewing ability*   The interviewers were, of course, also selected for their general interviewing ability.

Training

The social researcher does not pretend that he does not have feelings, hopes, inclinations, and expectations of his own. The training he receives teaches him to take his biases into account so that they will not interfere with the competency of his interviewing. Considerable attention was given to control over bias through selection and standardization of approach by the interviewers.

The training programme was aimed at giving a common approach, familiarization with questionnaires, theoretical understanding of the project, and help in rationalizing the interviewer's own biases and prejudices, not only towards the main focus of the study, but towards other areas about which the interviewers felt strongly. The intensive training proved to be very effective and indeed essential, particularly with a large team, where even in the same culture, problems of standardization will occur. The training programme was centred around the following:

1 Familiarity with the theoretical design and concepts of the study
2 Detailed knowledge of the questionnaires
3 Work in a language laboratory (or on tape-recorders) for standardization of approach and problems in phrasing and interpretation of questions
4 Piloting of questionnaires in an area similar to the areas to be investigated (1)
5 Discussion groups after each stage
6 Piloting of questionnaires in an area similar to the areas to be investigated (2)
7 Work in language laboratory as final trial run

The interview

The Dublin fieldwork was completed between March and May 1972. In the London areas, because of the criteria, a considerable amount of time was spent on the selection of applicable subjects to be interviewed, and the fieldwork was completed between May and September 1972.

The interview was usually carried out in private. This was necessary to achieve confidentiality, since in each household three interviews had to be undertaken. As far as possible all three interviews were held on the same night. It was through the cheerfulness, efficiency, and assiduity of the research team that this rather daunting task was accomplished. The parents' interview schedule took about half an hour to complete and the 18-21 year olds' took between an hour and an hour and a quarter to complete. The minimum amount of time spent in each household was between two to three hours. All those interviewed in the study were assured of the anonymity and confidentiality of the interview informa- tion, which proved to be a very effective way of obtaining the informa- tion required. Little hostility was evident from the young people or parents who were interviewed even though throughout the fieldwork we were besieged by a number of electricity and transport strikes causing difficulties in many of the homes visited. The interviews were carried out in the kitchen, frontroom or bedroom, some by candle-light. Because of such co-operation the resulting interviews were of a very high quality. At the end of each interview the interviewee received a brief account of the aims of·the study, so that each person interviewed was as clear as possible about the nature of the survey. When the questionnaires had been checked, a letter of thanks was delivered. When some of the young people or parents were reluctant to be interviewed, a special letter was sent to them asking for their co-operation. In most cases this proved very effective.

The interview schedules (see Appendix 2)

Both the parents' and 18-21 year olds' schedules were semi-structured, in that the order of topics was laid down to be followed by the interviewers. Because of the nature of the study, it was felt desirable to approach the topic of drinking within the broader context of leisure-time activities. The 18-21 year-old interview schedule was a lengthy document and most of the questions were open-ended. A schedule of this kind can and does create difficulties in analysis but it allows for more flexibility and originality on the part of the interviewee.

Where the response categories were long and complex, a card listing them was handed to the respondent. In this way interviewers were assisted during the interview to avoid tiring the interviewee. This approach was also used in the parents' questionnaire, especially as most of the questions were pre-coded.

In both schedules the order of presentation of questions was designed so that the questions directly relating to the drinking patterns and attitudes of respondents would come late in the interview after rapport had been well established. Questions of a general nature were asked at the beginning to help put respondents at their ease.

Questions were devised which could be used in an interview situation for each of the four areas investigated in the study (see Appendix 3) namely: (1) ethnic and cultural influences (including a picture of drinking among the Irish, Anglo-Irish, and English young people studied); (2) par- ental influences; (3) peers' influences; and (4) social and personal influences. The general approach was to consider each main area separately and to formulate numerous questions or items referring to them. Procedures used in previous research, were modified, the items were judged and revised, and measures were then incorporated into a draft form of the interview. The difficulty involved in including everything within the time limit, meant that this procedure went through many stages of revision.

Details of the response rate for the three groups under study are given below (see Appendix 4 for details and O'Connor 1976b).

Table 5   Response rate

	Inter-viewed	Refusals	Non-Contact	Deceased
Irish				
Fathers	301	17	37	45
Mothers	354	15	11	18
Males (18-21)	191*	3	6	–
Females (18-21)	188*	9	3	–
Anglo-Irish				
Fathers	134	54	9	13
Mothers	176	26	4	4
Males (18-21)	93	12	9	–
Females (18-21)	86	5	5	–
English				
Fathers	178	75	13	7
Mothers	217	50	2	4
Males (18-21)	119	27	4	–
Females (18-21)	99	21	3	–

*One interview not completed for the males, one for the females.

For Irish male 18-21 year olds the refusal rate was 1.5 per cent; for female 18-21 year olds 4.5 per cent; for fathers 4.25 per cent and mothers 3.75 per cent. The number interviewed compared to the number possible to interview also seemed quite satisfactory.

As can be seen the refusal rate was much higher among the Anglo-Irish and English groups than among the Irish group. *Table 5* shows that the Anglo-Irish male refusal rate was 11.4 per cent, female 5.5 per cent, fathers 28.7 per cent, and mothers 12.8 per cent. On the other hand, since coverage of all applicable families in the area was at least in principle complete, the higher refusal rate had less importance than if this had not been the case. *Table 5* also shows that for the English group the male 18-21 year olds' refusal rate was as high as 18.5 per cent, female 18-21 year olds 17.5 per cent, fathers 29.4 per cent and mothers 18.7 per cent. However, once again coverage at least in principle was complete.

Processing and analysis of the interview data

The interviews were all coded or scored and punched on IBM cards for the internal analysis of particular scales, for assessing intervariable relations, and for the description of ethnic group and sex differences on the various measures. The analysis of these factors served as preliminary or descriptive steps prior to applying the data to more complex analysis.

The reduction of the vast quantities of data was facilitated by the use of computer package programs (Nie, Bent, and Hull 1970; Goodman 1972a and b, 1973) as well as computer programs especially written for this study.*

Analysis of the data falls into three parts. In Chapters 5, 6, and 7, the data is mainly descriptive. In Chapters 8, 9, and 10, data is presented in a similar fashion, but is here followed by an assessment of a more analytical nature. The test employed is the Kolmogorov-Smirnov test (Siegel 1956: 47), which is concerned (in the one sample case) with the degree of agreement between the distribution of a set of observed scores and some specified theoretical distribution. This test does not provide estimates of the size of effects between variables, nor allow account to be taken of more than one variable at a time. This analysis enabled us to simplify the data by identifying statistically significant relationships. To provide more adequate measures of the effects of different variables taking into account their interrelations, Goodman's modified multiple regression method was used (Goodman 1972a and b, 1973). This method was used to give an assessment of the relative amount of variation in young people's drinking behaviour that is accounted for by the main effects of parental, peer, social and personal, and ethnic and cultural factors. (See Appendix 5 for a discussion of the statistical procedures used in the study, and O'Connor 1976a and b.)

Throughout the study the 18-21 year olds interviewed are referred to as males and females. Parents are referred to as fathers or mothers.

*Written by Mr Dan O'Shea, and Mr Michael Walsh, Computer Centre, University College, Dublin.

3
Drinking in English
and Irish societies:
an historical perspective

From the earliest times, the use of alcohol has been an integral part of the English and Irish cultural traditions. Its use and abuse has been celebrated by song and poetry. As was noted in Chapter 1, the Irish have won a reputation for being a hard drinking people, with a high rate of drink-related problems. The English on the other hand are viewed as moderate type drinkers, with relatively small numbers of problem drinkers. These images have been acquired over many years. The socio-cultural emphasis of this study seeks to establish the social meaning and function of alcohol, drinking, and drunkenness. Culture refers to man's entire social heritage, all the beliefs, skills, practices and attitudes he acquires as a member of the society he lives in. While a thorough historical treatment cannot be undertaken here, the ideas, practices, and attitudes about drinking presented to the generations now socialized in each culture, needs to be put in perspective by looking at historical material centred around the act of drinking.

Drinking in English society

When the Romans invaded England they brought with them many traditions and practices. Included among these were the drinking of wine and ale and the establishment of inns. The construction of roads throughout England meant that provision had to be made for the needs of workers and travellers. Accordingly, 'houses of entertainment for man and horse' were introduced all over the country (Hackwood 1909: 31). These were called *tabernae* (*tavernae*) and were the first of the road-side inns to provide food, drink, and a night's rest. They were not the equivalent of the English inn or 'drinking shop' which appeared in

England after the Anglo-Saxon invasion in the form of ale-houses. These Roman taverns were essentially places of entertainment and a refuge from travelling, where common drinking glasses were chained to posts and games were played, particularly chess. With the decline and fall of the Roman civilization, a change in beverage choice was affected by the invasion of the Anglo-Saxons. The German invaders were great lovers of malt beer. Indeed their mythology made frequent references to ale being the beverage of the Gods. The most popular drink with the Saxons was ale and mead. The Saxon mead was made from honey and was boiled with spices and then fermented (Rolleston 1933: 34; Ferguson 1975).

At this time drunkenness appeared to be widespread, the festivals of the time being characterized by drinking orgies. The Saxons however regarded drunkenness as a rather honourable feat. A man's standing, respectability, and indeed virility was ascertained by the amount of alcohol he could consume without surrendering to its intoxicating effects. The Saxons were believed to be one of the first to introduce the custom of drinking healths or toasts at public dinners. The passing round of a 'Loving Cup' was practiced in England from the earliest times and it was this practice that introduced the custom of drinking toasts (Hackwood 1909: 142).

Ale was still the most popular drink amongst the people, wine being the drink of the wealthier classes. At this time there were three kinds of drinking places open to the public, the eala-hus, win-hus, and the inn (Bretherton 1931). Allusions to the ale-house have been made frequently in English history. The regulation of such houses have ranged from the days of Ethelbert (616 AD) to the present day. In the early days the inns were not confined to drinking places as they are today. For example in London the Inns of Court were originally used for the lodging of law-students. The inns or halls in Oxford and Cambridge were used by students for lodging, and were under the regulation of the college authorities. Although the Roman *tavernae* laid the early foundations for the licensing trade, they were destroyed by the invaders, and monasteries acted as guest-houses, while the inns were run by religious orders (Hackwood 1909; French 1891: 134). The houses of the gentry also acted as inns for the accommodation of travellers. At these inns it was the custom to hang out signs of the arms of the owner and hence the origin of so many signs given to public houses (Hackwood 1909: 54).

Customs and usages

A review of the old customs reveals the place of drinking in the society. In old England no festive occasion from New Year to Christmas, from a christening to a funeral, could be properly celebrated without the consumption of cake and ale. Cake and ale was the Royal breakfast — the quantity consumed being quite considerable. French relates that the household books of the kings describe the allowance and rules of the table for the ladies of the household: 'A chin of beef, a manchet, and a cheft loaf was a breakfast for the three [three ladies of honour at court]. To these was added a gallon of ale' (French 1891: 135).

Ale was so much a drink in olden times that it gave its name to a number of festivals. All these were held with ecclesiastical sanction and were usually under their auspices or patronage. There were church-ales, help-ale, Whitson-ales, Easter-ale, clerk-ales, and bride-ales, give-ale, lamb-ale, scot-ale, weddyn-ale, among others. Ale signified a merry gathering, a feast. For example, scot-ale denoted a gathering at which drinking expenses were shared. French comments that scot signified payment, thus scot-free came to mean no payment (French 1891: 81, 123, 153). The clerk-ale usually referred to the custom in some places at Easter, where the ale officially brewed and sold in the churchyards was for the benefit of the parish. The bride-ale was a wedding custom, where the feast was celebrated by the consumption of specially provided ale. The custom of wakes still survives in some areas in England and Ireland and dates from that time. When a person died, the parish invited all friends and relations to make a tribute to the dead by the sale of wake-ales. These customs were so demanding in some areas, that special 'wardens' were appointed to look after the commercial side, and the task was seen as a legitimate church business (Longmate 1968: 3). The church wake, or vigil, kept before a major saint's day was also seen as a major occasion for 'glutony and sinne' and was a frequent cause of upset to the hierarchy.

One of the most important 'causes of every day drunkenness' was the system of drinking usages which had grown up in many trades, as well as the social role of the public house. Dunlop (1839) described in detail 300 usages in ninety-eight different trades. This study showed that the usages were universal and not peculiar to any particular occupation, and that the lower classes had a code of conduct and courtesy as binding on them as it was on the upper ranks of society. It was among skilled craftsmen with their exclusive initiation ceremonies that drinking customs had their strongest hold. The elaborate network of usages was maintained by a system of bullying (Thompson 1963: 243; Harrison, B. 1971). These usages were extended in the country to drinking during the harvest, or even when putting on runs, or tyres of cartwheels. Mayhew (1968, I: 246) commented that in the 1840s an introduction for a job was 'invariably, you know Mr so and so I am a good drinking man'.

Another system or usage was called the truck system. Hilton (1960: 81) and Thompson (1963) revealed that skilled wages often concealed a number of enforced payments, for example, rent of machinery, and fines for faulty work or indiscipline (Wright 1967: 86, 94, 98, 108). In industry, payment in goods and 'Tom and Jerry Shops' were often the practice. Seamen and waterside workers were subject to extortion at the hands of publicans. An extreme example of this were the Thames coal whippers, who until an act of government in 1843, could only gain employment through the publicans, who in their turn would only employ men who consumed up to 50 per cent of their wages in the public house. Drinking was an integral part of economic transactions and all deals were '..."sealed" or clenched by vendor or purchaser — either the one or the other, whichever was mutually agreed to have secured the advantage — paying for drinks' (Hackwood 1909: 151). The London coal and ballast beavers owed a lot to Mayhew's (1968: 243) work *London Labour and the London Poor* in their efforts to shake off the publicans' control over their livelihood.

In the days of statute hiring fairs, a servant usually enquired before agreeing to work if he would be allowed 'seals and meals' meaning the usual time for rest and refreshment. Refreshment was taken to mean liquid refreshment and was considered to be quite important. Another practice which Hackwood (1909: 151) comments on is the practice of treating another person to a drink or, as he refers to it, as 'standing treat' or 'standing sam'. A further indication of the importance of drink in the working life and recreational activities of skilled artisans was the custom called Saint Monday, which allowed a worker to extend his Sunday (Webb 1866: 143; Harrison, B. 1971: 40, 305). The Select Committee on Habitual Drunkards recorded witnesses complaining that the skilled worker was mainly responsible for the increase in drink consumption during the 1870s. One witness explained:

> 'In Lancashire which is the highest paid county in the kingdom, drinking exists to this terrible excess, because a workman can afford to lose one or two days a week, and can yet make a great deal more money than ordinary labourers.'   (Dingle 1972: 617)

A Select Committee set up in 1834 took anecdotal evidence from doctors, clergymen, officials, and interested citizens. It was badly received in Parliament and considered with ridicule. Many witnesses referred to the practice of paying men their wages in public houses, or giving one large note for the wages of five or six men, to be changed by the publican. It was expected that each man would buy a drink in the public house (Thompson 1963: 244).

The role of the public house in English society

The extent of drinking practices needs to be seen within a broader context, and account must also be taken of the publicans' extensive social and cultural role. From the earliest times inns, ale-houses, and taverns formed the basis of the economic and social life of the community. Reference to inns up to medieval times has been made in earlier sections, suffice it to say that they formed the basis of the social, cultural, and recreational life of a community (Bretherton 1931; Fryer 1963; Harrison, B. 1971). The transport system as we know it today did not exist, instead people travelled on foot or on horseback. The inns and ostlers were then indispensable to the traveller. When a road was turnpiked, inns sprang up as a matter of course (Hackwood 1909: 183). The inns also played a very important part in the evolution of the delivery of mail. Hackwood (1909) points out that it was not until 1784 that the roads were in any condition for the introduction of the fast mail-coach, as distinct from the much slower stagecoach. Prior to this mail was carried from inn to inn.

The inns pioneered commercial entertainment, and provided facilities for all sorts of games for people to amuse themselves. They were also to foster the beginnings of the music hall (Hackwood 1909: 188; Harrison, B. 1971: 46). At first it was more like a sing-song, but gradually the musical evenings became more commercial and professional. At this time inns were used as exhibition halls, and museums. Dog and poultry shows were put on regularly, together with bird judging contests and pipe smoking competitions. Some public houses acquired fame as museums of natural history. Licensed premises were often used for markets, exchanges, and other forms of trading.

Its important to remember that up until 1872 with the exception of London, there was no general legislation to prevent public houses opening all day every day. The Licensing Act of 1872 consolidated and tidied up the existing licensing system and introduced a number of new features (Monckton 1969: 84). Drinking places existed for all types of people. In order of respectability there was the 'inn', accommodating the traveller, the 'tavern' catering for the casual drinker, the 'ale-house', which unlike the inn and the tavern did not sell spirits and was under little or no control, and the 'gin shop' which supplied gin to the urban population. Ale-houses, beer shops, and gin shops differed from inns and taverns by the articles they sold and by the lower social class of their customers (Hackwood 1909: 183; Harrison, B. 1971: 46).

The public houses offered a refuge from the miserable social conditions of the poor, in that they provided facilities and opportunities for recreation, as well as a meeting place. As many commentators pointed out, Smiles (1875), Levy (1951), Askwith (1928), Zweig (1948), and

B. Harrison (1971), the working man's home was often cold, damp, overcrowded, and uncomfortable. Graphic and living pictures of the conditions of the poor emerge from the researches of Mayhew (1968), Engels (1958), Booth (1889-1903), Rowntree (1902), and Hyndman (1911). In fact, the poorer the man of the house was and the bigger his family, the more likely he was to resort to the relative comfort of the public houses. At a time when most people did not have lavatories, the publican was usually the only man in the neighbourhood to have one. Booth commented: 'Public houses play a larger part in the lives of the people than clubs or friendly societies, churches or missions or perhaps more than all put together' (Booth 1889-91: 113). The public house was the one place where there was gaiety, heat, light, and sometimes cooking facilities. In many ways, as B. Harrison (1971: 46) pointed out, '...drinking places mirrored the interests and needs of their localities'.

Public houses were also the local news centres. They provided newspapers for hire, and later employed newspaper readers for their customers. As they were one of the few public places where people could meet, associations of all kinds were based in their available rooms. Almost all the reforming campaigners met in public houses, as did election meetings, political gatherings, and trade unions (Thompson 1963: 616). Publicans did as much as any temperance society to prepare working men for public speaking, and in this way helped educate the working classes through the working men's debating societies which were formed on their premises (Harrison, B. 1971: 49).

The publican was often the treasurer for local friendly societies and for saving clubs. At one time, inn tokens or tavern tokens were used by publicans because of the shortage of coins of the realm (Monckton 1969: 60; Hackwood 1909: 274).

The public house acted as a centre for trade and a place for auctions. The original function of inns, that of lodging travellers was also still very much part of their function. For in many ways, the recreational activity grew naturally from the travellers' need for diversion when lodging away from home. The custom of paying wages in public houses, meant that the public houses were also embryo labour exchanges.

The publican, while portrayed by temperance tracts and also by some of his customers' wives as a villain (Mayhew 1968: 111, 265), was a popular and respected individual and often very well integrated into the power structure of the area. Booth noted that in the East End of London there were many respectable drinksellers: 'Behind the bar will be a decent middle aged woman ... respecting herself and respected by them [the customers]. The whole scene comfortable, quiet and orderly' (Booth 1889-91: 114).

B. Harrison (1971: 65) points out, that in the 1820s drink interests were allied with powerful agricultural interests. This fact may help to explain the temperance reformers' failure in the 1830s, and the regional variations in the support for the movement. In a society still basically agricultural the drink industry was very powerful and played an important role in the rural economy. In many cases the brewers and publicans were substantial landowners, and the system of manufacturing made for close co-operation with all sections of the trade (Mathais 1958). As the publicans were treasurers of local friendly and saving societies, there was also a strong association between banking and the drink industry. The importance of the drink revenue to the exchequer also helped to increase the political prestige of the drink interest at this time.

The role of the public house was to change with what Harrison calls the coming of the 'counter-attraction' (Harrison 1969: 204; Malcolmson 1973). It is important to remember that at that time, before the development of other entertainments, there was no place to go. The improved living standards and economic conditions, channelled off a great part of the population into football stadiums, theatres, and later cinemas.

Excessive drinking

In 81 AD the Emperor Domitian launched an attack on excessive drinking ordering half the vineyards to be destroyed, and no more to be planted without his permission. This edict was not formally revoked until 200 years later (French 1891: 6).

In the twelfth century drinking and fires were named as the only plagues of London. Rolleston comments that a '... striking indication of the intemperate habits of the Anglo-Saxons was that their drinking cups were so made that they could not stand upright, each guest being compelled to drink the glass off at one draught' (Rolleston 1933: 35). During this period university students, and members of the clergy were the chief drunkenness offenders. Coulton has documented the era and comments on the practices of the medieval clergy (Coulton 1907; Rolleston 1933: 38). He felt that they encouraged drunkenness among their parishioners.

The social commentators of the time, mainly the poets, Chaucer, Langland, and Fowler, denounced these drunken practices. There was little control over either the character and conduct of the license holder, the preservation of public order, or over the structure of licensed premises. It was only under the acts of 1495 and 1503 that the justices were able to suppress ale-houses (Monckton 1969). The only control on drunkenness or the sale of alcoholic drink was that relating to behaviour constituting a public nuisance. The Royalist preacher Thomas Reeve referred to England as the 'dizzy iland' whose population drank as if

'... we were nothing but spunges to draw up moisture, or we had tunnels in our mouths' (Fryer 1963: 129).

Drunkenness and insobriety continued well into the seventeenth century and it was not until the gin mania that more stringent legislative measures were taken. By the beginning of the seventeenth century some justices were using their power to revoke licenses as a sanction, laying down the time of closing, limiting the hours of opening on Sundays, and restricting the length of time a customer might stay tippling in an ale-house. An act of 1606 made public drunkenness a criminal offence, the penalty being a fine of five shillings or six hours in the stocks. Control of licenses remained strict until after the Restoration (The Departmental Committee on Liquor Licensing, (DCLL) 1972: 293).

Gin fever

After the restoration of Charles II in 1660, there were scenes of very heavy drinking. A spirit of laxness permeated all of English society. Taverns multiplied up and down the country and were granted licences almost on demand (DCLL 1972; Hackwood 1909: 127; Harrison, B. 1971: 46, 66, 82). Until this time, drinking in England had centred around wine, beer, mead, and cider. Spirits were now becoming popular (Ferguson 1975: 28). In 1690 distilling, until then a monopoly of Royal patentees, was thrown open. The government, concerned with the promotion of agriculture, helped create a market for low-grade corn unsuitable for brewing, by actively encouraging distilling and spirit selling. The retail sale of spirits was free from all licensing requirements and was subject to a low rate of excise duty. As Longmate (1968: 8) comments: 'Seldom can any policy have succeeded so completely.' It is not known exactly what the consumption of spirits was like at the time, but estimates ranged from 754,000 gallons to 810,000 gallons per annum. By 1736 the population was about six and a quarter million, but the consumption of spirits had rocketed to approximately six million gallons, which is roughly equivalent to one gallon a head per annum (Monckton 1969: 61).

Several decades passed before the tradition of clandestine distilling and unlicensed selling was brought under control. The advocates of tighter control made much of the evil effects of cheap gin and argued in favour of the use of the healthy traditional 'malt liquor'. Their attitude was reflected in Hogarth's engravings of the horrors of 'Gin Lane' and the relative happiness of 'Beer Street'.

Although drunkenness in the last half of the eighteenth century was less alarming than it had been, it was still a serious problem. Engels (1958) discussed the drink problem in his *Conditions of the Working*

Class in England. He commented among other things on the level of drunkenness in Manchester, where on Saturday nights he himself saw '...drunkards staggering in the road or lying helpless in the gutter' (1958: 143). Spirit drinking though still prevalent, was within bounds. Literature encouraged the people to drink ale rather than spirits. Magistrates now enforced the law more strictly, imposing a yardstick of one public house per village, insisting on 10 pm closing, and suppressing licences without compensation, which was to be of importance in the future (Longmate 1968: 12). The decrease in the general use of spirits seems to have resulted not so much from the pressures of legislation, as from changes in social habits, in attitudes, and in the policy of licensing justices.

Longmate commented that one of the few things that rich and poor had in common in the eighteenth century was excessive drinking. Things were to change with increasing urbanization and industrialization.

Although drunkenness in the first thirty years of the nineteenth century was less disturbing than that of the previous hundred years, the harmful consequences are depicted in many contemporary descriptions (Webb and Webb 1903: 98; Smollett 1848: 430). Other writers told of practices of giving gin in lieu of wages, of selling gin from market stalls and hawkers' barrows, and the free offering of gin to clients in chandlers' shops and brothels (Hackwood 1909). The act which was first passed with a view to checking this 'growing evil' was the act of 1729, which originated the system of licensing public houses at a general annual meeting of the justices. The government alarmed at the gin epidemic, imposed a high license duty on gin sellers by the Gin Act of 1736. It was unenforceable, there were public riots and in seven years only two licences were taken out and non-payment of excise duty went on unabated as did the illicit sales (Habitual Drunken Offenders 1971: 198). According to Hackwood, the brand of London gin known as 'Old Tom' came into vogue during the prohibition of gin being sold in less than two gallon quantities. An illicit outlet in the form of a vending machine was erected outside in the shape of an old tom cat cut out in wood or metal, and projecting into the street (Hackwood 1909: 127). By dropping a penny through a slot in the figure, a supply of gin to that value, could be made to trickle from a pipe concealed in the cat's forepaw. It was probably the first of the vending machines.

The Gin Act was repealed in 1743, before it was still a serious problem (Harrison, B. 1971: 64). In 1817 the Parliamentary Committee on the State of the Policy in the Metropolis came out strongly for free trade in liquor. They recommended that there be no licensing control by justices, and argued that under no circumstances should a publican be deprived of the right to trade in liquor without trial or jury. The public was in favour, and with the overall *laissez-faire* philosophy of the times it was bound to be upheld. In 1825, legislation was passed to reduce the licence fee. In 1828, the Licensing Act repealed the power to suppress unwanted beer-houses, and the Beer Act of 1830 temporarily increased drunkenness when it came into force: 'Everybody is drunk, noted Sydney Smith, those who are not singing are sprawling. The sovereign people are in a beastly state' (Longmate 1968: 23). Beer shops were freed from licensing control and beer from excise duty. 'Tom and Jerry shops' sprang up everywhere and the statutory closing hours were ignored. While overall consumption of spirits fell slightly for a year or two, the competition of the beer shops spurred the owners to refurbish the old licensed houses and draw customers back to their glittering 'gin palaces'. In 1834, it was for political rather than social reasons that beer housekeepers were required to obtain certificates of character, signed by six householders; their houses had become the meeting places of 'disaffected labourers' (Hammond and Hammond 1964: 144). Longmate (1968: 23) comments that a beer-house mania swept the country.

By 1834, for a population of fifteen million in England and Wales, there were now one million places at which one could obtain a drink, and almost half of these were under no public control. The Beer Act's supporters were unfortunate in that it came into operation at the same time as a wave of spontaneous riots, which had begun to sweep the whole of the south and west of England. As B. Harrison (1971: 85) showed, there was no direct evidence to prove that the beersellers participated in the riots, and he suggests that some opposed them. It was true that the beer shops had become meeting places where subversive literature could be distributed and riots planned. Thompson (1963: 616) commented that for many, the taverns or beer-houses were the only places for people to meet, and showed what an important part taverns had in the foundation of the trade union movement.*

Social historians saw the Beer Act as having broader implications, as a campaign against patronage, and as a way of helping the emancipation of popular culture from upper-class control (Harrison, B. 1971: 65 *et passim*). Other influences were at work to curb excessive drinking; temperance societies, inaugurated in the United States of America, crossed the Atlantic and the climate was right for a good reception (Ferguson 1975: 65).

*See B. Harrison (1976) 'Drink and sobriety in England 1815-1872: a critical bibilography'. *International Review of Social History*: 204-76. For a general discussion of works available on the public house in England see in particular p.211, pp.233-4.

Drinking in Irish society

'For Tyrone, as for his sons, so also for the race: drink has been their curse. It is the principal fact of Irishness that they have not been able to shake.' (Glazer and Moynihan 1963: 250)

From the earliest times drinking has been an integral part of the Irish cultural tradition. Unlike England where ale was popular, whisky or uische beatha was the main drink of the Irish, preferred by the population up until near the end of the nineteenth century (McGuire 1973; Wilson 1940: 9).* As far back as the fifteenth, sixteenth, and seventeenth centuries, travellers' accounts of Irish drinking emphasized the role it played in the life of the people; drunkenness was common and there appeared to be little or no strictures placed on its use (McManus 1939: 68; McCarthy 1911: 28; Lecky 1896: 32; Plunkett 1904: 113; Bales 1962: 157). The extensive usages and customs described in the section on drinking in English society were commonplace in Ireland. Drinking was a problem in both countries at the time. Dunlop's (1839) work showed that, contrary to what people thought, these customs were extensive and common in England, Ireland, and Scotland (Glover 1960).

The ale-houses, as they existed in England, were not as prevalent in Ireland, since whisky was the preferred drink. They provided accommodation and food for travellers. Legislation was passed in 1634-5, which set standards, and determined when the ownership and operation of these institutions was lawful. McManus in his book *Irish Cavalcade 1550-1850*, tells us about the Irish in the seventeenth century: '... they are of middle stature, strong of body, of a hotter and moister nature than many other nations ... given to fleshy lusts ... they will drink down very large quantities of Usquebah' (McManus 1939: 58).

Customs and usages

The customs and drinking usages associated with various occupational groups, often led to heavy drinking. These trade practices socialized the individual into hard drinking practices. If an individual did not comply with the wishes of the group his work and his social life suffered severely. The practice of giving domestic servants 'weekly money' for alcohol was discussed by the Select Committee on Drunkenness in 1834. Workmen were also paid in public houses, and the custom of 'treating' was associated with the payment of workmen.

*Longmate (1968: 13) remarks that 'porter' had begun to gain favour since around 1720.

This custom was further supported by the collusion of the owners of public houses with the people who paid the wages. The Committee pointed out that '… although there is no absolute law upon the subject, it is expected, as a matter of course, that each will drink a glass of spirit or liquor as a compensation to the master of the house for the change' (Select Committee on Drunkenness of the House of Commons, *Evidence on Drunkenness Presented to the House of Commons*, 1834: 98). The custom also made provision for the foreman to drink without being charged if he brought his men with him. This practice was still common in Ireland around the beginning of the twentieth century. Evidence of the custom in Dublin, in connection with the payment of dockers was given by James Larkin in his report to the Parliamentary Committee in 1907 which was investigating abuses on the docks in Dublin (Larkin 1968: 17).

Drinking played a prominent part in the economic life in Ireland during the eighteenth and nineteenth centuries. All economic deals were sealed by a drink. 'There are no dry bargains' — fair days, in consequence, were more of a social than an economic affair (McCarthy 1911: 28). As the whole day was usually spent at the fair selling cattle and goods, or meeting friends, an advanced stage of intoxication occurred. The solidarity and friendship implicit in 'treating' greatly facilitated the economic transactions, and as the main cash transactions of the small farmer were with 'strangers' or townsfolk, the custom was quite happily retained (Mooney 1850-65; Carleton 1846: 47). McCarthy (1911: 28) saw this practice as a form of 'social law — enforced with the vigour of a Coercion Act', and also commented that the towns were even worse than the country areas: 'Little fits of business get in, as if by stealth, between the drinks during the day' (McCarthy 1911: 119). It was a subject constantly being referred to in books and speeches in the eighteenth century (Maxwell 1936: 8).

Arensberg and Kimball (1940) pointed out that there was a strong sense of group solidarity among the men in rural Ireland in the 1930s. Within the group, men were seen to find companionship and security, and this was expanded and strengthened by the practice of 'treating'. The authors saw drinking in a group as a symbolic reaffirmation of solidarity and equality among males in the area that they investigated.

A reaction to the practice of treating was the formation of the Anti-Treating League by Fr Rossiter, Superior of the Missionaries in Enniscorthy, Co. Wexford (Plunkett 1904: 114), which Fr Cullen (1911) thought '…helped to eradicate the silly and deplorable habit of "treating" '. The success of the league, however, appeared to be limited.

Drink was also used as a substitute for food, as was noted by Bales (1962: 157) and McCarthy (1911: 295). More recently one poet commented:

'When food is scarce and your larder bare,
And no rasher grease on your pan,
When hunger grows as your meals are rare
A pint of plain is your man.'   (O'Hanlon 1976: 26)

McCarthy felt that this was one of the main differences between the English and Irish drinking habits: 'The main differences between the drinking habits of Ireland and Great Britain is that Irishmen drink fasting, while Englishmen drink with and after food' (McCarthy 1911: 295).

The medicinal use of alcohol has long been a custom in Ireland. Fr Cullen, founder of the Pioneer Total Abstinence Association, saw this practice as one that gave a bad example to children and also led to intemperance.

On a general level drinking appeared to be an integral part of the social and economic framework of the culture. Drunkenness was socially structured and accepted as a form of behaviour. In this culture there appeared to be no strictures placed on drinking. The situation however was not to remain unchallenged, and towards the 1900s measures were taken by the government and other sources to control drinking. Cullen (1968) comments that many visitors to the country in the eighteenth century noticed that the excessive drinking, which they were led to believe was part of the Irish culture, was not as prevalent as had been asserted. A somewhat ironic touch, however, in view of the government's efforts to control drinking, was the increasing success of the illegal production of alcohol, mainly of poteen.

Illicit distillation: poteen

Tom Kelly's Cow

There's a boy in our country he's proper but small
It's wee Tommy Kelly as do him call
It's him brews the cordial that exceeds them all
He can beat all the Doctors from this to Fingal.

If you were sick and was ready to die
One glass of Tom's poteen would raise your heart high
You could heave it up higher and nearer your nose
It's an Irishman's toast then wherever he goes.

(Morton 1973: 17)

Connell (1968) conducted a study of poteen-making from the eighteenth century to the early nineteenth century. Connell's evidence would seem to suggest that with the new legislation of the time which increased the price of whisky, the people, whose 'social life was hinged to cheap drink', began to make poteen. The advent of the poteen industry was understood by Connell to be one of the few pleasures of the Irish peasant. This industry, however, also served another purpose; it provided the peasantry with money for rent.

The magistrates as well as the excisemen were open to bribes. This fact alone increased the contempt of the people for the law. Whole areas were engaged in the illicit distillation of poteen. In areas where the local gentry stood to gain by the higher rents, they worked with the peasants. In cases like these, districts were protected by an elaborate guard system, in which the young boys often played an important part because of their speed and agility, which enabled them to outrun the 'guager' or exciseman.

By the 1830s when flax spinning was largely mechanized, there was probably no cottage industry that earned more than distilling. A Dublin distiller commented that poteen accounted for more than a half of all the spirit consumed in Ireland. More than 1,000 officers and men were recruited to restrict the production of poteen. The result of their endeavours reveals the extent of the industry: over 16,000 stills were discovered and confiscated in 1833 and 1834 (Connell 1968).

This illegal distillation was not only blamed for encouraging excessive drinking; it also brought the law into disrepute and put unnecessary taxes on the government. Connell (1968) quotes a reference to a Donegal rector's verdict: 'This baneful practice tends to promote dissipation, perjury, rebellion, revenge and murder.' The places for drinking poteen were seen as meeting places for all the loose and disorderly characters in the neighbourhood, where, half-intoxicated, they discussed politics and regulated rents, tithes, and taxes.

Ether drinking

Besides the poteen industry, Connell reports that ether drinking was very prevalent in Ulster, and, however exaggerated it may seem, warranted sufficient attention to be '... cursed by the priest, denounced by the Synod of the Church of Ireland, and investigated and restricted by Parliament' (Connell 1965: 629). He saw it as an unforeseen consequence of Fr Mathew's Temperence Campaign, as well as of the suppression of illicit distillation. By the end of the nineteenth century, with the sources of poteen drying up, and parliament whisky too dear to take its place, many disappointed spirit drinkers turned to ether as an alternative. Connell comments: 'No other people seem to have drunk ether so extensively or for so long a period as the 400,000 inhabitants of the 100 square miles of the North of Ireland ...' (Connell 1965: 629). Kerr (1894:

131, 135) reported that it was the general practice among all social classes, both males and females, and was particularly prevalent amongst farmers and labourers. It was also given to children, and hawkers who attended fairs and other social gatherings dispensed it in exchange for farm produce.

Perhaps one of the ironies of the situation was the contradiction between the spread of this type of drinking on the one hand, and the efforts of the temperance movement to control ordinary alcohol consumption on the other. Here, many commentators have pointed to the inadequate drinking legislation of the period. During the early part of the eighteenth century the licensing law apparently fell into disuse. Between 1759 and 1791, licensing questions were discussed in the Irish Parliament but nothing much was done. A large number of revenue acts were passed during this period, containing sections for the better regulation of liquor traffic or for fixing duties. Most of these acts were passed for one, two, or three years; sometimes they were renewed, and sometimes re-enacted with slight alterations, with the results that the law fell into great confusion, no reform was effected, and things went continually from bad to worse (Fitzpatrick 1970a and b).

Excessive drinking

The pervasiveness of drinking customs in the eighteenth and nineteenth centuries cannot be exaggerated. From the womb to the tomb, the Irish drank at christenings, weddings, and funerals. Every new stage of life was celebrated through the extensive use of alcohol, which almost took the form of an initiation rite. Many historians, McCarthy (1911), Lecky (1896), McLysaght (1911), saw drunkenness as a national weakness. Longmate (1968: 15) held that, although drunkenness appeared to be a more serious problem in the eighteenth century, the early nineteenth century still presented a picture of intemperance. That excessive drinking was causing some concern in the late seventeenth century is evident in Richard Lawrence's brave attempt to calculate the cost to the country of drinking, gaming, and swearing (see *Table 6*).

Larkin (1968) reports that although drunkenness appeared to be on the decline in Ireland in 1908, Dublin was 'still worse off than the general average for the whole of Ireland'. The picture he paints of Dublin evokes the feeling of the times, when unemployment, bad housing conditions, and utter poverty were coupled with despair. He reports:

'More disturbing ... were the figures involving the number of women and children who frequented public houses in Dublin. Twenty-two public houses in Dublin were observed for two weeks and 46,574 women and 27,999 children, of whom 5,807 were babies in arms went into them.'   (Larkin 1968: 41)

The drinking of methylated spirits, and sometimes of turpentine, was reported as one of the contributing factors for the high rate of mental illness in Dublin, which was 63.5 per 10,000 at that time.

Table 6   TO DRINKING, GAMING AND SWEARING
£246,000 (1682)

Richard Lawrence, Cromwellian adventurer and political economist, having settled in Ireland, calculates in round figures how much vice is costing the country.

GAMING INCLUDING peasantry and mechanick gamesters at Cards, Dice, Shovelboard, Bowling Alleys and Ninepins, say, 10,000 persons obstructing the wealth of the country to the extent of, per ann.:	£52,000
Profane swearing costs the country, per ann.:	£20,000
Drunkenness: 3 wine-bibbers to each parish at £10 per wine-bibber, per ann. 2,500 parishes:	£75,000
Ale-topers, 5 to a parish, at 4 each per ann.:	£50,000
Second set of ale-topers, or fuddlicups, generally artists or husbandmen, at £2 each per ann.:	£25,000
Tapsters and Drawers who might be employed in profitable arts cost the country per ann.:	£4,000
Loss through bad work of the sots, per ann.:	£20,000
	£246,000

Source: M. McManus (1939) *Irish Cavalcade 1550-1850*, London: Macmillan & Co. Ltd.

Brody (1973), in a study carried out in the late 1960s in the west of Ireland, found that drink was an integral part of the social life of a sector of the community — the traditionalists, farmers, and bachelors. The bar was seen as the 'province of men who are most committed to the land' (Brody 1973: 160). Here drinking was excessive and many of the men were seen to spend a considerable amount of money on it.

A follow-up study of Arensberg and Kimball's *Family and Community in Ireland* (1940) was carried out by Art Gallagher* between 1965 and mid-1966. Gallagher found that in the parishes where his studies were carried out, the attitudes toward drinking '... can only be defined as tolerant'. Drinking was condoned, censure being adopted only if one tended to spend too much on drink at the expense of the family, or if drinking interfered with the successful performance of functional tasks. Gallagher found that there were no moral sanctions invoked in the discussions about drinking, and that drinking was very often used to initiate social contact with strangers. The stereotype of the heavy drinking bachelor was also investigated, and its truth questioned. Gallagher found that people attributed many negative types of behaviour to bachelors. He explained drinking from a psychological standpoint: it was used as a mediator by the people who drank, in that it reduced psychological barriers. In this, his work supports that of Bales. The male drinking group, as he saw it, was an anticipated and enjoyable experience for the participants. There were three 'cliques' or groups in his study who had institutionalized their drinking, in that they met regularly for a drink and discussion. His data also lends support to Bales' finding of the institutionalized use of alcohol at fairs and wakes. He reported that '... when people would recount these kind of social situations, one of the most prominent elements in their definitions of structure and function was the "drink taken"' (ibid.).

The analysis of the attitudes and patterns of drinking of the English and Irish suggested that as far back as the sixteenth century and up to the early part of the twentieth century, English culture was quite like the Irish in relation to the use of alcohol. In both societies, the exchange of drink was a social ritual, implying interdependence and a continuing relationship. Both the English and the Irish drank heavily at funerals and other occasions, settled bargains over drinks at fairs, and drank for medicinal purposes. In both countries drinking was seen as a serious problem, and the evidence suggested that this continued up to the turn of the twentieth century. Legislation did little to help matters and temperance societies became active.

*Professor A. Gallagher, University of Kentucky, Lexington, Kentucky. Personal communication.

4
The temperance movement
in England and Ireland

Temperance movements are almost as old in the history of mankind as the use of alcohol itself. It is of interest to note that in nearly all societies in which alcohol was consumed attempts have been made to encourage or enforce temperance, if not prohibition. It is not the purpose of this chapter to discuss temperance movements in general but to look at the temperance movement in both Ireland and England. The main concern is analysis and interpretation, rather than a detailed description of the development of the movement in both countries.*

Using the concept of social movements in general, it is possible to analyze the temperance movement. A social movement tends by definition to affect directly or indirectly the social order. Smelser (1970) defines social movements as norm-oriented movements, where action is taken by a group, or groups, in the name of a generalized belief envisioning a reconstitution of norms.

Gusfield (1969) notes that three conditions are necessary for the development of a social movement: (1) a conscious indictment of whole or part of the social order, (2) a demand for change, and (3) a set of ideas which specify discontents, prescribed solutions, and justify change, which he calls 'sociological commitments'. All these three conditions were present in England and Ireland and facilitated the beginnings of the temperance movement (Ferguson 1975: 65).

As was noted in Chapter 3 drinking was seen as a serious problem in both English and Irish societies. Legislation did little to help matters and temperance societies began to become more active. English and Irish

*The amount written about the temperance movement in England is staggering to anyone who tries to read it. As Harrison comments there is '...if anything too much material'. See Harrison (1967: 215) for a discussion of the type of material available.

temperance movements were part of an overall reform movement. Like many social reform movements in the nineteenth century, they arose spontaneously and unpredictably from enthusiastic, charismatic, and eccentric individuals (Harrison, B. 1971: 147; Ferguson 1975: 66).

It is at this point that the difference between the English and Irish cultures emerged. Apart from the early stages, the temperance movements in England and Ireland developed in different ways; the trend and tactics used were in ways a reflection of the different social structures of both countries. *Table 7* shows the stages of development of the temperance movement in England and Ireland.

Free trade remedy

The free trade remedy for the drink problem, was symbolized in the policy of the free licensing movement, a movement to open up the licensing system and relax the existing laws. The free licensers saw drunkenness as an underlying problem in English society. The campaign was broadly based and concerned with excessive drinking, as well as class and religious oppression, administrative corruption, government expenditure, and illicit distilling. Education was seen as the means of bringing about change, rather than restrictive legislation (Harrison, B. 1971: 64). Drunkenness was only going to be removed gradually, as it was part of the social fabric. However, the free trade remedy did nothing to reduce the level of intemperance. Nevertheless, it was more flexible than its counterparts in later years, as its supporters were willing to try alternative solutions and were not sectarian in outlook. While this phase was common to both English and Irish societies, it was more important in England than in Ireland.

Anti-spirits movement

The first 'societies' in Ireland were 'moderation' societies, resembling the anti-spirits movement in England. It was a movement for moderation, not for total abstinence. The emphasis was on the harmful effects of drinking spirits and most of the reformers saw no objection to the moderate use of beer or wine (Rogers 1943: 31). *Table 8* shows the number of these moderation societies in Ireland. These reformers saw the 'evil' effects caused by the excessive drinking of cheap spirits by men, women, and children. The movement was initiated in Ireland by a 'reformed drunkard', Jeffrey Sedwards, of the 'respectable working class'. The moderationists were essentially led by non-Catholics, were members of

Table 7   Stages of development in the English and Irish temperance movements

Phase		Method
1	Free licensing; free trade remedy: mainly an English remedy; had some implications for the Irish as this philosophy was the basis of legislation.	Moral suasion. The emphasis was on moderation in the use of all alcoholic beverages.
2	Anti-spirit movement: advocated the moderate use of beer and wine, with total abstinence from spirits. This movement was more effective in England than in Ireland.	Moral suasion. The emphasis was on moderation.
3	Teetotalism: *England*	
	(1) Total abstinence for the excessive drinker and all people who wished to promote sobriety. There were two pledges: (i) short pledge – personal total abstinence, (ii) long pledge – personal total abstinence and refusal to serve and sell and offer alcohol to others.	Moral suasion.
	(2) Total abstinence through legislative reform – prohibition phase.	Prohibition.
	Ireland	
	(1) Fr Mathew Campaign: total abstinence for the excessive drinker.	Moral suasion.
	(2) Pioneer Total Abstinence Association: total abstinence from all alcohol for the non-drinker/moderate drinker, as a sacrifice, to make reparation to the Sacred Heart for the excessive drinker.	Moral suasion.
4	Total abstinence on dual basis: *England only* Moderationists following tradition of anti-spirits movement, and total abstainers. The emphasis was on (i) total abstinence, (ii) moderate use of beer and wine and total abstinence from all spirits.	Moral suasion.

Table 8   Irish temperance organizations 1817 – 1977

'Moderation' societies:	
1817	Abstinence Society, Skibbereen, Co. Cork
1829	New Ross Temperance Society, Co. Wexford
1829	Ulster Temperance Society
1829	Dublin Temperance Society
	From this date there were over twenty such societies scattered throughout the countryside
Change in perspective to total abstinence:	
1834	Cork Total Abstinence Society
1836	Dublin Total Abstinence Society
1838 to 1856	Fr Mathew Total Abstinence Association Established total abstinence associations all over the country
1838	Dublin Total Abstinence Society, a group independent of Fr Mathew, established by the Dublin Hierarchy under Dr York and Dr Spratt
	Metropolitan Society
1857	Irish Total Abstinence Association
1858	Pledge taken at Sacrament of Confirmation, not to drink until twenty-one years of age
Change in focus and orientation:	
1874	Temperance Movement Association of Prayer
1876	Wexford's Total Abstinence Society – League Fr Cullen
1898	Pioneer League. Branch League of the Sacred Heart (women only)
1899	Pioneer Battalion for Men
1901	Pioneer League of Total Abstinence of the Sacred Heart Association
1972	Renewal and Youth

the ruling class, and were therefore seen with suspicion by both the Catholic Church and the people. There were exceptions to this rule, in Cork City and County, where a number of moderation societies existed, which were run jointly by Catholic and Protestant clergy (Tynan 1908: 139). They had little following but did prepare the way for the Fr Mathew Temperance Campaign. With his campaign the movement took on a completely different perspective.

Explanations as to why a temperance movement, as distinct from attacks on drunkenness, began to appear in the 1820s in England are based on two factors: (1) the social situation; and (2) temperance personalities (Harrison, B. 1971: 87, 106; Ferguson 1975: 66).

The movement appeared independently over the country, promoted by Dr Edgar from Ulster, around 1829-30. It is reported that Dr Edgar launched The Ulster Temperance Society by pouring all the whisky in his house out of the window. It was a movement of its time in that it was only one of several contemporary attempts to emulate middle-class life-styles. The British and Foreign Temperance Society (1831) was founded in the same year as the Lords Day Observance Society. Efforts were being made by the middle class to 'bring up' the respectable working class, and to help them to the good life by encouraging imitation of their own middle-class behavioural patterns in all areas. At this time, co-operatives, friendly societies, and working men's institutions were flourishing.

The movement was also helped by the fact that drunkenness had begun prior to the 1820s. Drunkenness was now seen as a 'vulgar vice'. Leaders, both religious and lay, were campaigning for sobriety in 1820. Alongside the social situation of the time, four distinct influences prepared the ground for the temperance pioneers: (1) doctors; (2) coffee and tea traders; (3) industrialists; and (4) evangelicals.

(1) In both England and Ireland medical awareness of the nature of alcohol and drunkenness and the shedding of the myth that good health was linked with the use of alcohol, were important factors in preparing the ground for teetotalism at that time (Harrison, B. 1967, 1971: 90; Dingle 1972).

(2) In both England and Ireland it was far safer to drink alcohol than water (see *Figure 1*). The sanitary systems had not been developed, nor were there water purification plants. Water needed to be boiled. The introduction of cheap non-intoxicating hot drinks, in the form of coffee and tea was an important influence in the development of the third phase of teetotalism (Hartley 1964; Harrison, B. 1971: 90; Ferguson 1975: 38).

(3) In England industrialization and urbanization increased the need for precision and regularity of work patterns; this made existing levels of drunkenness less tolerable (Thompson 1963: 57).

(4) In England the evangelical tradition had a considerable influence. The early temperance movement was a child of late eighteenth-century humanitarianism. As B. Harrison (1971: 91) relates, the early temperance movement and the humanitarians had the same allies — women, quakers, and evangelicals — and the same enemies — sinners, 'irresponsible drink sellers, and sabbath breakers'.

The London Temperance Society was the first 'moderationist' group to appear in 1830. It changed its name to the British and Foreign Temperance Society in 1831; the anti-spirits movement was now in full swing.

In England, it was one of a number of movements for social reform. In an age of reform, one more crusading spirit was acceptable. It was to make society aware, through the distribution of large quantities of

TO THE CORPORATION OF THE CITY OF LONDON.

GENTLEMEN,

I am very sorry to say my father was a sad drunkard. I don't want to follow in his steps. I often have to be out in London streets during the hot weather. Many a time I have been parched with thirst, and I have panted for a drink. The temptation to go into a public-house has often been strong, but I have thought of what became of my father through going there, and God has helped me to keep *outside*. Scores of times I have caught a few drops from the street watering carts in the top of my leather cap, and have been thankful—even for this. Gentlemen, I hear that in a good many places the Corporations are putting up nice drinking fountains in the streets for folks, and I wish *you* would take pity on thousands of poor lads like myself in London. Do gentlemen! and you shall have the heartfelt thanks of many

A WORKING-MAN'S SON.

Figure 1   'The drunkard's son quenches his thirst.'

Source: *The British Workman*, 1858; cited in Ayles (1976) and reproduced by permission of The Mary Evans Picture Library.

literature and propaganda, that a drink problem existed. It tried to involve all sections of society, including the drink trade, to campaign for a sober society. It was not an extremist movement, and unlike the total abstinence and prohibition phase it had the support of the Church, mainly the Church of England, as well as the aristocracy. However, it failed to understand the nature of the problems posed by industrial and urban society, and was never really concerned with research into the problems of dealing with the broader social questions. It was one of several attempts to encourage the working class to emulate middle-class lifestyles; it encouraged example setting from above rather than self-help from below. It was also based in London, and had little impact in the north of England (Harrison 1971: 87).

The two early phases — (1) the free licensing campaign, and (2) the anti-spirits movement — helped prepare the way for the beginning of the teetotal movement. It is at this point that the English and Irish movements taken on very different forms.

Teetotalism: England

English teetotalism was divided into two phases: (1) total abstinence through moral suasion and (2) total abstinence through legislative reform. This was the prohibition phase.

Total abstinence through moral suasion

By 1829, tracts were appearing advocating the principle of total abstinence (Fryer 1963: 135). Preston in the north of England was the centre of teetotalism. This is where the Preston Seven, led by Joseph Livesay, established the first TT group in England. The early supporters came from the liberal/radical, non-conformist section of society. The teetotal support was in the north of England and its main supporters were dissenters rather than clergymen. Under the influence of the Preston Seven, a well organized system was developed to spread the word. So called 'missionaries' were sent to other areas, regular public meetings were held, as were 'experience' meetings where reformed drunkards told their story. Each town was divided into districts, each under a 'captain'. The pioneers of teetotalism were mostly manual workers, whose way of life and manners were considered coarse and insulting by the anti-spirits people.

The aims of the teetotal movement were different from those of the anti-spirits movement which preceded it. The teetotal movement sought the conversion of the intemperate and the drunkard. Long before

Alcoholics Anonymous or the World Health Organisation were founded, they viewed the drunkard as being a victim of alcohol, a diseased person who deserved sympathy and the right to redeem himself. In its beginnings, the teetotal movement was a scene for social mobility, a way for the respectable working class to parade its virtue. As Harrison comments:

> 'The early teetotal societies like so many non-conformists chapels of the day, were genuine communities, and the teetotalism constituted a form of free masonry among working men. In this way respectability was recruited.   (Harrison, B. 1971: 133)

After several conflicts in 1838 the total abstinence lobby had substantially captured the English temperance movement. It was not long however before divisions arose within the ranks of the total abstinence people themselves over the exact nature of the total abstinence pledge. There was a short pledge and a long pledge. The short pledge entailed total personal abstinence, the long pledge added the extra obligations to refrain from selling, giving, or offering alcohol to others. During the period from 1838 to 1870 various societies came into being, split, and amalgamated. By the end of the nineteenth century there were over seventy organizations all dedicated to the proposition that alcohol was poison (Fryer 1963: 135, 136).

The approach of the teetotal bodies up to 1850 was one of moral suasion, they did not try to force the issue through demands for public legislation. Their efforts were directed mainly towards education and the young. In 1887, The National Temperence Publication Department published a list of temperence works. Their educational approach was somewhat simplistic, using the media of the time, the tract and the pamphlet, to make an appeal to the public. In this way the temperance press won a battle for a free press, and could be seen as part of a general reform movement. When power was very much in the hands of the aristocracy, the reform movement saw itself in a perpetual state of siege and used the press to reach all corners of the country and all social classes (Harrison 1969b: 128, 1973).

By the mid 1870s a number of important changes had occurred in the temperance movement:

1 The Band of Hope was founded to help promote total abstinence in young people. The meetings were well organized and songs were encouraged, especially those condemning the 'demon drink'. For example,

> 'Dump him in the varnish,
> Pop him in the dye;

> Who wants alcoholic drinks
> Not I! Not I! Not I!   (Fryer 1963: 139)

2 The Prohibition phase was started by the United Kingdom Alliance in 1853.
3 The Church of England Temperance Society was established enlisting both moderationists and total abstainers.

With the formation of the United Kingdom Alliance the emphasis was to change to legislative reform. In this way the temperance movement turned to the law as a way of affirming its values.

Prohibition

Antagonism grew up between the prohibitionists and the moral suasionists, and reached its height in the 1860s. Many veterans looked on this new movement with scepticism, especially since the prohibitionists were engaging the help of non-abstainers. The public squabbles which followed had a damaging effect on the movement.

The main supporter of the prohibitionists' cause in Parliament was Sir Wilfred Lawson, called among other things the 'apostle of sops'. Many attempts to bring in prohibition by one means or another failed. The prohibitionists also attached themselves to individuals or political parties if they favoured their approach to a legislative solution to the drink problem. Although the Liberal Party incorporated the direct popular local veto for the use of alcohol in their programme, the prohibitionists never won full political support.

From time to time during the First World War, it looked as if prohibition in England was on the verge of success. The King and Lord Kitchener did not drink for the duration of the war. Lloyd George had declared that drink was doing more damage to the British than all the German submarines put together. 'We are fighting Germany, Austria, and drink and the greatest of these foes is drink' (Longmate 1968: 257).

During the First World War restrictive laws were enacted. Lloyd George introduced the Defence of the Realm Amendment Act in 1915, which was seen as an effective combination of moral suasion and legislation. The new laws led to sharp increases in taxation and shorter opening hours. Supplies of alcohol were limited and the absolute alcohol content of drink on sale was reduced. The success of this legislation indicated that alternative solutions could, in fact, be more effective than the extreme measure of prohibition. The experience of the failure of the American Prohibition Movement in the mid-1920s did little to help the movement in England. Today numbers are small, although local temperance organizations are still active, mainly with objections to licensing applications. Not only has there been a decline in members, but there has been a shift in focus. Efforts to oppose immorality and violence on the screen as well as gambling, are now emphasized; drugs receive a lot of attention. A chastity pledge was also proposed, by which young people would promise to abstain from pre-marital intercourse as well as alcohol (Harrison, B. 1971: 355).

To assess the strength of the temperance movements today is rather difficult. The most active bodies which aim to influence legislation are the United Kingdom Alliance and the National Temperance Federation. In an article in *Alliance News*, Robert Tayler advocated a new Citizens' Pledge which would produce a new kind of citizen, 'pledged not to self seeking and self indulgence, but to self discipline and service'. He notes the decline of the temperance movement:

'Nevertheless, in the last few years the temperance movement has been in decline, and there is no sign of a reversal in this process. It has been found very difficult to replace the full-time temperance advocates who have died or retired.'   Tayler 1973: 15)

Assessment and effects

The temperance movement on the whole had limited success. It had less of an impact on attitudes and behaviour in England than in Ireland. This may be accounted for by the diversification of effort, the numbers involved, and failure sufficiently to involve the institutionalized Church and the country as a whole. The English movement was essentially an urban one, strongest in the north of England where the working-class and non-conforming elements were strongest. Many members were lost because of its evangelical tradition, its hard-line approach, and at a later stage, because of its total inflexibility in political affairs. What Gusfield (1969) said of the Women's Christian Temperance Union in America was true of the prohibition phase, it was a 'symbolic crusade': the law must condemn harmful practices even if it can not prohibit or enforce them. The social situation of the time helped to create and destroy this movement.

As stated above the temperance movement in England appeared when the level of drunkenness was no longer considered acceptable. Drunkenness became unfashionable; because of industrialization and growth in urbanization, drunkenness was seen as dangerous, uneconomic, and socially explosive. The temperance followers failed to realize that drunkenness was a product of the complex interaction of a number of factors. By placing their attention on the 'trade', publicans and public houses, they failed to recognize the extensive role the public house played in the lives of the people. Instead of agitating for better public houses, more legislative control, and the support of the public house owners, they created a rift, and were in many ways responsible for making the public house a place of ill repute. While the temperance movement had a gradualist approach at the beginning, with the anti-spirits movement and the earlier teetotalers, it soon became hard-line, and alienated the aristocracy and the Church (Harrison, B. 1971: 348, 386). The concentration on one vice, drink, and not on others, was in some sense a convenient outlet for moral indignation. Booth (1889-1903) helped show that the temperance reformers' claim that drink was the root of all evil was an exaggerated one. His work clearly indicated that questions of family size, illness, and employment were of more relevance in understanding poverty. He found that only 13 per cent of the poor and 14 per cent of the very poor in his sample owed their position directly to drink. Temperance reformers were guilty of not sponsoring counter-attractions. The movement did provide an alternative lifestyle for the sober with temperance halls, hotels, and excursions; it did nothing for the 'others'. The 'us and them' philosophy was the principle on which the reformers operated and nothing was to change it. Drink was the root of all evil and only through total abstinence, and later through prohibition, would the better life be achieved.

Temperance movement growth in England affected change in many other ways, unintentional though this may have been. While it did bring public attention to the unacceptable level of drunkenness, it also brought about a change of attitude toward the 'drunkard' from one of rejection to compassion. On a broader level it raised the dignity of all human beings, and was instrumental in making the point that the humblest human being was worthy of consideration (Harrison, B. 1971: 348). It was a continuous thorn in the side of *laissez-faire* philosophy, and through its criticism brought the public's attention to this philosophy or way of life. In a society rigidly defined by the class system, it was one of many reform movements which helped create a more equitable social order. Instilling guilt in the aristocratic minority was the way to achieve this, rather than through the angry revolution of the oppressed majority.

Movements like the temperance movement in England, by creating small scale success systems, brought the working and middle classes together and enabled the underprivileged to adapt to their situation (Harrison, B. 1971). In this way English society was kept from splitting apart. It also created a sense of belonging and of solidarity among the members of the working class. Furthermore it helped to promote an elite of respectable working class, and gave a status to those who wanted it. Between 1830 and 1870, it was essentially a working-class, non-conformist movement. It thrived on the cult of respectability and self-reliance which was the ideal for many aspirant working-class people (Harrison 1968: 287, 1973: 178; Thale 1972). In one area its contribution was unique, the area of dietary reform. By concentrating on the dietary habits of the poor and the underprivileged, it helped to develop the flexibility in personal habits required by a rapidly changing society. It also helped bring about a free press, which could give support to the efforts of the working-class movement to form a lobby against the wealthy and aristocratic (Harrison 1969b: 127).

Other factors were also at work. As noted above, the 'counter-attraction development' took place. The improved living conditions, the change in lifestyle from a rural to an urban situation, the provision of public libraries, the parks, music halls, restaurants, and football clubs, were all alternatives to the public house (Malcolmson 1973). The improved affluence channelled off a great part of the population into football stadiums, theatres, and later, cinemas. The war-time legislation DORA in 1915, and other legislative control did help to bring about a change in consumption patterns. The most statistically verifiable reduction in the level of drinking occurred after the changes of the First World War. What is interesting is that temperance education was not established in England after the nineteenth century as it was in Ireland, with the introduction of the Confirmation Pledge. Abstinence as a value did not become institutionalized in English society and does not form part of the traditions and customs associated with drinking.

Teetotalism: Ireland

The Irish teetotalism phase was divided into two parts: (1) the Father Mathew Campaign and (2) the Pioneer Total Abstinence Movement.

The Father Mathew Campaign

The Father Mathew Campaign must be seen in the light of its leader. It was a charismatic movement in the classic Weberian sense, of the supernatural endowment of the leader; he was seen as having a divine gift of healing (Tynan 1908). It was also an ecumenical movement centred essentially on the lower classes, and 'native' Irish, and was aimed at changing drinking habits by a concentrated appeal to the excessive drinker to give up alcohol (Tackerary 1843: 115; Birmingham 1840: 42). When Fr Mathew OFM signed the pledge, something akin to temperance mania swept Cork (McKenna 1924: 301; Longmate 1968: 114). His movement, while being apolitical, helped to bring the people together, to unite them, and give the Irish a group consciousness, as had Daniel

O'Connell's Liberation Movement. Both men were leaders who believed that their cause would raise the people to the higher levels of respectability.

O'Connell did become a total abstainer himself but had to give up the pledge on doctor's orders. O'Connell addressed several marches in which temperance groups participated, although Fr Mathew forbade his members to take part. No drink was allowed at political meetings and at the Tara Monster Meeting over half a million people swore themselves to temperance (Longmate 1968: 114). The English parliament in 1840 saw the movement as a good thing as 'it improved the habits of the people and the diminution of outrages', and Fr Mathew's close co-operation with non-conformist teetotalers moderated anti-Catholic feeling among English Protestants at the time (Longmate 1968).

At the height of his campaign, Fr Mathew is credited with administering more than two million pledges to nearly a quarter of the population. Consumption of spirits fell as did the revenue from alcohol.

However, the movement failed for several reasons. It was a charismatic movement and after Fr Mathew's death in 1856 no one attempted to take it over. There was a complete lack of organization so that no structures existed within which to carry on the work. The movement had begun to wane around 1842 (Burns 1881: 241). Fr Mathew's charisma was wearing thin, his health failing, and some employers refused to employ pledge holders. Fr Mathew's lack of financial expertise meant that the movement was in dire financial trouble. The famine dealt it a severe blow, and famine relief works were set up in public houses, a somewhat ironic touch. Perhaps one of the main reasons for failure was that the movement was not linked directly to the Catholic Church. Few of its members were priests and the inclusion of all religious groups created a certain hostility. Of great importance, however, was the combination of Fr Mathew's failing health and his excursions out of the country. These two things left his group at home in total disarray.

Others factors were at work; Lecky (1896) reports that the work carried out by Fr Mathew was undermined by the constant political agitation and the increase of grocers' spirit licences. The sale of alcohol in the country shops intensified drinking, as it was 'for consumption on the premises', '… the demoralising effects of which are a hundredfold greater than those of the "grocers licences" which temperance reformers so strenuously denounce' (Lecky 1896: 32).

The Father Mathew Campaign did try to provide alternatives for the public, a token attempt in the provision of reading rooms, which were open to all. At the heights of his campaign, Fr Mathew certainly had an impact on the drinking habits of the people. At the end, however, little remained of his former work (Maguire 1865; Mathew 1890).

In Dublin, Dr Spratt had kept the temperance movement going at its former strength. He gave new life to the old Dublin Total Abstinence Society of 1836. This branch of the Irish Total Abstinence Association was to introduce coffee houses in Dublin. The Society was attached to several churches in the Dublin area and had quite good support (Rogers 1943: 116; McKenna 1924: 306). Pledges were given to children from the churches.

The movement lingered on, but the Catholic Church soon began to take a more active interest in temperance. In 1878, a bill was passed to introduce Sunday closing, which owed much to the Catholic Church's intervention. This had been introduced previously to Wexford in 1858 by Dr Furlong, who established Sunday and holy day closing of public houses throughout his diocese, and transferred public fairs and markets from holy days to week days. Dr Furlong also introduced the Confirmation Pledge, a pledge to abstain from taking a drink until the age of twenty-one years. This was taken at the Catholic confirmation ceremony. Dr Leahy, Archbishop of Cashel and Emly, also succeeded in having public houses closed in his diocese on holy days. He administered three year pledges; a pledge of total abstinence was given only to 'confirmed drunkards'. Further evidence of the Church's involvement was the institution of the National Crusade against Intemperance in 1905 (McKenna 1924: 307).

Pioneer Total Abstinence Association

The next phase of the total abstinence movement in Ireland was to begin in 1889, led by a Jesuit priest Fr J. Cullen. With it, the focus of the temperance movement in Ireland changed. While Fr Mathew concentrated on the excessive drinker, Fr Cullen took into his ranks, after a well-defined trial period, moderate drinkers, or people who never drank, who would give up the use of alcohol as a sacrifice to the Sacred Heart to make reparation for the sins of intemperance (McKenna 1924). If Fr Mathew was a charismatic figure, Fr Cullen was a bureaucratic one. The development and organization of the Pioneer Total Abstinence Association was well thought out and extremely well structured. The process of becoming a member was one in which the individual passed through a *rite de passage* after a probationary period. This being successful, membership of the group was for life.

Fr Cullen's work for temperance reflected in part the attitudes of his fellow priests. At first he administered pledges for 'not getting drunk' but no total abstinence pledges. However, in 1874 he pledged himself not to drink for life, and so began his mission of temperance. In its aspirations, values, and structures, it was deeply imbedded in the

Catholic Church. Unlike Fr Mathew's movement, Fr Cullen's work was ratified by the Church, and was finally to change the attitude of the clergy from one of apathy to commitment to total abstinence. Fr Cullen moved very slowly when organizing the new temperance movement. He was concerned that it should be successful and avoid the failings attributed to the Father Mathew Campaign. The 'societies' were well-structured with a hierarchy established in each group. The meetings were essentially religious in perspective and were on the whole organized by the clergy.

Fr Cullen's main influence was achieved by utilizing the power of the Church's institutions, such as ecclesiastical colleges and convents, to spread the message to young people. To the adults, his message was again passed through the local clergy (McKenna 1924: 123, 318). He also used church magazines to promote the ideals of his work, first of all in *The Messenger*, and later with a column in the *Irish Catholic*. After his death, the *Pioneer Magazine* was launched. Despite Fr Cullen's many visits outside the country, the movement went from strength to strength. It succeeded in turning the emblems of membership into symbols of honesty and integrity.

Unlike Fr Mathew, Fr Cullen used the political life of the people as a spur to changing their drinking habits. Drink was seen as the main enemy of the people and the reason for losing encounters with the British. His appeal was to the working class and was always sympathetic to their struggle against political or social oppression.

Fr Cullen welcomed legislation to combat the evil of drink, but never forced the issue; his method was one of moral suasion. He denounced the practice of doctors using alcohol for medicinal purposes, and of priests who used alcohol even in a moderate way. His organization was so thorough that if anyone fell away, he sent some of his followers along to encourage the 'weaky wobblers' to reconsider. If a 'society' was failing, his answer was to cut it off, as he felt it was not desirable to support it.

He concentrated on the young and wrote a *Temperance Catechism* in 1891 well before his work was fully underway. It did not get the approval of the Board of National Education because of its specific religious character. It was, however, well received, and was used in religious knowledge classes in several dioceses as well as in training colleges. It was finally approved by the Education Board in 1907 (McKenna 1924). Fr Cullen considered that the environmental conditions contributed significantly to intemperance and were a constant source of bad examples for children. With this in mind, the Juvenile Total Abstinence League of the Sacred Heart was established.

Fr Cullen's interest in developing the poorer classes' level of entertainment, led him to build the Pioneer Hall in Dublin in 1907. From his days as a curate he felt that the people had an '...inability to provide themselves with recreations and interests of a higher type than those to be found in public houses, and dancing saloons and at street corners' (McKenna 1924: 356). He wanted to foster their Gaelic culture and way of life. The Hall was only open to members of the Pioneer Club. There were a variety of clubs and societies, as well as reading and library rooms attached to the premises.

Fr Cullen was also involved in other works to encourage the spiritual education of the people. A list will give an idea of the scope and range of activities, all essentially religious in nature, but considered as ways of solving the drink problem. The works included the League of Daily Mass, League of the Holy Souls, Apostleship of Prayer, Apostleship of Cleanliness and Home Comfort, Apostleship of Study, Apostleship of Catholic Literature, Apostleship of Modesty in Dress, and League against Gambling. Fr Cullen was also involved in the work of a night shelter and a sailors' home, as well as a hostel for Roman Catholic female ex-prisoners (McKenna 1924: 363).

The Pioneer Total Abstinence Association grew and developed into a national organization. The movement was credited with 450,000 members in 1955 (Percevel 1955: 146). Today in Ireland there are over 2,000 branches of the Association and the membership runs into hundreds of thousands.*

Although the strength of the temperance movement has dwindled substantially from its earlier position, it has nevertheless had continuing importance for the growing ambivalence in attitudes to drinking. It is true to say that there has been a change of emphasis in the Pioneer Movement in the late 1960s, as can be seen from the following:

'One of the works of the Pioneer Association to-day is to promote a sense of responsibility as regards the use of alcohol. In 1970, a delegation from the Pioneer Assoication met the Minister for Education and urged the need for a policy of education as regards intoxicating drink. Young people must be helped to make right and responsible decisions about alcohol, its use, abuse, abstinence.'

(Personal communication)

The position as regards the Confirmation Pledge is also under review:

'At present, there is much re-thinking on the value of the Confirmation Pledge. In some dioceses (Armagh and Kerry) it has been discontinued. The problem, which has not yet been solved is to replace the

*Fr Dargan, S.J., Director, Pioneer Movement. Personal communication to the author.

Confirmation Pledge with something more effective and meaning-
ful.'   (ibid.)

And in 1972 a new branch of the movement was formed, Renewal and
Youth, aimed specifically at young people. Among its aims is the
development of responsible attitudes to drinking.

Historically, drink has been used freely in Ireland and to excess in
some cases, as is witnessed by the various commentators quoted above.
On the other hand, the emergence of the temperance movement and
specifically the Pioneer Total Abstinence Association has given rise to
two conflicting value systems operating in the culture. The result is a
culture which may be defined as ambivalent, in terms of the classification
of attitudes to drinking discussed in Chapter 1.

Assessments and effects

The Pioneer Movement was one of reform, the method was moral
suasion. It was essentially Catholic in perspective. The movement hoped
to change the lower classes' drinking habits not by the usual method of
concentrating on the excessive drinker, but by focusing on the person
who had no problem. The values of religion, sacrifice, and love of the
Sacred Heart were of utmost importance. In this way it was a specifically
religious contribution towards a solution. It was a form of Catholic
asceticism, otherworldly in its aims, and was confined to a spiritual elite.

Through these channels, excessive drinking could be stopped, and
reparation made for the excessive drinker. The movement was to help
institutionalize the value of abstinence in Irish culture. It linked religion,
sacrifice, and patriotism with abstinence, an ethic which was embodied in
the Pioneer Member and symbolized by the Pioneer Pin. It gave the
individual respectability, honesty, and integrity, and placed him in
society. The influence of the movement was pervasive. The temperance
movement in Ireland did affect drinking patterns, both behaviour and
attitudes. Its most profound effect was on attitudes towards drinking and
brought about a change in a cultural pattern where drinking was over-
permissive and part of the way of life. It replaced a drink-centred way of
life with a lifestyle which frowned on drink. The movement cannot be
credited with all the changes, but it was instrumental in bringing about a
change in cultural attitude — from an over-permissive attitude to drink to
an ambivalent one. Economic expansion came much later to Ireland
than to England, and when it did it offered counter-attractions to the
public houses. The change from a traditional type society to a society in
transition in the mid-1960s meant the adoption of a new lifestyle where
drink still played an important, though less dominant, part.

The Pioneer Total Abstinence Association failed to understand the system that produced excessive drinking. It never associated itself directly with the unsober, and its focus was on the sober; it was essentially a movement of abstainers, making a sacrifice and reparation for the excessive drinker. This position has changed slightly in that the organization does recognize alcoholism as a disease and works with Alcoholics Anonymous in their public meetings to promote the ideals of the organization.* While the movement's aims and goals have remained the same through to the present day, membership has fallen, and much of its influence has waned. However, recent studies have shown that abstinence is still very much part of the Irish drinking scene (Fitzpatrick 1972: 51; Brody 1973: 173), and appears to be an integral part of the traditions and customs associated with drinking.

The English and Irish temperance movements have been presented as norm-oriented movements, which had an impact not only on drinking habits, but also on the way people's attitudes to alcohol developed. It has been shown that the Irish movement was essentially a religious-oriented movement; it did affect attitudes to alcohol, helping create an ambivalent cultural attitude to drinking in Irish society. The English movement on the other hand did not do this, rather it was one of many factors helping to bring about sobriety.

*Minutes of Pioneer Association Central Council Meeting, March 22nd, 1970.

5

The young drinkers: prevalence
and extent of drinking behaviour

Many attempts have been made to account for differences in drinking behaviour among a wide array of cultural groups. The main focus of these studies has been a cultural one, stressing socialization into drinking patterns, the structure of social norms, and the prevalence of problem drinking among such groups as the Irish (Bales 1962; O'Connor 1975), French (Sadoun, Lolli, and Silverman 1965), Jews (Bales 1946; Glad, 1947-8; Snyder 1958, 1962), Italians (Lolli *et al.* 1957), and Chinese (Singer 1974). This literature stresses the social meaning and social function of drinking and drunkenness, and describes how different patterns of alcohol use have emerged in different societies.

Chapter 1 discussed the fact that theories and images of Irish drinking in Ireland and in England maintain that the Irish drink excessively, although explanations of this phenomenon differ. Despite this general agreement that the Irish drink a lot and get into trouble frequently as a result, some commentators question whether Irish drinking involves high levels of alcoholism. Many of the studies undertaken in this area are based on tenuous assumptions and on theories that have never been tested. A major reason for all this has been the way of gathering data, and the fact that little or no research has been carried out on the Irish in Ireland, or the Irish in England. Little effort has been devoted to the task of establishing quantifiable measures of alcohol consumption, or of measuring actual drinking patterns as opposed to the accumulation of statistics on the various indexes of alcoholism. Similar comments can be made about English drinking practices. The image of the English drinker and the statistics of various indicators of drink-related problems differ.

The main concern of this chapter is to describe the introduction to the use of alcohol and the extent and prevalence of present-day drinking.

Introduction to the use of alcohol

In both Irish and English societies children are normally expected to be abstinent. This is especially true of Irish young people, as abstinence from alcohol is part of the drinking tradition and is an institutionalized value in the society (O'Connor 1974).

It is the purpose of this section to focus attention on when, how, why, and where the abstinence of childhood was transformed into the drinking behaviour that is part of the lifestyle of Irish and English adults. The when and how of this transition is of interest to all those concerned with the use or non-use of alcohol in a particular culture. Besides the intrinsic interest in the circumstances of the first drink it reveals the nature of the socialization context in which drinking is learned. As Jessor, Collins, and Jessor comment, '... the most important issue to account for ... is not the occurrence — non-occurrence of the behaviour but rather the differential time of its occurrence or age of its onset' (Jessor *et al.* 1972: 199). By looking at the way a person is introduced to alcohol, one can learn about the cultural setting and the values and norms that are seen to be associated with it.

Becoming a drinker

The importance of abstinence in Irish culture was indicated by the fact that eight out of ten Irish males and nine out of ten Irish females took a pledge not to drink when they were ten to twelve years old. This held for seven out of ten Anglo-Irish males and females, who also took a pledge not to drink until they were twenty-one years of age. None of the English males and females took a pledge at this time.*

Age at first drink: 18-21 year olds

Nearly all the young people remembered the age at which they started to drink. *Figure 2* gives a more general picture of the 18-21 year olds' age at

---

*Reference will not be made explicitly to sampling error when reporting the data, but standard error of group differences should be kept in mind when reading the results, particularly when comparisons are made between the groups. Similarly, reference is not made continuously to tests of significance of difference between the data relating to the Irish, Anglo-Irish, and English young people and parents. Only differences which are significant are referred to in comparative analysis, with very occasional exceptions, which are identified as not being significant. All differences mentioned are significant at the 0.05 probability level. Tables not presented in the main text are given in Appendix 1.

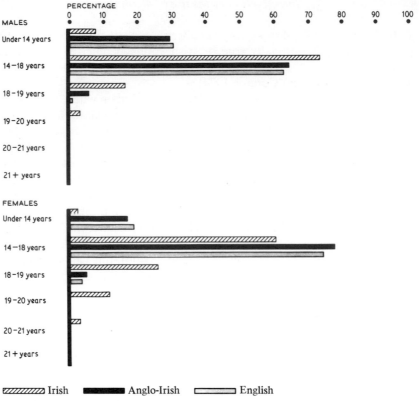

PERCENTAGE

Irish   Anglo-Irish   English

This convention will be observed throughout for the three ethnic groups.

Figure 2   18-21 year olds' age at first drink* (Q.26a)
*Based on number of respondents who have ever taken a drink.
Males   N: Irish = 174, Anglo-Irish = 92, English = 119
Females N: Irish = 151, Anglo-Irish = 85, English = 97

first drink. For the Irish group the introduction to the use of alcohol came much later than for the Anglo-Irish or English young people. Over half of the Anglo-Irish (53.3)* and English (54.7) males had taken their first drink before their fifteenth birthday, the corresponding figure for the Irish males was 16.7 per cent. By sixteen years of age over four-fifths of both Anglo-Irish and English males compared with nearly three-fifths of Irish males had taken their first drink. Differences between the groups at age of first drink was also found among the females. Over half of the English and two-thirds of the Anglo-Irish females, compared with

*The numbers in brackets refer to percentages throughout.

one-tenth of Irish females, had started to drink before their sixteenth birthday. At sixteen years of age four-fifths of the Anglo-Irish and English females, compared with three-tenths of the Irish females, were taking a drink. By eighteen years of age it was unusual for any male or female not to drink with the exception of the Irish females.

Age at first drink: parents

Eight out of ten Irish fathers and nine out of ten Irish mothers had taken the Confirmation Pledge (a pledge not to drink until they were twenty-one years of age) while at school. This applied to seven out of ten Anglo-Irish fathers and mothers. One-tenth of Irish fathers, and one-fifth of Irish mothers never took a drink. This applied to 1 per cent of the Anglo-Irish and English fathers and under 10 per cent of the Anglo-Irish and English mothers. Only one English mother took a pledge not to drink while at school, showing that abstinence played a very small part in the traditions associated with drinking for this group of English parents. That children appear to be drinking at an earlier age than their parents is shown when we examine parents' age at first drink. Here again differences emerged.

Anglo-Irish parents like English parents had their first drink much earlier than Irish parents. This may be accounted for by the fact that nearly all of these Anglo-Irish parents came to England at fifteen years of age or over, where the overall cultural attitude to drink was favourable and they were free from cultural and social constraints not to drink. Two-fifths of the Anglo Irish and English (37.6) fathers, compared with one-fifth of Irish fathers, had their first drink between fifteen and eighteen years of age. By the age of twenty-one to twenty-five, over four-fifths of the Anglo-Irish fathers and nine-tenths of the English fathers, compared with seven-tenths of the Irish fathers, had started to drink. Irish and Anglo-Irish mothers started to drink at a later age than English mothers. Two-fifths of the English mothers, compared with less than one-tenth of the Irish (4.2) and Anglo-Irish (7.4) mothers had their first drink between fifteen and eighteen years of age. By the age of eighteen to twenty-one, four-fifths of English mothers, compared with two-fifths of the Anglo-Irish and less than one-fifth of the Irish mothers, had started to drink. The difference in ages at which they started to drink was highlighted when we examined the percentage of mothers who first started to drink at twenty-five years and over. Two-fifths of the Irish mothers, compared with one-fifth of the Anglo-Irish and less than one-twentieth of the English mothers, started to drink at this age.

Type and amount of drink taken on first drinking occasion:
18-21 year olds

Approximately half of the Irish males and females did not like their first taste of alcohol. English and Anglo-Irish males and females were rather undecided about it in that they either found it pleasant or were uncommitted about it. Three-tenths of the English males and half of the English females said they found it pleasant. This applied to approximately half of both Anglo-Irish males and females. Approximately one quarter of the Irish males and females said that their first taste of alcohol was pleasant. A further one-fifth of both males and females said that it was neither pleasant nor unpleasant. The type and amount of drink taken on the first drinking occasion was shown to vary by sex and by ethnic status.

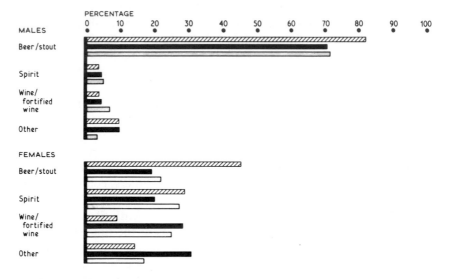

Figure 3   Type of alcoholic beverage first taken* (Q.26e)
  *Based on the replies of respondents who had ever taken a drink.
  Males   N: Irish = 174, Anglo-Irish = 92, English = 119
  Females N: Irish = 151, Anglo-Irish = 85, English =   97

As can be seen in *Figure 3* on the first drinking occasion beer/stout was the most popular drink for the males. More of the Irish males (82.1) and females (45.1) drank beer/stout than the Anglo-Irish (males 70.7, females 18.8) and English (males 71.4, females 21.6) young people. Females in all groups had a more varied choice of first drink than the males. Females' first preference was beer, spirits, wine/fortified wine, or cider. More of the English and Anglo-Irish than Irish females drank wine/fortified wine (English 24.8, Anglo-Irish 28.2, Irish 8.6) or cider and babycham (English 15.5, Anglo-Irish 28.3, Irish 12.6) on this occasion. The amount of alcohol taken on this first drinking occasion tended to be smaller for the females than for the males in all groups. More Irish males (70.6) than Anglo-Irish (58.1) or English males (36.9) drank one pint or more of beer/stout. Over one-third of the Irish females and two-fifths of the Anglo-Irish females drank one pint or more of beer. This applied to one quarter of the English females.

Company and location on first drinking experience

The social context of the first drink experience differed for the Irish males and females on the one hand, and for the Anglo-Irish and English males and females on the other. Three-quarters of the Irish males (75.3) and females (73.0) were in the company of friends, with less than one-fifth with parents, family, or relatives. The first drink for Irish young people took place either in a pub (males 56.3, females 44.4), at home (males 12.6, females 11.3), or on a special occasion (males 19.4, females 33.8). Half of the Anglo-Irish and English males were with friends on the occasion of their first drink, a third were with their parents or family. Over half of the English and three-tenths of the Anglo-Irish females were at home or with relatives, with a further two-fifths of the English and half of the Anglo-Irish females in the company of friends. The location of the first drink for the Anglo-Irish and English males was either in a pub (Anglo-Irish 44.6, English 38.7), at home (Anglo-Irish 26.1, English 21.8), or at a party, wedding, or dress dance (Anglo-Irish 18.5, English 16.0). The location in order of rank for the Anglo-Irish females was on a special occasion, at a party, wedding, or dress dance (37.7), at a pub (24.7), and at home (21.2). For the English females it was at home (30.9), on a special occasion (30.8), and in a pub (22.7).

Reasons for taking first drink

The reasons given for starting to drink centred around three themes: (1) anticipatory socialization, (2) celebration, (3) social pressure. A sizeable percentage in all groups gave other miscellaneous reasons for taking their first drink, which could not be categorized. More of the Irish (males 71.2, females 58.3) than Anglo-Irish (males 36.0, females 32.9) or English (males 30.2, females 28.3) drank in anticipation of adulthood. English (males 26.1, females 41.4) and Anglo-Irish (males 23.9, females 36.5) young people, particularly the females, first drank to celebrate on a special occasion; the corresponding figures for the Irish were 8.0 per cent of males and 14.0 per cent of females having their first drink at a celebration or special occasion.

Parental knowledge of first drink

More of the Irish males (46.5) and females (35.1) than the Anglo-Irish (males 30.5, females 17.6) and English males (13.5) and females (10.4) said that their parents did not know about their first drink until six months or more had elapsed. Twelve per cent of the Irish males and 40 per cent of the Irish females, said that their parents did not know, at the time of the study, that they took a drink. This applied to approximately 2 per cent of all the other young people. A quarter of the Irish males and females, compared with less than one-tenth of the Anglo-Irish and English males and females said that they felt a little or pretty guilty about taking their first drink. A third of the Irish males and females and over one-fifth of Anglo-Irish males, compared with under one-tenth of the Anglo-Irish females and English males and females, felt a little or very worried, or apprehensive, about getting caught after having their first drink.

We have seen that the manner in which these young people were introduced to the use of alcohol gave us some understanding of the way in which drinking was learned in each culture. For the Irish group the introduction to the use of alcohol came much later than for the Anglo-Irish or English young people. The modal age of first drink was sixteen for Irish males and fourteen years of age for both Anglo-Irish and English males. The modal age for Irish females was seventeen years, fifteen for Anglo-Irish females, and sixteen for English females. By eighteen years of age it was unusual for any male or female not to drink with the exception of the Irish females. While most of the Irish males and females were not guilty or apprehensive about taking their first drink, sizeable percentages were. Parental lack of awareness of their children's first use of alcohol seems to suggest that Irish young people had to make their own rules in relation to drinking. The only direct guide to the use of alcohol would appear to be the taking of the Confirmation Pledge, a pledge not to drink until they were twenty-one years of age. This general ambivalent cultural attitude to the use of alcohol noted previously seemed to make the introduction to alcohol an activity centred away from parents but within the context of friends. Friends could be considered to have provided support for an activity that was seen as an anticipation of adult-type behaviour.

On the other hand, for English and Anglo-Irish young people, the experience was one of which their parents were aware. The introduction appeared to be both open and sanctioned. From fourteen years of age onwards, Anglo-Irish and English young people were more likely to be with friends and as they got nearer to sixteen years of age, to have their first drink in a public house. Reasons for starting to drink were centred on social pressure and celebration, very few felt guilty or apprehensive about it.

Prevalence and extent of drinking

Young people learn to drink in a society in which adults in general and parents in particular are seen to drink. Irish young people learned to drink in a culture which appeared to be somewhat ambivalent towards alcohol. English and Anglo-Irish young people were introduced to alcohol in a society that appeared to have no ambivalence towards the use of alcohol. This study showed that fewer of the Irish people interviewed drank compared with Anglo-Irish and English people. As *Figure 4* shows, at the time of interview nearly all Anglo-Irish (95.5) and English (94.4) fathers drank compared with 84.7 per cent of Irish fathers. Over 15 per cent of Irish fathers were non-drinkers.

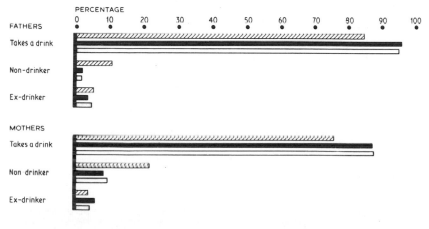

Figure 4   Whether respondent takes a drink at time of interview (Q.11b)
         Fathers N: Irish = 301, Anglo-Irish = 134, English = 178
         Mothers N: Irish = 354, Anglo-Irish = 176, English = 217

A similar pattern was found for the mothers. Over four-fifths of Anglo-Irish (86.9) and English (87.1) mothers compared with three-quarters of Irish mothers drank at the time of interview. A quarter of Irish mothers were non-drinkers at the time of interview. A similar pattern was found for their children. As is shown in *Figure 5* fewer Irish males and females drank compared with Anglo-Irish and English young people. Nine out of ten Anglo-Irish and English drank compared with eight out of ten Irish males and seven out of ten Irish females. Over a quarter of Irish females and one-tenth Irish males compared with less than one-twentieth of either Anglo-Irish or English young people were non-drinkers.

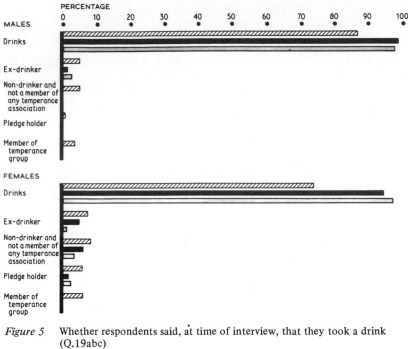

Figure 5   Whether respondents said, at time of interview, that they took a drink
(Q.19abc)
Males   N: Irish = 190, Anglo-Irish = 93, English = 119
Females N: Irish = 187, Anglo-Irish = 86, English = 99

Extent of drinking

Parents and young people's drinking was measured by a 'type of drinker' index. As *Table 9* shows this is a five point drinking index which distinguishes between different types of drinkers. It indicates also how much one needs to consume as well as the way one needs to drink to be classified on the type of drinker index. Using the index, more Anglo-Irish fathers (35.8) than Irish fathers (25.2) or English fathers (18.5) were classified as very heavy type drinkers (*Figure 6*). Differences between the Irish and English fathers were not significant and could be accounted for by sampling error. Over one-fifth of Anglo-Irish and Irish fathers and less than one-tenth English fathers (6.6) drank the equivalent on average of five pints (4.46 pints) of beer per day. If the very heavy and heavy drinking categories are grouped, over half of the Anglo-Irish (56.7), two fifths of the Irish (43.5), and a third of the English (37.6) fathers were in

Table 9   Type of drinker index[1]
(Q.22§, Q.24§, parents, Qs.17, 18, 19, 20, 23, 33)
(Q.50§, Q.53§, 18-21 year olds, Qs.42, 43, 51, 54, 59a)

Abstainers and virtual abstainers	People who do not drink; people who drink less than once a month but more than once a year, and when they do drink, drink less than 1 to 2 drinks at a sitting.
Light drinker	Usually drinks 1 to 2 drinks at a sitting, never 3 to 4 drinks, and drinks up to 20 fluid ounces of absolute alcohol per month, which is equivalent to 25 pints of beer per month.
Moderate drinker	Usually drinks 3 to 4 drinks at a sitting, never 5 to 6 drinks and drinks up to 10 to 60 fluid ounces of absolute alchohol per month, which is equivalent to 12.5-75 pints of beer per month.
Heavy drinker	Usually drinks 5 to 6 drinks at least once in a while[2] and always 3 to 4 drinks at a sitting, and drinks up to 20 to 60 fluid ounces of absolute alcohol per month, which is equivalent to 25-75 pints of beer per month.
Very heavy drinker	Usually drinks 5 to 6 drinks at least once in a while and always 3 to 4 drinks at a sitting, and drinks up to 60 to 200+ fluid ounces of absolute alcohol per month, which is equivalent to 75 to 250+ pints of beer per month.

[1]Type of drinker index: it takes into account the *amount* of alcohol consumed, the *frequency* of drinking and the *variability* of drinking, i.e. whether one drinks one, two drinks, three or four drinks, or five or six drinks at one sitting. Amount, frequency and variability of drinking were analyzed with other factors and out of this analysis the 'drinking index' was devised. (*See* Appendix 6 for details; *see* also *Table A.1.17*)

[2] See *Table A.1.17*.

these two categories. Mothers drank less in all groups. Irish mothers drank the least, as over half of them compared with two-fifths of the English mothers and one-third of the Anglo-Irish mothers were classified as abstainers or virtual abstainers. More of the Anglo-Irish (18.8) than English (12.0) and Irish (5.6) mothers were classified as heavy type drinkers. Approximately 1 per cent of all mothers who drank, drank the equivalent of five pints (4.46 pints) of beer per day.

The study supports the image of the Irishman in England as a heavy type drinker. However, while more Irish fathers than English fathers were classified as heavy or very heavy drinkers, the differences between these two groups could be accounted for by sampling error. The results also show that less Irish people drank than either the Anglo-Irish or the English. Irish mothers were much less likely to take a drink than were either the Anglo-Irish or English mothers.

Differences found between the groups might be expected to persist from one generation to the next if ethnicity is a major factor. The results showed that this was not the case. *Figure 7* shows that one-third of Irish

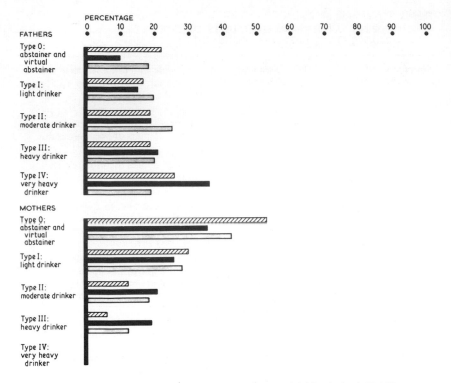

Figure 6   Respondents' type of drinker as classified on drinking index* (Q.22§, Q.24§)
*Based on modified form of the volume variability index and absolute alcohol content index
Fathers N: Irish = 301, Anglo-Irish = 134, English = 178
Mothers N: Irish = 354, Anglo-Irish = 176, English = 217

males were classified as very heavy type drinkers compared with nearly three-fifths of Anglo-Irish males (57.0) and just over two-fifths of English males. Twenty-five per cent of the Anglo-Irish males, 18 per cent of the English males, and 14.2 per cent of the Irish males drank an average of five pints (4.46 pints) of beer per day. Differences were small and could be accounted for by sampling error. Taking the two heavy drinking categories together over four-fifths of Anglo-Irish males, compared with seven-tenths of English males and two-thirds of Irish males were classified as heavy and very heavy type drinkers. Irish females also drank the least, with one-fifth categorized as heavy type drinkers, compared with over a quarter of English females (28.3) and over half the Anglo-Irish females (52.0). Just over 5.8 per cent of Anglo-Irish females and 1 per cent of English females drank the equivalent of five pints (4.46

pints) of beer per day. A small percentage of all females were very heavy type drinkers, more of the Anglo-Irish (9.3) than English (5.1) or Irish (2.6) females were classified as very heavy type drinkers. The differences between the English and Irish, and English and Anglo-Irish are small and could be accounted for by sampling error.

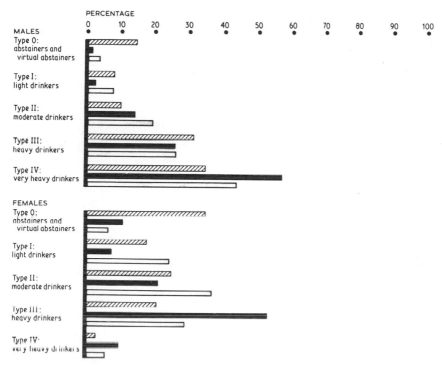

Figure 7   Respondents' type of drinker as classified on type of drinker index
(Q.50a§, Q.53§)
Males   N: Irish = 190, Anglo-Irish = 93, English = 119
Females N: Irish = 187, Anglo-Irish = 86, English = 99

Contrary to what had been accepted this study found that of all the groups, fewer Irish drank compared with the Anglo-Irish and English. There was a much higher proportion of abstainers among the Irish than among the English under study. In relation to the amount of alcohol consumed, the Anglo-Irish were the heaviest types of drinkers. This held true for fathers, mothers, and young people. Nearly all English parents and young people drank, with most fathers and mothers being classified as lighter type drinkers. However, English young people, particularly males, were classified as heavy or very heavy drinkers. Less Irish parents and young people took a drink compared with the other groups. While Irish fathers tended to be heavy or very heavy type drinkers, mothers were classified as abstainers, virtual abstainers, and light drinkers. Of all the young people in the study, Irish males and females were the least heavy type of drinkers.

6

Customs and patterns of drinking
and the social meaning
and function of alcohol

This chapter looks at how drinking is integrated into the lifestyle of the young people under study. It also looks at patterns of drinking, with whom, where, why, and what young people drink. The chapter concludes with a descriptive analysis of the social meaning and function of alcohol, among the Irish, Anglo-Irish, and English young people interviewed.

Present-day customs and patterns of drinking

Drinking and recreational activities

The young people had a very varied recreational pattern, of which drinking formed an integral part. The extent and range of activities varied with sex and ethnic group. More of the Anglo-Irish (97.8) and English (89.1) than Irish (80.5) males drank once a month or more with friends, and drank specifically with male friends once a month or more (English 96.8, Anglo Irish 94.1, Irish 81.6). When going out with friends, the usual recreational activity was drinking for three-quarters of the Anglo-Irish males, compared with two-thirds of the English males, and nearly three-fifths of the Irish males (54.8).

More Anglo-Irish (47.3) males than English (24.4) and Irish (21.1) drank with their parents once a month or more. Females' recreational activities were also very varied, going out drinking with friends being a monthly activity for over four-fifths of all the Anglo-Irish and English females and two-thirds of the Irish females. Over two-thirds of the Anglo-Irish, three-fifths of the English females, and just under half of the Irish females drank with their girl-friends once a month or more. When going out with friends, the usual recreational activity was drinking for over half of the Anglo-Irish and two-fifths of the English females (45.4), compared with less than three-tenths of the Irish females. Drinking with parents was a regular activity once a month or more for three-tenths of the Anglo-Irish and English (30.3), compared with over one-tenth of the Irish (15.5) females.

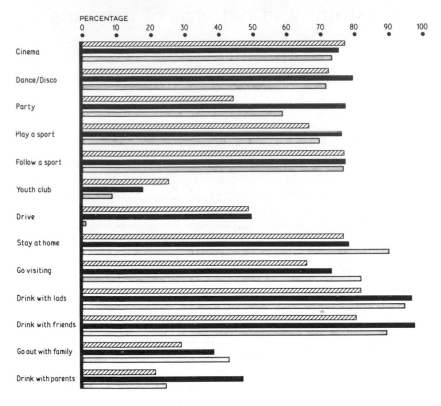

Figure 8   General profile of respondents' recreational activities once a month or more: Males (Q.2§)
N: Irish 190, Anglo-Irish = 93, English = 119

Weekly expenditure on alcohol   Nine out of ten Irish, and Anglo-Irish, and English males spent part of their weekly income on alcohol. This applied to three out of ten Irish, four out of ten English, and five out of ten Anglo-Irish females. In both the Irish and English male groups, there was a low correlation (Irish 0.1977, English 0.1836) between weekly income and expenditure on alcohol. No such relationship was found for Irish or English females. The relationship was slightly higher for the Anglo-Irish males (0.3082) and females (0.1322). Of the males who spent

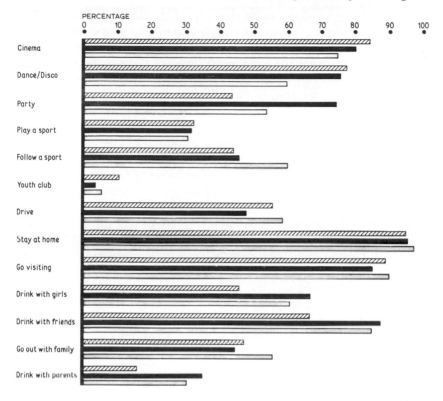

PERCENTAGE

Cinema

Dance/Disco

Party

Play a sport

Follow a sport

Youth club

Drive

Stay at home

Go visiting

Drink with girls

Drink with friends

Go out with family

Drink with parents

Figure 9   General profile of respondents' recreational activities once a month or more:
Females (Q.22§)
N: Irish = 187, Anglo-Irish = 86, English = 99

a weekly sum on alcohol 44 per cent of the Irish, 50 per cent of the
Anglo-Irish, and 35 per cent of the English males spent between £1 and
£3 a week on alcohol. Just over 30 per cent of the Irish and Anglo-
Irish males had a weekly expenditure of between £3 and £6; this applied
to 40 per cent of the English males. Between 9 and 13 per cent of all males
spent £6 to £9, with 14 per cent of the Anglo-Irish males, 5 per cent of the
English males, and 3 per cent of the Irish spending between £9 and £12 a
week on alcohol. Two Irish and Anglo-Irish males spent £12 to £15 a week.

Of the females who spent a weekly sum on alcohol, between 57 and 62
per cent of all groups spent between £1 and £3 weekly. Twenty-two to 29
per cent spent less than £1, and a further 9 to 15 per cent spent between
£3 and £6. One Irish female spent £9 to £12 a week on alcohol.

Days associated with drinking   Approximately 70 per cent of all males associated drinking with a particular day of the week. This applied to approximately 60 per cent of Irish females, compared with 70 per cent of Anglo-Irish and 61 per cent of English females. For both males and females weekends were the most usual time for them to take a drink. Between 1 and 5 per cent of the males drank every day. This applied to 1 per cent of English females.

Drinking with meals   The integration of alcohol with everyday activities can be understood in part by describing the use of alcohol with meals. Drinking with meals was not a frequent occurrence for either the Irish, Anglo-Irish, or English young people. However, if eating was at home, more of the English (41.4) males than either the Anglo-Irish (15.2) or Irish (13.9) males said they occasionally/rarely took a drink with their meals. More of the English females (32.3) and Anglo-Irish (29.6) than Irish (13.3) females drank occasionally/rarely with meals at home. More young people took a drink with a meal if they were eating out, although it was still not a frequent activity. Over two-thirds of the English (males 64.6, females 63.5) and three-fifths of the Anglo-Irish (males 60.8, females 71.5), compared with three-tenths of the Irish (males 30.7, females 33.3) young people, took a drink on occasions when dining out.

Location of drinking   Young people were asked how frequently they drank in a pub, at parties, at stag/hen parties, clubs, restaurants, at home or at a friend's home (*Figure 10*). The pub and parties were the most popular places to drink. Nine out of ten Anglo-Irish and English males, eight out of ten Irish males, seven out of ten English females, and six out of ten Irish females drank frequently in a pub. Over 80 per cent of Anglo-Irish males and females and 70 per cent Irish and English males drank frequently at parties. Approximately 60 per cent of the English and Irish females drank frequently at parties. Nearly three-fifths of all males drank frequently at stag parties, with over one-third of the Irish females and approximately three-tenths of Anglo-Irish and English females drinking frequently at hen parties. More of the Anglo-Irish males (76.0) and females (53.1) than English males (46.6) and females (30.0) drank in a club; and less than 10 per cent of Irish males and females drank frequently in a club. Drinking in a restaurant was a more frequent activity for English males (20.7) and females (20.0) and for Anglo-Irish females (20.9) than for Anglo-Irish males (11.9). Less than 5 per cent of Irish young people drank frequently in a restaurant. A very small percentage of all males and females drank frequently at home or in a friend's home.

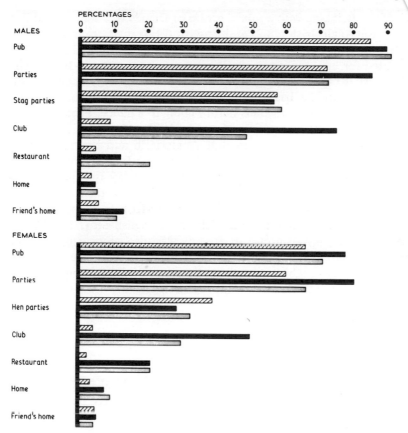

PERCENTAGES

MALES
Pub
Parties
Stag parties
Club
Restaurant
Home
Friend's home

FEMALES
Pub
Parties
Hen parties
Club
Restaurant
Home
Friend's home

Figure 10 General profile of places where respondent frequently takes a drink* (0.438)
  *Refers to respondents who, at time of interview, said they took a drink.
  Males N: Irish = 165, Anglo-Irish = 92, English = 119
  Females N: Irish = 138, Anglo-Irish = 81, English = 96

Company while drinking Drinking took place almost exclusively with friends in three types of situations: (1) with a particular boy/girl-friend; (2) with a mixed group of friends, and (3) with a group of friends of the same sex, all male or all female. It is important to remember that these were the situations in which most young people drank, and it was the frequency with which they drank in these situations that showed differences both in terms of sex and of ethnic status.

More of the Anglo-Irish and English than Irish males drank frequently with their particular girl-friend, on a date (Anglo-Irish 62.0, English 65.0, Irish 36.9), with entertainment (Anglo-Irish 40.2, English 50.9, Irish 32.1), or at a party (Anglo-Irish 82.6, English 75.0,

Irish 68.5). Drinking with a mixed group of friends was a more frequent activity for Anglo-Irish (78.2) and English (71.5) males than it was for Irish (60.0) males. The difference between the English and Irish could be accounted for by sampling error. While more of the Anglo-Irish (91.3) and English (83.6) than Irish (79.4) males drank frequently in an all male context, more of the Irish (58.2) and Anglo-Irish (62.0) than English (36.2) males drank with the lads before going to a dance. Females drank less frequently in the company of their friends. However, differences emerged between the groups, in that Anglo-Irish and English females drank more frequently with boy-friends than did Irish females. Nearly three-fifths of the Anglo-Irish (58.0) and English (56.3) females, compared with two-fifths of the Irish females, drank with their boy-friends on a date, and with other entertainment (Anglo-Irish 35.8, English 40.6, Irish 31.2), or at a party (Anglo-Irish 75.3, English 66.7, Irish 65.2). Drinking with a mixed group of friends was also more usual for the Anglo-Irish (60.5) and English (55.3) females than it was for Irish females (46.3). A sizeable percentage of females from all groups (Anglo-Irish 44.4, English 39.6, Irish 35.5) drank frequently with a group of females or with their girl-friends before going to a dance (Anglo-Irish 23.4, English 20.9, Irish 32.6).

Round drinking   Young people in all groups were asked if round drinking was a custom peculiar to their country of residence. Over two-thirds of the Irish young people felt it was a peculiarly Irish custom. More English males (35.3) and females (44.4) than Anglo-Irish males (23.7) and females (18.6) felt that it was a peculiarly English custom. However, approximately four-fifths of Anglo-Irish males and females and three-quarters of the English young people, compared with three-fifths of Irish males and two-fifths of Irish females, gave qualified support to round drinking. In keeping with this sentiment, more Anglo-Irish (92.4) and English males (84.9) than Irish males (81.1) took part in round drinking. Less females than males took part in round drinking. Three-quarters of the Anglo-Irish and two-thirds of the English females, compared with over two-fifths of the Irish females, took part in round drinking.

Type of alcohol usually taken by respondents   Males in all groups usually drank beer/stout or lager (*Figure 11*). Over half of the Irish males and two-thirds of the Anglo-Irish and English males usually drank beer, with over one-third of the Irish males usually drinking stout, compared with less than one-tenth of both Anglo-Irish and English males. More of the Anglo-Irish males (20.7) than Irish (6.1) or English males (11.2) usually drank lager. Approximately 5 per cent of all males usually drank spirits. Female preferences in beverage choice were more varied, spirits being the most usual type of drink for all groups. Half of the Irish and two-fifths of the Anglo-Irish and English females usually drank spirits. One-fifth of the Anglo-Irish and English females, compared with less than one-tenth of the Irish females, said wine was their usual drink. Lager was the choice of 23.2 per cent of the Irish, 18.5 per cent of the Anglo-Irish, and 14.6 per cent of the English females. Beer/stout accounted for 15.9 per cent of the Irish females, 11.2 per cent of the Anglo-Irish and 6.2 per cent of the English females' beverage choice.

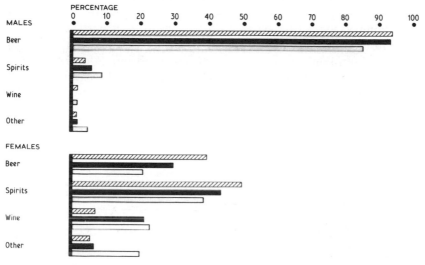

Figure 11 Type of drink respondent usually has* (Q.49)
          *Refers to respondents who, at time of interview, said they took a drink.
          Males N: Irish = 165, Anglo-Irish 92, English 119
          Females N. Irish = 138, Anglo-Irish 81, English 96

Social meaning and function of alcohol

Image of drinking

Expectations, attitudes, and particular patterns of behaviour in relation to drinking and other behaviours are developed through contact with society over a period of time. An understanding of the individual's reaction to any object in his external environment can only be ascertained if one understands the traditional meanings which it has come to have for him. The socio-cultural approach emphasizes that within a cultural system there is a common fabric of meanings shared by a group which governs who drinks as well as drinking styles. Explanations of an individual's use or non-use of alcohol can thus be defined by the cultural prescriptions for drinking that are part of the particular social group to which he belongs.

Parents and children in all groups agreed that most adults and young people drink. Not only was drinking seen as an established practice, but parents felt that young people in general drank more than they had done at their age. This held for nine out of ten Irish fathers and mothers, compared with seven out of ten Anglo-Irish and English fathers and eight out of ten Anglo-Irish and English mothers (*Figure 12*).

When parents were asked to mention the most serious problem in their country, more Irish parents (fathers 18.0), and particularly Irish mothers (30.0), than Anglo-Irish or English parents (less than 10.0) mentioned drinking as the most serious problem. Alcoholism was defined as a serious problem by over 70 per cent of the Irish (fathers 70.0, mothers 80.0) compared with over 40 per cent of the Anglo-Irish and 20 per cent of the English parents (*Figure 12*).

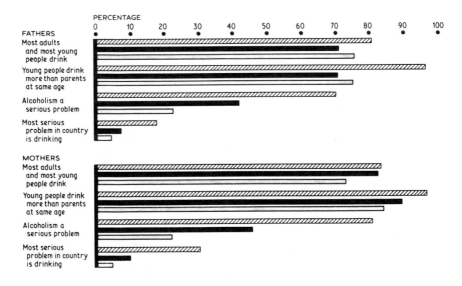

Figure 12   Perception of drinking in the three groups under study (Q.30, Q.36, Q.37, Q.38)
Fathers N: Irish = 301, Anglo-Irish = 134, English = 178
Mothers N: Irish = 354, Anglo-Irish = 176, English = 217

Figure 13 shows that over half of the Irish males and 70 per cent of the Irish females, compared with 20 per cent of the Anglo-Irish and English males, and 30 per cent Anglo-Irish and English females, said that drinking was a problem among the young. The Irish were also more likely to see alcoholism as a serious problem in their country, when compared with either the Anglo-Irish or English young people. Four-fifths of the Irish males and females, compared with three-fifths of the Anglo-Irish, two-fifths of the English males, and half of the English females felt alcoholism was a problem in their country.

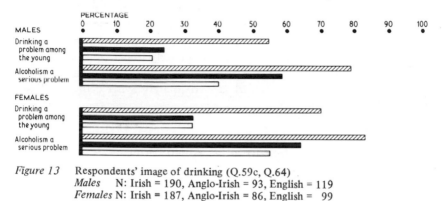

Figure 13   Respondents' image of drinking (Q.59c, Q.64)
          Males   N: Irish = 190, Anglo-Irish = 93, English = 119
          Females N: Irish = 187, Anglo-Irish = 86, English = 99

Why other people drink   It is possible to learn something about the role of alcohol in society by asking young people why others drink. What an individual assumes drinking to mean to others is likely to indicate the meaning it has for the society in which he lives. It also suggests how alcohol comes to be integrated into his own lifestyle.

Why adults drink   All the young people associated adult drinking with sociability. Three-fifths of the Irish and Anglo-Irish males, and two-thirds of the English males emphasized social and recreational reasons for adults drinking. The corresponding figures for the females were nearly half of the Irish females, and three-fifths of the Anglo-Irish and English females. While emphasis was placed on drinking as a part of the social life of adults, over two-fifths of the Irish females compared with one-third of the English and three-tenths of the Anglo-Irish females associated its use for adults with the reduction of anxiety. The corresponding figures given for the males were one-third of Irish males, three-tenths of Anglo-Irish, and one-fifth of the English males.

Why lads drink   Three themes emerged when young people were asked why lads drank: (1) sociability, (2) anxiety reduction, and (3) anticipatory socialization. More males than females gave sociability as the main reason for lads drinking. More Anglo-Irish (86.0) and English (87.4) than Irish (76.8) males gave this reason. A similar pattern was found among the females. Seventy-eight per cent of Anglo-Irish females and 70 per cent of English females, compared with 59 per cent of Irish females, said lads drank for social reasons.

More Irish males (14.7) and females (19.3) mentioned anxiety reduction as a reason, than either Anglo-Irish (males 7.6, females 3.5) or English (males 0.8, females 4.0) young people. It is also worth noting that more of the females than males gave anticipation of adulthood as the main reason for lads drinking. Approximately 15 per cent of the Irish and English females and 10 per cent of the Anglo-Irish females mentioned this reason, compared with approximately 5 per cent of all the males under study.

Why girls drink   Over four-fifths of Anglo-Irish and English young people, compared with seven-tenths of Irish young people, gave sociability as the main reason for girls drinking. More Irish females (16.0) and males (7.3) than Anglo-Irish (males 1.1, females 8.2) or English (males 0, females 2.0) young people mentioned alcohol as a means to reduce anxiety. A small percentage of all young people mentioned females using alcohol as a way of preparing for adult status. Ten per cent of English and 5 per cent of Anglo-Irish and Irish females gave this reason; 5 per cent of Irish males, 4.3 per cent of Anglo-Irish males, and 1.7 per cent of English males associated females drinking with anticipation of adult-type roles.

Definitions of different types of drinkers

This section looks at how the young people defined and came to recognize alcohol-related problems. They were asked what they meant when they said a person was (1) drunk, (2) had a drinking problem, and (3) was an alcoholic. There were little or no differences between the different groups when the definitions of a person who was drunk were examined. A person who was drunk was seen by approximately two-thirds of all males and three-fifths of all females as having no control over sensory and bodily functions. Approximately one-fifth of the Irish, compared with one-tenth of the English males and females, and over one-tenth of the Anglo-Irish males (16.2) and females (10.5), saw him as irrational and aggressive in his behaviour. More of the English males

(16.0) and females (18.1) than Irish (males 9.5, females 4.3) and Anglo-Irish (males 2.2, females 9.3) young people, said he was someone who had taken too much to drink. When looking for problem drinking emphasis was placed on (1) having no control over drinking, (2) physical appearance, (3) behaviour, and (4) social and health problems attributed to drink. Approximately three-tenths of all males and Anglo-Irish and Irish females looked for evidence of no control over drinking; this applied to one-fifth of English females. More of the Anglo-Irish (26.0) and English (21.9) males than Irish (13.7) would consider an unruly appearance as a sign to look for if a person had a drink problem. Over three-tenths of English females and one-fifth of Anglo-Irish females compared with over one-tenth of Irish females would look at a person's appearance. A person's behaviour whether disorderly, aggressive, nervous, or subdued would be an indication of a drink problem for approximately 13 per cent of all of the males. A quarter of the Anglo-Irish females and one-fifth of English females, compared with one-tenth of Irish females, would look at a person's behaviour. More Irish males (20.1) than Anglo-Irish (11.9) or English males (8.6) would consider social and health problems. Differences between the Irish and Anglo-Irish males could be accounted for by sampling error. Approximately 10 per cent of all Irish (12.3) and Anglo-Irish females (10.8) and 7 per cent of the English females would look at social and health problems associated with a person's drinking. It is worth noting that a sizeable percentage would not know what to look for if someone had a drink problem. This was true for more of the English (18.5) than Irish (11.6) or Anglo-Irish (10.8) males, and for more of the Irish females (20.3) than English (13.1) or Anglo-Irish (10.8) females.

Young people in all groups defined an alcoholic in terms of a peson being addicted to drink, having no control over drinking, or drinking all the time. Over four-fifths of all males and females gave this as their definition of an alcoholic. Approximately 5 per cent of all males mentioned personal, social, and economic consequences, and the use of drink under anxiety or pressure. Ten per cent of the Irish females and 3 per cent of the English females gave this definition. A small percentage of males (Irish 4.2, English 2.5, Anglo-Irish 1.1) and 6 per cent of English females said alcoholics were people who drank under pressure or because of anxiety.

Reasons for drinking

It has been shown that Irish young people viewed drinking by adults and other young people as an essentially social act. However, a sizeable percentage saw its use as associated with the reduction of anxiety. Anglo-

Irish young people, like the Irish, viewed the use of alcohol as a social and recreational act, but a sizeable percentage of them also saw it as a means of reducing anxiety. English young people defined drinking by adults and young people as a social activity. It was felt desirable to move from the sphere of the general to an assessment of personal reasons for taking a drink. The following focuses on the reasons respondents gave for taking a drink.

Young people were handed a pre-coded card containing a number of items which were used to measure their main reasons for drinking. These individual items were combined to form four scales or indexes. In general indexes are used to gauge or predict some underlying continuum which can only be partially measured by any single item which is included in the index. It therefore combines items into a composite measure. There are many ways of doing this; one of these techniques, called Guttman Scaling after its originator, is the one that is used here. Guttman based his scale on the idea of the measurement of an unidimensional area, i.e. the component items must all measure movement toward or away from the same single underlying object to be measured. Guttman scales must then be cumulative, and it is this property that differentiates these scales from almost all other types of scales and indexes. This means that the items in the scale arrange themselves in certain specified ways. In particular it must be possible to order the items so that *ideally* all interviewees who answer a given question favourably will have higher scores than those who answer the same questions unfavourably. From a person's scale score we know exactly which items he has endorsed. In this way, we can say that the response to any item provides a definition of the person's attitude (Oppenheim 1966: 120; Moser and Kalton 1971: 350).

Four Guttman type scales were devised to measure reasons for drinking (for details see Appendix 3): (1) festive and social pleasure, (2) social conforming, drinking from a sense of obligation to meet group pressures, (3) personal effects, drinking to resolve problems or inadequacies, and (4) mood changing, drinking to affect a change in mood. *Figure 14* summarizes the data from the scales and shows that over 90 per cent of all young people under study associated the use of alcohol with festive and social reasons.

More of the Anglo-Irish (85.8) and English (87.7) males than Irish males (69.7) drank under group pressure. Over 70 per cent of all females drank as a reaction to group pressure. More of the males than females in all groups drank for personal effect reasons, to resolve problems or inadequacies. Approximately 17 per cent of the Irish and Anglo-Irish males compared with 8 per cent of the English males said they drank when feeling lonely, tense and nervous, under pressure, to forget worries, or simply to forget. This applied to one-fifth of the Anglo-Irish females,

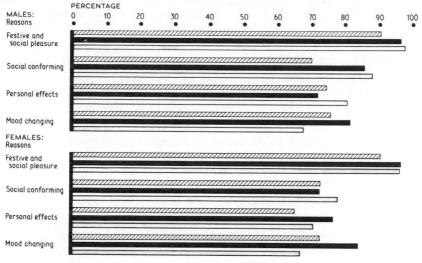

Figure 14   Reasons for taking a drink (Q.51§, Q.54§)
Response indicates that respondents agreed to at least one item on the
scale, and, at the time of interview, said they took a drink.
Males   N: Irish = 165, Anglo-Irish = 92, English = 119
Females N: Irish = 138, Anglo-Irish = 81, English = 96

one-tenth of the Irish females, and one-twentieth of the English females.
Two-fifths of the Anglo-Irish males, over one-third of the Irish males
and three-tenths of the English males agreed with three or more items on
the scale. The corresponding proportions for the females were half of the
Anglo-Irish females and approximately one-quarter of the Irish (26.2)
and English (23.9) females. More English males (80.7) than Anglo-Irish
(71.7) or Irish (74.6) males agreed to one item on the scale indicating that
they drank to resolve problem or inadequcy. This applied to more Anglo-
Irish females (76.5) than Irish (64.9) or English (68.7) females.
    More Anglo-Irish young people than Irish or English young people
drank to effect a change in mood. Seventeen per cent of the Anglo-Irish
males and females, compared with 10 per cent of the Irish and 7 per cent
of the English young people, drank to get some energy or pep, to cheer
up when in a bad mood, and to make themselves feel good. Over half of
the Anglo-Irish males (57.6) and females (54.3), compared with two-
fifths of the Irish (males 47.5, females 43.7) young people, drank for two
or more reasons given on the scale. This applied to two-fifths of the
English males and one-fifth of the English females. Four-fifths of the
Anglo-Irish males and females, three-quarters of the Irish, and two-
thirds of the English young people agreed to at least one item on the
scale.

This chapter looked at the customs and patterns of present-day drinking among the three groups. The description was concerned with where, with whom, and why young people drink. Drinking was shown to be part of the society in which they lived, and to form an integral part of the lifestyle of the young people under study. The analysis indicated that while drinking was essentially a peer group activity for all groups, both English and Anglo-Irish young people drank more frequently in these situations than did Irish males and females.

The social meaning and function of alcohol differed for the Irish and for the English young people studied. The Irish view of drinking was problematic, and, while being seen essentially as a social act, its use was also associated with the reduction of anxiety. More of the Irish parents and young people than either the English or the Anglo-Irish under study, considered alcoholism a very serious problem in their country. The English young people interviewed saw drinking in a more positive light, placing little emphasis on drink as a problem. For them, drinking by adults and other young people was a social activity. The Anglo-Irish were like the English in placing little emphasis on drink as a problem. However, while they too considered drinking a social and recreational act, a sizeable percentage also saw it as a means of reducing anxiety. The problem aspects of the use of alcohol in England were acknowledged by more of the Anglo-Irish than the English under study.

Reasons associated with drinking centred around four themes: (1) festive and social pleasure, (2) social conforming, (3) personal effects, and (4) mood changing. In all the groups both males and females drank as a means of sociability, and as a recreational outlet. Anglo-Irish young people were more likely than the Irish or English young people to drink as a means of altering their mood. On the other hand, more of the Anglo-Irish young people and Irish males, compared with the English males and females, drank to resolve personal problems or inadequacies.

The young people's definitions of a drunk person, a person with a drinking problem, and an alcoholic, were similar in all groups. The only area where there appeared to be some difference was on the priority given to signs indicating that a person has a problem with drink. It is worth noting that being drunk was defined in behavioural terms of having no control over sensory or bodily functions. Overall, the vast majority of all groups defined an alcoholic in the traditional terms of control over drinking.

7

Social rules
surrounding drinking behaviour

Social rules

The social rules surrounding drinking behaviour is the concern of this chapter. Each situation in which people interact socially is made up of typical expectations to which people are expected to respond in a typical way. Social norms or rules can be seen to define appropriate behaviour, the kind of behaviour that is considered 'normal'. It is largely due to the sociologist Max Weber that we have become aware of the importance of paying attention to the meaning of social actions. If we are to understand what goes on in a particular social situation, then we must understand how the people in that social situation make sense of it, what their motives and intentions are, and how they judge the implications of what they and others are doing. Just as individuals who partake in a social situation jointly define what that situation means, so entire societies will produce 'definitions of reality' which serve as the taken-for-granted context of all social situations in that society. Social norms are based on cultural values, and can be viewed as society 'living in us'. These norms or rules are not usually completely rigid and closed to interpretation, there is a latitude of acceptable behaviour which allows for variations and alternative actions within certain bounds (Sherif and Sherif 1964: 62).

The social rules or norms of drinking found in this study are described here. The main foci of this description centres around three themes: (1) norms for children drinking as reported by parents, (2) norms defined by young people for young people of their age drinking, and (3) levels of permissiveness. An account of respondents' exposure to and experience of drink-related problems is also included.

Norms for children as reported by parents: 'what ought to be'

English and Anglo-Irish parents were significantly more likely than Irish parents to approve of their children drinking. Eight out of ten of the Anglo-Irish and English parents felt that it was a good thing for their children to drink. Irish parents had mixed feelings about their children drinking. Over two-fifths of Irish mothers and one-third of Irish fathers strongly disapproved of their children drinking. Parents were also asked, more specifically, to define the social rules for their 18-21 year olds drinking: (1) in a family and peer group context, (2) being drunk at home, being drunk in a mixed group of friends, visibly affected by drink without being drunk, and (3) mixing drinks, drinking six or more drinks on one occasion. The results of these questions are given in cumulative tables scaled by Guttman techniques (see Appendix 3 for details).

The results showed again that in these specified areas both Anglo-Irish and English parents were more favourable to their children drinking than were Irish parents. Anglo-Irish and English parents seemed to discriminate between the drinking situation or context, amount of alcohol taken, and the effects on the drinker. Irish parents, particularly Irish mothers, tended to have consistently negative attitudes to their children drinking, irrespective of the situation and other factors mentioned above. Thus, English and Anglo-Irish parents were more permissive in their attitudes to their children drinking, although they also appeared to have defined areas of acceptable behaviour. The detailed results show this pattern more clearly.

In relation to their 18-21 year olds drinking in a family and peer group context, one-fifth of Irish fathers (18.9) and one-third of Irish mothers (34.7) did not give general approval. Irish parents were the least permissive of all parental groups, they disapproved of their children being drunk at home or in a mixed group, and being visibly affected by drink (fathers 92.1, mothers 92.6). In keeping with this attitude, half of the Irish fathers (53.5) and two-thirds of the Irish mothers disapproved of their 18-21 year olds mixing their drinks and drinking three or more drinks on one occasion. Two-fifths of Irish fathers and one-third of Irish mothers approved of their children drinking three or four drinks at one sitting.

English parents presented a contrast to Irish parents. They approved of their children drinking and drinking in a family and peer group context (fathers 98.3, mothers 96.2). English fathers and mothers appear to have set limits in that they did not approve of their children being drunk in mixed company or at home, or mixing drinks, and drinking six or more drinks. However, approximately one quarter of both fathers and mothers approved of their children being visibly affected by drink. Over

70 per cent of English fathers (73.6) and mothers (70.3) approved of their 18-21 year-old children drinking three or four drinks on one occasion. In this they were more permissive than Irish parents.

Anglo-Irish parents' attitudes lay between the restrictive attitudes of the Irish and the permissive attitudes of English parents. They approved of their children drinking, and drinking in a family and peer group context (fathers 91.7, mothers 94.2). They also set limits and did not approve of drunkenness at home or in mixed company, or mixing drinks, or drinking six or more drinks at a time. One-fifth of fathers and mothers approved of their children being visibly affected by drink. Eight out of ten Anglo-Irish fathers and six out of ten Anglo-Irish mothers approved of their children drinking three or four drinks on one occasion. Anglo-Irish parents appeared to be adopting the social rules of drinking of the host society.

Norms defined by young people for their peers drinking:
'what ought to be'

The norms were concerned with (1) young people of their own age drinking, (2) drinking in a mixed group, and (3) drinking in a single sex context. The data suggested that Irish males had a double standard approach to male and female drinking (*Tables 10 and 11*). Drinking was seen as more appropriate for males (60.0) than for females (39.5), or for their own girl-friends (40.9). Fewer Irish females were favourable to all young people drinking, whether they were male (40.1) or female (40.6). More Irish young people felt that boys and girls drinking in a mixed group (male 78.9, female 62.0), and boys/girls drinking with their boy/girl-friends (male 70.5, female 65.3) was a good thing, than they felt it was for young people to drink in general. Irish males gave general approval to all male group drinking (60.1), but girls drinking in an all female group (33.2), or in a pub by themselves (55.8) was seen to be 'undesirable'. More Irish females approved of all male group drinking (35.4) than all female group drinking (25.2), or girls drinking in a pub on their own (14.9).

English males and females were more favourable in their attitudes to young people drinking than were Irish or Anglo-Irish young people. Four-fifths of the English males felt that drinking by males and females of their own age and by their own boy/girl friends, was a good thing. This applied to approximately two-thirds of the English females. Drinking in mixed groups of friends and by boys/girls with their girl/boy-friends was also considered to be a desirable practice (males 83.2, females 79.8). Their attitudes shifted when asked about young people drinking in a single sex context. All male group drinking (79.0) was considered more

Table 10 General profile of respondents' attitudes to people taking a drink in different situations:* Males (Q.59a)

Situations	Good			Fair			Undesirable		
	Irish %	Anglo-Irish %	English %	Irish %	Anglo-Irish %	English %	Irish %	Anglo-Irish %	English %
Girls of your age taking a drink	39.5	59.2	76.5	37.4	34.4	20.2	20.5	4.3	–
Lads of your age taking a drink	60.0	76.4	81.5	33.7	21.5	17.6	4.2	–	–
Your girl-friend taking a drink	40.9	53.7	75.6	40.0	40.9	19.3	16.3	2.2	2.5
In mixed group	78.9	81.8	83.2	18.4	16.1	15.1	2.1	–	0.8
Boys with their girl-friends	70.5	67.7	82.4	24.7	23.8	15.1	4.2	2.2	0.8
In an all male group	60.1	68.8	79.0	28.9	28.0	18.5	10.0	1.1	0.8
In an all female group	27.3	39.8	55.5	37.4	39.8	31.9	33.2	17.2	10.1
Girls in a pub on their own taking a drink	16.3	21.5	42.0	27.4	38.7	31.9	55.8	36.6	24.4
N =	190	93	99	190	93	99	190	93	99

*Does not include percentage of those who did not answer items.

Table 11 General profile of respondents' attitudes to people taking a drink in different situations:* Females (Q.59a)

Situations	Good			Fair			Undesirable		
	Irish %	Anglo-Irish %	English %	Irish %	Anglo-Irish %	English %	Irish %	Anglo-Irish %	English %
Girls of your age taking a drink	40.6	68.6	52.6	43.3	31.4	31.3	15.5	–	6.1
Lads of your age taking a drink	40.1	73.3	55.6	45.5	25.6	29.3	13.4	1.2	3.0
Your boy-friend taking a drink	47.1	73.3	54.6	41.2	22.1	32.3	11.2	4.7	2.0
In a mixed group	62.0	81.4	79.8	32.1	17.4	20.2	4.3	–	–
Girls with their boy-friends	65.3	82.5	81.8	28.9	16.3	18.2	5.3	–	–
In an all male group	35.4	61.6	50.5	48.1	36.0	44.4	15.5	1.2	4.0
In an all female group	25.2	47.6	43.5	45.5	47.7	40.4	28.3	3.5	16.2
Girls in a pub on their own taking a drink	14.9	29.1	16.1	20.3	25.6	33.3	64.2	45.3	50.4
N=	187	86	99	187	86	99	187	86	99

*Does not include percentage of those who did not answer items.

101

appropriate by English males than all female group drinking (55.5), especially for females drinking in a public house on their own (42.0). Fewer English females approved of single sex drinking, and did not distinguish significantly between all male (50.5) and all female (43.5) group drinking. However, girls drinking on their own in a pub was considered to be an undesirable practice by half of the English females.

Anglo-Irish males and females presented a more complex picture. Anglo-Irish young people held more favourable attitudes to drinking by peers than did Irish young people. However, more Anglo-Irish males approved of lads of their own age drinking (76.4) than girls of their age drinking (59.2), or of their own girl-friends drinking (53.7). On the other hand, Anglo-Irish females gave general approval to lads (73.3) and girls (68.6) of their own age, as well as to their boy-friends drinking (73.6). Four-fifths of Anglo-Irish males and females felt drinking in a mixed group of friends was a good thing. Drinking by boys/girls with their girl/boy-friends was considered a good thing by over two-thirds of the Anglo-Irish males (67.7) and four-fifths of Anglo-Irish females (82.5). Single sex drinking was seen as more appropriate for males (males 68.8, females 61.6) than for females (males 39.8, females 47.6), especially females drinking on their own in a public house (males 21.5, females 29.1).

Compared with the other females interviewed, the Anglo-Irish held more favourable attitudes to females drinking in a pub on their own.

Levels of permissiveness

In any society that uses alcohol there is a wide variety of social rules and conventions concerning both its appropriate and inappropriate use. This section looks at young people's levels of permissiveness in relation to the use of alcohol and gives a description of (1) their attitudes to drunkenness in general, and (2) their acceptance and tolerance of a person who was drunk in a group of people with whom they were drinking. Irish young people were the least permissive and Anglo-Irish the most permissive in relation to the use of alcohol.

Fifty-one per cent of English females agreed with the statement, 'drunkenness is a sign of immaturity'. Over two-fifths of English and Anglo-Irish males, compared with three-tenths of Irish males, felt that excessive drinking was appropriate as long as a person kept out of trouble. More of the English females approved of this statement (39.4), than Anglo-Irish (30.2), or Irish (27.3) females. Approximately two-fifths of all 18-21 year olds agreed with the statement, 'drunkenness is excusable under many circumstances'.

All groups were more likely to tolerate than accept the company of a drunk person. This was especially true of the Irish young people, of whom only 42.6 per cent of the males and 16.6 per cent of the females were seen to accept a drunk person in a group with whom they were drinking, while 59.5 per cent and 28.9 per cent respectively were prepared to tolerate him. Anglo-Irish young people were the most permissive in their attitudes to excessive drinking. Two-thirds of the Anglo-Irish males said they would accept, and three-quarters tolerate, a person who was drunk in a group of people that were drinking, compared with half of the English males accepting, and three-fifths tolerating, a drunk person. Anglo-Irish females were the most permissive of the females, one-third of them stated that they would accept and tolerate a person who was drunk in a group that was drinking. One-fifth of the English females said they would accept, and two-fifths tolerate, a drunk person while out drinking in a group. As was shown, compared to the males, females under study were less likely to accept or tolerate a person who was drunk in a group of people with whom they were drinking.

Exposure to and experience of
drink-related problems

Parents*

Figure 15 shows that more of the Irish and Anglo-Irish parents than English parents had been exposed to problem drinking in their parental home, and had a relative or close friend with a drinking problem. Approximately 10 per cent of the Irish and Anglo-Irish parents, 10 per cent of the English mothers, and 5 per cent of the English fathers, had problems in their parental home due to drink. These differences were small and could be accounted for by sampling error. However, three-tenths of the Irish mothers and fathers, a quarter of the Anglo-Irish fathers and three-tenths of the Anglo-Irish mothers, compared with one-tenth of English fathers and one-fifth of English mothers, had a close relative with a drinking problem.

More of the Irish fathers (30.0) than Anglo-Irish (20.0) or English (8.0) fathers had a close friend with a drinking problem. Approximately 10 per cent of the Irish and Anglo-Irish mothers and 5 per cent of English mothers had close friends with a drinking problem. There was no difference between groups in the percentage who admitted to drink-related problems in their own lives. Less than 10 per cent of all fathers

---

*The definition of problem was both the parents' and 18-21 year olds' definition of what 'problem' meant to them.

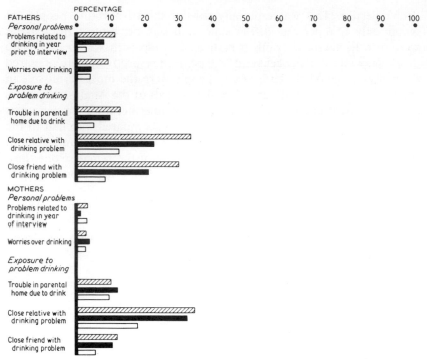

Figure 15   Problem drinking in the lives of respondents* (Q.27, Q.28abc)
*Based on the replies of those respondents who answered yes to these questions.
Fathers N: Irish = 301, Anglo-Irish = 134, English = 178
Mothers N: Irish = 354, Anglo-Irish = 176, English = 217

and 5 per cent of all mothers experienced problems related to their own drinking in the year prior to interview. It would appear that all parents under study, particularly the Irish and Anglo-Irish fathers and mothers, were more likely to mention close relatives or close friends than their parental home or themselves as experiencing problems related to drinking. This may reflect the actual situation, or perhaps a certain reluctance to specify drink-related problems within the family circle.

18-21 year olds' exposure to drink-related problems

Thirty per cent of Irish males and 16.6 per cent of Irish females said that there was trouble in their home due to drink. The corresponding figures for the Anglo-Irish were just under 10 per cent for the males, and 15 per cent for the Anglo-Irish females; less than 8 per cent of English males (7.5) and females (5.0) experienced trouble in their home due to drink. Just under one-fifth of the Irish and Anglo-Irish males and females, compared with under one-tenth of the English females and one-twentieth of the English males, had a close relative with a drinking problem. Approximately 10 per cent of Irish and Anglo-Irish young people, compared with 4 per cent of English males and females, had a close friend with a drinking problem.

18-21 year olds' experience of drink-related problems

Few researchers are in total agreement about the definitions of problem drinking and/or drink-related problems. Researchers who have looked at problem drinking and the young, have used a variety of measures and indexes to look at a syndrome of behaviour which might indicate the development of a pathological pattern of drinking behaviour (O'Connor 1976a and b, 1977; Moser 1974). Recent research approaches problem drinking as a multivariate network of personality, social, and behavioural characteristics (O'Connor 1976a and b; Robinson, 1976).

This study sees problem drinking as more than a problem of aetiology and current drinking patterns. It involves a response on the part of the community. In this instance attention was given to the extent to which drinking was an issue for the community. It follows Knupfer's (1967: 974) definition of what constitutes a drinking problem, namely that 'a problem, any problem connected fairly closely with drinking constitutes a drinking problem'. A description of problems related to drinking within the three groups interviewed follows.

A number of indicators were taken to look at the extent of problem drinking in the groups under study. They were:

1 Defined limits in relation to drinking
2 Frequency of drunkenness in year prior to interview
3 Problems related to drinking in year prior to interview
4 Concern over drinking

Two other factors have already been discussed:

5 Alcohol intake capable of resulting in problems, i.e. drinking the equivalent of five pints (4.46 pints) of beer per day (Davies 1977)
6 Image of drinking among the groups

1. *Defined limits in relation to drinking* Over two-thirds of the Irish, half of the Anglo-Irish, and three-fifths of the English males said that they had a limit in relation to their drinking. This applied to over four-fifths of the Irish and Anglo-Irish females and three-fifths of the English females. Half of the Irish males, two-fifths of the Anglo-Irish (39.1) and English (46.5) males had exceeded their defined limit. This applied to

two-fifths of the Irish, three-fifths of the Anglo-Irish, and three-tenths of the English females. Between 11 and 13 per cent of the males had not exceeded their defined limit in relation to drinking. More of the Irish females (44.1) than Anglo-Irish (22.2) or English females (30.2) had not exceeded their limit. Thirty-three per cent of the Irish (33.3) and English (35.3) males, compared with 46 per cent of the Anglo-Irish males, said that they did not consider themselves to have a limit. This applied to 14 per cent of the Irish females, 20 per cent of the Anglo-Irish females and 35 per cent of the English females.

2. *Frequency of drunkenness in year prior to interview* More of the Anglo-Irish (55.4) and Irish (46.7) males than English males (28.4) had been drunk ten times or more in the year prior to interview. A quarter of the Anglo-Irish females, compared with just over 10 per cent of Irish and English females, were drunk ten or more times in the year prior to interview.

3. *Problems related to drinking in year prior to interview* Problems related to drinking in year prior to interview are shown in *Table 12*, which is a cumulative table. The data records problems experienced by the young people in the year prior to interview, and do not indicate the frequency with which these problems occurred. Experience of drink-related problems was highest for the Irish (45.2) and Anglo-Irish males (48.9) and females (30.9), and lowest for the English males (26.7) and females (11.5), as well as the Irish females (17.5). The table shows that of all problems given, arguments with friends and money problems were the most frequently mentioned by respondents. The index shows that one English 18-21 year old experienced job difficulties, health problems, police trouble, family arguments, money problems, and arguments with friends due to drink. Three Irish males and one Irish female, three Anglo-Irish males and one English male and one female, had experience of four problems in relation to their drinking during the year prior to interview. One-fifth of the Irish and Anglo-Irish males and one-tenth of the English males had money problems and arguments with friends due to drink. This applied to apprxoimately 5 per cent of the Irish and English females and 7 per cent of the Anglo-Irish females.

4. *Concern over drinking* More of the Irish (15.7) and Anglo-Irish (17.4) than English (8.6) males said that they were worried over their drinking. More Irish females (7.2) than either the Anglo-Irish (2.5) or English (3.1) said they worried over their drinking.

Table 12 Problems related to respondents' drinking in the year prior to interview (Q.56)

	Males			Females		
	Irish *164*	*Anglo-Irish* *92*	*English* *116*	*Irish* *137*	*Anglo-Irish* *81*	*English* *96*
No experience of problems	100% 90 (54.9)	100% 47 (51.1)	100% 85 (73.4)	100% 113 (82.5)	100% 56 (69.1)	100% 85 (88.5)
Friend's arguments due to drink	45.2 38 (23.2)	48.9 26 (28.2)	26.7 19 (16.3)	17.5 17 (12.4)	30.9 19 (23.5)	11.5 7 (7.3)
Money problems due to drink	22.0 28 (15.9)	20.6 12 (13.0)	10.3 5 (4.3)	5.1 5 (3.7)	7.4 6 (7.4)	4.2 3 (3.1)
Family arguments	6.1 5 (3.0)	7.6 4 (4.3)	6.0 5 (4.3)	1.4 1 (0.7)	0 0 (0.0)	0 0 (0.0)
Police trouble due to drink	3.0 3 (1.8)	3.3 3 (3.3)	1.7 1 (0.9)	0.7 1 (0.7)	0 0 (0.0)	1.0 1 (1.0)
Health problems due to drink	1.2 2 (1.2)	0.0 0 (0.0)	0.9 0 (0.9)	0.0 0 (0.0)	0 0 (0.0)	0.0 0 (0.0)
Job/work difficulties due to drink	0 (0.0)	0 (0.0)	1 (0.9)	0 (0.0)	0 (0.0)	0 (0.0)
N=	164	92	116	137	81	96

This chapter outlined the social rules surrounding drinking behaviour, through an examination of (1) norms for children drinking as reported by parents, (2) norms defined by young people for peers drinking, and (3) levels of permissiveness. An account was also given for all those studied of their experience of and exposure to drink-related problems.

The attitudes of Irish parents to their children were in general negative. The social rules of drinking they adopted for their children were restrictive, with little distinction being made between social and excessive type drinking. The Irish males and females interviewed appeared to have slightly more favourable attitudes to drinking than their parents. However, Irish males had a double standard approach to drinking for males and females, approving more of males than of females of their age drinking, and of all male group than of all female group drinking. The inconsistency in the Irish females' attitudes was evident when more appeared to approve of males and females drinking together than of the whole idea of drinking itself. Irish 18-21 year olds generally, were not tolerant of drunkenness.

English parents and young people held more positive and permissive attitudes to the use of alcohol. Parents were favourable to their 18-21 year-old children drinking in a family and peer group context, although they set limits in that general approval was not given to being drunk, or to drinking six or more drinks on one occasion. English 18-21 year olds under study showed that they held more favourable attitudes to their peers drinking than either the Irish or the Anglo-Irish young people. Although both males and females had a double standard approach in that they approved more of all male than of all female group drinking, compared with the Irish and Anglo-Irish, more of the English males felt that girls drinking in a pub on their own was a good thing. English 18-21 year olds were also more tolerant of drunkenness than the Irish.

The information obtained from the Anglo-Irish under study is more complex. It is of interest to keep in mind that the Anglo-Irish parents interviewed had common cultural origins with the Irish parents, for there appeared to be a change or shift in attitude from the restrictive cultural norms and social rules of drinking given by the Irish to the more permissive customs of the English parents under study. They seemed to be adopting the social rules of drinking of their host culture. Parents were favourable to their 18-21 year-old children drinking in a family or peer group context, although, like the English, they did not approve of them being drunk. While the Anglo-Irish 18-21 year olds were more favourable to their peers drinking than the Irish, their attitudes were not as clear-cut and consistent as those of the English young people. Anglo-Irish males approved more of males than of females of their age drinking, while Anglo-Irish females gave general approval to both males and females drinking. While they approved more of all male than of all female group drinking, more Anglo-Irish females than other females under study gave approval to females drinking in an all female group, or in a public house on their own. Of all the 18-21 year olds interviewed, the Anglo-Irish were the most permissive to drunkenness.

English young people were more likely than Irish 18-21 year olds to drink the equivalent of five pints (4.46) of beer per day, an amount which has been shown to be capable of resulting in problems (Davies 1977). Yet among the 18-21 year olds interviewed, experience of drink-related problems was highest for the Irish and Anglo-Irish males and Anglo-Irish females, who were also shown to have been more exposed to problem drinking. Less than 10 per cent of all parents under study had problems relating to their own drinking. However, more Irish and Anglo-Irish than English fathers had an average daily intake capable of resulting in problems.

The next part of the present study, as described in Chapter 2, is concerned with influences in the transmission of drinking behaviour. Four mechanisms through which influence may be exerted on the drinking behaviour of the young, are assessed, both individually and in interaction. These mechanisms are: (1) parental influences, (2) peer group influences, (3) social and personal influences, and (4) ethnic and cultural influences.

There are four main chapters in this third part of the study. The first three deal respectively with parental, peer group, and social and personal influences. In this way it is hoped to isolate and clarify what appear to be the relevant factors associated with young people's drinking behaviour viewed from a sociological perspective. The fourth, Chapter 11, using modified multiple regression analysis (Goodman 1972a: 28, 1972b: 1035, 1973: 1135), illustrates how culture, parents, and peers interact in influencing a young person's drinking.

The analysis in Chapters 8 to 10 is divided into three stages. First, additional survey data is presented, similar in nature to that of Chapters 5, 6, and 7. The second section deals with an intermediary stage in the analysis, which specifies statistically significant relationships between variables and the 18-21 year olds' drinking behaviour (Siegel 1956: 47). This procedure, using the Kolmogorov-Smirnov test, helped organize the data for the final stage of multiple regression analysis. And this, in turn, assisted in the construction of a general model of the development of drinking behaviour, which is the subject of Chapter 11. Chapter 12 presents a summary of the major findings of the study as a whole.

8
Parental influences

Influential factors

The way in which a society transmits its culture to its members is through the process of socialization, and the family is the critical socializing agent for the society. Research shows that parental influence on all forms of behaviour is considerable. In this chapter an attempt is made to define the importance and interrelationships of parental influences in the transmission of drinking behaviour from parent to child. The influences may be described in terms of (1) general family relationships, (2) parental drinking behaviour, and (3) parental social rules for children drinking.

General family relationships

The family can be seen to have a wide variety of functions. One important consideration is the relationship between parents and their children. A number of indicators were used to assess the young people's relationships with their parents, and to look at their influence on drinking behaviour.

Nearly all young people felt that their family life to date was either happy, or moderately happy with ups and downs. Under 5 per cent of all 18-21 year olds under study said that their family life was unhappy, with upsets and serious difficulties. Perceived parental support was measured, using a cumulative type scale. More females than males in all groups felt that they received a high level of social support from their parents. Three-tenths of the Irish males and one quarter of the English males, compared with one-fifth of the Anglo-Irish males, felt that their parents helped them when worried, gave them general encouragement, and were interested in their school/college or work. This applied to over two-fifths of all the female groups. Two-thirds of the Irish, three-fifths of the English, compared with half of the Anglo-Irish males, said parents gave them encouragement and were interested in their school/college/work situation. Approximately three-quarters of both Irish and English females, compared with two-thirds of Anglo-Irish females, said their parents gave them this type of social support. Over 90 per cent of the Irish males and females, compared with 80 per cent of the English and Anglo-Irish young people, said that their parents were interested in their school/college or work.

Besides these feelings of general parental support and interest, eight in every ten of the males and females interviewed said that their parents never made promises that did not materialize. Seven-tenths of the Irish males and females, with two-thirds of the Anglo-Irish males and females, and four-fifths of the English females, and seven-tenths of the English males, said their parents never said one thing and did another. A further indication of their general relationship with their parents was that nine out of ten of the 18-21 year olds under study felt that there was some level of agreement between parents and their friends.

Research in general and in the area of deviance has shown the importance of family relationships in the development of the individual. Stacey and Davies commenting on parental influences on drinking behaviour, state:

> '...the alienation or anomie often felt by young problem drinkers might well be related to the degree of guidance, interest and encouragement shown by parents in relation to a wide range of activities of which the supervision of drinking behaviour would be only one aspect.'   (Stacey and Davies 1970: 203)

The evidence from this study was that no association existed between having an unhappy family life, a low level of parental support, inconsistent behaviour by parents, and heavy or very heavy drinking behaviour. However, while the evidence* was weak, parental social support and the level of agreement between parents and friends were found to be significantly related to heavy type drinking. Males who were categorized as heavy or very heavy types of drinkers, had lower levels of parental support compared to males who were classified as lighter types of drinkers. English males who felt that there was a low level of agreement between parents and their friends were heavy type drinkers.

*The detailed tables relating to these findings are contained in J. O'Connor (1976a and b: 419-44) and are available for examination at the library of the Medical Council on Alcoholism, London, or by writing to the National University of Ireland, Department of Social Sciences, University College, Dublin.

Parental drinking behaviour

In view of the suggestions in the literature that the most accurate basis for predicting whether a young person will drink or not is to know whether his parents drink, our next concern was an examination of parents' drinking behaviour and that of their children. The results showed that it was not enough to know whether a parent drank or not. It was necessary (1) to differentiate the contributions of fathers and mothers, and (2) to classify each parent on how much he/she consumed on each drinking occasion, as well as the frequency of their drinking. The following significant patterns* emerged:

1   Fathers had more influence on children's drinking behaviour than mothers.
2   Fathers influenced daughters more than sons.
3   Fathers and mothers who were abstainers, virtual abstainers, light drinkers or moderate drinkers, had sons and daughters who were also abstainers, virtual abstainers, light drinkers or moderate drinkers.
4   The reverse was also true, in that sons and daughters who were abstainers, virtual abstainers, light drinkers, had parents in these light drinking categories.
5   More sons and daughters who were moderate drinkers had fathers and mothers who were abstainers, virtual abstainers or moderate drinkers, than did sons and daughters who were classified as heavy or very heavy type drinkers.

Parental social rules for drinking

It has been noted that the culture in which we live establishes what is right and wrong by defining rules of conduct called norms. Parents' social rules relating to their children's drinking, defined the norms for the young people interviewed. The analysis highlighted the necessity of looking at parental attitudes towards their children drinking in different kinds of situations, to the amount of alcohol they consume, and how and what they drink. These definitions not only influenced the drinking behaviour of their children but also influenced the development of their general attitudes to drink.

Parents were asked separately what their attitudes were to three particular social rules, and their children in turn were asked what they perceived these attitudes would be. The three social rules were:

*See O'Connor (1976a and b: 419-44) for details.

(1) drinking in a family and peer group context, (2) being drunk or visibly affected by drink, and (3) mixing drinks and the amount of alcohol consumed. In the detailed analysis it was shown that parents' social rules as reported by children, emerged as better predictors of children's drinking behaviour than did the social rules of drinking as reported by parents themselves. The measure used therefore was children's perception of their parents' social rules in relation to drinking (see Appendix 3 for details). The analysis identified the following significant relationships:

1 While fathers' and mothers' social rules for their children drinking in a family and peer group context had little influence on their children's drinking, more fathers, who were seen to approve of their sons drinking in a family and peer group context, had sons who were moderate types of drinkers, than did fathers who were seen to hold unfavourable attitudes.

2 It will be remembered that more Irish than Anglo-Irish or English parents tended to disapprove of their children drinking in this situation. More Irish fathers and mothers who disapproved rather than approved of their sons and daughters drinking in a family and peer group context, had children who were classified as abstainers and virtual abstainers.

3 Irish sons and daughters who were abstainers or virtual abstainers had fathers and mothers who disapproved of their children drinking in a family and peer group context.

4 Fathers and mothers who were seen to be permissive in the scope and limits of their views on the appropriate drinking behaviour for their children, had children who were classified as heavy or very heavy types of drinkers. More fathers and mothers who were seen to approve, than those who were seen to disapprove, of the effect of excessive drinking on their children, had sons and daughters who were heavy or very heavy drinkers.

5 More fathers and mothers who approved, than those who disapproved, of their children mixing their drinks, drinking three or more drinks on one occasion, had sons and daughters in the heavy or very heavy drinking categories. The results also showed that sons appeared to discriminate between fathers' very favourable and favourable attitudes.

Besides influencing children's drinking behaviour, children's perceptions of parental definitions of appropriate drinking behaviour, also influenced their attitudes to peers drinking, in the following way:

1 Parents who were seen to hold very favourable or favourable

attitudes to their children drinking in a family and peer group context, had sons and daughters who themselves held favourable or very favourable attitudes to (i) young people of their own age drinking, (ii) young people drinking in a mixed group context, and (iii) young people drinking in a single sex context.

2 Fathers who were seen to hold very favourable or favourable attitudes to their children mixing drinks and drinking three or more drinks at one sitting, had sons and daughters who held favourable or very favourable attitudes to peers of their age drinking.

3 Fathers and mothers who held very favourable attitudes to sons and daughters mixing drinks and drinking three or more drinks on one occasion, had children who held favourable or very favourable attitudes to young people drinking in a single sex context.

It is worth noting that the drinking behaviour of parents did not emerge as having any influence on children's attitudes to social rules for peers drinking.

Interrelationships and relative importance of parental influences

To look at the importance and interrelationships of (1) general family relationships, (2) parental drinking behaviour, and (3) parental social rules for their children's drinking, further analysis was undertaken. This analysis is called Goodman's (1972a: 28, 1972b: 1035, 1973: 1135) modified multiple regression analysis.* When the interrelationships and and relative importance of these influences were ascertained, it was shown that of all the influences investigated the following four were the most important (O'Connor 1976a and b):

1 Fathers' drinking behaviour
2 Mothers' drinking behaviour
3 Fathers' attitude to children drinking six or more drinks, three or more drinks, and mixing drinks
4 Mothers' attitude to children drinking six or more drinks, three or more drinks, and mixing drinks

The evidence from this study showed that parental attitudes, particularly those of the father, rather than parental drinking behaviour or general family relationships, were the most important influences on children's

*A more detailed discussion of how this method was used, is given in O'Connor (1976a and b: 224-31). For a definition of the 'odds ratio' see p. 116.

drinking behaviour. The influence of parental drinking behaviour and general family relationships was diminished.

Of all parental attitudes, fathers' attitudes to children mixing drinks and drinking three or more drinks at a sitting, were the most important. The influence of parental behaviour, especially that of the mother, was diminished when the relative importance and interaction of parental behaviour and attitudes was investigated. The differential effects of fathers' and mothers' attitudes, as well as behaviour, were especially pronounced. However, there was evidence of some interaction effects among the variables. Fathers' and mothers' drinking behaviour, and mothers' attitudes to the amount of alcohol consumed by their children, while not highly significant, did appear to contribute to the development of their children's drinking behaviour.

Table 13 reveals the 'odds ratio' of a child being classified as a light or heavy type drinker depending on the relative interaction of the four main parental influences discussed above. The odds ratio was 2.5 to 1 that the child would be a light type of drinker if both parents were light types of

Table 13 Estimate of the odds for becoming a light or heavy type of drinker depends on fathers' behaviour, mothers' behaviour, fathers' attitude to amount of alcohol consumed by their children and mothers' attitude to amount of alcohol consumed by their children.

Fathers' behaviour	Mothers' behaviour	Fathers' attitude	Mothers' attitude	ODDS RATIO Children's type of drinker	
				Light drinker	Heavy drinker
Light	Light	Disapprove	Disapprove	2.5 to 1	0.4 to 1
Light	Light	Disapprove	Approve	1.2 to 1	0.83 to 1
Light	Light	Approve	Disapprove	1.0 to 1	0.9 to 1
Light	Light	Approve	Approve	0.5 to 1	2.0 to 1
Heavy	Heavy	Disapprove	Disapprove	1.5 to 1	0.7 to 1
Heavy	Heavy	Disapprove	Approve	0.7 to 1	1.4 to 1
Heavy	Heavy	Approve	Disapprove	0.6 to 1	1.6 to 1
Heavy	Heavy	Approve	Approve	0.3 to 1	3.3 to 1
Light	Heavy	Disapprove	Disapprove	2.5 to 1	0.40 to 1
Light	Heavy	Disapprove	Approve	1.2 to 1	0.83 to 1
Light	Heavy	Approve	Disapprove	1.0 to 1	0.9 to 1
Light	Heavy	Approve	Approve	0.5 to 1	2.0 to 1
Heavy	Light	Disapprove	Disapprove	1.5 to 1	0.7 to 1
Heavy	Light	Disapprove	Approve	0.7 to 1	1.4 to 1
Heavy	Light	Approve	Disapprove	0.6 to 1	1.6 to 1
Heavy	Light	Approve	Approve	0.3 to 1	3.4 to 1

drinkers, and both disapproved of their children drinking three or more drinks on one occasion and mixing drinks. As fathers' and mothers' attitudes changed and became more approving of this behaviour, and both were light types of drinkers, the odds ratio* was shortened, to an even chance of being a light type of drinker when one parent approved, and the other disapproved. The odds ratio was 2 to 1 against a young person being classified as a light type of drinker when both parents approved of mixing drinks, drinking three or more drinks on one occasion, and were light type drinkers. The odds ratio of a young person being a light type of drinker was 3 to 1 against, when both parents were heavy type drinkers and both had approving attitudes, as well as when the father was a heavy type, but the mother a light type drinker, thus showing the differential influence of fathers' and mothers' drinking behaviour.

Parents play a major role in the transmission of drinking behaviour. The differential effects of their drinking behaviour, attitudes to alcohol, involvement and interest in their children's activities, their consistency in dealing with them, and their relationship with their children's friends, were related here to the development of the drinking practices and attitudes of young people. It was shown that parental attitudes, rather than parental drinking behaviour and general family relationships, were the most important influences. While the mothers' influence was evident, the fathers' was greater.

Family relationships were related to children's drinking behaviour, but their effect was diminished when parental drinking behaviour and attitudes to drink were taken into account. The most important of all parental influences were the children's perceptions of their parents' attitudes towards drinking. These perceptions influenced not only their actual drinking behaviour, but also the development of their own attitudes in relation to drinking. The fathers' attitude to children drinking three or more drinks on one occasion, and mixing their drinks, was the most powerful explanatory variable in determining whether a child would be classified as a light or heavy type of drinker.

---

*The odds ratio for a two cell table is the ratio of the number in the first cell to the number in the second cell. Thus if there are 20 in the first cell and 5 in the second, the odds ratio (or the odds) for the two cells is $\frac{20}{5}$ or 4 to 1. This can also be described as an odds of 4 to 1 against being in the second cell.

9
Peer group influences

One favourite explanation of young people's drinking behaviour is that it is the result of social pressure from other young people, namely, their peer group. The general population and the media have come to accept the term 'youth culture' as an adequate description of what is going on. The most active research controversy has centred around the interrelated pressures from parents and peers, and their influence on the behaviour of the young. The evidence suggests that while a major portion of what we learn occurs at a young age, social learning is a continuous process and takes place in a variety of settings outside the family. Peers are seen to influence young people in such areas as educational aspirations, dress, smoking, drug taking, sexual behaviour, and dating patterns. Peer groups teach new skills and new attitudes that are sometimes different from those learnt from the family. Peer influence appears to be especially high during adolescence but continues throughout life.

Research has shown that peers are important in how, when, and where drinking is integrated into the lifestyle of the individual. The results of the present study showed that drinking was essentially a peer group activity. This chapter looks at peer group influences in more detail. Certain findings already described in Chapters 6 and 7 are brought together and their relative influence on young people's drinking is specified. There are three sections in this chapter. The first part, descriptive in nature, deals with general friendship patterns and overall peer group support for drinking; in the second part, peer group influences on young people's drinking behaviour and attitudes are specified; and in the third, interrelationships of all these variables, as well as their relative influence on young people's drinking behaviour are explored. (Details relating to the analysis can be found in O'Connor 1976 a and b: 241-61.)

Influences

General friendship patterns

All young people under study had a group of friends or a particular friend with whom they usually went out. General social support was measured by whether the young people under study felt free to talk to their friends about personal problems. Overall social support from friends was found to be medium to high for the majority of males and females under study. Over half of the Irish (56.6) and English (56.5) females and two-thirds of the Anglo-Irish females, felt that they received a high level of social support from their friends. The corresponding figures for the males were slightly lower, with over two-fifths of the Irish and Anglo-Irish males and half of the English males receiving a high level of social support from friends. A quarter of both Irish (25.1) and English (26.3) females and one-fifth Anglo-Irish females, reported a medium level of social support; this was true for two-fifths of the Anglo-Irish males, one-third of the Irish, and under three-tenths of the English males. Between 11 and 17 per cent of the females and 17 and 21 per cent of the males, said that their friends gave them a low level of social support.

Overall peer group support for drinking

Chapter 6 gave us some indication of peer group support for drinking. *Table 14* gives us a more concise picture of this support; it is a cumulative index, based on the replies of those who said they took a drink at the time of the study. Eight items were selected, stated in increasing order of 'difficulty', from the support most frequently found to the one that was least frequently found, or the most 'difficult' support to obtain from peers. This was a measure indicating a young person's immersion in a context of peer group support for drinking.

Irish males and females appeared to have less support for drinking than did either the Anglo-Irish or English young people. In all groups peer group support for drinking was higher among the males than among the females. A quarter of the Anglo-Irish males, compared with one-fifth of the Irish and English males, and 5 per cent of all the females, said that they drank frequently with lads/girls before going dancing, drank frequently on a date, with a group of mixed friends, with an all male/female group, with their friends once a month or more, with the lads/girls once a month or more, usually met friends in a pub, and said that their friends drank regularly. Three-fifths of the Anglo-Irish males, half of the English, and two-fifths of the Irish males, agreed with seven of the

Table 14 Overall peer group support for drinking as measured by 18-21 year olds' responses (Q.2, Q.41ab, Q.42)

	Males			Females		
	Irish	*Anglo-Irish*	*English*	*Irish*	*Anglo-Irish*	*English*
Negative to all items	100%	100%	100%	100%	100%	100%
	1 (0.8)	0 (0.0)	1 (1.1)	10 (9.9)	1 (1.6)	10 (1.4)
Friends drink regularly	99.2	100	98.9	91.1	98.4	98.6
	6 (4.6)	0 (0.0)	2 (2.1)	14 (13.9)	4 (6.5)	4 (6.3)
Usual place to meet friends: pub	94.6	100	96.8	76.2	91.6	92.3
	8 (6.2)	0 (0.0)	1 (1.1)	18 (17.8)	8 (12.9)	9 (14.1)
Drinks with a group of friends lads/girls once a month or more	88.4	100	95.7	58.4	79.0	78.2
	7 (5.4)	3 (3.8)	5 (5.4)	13 (12.9)	11 (17.7)	6 (9.4)
Go for a drink with friends once a month or more	83	96.2	90.3	45.5	61.3	68.8
	16 (12.3)	7 (8.6)	6 (6.5)	10 (9.9)	7 (11.3)	10 (15.6)
Go out for a drink with the lads/girls frequently	70.7	87.6	83.8	35.6	50.0	53.2
	16 (12.3)	4 (4.9)	7 (7.5)	13 (12.9)	9 (14.5)	12 (18.8)
Drinks with a group of mixed friends frequently	58.4	82.7	76.3	22.7	35.5	34.4
	22 (16.9)	16 (19.8)	23 (24.7)	11 (10.9)	9 (14.5)	7 (10.9)
Drinks when on a date frequently	41.5	62.9	51.6	11.8	20.9	23.5
	28 (21.5)	30 (37.0)	29 (31.2)	8 (7.8)	10 (16.1)	11 (17.2)
Drinks with lads or girls before dancing frequently	20.0	25.9	20.4	4.0	4.8	6.3
	26 (20.0)	21 (25.9)	19 (20.4)	4 (4.0)	3 (4.8)	4 (6.3)
N =	130	81	93	101	62	73

eight items on the scale. The corresponding figures for the females were one-fifth for the Anglo-Irish and English females, and one-tenth for the Irish females. Four-fifths of the Anglo-Irish, three-quarters of the English and three-fifths of the Irish males drank frequently with a mixed group of friends, when out with lads/girls, went for a drink with friends once a month or more, and with a group of lads/girls once a month or more, usually met friends in a pub, and had friends, all or most of whom drank regularly. This held for over one-third of the Anglo-Irish and English females and one-fifth of the Irish females.

Irish females had the lowest level of overall peer group support for drinking. Ten per cent of the Irish females, compared with under 2 per cent of the English and Anglo-Irish females, had no peer group support for drinking; this held for approximately 1 per cent of the Irish and English males.

Peer group support for non-drinking patterns

A separate analysis was undertaken on the group of non-drinkers. The purpose of this analysis was to see whether social support existed for their non-drinking pattern. The number of non-drinkers in both the Anglo-Irish and English groups, was too small for further analysis, so analysis was confined to Irish males and females who said they did not drink at the time of interview. Over 80 per cent of Irish non-drinkers said that their friends took a drink, with over half of them (56.8) drinking on a regular basis. More Irish males (76.0) than females (46.9) had friends who drank on a regular basis. Just over a third of all Irish non-drinkers (36.4) had felt pressure to drink from friends. Half of these non-drinkers stated that their friends had been quite direct in suggesting that they should take a drink. More of the females (55.1) than males (32.0) stated that their friends had suggested they should drink. A third of the males (32.0) and one-fifth of the females said that friends had supported their non-drinking pattern, in that their friends had not suggested that they should drink.

Their recreational pattern was shown to be varied. More of the males (32.0) than females (14.3) said they went out with a group of lads/girls and with a mixed group of friends for a drink at least once a month (males 40.0, females 34.7). One-fifth of both males and females specified the public house as the place they usually went to with their friends.

Of all the Irish non-drinkers, one-third said that they might drink in the future, a half (51.4) said that they would never drink, and one-tenth said that they did not know. More of the males (40.2) than females (30.6) said that they would drink in the future, and they were also more likely to say that they had felt pressure to drink from friends, and had friends who drank on a regular basis. The association was moderate but did lend some support to the prediction of future drinking behaviour. Further analysis showed that a significant relationship existed (though weak) beween males' perceived pressure to drink and the decision to drink in the future. These associations did not operate for the female non-drinkers. It should be remembered however that the numbers in this group are very small.

Overall peer group support for drinking and type of drinker

How often friends drank, and how frequently the young people under study themselves drank in the company of their friends, was highly associated with heavy and very heavy type drinking. Relationships found to be significant were as follows (see O'Connor 1976a and b: 241-42):

1 Males, who were heavy type drinkers had a higher level of peer group support for drinking than did males who were classified in the lower drinking categories.
2 Young people, males and females, who drank frequently with (i) a particular girl/boy friend, (ii) with a mixed group of friends, (iii) with a group of friends of the same sex, (iv) in a pub, (v) at parties, and (vi) at stag/hen parties, had a higher level of peer group support for drinking than those young people who occasion-ally or never drank on these occasions.
3 Young people who had friends who drank regularly, tended to be classified as heavy type drinkers.
4 Young people who drank frequently with a particular boy/girl friend, with a mixed group of friends, with a group of friends of the same sex, tended to be classified as heavy type drinkers.
5 Young people who drank occasionally, compared with those who drank frequently in these situations were moderate or light types of drinkers.

Interrelationships and relative importance of peer group influences

Peer group contexts for drinking (O'Connor 1976a and b: 245-49)

When all the situations in which these young people drank were analyzed together and their interrelations taken into account, drinking in a single sex context was shown to be the most highly related to heavy type drinking. Its effect was twice as great as that of drinking with a mixed group of friends. Drinking frequently with a 'significant other' or boy/girl-friend, was also associated with heavy type drinking behaviour. The frequency of drinking with a mixed group of friends appeared to have little impact on young people's drinking behaviour.

It will be remembered that young people were asked how frequently they drank in a pub, in a pub with parents, at parties, stag/hen parties, in a club, a restaurant, at home, or at a friend's home. Of all these settings used for drinking, the analysis showed that drinking frequently in a pub was highly associated with being classified as a heavy or very heavy type of drinker. This was not found for drinking with parents in a pub, or at a stag or hen party. However, drinking in a single sex setting at a stag/hen party was associated, though not very significantly, with heavy type drinking.

Social rules for peers drinking (O'Connor 1976a and b: 243-44, 250-56)

The importance of social rules in relation to drinking has been noted. These rules helped define appropriate behaviour for young people and were an important factor in the development of drinking behaviour.

The relationships found to be significant were as follows:

1 Young people who held very favourable attitudes to (i) young people of their own age drinking, (ii) young people drinking in a single sex context, and (iii) young people drinking in a mixed group context, tended to be classified as heavy or very heavy type drinkers. This was especially true of the males under study.
2 Irish abstainers and virtual abstainers, were more likely to hold unfavourable attitudes to young people drinking than were Irish people in other drinking categories.

The interrelationships and relative importance of these three social rules for peers drinking were ascertained. Favourable attitudes to drinking in a single sex context was highly associated with heavy type drinking. Attitudes to peers drinking and to drinking in a mixed group of friends appeared not to be associated with young people's drinking behaviour.

Levels of acceptance and tolerance of behaviour associated with excessive drinking while drinking with peers, were seen to affect drinking styles. Heavy and very heavy type drinkers had higher levels of both acceptance and tolerance of excessive drinking among peers. The results indicated, however, that a young person's level of acceptance of excessive drinking had a much greater effect than the corresponding level of tolerance.

Interrelationships among all peer group influences

Of all peer group influences, peer group support for drinking was the most powerful explanatory variable, with level of acceptable behaviour also showing a highly significant relationship with young people's drinking behaviour. The influence of attitudes to peers drinking in a single sex context was diminished when account was taken of its relative importance and interaction with level of acceptable behaviour and overall peer group support for drinking (O'Connor 1976a and b: 256-61).

An assessment was also made of the relative amount of variation in young people's drinking that was accounted for by the main effects of level of acceptable behaviour while drinking with a group of friends, attitudes to peers drinking in a single sex context, and overall peer group support for drinking. A description is now given of how the odds ratio of a young person being a light or heavy type of drinker was changed by the main and interaction effects of the variables described above.

As *Table 15* indicates, for every 7 young people, 6 would be light types of drinkers if he or she had a low level of acceptance of people showing signs of excessive drinking, disapproved of single sex drinking, and had low peer group support for drinking. This odds ratio (6 to 1) was the same when both the level of acceptance of excessive drinking and peer group support for drinking were low. If a young person's level of acceptance of excessive drinking was low, peer group support for his drinking high, and he disapproved or approved of single sex drinking, there was an even chance of his being classified as a light or heavy type of drinker.

When these young people accepted permissive behaviour while drinking, had high peer group support for drinking, and disapproved of drinking in a single sex context, the odds ratio was 4 to 1 that they would be heavy type drinkers — for every 5, 4 would be light type drinkers.

The evidence from this study is at one with previous findings which showed that as the child grows older, friends provide the overall context and location of drinking. On an index that measured peer group support for drinking, the Irish males and females appeared to have less support than did either the Anglo-Irish or English young people. In all groups peer group support for drinking was higher among the males than among the females. Overall social support from friends was found to be medium to high for the majority of the males and females under study. How often friends drank and how frequently the young people themselves drank in the company of their friends, was highly associated with heavy and very heavy type drinking.

When all the situations in which these young people drank were analyzed together and their interrelations taken into account, drinking in

Table 15   Estimate of the odds for becoming a light or heavy type of drinker depends on level of acceptable behaviour while drinking, attitude to single sex drinking, and peer group support for drinking

Level of acceptance	Attitude to single sex drinking	Peer group support for drinking	ODDS RATIO	
			Light type drinker	Heavy type drinker
Low	Disapprove	Low	5.8 to 1	0.17 to 1
High	Disapprove	Low	1.3 to 1	0.74 to 1
Low	Approve	Low	5.8 to 1	0.17 to 1
High	Approve	Low	1.3 to 1	0.74 to 1
Low	Disapprove	High	1.0 to 1	0.96 to 1
High	Disapprove	High	0.24 to 1	4.10 to 1
Low	Approve	High	1.03 to 1	0.96 to 1
High	Approve	High	0.24 to 1	4.0 to 1

a single sex context was shown to be the most highly related to heavy type drinking. Drinking frequently with a significant other or boy/girl friend was also highly related to heavy type drinking. Of all the settings used for drinking, the analysis showed that drinking frequently in a pub was the most highly associated with being classified as a heavy or very heavy type of drinker.

The importance of social rules in relation to drinking was very evident. Of all social rules for peers, favourable attitudes to drinking in a single sex context was highly associated with heavy type drinking. Attitudes to peers drinking and drinking in a mixed group context appeared not to be associated with young people's drinking behaviour. Levels of permissiveness were seen to affect drinking styles. Young people who had a high level of acceptance of behaviour associated with excessive drinking were heavier types of drinkers than those who had a low level of acceptance.

Using Goodman's analysis, the interaction of all these variables was ascertained. Of all peer group influences, overall peer group support for drinking was the most powerful explanatory variable. The results appeared to indicate that social pressure from friends *per se* was not the most important factor in whether young people developed a heavy type drinking pattern, although it did seem to influence the Irish male non-drinkers' decision to drink at some stage in the future.

Thus the complex interaction of the frequency of drinking in certain peer group contexts, the social rules of and permissive attitudes to drinking, drinking behaviour, and overall peer group support for drinking, needs to be considered when examining peers' influence on drinking behaviour. Account also needs to be taken of the general latitude of acceptable behaviour. However, it is worth remembering that for some young people, the verbalization of the various rules is not reflected in actual behaviour.

10
Social and personal influences

Social and personal variables

This chapter is concerned with social and personal influences and drinking behaviour. It aims at bringing together some of the descriptive data presented in Chapters 5, 6, and 7, to provide a more adequate analysis of the development of drinking behaviour among the young. The main focus of the discussion is an examination of how the young people under study define and interpret their social situation. To provide a general profile of the impact of young people's definition of their social situation, selected values and perceptions are investigated. These include the psychological aspects of anomie, and perceptions of the social environment in terms of opportunities, general attitude, areas of concern, and feelings of control over the future. Church membership and attendance at religious services, as well as the importance of religious beliefs in the lives of the young people under study, are also examined.

Perception of the social environment

A great deal of the early elaboration of the concept of alienation was the work of sociologists, who emphasized the societal nature of the condition. An emphasis on the psychological aspects followed and contemporary writers have attempted to integrate the two perspectives. It is not the purpose of this chapter to give an extensive review of the literature, or to reconcile the two differing perspectives, but rather to make clear the conceptual usage and empirical specification of the measures used, in order to gain a general profile of the world as viewed by the young people under study.

The term alienation is usually used to identify feelings of estrangement or detachment from self, others, or from society in general. However, it has also been used to refer to feelings of anomie, loss of self, despair, loneliness, rootlessness, powerlessness, pessimism, apathy, disaffection, withdrawal, disengagement, indifference, isolation, depersonalization, atomization, and meaninglessness (Josephson 1962). This list is not complete, for alienation is a word that lends itself to a wide variety of meanings. Fischer comments that there are

> '...a number of divisions in the study of alienation: between Durkheimians for whom man is alienated from society and Marxists for whom society is alienated from man; between subjectivists for whom alienation is a state of mind and objectivists for whom the mind's state can control true alienation...'   (Fischer 1976: 35)

The concept has received extensive treatment in the literature of social philosophy, psychology, and sociology over the years. It remains a dominant topic in both contemporary theoretical discussion and empirical research (Fischer 1976: 35). Empirical studies have focused on the alienation of the worker (Seeman 1959; Aiken and Hage 1966), of the voter (Dean 1960; Ghaem-Maghami 1973), of the young (Hoy 1972), of the elderly (Rosow 1967), and of the coloured person (Bullough 1967; Hiro 1973). Many researchers have applied the concept to the study of suicide and crime rates (Bagley 1967; Bernstein 1967). Some have found it mostly characteristic of the socio-economically deprived individuals in society. Others with different perspectives have used alienation to describe the attitude of social groups, such as intellectuals and white-collar workers in modern society (Fischer 1976: 35). The psychologist has tended to neglect the moulding power of the social context, while the sociologist in turn does not take the personal dimensions of the problem sufficiently into account. Increasingly, however, attention has been given to the socio-psychological approach.

It was noted in Chapter 1, that the concept of alienation has been used in the study of alcoholism and problem drinking, as well as in the enquiry into the development of problem drinking among the young. There are two ways in which the concept tends to have been used: (1) as a condition existing prior to the onset of alcoholism, or (2) as a condition which develops along with alcoholism. In this study the concept is explored in a number of ways. First the psychological aspect is examined, using a modified version of the anomie scale developed by McCloskey and Schaar. McCloskey and Schaar (1965: 14) defined anomie as 'a state of mind, a cluster of attitudes, beliefs and feelings in the mind of individuals'. They defined it as 'moral emptiness'. Anomie appears if the learning of the norms of a society is impaired. The personal factors that impede the learning of societal norms are cognitive, emotional, and substantive beliefs and attitudes. Briefly, the authors saw the situation as one where cognitive factors impair one's learning and comprehension ability, emotional factors lessen one's perception of reality, and substantive beliefs and attitudes impede both communication and interaction. Inability to learn and understand may be the result of a lack of innate ability, but it may also be due to social conditions. Failure at the emotional level may be due in many circumstances to inadequate socialization. If one's beliefs and values are not the predominant ones held by the group, their acceptance by the other members will be difficult. Responses to the social and political community were measured by the anomie scale as designed by McCloskey and Schaar (1965: 23). 'Other measures in this set', they note, 'included bewilderment, pessimism, alienation, and a sense of political futility'.

Modified anomie scale   The modified McCloskey and Schaar scale (see Appendix 3) was divided into three parts, and the young people were designated as having a high, medium, or low anomie score. Using this scale, it can be seen that more of the Irish males (36.2) and females (46.6) than either the Anglo-Irish (males 19.4, females 30.2), or English (males 21.0, females 37.4) young people had a high score on the anomie scale. Two-fifths of the Anglo-Irish and one-third of the English males, compared with a quarter of the Irish males, were designated as low on this scale. The corresponding figures for the females were over one-tenth of the Irish and a quarter of both English and Anglo-Irish females. In all groups more of the females than the males were high on this scale.

Perceived opportunity in country of origin

An index was devised consisting of four items which were concerned mainly with the image of various aspects of perceived opportunities available in, as well as general feelings about, the country in which the 18-21 year olds lived. Twenty-three per cent of Anglo-Irish and 17 per cent of Irish and English males agreed with all of the four items; they had a favourable image of the country in which they lived, where with hard work one could make a good career, which was preferable for bringing up children, and was a good place to live in. This was found for between 11 and 19 per cent of the females. Nearly all of the Irish and English males and females agreed with one statement on the index — that their country was a good place to live in. This was found for seven-tenths of the Anglo-Irish males and four-fifths of the Anglo-Irish females. More of the Irish (males 55.4, females 49.2) than either the Anglo-Irish (males 38.5, females 37.0) or English (males 35.3, females 35.8) young people agreed with three of the items, namely that their country was a preferable place to bring up children, to make a good career, and was a good place to live in. Thirty per cent of the Anglo-Irish males and 16.1 per cent of the Anglo-Irish females, disagreed with all the items on the scale. This applied to under 10 per cent of all the other young people under study. Certain inconsistencies arose in that, although more of the Irish than Anglo-Irish or English young people scored higher on the index used to measure conditions resulting from certain stresses in the social system, they also had a more positive view of the social situation in which they found themselves, in terms of opportunities and general attitude to their country.

All the males and females under study felt that there were problems in their country. The Irish conception of the major areas of concern was different from that of the Anglo-Irish and English. This reflected in part the different cultural settings. Priority was given by the Irish to political, economic, and social problems, while both the Anglo-Irish and English specified (1) economic, (2) housing, and (3) race relations, as the major problems in their country.

When they were asked how changes could be brought about, over two-thirds of the Irish, seven-tenths of the Anglo-Irish, and three-fifths of the English males, said it could be brought about by democratic means. This applied to over three-fifths of the Irish females; half of both Anglo-Irish and English females said that the desired change could be brought about by democratic means but added by political pressure, or change of government. A small percentage, 6.8 per cent of Irish and 4.3 per cent of Anglo-Irish males, felt that changes could only be brought about by revolutionary methods. This applied to 17 per cent of the Anglo-Irish females. While between 4 and 7 per cent of all groups felt that change could not be brought about, between 17 and 25 per cent of the males, and 17 and 30 per cent of the females, did not know how change could be brought about. Over half of all groups felt that they themselves would not be involved in bringing about change. Slightly under one-fifth of the Irish (16.8) and Anglo-Irish males (18.6), and over one-tenth of the English (13.5), felt that they could be involved through political measures. The corresponding figures for the females were 17 per cent of the Anglo-Irish, 13 per cent of the Irish females, and 7 per cent of the English females.

Values important in family life

The young people were asked if the values of affection, dependence, independence, and recognition were important in family life. A cumulative index was devised which placed these values in order of importance. *Table 16* shows that between 27 and 33 per cent of the males, and 31 to 36 per cent of the females, said that recognition, independence, dependence, and affection were all important in family life. The value agreed on by most young people as being of the greatest importance was affection: over 95 per cent of all females, and 94 per cent of Irish, 80 per cent of Anglo-Irish, and 87 per cent of English males gave this answer. One-fifth of the Anglo-Irish males and one-tenth of the English males felt that these values were not important in family life. This was found for 6 per cent of Irish males and between 2 and 3 per cent of all the females under study.

Of all the indicators (see O'Connor 1976a and b: 278-84) used to look at the world view of those under study, the perceived opportunity system in and attitude to their country were the only measures associated with the amount of alcohol consumed by young people. More young people classified in the lighter than in the heavier drinking categories had positive feelings for their country in general, as well as for the opportunity structure.

Religious practice and religiosity

This section looks at church membership and attendance at religious services, as well as the importance of religious beliefs in the lives of the young people interviewed.

Over 90 per cent of Irish and Anglo-Irish males and females were members of the Roman Catholic Church. Seventy per cent of the English females and 55 per cent of the English males were members of the Church of England. However, attendance at religious services indicated that Irish males (57.3) and females (86.1) were more involved in the formal aspects of church membership (going to church once a week or more) than were the Anglo-Irish males (31.2) and females (49.0). Very few English females (6.1) and males (4.2) attended church services once a week or more, while two-thirds of the males and nearly three-fifths of the females never went to church or religious services at all (see Appendix 3).

A four-item cumulative scale was devised on religiosity. This was aimed at seeing whether prayer, belief in God, religious advice, and going to church, were important in the young people's lives. A second measure was concerned with how religion was seen to influence their everyday activities. Two-fifths of Irish males, compared with one-tenth of Anglo-Irish and English males, said that going to church regularly, reliance on religious advice, belief in God, and prayer, were important in their lives (*Table 17*). These four items were found to be important for three-fifths of the Irish, two-fifths of the Anglo-Irish, and one-fifth of the English

Table 16 Values perceived to be important in family life as measured by the 18-21 year olds' responses (Q.788)

	Males			Females		
	Irish 187	*Anglo-Irish* 93	*English* 117	*Irish* 184	*Anglo-Irish* 85	*English* 98
Negative to all items	100% 11 (5.9)	100% 18 (19.4)	100% 15 (12.8)	100% 6 (3.3)	100% 2 (2.4)	100% 2 (2.1)
Affection	94.1 21 (11.2)	80.6 18 (19.5)	87.2 16 (13.7)	96.7 10 (5.4)	97.6 11 (12.9)	97.9 8 (8.2)
Dependence	82.8 48 (25.7)	61.3 14 (15.1)	73.5 20 (17.1)	91.3 42 (22.8)	84.7 21 (24.7)	89.8 21 (21.4)
Independence	57.2 56 (29.9)	46.2 14 (15.1)	56.4 27 (23.1)	58.5 58 (31.5)	59.9 24 (28.2)	68.4 31 (31.6)
Recognition	27.3 51 (27.3)	31.2 29 (31.2)	33.3 39 (33.3)	36.9 68 (36.9)	31.8 27 (31.8)	36.7 36 (36.7)
Total	187	93	117	184	85	98

Table 17 Religiosity Guttman scale: percentage frequency distribution of items considered to be important as measured by 18-21 year-olds' responses and scaled by Guttman techniques (Q.74§)

Scale type cumulative	Items	Males			Females		
		Irish	Anglo-Irish	English	Irish	Anglo-Irish	English
1	Does not consider any item important	100% 14 (7.6)	100% 24 (25.1)	100% 53 (44.9)	100% 7 (3.8)	100% 7 (8.2)	100% 23 (23.7)
2	Prayer important	92.4 29 (15.6)	73.8 21 (22.8)	55.1 27 (22.8)	96.2 10 (5.3)	91.8 10 (11.7)	75.9 15 (15.4)
3	Believing in God important	76.7 22 (11.8)	51.0 18 (19.5)	32.1 18 (15.2)	90.8 15 (8.0)	79.9 18 (21.1)	60.7 19 (19.5)
4	Reliance on religious advice, counsel or teaching when he has a problem, important	64.8 47 (25.4)	31.5 19 (20.6)	16.9 11 (9.3)	82.7 40 (21.5)	58.8 17 (20.0)	41.2 20 (20.6)
5	Going to church regularly important	39.4 73 (39.4)	10.8 10 (10.8)	7.6 9 (7.6)	61.2 114 (61.2)	38.8 33 (38.8)	20.6 20 (20.6)
	N =	185	92	118	186	85	97
	Coefficient of reproducibility	0.7919	0.7880	0.8602	0.9113	0.8176	0.8814
	Minimal margin reproducibility	0.6838	0.6576	0.7203	0.8230	0.6735	0.6134
	Percentage improvement	0.1081	0.1304	0.1398	0.0833	0.1441	0.2680
	Coefficient of scalability	0.3419	0.3810	0.5000	0.4844	0.4414	0.6933

females. Two-thirds of the Irish males, three-tenths of the Anglo-Irish, and under one-fifth of the English males, said that reliance on religious advice, belief in God, and prayer, were important in their lives. The corresponding figures for the females were four-fifths for the Irish, three-fifths for the Anglo-Irish, and two-fifths for the English females. At the other end of the scale, a quarter of the Anglo-Irish and over two-fifths of the English males, compared with under one-tenth of the Irish males, said they did not consider any of the items to be important. This also applied to a quarter of the English females, 8 per cent of the Anglo-Irish, and 4 per cent of the Irish females.

Religious beliefs or teachings were a continuous, very frequent, or frequent influence on the actions of 43 per cent of the Irish males, 28 per cent of the Anglo-Irish, and 15 per cent of the English males. The corresponding figures for the females were three-fifths of the Irish females, two-fifths of the Anglo-Irish, and one-fifth of the English females. Religious beliefs or teachings were said never to influence the actions of nearly half of the English males (47.9) and three-tenths of the English females (27.3). One-fifth of Anglo-Irish males, one-tenth of Anglo-Irish females, nearly one-fifth of Irish males, and under 5 per cent of Irish females, said religion never influenced their actions.

Over nine out of ten Irish and Anglo-Irish young people, compared with six out of ten English males and seven out of ten English females, were members of the same church as their parents.

An examination was made of the relationship between drinking behaviour and the importance of religion in the young people's lives, as well as the frequency with which their religious beliefs or teachings influenced their actions. No association was found between these variables for the Anglo-Irish or English young people. The numbers of abstainers/virtual abstainers were too small in the English and Anglo-Irish groups to make any meaningful analysis. As religious affiliation followed ethnic lines it was not possible to make meaningful comparisons in relation to drinking behaviour and religious affiliation. The following statistically significant relationships were found for the Irish groups (see O'Connor 1976a and b: 458):

1 Irish abstainers and virtual abstainers felt that religious values were more important in their lives than did the other types of Irish drinkers.
2 Irish abstainers and virtual abstainers were more frequently influenced by their religious beliefs than were the young people in the heavier drinking categories.

Social and personal correlates of drinking behaviour

This analysis brings together some of the descriptive data from Chapters 5, 6, and 7, which have not already been discussed.

Influence of drinking practices (see O'Connor 1976a and b: 459-62)

1 There was some evidence to suggest that heavier drinking young people started to drink at an earlier age than did young people who were classified as lighter types of drinkers.
2 Young people who drank to effect a change in mood tended to be heavy type drinkers.
3 Young people who experienced one or more problems related to their drinking tended to be heavier type drinkers.
4 More young people who experienced three or more types of behaviour associated with sensation excitement seeking were classified in the heavy or very heavy drinking category.

Personal influences on drinking behaviour
(see O'Connor 1976a and b: 463-65)

1 There was a general tendency for alcohol consumption to increase with age for Irish males and females. This pattern was weak and was weaker still for both Anglo-Irish and English young people.
2 While the relationship was weak, Irish males who were abstainers or light types of drinkers had jobs of high rather than low occupational status.
3 Young people whose net income was £25 a week or more were heavier types of drinkers than those who earned £25 or less.
4 Males who were classified as heavy or very heavy types of drinkers tended to spend more money on alcohol than those males who were classified as lighter type drinkers.

Interrelationships and relative importance of variables
(details in O'Connor 1976a and b: 281-91)

A number of variables were taken together — age at first drink, age at time of interview, experience of sensation excitement seeking behaviour, and religiosity — and their relative influence on young people's drinking behaviour, as well as the interaction between the variables, was ascertained. The results suggested that age at first drink and age at time of interview did not appear to influence the development of drinking behaviour. Of the four variables, experience of sensation excitement seeking behaviour was the most highly related to the development of drinking behaviour. More young people who partook in three or more, than in two or less of the behaviours included in the sensation excitement seeking index were heavy type drinkers. There was a strong relationship between those young people with a high level of religiosity, as measured by the importance of religion in their lives, and drinking behaviour. The effect was negative, showing that those with a high level of religiosity tended to be categorized in the lighter drinking categories.

Further analysis revealed the main and interaction effects of perceived opportunities in and attitudes towards country of origin, occupation and income. The evidence was that of all these variables, level of income was the most highly significant in relation to drinking behaviour. The results suggested that those young people with £25 net income (at 1972 prices) or more a week were classified in the heavier drinking categories. Young people who perceived the opportunity structure in their country as low, were more likely to be in the heavy or very heavy type drinking categories. However, the interaction effect between the perceived opportunities in country of origin, income level, and drinking behaviour, is worthy of note. Positive attitudes towards country of origin tended to be related to lighter type drinking, but when these were allied to high levels of income, the income effect took over.

Interrelationships

To synthesize and pinpoint the main social and personal influence/s, the most powerful explanatory variables that emerged from the data discussed above were further analyzed. These were, income level, experience of sensation excitement seeking, perceived opportunities, and attitudes towards their country. Sex status and weekly expenditure on alcohol were added to the list.

Table 18 showed that the only variables affecting the odds ratio of being a light or heavy type drinker, were sex status and expenditure on alcohol. The strongest effect was sex status, which had a highly significant direct effect on drinking behaviour. This reflected the fact that heavy and very heavy type drinking was sex related, males being heavier type drinkers than females. The next biggest effect was weekly expenditure on alcohol. This result indicated that heavier drinkers spent more than £3 a week on alcohol, a not unexpected result. The odds ratio was 7 to 1 of being classified as a heavy type drinker if the young person was male and spent £3 or over a week on alcohol. As approximately 85 per cent of all females who spent money on alcohol spent less than £3 a

Table 18 Estimate of the odds for becoming a light or heavy type of drinker depends on income level, perceived opportunity in and attitude towards country, sex status, sensation excitement seeking behaviour, and level of expenditure on alcohol

Income level per week (net)	Perceived opportunity attitude to country	Sex status	Sensation excitement seeking	Expenditure on alcohol per week	ODDS RATIO	
					Light type drinker	Heavy type drinker
£25 or less	Low	Male	Low	Less than £3	0.80 to 1	1.20 to 1
£25 or more	Low	Male	Low	Less than £3	0.80 to 1	1.20 to 1
£25 or less	High	Male	Low	Less than £3	0.80 to 1	1.20 to 1
£25 or more	High	Male	Low	Less than £3	0.80 to 1	1.20 to 1
£25 or less	Low	Female	Low	Less than £3	2.00 to 1	0.50 to 1
£25 or more	Low	Female	Low	Less than £3	2.00 to 1	0.50 to 1
£25 or less	High	Female	Low	Less than £3	2.00 to 1	0.50 to 1
£25 or more	High	Female	Low	Less than £3	2.00 to 1	0.50 to 1
£25 or less	Low	Male	High	Less than £3	0.80 to 1	1.20 to 1
£25 or more	Low	Male	High	Less than £3	0.80 to 1	1.20 to 1
£25 or less	High	Male	High	Less than £3	0.80 to 1	1.20 to 1
£25 or more	High	Male	High	Less than £3	0.80 to 1	1.20 to 1
£25 or less	Low	Female	High	Less than £3	2.00 to 1*	0.50 to 1
£25 or more	Low	Female	High	Less than £3	2.00 to 1*	0.50 to 1
£25 or less	High	Female	High	Less than £3	2.00 to 1*	0.50 to 1
£25 or more	High	Female	High	Less than £3	2.00 to 1*	0.50 to 1

Table 18 continued

£25 or less	Low	Male	Low	More than £3	0.14 to 1	7.10 to 1
£25 or more	Low	Male	Low	More than £3	0.14 to 1	7.10 to 1
£25 or less	High	Male	Low	More than £3	0.14 to 1	7.10 to 1
£25 or more	High	Male	Low	More than £3	0.14 to 1	7.10 to 1
£25 or less	Low	Female	Low	More than £3	0.90 to 1*	1.10 to 1
£25 or more	Low	Female	Low	More than £3	0.90 to 1*	1.10 to 1
£25 or less	High	Female	Low	More than £3	0.90 to 1*	1.10 to 1
£25 or more	High	Female	Low	More than £3	0.90 to 1*	1.10 to 1
£25 or less	Low	Male	High	More than £3	0.14 to 1	7.10 to 1
£25 or more	Low	Male	High	More than £3	0.14 to 1	7.10 to 1
£25 or less	High	Male	High	More than £3	0.14 to 1	7.10 to 1
£25 or more	High	Male	High	More than £3	0.14 to 1	7.10 to 1
£25 or less	Low	Female	High	More than £3	0.90 to 1*	1.10 to 1
£25 or more	Low	Female	High	More than £3	0.90 to 1*	1.10 to 1
£25 or less	High	Female	High	More than £3	0.90 to 1*	1.10 to 1
£25 or more	High	Female	High	More than £3	0.90 to 1*	1.10 to 1

*There were very few in these categories.

week, inclusion of the odds ratio for them was really unnecessary, the numbers being too small for meaningful analysis. The odds ratios of a male being a heavy or light drinker were almost equal when weekly expenditure on alcohol was less than £3, irrespective of income level or perceived opportunity structure and attitudes towards his country.

In the attempt to understand how social and personal influences are related to drinking behaviour, an examination was made of how the young people under study defined and interpreted their social situation. Of all the indicators used to look at these definitions, young people's perceptions of the opportunity structure in and their attitudes towards their country of origin were found to be associated with the amount of alcohol consumed. Also related to their drinking behaviour were a number of social and personal variables, such as age at first drink, age at time of interview, occupation, income, experience of drink-related problems, and expenditure on alcohol; other influences included certain reasons associated with drinking, sensation excitement seeking behaviour, and young people's level of religiosity.

Further analysis was undertaken to assess the interrelationships between variables (age at first drink, age at time of interview, experience of sensation excitement seeking behaviour, and religiosity) and their relative importance on the young people's drinking behaviour. Experience of three or more behaviours associated with sensation excitement seeking was highly related to heavy type drinking. The effect of religiosity was next, it was negative, showing that those with a high level of religiosity tended to be classified in the lighter drinking categories. The relative influence of age at first drink and age at time of interview, was diminished.

Under another model, the main and interaction effects of perceived opportunities in and attitudes towards country of origin, occupation, and level of income, were assessed. Income level and perceived opportunities in country of origin were found to be highly related to drinking behaviour. An interaction effect existed between these two variables, and although positive attitudes towards country of origin were associated with lighter type drinking, when they were allied to high level of income, the income effect took over. The influence of occupational level was diminished, and appeared to have no significant effect on drinking behaviour.

In an effort to synthesize the vast amount of data and variables in this section, further analysis was undertaken which showed that of all the powerful variables in the preceding analyses, the sex of the drinker was the most important predictive variable in relation to young people's drinking behaviour.

11

The development of drinking
behaviour among young people:
a general model

The main findings relating to the use of alcohol among the Irish, Anglo-Irish, and English young people studied, as well as in the transmission of drinking behaviour have been presented. It is the purpose of this final chapter of results to present a general model of the development of drinking among young people.

Several stages of analysis were involved in the construction of the model. In Chapters 5, 6, and 7 the data analyses were mainly descriptive. Following this, the material was organized into four main areas: (1) parental influences, (2) peer group influences, (3) social and personal influences, and (4) ethnic and cultural influences. To provide more adequate measures of the effects of different variables, taking into account their interrelations, Goodman's modified multiple regression analysis was used (1972a, b, and c). Within each group the main and interaction effects of the variables were estimated, and the most powerful explanatory or classificatory variable was selected to go forward into the general model. In this model* the four most powerful variables were: fathers' attitude to mixing drinks and drinking three or more drinks on one occasion, peer group support for drinking, sex status, and ethnic status. Other variables were relatively unimportant, having little or no effect on the dependent variable — young people's drinking behaviour — once these four variables were taken into account (O'Connor 1976a and b: 295-97).

To simplify the presentation of results, the three groups of young people were examined in pairs. This is equivalent to examining the three

*As there were a number of missing values in some of the variables, the possibility of getting low numbers in some of the categories had to be considered. Since this was a general model the number of variables that could have emerged were quite considerable.

groups together, but is easier to interpret (O'Connor, 1976a and b: 297-315).

Among the Irish and English groups, the largest main influence was that of sex, indicating that males were heavier type drinkers than females. The next most important effect was that due to peer group support for drinking; young people who were heavy type drinkers tended to have high peer group support for drinking, and light drinkers tended to have friends who did not give this kind of support. The smallest main effect was due to fathers' attitude. In this analysis, ethnic status was not used as a variable related to young people's type of drinking, as it had no direct effect on their drinking behaviour. However, this result should be interpreted with care and will be discussed below.

The Anglo-Irish and English groups were examined next. The results suggested that the order of importance of the main influences was somewhat different from that of the results presented for the Irish and English young people. Peer group support was the most important, with fathers' attitude marginally less important. The evidence also suggested that there was less of a difference in the drinking habits of males and females in these groups compared with the Irish males and females. In this case the data showed a weak ethnic effect, reflecting the fact that, all other things being equal, the Anglo-Irish young people drank more heavily than the English under study.

The comparison between the Irish and the Anglo-Irish indicated interaction effects between ethnic status and fathers' attitude, as well as between ethnic status and sex status. The influence of sex was marginally more important than that of peer group support. Fathers' attitude, though not as important as these two influences, was still more important than when the Irish and English young people were compared. Here again the influence of ethnic status was evident, in that the Anglo-Irish tended to be heavier type drinkers than the Irish 18-21 year olds.

The interaction effect between ethnic status and sex substantiates the earlier results that there were greater differences between the drinking habits of the two sexes among the Irish, than among the Anglo-Irish. The interaction effects between fathers' attitude and ethnic status indicate quite clearly that fathers' attitude was more important in the Anglo-Irish than in the Irish group under study.

Drawing together the results from the three groups of young people interviewed, the largest main effect was due to sex, reflecting the fact that males were heavier type drinkers than were females. The most important explanatory variable to emerge in all groups was peer group support for drinking. Fathers' attitude to drinking was of most importance in the Anglo-Irish group and least in the Irish group. In no case was there a statistically significant direct effect due to the ethnic variable. From this, one may be tempted to conclude that the ethnic variable had no effect on young people's drinking behaviour.

However, this is not altogether correct. The results that we have examined gave the effects of the independent variables, fathers' attitude, peer-group support for drinking, and sex status, on young people's classification as a type of drinker, for each of the three groups under study. In order to consider the ethnic effect more closely, it was necessary to examine the interactions between the ethnic variable and the other variables, in particular peer group support for drinking and fathers' attitude (see O'Connor, 1976a and b: 303).

The interpretation of these effects is of some interest. The results showed that more Irish than Anglo-Irish fathers had negative attitudes to heavy drinking. In turn, more Anglo-Irish fathers had negative attitudes than English fathers. Again, more of the Irish young people had low peer group support for drinking than either of the other two groups. These figures confirm that while ethnic status does not itself have a direct effect on drinking behaviour, it does very strongly influence fathers' attitude, and in the case of Irish males and females, it influences peer group support for drinking.

It was decided to test the validity of the general overall model by considering very heavy drinkers and the other types of drinkers. It will be remembered that the type of drinker index showed that slightly over two-thirds of the Irish, four-fifths of the Anglo-Irish, and seven-tenths of the English males were heavy type drinkers. The corresponding figures for the females were slightly over one-fifth of the Irish, three-fifths of the Anglo-Irish, and one-third of the English. Very few of these females were very heavy type drinkers (see *Table A.1.15*). As expected, the pattern found in the overall model, between the independent variables discussed above and young people's drinking behaviour, was also seen to hold in this case.

The results showed that by changing the definition of light and heavy drinking to include

light drinkers = abstainer/virtual abstainer, light drinker,
                     moderate drinker and heavy drinker
heavy drinkers = very heavy drinker

the model was similar, but the effect of fathers' attitude to mixing drinks and drinking three or more drinks on one occasion and ethnic status (which was weak in the other model) was further weakened in this model. The most significant effect here too was the sex difference, which emerged even more strongly. The next effect which was important was that due to peer group support for drinking. Young people who were very heavy drinkers had a high level of peer group support for drinking, while lighter drinkers did not. In all three groups, the main effects due to both peer group support and to sex were strengthened but their relative importance remained the same. However, in the comparison between the Irish and the Anglo-Irish, it was necessary to include the effect due to fathers' attitude. Thus, under this model, Irish and Anglo-Irish young people who had fathers who disapproved of mixing drinks and drinking three or more drinks, tended to be light type drinkers. This effect was not found between the Irish and English, or Anglo-Irish and English i.e. fathers' attitude had no statistically significant effect. As in the previous model in no case was it necessary to include a direct effect due to the ethnic variable.

A second interpretation of these results (Goodman 1972b: 1080) explains the amount of variation in young people's drinking behaviour that was accounted for by the main effects of fathers' attitude to mixing drinks and amount of alcohol consumed, peer group support for drinking, sex status, and ethnic status. In this way a description was made of how the odds of a young person being a light or heavy type drinker were changed by the main and interaction effects of the variables described above, and how the proportion in the light or heavy type drinking categories were changed by these effects (*Tables 19 and 20*).

The results for the Irish and English males show that when peer group support was low the odds ratio was approximately 5 to 1 that the young male would be a light type of drinker, irrespective of fathers' attitude or ethnic status. However, if peer group support was high, it was nearly 2 to 1 against him being classified as a light type of drinker.

When the Irish and Anglo-Irish males were considered, it was necessary to take into account fathers' attitude, as well as peer group support for drinking. If peer group support was low and fathers' attitude disapproving, the odds ratio was high (7 to 1) that the young person would be a light type drinker. However, if fathers' attitude was approving, and peer group support low, the odds ratio shortened to nearly 3 to 1 that the male would be a light type of drinker. The chances of a male being a light or heavy type of drinker were about even, when peer group support for drinking was high, and fathers' attitude not approving. If, on the other hand, both peer group support for drinking was high and fathers' attitude approving, the odds ratio was 2 to 1 against the young male being a light type of drinker. The odds ratio of being a light type of drinker when peer group support was low, was 3 to 1 for the Anglo-Irish and English males taken together, irrespective of fathers' attitude. (It will be remembered here, that fathers' attitude, and ethnic status had no direct effect.) If peer group support for drinking was high, the odds ratio was nearly 2 to 1 against being classified as a light type of drinker.

Table 19   Estimate of the odds for becoming a light or heavy type drinker, depending on fathers' attitude to the amount of alcohol consumed by his children, peer group support for drinking, sex status, and ethnic status

			ODDS RATIO	
Fathers' attitude	*Peer group support*	*Ethnic*	*Light type drinker*	*Very heavy type drinker*
Males — Irish and English				
Disapprove	Low	Irish	4.8 to 1	0.20 to 1
Approve	Low	Irish	4.7 to 1	0.20 to 1
Disapprove	Low	English	4.8 to 1	0.20 to 1
Approve	Low	English	4.7 to 1	0.20 to 1
Disapprove	High	Irish	0.7 to 1	1.50 to 1
Approve	High	Irish	0.7 to 1	1.40 to 1
Disapprove	High	English	0.7 to 1	1.50 to 1
Approve	High	English	0.7 to 1	1.40 to 1
Males — Irish and Anglo-Irish				
Disapprove	Low	Irish	7.0 to 1	0.14 to 1
Approve	Low	Irish	2.8 to 1	0.35 to 1
Disapprove	Low	Anglo-Irish	6.7 to 1	0.14 to 1
Approve	Low	Anglo-Irish	2.8 to 1	0.34 to 1
Disapprove	High	Irish	1.2 to 1	0.83 to 1
Approve	High	Irish	1.7 to 1	2.11 to 1
Disapprove	High	Anglo-Irish	1.9 to 1	0.83 to 1
Approve	High	Anglo-Irish	0.5 to 1	2.10 to 1
Males Anglo-Irish and English				
Disapprove	Low	Anglo-Irish	3.1 to 1	0.31 to 1
Approve	Low	Anglo-Irish	3.1 to 1	0.31 to 1
Disapprove	Low	English	3.1 to 1	0.32 to 1
Approve	Low	English	3.1 to 1	0.32 to 1
Disapprove	High	Anglo-Irish	0.6 to 1	1.59 to 1
Approve	High	Anglo-Irish	0.6 to 1	1.59 to 1
Disapprove	High	English	0.6 to 1	1.59 to 1
Approve	High	English	0.6 to 1	1.59 to 1

The females under study presented a somewhat different pattern. It will be remembered that fathers' attitude to drinking was included in the overall model for all groups; ethnic status was also included but it had no direct effect. Under the model used, when Irish and English females had

Table 20   Estimate of the odds for becoming a light or heavy type drinker, depending on fathers' attitude to the amount of alcohol consumed by his children, peer group support for drinking, sex status, and ethnic status

			ODDS RATIO	
Fathers' attitude	*Peer group support*	*Ethnic*	*Light type drinker*	*Very heavy type drinker*
Females – Irish and English				
Disapprove	Low	Irish	7.1 to 1	0.13 to 1
Approve	Low	Irish	3.3 to 1	0.30 to 1
Disapprove	Low	English	7.1 to 1	0.13 to 1
Approve	Low	English	3.3 to 1	0.30 to 1
Disapprove	High	Irish	1.8 to 1	0.54 to 1
Approve	High	Irish	0.9 to 1	1.17 to 1
Disapprove	High	English	1.8 to 1	0.54 to 1
Approve	High	English	0.9 to 1	1.17 to 1
Females – Irish and Anglo-Irish				
Disapprove	Low	Irish	7.3 to 1	0.13 to 1
Approve	Low	Irish	3.7 to 1	0.27 to 1
Disapprove	Low	Anglo-Irish	3.5 to 1	0.28 to 1
Approve	Low	Anglo-Irish	0.6 to 1	1.59 to 1
Disapprove	High	Irish	1.8 to 1	0.53 to 1
Approve	High	Irish	0.9 to 1	1.05 to 1
Disapprove	High	Anglo-Irish	0.9 to 1	1.09 to 1
Approve	High	Anglo-Irish	0.16 to 1	6.19 to 1
Females – Anglo-Irish and English				
Disapprove	Low	Anglo-Irish	3.8 to 1	0.26 to 1
Approve	Low	Anglo-Irish	0.8 to 1	1.24 to 1
Disapprove	Low	English	7.7 to 1	0.12 to 1
Approve	Low	English	1.7 to 1	0.58 to 1
Disapprove	High	Anglo-Irish	1.1 to 1	0.87 to 1
Approve	High	Anglo-Irish	0.2 to 1	4.08 to 1
Disapprove	High	English	2.4 to 1	0.41 to 1
Approve	High	English	0.5 to 1	1.96 to 1

low peer group support for drinking and fathers' attitude was disapproving, the odds ratio was 7.1 that they would be light type drinkers. The odds ratio was reduced by half (approximately 3 to 1) if fathers' attitude was approving and peer group support low. If on the other hand fathers' attitude was approving and peer group support was high, the odds ratios were (approximately) equal for the young female being either a light or heavy type of drinker.

A slightly different picture arises when we look specifically at the Irish and Anglo-Irish females. When fathers' attitude was approving and peer group support for drinking was low, the odds ratio was 4 to 1 that an Irish female would be a light type drinker, but nearly 2 to 1 against an Anglo-Irish female being a light type of drinker. If peer group support was high and fathers' attitude approving, the Irish females had an even chance of being a light drinker; however, the odds ratio was 6 to 1 against an Anglo-Irish female being a light type of drinker.

The pattern was somewhat similar for the Anglo-Irish and English females. If the father disapproved and there was low peer group support for drinking, the odds ratio was about 8 to 1 that an English female would be a light type of drinker, and approximately 4 to 1 for an Anglo-Irish female. When both the father approved and peer group support for drinking was high, the odds ratio was nearly 4 to 1 that an Anglo-Irish female would be a heavy type of drinker, and 2 to 1 for an English female.

The most powerful explanatory model of the data has been presented in this chapter which illustrated how culture, parents, and peers interact in influencing the development of young people's drinking behaviour. The implications to be drawn from these results are discussed in the next chapter.

12
Summary and conclusion

This book is about drinking and the young. It is a study of the importance and interaction of factors which influence patterns of drinking behaviour and attitudes among young people. The four central areas of study were:

1 Ethnic and cultural influences
2 Parental influences
3 Peer group influences
4 Social and personal influences

The research design provided for a detailed description of drinking behaviour and attitudes, and a comparative study of (1) parents and children and (2) young people differing in country of origin and parental ethnic background. The general model of the development of drinking behaviour presented, indicated how culture, parents, and peers interact in influencing the development of a young person's drinking behaviour.

To look at ethnic influences it was decided to take two ethnic groups, the Irish and English, known to have different rates of drinking problems. This assertion is based partly on research indicators and partly on the images of both groups as particular types of drinkers. An historical analysis of the attitudes and patterns of drinking of the Irish and English suggests that, as far back as the sixteenth and up to the early part of the twentieth century, English culture was quite like the Irish in relation to the use of alcohol. However, the stereotype image of the Irishman as a humorous and boisterous drunk has become a legend both abroad and in Ireland itself. The stereotype image of the Englishman, on the other hand, is one of a moderate drinker, even though epidemiological studies have shown that the English do have a drink problem and that their rates of alcoholism are high.

The selection of these ethnic groups was dictated in part by their close proximity to one another. The fact that there was a large section of Irish people living in England also made it possible to look at people of Irish origin living in another cultural setting. As a third group was required to assist in the assessment of the relative importance of ethnic and cultural, parental, peer, and social and personal influences, the group to be chosen were those referred to throughout the study as the Anglo-Irish. This group consisted of 18-21 year olds born in England, and socialized in an English cultural environment by Irish parents, who were born and reared in the Republic of Ireland, had emigrated to England, and had married, and settled down there. They provided a valuable comparative group.

Empirical data was obtained through interviews with samples of Irish, Anglo-Irish, and English 18-21 year olds of both sexes, and their parents. Altogether 774 18-21 year olds, 613 fathers and 747 mothers were interviewed and among them there were 545 family units consisting of a father and a mother, and a son or a daughter. Parents and children were interviewed separately.

A brief overview of the main findings of the study and an examination of some of the results will be discussed here.

Ethnic and cultural influences

It appears to be an established fact that different groups and societies have different drinking practices and different rates of alcoholism. Many attempts have been made to explain these differences. One of the main explanations put forward is the cultural one. Studies using this perspective stress the social meaning and function of alcohol, drinking, and drunkenness. They describe how different patterns of alcohol use have emerged in different societies. The focus of these studies has been on the socialization into drinking patterns, the structure of social norms, and the rates of drinking problems.

From these studies sociologists have endeavoured to define the role and function of alcohol in society, as well as the more complex everyday social rules of drinking behaviour. The socio-cultural emphasis of this study seeks to establish the social meaning and function of alcohol, drinking, and drunkenness among the young people under study. Culture refers to a man's entire social heritage, all the beliefs, skills, practices, and attitudes he acquires as a member of the society in which he lives.

The Irish and the English

A brief historical analysis helped put into perspective the ideas, practices, and attitudes presented to the generations now socialized in each culture. Originally, the English and Irish cultures seem to have been quite similar with regard to their use of alcohol. In both societies the exchange of drink was a social ritual, implying interdependence and a continuing relationship. Both the English and Irish drank heavily at funerals and other occasions, settled bargains over drinks at fairs, and drank for medicinal purposes. In both countries drinking was seen as a serious problem and the evidence suggested that this continued up to the turn of the twentieth century. Legislation did little to help matters and temperance societies became active. The English and Irish temperance movements were norm-oriented, and had an impact not only on drinking habits, but also on the way people's attitudes to alcohol developed. The Irish temperance movement was essentially a religious-oriented movement affecting attitudes to alcohol, and helping to create an ambivalent cultural attitude to drink. The English movement did not have this particular effect, although it was one of many factors which helped to bring about sobriety.

The evidence from this study suggested that there were differences between the drinking patterns and attitudes towards drinking of the Irish and English young people interviewed. The differences centred around:

1 Extent and prevalence of drinking
2 Customs and patterns of drinking
3 Social meaning and function of alcohol
4 Social rules of drinking
5 Exposure to drink-related problems
6 Experience of drink-related problems

(1) There was a much higher proportion of abstainers among the Irish 18-21 year olds than among the English young people under study. In relation to the amount of alcohol consumed, the findings showed that nearly all the English parents and 18-21 year olds drank, with 62 per cent of the English fathers and 88 per cent of the English mothers being classified as abstainers/virtual abstainers, light, or moderate type drinkers. However, 70 per cent of all English males, and 33 per cent of English females, were classified as heavy or very heavy type drinkers. Less of the Irish parents and young people drank, compared with the English under study. Over half of the Irish fathers were abstainers/ virtual abstainers, light or moderate type drinkers, and this held for 94 per cent of Irish mothers. Of all young people under study, Irish 18-21 year olds were categorized as the least heavy type of drinkers, 66 per cent of the males and 22 per cent of the Irish females being heavy or very heavy type drinkers. Differences between the English and Irish parents and young people in relation to their type of drinker classification were not statistically significant.

Introduction to the use of alcohol for the Irish young people interviewed was an activity centred away from parents, and in the context of friends. Their only direct guide to the use of alcohol would appear to be the taking of the Confirmation Pledge, a pledge not to drink until they were twenty-one years of age. In this setting of cultural ambivalence to the use of alcohol, friends seem to have provided support for an activity which was considered an anticipation of adult-type behaviour. For English young people the introduction to alcohol appeared to be both open and sanctioned.

(2) Present-day drinking was essentially a peer group activity for all the 18-21 year olds under study. English young people drank more frequently in these situations than did Irish males and females. Drinking with meals was not a frequent occurrence for either the Irish or English young people, although more of the English than Irish males and females took a drink on occasions when eating out or at home.

(3) Drinking was seen as a means of sociability and as a recreational outlet, by both Irish and English young people. However, more of the English than Irish males drank under group pressure, whereas more of the Irish than English males drank for several reasons indicating drinking for personal effects.

Both Irish and English young people under study felt that drinking was part of the society in which they lived. However, the social meaning and function of alcohol was shown to be different for the two ethnic groups studied. The Irish viewed drinking as a problematic area, while considering it essentially a social act. A sizeable percentage saw its use as associated with the reduction of anxiety. While they produced similar definitions of different types of drinkers, over half of the Irish males and 70 per cent of the Irish females, compared with 20 per cent of the English males and 50 per cent of the English females, said that drinking was a problem among the young. Alcoholism was seen by approximately eight out of ten Irish parents and children as a very serious problem in their country. The Irish 18-21 year olds were the least permissive in their attitudes to drunkenness, and the least likely to accept or tolerate a drunk person in a group with whom they were drinking.

The English 18-21 year olds viewed drinking in a more positive light, with little emphasis being placed on drink as a problem area. Drinking by adults and young people was seen as a social activity. Alcoholism was defined as a very serious problem in England by approximately one-fifth of the parents, half of the English males, and two-fifths of the English females.

(4) Irish parents' attitude to their children drinking was in general mixed, with a relatively high percentage (over two-fifths) of Irish mothers strongly disapproving of this practice. Little distinction

appeared to be made between attitudes to drinking, drunkenness, and alcoholism. Irish parents' and young people's rules for drinking were restrictive and less favourable compared to the English under study. These rules could be considered to place constraints on males not to drink, and for those who did, not to be heavy or very heavy type drinkers.

Females were also exposed to the restrictive rules surrounding the use of alcohol; there appeared to be more pressure placed on females not to drink. Both males' and females' attitudes to peers drinking seem to suggest that drinking was considered more appropriate for boys than for girls. Both males and females could be seen to reinforce the restrictive norms of their parents. These factors, together with the emphasis given to abstinence from alcohol in the cultural setting, may be seen to contribute in part to the fact that less Irish young people under study drank, and of those who did less were categorized as heavy type drinkers.

English parents did not lay down restrictive rules on drinking. Parents, and the young people's girl/boy-friends and friends in general, could be seen to support drinking behaviour, and drinking formed an integral part of their recreational and social activities. English parents' social rules were favourable to drinking in general, as well as to their children drinking in a family and peer group context. While they set limits in that general approval was not given to being drunk, or mixing drinks, or drinking six or more drinks on one occasion, they were more permissive in relation to their children's drinking three or four drinks on one occasion, than were Irish parents under study.

English 18-21 year olds showed that they held similar attitudes to their parents when they were asked about their attitudes to peers drinking. They were very favourable to boys and girls of their age drinking, and to friends and boy/girl-friends drinking together. They did not approve as much of single sex drinking, and particularly to girls drinking on their own in a public house. In this respect they held a double standard, in that they approved more of all male group than of all female group drinking. However, compared with other males and females interviewed, more English males felt that girls drinking in a pub on their own was a good thing. English 18-21 year olds were more permissive in their attitudes to drunkenness than were the Irish males or females under study.

(5) The results indicated that more of the Irish than English males and females under study were exposed to problem drinking. Exposure to problem drinking was either among parents, relatives, or parents' close friends, or their own close relatives or close friends. While less than 10 per cent of all parents admitted to having drink-related problems of their own, over 20 per cent of Irish fathers compared with 6 per cent of English fathers had an average daily alcohol intake capable of resulting in problems.

(6) Among the 18-21 year olds interviewed, experience of drink-related problems was higher for the Irish males than for the English males or females. This also held for being drunk ten times or more in the year prior to interview. The Irish young people interviewed manifested problems related to consumption of alcohol, especially in the form of drunkenness and attendant problems such as arguments with friends, money problems, and family arguments. Episodes of drunkenness, while recurring, were intermittent, and occurred within a context of an overall consumption level that was below that of the English. Fourteen per cent of Irish males and no Irish females drank approximately the equivalent of five pints (4.46 pints) of beer per day, compared with 18 per cent of the English males and 1 per cent of the English females.

Two things need to be considered when looking at drink-related problems: (1) the socio-cultural climate in which drinking takes place, i.e. the social meaning, norms surrounding the use of alcohol, and the function of alcohol in the society, and (2) the complications associated with the level of consumption of alcohol, on both a societal and individual level (Whitehead and Harvey 1974). Negative consequences due to drinking seem to be related to social reactions to the use of alcohol, as well as drinking behaviour *per se*. It has been suggested, for example, that the Irish have an ambivalent attitude to the use of alcohol. Irish 18-21 year olds and their parents viewed drinking both as a problematic area, and as an essentially social act. Parental attitudes to drinking tended to be negative, making little distinction between attitudes to drinking, drunkenness, and alcoholism. In general, drinking for the Irish was associated with negative results. It is likely that these definitions of drinking affected the expectations of drinkers, and contributed in some way to the very problems the definition recognized.

The Anglo-Irish

Of all those under study, Anglo-Irish young people and their parents were categorized as the heaviest types of drinkers. Over half of the Anglo-Irish fathers (56.7) and one-fifth of Anglo-Irish mothers were classified as heavy or very heavy type drinkers. Over four-fifths of the 18-21 year-old males and three-fifths of the Anglo-Irish females were classified as heavy or very heavy type drinkers.

On a general level it has been pointed out that children of immigrants, while not exposed to the disruption of immigration, are nevertheless placed in an ambiguous and difficult situation of dual culture. They are exposed to the culture of their parents' ethnic group and also to the cultural symbols and behaviour patterns of the host culture, through the school system, through peer group contacts outside the ethnic community, and later in employment.

It might be that the Anglo-Irish young people were heavy type drinkers because, being children of Irish immigrants, they had developed a distinct culture in conflict with that of their parents, and/or hostile to that of the host society. This point was investigated. As some of the information has not been given before, the details are given here. While the fathers (88.9) and mothers (75.6) of the Anglo-Irish young people (first generation English) considered themselves to be Irish, only half of them said that their children felt themselves to be so. The study was undertaken in a London area five miles square, which was ethnically heterogeneous. Half of the young people mentioned that it was a specifically 'Irish' area, and over 80 per cent of those studied went to separate Catholic schools in their immediate areas. However, while there were a number of Irish social clubs, some of them attached to the local parish churches, very few of the young people under study were active members, only four of the males and two of the females. Their friends were nearly all English. On a more personal level, 38.7 per cent of the males and 64.0 per cent of the females had a regular girl/boy-friend. Of the males who had regular girl-friends, 19.4 per cent were Irish and 13.9 per cent were first generation English of Irish parents. Of the females who had regular boy-friends, 14.5 per cent were Irish and 11 per cent were first generation English. Thus most of the males and females under study did not associate on a general or on a particular level with Irish or first generation English friends.

Ethnic identity was measured in terms of emotional, or historical identification with Ireland, and republican nationalist sympathies in relation to the political problems in Northern Ireland. The holiday patterns of these young people were ascertained for the years 1969, 1970, and 1971. Approximately one-third of the males went to the Republic of Ireland for their holidays in 1969, a quarter in 1971. Two-fifths of the females went to Ireland in 1969, and in 1971 a quarter went there for holidays. Attitudes on the Northern Ireland situation indicated that a quarter of the males and one-fifth of the females held strong republican nationalist sympathies. However, there was no evidence of a core of young people with a strong Irish orientation/identification.

As was shown in Chapter 10, relationships with their parents were seen to be good. However, approximately 20 per cent of both males and females felt that they received no parental support.

While over 90 per cent of the 18-21 year-old Anglo-Irish interviewed adhered to the same religious group as their parents, only 30 per cent of the males and 50 per cent of the females were involved in some of the formal aspects of church membership (i.e. going to church once a week or more). One quarter of the males did not consider any of the items on the religiosity scale to be important in their lives. This held for under

10 per cent of the Anglo-Irish females.

Anglo-Irish 18-21 year olds were not as positive in their attitudes towards England as were the English young people interviewed, although their listing of the biggest problems in England showed that they had similar concerns.

There was evidence also that these young people indulged in a mild form of sensation excitement seeking behaviour. Three-tenths of the males and one-tenth of the females had driven a car without a licence, one-third of the males and one-fifth of the females had driven a car recklessly, over 70 per cent of the males and 30 per cent of females had got into a place of entertainment without paying, and 60 per cent of the males and 30 per cent of the females had crashed a party. These activities were similar to those of the other young people under study, and there was no indication that they formed part of a syndrome of anti-social behaviour.

Analysis of the variables described failed to find a core of young Anglo-Irish who were hostile either to parents or to the society in which they lived. It may have been that the numbers involved were too small to isolate, or that those who showed signs of being hostile to parents or to England were randomly distributed among those under study. On the basis of this evidence it is tentatively suggested that this group of first generation English children had not developed a distinct culture in conflict with that of their parents or hostile to that of the host society.

The findings in relation to the drinking behaviour of Anglo-Irish 18-21 year olds under study were more complex. It is worth noting again, that the Anglo-Irish parents had common cultural origins with the Irish parents interviewed. Anglo-Irish data can therefore be taken to indicate a change or shift in an established cultural behaviour pattern to an English cultural pattern. It has been shown that of all the groups, Anglo-Irish parents and 18-21 year olds were categorized as the heaviest types of drinkers. Parents were part of the sub-culture of abstinence from drinking, having taken the Confirmation Pledge at ten or twelve years of age, as they were born and reared in Ireland where abstinence from alcohol forms part of the traditions of drinking.

During childhood over 70 per cent of the Anglo-Irish males and females took a pledge not to drink until they were twenty-one years of age. Their introduction to the use of alcohol was different from that of the Irish and similar to the experience of English young people. Like the English, they drank more frequently in peer group contexts than the Irish young people under study. Drinking was an integral part of their recreational activities. Like the other males and females interviewed, the Anglo-Irish drank as a means of sociability and as a recreational outlet. They resembled the English males, in that more of the Anglo-Irish than

Irish males interviewed drank under group pressure. One the other hand more of the Anglo-Irish males and females than Irish or English young people drank as a means of effecting a change in mood. The results showed that more of the Anglo-Irish and Irish than English males drank for several reasons suggesting drinking for personal effects. This held for Anglo-Irish females also, with over half giving three or more reasons that suggested that they drank to resolve personal problems or inadequacies.

The Anglo-Irish males and females were like the English in placing little emphasis on drink as a problem area. While they viewed drinking as a social and recreational act, as did the Irish, a sizeable percentage also saw it as a means of reducing anxiety. The problem aspects of alcohol use in England were acknowledged by more of the Anglo-Irish than the English males and females under study. This may reflect the fact that, like the Irish, more of the Anglo-Irish males and females said that their parents' relatives or close friends or their own close relatives and friends had drink-related problems. Furthermore over 20 per cent of Anglo-Irish fathers had an average daily alcohol intake capable of resulting in problems.

Anglo-Irish males and females were like Irish males in that their experience of drink-related problems was higher than that of English young people under study. This held for being drunk ten times or more in the year prior to interview, as well as having problems relating to their own drinking.

The data on their attitudes showed that while the Anglo-Irish young people were more favourably disposed towards drinking than the Irish, their attitudes were not as clear-cut and consistent as those of their English peers. For example, Anglo-Irish males had a double standard approach to males and females of their own age drinking. On the other hand, both males and females felt that mixed group drinking and boys/girls drinking with their girl/boy-friends was a good thing. Females gave general approval to boys and girls drinking, to drinking in mixed groups, and to boy/girl-friends drinking together. More Anglo-Irish females approved of all male group drinking, than of all female group drinking, but, compared to other females, more approved of girls drinking in an all female group or in a public house on their own. Anglo-Irish males and females were the most permissive in relation to drunkenness, and had a higher level of tolerance and acceptability of a drunk person than the English or Irish 18-21 year olds under study.

The research findings suggest that the Anglo-Irish young people under study were placed in an ambiguous and dual situation for the following reasons:

1 They socialized with English friends, who could be seen to hold

positive attitudes to drinking with little emphasis being placed on drink as a problem area, and were somewhat permissive in relation to drunkenness.

2 Anglo-Irish parents' attitudes towards their 18-21 year-old children drinking lay between the negative restrictive attitudes of the Irish parents and the positive permissive attitudes of the English parents under study.

3 Anglo-Irish males and females under study were presented with a heavy drinking pattern from parents, and were more likely to be exposed to problem drinking than were the English young people.

4 They were also presented with the idea of abstinence from alcohol in a society where it does not appear to be part of the traditions of drinking.

5 Anglo-Irish young people were not as clear-cut and consistent in their attitudes to drinking as were the English 18-21 year olds, nor as negative as the Irish 18-21 year olds under study. They were the most permissive in relation to their attitudes towards drunkenness.

Since the Anglo-Irish young people had not completely assimilated the social rules and norms of their hosts, nor of their parents in relation to drinking, constraints failed to operate, giving rise to heavy type drinking. Their drinking behaviour coupled with their social environment in relation to drinking, contributed to the development of drink-related problems.

The question of the influence of ethnic status remains open. Does the fact of being Irish or of Irish origin mean that one develops a particular type of drinking behaviour, different from English drinking behaviour? This question is dealt with in a later section.

Parental influences

The general influence of parents on the development of their children's attitudes and behaviour has been well documented. The evidence from this study supports findings elsewhere, that parents have a major influence in the transmission of drinking behaviour. The relative importance and interrelationships of parental influences were ascertained. The results indicated that it is necessary to differentiate the influence of fathers and mothers in order to understand the socialization process within the family circle. Parental attitudes towards drinking, rather than parental drinking behaviour or general family relationships, were the most important influence on children's drinking behaviour. The influence of family relationships was diminished when these factors were taken into account. Fathers' attitude to children mixing drinks and drinking three or more drinks on one occasion, was found to be the most powerful explanatory variable in relation to a child being classified as a light or heavy type of drinker. While the influence of the mother was evident, the father's influence on children's drinking appeared to be greater.

Peer group influences

Peers like parents are important figures in whether, when, and where, drinking behaviour becomes integrated into the lifestyle of a young person. The results are at one with findings in relation to other drug use which indicate the importance of peer group influence. The evidence is similar to previous research which showed that as the child grows older, friends provide the overall context and location for drinking. On an index that measured peer group support for drinking, the Irish males and females appeared to have less support than did either the Anglo-Irish or English young people. In all groups, peer group support for drinking was higher among the males than the females. Overall social support from friends was found to be medium to high for the majority of the males and females under study.

The results indicated that social pressure from friends *per se* was not an important factor in whether young people developed a heavy type drinking pattern. However, for Irish males who were non-drinkers, social pressure from friends to drink did appear to influence the decision to drink at some stage in the future. This decision was also influenced by friends who drank on a regular basis. The results suggested a complex interaction of peer group influences. How often drinking took place in certain peer group contexts, the social rules for peers drinking, permissive attitudes to drinking in a mixed peer group context, and overall peer group support for drinking, all needed to be considered when looking at peer group influences. Using Goodman's analysis, the relative importance and interrelationships of all these variables was ascertained; and peer group support for drinking was found to be the most powerful explanatory variable.

Account also needs to be taken of the general level of contradiction that existed between stated rules and actual behaviour. This is relevant for the young people and parents alike. It is of interest to note that young people's attitudes and rules in relation to drink mirrored parental rules. If youth is seen as a 'connective tissue' that holds the generations together, the idea of young people being early adapters of rules or norms, rather than the generators or innovators of new rules of behaviour, seems quite appropriate (Spindler 1963). It would appear that, in relation to drinking behaviour, these young people are carriers of both emergent patterns as well as traditional ones, their friends providing the company and context, as well as overall support for their particular patterns of drinking. The overall influence of significant others, whether they were particular boy/girl-friends or parents, was evident. The interplay of parental, peer, and cultural influences is illustrated at the end of this chapter.

Social and personal influences

Sociological investigations of drinking in complex societies have shown that drinking is related to a wide variety of social and personal factors.

To provide a more adequate analysis of the correlates of young people's drinking behaviour an attempt was made to bring together some of the descriptive data on present-day drinking practices presented in Chapters 5, 6, and 7. There were two findings common to many studies. The consumption of alcohol was related to sex and age. More males drank than females, in terms both of quantities consumed and frequency of drinking. The analysis showed that alcohol consumption increased with age, although the association was rather weak. A male's occupation and income level was related to the type of drinker he became. There was some evidence, although the association was weak, that heavier drinking young people started to drink at an earlier age than did young people who were classified as lighter types of drinkers. Further attention needs to be given to the onset of drinking behaviour and its possible association with later drinking behaviour.

A relationship was found between certain reasons for drinking and type of drinking behaviour. More heavier type drinkers from all groups tended to drink to effect a change in mood, than did those young people in lighter drinking categories. As might be expected, heavier type drinkers had a greater probability of having drink-related problems than those who were classified as lighter types of drinkers.

An examination was made of how the young people under study interpreted their social situation. Using a modified anomie scale (McCloskey and Schaar 1965) it was found that more of the Irish young people were given a high score than the Anglo-Irish or English young people under study. A somewhat contradictory finding was that more of the Irish, than either the English or Anglo-Irish young people, had a positive view of the social situation in which they found themselves, in terms of opportunities and general attitude to their country. The Anglo-Irish 18-21 year olds did not hold as positive an attitude to England as a place to live in, as did the English. While all the males and females under study felt that there were specific problems in their country, over half of all 18-21 year olds felt that they themselves would not be involved in bringing about change. Of all the indicators used to look at the world view of those under study, the perceived opportunity system in, and attitude towards their country emerged as the only ones associated with the amount of alcohol consumed. This reinforces the point that the 'whole' person, with all his attitudes and relationships and views, must be considered.

Taking a number of variables together, an assessment was made of the interrelationships between variables and their relative importance on young people's drinking behaviour: age at first drink, age at time of interview, experience of sensation excitement seeking behaviour, and religiosity. When taken together with other variables, the results showed that the influence of age at first drink, and age at time of interview, was diminished. Experience of three or more behaviours associated with sensation excitement seeking was highly related to heavy type drinking. The effect of religiosity was next, it was negative, showing that those with a high level of religiosity tended to be categorized in the lighter drinking categories.

The main and interaction effects of perceived opportunities in and attitude towards country of origin, occupation, and income, were ascertained. Of these variables, the influence of occupational level was diminished, it appeared to have no significant effect, whereas income level and perceived opportunities in country of origin were highly related to drinking behaviour. Young people with £25 or more a week tended to be heavy types of drinkers. Those who perceived that opportunities in their country were low were also heavy type drinkers. An interaction effect existed between these two variables. Although positive attitudes towards country of origin were associated with lighter type drinking, when they were allied to a high level of income, the income effect took over.

Further analysis was undertaken to synthesize the data in this section. The most powerful variables from the previous analysis, were selected to go into a model by themselves. These were income level, perceived opportunities in and attitudes towards country of origin, sensation excitement seeking, and sex status; expenditure on alcohol was also included. The findings showed that of all these variables, the sex of the drinker was the most important predictive variable in relation to young people's drinking behaviour.

The development of drinking behaviour among young people:
a general model

The main findings of the use of alcohol among the young people studied, as well as influences in the transmission of drinking behaviour have been presented. The four most powerful variables to emerge from the detailed analysis undertaken in the previous chapters were sex status, peer group support for drinking, fathers' attitude to mixing drinks and drinking three or more drinks on one occasion, and ethnic status. This analysis illustrated how culture, parents, and peers, interact in influencing a young person's drinking behaviour.

The greatest influence was the sex of the drinker. This finding reflected the fact that males were heavier type drinkers than were female, a not unexpected result. Using the type of drinker index developed for the study, it was shown that different types of drinking behaviour were found among, as well as between the sexes.

It is worth recalling at this point that while less of the females under study drank or were classified as heavy type drinkers, the social rules of drinking for peers would suggest that this was both an expected and accepted role for females. Drink did not play such an integral part in their lifestyles, or in their recreational activities, as it did for the males under study. Less of the females than the males associated a particular day with taking a drink. While they drank in the same peer group contexts as the males, they did so less frequently. They spent much less of their weekly income on alcohol and were less likely to take part in round drinking. This may reflect in part the practice of males rather than females paying for drinks. While both males and females did not drink frequently at home, less of the females than the males drank occasionally with their meals at home. Both males and females under study did not approve of females drinking in an all female group. Double standards were held by both sexes, in that drinking in a single sex group was felt to be more appropriate for males than for females. Females were more likely to have a limit in relation to drinking, and less likely than the males to exceed it. Females were less tolerant than males of a drunk person in a groups with whom they were drinking. While both Irish and Anglo-Irish females gave approval to males and females of their age drinking, the Irish females approved less of females than of males of their age drinking. Account needs to be taken of the general level of contradiction between stated rules and actual behaviour. Although they did not approve of all female group drinking, over two-thirds of the Anglo-Irish, three-fifths of the English females, and under half of the Irish females, drank with their girl-friends once a month or more.

The evidence from this study is similar to that of other studies of drug use in general and of drinking behaviour in particular. The peer group was generally found to be a powerful influence on drinking behaviour.

The most important explanatory variable of heavy and very heavy type drinking to emerge in all groups, was high peer group support for drinking. This was a measure indicating a young person's immersion in a context of peer group support for drinking, i.e. having friends who were regular drinkers, usually drinking in the course of socializing with friends, drinking frequently with a significant other (girl/boy-friend), with friends of the same sex, and in a mixed group of friends. By placing the study within a broader social context rather than in a school or college environment, it was possible to look at young people who assumed adult-type roles, while still remaining in the sphere of influence of the home and parents. Parental influences, however, were not as strong as those of the peer group.

While the results showed that drinking took place out of the home, away from adult supervision, it was also found that parental influences still operated. Parents' involvement and interest in their children's activities was significantly related to their children's drinking; the effect, however, was diminished when parental drinking behaviour and attitudes towards drinking were considered. It has been shown that in relation to parental drinking behaviour and attitudes towards their children drinking, it was necessary to differentiate the contributions of fathers and mothers. Here again the type of drinker index helped to distinguish between the different types of drinking behaviour of fathers and mothers, as well as to measure the differences among the fathers and mothers separately. There was a strong relationship between heavy drinking fathers and heavy drinking children. Mothers' influence was not as strong but followed the same pattern.

The most important of all parental influences were children's perceptions of fathers' attitudes to mixing drinks and drinking three or more drinks on one occasion. This showed that it was not enough only to know fathers' and mothers' general attitudes to their children drinking or to children drinking with friends and with family, or their attitudes to their children being drunk. Fathers' attitudes to drinking were of most importance in the Anglo-Irish group and least in the Irish group. The finding that it was the children's perception of parental attitudes, rather than attitudes reported by parents themselves, that was of more importance, may suggest that future studies will need to have children's reports on their parents' attitudes, as well as take into account parents' reports of their own attitudes.

In no case was it necessary to include a direct effect due to the ethnic variable. From this it might be concluded that the ethnic variable had no effect on young people's drinking behaviour. This is not correct. The study indicated that the prevalence and extent of drinking, the social meaning and function of alcohol, drinking, and drunkenness, were different among the Irish and English young people under study. The results showed that while ethnic status did not have a direct effect on drinking behaviour, it did have a very strong influence on fathers' attitudes to mixing drinks and drinking three or more drinks at one sitting. In the case of Irish males and females, it also influenced peer group support for drinking. Thus, ethnic origin, though influential, has not sufficient effect to be counted on its own as an explanatory variable in the study of drinking behaviour.

The results underline the importance of looking at the interaction of a number of influences, rather than relying on one particular influence to account for a young person's drinking behaviour. The main point of the general model was to show this interaction effect. While some factors appeared to have more influence than others, their real effect was shown in the context of a number of variables which emphasized the interplay of culture, peers, and parents as influences on young people's drinking behaviour. This process is best illustrated by the odds ratio of an Irish or English male being classified as a light or very heavy type drinker. The results showed that, when the two ethnic groups were considered together, the odds ratios varied with the level of peer group support for drinking, while fathers' attitude had no direct effect. When peer group support for drinking was low, the odds ratio was approximately 5 to 1 that the Irish or English male would be a light type of drinker, irrespective of fathers' attitudes to mixing drinks and drinking three or more drinks on one occasion. If, on the other hand, peer group support for drinking was high, again, irrespective of fathers' attitude, the odds ratio was reduced to an approximately even chance of the Irish or English male being a light type of drinker.

When the interplay of influences for the Anglo-Irish and the Irish males and the Anglo-Irish and English males were considered, the odds ratios presented were somewhat different from those presented for the Irish and the English males. If the Anglo-Irish and Irish males had fathers whose attitudes were disapproving (in this model, fathers' attitude had a direct effect) and had low peer group support for drinking the odds ratio was 7 to 1 that they would be classified as light type drinkers. In the same situation, when the Anglo-Irish and English males were analyzed together, the odds ratio was 3 to 1 that the young male was a light type of drinker. If on the other hand fathers' attitudes were approving and peer group support for drinking was high, the odds ratio of an Irish and Anglo-Irish male being a light type of drinker in these circumstances was 2 to 1 against. There were approximately the same odds ratios for the Anglo-Irish males and English males under study, being classified as light types of drinkers.

Since it has been suggested that the ethnic variable is inadequate to account alone for the differences in type of drinking behaviour, one may ask whether there are any particular reasons why the Anglo-Irish young people appear to react differently to influences that have been shown to affect the Irish and the English, and why they also have the greatest number of heavy and very heavy type drinkers among both males and females. The present study suggests that this arose in part because the Anglo-Irish young people were exposed to a dual culture in relation to drinking behaviour and attitudes towards drinking. The fact that they had not assimilated the constraints of either culture appears to have given rise to a heavy drinking behaviour pattern.

The overall results suggest that a number of factors — some of more importance than others — are involved in the development of a young person's drinking behaviour. The analysis of these factors demonstrated that the transmission of drinking behaviour to the young is helped by the interplay of the following four influences: (1) ethnic and cultural, (2) parental, (3) peer group, and (4) social and personal influences. The evidence indicates that a comprehensive understanding of alcohol use requires knowledge of how it is learned, the context of its use, the amount drank, the social meaning and function of alcohol, as well as the consequences of its use.

Appendices

Appendix 1

Additional tables
relating to Chapters 5 to 10

Table A.1.1   Whether respondent took a pledge not to drink during childhood* (Q.20a)

Pledge	Male			Female		
	Irish %	Anglo-Irish %	English %	Irish %	Anglo-Irish %	English %
Took it	82.4	71.0	–	91.0	75.9	–
Never took it	17.7	29.0	100.0	9.0	24.0	99.0
Cannot remember	–	–	–	–	–	1.0
N =	190	93	119	187	86	99

*Table refers to the taking of Confirmation Pledge for the Irish and Anglo-Irish group. For the English group it could be the Band of Hope.

Table A.1.2   Respondents' age at first drink* (Q.26a)

Age	Male			Female		
	Irish %	Anglo-Irish %	English %	Irish %	Anglo-Irish %	English %
Under 14 years	7.5	29.3	30.3	2.0	16.5	18.6
14- under 15 years	9.2	24.0	24.4	1.3	15.3	20.6
15- under 16 years	15.5	15.4	15.1	6.0	30.6	14.4
16- under 17 years	26.4	16.5	15.1	21.5	20.0	26.8
17- under 18 years	22.4	8.8	7.6	29.3	11.8	12.4
18- under 19 years	16.1	5.4	0.8	25.4	4.7	3.1
19- under 20 years	2.9	–	–	11.4	–	–
20- under 21 years	–	–	–	2.6	–	–
21 years	–	–	–	–	–	–
Cannot remember	–	–	6.7	1.4	–	4.1
N =	174	92	119	151	85	97

*Based on number of respondents who had ever taken a drink.

Table A.1.3   Whether respondents took pledge at school (Q.12: parents)

Category	Fathers			Mothers		
	Irish %	Anglo-Irish %	English %	Irish %	Anglo-Irish %	English %
Took pledge	83.4	70.0	–	91.6	76.1	0.5
Never took it	13.2	25.4	100.0	6.8	20.4	98.7
Can't remember	3.0	4.5	–	1.7	3.4	0.5
No answer given	0.3	–	–	–	–	0.5
N =	301	134	178	354	176	217

Table A.1.4   Age at first drink (Q.15: parents)

Age	Fathers			Mothers		
	Irish %	Anglo-Irish %	English %	Irish %	Anglo-Irish %	English %
14- under 15	3.0	10.4	20.8	0.6	3.4	9.7
15- under 18	21.3	39.6	37.6	4.2	7.4	41.0
18- under 21	29.2	25.4	30.9	11.9	29.0	30.4
21- under 25	17.9	11.9	2.8	14.4	25.0	4.6
25- under 30	6.3	3.0	–	14.1	11.9	1.8
30- under 40	6.6	2.2	0.6	16.4	8.0	0.5
40- under 50	2.7	0.7	–	8.2	1.1	0.5
50 and over	1.7	–	–	2.5	0.6	–
Can't remember	0.3	4.5	5.1	6.5	5.7	2.3
Never took a drink	10.3	1.5	1.1	21.2	8.0	9.2
No answer	0.7	0.7	1.1	–	–	–
N =	301	134	178	354	176	217

Table A.1.5   Respondents' perception of taste of alcohol at first drinking experience* (Q.29b)

Taste	Males			Females		
	Irish %	Anglo-Irish %	English %	Irish %	Anglo-Irish %	English %
Pleasant	25.9	50.0	31.9	26.5	45.9	49.5
Neither pleasant nor unpleasant	22.4	25.0	28.6	22.5	32.9	19.6
Unpleasant	51.7	23.9	31.1	50.3	20.0	29.9
Do not remember	0.0	1.1	8.4	0.7	1.2	1.0
N =	174	92	119	151	85	97

*Based on replies of respondents who had ever taken a drink.

Table A.1.6   First drink taken* (Q.26e)

Type of drink	Males			Females		
	Irish %	Anglo-Irish %	English %	Irish %	Anglo-Irish %	English %
Beer						
Beer, ale, bitter	51.1	57.6	70.6	41.1	18.8	21.6
Stout, Guinness	31.0	13.1	0.8	4.0	0.0	0.0
Spirit						
Vodka, gin, scotch, whisky, rum, brandy	3.5	6.5	5.0	28.4	20.0	26.8
Wine/fortified wine						
Wine	1.7	2.2	3.4	6.0	15.3	9.3
Fortified wine	1.7	2.2	3.4	2.6	12.9	15.5
Other						
Cider	8.0	7.6	2.5	2.0	22.4	10.3
Babycham	0.0	0.0	0.0	10.6	5.9	5.2
Cannot remember	2.8	10.9	14.2	4.6	4.8	11.3
N =	174	92	119	151	85	97

*Based on the replies of respondents who had ever taken a drink.

Table A.1.7   Amount of drink taken on first drinking experience* (Q.26f)

Amount taken	Males			Females		
	Irish %	Anglo-Irish %	English %	Irish %	Anglo-Irish %	English %
Less than 1 glass/bottle	6.9	6.7	4.2	9.3	3.5	4.1
1 glass	17.2	23.9	42.0	44.4	40.0	54.6
1 pint	29.3	19.8	21.9	33.8	34.1	23.7
1-2 pints	23.5	21.8	11.7	4.6	11.8	3.1
3 pints or more	17.8	16.5	3.3	0.0	0.0	2.1
Cannot remember	4.6	11.0	16.8	8.0	10.6	12.4
N =	174	92	119	151	85	97

*Based on the replies of respondents who had ever taken a drink.

Table A.1.8 Person/s with whom respondents took their first drink* (Q.26c)

Persons	Males			Females		
	Irish %	Anglo-Irish %	English %	Irish %	Anglo-Irish %	English %
Male friend/s only	38.5	26.1	18.5	–	–	–
Female friend/s only	–	–	–	21.9	11.8	10.3
Group of friends mixed	7.5	2.2	3.4	31.1	21.2	8.2
Friends sex not specified	29.3	25.0	26.9	19.9	18.8	23.7
Parents at home	0.6	21.7	21.8	4.6	14.1	25.8
Family	11.5	12.0	16.0	11.3	18.8	26.8
Relatives	3.4	5.4	3.4	4.0	5.9	2.1
Wedding	1.1	–	–	1.3	1.2	1.0
Party	–	2.2	0.8	0.7	1.2	–
Other person(s) not specified	5.7	1.1	–	0.7	–	–
Cannot remember	2.3	4.3	9.2	4.0	7.1	2.1
N =	174	92	119	151	85	97

*Based on replies of those who had ever taken a drink.

Table A.1.9 Place of first drink* (Q.26b)

Category	Males			Females		
	Irish %	Anglo-Irish %	English %	Irish %	Anglo-Irish %	English %
Pub	56.3	44.6	38.7	44.4	24.7	22.7
Home	12.6	26.1	21.8	11.3	21.2	30.9
Relative's house	–	–	3.4	0.7	–	1.0
Friend's house	3.4	1.1	1.7	2.7	3.5	3.1
Party	10.9	7.6	7.6	19.2	22.4	19.5
Wedding	2.8	3.3	4.2	5.3	8.2	10.3
Holiday/dress dance	5.7	7.6	4.2	9.3	7.1	1.0
Social club	–	1.1	3.4	–	3.5	1.0
Place not specified	6.9	5.4	5.9	1.3	5.9	8.2
Cannot remember	1.3	3.2	9.1	5.8	3.5	2.2
N =	174	92	119	151	85	97

Note: Party, Wedding, and Holiday/dress dance are grouped as "Special occasion".

*Based on replies of respondents who had ever taken a drink.

Table A.1.10   Reasons for taking first drink* (Q.26d)

Reason	Males			Females		
	Irish %	Anglo-Irish %	English %	Irish %	Anglo-Irish %	English %
Anticipatory socialization						
Wanted to try it	26.4	10.9	9.2	23.2	9.4	7.1
Everyone else was taking it	17.8	17.4	10.1	12.6	14.1	10.1
Natural thing to do	2.9	1.1	1.7	–	–	–
Curiosity	15.5	3.3	5.9	13.9	3.5	2.0
To experiment	5.7	2.2	0.8	6.6	2.4	6.1
To be big	2.9	1.1	2.5	2.0	3.5	3.0
Social pressure	8.0	10.9	9.2	7.3	8.2	10.1
To celebrate, special occasion	8.0	23.9	26.1	14.0	36.5	41.4
Other reason/s	10.9	23.9	21.0	16.0	17.6	11.1
Cannot remember	1.7	5.4	13.4	4.0	4.7	9.1
N =	174	92	119	151	85	97

*Based on the replies of those who had ever taken a drink.

Table A.1.11   Parents' knowledge of first drink* (Q.27a)

They knew	Males			Females		
	Irish %	Anglo-Irish %	English %	Irish %	Anglo-Irish %	English %
Gave it to me/knew immediately afterwards	19.5	55.5	54.6	25.8	64.7	74.2
Knew 6 months or less afterwards	19.5	7.6	16.0	10.6	7.1	8.2
6 months, up to 1 year later	13.2	13.0	5.9	17.9	9.4	5.2
Over 1 year later	33.3	17.4	7.6	17.2	8.2	5.2
Do not know	12.5	2.2	1.6	41.0	2.4	2.0
Cannot remember/do not know	7.5	5.5	15.1	6.6	9.4	6.2
N =	174	92	119	151	85	97

*Based on the replies of respondents who had ever taken a drink.

Table A.1.12   Whether respondent felt guilty about first drinking experience* (Q.28b)

Guilty	Males			Females		
	Irish %	*Anglo-Irish* %	*English* %	*Irish* %	*Anglo-Irish* %	*English* %
Not at all	75.3	90.2	89.1	73.5	88.2	90.7
A little	21.3	4.3	5.9	18.5	10.6	7.2
Pretty guilty	3.4	4.3	0.8	6.6	–	–
Cannot remember	–	1.1	4.2	1.3	1.2	2.1
N =	174	92	119	151	85	97

*Based on the replies of respondents who had ever taken a drink.

Table A.1.13   Whether respondent worried about getting caught at first drinking experience* (Q.28c)

Worried	Male			Female		
	Irish %	*Anglo-Irish* %	*English* %	*Irish* %	*Anglo-Irish* %	*English* %
Not at all	64.9	75.0	86.6	64.9	89.4	93.8
A little	21.8	17.4	6.7	15.9	5.9	5.2
Very much	13.2	6.5	2.5	17.9	3.5	–
Cannot remember/don't know	–	1.1	4.2	1.4	1.2	1.0
N =	174	92	119	151	85	97

*Based on the replies of respondents who had ever taken a drink.

Table A.1.14   Respondents' type of drinker as classified on drinking index* (Q.22§, Q.24§)

	Fathers			Mothers		
	Irish %	Anglo-Irish %	English %	Irish %	Anglo-Irish %	English %
Abstainer and virtual abstainer	21.9 (66)	9.7 (13)	18.0 (32)	52.8 (187)	35.2 (62)	42.4 (92)
Light drinker	16.3 (49)	14.9 (20)	19.7 (35)	29.7 (105)	25.6 (45)	27.6 (60)
Moderate drinker	18.3 (55)	18.7 (25)	24.7 (44)	11.9 (42)	20.5 (36)	18.0 (39)
Heavy drinker	18.3 (55)	20.9 (28)	19.1 (34)	5.6 (20)	18.8 (33)	12.0 (26)
Very heavy drinker	25.2 (76)	35.8 (48)	18.5 (33)	–	–	–
N =	301	134	178	354	176	217

*Based on modified form of the volume variability index and absolute alcohol content index. *See* Appendix 6.

Table A.1.15   Respondents' type of drinker as classified on drinking index (Q.50a§, Q.53§)

	Males			Females		
	Irish %	Anglo-Irish %	English %	Irish %	Anglo-Irish %	English %
Abstainers	13.1 (22)	1.1 (1)	2.5 (3)	25.1 (47)	5.9 (5)	3.1 (3)
Virtual abstainers	3.2 (9)	–	0.9 (1)	9.6 (18)	4.6 (4)	3.0 (3)
Light drinkers	7.9 (15)	2.2 (2)	7.6 (9)	17.6 (33)	7.0 (6)	24.2 (24)
Moderate drinkers	10.0 (19)	14.0 (13)	19.3 (23)	24.6 (46)	20.9 (18)	36.4 (36)
Heavy drinkers	31.3 (59)	25.8 (24)	26.1 (31)	20.3 (38)	52.3 (45)	28.3 (28)
Very heavy drinkers	34.7 (66)	57.0 (53)	43.7 (52)	2.6 (5)	9.3 (8)	5.1 (5)
N =	190	93	119	187	86	99

Table A.1.16 Amount of drinking – Overall absolute alcohol content index* (Q.228, Q.248)

Pints per week	Overall absolute alcohol content index	Fathers				Mothers			
		Irish %	Anglo-Irish %	English %		Irish %	Anglo-Irish %	English %	
0 – 3 pints	0 – 9 fluid ounces	12.5	14.1	36.3		54.9	48.4	51.9	
3 – 6.2 pints	10 – 19 fluid ounces	8.6	11.7	16.1		19.0	20.3	17.5	
6.2 – 12.5 pints	20 – 39 fluid ounces	25.9	21.9	20.2		15.7	22.2	14.8	
12.5 – 18.7 pints	40 – 59 fluid ounces	12.9	12.5	8.3		4.9	5.2	3.2	
18.7 – 25 pints	60 – 79 fluid ounces	10.2	9.4	6.0		0.4	2.0	1.1	
25 – 31.25 pints	80 – 99 fluid ounces	8.6	9.4	4.8		1.5	–	3.2	
31.25 – 50 pints	100 – 159 fluid ounces	13.3	10.9	4.8		1.1	0.7	1.1	
	160 – 199 fluid ounces	3.5	4.7	0.6		0.4	–	0.5	
50 – 62.5 pints	200 fluid ounces	4.3	6.5	1.2		–	–	–	
	Virtual abstainers	–	–	1.8		2.2	1.3	6.9	
N =		255	128	168		268	153	189	

*Based on replies of those respondents who, at time of interview, said they took a drink.

Table A.1.17   Respondents drinking over 60 fluid ounces of absolute alcohol and usually drinking 5 – 6 drinks on a drinking session (Q.50a§, Q.53§)

Total % in sample	Pints per week	Pints per month	Males						Females					
			Irish Overall % 35.7% (68)		Anglo-Irish Overall % 57.0% (53)		English Overall % 43.7% (52)		Irish Overall % 2.2% (4)		Anglo-Irish Overall % 9.3% (8)		English Overall % 5.0% (5)	
60 – 80 fluid ounces	18.5 – 25	75 – 100	13.7 (26)	38.3	17.2 (16)	30.2	15.9 (19)	36.5	1.6 (3)	75.0	2.3 (2)	25.0	2.0 (2)	40.0
80 – 100 fluid ounces	25 – 31.25	100 – 125	7.8 (15)	22.1	15.1 (14)	26.4	10.1 (12)	23.1	0.5 (1)	25.0	1.2 (1)	12.5	2.0 (2)	40.0
100 – 160 fluid ounces	31.25 – 50	125 – 200	10.0 (19)	27.9	11.8 (11)	20.8	10.1 (12)	23.1	0.0 (0)	0.0	3.5 (3)	37.5	1.0 (1)	20.0
160 – 200 + fluid ounces	50 – 62.5	200 – 250+	4.2 (8)	11.7	12.9 (12)	22.6	7.7 (9)	17.3	0.0 (0)	0.0	2.3 (2)	25.0	0.0 (0)	0.0

Table A.1.18   Usual recreational activities with friends (Q.16a)

Category	Males			Females		
	Irish %	Anglo-Irish %	English %	Irish %	Anglo-Irish %	English %
Drinking:						
Pub/drink and other activities	21.6	39.8	25.2	11.8	29.1	21.2
Drinking and dancing	11.6	15.1	6.7	10.7	16.3	4.0
Pub	21.6	20.4	34.5	6.4	8.1	20.2
Other:						
Dance	8.9	7.5	3.4	23.5	11.6	5.1
Club of any sort	6.8	2.2	2.5	4.3	1.2	4.0
Pictures/theatre	2.1	1.1	0.8	6.4	4.7	6.1
Visiting	3.2	–	0.8	3.7	3.5	3.0
No place in particular	1.1	1.1	4.2	1.1	1.2	1.1
Other	2.1	1.1	4.2	2.1	3.5	3.0
Does not have any particular group of friends	21.1	11.8	17.6	29.4	20.9	32.3
Information incomplete	–	–	–	0.5	–	–
N =	190	93	119	187	86	99

Table A.1.19   Usual recreational activities with friends* (Q.16a)

Activity	Males			Females		
	Irish %	Anglo-Irish %	English %	Irish %	Anglo-Irish %	English %
Pub/drink and other activities	22.4	40.2	25.9	13.8	29.6	21.9
Drinking and dancing	13.3	15.2	6.9	12.3	14.8	4.2
Pub	24.8	20.7	35.3	7.2	7.4	20.8
Dance	9.1	7.6	3.4	23.9	12.3	5.2
Club of any sort	6.1	1.1	2.6	4.3	1.2	4.2
Pictures/theatre	–	1.1	–	5.1	4.9	6.3
Visiting	1.2	–	0.9	2.2	3.7	3.1
No place in particular	1.2	1.1	4.3	1.4	1.2	1.0
Other	1.8	1.1	3.4	2.9	3.7	3.1
Does not have any particular group of friends	20.0	12.0	14.7	26.8	21.0	30.2
Information incomplete	–	–	2.6	–	–	–
N =	165	92	116	138	81	96

*Refers to respondents who, at time of interview, said they took a drink.

Table A.1.20   General profile of respondents' recreational activities once a month or more (Q.2 favourable responses)

Males

Activity	Never			Once or twice			Three or four times			Once a week +		
	Irish %	Anglo-Irish %	English %	Irish %	Anglo-Irish %	English %	Irish %	Anglo-Irish %	English %	Irish %	Anglo-Irish %	English %
Cinema	22.6	24.7	26.9	31.1	55.9	53.8	12.1	7.5	8.4	34.2	11.8	10.9
Dance/disco	27.4	20.4	28.6	21.1	28.0	32.8	5.8	7.5	7.6	45.8	44.1	31.1
Party	55.8	22.6	41.2	40.0	61.3	52.9	1.6	10.8	1.7	2.6	5.4	4.2
Play a sport	33.2	23.7	30.3	11.1	18.3	10.9	3.2	5.4	5.0	52.6	52.7	53.8
Follow a sport	23.2	22.6	22.7	10.0	10.8	13.4	1.6	4.3	2.5	65.3	62.4	61.3
Youth club	74.7	88.2	91.6	3.2	3.2	–	–	–	0.8	22.1	8.6	7.6
Bingo	95.3	100.0	99.2	4.2	–	–	–	–	–	0.5	–	0.8
Drive	51.6	50.5	41.2	15.3	11.8	23.5	4.7	5.4	5.0	28.4	32.3	80.3
Stay at home	23.7	21.5	10.1	7.4	4.3	7.6	5.3	3.2	5.0	63.7	71.0	77.3
Go visiting	34.2	26.9	18.5	23.7	25.8	22.7	6.3	6.5	6.7	35.8	40.9	52.1
Drink with lads	18.4	3.2	5.9	12.6	5.4	11.8	5.3	2.2	2.5	63.7	89.2	79.8
Drink with friends	19.5	2.2	10.9	24.7	14.0	11.8	4.7	3.2	5.0	50.5	80.6	73.1
Go out with family	71.1	61.3	57.1	20.0	30.1	29.4	2.1	5.4	0.8	6.8	3.2	12.6
Drink with parents	78.9	52.7	75.6	12.6	26.9	15.1	1.1	2.2	–	6.8	17.2	9.2
N =	190	93	119	190	93	119	190	93	119	190	93	119

Table A.1.21 General profile of respondents' recreational activities once a month or more (Q.2 favourable responses)

Females

Activity	Never			Once or twice			Three or four times			Once a week +		
	Irish %	Anglo-Irish %	English %	Irish %	Anglo-Irish %	English %	Irish %	Anglo-Irish %	English %	Irish %	Anglo-Irish %	English %
Cinema	16.0	19.8	27.3	31.6	54.7	47.5	17.6	14.0	9.1	34.2	11.6	16.2
Dance/disco	28.9	24.4	40.4	23.0	22.1	29.3	5.9	8.1	5.1	41.7	45.3	25.3
Party	56.7	25.6	46.5	40.1	53.5	44.4	1.6	11.6	5.1	1.1	9.3	4.0
Play a sport	67.9	68.6	69.7	8.0	12.8	13.1	2.7	3.5	2.0	20.9	15.1	15.2
Follow a sport	56.1	54.7	40.4	13.4	11.6	12.1	2.7	4.7	2.0	27.3	29.1	45.5
Youth club	89.8	96.5	94.9	–	–	1.0	0.5	–	–	9.1	3.5	4.0
Bingo	81.8	98.5	92.9	9.6	3.5	4.0	1.1	–	–	7.0	7.0	3.0
Drive	44.4	52.3	41.4	18.2	15.1	21.2	7.5	10.3	2.0	29.4	22.1	35.4
Stay at home	5.3	4.7	3.0	3.2	7.0	4.0	2.1	4.7	6.1	88.8	83.7	86.9
Go visiting	11.2	15.1	10.1	27.3	23.3	30.3	5.9	15.1	8.1	55.1	46.5	51.5
Drink with girls	54.5	33.7	39.4	15.0	19.8	14.1	4.3	9.3	2.0	25.7	37.2	44.4
Drink with friends	33.7	12.8	15.2	24.1	17.4	14.1	7.0	15.1	4.0	34.8	54.7	66.7
Go out with family	52.9	55.8	44.4	29.4	34.9	38.4	4.8	3.5	4.0	12.3	5.8	13.1
Drink with parents	84.5	65.1	69.7	9.6	25.6	23.2	1.1	3.5	2.0	4.3	5.8	5.1
N =	187	86	99	187	86	99	187	86	99	187	86	99

Table A.1.22 Respondents' expenditure on alcohol by income (Q.13, Q.14)
Irish males

Income	Less £1	£1 – £3	£3 – £6	£6 – £9	£9 – £12	£12 – £15	N	Total %
Up to £10	2 10.5%	11 57.9%	5 26.3%	1 5.3%	0 0%	0 0%	19	14.0
£10 – £20	5 5.5%	42 46.2%	33 36.3%	10 11.0%	0 0%	1 1.1%	91	66.9
£20 – £30	0 0%	7 31.8%	4 18.2%	7 31.8%	3 13.8%	1 4.4%	22	16.2
£30 and over	0 0%	1 25%	2 50%	0 0%	1 25%	0 0%	4	2.9
							N = 136	
% spent on alcohol	5.1	44.3	32.3	13.2	2.9	0.73		

Kendalls Tau C = 0.19778 significant at 0.05 level. Based on those who spent money on alcohol.

Table A.1.23   Respondents' expenditure on alcohol by income (Q.13, Q.14)
Anglo-Irish males

Income	Less £1	£1 – £3	£3 – £6	£6 – £9	£9 – £12	£12 – £15	N	Total %
Up to £10	2 28.8%	5 71.4%	0 0%	0 0%	0 0%	0 0%	7	8.2
£10 – £20	2 2.3%	33 50%	12 27.3%	4 9.1%	4 9.1%	1 2.3%	44	52.0
£20 – £30	0 0%	4 15.4%	13 50%	1 3.8%	7 26.9%	1 3.8%	26	30.5
£30 and over	0 0%	1 12.5%	3 37.5%	3 37.5%	1 12.5%	0 0%	8	9.4
							N = 85	
% spent on alcohol	4.7	50.5	32.9	9.4	14.1	2.3		

Kendalls Tau C = 0.30827 significant at 0.01 level. Based on those who spent money on alcohol.

Table A.1.24   Respondents' expenditure on alcohol by income (Q.13, Q.14)
English males

Income	Less £1	£1 – £3	£3 – £5	£6 – £9	£9 – £12	£12 – £15	N	Total %
Up to £10	2 50%	2 50%	0 0%	0 0%	0 0%	0 0%	4	4.1
£10 – £20	5 10.8%	20 40.2%	18 36.2%	4 8.6%	2 4.2%	0 0%	49	50.0
£20 – £30	2 5.1%	12 30.8%	19 48.7%	5 12.8%	1 2.6%	0 0%	39	39.7
£30 and over	0 0%	1 12.5%	3 50%	1 12.5%	2 25%	0 0%	6	6.1
							N = 98	
% spent on alcohol	9.1	35.7	40.8	10.2	5.1	0		

Kendalls Tau C = 0.18368 significant at 0.05 level. Based on those who spent money on alcohol.

Table A.1.25   Respondents' expenditure on alcohol by income (Q.13, Q.14)
Irish females

Income	Less £1	£1 – £3	£3 – £6	£6 – £9	£9 – £12	£12 – £15	N	Total %
Up to £10	2 40%	3 60%	0 0%	0 0%	0 0%	0 0%	5	10.6
£10 – £20	11 26.8%	23 56.1%	6 14.6%	0 0%	1 2.4%	0 0%	41	87.2
£20 – £30	0 0%	1 100%	0 0%	0 0%	0 0%	0 0%	1	2.1
£30 and over	0 0%	0 0%	0 0%	0 0%	0 0%	0 0%	0	0.0
							N = 47	
% spent on alcohol	27.6	57.4	12.7	–	2.1	–		

Kendalls Tau C. N.S. Based on those who spent money on alcohol.

Table A.1.26   Respondents' expenditure on alcohol by income (Q.13, Q.14)
Anglo-Irish females

Income	Less £1	£1 – £3	£3 – £6	£6 – £9	£9 – £12	£12 – £15	N	Total %
Up to £10	2 100%	0 0%	0 0%	0 0%	0 0%	0 0%	2	5.0
£10 – £20	5 16.7%	21 70%	4 13.3%	0 0%	0 0%	0 0%	30	75.0
£20 – £30	2 25%	4 50%	2 25%	0 0%	0 0%	0 0%	8	20.0
£30 and over	0 0%	0 0%	0 0%	0 0%	0 0%	0 0%	0	0.0
							N = 40	
% spent on alcohol	22.5	62.5	15.0	–	–	–		

Kendalls Tau C = 0.13227 significant at 0.05 level. Based on those who spent money on alcohol.

Table A.1.27 Respondents' expenditure on alcohol by income (Q.13, Q.14)
English females

Income	Less £1	£1 – £3	£3 – £6	£6 – £9	£9 – £12	£12 – £15	N	Total %
Up to £10	1 50%	1 50%	0 0%	0 0%	0 0%	0 0%	2	4.5
£10 – £20	8 21.6%	25 67.6%	4 10.8%	0 0%	0 0%	0 0%	37	84.1
£20 – £30	3 75%	1 25%	0 0%	0 0%	0 0%	0 0%	4	9.1
£30 and over	1 100%	0 0%	0 0%	0 0%	0 0%	0 0%	1	2.3
							N = 44	
% spent on alcohol	29.5	61.3	9.1	–	–	–		

Kendalls Tau C. N.S. Based on those who spent money on alcohol.

Table A.1.28   Particular days on which respondent will usually have a drink* (Q.44)

Category	Males			Females		
	Irish %	Anglo-Irish %	English %	Irish %	Anglo-Irish %	English %
Every day	1.8	4.3	5.2	–	–	1.0
One day during the week	0.6	3.3	12.9	1.4	4.9	5.2
Weekends:						
Weekends, two to three days during the week	3.6	7.6	6.9	–	4.9	5.2
Weekends, one day during the week	4.2	15.2	8.6	2.9	11.1	5.2
Weekends	47.3	38.0	23.3	31.2	43.2	31.3
One day at the weekend	17.6	9.8	11.2	21.7	12.3	13.5
Other:						
Anytime I have the money	1.2	–	–	–	–	–
It depends, no particular day	23.6	21.8	32.1	42.7	28.4	38.6
N =	165	92	116	138	81	96

*Based on the replies of respondents who, at the time of the study, said they took a drink.

Table A.1.29   Whether respondent takes a drink with a meal at home* (Q.46)

Category	Males			Females		
	Irish %	Anglo-Irish %	English %	Irish %	Anglo-Irish %	English %
Frequently	–	–	3.4	0.7	2.5	1.0
At meals on a Sunday	0.6	2.2	10.3	1.5	1.2	3.1
Special occasions	0.6	–	2.6	1.5	2.5	6.3
Christmas	2.4	1.1	5.2	2.9	6.2	5.2
Occasionally	3.0	7.6	7.8	1.5	12.3	6.3
Rarely	6.7	4.3	10.3	5.2	3.7	9.4
Yes	0.6	–	1.7	0.7	1.2	1.0
No	85.5	84.8	58.6	85.6	70.4	67.7
N =	165	92	119	138	81	96

*Refers to respondents who, at time of interview, said they took a drink.

Table A.1.30   Whether respondent takes a drink when out for a meal* (Q.46)

Category	Males			Females		
	Irish %	Anglo-Irish %	English %	Irish %	Anglo-Irish %	English %
Frequently	1.8	6.5	12.1	0.7	4.9	5.2
Nearly always	4.8	4.3	18.1	2.2	22.2	16.7
Special occasions	–	1.1	1.7	0.7	1.2	3.1
Christmas	–	1.1	–	–	–	–
Dress Dance	2.4	–	–	–	–	–
Occasionally	11.4	30.4	19.8	17.4	28.4	19.8
Rarely	9.7	12.0	12.9	12.3	11.1	17.7
Yes	0.6	5.4	–	–	3.7	1.0
No	68.5	39.1	35.3	65.9	28.4	36.5
N =	165	92	119	138	81	96

*Refers to respondents who, at time of interview, said they took a drink.

Table A.1.31 Places where respondent drinks* – Males (Q.43§ favourable responses)

Place	Frequently			Occasionally			Never		
	Irish %	Anglo-Irish %	English %	Irish %	Anglo-Irish %	English %	Irish %	Anglo-Irish %	English %
Pub	84.8	90.2	89.7	9.7	7.6	6.9	5.5	2.2	3.5
Home	3.0	4.3	5.1	20.6	41.3	32.8	76.3	54.4	61.2
Restaurant	4.2	11.9	20.7	8.5	38.0	41.4	87.2	50.0	37.9
Friend's home	5.4	13.0	10.3	24.2	35.9	32.8	70.3	51.1	56.0
Parties	72.2	85.9	72.4	16.4	9.8	13.8	11.5	4.4	13.7
Parties 'stag'	57.5	56.6	58.6	9.1	15.2	10.3	33.3	28.3	31.0
Club – general	8.5	67.4	46.6	6.7	10.9	9.5	84.8	21.8	43.9
Club – Irish club	–	8.6	–	–	3.3	–	–	87.0	–
N =	165	92	119	165	92	119	165	92	119

Table A.1.32 Places where respondent drinks* – Females (Q.43§ favourable responses)

Place	Frequently			Occasionally			Never		
	Irish %	Anglo-Irish %	English %	Irish %	Anglo-Irish %	English %	Irish %	Anglo-Irish %	English %
Pub	65.2	77.8	70.3	21.7	13.6	20.8	12.3	8.7	7.3
Home	1.4	7.4	8.3	17.4	30.9	20.8	80.4	61.7	69.8
Restaurant	2.1	20.3	20.3	13.0	29.6	32.3	84.1	49.4	46.9
Friend's home	3.6	4.3	4.1	16.7	34.6	28.1	79.0	60.5	66.6
Parties	60.2	80.2	65.7	28.3	11.1	19.8	10.9	8.7	14.6
Parties 'hen'	38.4	28.4	32.3	24.6	22.2	19.8	36.2	49.4	45.8
Club – general	3.6	49.4	29.2	8.7	25.9	10.4	84.8	24.7	60.4
Club – Irish club	–	3.7	–	–	–	–	–	96.3	–
N =	138	81	96	138	81	96	138	81	96

Table A.1.33   General profile of drinking situations* – Males (Q.42§ favourable responses)

Category	Frequently			Occasionally			Rarely/Never		
	Irish %	Anglo-Irish %	English %	Irish %	Anglo-Irish %	English %	Irish %	Anglo-Irish %	English %
On a date	36.9	62.0	65.6	35.2	33.7	25.9	27.9	4.4	8.6
On a date with some other entertainment	32.1	40.2	50.9	27.3	40.2	32.8	40.6	19.5	16.4
Party with girl-friend	68.5	82.6	75.0	15.8	10.9	12.1	15.2	6.5	11.2
With a group of lads	79.4	91.3	83.6	14.5	7.6	13.8	6.1	1.1	2.6
With a group of lads before dancing	58.2	62.0	36.2	13.3	12.0	20.7	28.5	26.1	40.5
Mixed group of friends	60.0	78.2	71.5	27.3	20.7	20.7	12.8	1.1	7.7
After a match	30.9	48.9	41.3	11.5	13.0	6.9	56.9	38.0	50.9
Anywhere at all	26.0	22.0	13.8	13.9	18.5	19.8	59.4	55.4	64.7
With parents at home	3.6	2.2	6.9	21.8	38.0	37.1	73.4	59.8	55.1
With parents in a pub	13.4	16.3	16.4	14.5	34.8	19.8	70.9	47.8	63.0
With relatives	15.2	13.1	10.3	13.9	26.1	19.8	70.9	59.8	69.9
N =	165	92	119	165	92	119	165	92	119

*Refers to respondents who, at time of interview, said they took a drink.

Table A.1.34 General profile of drinking situations* – Females (Q.42§ favourable responses)

Category	Frequently			Occasionally			Rarely/Never		
	Irish %	Anglo-Irish %	English %	Irish %	Anglo-Irish %	English %	Irish %	Anglo-Irish %	English %
On a date	42.1	58.0	56.3	31.2	37.0	31.3	26.8	5.0	12.5
On a date with some other entertainment	31.2	35.8	40.6	34.1	43.2	32.3	34.8	21.0	26.1
Party with boy-friend	65.2	75.3	66.7	18.1	16.0	21.9	15.9	8.6	11.5
With a group of girls	35.5	44.4	39.6	26.1	37.0	32.3	37.7	18.5	28.1
With a group of girls before dancing	32.6	23.4	20.9	15.2	16.0	9.4	50.0	59.3	69.8
Mixed group of friends	46.3	60.5	55.3	39.1	37.0	29.2	14.5	2.4	13.6
After a match	15.2	11.1	12.5	7.2	12.3	9.4	77.5	76.5	75.1
Anywhere at all	10.8	9.9	11.5	12.3	21.0	9.4	73.9	69.1	77.1
With parents at home	1.4	7.4	7.3	14.5	32.1	27.1	83.4	60.5	64.6
With parents in a pub	8.6	22.2	14.6	18.1	24.7	25.0	72.4	53.1	60.5
With relatives	6.5	13.6	8.4	13.8	30.9	21.9	79.0	55.5	69.8
N =	138	81	96	138	81	96	138	81	96

*Refers to respondents who, at time of interview, said they took a drink.

189

Table A.1.35   Whether respondent considers round drinking to be a custom peculiar to country of residence (Q.62d)

Category	Males			Females		
	Irish %	Anglo-Irish %	English %	Irish %	Anglo-Irish %	English %
Is peculiarly Irish custom	69.5	8.6	–	68.4	4.7	–
Is not peculiarly Irish custom	21.6	–	–	21.4	–	–
Every country does it	1.6	4.3	1.7	1.6	1.2	–
Is peculiarly English custom	–	23.7	35.3	–	18.6	44.4
Is not peculiarly English custom	–	47.3	36.1	–	65.1	22.2
Is a British custom/Scots custom	–	1.1	–	–	2.3	–
Do not know	6.8	15.1	25.2	7.0	7.0	32.3
Other answer	–	–	1.7	1.1	1.2	1.0
No answer given	0.5	–	–	0.5	–	–
N =	190	93	119	187	86	99

Table A.1.36   Respondents' attitudes to round drinking (Q.62a)

Attitude	Males			Females		
	Irish %	Anglo-Irish %	English %	Irish %	Anglo-Irish %	English %
Good thing, agree with it	42.1	71.0	57.9	32.6	68.6	65.6
Good, with qualification	21.6	14.0	17.6	8.6	9.3	12.1
Bad thing	33.7	12.9	20.1	47.0	9.3	17.2
Pooling is better	0.5	–	–	3.7	–	–
Men and women should join in round	0.5	–	–	–	1.2	–
Other answer	1.1	2.2	1.7	4.2	9.3	3.0
No answer	0.5	–	2.5	3.7	2.3	2.0
N =	190	93	119	187	86	99

Table A.1.37   Whether respondent takes part in round drinking (Q.62b)

Category	Males			Females		
	Irish %	Anglo-Irish %	English %	Irish %	Anglo-Irish %	English %
Yes	60.0	80.6	70.6	28.9	57.0	44.4
Yes, in small groups	4.7	–	0.8	1.6	1.2	3.0
Yes, but do not like it	2.7	–	3.4	–	–	–
Sometimes	13.7	11.8	10.1	7.0	3.5	10.1
Yes, with girl-friends only	–	–	–	5.3	11.6	8.1
Husband, boy-friend does	–	–	–	2.1	5.8	6.1
Has never been in that situation	–	–	–	1.6	–	1.0
No	18.4	6.5	15.1	51.3	20.9	27.3
No, pool it	–	–	–	1.6	–	–
No answer given	0.5	1.1	–	0.5	–	–
N=	190	93	119	187	86	99

Table A.1.38   Type of drink respondent usually has* (Q.49)

Type of drink	Males			Females		
	Irish %	Anglo-Irish %	English %	Irish %	Anglo-Irish %	English %
Beer	50.9	66.3	67.2	12.3	9.9	5.2
Stout	37.0	6.5	6.9	3.6	1.2	1.0
Lager	6.1	20.7	11.2	23.2	18.5	14.6
Cider	–	1.1	2.6	–	1.2	10.4
Wine	1.2	–	1.7	6.5	21.0	22.9
Babycham	–	–	–	2.9	3.7	4.2
Spirits of any kind	3.6	5.4	8.6	49.3	43.2	38.5
It depends, no particular drink	1.2	–	1.8	2.1	1.2	3.1
N =	165	92	116	138	81	96

*Refers to respondents who, at time of interview, said they took a drink.

Table A.1.39   Why adults drink (Q.58a)

	Males			Females		
	Irish %	Anglo-Irish %	English %	Irish %	Anglo-Irish %	English %
Sociability	38.4	37.6	55.5	28.3	44.2	49.5
Recreation	21.6	23.6	10.9	18.7	16.3	12.2
Anxiety reduction	33.2	29.1	22.7	46.1	31.4	36.4
Other reasons	2.6	7.6	5.0	2.6	5.8	0.0
Do not know	4.2	2.2	5.9	4.3	2.3	2.0
N =	190	93	119	187	86	99

Table A.1.40   Why lads drink (Q.58b)

	Males			Females		
	Irish %	Anglo-Irish %	English %	Irish %	Anglo-Irish %	English %
Sociability	68.9	78.5	78.2	52.9	71.0	60.6
Recreation	7.9	7.5	9.2	5.9	7.0	10.1
Anxiety reduction	14.7	7.6	0.8	19.3	3.5	4.0
Anticipatory socialization	6.3	4.3	5.0	15.0	10.5	17.2
Other reasons	2.1	2.2	6.7	6.9	8.1	8.1
N =	190	93	119	187	86	99

Table A.1.41   Why girls drink (Q.58c)

	Males			Females		
	Irish %	Anglo-Irish %	English %	Irish %	Anglo-Irish %	English %
Sociability	71.6	78.5	82.3	67.0	75.6	71.7
Recreation	3.2	5.4	4.2	5.9	5.8	12.1
Anxiety reduction	7.3	1.1	0.0	16.0	8.2	2.0
Anticipatory socialization	5.3	4.3	1.7	6.4	4.7	10.1
Other reasons	12.5	10.8	11.8	4.8	5.8	4.0
N =	190	93	119	187	86	99

Table A.1.42 Respondents' definitions of a person who is drunk (Q.64)

Category	Males			Females		
	Irish %	Anglo-Irish %	English %	Irish %	Anglo-Irish %	English %
No control over sensory and bodily functions	61.5	69.9	58.8	68.4	69.8	68.7
Talks too much	5.3	3.2	1.7	5.3	8.1	5.1
Had more to drink than he should	9.5	2.2	16.0	4.3	9.3	18.1
Unpredictable, irrational behaviour	12.1	9.7	5.0	9.6	5.8	4.0
Aggressive behaviour	6.3	6.5	7.6	10.2	4.7	7.1
Enjoying himself	1.1	3.2	5.9	0.5	–	1.0
Affects different people in different ways	1.6	4.3	2.5	–	2.3	5.1
Difficult to explain	–	1.1	–	–	–	–
No answer given	0.5	–	0.8	0.5	–	–
Other answer	2.1	–	1.7	1.1	–	1.0
N =	190	93	119	187	86	99

Table A.1.43 The first sign respondent would look for if someone had a drink problem (Q.70)

Category	Males			Females		
	Irish %	Anglo-Irish %	English %	Irish %	Anglo-Irish %	English %
Way of drinking and No control over drinking	35.0	30.4	31.0	32.5	31.3	21.2
Appearance	13.7	26.0	21.9	15.7	19.3	31.3
Behaviour	3.7	5.9	3.3	4.2	9.3	8.1
Aggressive behaviour	2.6	3.3	4.2	3.7	3.8	5.1
Becomes nervous, subdued	6.8	4.3	4.2	4.8	12.8	7.1
Social and health problems	20.1	11.9	8.6	12.3	10.8	7.0
Don't know what to look for	11.6	10.8	18.5	20.3	10.8	13.1
Other answer	5.8	7.5	9.2	5.9	1.2	7.1
No answer	1.6	–	–	0.5	1.2	–
N =	190	93	119	187	86	99

Table A.1.44   Respondents' definitions of an alcoholic (Q.69a)

Definition	Males			Females		
	Irish %	Anglo-Irish %	English %	Irish %	Anglo-Irish %	English %
Someone addicted to drink	35.3	51.6	42.9	42.3	54.7	45.5
Lack of control over drinking	34.5	24.7	31.0	34.2	23.3	27.2
Drinking all the time	10.5	12.9	11.7	7.5	14.0	12.1
Personal, social and economic consequences	5.8	3.3	5.9	9.7	–	3.0
Instrumental use of alcohol	4.2	1.1	2.5	0.5	–	6.1
Do not know what to look for	0.5	1.1	2.5	1.6	2.3	3.0
Other answers	8.4	5.4	3.4	3.7	4.7	3.0
No answer	1.1	–	–	0.5	1.2	–
N =	190	93	119	187	86	99

Table A.1.45 Percentage frequency distribution of respondents' reasons for drinking scaled by Guttman techniques – Drinking for festive and social pleasure (Q.518, 1,2,8)

Category	Males			Females		
	Irish *165* *100%*	*Anglo-Irish* *92* *100%*	*English* *114* *100%*	*Irish* *137* *100%*	*Anglo-Irish* *81* *100%*	*English* *96* *100%*
Does not drink for any of these reasons	16 (9.7)	3 (3.3)	3 (2.6)	13 (9.5)	3 (3.7)	4 (4.2)
Drink to celebrate special occasions	90.3 35 (21.2)	96.7 25 (27.1)	97.4 31 (27.1)	90.5 42 (30.6)	96.3 25 (30.8)	95.8 25 (26.0)
Drink to be sociable	69.0 66 (40.0)	69.5 42 (45.6)	70.1 45 (39.4)	59.8 46 (33.5)	65.4 31 (38.2)	69.8 46 (47.9)
Helps me to relax	29.1 48 (29.1)	23.9 22 (23.9)	30.7 35 (30.7)	26.3 36 (26.3)	27.2 22 (27.2)	21.8 21 (21.8)
N =	165	92	114	137	81	96
Coefficient of reproducibility	0.8626	0.9203	0.9298	0.8540	0.9012	0.9167
Minimum marginal reproducibility	0.6545	0.7500	0.7368	0.6569	0.7078	0.7500
Percentage improvement	0.2081	0.1703	0.1930	0.1971	0.1934	0.1667
Coefficient of scalability	0.6023	0.5812	0.7333	0.5745	0.6620	0.6667

Table A.1.46   Percentage frequency distribution of respondents' reasons for drinking scaled by Guttman techniques – Drinking for social conforming, for a sense of obligation for meeting group pressures (Q.518, 9, 6, 5)

Category	Males			Females		
	Irish 165 100%	Anglo-Irish 92 100%	English 114 100%	Irish 137 100%	Anglo-Irish 81 100%	English 96 100%
Does not drink for any of these reasons	50 (30.3)	13 (14.2)	14 (12.3)	38 (27.7)	22 (27.2)	21 (21.9)
Because the people I know drink	69.7 30 (18.1)	85.8 30 (32.6)	87.7 19 (16.7)	72.3 29 (21.1)	72.8 33 (40.7)	78.1 26 (27.0)
A man or woman is expected to	51.5 46 (27.9)	53.3 27 (29.3)	71.0 43 (37.7)	51.0 44 (32.1)	32.0 15 (18.5)	51.0 28 (29.1)
One way of being part of a group	23.6 39 (23.6)	23.9 22 (23.9)	33.3 38 (33.3)	18.9 26 (18.9)	13.6 11 (13.5)	21.9 21 (21.9)
N =	165	92	114	137	81	96
Coefficient of reproducibility	0.8545	0.8623	0.8713	0.8248	0.8683	0.8750
Minimum marginal reproducibility	0.5596	0.6449	0.6404	0.5718	0.6667	0.6076
Percentage improvement	0.2949	0.2174	0.2310	0.2530	0.2016	0.2674
Coefficient of scalability	0.6697	0.6122	0.6423	0.5909	0.6049	0.6814

Table A.1.47 Percentage frequency distribution of respondents' reasons for drinking scaled by Guttman techniques – Personal effect reasons, drinking to resolve problems or inadequacies (Q.518, 7; Q.548, 1, 2, 4, 10)

Category	Males			Females		
	Irish 162	Anglo-Irish 92	English 114	Irish 137	Anglo-Irish 81	English 96
Does not drink for any of these reasons	100% 41 (25.4)	100% 26 (28.2)	100% 22 (19.3)	100% 48 (35.3)	100% 19 (23.4)	100% 30 (31.3)
When I want to forget anything	74.6 42 (25.9)	71.7 15 (16.3)	80.7 46 (40.3)	64.9 31 (22.6)	76.5 14 (17.2)	68.7 32 (33.3)
When I am under pressure	48.7 21 (12.9)	55.4 13 (14.1)	40.3 13 (11.4)	42.3 22 (16.0)	59.2 6 (7.4)	35.4 11 (11.4)
To forget my worries	35.8 16 (9.9)	41.3 8 (0.6)	28.9 13 (11.4)	26.2 11 (8.0)	51.8 11 (13.6)	23.9 10 (10.4)
Drink because I need it when tense and nervous	25.9 15 (9.2)	32.6 14 (15.2)	17.5 11 (9.6)	18.2 9 (6.6)	38.3 14 (17.3)	13.5 8 (8.3)
When I am feeling lonely	16.6 27 (16.6)	17.4 16 (17.9)	7.8 9 (7.8)	11.6 16 (11.6)	20.9 17 (20.9)	5.2 5 (5.2)
N =	162	92	114	137	81	96
Coefficient of reproducibility	0.8321	0.8348	0.8316	0.8569	0.8321	0.8667
Minimum marginal reproducibility	0.6012	0.5630	0.6877	0.6730	0.5457	0.7104
Percentage improvement	0.2309	0.2717	0.1439	0.1839	0.2864	0.1563
Coefficient of scalability	0.5789	0.6219	0.4607	0.5625	0.6304	0.5396

Table A.1.48 Percentage frequency distribution of respondents' reasons for drinking scaled by Guttman techniques – Mood changing reasons, drinking to affect a change in mood (Q.54§, 3, 9, 12)

Category	Males			Females		
	Irish 164	*Anglo-Irish* 92	*English* 116	*Irish* 134	*Anglo-Irish* 81	*English* 96
Does not drink for any of these reasons	100% 40 (24.4)	100% 17 (18.5)	100% 38 (32.8)	100% 38 (27.8)	100% 13 (16.1)	100% 32 (33.3)
To make me feel good	75.6 46 (28.0)	81.5 22 (32.9)	67.2 31 (26.7)	72.2 39 (28.5)	83.9 24 (29.6)	66.6 41 (42.7)
A drink helps to cheer me up when I'm in a bad mood	47.5 60 (36.6)	57.6 37 (40.2)	40.5 38 (32.8)	44.7 45 (32.8)	54.3 30 (37.0)	23.9 17 (17.7)
I drink to get some energy or pep	10.9 18 (10.9)	17.3 16 (17.3)	7.7 9 (7.7)	10.9 15 (10.9)	17.3 14 (17.3)	6 (6.3)
N =	164	92	116	134	81	96
Coefficient of reproducibility	0.8780	0.9565	0.9368	0.8881	0.9177	0.8958
Minimum marginal reproducibility	0.6626	0.7319	0.6724	0.6545	0.7119	0.6979
Percentage improvement	0.2154	0.2246	0.2644	0.2336	0.2058	0.1979
Coefficient of scalability	0.6386	0.8378	0.8070	0.6761	0.7143	0.6552

Table A.1.49   Attitude of respondents to their children taking a drink — 1st mention
(Q.31)

	Fathers			Mothers		
	Irish %	Anglo-Irish %	English %	Irish %	Anglo-Irish %	English %
Approve	16.9	29.1	29.2	8.5	23.9	21.7
Approve in moderation	31.9	41.0	49.9	28.0	52.3	53.0
Approve if old enough	7.6	6.7	2.8	6.8	4.0	6.0
It's alright for boys — not for girls	3.0	2.2	0.6	2.0	0.6	0.5
It depends on the circumstances	0.3	0.7	–	0.6	–	0.5
It's up to themselves	2.3	3.0	11.8	1.1	2.8	6.0
Leads to all kinds of improper behaviour	–	–	–	0.8	–	–
Don't like it, but can't stop them	9.6	1.5	3.9	5.9	2.3	4.1
Strongly disapprove	24.6	8.2	2.8	43.8	10.8	6.0
Other answer	3.3	6.7	–	2.5	3.4	1.4
No answer	0.3	0.7	–	–	–	0.5
N =	301	134	178	354	176	217

Table A.1.50 Percentage frequency distribution of respondents' attitudes towards their 18-21 year-old children drinking in a family and peer group context as measured by fathers' and mothers' responses and scales by Guttman techniques (Q.33§, 1,2,3,4,5; Q.34§, 1,2,3,4,5)

Scale type cumulative	Fathers			Mothers		
	Irish 296	Anglo-Irish 133	English 177	Irish 345	Anglo-Irish 173	English 215
Negative attitudes to their children drinking in peer group and family context	100.0 56 (18.9)	100.0 11 (8.2)	100.0 3 (1.7)	100.0 120 (34.7)	100.0 10 (5.7)	100.0 8 (3.8)
Drink in a mixed group (of friends) in a pub	81.1 66 (22.2)	91.7 39 (29.3)	98.3 19 (10.7)	65.2 64 (18.5)	94.2 31 (17.9)	96.2 31 (14.4)
Take a drink at home	58.8 33 (11.1)	62.4 10 (7.5)	87.6 12 (6.7)	46.6 42 (12.1)	76.3 15 (8.6)	81.8 17 (7.9)
Drink in a pub with your husband/wife	47.6 36 (12.1)	54.8 7 (5.3)	81.0 7 (3.9)	34.5 38 (11.0)	67.6 18 (10.4)	73.9 12 (5.5)
Drink with a girl- or boy-friend in a pub	35.5 36 (12.1)	49.6 17 (12.7)	76.8 20 (11.2)	23.5 31 (8.9)	57.2 21 (12.1)	68.3 18 (8.3)
Drink in a pub with friends same sex	23.2 69 (23.3)	36.8 49 (36.8)	65.5 116 (65.5)	14.5 50 (14.5)	45.0 78 (45.0)	60.0 129 (60.0)
N =	296	133	177	345	173	215
Coefficient of reproducibility	0.8000	0.8917	0.9299	0.8261	0.8936	0.9423
Minimum marginal reproducibility	0.5264	0.6000	0.8181	0.6313	0.6775	0.7609
Percentage improvement	0.2736	0.2907	0.7119	0.1943	0.2162	0.1814
Coefficient of scalability	0.5777	0.7293	0.6149	0.5283	0.6703	0.7588

Table A.1.51 Percentage frequency distribution of respondents' attitudes towards the effects of excessive drinking on their 18-21 year-old children as measured by fathers' and mothers' responses and scaled by Guttman techniques (Q.33§, 8, 9, 10; Q.34§, 8, 9, 10)

Scale type cumulative	Fathers			Mothers		
	Irish 300	Anglo-Irish 134	English 178	Irish 353	Anglo-Irish 175	English 217
Negative attitudes to the effects of excessive drinking	100 277 (92.1)	100 106 (79.1)	100 128 (71.9)	100 328 (92.6)	100 140 (79.5)	100 161 (74.2)
Be visibly affected by drink without being drunk	7.6 16 (5.3)	20.9 17 (12.7)	28.1 37 (20.8)	7.1 22 (6.2)	20.5 26 (14.8)	25.8 38 (17.5)
Be what you describe as drunk at home	2.3 4 (1.3)	8.2 4 (3.0)	7.3 7 (3.2)	0.85 3 (0.85)	5.7 7 (4.0)	8.3 7 (3.2)
Be what you describe as drunk in mixed company	1.0 3 (1.0)	5.2 7 (5.2)	3.4 6 (3.4)	0.0 0 (0.0)	1.7 3 (1.7)	5.1 11 (5.1)
N =	300	134	178	353	176	217
Coefficient of reproducibility	0.9889	0.9751	0.9888	0.9868	0.9811	0.9908
Minimum marginal reproducibility	0.9533	0.8856	0.8708	0.9736	0.9072	0.8694
Percentage improvement	0.0256	0.0896	0.1180	0.0132	0.0739	0.1214
Coefficient of scalability	0.6970	0.7826	0.9130	0.5000	0.7959	0.9294

201

Table A.1.52 Percentage frequency distribution of respondents' attitudes towards their 18-21 year-old children mixing their drinks, drinking 3 or 4 drinks or 6 or more drinks on a drinking occasion as measured by fathers' and mothers' responses and scaled by Guttman techniques (Q. 33§, 6, 7, 11; Q.34§, 6, 7, 11).

Scale type cumulative	Fathers			Mothers		
	Irish 300	*Anglo-Irish* 134	*English* 178	*Irish* 353	*Anglo-Irish* 176	*English* 217
Would not agree to statements	100 161 (53.5)	100 30 (22.4)	100 47 (26.4)	100 235 (66.4)	100 59 (33.6)	100 62 (28.7)
Drink 3 or 4 drinks on one occasion	45.8 112 (37.2)	87.6 71 (53.0)	73.6 80 (44.9)	33.3 104 (29.4)	66.4 89 (50.5)	70.3 104 (47.9)
Drink 6 or more drinks on one occasion	8.6 21 (7.0)	24.6 24 (17.9)	28.7 40 (22.5)	3.9 13 (13.8)	15.9 23 (13.1)	23.4 38 (17.5)
Mix their drinks	1.6 5 (1.6)	6.7 9 (6.7)	6.1 11 (6.1)	0.3 1 (0.3)	2.8 5 (2.8)	5.9 13 (5.9)
N =	300	134	178	353	176	217
Coefficient of reproducibility	0.9532	0.9602	0.9588	0.9849	0.9659	0.9570
Minimum marginal reproducibility	0.8116	0.8109	0.7959	0.8744	0.8144	0.7942
Percentage improvement	0.1416	0.1493	0.1629	0.1105	0.1515	0.1628
Coefficient of scalability	0.7515	0.7895	0.7982	0.8797	0.8163	0.7910

Table A.1.53 Respondents' attitudes to drunkenness (Q.59ᴄ)

Category	Irish				Anglo-Irish				English			
	Males	Females	Males	Females	Males	Females	Males	Females	Males	Females	Males	Females
	Approve %	%	Disapprove %	%	Approve %	%	Disapprove %	%	Approve %	%	Disapprove %	%
Drunkenness is a sign of immaturity	46.8	57.2	42.2	31.0	21.6	31.4	61.2	55.8	25.2	51.5	57.9	37.4
Drunkenness is excusable under many circumstances	45.3	42.8	44.7	45.4	50.5	47.7	33.4	33.7	46.2	38.4	40.3	49.5
As long as a person keeps out of trouble it is alright for him to drink to excess	31.6	27.3	63.7	67.9	44.1	30.2	48.4	57.0	47.9	39.4	37.8	50.5
N =	190	187	190	187	93	86	93	86	119	99	119	99

Table A.1.54   Respondents' definitions of acceptable behaviour while drinking in a group (Q.63)

Category	Males			Females		
	Irish %	*Anglo-Irish* %	*English* %	*Irish* %	*Anglo-Irish* %	*English* %
Being happy	94.7	100.0	98.3	92.5	100.0	98.0
Being very talkative	80.5	83.9	89.9	82.9	93.0	87.9
Being merry	94.7	100.0	99.2	91.4	98.8	99.0
Being amorous	48.9	68.8	64.7	30.5	53.5	27.3
Being drunk	42.6	65.6	48.7	16.6	34.9	19.2
N =	190	93	119	187	86	99

Table A.1.55   Respondents' definitions of tolerable behaviour while drinking in a group (Q.63)

Category	Males			Females		
	Irish %	*Anglo-Irish* %	*English* %	*Irish* %	*Anglo-Irish* %	*English* %
Being happy	95.8	96.8	97.5	95.7	98.8	98.0
Being very talkative	90.0	91.4	95.0	90.9	90.7	90.9
Being merry	96.3	97.8	96.6	93.0	98.8	96.0
Being amorous	63.2	74.2	73.1	38.5	55.8	43.4
Being drunk	59.5	76.3	60.5	28.9	36.0	38.4
N =	190	93	119	187	86	99

Table A.1.56   Exposure to problem drinking* (Q.40a, Q.67b, Q.67c favourable response)

	Males			Females		
	Irish %	Anglo-Irish %	English %	Irish %	Anglo-Irish %	English %
Trouble in respondents' home due to drink	30.0	9.7	7.5	16.6	15.2	5.0
Close relative with drinking problem	17.8	19.3	5.0	19.3	19.7	8.1
Close friend with drinking problem	14.8	10.8	3.4	7.0	8.2	4.0
N =	190	93	119	187	86	99

*Based on replies of respondents who answered yes to the above questions.

Table A.1.57   Whether respondent considers that he has a limit to his drinking* (Q.48e)

	Males			Females		
	Irish %	Anglo-Irish %	English %	Irish %	Anglo-Irish %	English %
Has limit in terms of volume taken, has exceeded it	25.5	14.1	31.0	20.3	24.7	22.9
Has limit in terms of finance, has exceeded it	0.6	5.4	6.0	0.7	3.7	2.1
Has limit and exceeded it	26.1	19.6	9.5	19.6	29.6	6.3
Has limit and has not exceeded it	9.7	4.3	7.8	26.8	7.4	15.6
Has limit in terms of volume, has not exceeded it	3.6	4.3	1.7	15.9	13.6	14.6
Has limit in terms of finance, has not exceeded it	—	3.3	4.3	1.4	1.2	—
No limits	33.3	46.7	35.3	13.8	19.8	35.4
Ambiguous answer	1.2	2.2	4.3	0.7	—	3.1
No answer	—	—	—	0.7	—	—
N =	165	92	116	138	81	96

*Refers to respondents who, at the time of interview, said they took a drink.

Table A.1.58   Problem drinking in the lives of respondents* (Q.48d, e, Q.55, Q.56, Q.56f favourable response)

	Males			Females		
	Irish %	Anglo-Irish %	English %	Irish %	Anglo-Irish %	English %
Misappropriate behaviour:						
Merry in past year, several times, 10 times or more	67.9	79.2	65.5	48.5	61.7	41.7
Drunk in past year, several times, 10 times or more	46.7	55.4	28.4	12.3	24.7	10.4
Personal problems:						
Problem(s) related to drinking in year prior to interview	45.2	49.0	26.7	17.5	30.9	11.5
Worries over drinking	15.7	17.4	8.6	7.2	2.5	3.1
N =	165	92	116	138	81	96

*Based on replies of respondents who answered yes to the above questions and who, at the time of interview, said they took a drink.

Table A.1.59   Respondents' assessment of family life to date (Q.77a)

Assessment	Males			Females		
	Irish %	Anglo-Irish %	English %	Irish %	Anglo-Irish %	English %
Happy	41.1	45.2	42.9	47.6	34.9	47.5
Moderately happy with ups and down	53.7	53.8	53.8	44.4	58.1	47.5
Unhappy with frequent upsets	2.1	1.1	0.8	4.8	2.3	2.0
Serious difficulties	1.1	–	0.8	1.6	–	1.0
Serious difficulties with long periods of separation	1.1	–	–	0.5	2.3	2.0
Serious difficulties without long periods of separation	–	–	–	–	1.2	–
Unclear ambiguous answer	1.1	–	1.7	1.0	1.2	–
N =	190	93	119	187	86	99

Table A.1.60 Perceived parental support as measured by 18–21 year olds' responses and scaled by Guttman techniques (Q.79§, 1,2; Q.80§, 2)

	Males			Females		
	Irish 188	Anglo-Irish 93	English 119	Irish 185	Anglo-Irish 85	English 99
Negative to all items	100% 10 (5.3)	100% ...9 (20.4)	100% 19 (15.9)	100% 12 (6.5)	100% 15 (17.6)	100% 12 (12.2)
Whether parents are interested in school, college, work	94.7 52 (27.7)	79.7 25 (27.9)	84.1 29 (24.4)	93.6 38 (20.5)	82.4 15 (17.6)	87.87 10 (10.1)
Encouragement to do things in which respondent has interest	67.1 70 (37.2)	51.6 29 (31.2)	59.7 41 (34.5)	73.1 51 (27.6)	64.7 17 (20.0)	77.8 29 (29.3)
Whether parents help him when he is worried about something	29.8 56 (29.8)	20.4 19 (20.4)	25.2 30 (25.2)	45.4 84 (45.4)	45.4 38 (44.7)	48.5 48 (48.5)
N =	188	93	119	185	85	99
Coefficient of reproducibility	0.8759	0.8710	0.7815	0.8703	0.8824	0.8653
Minimum marginal reproducibility	0.6915	0.6272	0.5826	0.7063	0.6392	0.7138
Percentage improvement	0.1844	0.2437	0.1989	0.1640	0.2431	0.1515
Coefficient of scalability	0.5977	0.6538	0.4765	0.5583	0.6739	0.5294

Table A.1.61   Inconsistency in parental behaviour as perceived by respondents (Q79§, 2, 4)

Inconsistency	Males								
	High			Medium			Low		
	Irish %	Anglo-Irish %	English %	Irish %	Anglo-Irish %	English %	Irish %	Anglo-Irish %	English %
Made promises, but never materialized	1.6	2.2	3.4	8.9	15.1	8.4	87.4	82.8	88.2
Saying one thing and doing another	6.8	5.4	2.5	18.4	30.1	26.9	73.1	64.5	69.8
N =	190	93	119	190	93	119	190	93	119

Table A.1.62   Inconsistency in parental behaviour as perceived by respondents (Q.79§, 2, 4)

Inconsistency	Females								
	High			Medium			Low		
	Irish %	Anglo-Irish %	English %	Irish %	Anglo-Irish %	English %	Irish %	Anglo-Irish %	English %
Made promises, but never materialized	4.2	4.6	3.0	9.6	9.3	8.1	85.5	83.7	88.9
Saying one thing and doing another	4.8	7.0	5.1	20.9	22.1	15.2	73.8	68.6	79.8
N =	187	86	99	187	86	99	187	86	99

Table A.1.63   Agreement between respondents' parents and friends (Q.81a)

Agreement	Males			Females		
	Irish %	*Anglo-Irish* %	*English* %	*Irish* %	*Anglo-Irish* %	*English* %
Almost complete agreement	6.3	5.4	4.2	11.8	4.7	7.1
A lot of agreement	15.8	17.3	14.3	19.3	20.9	23.2
A fair amount of agreement	32.6	28.0	28.6	38.5	34.9	33.3
Some agreement	32.1	41.9	42.0	25.7	32.6	33.3
No agreement at all	11.1	7.5	8.4	2.7	5.8	3.0
Do not know	1.1	–	–	2.2	–	–
Information incomplete	0.1	–	2.5	–	1.2	–
N =	190	93	119	187	86	99

Table A.1.64   General social support from respondents' friends (Q.80 favourable response)

	Males			Females		
	Irish %	*Anglo-Irish* %	*English* %	*Irish* %	*Anglo-Irish* %	*English* %
High level of perceived social support	45.0	42.0	52.1	55.6	66.3	56.5
Medium level of perceived social support	32.6	40.9	28.6	25.1	20.9	26.3
Low level of perceived social support	21.0	16.1	16.8	17.1	11.7	16.2
Information incomplete	1.6	1.1	2.5	2.2	1.2	1.0
N =	190	93	119	187	86	99

Table A.1.65   General profile of overall exposure to drinking: peer group support for non-drinking pattern * (Q.16, 2; Q.23ab favourable responses)

	Irish		
	Males %	Females %	Total %
Friends take a drink	80.0	83.7	82.4
Friends take a drink regularly	76.0	46.9	56.8
Pressure to drink by friends at any time	36.0	32.7	36.4
Friends suggested to drink at any time	32.0	55.1	54.1
Friends suggested not to drink at any time	32.0	20.4	24.3
Recreational activities once a month or more:			
Drinking with girls/lads	32.0	14.3	20.3
Drink with friends	40.0	34.7	36.5
Pub usual place respondent goes with friends	21.1	21.4	21.2
N =	25	49	74

*This refers to non-drinkers at time of interview.

Table A.1.66 Recreational activities once a month or more – Irish non-drinkers (Q.28)

Activity	Irish											
	Never			*Once or twice*			*3 or 4 times*			*Once a week +*		
	Males %	*Females* %	*Total* %	*Males* %	*Females* %	*Total* %	*Males* %	*Females* %	*Total* %	*Males* %	*Females* %	*Total* %
Cinema	12.0	20.4	17.6	36.0	30.6	32.4	12.0	14.3	13.5	40.0	34.7	36.5
Dance/disco	52.0	38.8	43.2	24.0	26.5	25.7	4.0	2.0	2.7	20.0	32.7	28.4
Party	68.0	67.3	67.6	32.0	30.6	31.1	–	2.0	1.4	–	–	–
Play a sport	24.0	61.2	48.7	20.0	12.2	14.9	4.0	2.0	2.7	52.0	24.5	36.5
Follow a sport	40.0	53.1	48.7	12.0	12.2	12.2	–	4.1	2.7	48.0	30.6	33.8
Youth club	84.0	93.9	90.5	4.0	–	1.4	–	2.0	1.4	12.0	4.1	6.7
Bingo	92.0	83.7	86.5	8.0	10.2	9.5	–	2.0	1.4	–	4.1	2.7
Drive	40.0	49.0	46.0	28.0	16.3	20.3	4.0	10.2	8.1	28.0	24.5	25.7
Stay at home	20.0	6.1	10.8	8.0	–	2.7	–	2.0	1.4	72.0	91.8	85.4
Go visiting	28.0	10.2	16.2	28.0	26.5	27.0	8.0	4.1	5.4	36.0	59.2	51.4
Go out with the family	68.0	55.1	59.5	20.0	26.5	24.3	–	8.2	5.4	12.0	10.2	10.8
Drink with girls/lads	68.0	85.7	79.7	4.0	2.0	2.7	8.0	–	2.7	20.0	12.2	14.7
Drink with friends	60.0	65.3	63.5	24.0	18.4	20.3	4.0	4.1	4.1	12.0	12.2	12.2
Drink with parents	96.0	93.9	94.6	–	4.1	2.7	–	–	–	4.0	1.0	2.7
N =	25	49	74	25	49	74	25	49	74	25	49	74

Table A.1.67   Respondents' attitudes to young people of their own age drinking as measured by 18-21 year olds' responses and scaled by Guttman techniques (Q.59a)

Scale type cumulative	Males						Females					
	Irish		Anglo-Irish		English		Irish		Anglo-Irish		English	
Negative attitude to all items	100% 12	(100.0)	100% 17	(19.1)	100% 16	(14.1)	100% 12	(6.4)	100% 18	(20.9)	100% 21	(22.1)
Lads of your age taking a drink	93.2 24	(13.2)	82.9 16	(18.0)	85.9 4	(3.5)	93.6 14	(76.0)	79.1 5	(5.8)	77.9 11	(11.6)
Girl/boy-friend taking a drink	80.2 53	(29.1)	63.9 10	(11.2)	82.4 10	(8.9)	86.0 11	(6.0)	73.3 9	(10.5)	66.3 12	(12.6)
Girls of your age taking a drink	51.1 93	(51.1)	51.7 46	(51.7)	73.5 83	(73.5)	80.0 148	(80.0)	62.8 54	(62.8)	53.7 51	(53.7)
N =	182		89		113		185		86		95	
Coefficient of reproducibility	0.7619		0.9251		0.9469		0.9387		0.9225		0.8807	
Minimum marginal reproducibility	0.7491		0.6517		0.8053		0.8649		0.7171		0.6596	
Percentage improvement	0.0128		0.2737		0.1416		0.0739		0.2054		0.2211	
Coefficient of scalability	0.0511		0.7849		0.7273		0.5467		0.7260		0.6495	

Table A.1.68 Respondents' attitudes to single-sex drinking among young people as measured by 18-21 year olds' responses and scaled by Guttman techniques (Q.59a8)

Type cumulative	Males			Females		
	Irish	Anglo-Irish	English	Irish	Anglo-Irish	English
Negative to all items	100% 24 (13.0)	100% 2 (2.2)	100% 8 (7.0)	100% 35 (18.9)	100% 2 (2.3)	100% 8 (8.1)
Drinking in all female group	87.1 51 (27.6)	97.8 20 (22.5)	93.0 28 (24.6)	81.1 61 (33.0)	97.7 16 (18.8)	91.9 27 (27.6)
Drinking in all male group	59.5 64 (34.6)	75.3 30 (33.7)	68.4 17 (14.9)	48.1 64 (34.6)	78.9 36 (42.4)	64.3 35 (35.7)
Girls in a pub on their own taking a drink	24.9 46 (24.9)	41.6 37 (41.6)	53.5 61 (53.5)	13.5 25 (13.5)	36.5 31 (36.5)	28.6 28 (28.6)
N =	185	89	114	185	85	98
Coefficient of reproducibility	0.7658	0.7978	0.7661	0.8054	0.8745	0.8231
Minimum marginal reproducibility	0.6090	0.7154	0.7164	0.6667	0.7096	0.6156
Percentage improvement	0.1568	0.0824	0.0497	0.1387	0.1647	0.2076
Coefficient of scalability	0.4009	0.2894	0.1753	0.4162	0.5676	0.5398

Table A.1.69 Level of tolerable behaviour while drinking in a group as measured by 18-21 year olds' responses (Q.63)

	Males			Females		
	Irish %	*Anglo-Irish* %	*English* %	*Irish* %	*Anglo-Irish* %	*English* %
Negative to all items	100			100		
	2 (1.1)	0 (0.0)	0 (0.0)	4 (2.3)	0 (0.0)	0 (0.0)
To be happy	98.9			97.7		100
	1 (0.5)	0 (0.0)	0 (0.0)	7 (3.9)	0 (0.0)	2 (3.1)
To feel merry	98.3	100	100	93.8	100	96.9
	13 (7.1)	1 (1.7)	2 (2.6)	18 (10.1)	2 (3.9)	3 (4.6)
To be very talkative	91.1	98.3	97.4	83.6	96.1	92.1
	39 (21.5)	6 (10.0)	12 (15.3)	75 (42.1)	10 (19.2)	32 (50.0)
To be jarred	69.5	88.3	82.0	41.5	76.9	42.1
	50 (27.6)	7 (11.6)	15 (19.2)	35 (19.6)	15 (28.8)	12 (18.7)
To be amorous	41.9	76.6	62.8	21.9	48.0	23.4
	28 (15.4)	11 (18.3)	14 (17.9)	16 (3.9)	14 (26.9)	6 (9.3)
To be drunk	26.5	58.3	44.8	12.9	21.1	14.0
	48 (26.5)	35 (58.3)	35 (44.8)	23 (12.9)	11 (21.1)	9 (14.0)
N =	181	60	78	178	52	64

214

Table. A.1.70   Level of tolerable behaviour while drinking in a group as measured by 18-21 year olds' responses (Q.63)

	Males			Females		
	Irish %	Anglo-Irish %	English %	Irish %	Anglo-Irish %	English %
Negative to all items	100 1 (0.5)	0 (0.0)	0 (0.0)	100 2 (1.2)	0 (0.0)	0 (0.0)
To feel merry	99.4 1 (0.5)	100 0 (0.0)	100 1 (1.4)	98.8 4 (2.2)	0 (0.0)	0 (0.0)
To be happy	98.8 9 (5.0)	100 1 (1.6)	100 0 (0.0)	96.5 12 (6.7)	100 4 (7.9)	100 2 (3.3)
To be very talkative	93.8 22 (12.2)	99.0 5 (8.4)	98.6 8 (10.8)	89.8 62 (35.0)	92.1 11 (21.5)	96.7 18 (30.0)
To be jarred	81.6 34 (18.3)	90.6 3 (5.8)	87.8 12 (16.2)	54.7 36 (20.3)	70.5 8 (15.6)	6.6 18 (30.0)
To be amorous	62.7 36 (20.0)	84.7 7 (11.8)	71.6 6 (8.1)	34.5 26 (14.7)	54.9 13 (25.5)	36.6 7 (11.6)
To be drunk	42.7 77 (42.7)	72.8 43 (72.8)	63.5 47 (63.5)	19.7 35 (19.7)	29.4 15 (29.4)	25.0 15 (25.0)
N =	180	59	74	177	51	60

Table A.1.71 Positive view of the social context in which respondent lives as measured by 18-21 year olds' responses and scaled by Guttman techniques (Q.82, Q.85ab)

	Males			Females		
	Irish 146	Anglo-Irish 65	English 82	Irish 122	Anglo-Irish 56	English 67
Negative to all items	100% 5 (3.5)	100% 20 (30.8)	100% 8 (9.8)	100% 12 (9.9)	100% 9 (16.1)	100% 6 (8.9)
Ireland/England is a good place to live in	96.5 22 (15.1)	69.2 9 (13.8)	90.2 19 (23.1)	90.2 22 (18.0)	83.9 15 (26.8)	91.1 18 (26.9)
Hard work can make a good career in Ireland/England	81.4 38 (26.0)	55.4 11 (16.9)	66.9 26 (31.7)	72.1 28 (22.9)	57.1 11 (19.6)	64.2 19 (28.4)
Ireland/England as it is now is the place I would prefer to bring up my children	55.4 55 (37.6)	38.5 10 (15.4)	35.3 15 (18.3)	49.2 37 (30.3)	37.0 14 (25.0)	35.8 16 (23.8)
Image of Ireland/England favourable	17.8 26 (17.8)	23.1 15 (23.1)	17.0 14 (17.0)	18.8 23 (18.8)	12.5 7 (12.5)	11.9 8 (11.9)
N =	146	65	82	122	56	67
Coefficient of reproducibility	0.7397	0.8308	0.7866	0.7746	0.7589	0.7313
Minimum marginal reproducibility	0.6284	0.5577	0.6280	0.6004	0.6205	0.5821
Percentage improvement	0.1113	0.2731	0.1585	0.1742	0.1384	0.1493
Coefficient of scalability	0.2995	0.6174	0.4262	0.4359	0.3647	0.3571

Table A.1.72 Score on scale of anomie (Q.82)

Score	Males			Females		
	Irish %	Anglo-Irish %	English %	Irish %	Anglo-Irish %	English %
High anomie	36.2	19.4	21.0	46.6	30.2	37.4
Medium anomie	37.3	39.8	42.9	39.6	41.8	36.3
Low anomie/Non-anomic	25.2	40.9	35.3	12.8	26.8	26.2
No information	1.1	—	0.8	1.1	1.2	—
N =	190	93	119	187	86	99

Table A.1.73 Areas of concern in country of origin* (Q.83a)

Category	Males			Females		
	Irish %	Anglo-Irish %	English %	Irish %	Anglo-Irish %	English %
Economic	21.1	34.4	28.6	21.4	32.6	23.2
Housing and overpopulation	4.2	11.8	22.7	4.8	29.1	23.2
Immigration, race relations	—	17.2	17.6	—	8.1	21.2
Political	39.5	12.9	7.6	37.4	1.2	7.1
Education			—	0.5	—	—
Educational and religious	5.8	1.1	—	2.1	—	1.0
Social and moral pollution	20.5	3.2	7.6	23.0	14.0	6.1
No problem	—	—	—	—	1.2	—
Other answer	7.4	17.2	13.4	7.5	11.6	13.1
Don't know	1.6	2.2	2.5	3.2	2.3	5.1
N =	190	93	119	187	86	99

*This refers to the biggest perceived problem in country of origin.

Table A.1.74   Respondents' perception of how changes can be brought about (Q.84c)

	Males			Females		
	Irish %	Anglo-Irish %	English %	Irish %	Anglo-Irish %	English %
Democratic means	68.4	72.1	62.1	62.5	50.0	52.5
Revolution	6.8	4.3	–	0.5	17.5	–
Change cannot be brought about	4.8	6.5	5.0	4.8	15.1	7.0
Do not know	18.4	17.2	25.2	29.9	17.4	29.3
No answer	1.6	–	7.6	2.1	–	11.1
N =	190	93	119	187	86	99

Table A.1.75   Respondents' participation in bringing change to country of origin (Q.84d)

Category	Males			Females		
	Irish %	Anglo-Irish %	English %	Irish %	Anglo-Irish %	English %
Yes, through political measures	21.0	18.3	13.5	13.9	17.4	7.1
Nothing I can do	55.4	55.9	59.7	63.1	53.5	61.7
Other answer	13.7	12.9	9.2	10.2	15.1	6.1
No answer given	1.1	3.2	5.0	1.6	10.5	19.2
Do not know	8.9	9.7	12.6	11.2	3.5	6.1
N =	190	93	119	187	86	99

Table A.1.76 Respondents' membership of religious group (Q.76a)

Religion	Males			Females		
	Irish %	Anglo-Irish %	English %	Irish %	Anglo-Irish %	English %
Roman Catholic	91.5	93.5	7.6	99.0	97.6	3.0
Church of Ireland	1.1	–	–	–	–	–
Church of England and Anglican	–	–	55.5	–	–	70.7
Baptist	–	–	2.5	–	–	5.1
Methodist	–	–	0.8	–	–	6.1
Presbyterian	–	–	–	–	–	1.0
Salvation Army	–	–	–	–	–	–
Congregationalist	–	–	–	–	–	–
Jehovah's Witness	–	–	–	0.5	–	–
Christian	2.1	–	1.6	–	–	3.0
Atheist	1.1	1.1	6.8	–	–	3.0
Other	–	–	6.8	–	–	3.0
Not a member of any religious group	3.2	5.4	18.5	–	1.2	5.1
No answer given	1.1	–	–	0.5	1.2	–
N =	190	93	119	187	86	99

Table A.1.77 Attendance at religious services (Q.73)

Attendance	Males			Females		
	Irish %	Anglo-Irish %	English %	Irish %	Anglo-Irish %	English %
More than once a week	2.6	2.2	1.7	9.1	3.5	1.0
Once a week	54.7	29.0	2.5	77.0	46.5	5.1
Once or twice a month	7.9	7.5	–	3.7	8.1	4.0
About once a month	3.2	3.2	–	3.2	1.2	1.0
A few times during the year	6.3	16.1	8.4	1.6	9.3	9.1
Only rarely	6.0	14.0	21.0	2.7	16.3	23.2
Never	17.9	28.0	66.4	1.6	14.0	56.6
Unclear answer	1.1	–	–	1.1	1.2	–
N =	190	93	119	187	86	99

Table A.1.78　Influence of religious beliefs on way in which respondent acts (Q.75)

Influence	Males			Females		
	Irish %	Anglo-Irish %	English %	Irish %	Anglo-Irish %	English %
Continuous	5.8	4.3	2.5	17.1	5.8	4.0
Very frequent	9.5	8.6	4.2	11.8	12.8	6.1
Frequent	27.9	15.1	8.4	33.2	24.4	8.1
Occasional	24.2	30.1	11.8	24.1	31.4	28.3
Rarely	14.2	20.4	22.7	7.5	14.0	25.3
Never	17.4	21.5	47.9	4.8	10.5	27.3
Unclear answer	1.1	–	0.8	1.1	1.2	–
Do not know	–	–	1.7	–	–	1.0
N =	190	93	119	187	86	99

Table A.1.79　Religious discrepancy (Q.76b)

Category	Males			Females		
	Irish %	Anglo-Irish %	English %	Irish %	Anglo-Irish %	English %
Same as parents	93.2	92.5	58.0	97.9	97.7	74.7
Same as mother, not father	1.1	1.1	2.5	0.5	1.2	2.0
Same as father, not mother	–	–	1.7	1.1	–	3.0
Not the same religion as parents	4.7	6.5	25.2	–	–	15.2
No answer given	1.1	–	9.2	0.3	1.2	5.0
Do not know	–	–	3.4	–	–	–
N =	190	93	119	187	86	99

Appendix 2
Questionnaires

Instruction to interviewers

Interviewers should emphasize that those who are interviewed remain absolutely anonymous — even the areas in which the interviews take place will be anonymous. Interviewers should also explain that the focus of the survey is on general patterns among those interviewed, not on replies of particular individuals.

Care should be taken to satisfy respondents as to the purpose of the survey as a whole, and the reasons for the inclusion of particular questions. Interviewers must, therefore, be familiar with the necessary explanations. The interview schedule should be known thoroughly along with the introduction to the various sections.

Interviewers should fill in the date of the interview and the time taken, in the appropriate space provided at the top of the schedule. Words in capitals indicate instructions to the interviewers. *All responses* should be recorded fully and *verbatim*, as the aim of the interviewer is to get the person to talk freely, not merely to complete the schedule.

Questions marked thus: Q.§, are to be given to respondents on a prompt card, and read to them at the same time. The type of question to be asked when using the cards should be: 'Now there are five possible answers to this question ... (name them) ... could you tell me which one best applies to you?'

At the end of the interview, check your schedule and make sure that there is an answer to each question. Before you leave, make sure that your respondent is happy about what you are doing, and is as clear as possible about the nature of the survey.

After the questionnaire/s have been checked a letter of thanks is to be delivered to each of the respondents interviewed. This applies to both 18-21 year olds and parents. Each parent is to receive a separate thank you letter.

COVER SHEET CENSUS FORM

Department of Social Science
University College   Schedule No . . . .
Social Research Organisation

INTERVIEWER:
                              DATE: TIME: From . . . . To . . .

1. Total number of children in family . . . .

2. Where parents were born:

	Town	County	Country
Mother			
Father			

3. Number of children living in the
   house between the ages of 18-21   . . . .

   Dates of birth of 18-21 year olds

Name	Male	Female	Date of birth

4. Where 18-21 year old to be interviewed was born:

	Town	County	Country
NAME:			

5. Time available for interview:

No contact made . . . . Mother . . . .

Refusals (details) . . . . Father . . . .

                                                         18-21 year old . . . .

                                                         Not applicable . . . .

18-21 year-old questionnaire

Questionnaire design

The questionnaire was designed to elicit information on the attitudes and patterns of drinking of 18-21 year olds. To structure and facilitate the collection and analysis of data, a theoretical framework was designed. The facts deemed necessary for this theoretical framework are as follows (see O'Connor 1976a and b for details):

Socio-economic characteristics
Income and expenditure
Recreational activities
Friendship patterns and perceived social support
Ethnic identification
Religion
Excitement and sensation seeking
General profile of drug taking
Alcoholism
Social support for drinking
Patterns of abstinence
Social support for drinking (non-drinkers)
Ex-drinker pattern
Learning to drink: first drinking experience
Parental practices and attitudes
Family life and satisfaction
Problem drinking
Present pattern of drinking
Attitudes towards drinking
Reasons for 'others' taking a drink
Role of public house and round drinking

Sample questionnaire

INTERVIEWER . . . . DATE . . . . TIME: FROM . . . . . . TO . . . .

Q. 1   What do you think of the opportunities in this area for free time activities?

Q. 2§   I have listed a number of activities which some people enjoy. As I read each
          one out would you tell me how often you do any of them in your free time
          in a month?

CARD

	Never	*Once or twice a month*	*Three or four times a month*	*Once a week or more*
1. Go to the pictures	1	2	3	4
2. Play a sport (please specify)	1	2	3	4
3. Follow a sport	1	2	3	4
4. Stay at home all evening	1	2	3	4
5. Go to bingo	1	2	3	4
6. Go for a drink with the lads/girls	1	2	3	4
7. Go visiting	1	2	3	4
8. Go for a drink with your parents	1	2	3	4
9. Go for a drive	1	2	3	4
10. Go to a dance	1	2	3	4
11. Go to a youth club	1	2	3	4
12. Go out with the family	1	2	3	4
13. Go to a party	1	2	3	4
14. Go for a drink with friends	1	2	3	4
15. Other (please specify)				

Q. 3a   At present are you an active member of any club or association?
          IF YES   Yes 2   No 1

Club	*Organization*	*Activities*
b	c	d

Q. 4a   Would you tell me about the free-time activities you were engaged in during
          the last week?

Day	*Activities*	*With whom*
a	b	c

b   Would you say this was a typical week?

c   Could you tell me where you spent your holidays for the last three years?

Year	Place
1971	
1970	
1969	

INTRODUCTION

Q. 5   About how many years have you lived in this area?

1	2	3
Under 6 years	6-under 11 years	11-under 16 years
4	5	6
16-under 21 years	21 years or more	Don't know

Q. 6   What age are you?

           18 years 1
           19 years 2
           20 years 3
           21 years 4

Q. 7   Could you tell me, are you:

           Married 1
           Single 2

           ....
           Other (please specify)

IF SINGLE:

Q. 8   Have you got a regular/steady boy/girl friend? Yes 2 No 1

Q. 9a   How many brothers and sisters have you?

Brothers   0   1   2   3   4   5   6   7   8   9   10 or more

Sisters   0   1   2   3   4   5   6   7   8   9   10 or more

b   What place do you come in the family?

1   2   3   4   5   6   7   8   9   10 11 12 13 14 15 or more

           Eldest (   )   Youngest (   )

Q.10a   Do you currently have a full-time or part-time job for which you are paid?

Yes 2 No 1

IF YES:

b   Full-time (   )   Part-time (   )

c   What kind of work do you do?

DETAILS OF OCCUPATION

Q.11a   Have you ever had any long illness, i.e. been sick for six weeks or more?

Yes 2 No 1

IF YES:

b   Were you in hospital? ....

IF YES:

c   What kind of hospital? ....

Q.12   What is/was the last type of school/college you attended?
       DETAILS

Q.13   It is difficult, I know, to get exact amounts spent per week, but could you tell
       me in what way your money goes during the week?

       Give up in the house . . . .
       About how much on records . . . .
       Cigarettes/tobacco . . . .
       Save . . . .
       Alcohol . . . .
       Recreation . . . .
       Travelling to work . . . .
       Other (please specify) . . . .

       IF WORKS:

Q.14§ Could you tell me what your take home money is per week?

       CARD   Under £10   1
              £10-under £16   2
              £16-under £20   3

              £20-under £25   4
              £25-under £30   5
              £30 and over   6

              Other   7
              Don't know   8

INTRODUCTION

Q.15   Where would you say is the easiest place to make friends?

Q.16a Do you have a special group of friends with whom you usually go out?
       IF YES:

   b   Where do you usually go?

Q.17   Could you tell me, what are your views on young people's drinking?

Q.18a Do you think lads between the ages of 18-21 years take a drink?
   b   Do you think girls between the ages of 18-21 years take a drink?

Q.19a Have you ever taken a drink – not just a sip or taste? Yes 2 No 1

       IF YES → Q.19b   IF NO → Q.20a

   b   Have you had a drink of beer, stout, wine, spirits or cider more than two or
       or three times in your life? Yes 2 No 1

       IF YES → Q.19c   IF NO → Q.20a

   c   Do you take a drink now? Yes 2 No 1
       IF YES → Q.20a
       IF NO:

   d   What age would you say you were when you stopped drinking?

   e   Could you tell me, was there any reason for this?
       DETAILS

ALL:

Q.20a   At school did you take any pledge not to drink until a certain age?
         Yes 2 No 1
         IF YES:

Name	Age	Reasons	Still a member
b	c	d	e

IF NO:
REASONS

IF NO: A PERSON WHO DRINKS → Q.26
NON-DRINKER OR EX-DRINKER:

Q.21a   Are you a member of a temperance group/total abstinence association?
         IF YES:

Name	Reasons	Age
b	c	d

IF NO: ALL NON-DRINKERS → Q.22
OTHERS → Q.25

NON-DRINKERS:

Q.22   Do you think that you will ever take a drink?

Q.23§

CARD	Never	Once or twice	Several times	Often
a Have you ever felt that any of your friends were putting pressure on you to drink?	0	1	2	3
b Have any of your friends suggested that you should try taking a drink?	0	1	2	3

c   Have any of your friends told you that you should not drink? Yes 2 No 1

Q.24a   About how many of your friends take a drink?

1	2	3	4
None	One or two	Several	Most of them

b   Do you have any close friends who drink fairly regularly, i.e. at least once a
         week?

c   IF YES:
         How many?

Q.25a　There are a number of reasons people have given for not taking a drink. Could you tell me if any of the following are true for you?

	Yes	No	Partly
1. Do not want to take a drink	2	1	0
2. As a sacrifice for those who drink excessively	2	1	0
3. Because drinking leads to being loud and rowdy	2	1	0
4. It is against my religion	2	1	0
5. The people I go around with are against it	2	1	0
6. Because it gets to be a bad habit	2	1	0
7. Health reasons	2	1	0
8. It is just an artificial way of solving your problems	2	1	0
9. Saw the effects of drink on other people	2	1	0
10. Don't want to lose my self control	2	1	0
11. Parents did not want me to take a drink	2	1	0

　　b　Have you ever felt after watching people drinking in the films or on TV or after reading about people drinking in books or magazines, that it might be fun to drink or to try drinking?

0	1	2	3
Never	Once or twice	Several times	Often

NON-DRINKERS → Q.32

FOR THOSE WHO HAVE EVER TAKEN A DRINK:

Q.26　When did you have your first drink?

Age	Where	With whom	Reasons	Type of drink	Amount
a	b	c	d	e	f

Q.27a　When did your parents know that you were having a drink?

　　b　How did your parents feel about you having your first drink?

Q.28a　How did you feel at that time about having a drink?

0	1	2

　　b　Did you feel: Not at all guilty　　A little guilty　　Pretty guilty

　　c　At that time do you remember worrying about getting caught drinking?

0	1	2
Not at all	A little	Very much

Q.29a　How did you feel about the taste of alcohol that first time?

　　b　Overall, would you say your first drink was:

0	1	2
Pleasant	Neither pleasant nor unpleasant	Unpleasant

Q.30　Did you get into trouble of any kind because of drinking that first time?

0	1	2
Not at all	Just a little	Quite a bit

Q.31   How long after was it until your next drink?

ALL:

Q.32   As far as recreation is concerned what do your parents usually do at the weekends?

Q.33   Does your father/mother take a drink?

Father − Yes 2   Mother − Yes 2
               No 1   No 1
Father deceased ( )   Mother deceased ( )

FOR THOSE WHOSE PARENTS TAKE A DRINK:

CARD

Q.34a§   Do you consider your father to be a:

1	2	3
Hard drinker	Moderate drinker	Light drinker
4	5	6
Non-drinker	Abstainer	Don't know

b§   Do you consider your mother to be a:

1	2	3
Hard drinker	Moderate drinker	Light drinker
4	5	6
Non-drinker	Abstainer	Don't know

INTRODUCTION   Could we talk about where your parents usually take a drink?

INSTRUCTIONS

Q.35

Father	*Where*	*With whom*	*Occasions*
	a	b	c
Mother	*Where*	*With whom*	*Occasions*
	d	e	f

Q.36   How do your parents feel about young people of your age taking a drink?

DETAILS

Q.37   Were you ever offered a drink at home by your parents? Yes 2 No 1

FOR THOSE WHO DRINK:

Q.38a   Could you tell me, what does your father think of you taking a drink?

b   What does your mother think of you taking a drink?

FOR NON-DRINKERS:

c   Could you tell me what your father would think if you took a drink?

d   What your mother would think if you took a drink?

Q.39§   I have a list of statements here and perhaps you would tell me how *you* feel what each of your parents' attitudes would be if you were to do any of the things mentioned? Could you take each parent separately? Each statement has six possible answers − strongly approve, moderately approve, neither approve nor disapprove, uncertain, moderately disapprove, strongly disapprove.

Q.39 (cont.) CARD

a §

FATHER

	Strongly approve	Moderately approve	Neither approve nor dis-approve	Uncertain	Moderately disapprove	Strongly disapprove
1. Take a drink at home	5	4	3	2	1	0
2. Drink in a pub with friends (all the same sex)	5	4	3	2	1	0
3. Drink alcohol in a pub with them, i.e. your parents	5	4	3	2	1	0
4. Drink with your girl/boy friend in a pub	5	4	3	2	1	0
5. Drink in a mixed group in a pub	5	4	3	2	1	0
6. Drink three or four drinks on one occasion	5	4	3	2	1	0
7. Drink six or more drinks on one occasion	5	4	3	2	1	0
8. Be visibly affected by drink without being drunk	5	4	3	2	1	0
9. Be what you describe as drunk at home	5	4	3	2	1	0
10. Be what you describe as drunk in mixed company	5	4	3	2	1	0
11. Mix your drinks	5	4	3	2	1	0
12. Drive a car after being affected by drink	5	4	3	2	1	0

Q.39 (cont.) CARD

b§   MOTHER

	Strongly approve	Moderately approve	Neither approve nor disapprove	Uncertain	Moderately disapprove	Strongly disapprove
1. Take a drink at home	5	4	3	2	1	0
2. Drink in a pub with friends (all the same sex)	5	4	3	2	1	0
3. Drink in a pub with them, i.e. your parents	5	4	3	2	1	0
4. Drink with your girl/boy friend in a pub	5	4	3	2	1	0
5. Drink in a mixed group in a pub	5	4	3	2	1	0
6. Drink three or four drinks on one occasion	5	4	3	2	1	0
7. Drink six or more drinks on one occasion	5	4	3	2	1	0
8. Be visibly affected by drink without being drunk	5	4	3	2	1	0
9. Be what you describe as drunk at home	5	4	3	2	1	0
10. Be what you describe as drunk in mixed company	5	4	3	2	1	0
11. Mix your drinks	5	4	3	2	1	0
12. Drive a car after being affected by drink	5	4	3	2	1	0

231

Q.40a   Was there ever any trouble in your home because of drink? Yes 2   No 1

   IF YES:

   DETAILS

   b   How did/do you feel about this?

THOSE WHO DRINK → Q. 41a   ALL → Q.57

Q.41a   About how many of your friends take a drink?

1	2	3	4
None	One or two	Several	Most of them

   b   Do you have any close friends who drink fairly regularly, i.e. at least once a week?

   IF YES:

   c   How many?

Q.42§   In what situations do you drink? I have a list of situations. Could you tell me whether you take a drink in these situations. Answer in terms of: very frequently, frequently, occasionally, rarely, never.

   CARD

	Very frequently	Frequently	Occasionally	Rarely	Never
1. When you are out on a date	4	3	2	1	0
2. When you are out on a date with some other entertainment	4	3	2	1	0
3. With a group of friends – lads	4	3	2	1	0
4. With a group of friends – girls	4	3	2	1	0
5. With a group of friends – mixed	4	3	2	1	0
6. After a match	4	3	2	1	0
7. When you go to a party with a girl/ boy friend	4	3	2	1	0
8. With the lads before you go dancing	4	3	2	1	0
9. With the girls before you go dancing	4	3	2	1	0
10. With your parents at home	4	3	2	1	0
11. With your parents in a pub	4	3	2	1	0
12. With your relatives	4	3	2	1	0
13. Anywhere at all you can	4	3	2	1	0
14. Other (please specify)	4	3	2	1	0

Q.43§ How often do you take a drink in the following places? Answer again in terms of: very frequently, frequently, occasionally, rarely, never.

CARD

	Very frequently	Frequently	Occasionally	Rarely	Never
1. Pub	4	3	2	1	0
2. Restaurant	4	3	2	1	0
3. Home	4	3	2	1	0
4. Friend's home	4	3	2	1	0
5. Parties — stag	4	3	2	1	0
6. Parties — hen	4	3	2	1	0
7. Parties	4	3	2	1	0
8. Club — specify type of club	4	3	2	1	0

. . . .

9. Other (please specify) . . . .

Q.44 Are there any particular days when you usually have a drink?

Q.45a I wonder, if you went through the last week could you tell me what you had to drink?

Day a	Type of drink b	Where c	With whom d	Amount e

b Do you feel this was a typical week?

Q.46 Do you ever take a drink with your meals at home — 1; when out for a meal — 2

DETAILS OF FREQUENCY

Q.47a What is your attitude to members of temperance groups/total abstinence associations?

b Do you feel they have any effect on the enjoyment of a group who are drinking?

DETAILS

Q.48a When you are drinking do you have a certain limit you do not cross?

b Do your friends feel this way too? Yes 2 No 1

c Have you ever exceeded this limit? Yes 2 No 1

d How many times were you ever drunk in the last year?

e How many times were you merry in the last year?

Q.49 When you do go out for a drink what kind do you usually have?

Q.50a⸍   If I read the following to you, could you tell me how often you usually have/
had wine/stout/beer/spirits?

CARD

	Wine	Stout	Beer	Spirits
1. Three or four times a day	1	1	1	1
2. Twice a day	2	2	2	2
3. About once a day	3	3	3	3
4. Three or four times a week	4	4	4	4
5. Once or twice a week	5	5	5	5
6. Twice a month	6	6	6	6
7. About once a month	7	7	7	7
8. Less than once a month but at least once a year	8	8	8	8
9. Less than once a year	9	9	9	9
10. Never	10	10	10	10

b   After watching people drinking in the films or TV or after reading about
people drinking, do you ever feel like taking a drink?

1	2	3	4
Never	Once or twice	Several times	Often

Q.51§   People take a drink for different reasons. Here are some statements people
have made about why they take a drink. Could you tell me how important
any of the following reasons are *to you* for taking a drink? There are four
possible answers to this question: very important, pretty important, not too
important, not at all important.

CARD

	Very important	Pretty important	Not too important	Not at all important
1. To be sociable	3	2	1	0
2. Because it helps me relax	3	2	1	0
3. I like the taste	3	2	1	0
4. Just to have a good time	3	2	1	0
5. It is one way of being part of a group	3	2	1	0
6. Because a man/woman is expected to	3	2	1	0
7. When I want to forget anything	3	2	1	0
8. To celebrate special occasions	3	2	1	0
9. Because the people I know drink	3	2	1	0

Q.52a   Do you consider yourself a person who drinks? Yes 2 No 1

b   Do you consider yourself to be a

1	2	3	4	5	6
Hard drinker	Moderate drinker	Light drinker	Non-drinker	Abstainer	Don't know

Q.53§ When you take a drink, could you tell me on a single occasion how often would you have the following amount:

CARD

		5 to 6 glasses	*3 to 4 glasses*	*1 to 2 glasses*
a	*Wine*			
	Nearly every time	1	1	1
	More than half the time	2	2	2
	Less than half the time	3	3	3
	Once in a while	4	4	4
	Never	5	5	5
b	*Spirits*			
	Nearly every time	1	1	1
	More than half the time	2	2	2
	Less than half the time	3	3	3
	Once in a while	4	4	4
	Never	5	5	5

		5 to 6 pints	*3 to 4 pints*	*1 to 2 pints*
c	*Stout*			
	Nearly every time	1	1	1
	More than half the time	2	2	2
	Less than half the time	3	3	3
	Once in a while	4	4	4
	Never	5	5	5
d	*Beer*			
	Nearly every time	1	1	1
	More than half the time	2	2	2
	Less than half the time	3	3	3
	Once in a while	4	4	4
	Never	5	5	5

Q.54§ I have another list of reasons why people take a drink. Could you tell me how important any of the following reasons are to you for taking a drink?

CARD

	Very important	*Pretty important*	*Not too important*	*Not at all important*
1. To forget my worries	3	2	1	0
2. When under pressure	3	2	1	0
3. To feel good	3	2	1	0
4. When feeling lonely	3	2	1	0
5. Nothing else to do	3	2	1	0
6. A small drink improves appetite for food	3	2	1	0
7. Like it	3	2	1	0
8. Accept a drink because it is the polite thing to do in certain situations	3	2	1	0
9. A drink helps me cheer up when in a bad mood	3	2	1	0
10. When tense and nervous	3	2	1	0
11. To stop aches and pains	3	2	1	0
12. To get some energy or pep	3	2	1	0

Q.55　　Some people worry about their drinking habits. Do you worry about your drinking?

3	2	1	0
A lot	Some	A little	Not at all

INTRODUCTION

Q.56

	Yes	No	Partly
1. In the past year or so, have you ever had health problems because of drinking?	2	1	0
2. In the past year or so, have you ever had difficulty with your job/work because of drinking?	2	1	0
3. In the past year or so, have you ever had money problems because of drinking?	2	1	0
4. In the past year or so, have you ever had family arguments because of drinking?	2	1	0
5. In the past year or so, have you ever had arguments with friends because of drinking?	2	1	0
6. In the past year or so, have you ever had trouble with police, either in connection with drunken driving or other behaviour resulting from drinking?	2	1	0
7. Have you ever in your life, *before* the past year, had any difficulties at all because of drinking?	2	1	0

FOR ALL:

INTRODUCTION

Q.57a　　What changes if any have you noticed in people's drinking in the last five years?

   b　　In your opinion would you say:
Most adults drink — Yes 2 No 1
Most young people drink — Yes 2 No 1

Q.58　　What do you think are the main reasons for:

   a　Adults drinking
   b　Lads of your age drinking
   c　Girls of your age drinking

Q.59a§　　What do you think of people taking a drink in the following situations:

CARD

	Very Good	Good	Fair	Undesirable
1. Drinking in an all male group	3	2	1	0
2. Drinking in an all female group	3	2	1	0
3. Drinking in a mixed group	3	2	1	0
4. Girls going into a pub with their boy-friends	3	2	1	0

Q.59a§ (cont.)

	Very Good	Good	Fair	Undesirable
5. Girls of your age taking a drink	3	2	1	0
6. Lads of your age taking a drink	3	2	1	0
7. Girls in a pub on their own taking a drink	3	2	1	0
8. How do you feel about your girl-friend/boy-friend taking a drink	3	2	1	0

b   I have here a few statements that other people have made about drinking. There are five possible answers, could you pick one of the five possible answers which best describe how you feel about it?

CARD

	Strongly agree	Agree	Unde-cided	Dis-agree	Strongly disagree
1. Drinking in groups and having a good laugh is one of the best forms of recreation	4	3	2	1	0
2. Drunkenness is a sign of immaturity	4	3	2	1	0
3. Drunkenness is excusable under many circumstances	4	3	2	1	0
4. As long as a person keeps out of trouble, it is alright for him to drink to excess	4	3	2	1	0

Q.59c   Do you think drinking by young people is a problem?

INTRODUCTION

Q.60a   What do you consider to be the main function/s of a public house?

b   Could you describe the kind of pub you usually go to?

Q.61   Do you like going out drinking in a pub/lounge on a date?

Q.62a   How do you feel about the custom of 'round' drinking — of buying 'rounds'?

b   Do you take part in this custom?

c   Do you think it is a sign of being mean if you won't join in? Yes 2 No 1

d   Do you think it is a peculiarly Irish/English custom?

Q.63   If any of the following happened to a member of a group you were drinking with, would you personally find it acceptable and tolerable?

	Acceptable Yes	No	Tolerable Yes	No
1. To feel merry	2	1	2	1
2. To be very talkative	2	1	2	1
3. To be happy	2	1	2	1
4. To be jarred	2	1	2	1
5. To be amorous	2	1	2	1
6. To be drunk	2	1	2	1

Q.64   Could you explain to me what you mean when you say a person is drunk?

Q.65   How serious a problem do you think alcoholism is in this country?

Not at all serious	1
Slightly serious	2
Fairly serious	3
Very serious	4
No opinion	0

Q.66   Would you use any of the following terms when talking about an alcoholic?

	Yes	No	Don't Know
Weak-willed	2	1	0
Criminal	2	1	0
Sick person	2	1	0
Morally weak	2	1	0
Waster	2	1	0

Other (please specify) . . . .

Q.67a   Do you think alcoholics need help to stop drinking? Yes 2 No 1
         IF YES:

    b   What kind of help?

    c   Have you ever had a relative or close friend with a serious drinking problem?
         Yes 2 No 1
         IF YES:
         DETAILS

Q.68a   If there was a problem with drink in your family would you try to solve the
         problem within the family or would you seek outside help or advice?

Within family	Yes 2 No 1
Outside help	Yes 2 No 1
Within family + outside help	Yes 2 No 1

FOR THOSE WHO WOULD SEEK OUTSIDE HELP:

    b   Would you tell me where and to whom you would go for help?

Place	*Person*

Q.69   What do you mean when you describe a person as an alcoholic?

Q.70   What three signs would you look for if you thought someone had a drink
        problem?
        1.
        2.
        3.

Q.71   Do you know of any facilities for the treatment of alcoholics in this country?

Q.72§   The following is a list of things which are often associated with young people
        today. Could you tell me if you have ever done or taken any of these things?

CARD

	Never	Once or twice	Several times	Often	Very often
1. Crashed a party	0	1	2	3	4
2. Sneaked/got into a place of entertainment without paying	0	1	2	3	4
3. Gone speeding or driving recklessly	0	1	2	3	4
4. Driven a car without a driver's licence	0	1	2	3	4
5. Have you ever taken tranquillizers?	0	1	2	3	4
6. Have you ever taken sleeping pills?	0	1	2	3	4
7. Have you ever taken stimulants or pep pills	0	1	2	3	4
8. Have you ever smoked marijuana	0	1	2	3	4
9. Other drugs (please specify)	0	1	2	3	4

Q.73 Today there is a lot of talk about young people and religion. Could you tell me a little about yourself? Do you attend religious services?

More than once a week	7
Once a week	6
Once or twice a month	5
About once a month	4
A few times during the year	3
Only rarely	2
Never	1

Q.74§ Please indicate how important you think the following ideas are:

CARD

	Not important	Slightly important	Important	Very important
1. To be able to rely on religious advice, counsel or teachings when you have a problem	0	1	2	3
2. To believe in God	0	1	2	3
3. To be able to turn to prayer when you are facing a personal problem	0	1	2	3
4. To go to church regularly	0	1	2	3

Q.75 How often would you estimate that either your religious beliefs or teaching influence the way in which you act?

READ OUT

6	5	4	3	2	1
Continuously	Very frequently	Frequently	Occasionally	Rarely	Never

Q.76a To what religion do you belong?

b Do your parents belong to this religion? Yes 2 No 1

Q.77a§   What would you say your family life to date was?

CARD   Happy   1
       Moderately happy with normal ups and downs   2
       Unhappy with frequent upsets   3

       Serious difficulties   4
       Serious difficulties, parents had long periods of separation   5
       Serious difficulties without long periods of separation   6

       Other (please specify)   7

b   If with difficulties, could you give me some examples please?

Q.78§   Below is a list of things that are said to be satisfying in family life. Could you
        tell me how important you feel they are? The four possible answers to this
        question are: very important, pretty important, not too important, not
        important at all.

CARD

	Very important	Pretty important	Not too important	Not impor- tant at all
1. The love and affection you get in the family	4	3	2	1
2. Having somebody in the family you can count on to help out	4	3	2	1
3. Being able to do things in the family your own way	4	3	2	1
4. The good opinion of the family for the things you do well	4	3	2	1

Q.79§   Now, I would like to talk a little about your relationship with your parents:

CARD

	Always	Often	Sometimes	Hardly ever	Never
1. Do your parents help you when you are worried about some problem	4	3	2	1	0
2. Do they promise something to you but you never get it	4	3	2	1	0
3. Are/were they interested in your school/college work or work plans	4	3	2	1	0
4. Do they say one thing and do another	4	3	2	1	0

Q.80§   I have two statements here. One is about your friends, the other about your
        parents. Again there are five possible answers: hardly ever, not too often,
        sometimes, very often, almost always. Could you tell me which one best
        applies to you?

Q.80§ (cont.)

CARD

	Hardly ever	Not too often	Some-times	Very often	Almost always
1. Do you feel free to talk to your friends about personal problems when you want to?	1	2	3	4	5
2. Would you say that your parents generally encourage you to do things you are interested in doing?	1	2	3	4	5

Q.81a With respect to the sort of things you personally think are important in life, would you say that your parents and your friends are really pretty much in agreement about these things?

0	1	2	3	4
No agreement at all	Some agreement	A fair amount of agreement	A lot of agreement	Almost complete agreement

LONDON ONLY:

b Certain parts of London are labelled in various ways. Is this true for this area? What sort of area would you say this is?

IF YES:

c How do you feel about this?

ALL:

Q.82§ And now finally, I'd like to talk to you about your views on life in general and on England/Ireland in particular. I have a list of statements below which have been used in other studies. I'd like you to tell me whether you agree, disagree, or don't know about each of the following statements.

CARD

	Agree	Dis-agree	Don't know
1. With everything so uncertain these days it almost seems as though anything could happen	2	1	0
2. Ireland/England is a good place to live in	2	1	0
3. The trouble with the world today is that most people don't believe in anything	2	1	0
4. Having a religion is a great help in coping with life's problems	2	1	0
5. With everything in such a state of disorder, it is hard for a person to know where he stands from one day to the next	2	1	0
6. Ireland/England as it is now is the place I would prefer to bring up my children	2	1	0
7. People were better off in the old days when everyone knew just how he was expected to act	2	1	0
8. Anyone who is willing to work hard can make a good career in Ireland/England today	2	1	0

Q.82§ (cont.)

	Agree	Dis-agree	Don't Know
9. Everything changes so quickly these days that I often have trouble deciding which are the right rules to follow	2	1	0
10. The changes in the Catholic Church since the Vatican Council have done more good than harm	2	1	0
11. I often feel that many things our parents stood for are just going to ruin before our very eyes	2	1	0
12. The values people hold nowadays are more real than those held previously	2	1	0

Q.83a   In general what do you think are the two biggest problems in Ireland/England today?

b   How do you think the problem will be solved?

Problem a	How to solve problem b
1.	
2.	

c   A problem in another sphere is the Northern Ireland situation, would you give me a *quick* three sentence comment on it?

Q.84a   What are the two biggest changes that have occurred in Ireland/England during the past three years?

b   What two changes would you most like to see in Ireland/England in the next three years?

c   How do you think these changes can be brought about?

d   Are you going to do anything to help bring them about?

Q.85   Can you tell me briefly your image of England, Ireland and France?

England a	Ireland b	France c

Could you tell me your image of England, Ireland and France in say ten years time?

England a	Ireland b	France c

Q.86   When would you say Ireland became independent of England?

Q.87   We have covered a wide range of topics, is there anything else you would like to talk about?

Notes to interviewers

Q. 2   Statement 6 — when asked to males: 'go for a drink with the lads'; when asked to females: 'go for a drink with the girls'.

Q. 3a   An active member of any organization or club, is a member who goes to that club/organization at least once a month, and whatever applied in parents' questionnaire for this question. Get as many details as possible.

b   Get name and type of club/organization and activity carried out.

c   Try to find out if there is a drinking licence attached to the club.

d   For England enquire if it is an Irish club, or 'mixed', or a church sponsored one.

Q. 4a   Give introduction as written on paper. The procedure of asking this
+ b   question is: 'Now if we go through every day of last week starting yesterday, could you tell me what you did each day, where you were, and what you did and with whom — in terms of free-time activities?' Typical week — write in full. If *no* why?

Q. 4c   FOR ANGLO-IRISH: Who they went with or to. Look for those who went on holidays or to visit relatives.

Q. 5   INTRODUCTION: I would like to talk to you about yourself and how long you have lived in this area.

Q. 7   If possible find out if married, are they living with husband; deserted; separated; etc. If single, find out if they are co-habiting.

Q. 8   A regular steady/girl/boy-friend is one whom they go out with *at least* once a week. Probe for *nationality*.

Q. 9b   Place: Count all children who were *alive at birth*, and write.

Q.10a   Get exact details of occupation — not just title but actual work carried
+ b + c out. Find out, are they self-employed; what they make on the job; do they supervize other people — if so how many?

Q.12   Get *exact* details of type of school/college they are attending/attended, and get *age* when left full-time education — not extra mural or general interest. Will include sandwich courses, block release.

Q.13   I am looking for the general pattern of expenditure by these young people. Try to get amount of £s/new pence from respondents. Write everything in full that they say but encourage them to give each item in terms of money.

Q.14   Take-home money — includes everything i.e. overtime but *excludes* tax and insurance. If grant, write down amount spread over fifty-two weeks of year.

Q.15   INTRODUCTION: Could we talk a little bit about your friends and young people in general.

Q.16   Ask question open-ended and probe for type of group, e.g. mixed group of friends, the lads, etc. Specify type of group. For Anglo-Irish group, friends' nationality.

Q.19   Looking for ex-drinker category — i.e. a person who drinks up to a period of six months in all, and then stopped for one reason or another.

Q.20a   In Ireland — Confirmation Pledge. *Write in if had not heard of pledge,* and same if non-drinkers.

   b   Name

   b   What age were you . . . .

   d   Could you tell me why you took it (the pledge)?

   e   Do you still hold the pledge?

     Whether or not they took the Confirmation Pledge — get reasons for this. Distinguish between never heard of it and don't believe in it.

Q.21a   All current non-drinkers → Q.23.

Q.23   Whether male or female friends.

Q.25   All non-drinkers → Q.32.

Q.26   This question is for everyone who HAS EVER TAKEN A DRINK. What age were you when you had your first drink?

Q.27   Find out when parents *knew* about *first* drinking experience as accurately as possible.

Q.32   INTRODUCTION: I would like to talk to you about what your parents do in their free time. If one parent is non-drinker ask questions for parents who drink. Ask all attitude questions about both parents even if one parent is deceased. Ask first four statements and if it emerges they can't remember or can't say, stop. As a general rule ask *everyone*.

Q.35   Where does your father/mother usually take a drink? With whom does your father/mother usually take a drink? On what occasion does your father/mother usually take a drink?

Q.36   Get mother's and father's attitudes separately.

Q.37   Try to find if occasionally on special occasions, or very frequently e.g. meals.

Q.40   If there was/is trouble in the home due to drink, try to get exact nature of trouble — whether financial, tension, rows, etc., and who caused the trouble — mother/father, respondent, brother, sister.

Q.41b   Get details of type of group e.g. mixed, male, or female.

Q.43   Statement 5, ask to lads — statement 6, ask to girls.

     Statement 8 — get type of club, activities, if drinking licence; English if Irish club, church club or whatever else.

Q.45a   Same procedure as question 4a.

Q.46   Get details of what they drink with meals at home, what they drink with meals when they are out. Give details of frequency.

Q.47a   In Ireland, you can use members of the Pioneer Total Abstinence Association to non-Catholics etc. In England, use temperance group/ total abstinence associations. Get type of *effect* they have on group who are drinking.

Q.48a   Get limit in terms of money, drinks or whatever.

Q.49 Get usual type, and if individual drinks in combination.

Q.52a Ask in exact words.

Q.53 Let us take wine first — would you take wine three to four times a day, twice a day, etc. Follow the same procedure for each beverage drunk. If cider is mentioned write in.

Q.55 *Not* open-ended.

Q.57 INTRODUCTION: 'I would like to talk to you about drinking in general and young people's drinking in particular'.

Q.58 Try for three reasons.

Q.60a What sort of people go *there*? Probe type of people who go to pub — young/old/Irish/English/Pakistani etc.

Q.62a The next few questions concern the pub and buying rounds.

  b Do you do this yourself?

  d In England — English custom.
    In Ireland — Irish custom.

Q.63 Take tolerable first — then acceptable. Note reaction to these words.

Q.67c Try to get relationship if at all possible. Get if friends or relatives and get as much information especially *re relative*.

Q.70 Look for three signs — but try in *all* cases to get one.

Q.72 Statement 9 — Have you ever taken other kinds of drugs?

Q.77 Enquire *re* difficulties from code 3-6. Probe for problems due to drink.

Q.81bc Describe type of people, probe for details.

Q.82 Statement 2 in Ireland, Ireland is used.
    Statement 6 in Ireland, Ireland is used.

Q.83ab (a) get problem; (b) and ask for each problem mentioned: 'How do you think the problem will be solved?'

Q.83a In Ireland use Ireland, in England use England, for both Anglo-Irish and English.

Q.83c N.B. If Ulster or Northern Ireland is mentioned as a second problem, ask second half of 83c i.e.: 'Could you give me a quick three sentence comment on it?' If Ulster or Northern Ireland is not given as a problem ask 83c in full.

Parents' questionnaire

Questionnaire design

The questionnaire was designed to elicit information on the attitudes and patterns of drinking of parents. To structure and facilitate the collection and analysis of data, a theoretical framework was designed. The facts deemed necessary for this theoretical framework are as follows (O'Connor 1976a and b for details):

Socio-economic characteristics
Income and expenditure
Recreational activities
Use of other drugs
Ethnic identification
Pattern of abstinence
Learning to drink
Present patterns of drinking
Attitudes towards drinking
Problem drinking
Family life and satisfaction
Religion
Alcoholism

Sample questionnaire

INTERVIEWER...................................DATE...................TIME: FROM..............TO........

INTRODUCTION

Q. 1   What do you think of the opportunities in this area for free/leisure-time activities?

Q.2a§   I have here a number of activities which some people enjoy. Could you tell me how often in a month do you do any of them in your free time?

CARD

	Never	Once or twice a month	Three or four times a month	Once a week or more
1. Go to the pictures	1	2	3	4
2. Follow a sport	1	2	3	4
3. Stay at home all evening	1	2	3	4
4. Go to bingo	1	2	3	4
5. Go visiting	1	2	3	4
6. Go for a drive	1	2	3	4
7. Mothers/women's club (women only)	1	2	3	4
8. Go for a drink with husband/wife	1	2	3	4
9. Go for a drink with your children	1	2	3	4
10. Go for a drink with your friends	1	2	3	4
11. Other (please specify)	1	2	3	4

b§   When you go out to any of the places that we have just talked about, could you tell me how often do you go out with:

CARD

	Never	Once or twice a month	Three or four times a month	Once a week or more
1. Your husband (for wife)	1	2	3	4
2. Your wife (for husband)	1	2	3	4
3. Your family	1	2	3	4
4. An all male group	1	2	3	4
5. An all female group	1	2	3	4
6. Male and female group	1	2	3	4

Q.3a   Are you an active member of any club or organization? Yes 2 No 1

IF YES:

DETAILS

b   Could you tell me to what club/s or organization/s you belong?

Club/s
Organization/s

Q. 4   Would you like to see a community centre in this area? Yes 2 No 1

INTRODUCTION

Q. 5   How many years have you lived in this area?
    1. 0-under 6 years   2. 6-under 11 years   3. 11-under 16 years
    4. 16-under 20 years   5. 20-under 25 years   6. 25 years and over

Q. 6a   Could you tell me where you were born?
    Town   County   Country

    BORN OUTSIDE ENGLAND:

b   Do you consider yourself Irish?

c   Would you say your children consider themselves to be Irish?

    BORN IN ENGLAND:

d   Do you consider yourself British or English?

e   Would you say your children consider themselves to be British or English?

Q. 7   Could you tell me how many are in your family including yourself and your wife/husband?
    0   1   2   3   4   5   6   7   8   9   10 11 12+

Q. 8a   Do you currently have a full-time or part-time job for which you are paid?
    Yes 2 No 1

    IF YES GO TO QUESTIONS 8b, c, d.

b   Do you work part-time or full-time?   Part-time 2   Full-time 1

c   What kind of work do you do? . . . .
    DETAILS

Q. 9   It is difficult, I know, to get exact amounts spent per week, but could you tell me in what way the money goes during the week?
    About how much on food?   . . . .
    About how much on cigarettes?   . . . .
    About how much on alcohol?   . . . .
    About how much on recreation?   . . . .
    If other, please specify   . . . .

    IF WORKS:

Q.10a§ Could you tell me what take-home money you get a week?
    CARD   Up to £10   1
                £10-under £16   2
                £16-under £20   3
                £20-under £25   4
                £25-under £30   5
                £30+   6
                Don't know   7

INTRODUCTION

Q.11a   I am interested in whether you smoke cigarettes or tobacco of any sort?
    DETAILS

Q.11b   Have you ever taken an alcoholic drink? Yes 2 No 1
          IF YES → Q.11c   IF NO → Q.12

    c   Do you take a drink now? Yes 2 No 1
        IF NO:

    d   At what age did you stop drinking? ....

    e   Could you tell me, was there any reason for this? ....
        ALL:

Q.12   At school did you take any pledge not to drink until a certain age? Yes 2 No 1
        REASONS

Q.13a   Do you still hold that pledge? Yes 2 No 1
        ALL WHO DO NOT DRINK AT TIME OF SURVEY → Q.13b
        THOSE WHO HAVE EVER TAKEN A DRINK → Q.15

    b   Are you a pioneer/member of a temperance society? Yes 2 No 1
        IF YES:

    c   Name of association ....

        NON-DRINKERS AT TIME OF INTERVIEW:
Q.14   There are a number of reasons people have given for why they do not drink.
        As I read them out would you tell me which are your reasons, please?

	Yes	No	Partly
1. Do not want to take a drink	2	1	0
2. As a sacrifice for those who drink excessively	2	1	0
3. Because drinking leads to being loud and rowdy	2	1	0
4. It is against my religion	2	1	0
5. The people I go around with are against it	2	1	0
6. Because it gets to be a bad habit	2	1	0
7. It is not good for your health	2	1	0
8. It is just an artificial way of solving problems	2	1	0
9. Saw the effects of drink on other people	2	1	0
10. I don't want to lose my self-control	2	1	0
11. Took a pledge not to drink	2	1	0

        ALL WHO HAVE EVER TAKEN A DRINK:

Q.15   What age were you when you had your first drink? Age ....
        ALL NON-DRINKERS I.E. PLEDGE HOLDERS AND EX-DRINKERS → Q28a

        FOR THOSE WHO TAKE A DRINK AT THE TIME OF STUDY:

Q.16   Would you consider yourself 'a person who drinks'? Yes 2 No 1

Q.17   When you go out for a drink where do you usually go?
        DETAILS

Q.18   When you go out for a drink whom do you go with?
        DETAILS

Q.19   On what occasions do you usually drink?
        DETAILS

Q.20   People take a drink for different reasons. Here are some statements people have made about why they drink. Do you drink for any of the following reasons?

	Yes	No	Partly
1. To be sociable	2	1	0
2. Because it helps me to relax	2	1	0
3. I like the taste	2	1	0
4. Just to have a good time	2	1	0
5. It is one way of being part of a group	2	1	0
6. Somewhere to go	2	1	0
7. Because a man is expected to (men only)	2	1	0
8. Because a woman is expected to (women only)	2	1	0
9. When I want to forget anything	2	1	0
10. To celebrate special occasions	2	1	0
11. Because the people I know drink	2	1	0

Q.21   When you go out for a drink what kind do you usually have?
DETAILS

Q.22§   Could you tell me how often you usually have/had wine/stout/beer/spirits?
CARD

	Wine	Stout	Beer	Spirits
Three or four times a day	1	1	1	1
Twice a day	2	2	2	2
About once a day	3	3	3	3
Three or four times a week	4	4	4	4
Twice or once a week	5	5	5	5
About twice a month	6	6	6	6
About once a month	7	7	7	7
Less than once a month but at least once a year	8	8	8	8
Less than once a year	9	9	9	9
Never	10	10	10	10

Q.23   Now I have another list of reasons why people take a drink. Do you drink for any of the following reasons?

	Yes	No	Partly
1. To forget worries	2	1	0
2. When under pressure	2	1	0
3. To feel good	2	1	0
4. When feeling lonely	2	1	0
5. Nothing else to do	2	1	0
6. A small drink improves appetite for food	2	1	0
7. Accept a drink because it is the polite thing to do in certain situations	2	1	0
8. A drink helps me cheer up when I am in a bad mood	2	1	0
9. When tense and nervous	2	1	0
10. To stop aches or pains	2	1	0
11. To get some energy or pep	2	1	0

Q.24§ When you take a drink, could you tell me on a single occasion how often would you have the following amount:

CARD

Wine:	5 to 6 glasses	Nearly every time	1
		More than half the time	2
		Less than half the time	3
		Once in a while	4
		Never	5
	3 to 4 glasses	Nearly every time	1
		More than half the time	2
		Less than half the time	3
		Once in a while	4
		Never	5
	1 to 2 glasses	Nearly every time	1
		More than half the time	2
		Less than half the time	3
		Once in a while	4
		Never	5
Spirits:	5 to 6 glasses	Nearly every time	1
		More than half the time	2
		Less than half the time	3
		Once in a while	4
		Never	5
	3 to 4 glasses	Nearly every time	1
		More than half the time	2
		Less than half the time	3
		Once in a while	4
		Never	5
	1 to 2 glasses	Nearly every time	1
		More than half the time	2
		Less than half the time	3
		Once in a while	4
		Never	5
Guinness/ Stout:	5 to 6 pints	Nearly every time	1
		More than half the time	2
		Less than half the time	3
		Once in a while	4
		Never	5
	3 to 4 pints	Nearly every time	1
		More than half the time	2
		Less than half the time	3
		Once in a while	4
		Never	5
	1 to 2 pints	Nearly every time	1
		More than half the time	2
		Less than half the time	3
		Once in a while	4
		Never	5
Beer:	5 to 6 pints	Nearly every time	1
		More than half the time	2
		Less than half the time	3
		Once in a while	4
		Never	5

Beer	3 to 4 pints	Nearly every time	1
(cont.)		More than half the time	2
		Less than half the time	3
		Once in a while	4
		Never	5
	1 to 2 pints	Nearly every time	1
		More than half the time	2
		Less than half the time	3
		Once in a while	4
		Never	5

Q.25 Some people worry about their drinking even though they may not be really heavy drinkers. How much do you worry about your drinking?

A lot 3;   Some 2;   A little 1;   Not at all 0;

CARD

Q.26§ Do you consider yourself to be: (Circle one)

Hard drinker 1; Moderate drinker 2; Light drinker 3; Non-drinker 4;

Don't know 5;

Q.27

	Yes	No	Partly
1. In the past year or so, have you ever had health problems because of drinking?	2	1	0
2. In the past year or so, have you ever had difficulty with your job/work because of drinking?	2	1	0
3. In the past year or so, have you ever had money problems because of drinking?	2	1	0
4. In the past year or so, have you ever had family arguments or trouble over drinking?	2	1	0
5. In the past year or so, have you ever had arguments with friends because of drinking?	2	1	0
6. In the past year or so, have you ever had trouble with police, either in connection with drunken driving or other behaviour resulting from drinking?	2	1	0
7. Have you ever in your life, *before the past year*, had any difficulties at all because of drinking?	2	1	0
8. Have you ever had a drink or two before breakfast?	2	1	0
9. Have you ever drunk so much that you could not remember afterwards some of the things you had done?	2	1	0
10. Have you ever driven a car while drunk?	2	1	0

ALL:

Q.28a Have you ever had a close relative with a serious drinking problem? Yes 2 No 1

IF YES:

b How is this person related to you? ....

c Were there ever any problems with drink in your own home? Yes 2 No 1

Q.29 Have you ever had a close friend with a serious drinking problem? Yes 2 No 1

INTRODUCTION

Q.30 From your experience would you say: Most adults drink Yes 2 No 1
Most young people drink Yes 2 No 1

Q.31 What is your attitude to your children taking a drink?

Q.32 What are the things you would like your children to know about drinking?
Could you answer yes or no to the following?

	Yes	No	Partly
Alcohol is good in moderation	2	1	0
It is better to drink beer than spirits	2	1	0
Alcohol is a bad habit	2	1	0
Alcohol leads to all kinds of improper behaviour	2	1	0
Alcohol is good	2	1	0

Q.33§ Could you tell me what your attitude would be if your children who are aged between 18-21 were to drink in the following ways? Could you answer in terms of the following: strongly approve, moderately approve, neither approve nor disapprove, uncertain, moderately disapprove, strongly disapprove.

CARD

	Strongly approve	Moderately approve	Neither approve nor disapprove	Uncertain	Moderately disapprove	Strongly disapprove
1. Take a drink at home	5	4	3	2	1	0
2. Drink alcohol in a pub with friends (same sex)	5	4	3	2	1	0
3. Drink alcohol in a pub with your wife/husband	5	4	3	2	1	0
4. Drink with his/her girl/boy-friend in a pub	5	4	3	2	1	0
5. Drink in a mixed group in a pub	5	4	3	2	1	0
6. Drink three or four drinks on one occasion	5	4	3	2	1	0
7. Drink six or more drinks on one occasion	5	4	3	2	1	0
8. Be visibly affected by drink without being drunk	5	4	3	2	1	0
9. Be what you describe as drunk at home	5	4	3	2	1	0
10. Be what you describe as drunk in mixed company	5	4	3	2	1	0
11. Mix their drinks	5	4	3	2	1	0
12. Drive a car after being affected by drink	5	4	3	2	1	0

Q.34§   I have here a list of statements that other people have made about drinking. As
I read out each one would you tell me please whether you: strongly agree,
agree, undecided, disagree, strongly disagree, with the following?

CARD

	Strongly agree	Agree	Unde-cided	Dis-agree	Strongly disagree
1. Drinking in groups and having a good laugh is one of the best forms of recreation	4	3	2	1	0
2. Drunkenness is a sign of immaturity	4	3	2	1	0
3. Drunkenness is excusable under many circumstances	4	3	2	1	0
4. As long as a person keeps out of trouble, it is alright for him to drink to excess	4	3	2	1	0

Q.35   What changes, if any, have you noticed in people's drinking in the last five
years?

Q.36   Do you think young people are drinking more or less now than they were
when you were 18-21 years of age?

More 3
Less 2
About the same 1
No opinion 0

Q.37   How serious a problem do you think alcoholism is in this country?

Not at all serious 1
Slightly serious 2
Fairly serious 3
Serious 4
Very serious 5
No opinion 6

Q.38   In general, what would you consider to be the most serious problem in this
country?

Q.39a   Have you ever had any long illness, i.e. been sick for six weeks or more?
Yes 2 No 1

IF YES:

b   Have you been in a medical hospital for six weeks or more? Yes 2 No 1

c   Have you been in a psychiatric hospital for six weeks or more? Yes 2 No 1

Q.40§   CARD

	Never	Once or twice	Several times	Often	Very often
Have you ever taken tranquillizers?	1	2	3	4	9
Have you ever taken stimulants or pep pills?	1	2	3	4	9
Have you ever taken barbiturates or sleeping pills?	1	2	3	4	9
Have you ever taken other tablets	1	2	3	4	9
(Please specify type of tablets)					

Q.41a   There is a lot of discussion about religion today. Could I discuss some aspects with you? Do you attend religious services?

More than once a week	7
Once a week	6
Two or three times a month	5
Less than once a month	4
A few times during the year	3
Very occasionally	2
Never	1

   b   Could you tell me to what religion you belong?

Q.42§   CARD

Would you say that your family life to date was:

Happy	1
Moderately happy with ups and downs	2
Unhappy with frequent upsets	3
Serious difficulties	4
Serious difficulties with long periods of separation	5
Serious difficulties but without long periods of separation	6

   b   If there are/have been some difficulties please give some examples.

. . . .

Q.43§   I would like to talk with you about your relationship with your children. I have a number of things which involve parents. Could you tell me what you usually do? Answer in terms of always, often, sometimes, hardly ever, never.

CARD

	Always	Often	Some-times	Hardly ever	Never
1. When your children are in trouble do you help them?	4	3	2	1	0
2. Do you promise something to them but they never get it?	4	3	2	1	0
3. Were you interested in their school/ college work or work plans	4	3	2	1	0
4. Do you say one thing and do another	4	3	2	1	0

Q.44§   I have a list of things here that have been said to be important in family life. There are four items. Could you tell me how important you feel they are? The four possible answers to this question are: very important, pretty important, not too important, and not important at all.

CARD

	Very important	Pretty important	Not too important	Not impor-tant at all
1. The love and affection you get in the family	4	3	2	1
2. Having somebody in the family you can count on to help out	4	3	2	1
3. The good opinion of the family for the things you do well	4	3	2	1
4. Being able to do things in the family in your own way	4	3	2	1

Q.45   We have talked about a lot of things. Is there anything else you would like to talk about?

Notes to interviewers

Q. 1   Opportunities for free-time activities for *everyone*: not a particular age-group. Question is open-ended but if respondent asks for clarification say 'in general'.

Q. 2a   Statement 2. 'Follow a sport'. This includes watching on TV, going to sporting events, following a particular team, e.g. generally taking an interest in a sport.

Statement 3. 'Stay at home all evening'. This is spending the evening at home; maybe night will be used by some respondents.

Statement 6. 'Go for a drive'. This does not include driving to work or to do the shopping or with the intention of getting to a place of entertainment. Meant as a recreational activity in itself.

Statement 7. Ladies club/women's club for use in England.

Statement 8. 'Go for a drink with husband/wife' includes going out for a drink with her husband even if the wife herself does not take a drink.

Statement 9. i.e. immediate family.

Statement 8, 9, 10. 'Go for a drink' — interpret as going out for a drink.

Q. 2b   There may be some difficulty as respondent perhaps feels you are going to go through the previous list again. (Question is not necessarily verbatim and statements might be prefaced with 'Could you tell me how often you go with. . . .?')

Statement 3. Nuclear family.

Statement 4. With a group of men (for men).

Satement 5. With a group of women (for women).

Statement 6. Other — to be asked e.g. 'anyone else you go out with?' Specify e.g. colleagues, mixed group.

Q. 3a   An active member of any organization or club is a member who goes to that club/organization at least once a month.

Q. 3b   Get name and type of club/organization activity carried out. Try to find out if there is a drinking licence attached to the club. For England try to find out if it is an Irish club or 'mixed' — or a church sponsored club. Details e.g. name of club and activities.

Q. 6   Introduction: 'I would like to talk to you about yourself and how long you have lived in this area.' Ask this question open-ended and fill in appropriate information for example, 'I was born in Dublin' would code as:

Country	County	Town
Ireland	Dublin	Dublin

Record all live births.

Q. 7   Try to find out if person is married, single, separated, deserted, divorced, co-habiting.

Q. 7   For Irish: If husband is 'in England' or 'working in England' ask frequency of visits home. Want to ascertain the quality of relationship between husband and wife, e.g. separated because husband has to work in England, seasonally or otherwise, or a real separation and estrangement.

For English, Anglo-Irish: the same applies if the answer is 'working away' from home.

Family does not include *foster children*. Legal definition of child. If child is illegitimate and is brought up in the family and is seen as one of the family, include as respondents will automatically include.

Q. 8a   Get exact details of job — not just title but work carried out, type and
+ b + c   location of industry. Find out if they are self-employed; what they make on the job; do they supervize other people; if so, how many.

Q. 9   I am looking for the general pattern of expenditure by the parents. Try to get amount of money from the parents, write everything in full that they say, but encourage them to give each item in terms of money.

Q. 9   Food refers to household expenditure on food. Cigarettes, alcohol, and recreation refers to personal expenditure. These items do not include money given to children for their recreation. Recreation *excludes* alcohol. Other items, record in space provided, e.g. rent, maintenance of car and petrol expenditure, savings for holidays, etc. Get *actual money* spent, *not* percentage of income.

Q.10a   Take home money, i.e. it *excludes* tax and insurance.

INTRODUCTION: 'I'd like to talk to you about whether you smoke cigarettes or tobacco.'

Q.11   Tobacco refers to cigarettes. Note those who smoke a pipe or cigars. Get quantity smoked, e.g. twenty cigarettes a day or tobacco in ounces.

Q.11d   This question is designed to get at category of ex-drinker, i.e. a person who took a drink for a period of six months and then decided to stop taking a drink. Therefore, be especially careful in asking this question. Get reasons for stopping to take a drink, get in as much detail as possible.

Q.12   Get reasons for taking Confirmation Pledge, enquire about temperance groups they may have joined. In England, ask if they have ever taken a pledge of any sort not to drink.

Q.13a   In Ireland ask both, in England ask if member of temperance society.

Q.15   Ask ex-drinkers as well as those who take a drink. Try to get precise ages, not mid-twenties or late twenties, etc. If respondent can't remember, record this. If estimates or guesses indicate respondent is not very sure.

Q.16   Ask those who take a drink at the present time.

Qs.17,   When, with whom and what the occasions of drinking are; get all details
18, 19   on these questions.

Q.17   If drinks in a club get exact nature of club i.e. Irish, Church, Workmen's club?

Q.17   This is go out for a drink; if respondent does not go out for a drink, as may have emerged from previous questions, *record an answer* to show the question has been asked, even if interviewer has chatted over the question.

Q.20   Each statement can be seen as a factor in the total rationale of why people take a drink. Statements should not be rephrased.

Q.21   Try to get those who take a drink, one kind of drink *only* and those who have a combination of drinks, e.g. beer and spirits.

Q.22   Let's take *wine* first: would you take wine 3-4 times a day, 2 times etc. 'Now let us take *stout*' and follow same procedure all the way through.

Q.22   If respondent does not drink a beverage type, code 'never' for all three quantities.

Q.24   Could you tell me on a single occasion how often you would have the following amount. I will take wine/spirits/stout/beer/separately. Let us take wine first ... When you are out would you ever take 5-6 glasses of wine on a single occasion? If respondent answers either code 1 or code 2, skip to next beverage which is spirits. If she answers code 3,4,5 ask 'Would you ever have 3-4 glasses of wine on a single occasion?' If she says code 1 or code 2 skip to spirits, if not go to 1-2 glasses and so on for each beverage type.

Q.27   Keep to the exact wording of the statements.

Q.28a   Try to get as much detail as possible on person related to them.

Q.28c   'In your own home' i.e. *their* parental home.

Q.30   Introduction: 'I would like to talk to you about young people in general, but especially about your own children.'

Q.27   Job — for women use job/work (indicate on questionnaire when you use the word 'work').

        Statement 4. Respondent's perception of definition of 'trouble' and 'arguments'.

        Statement 5. Any arguments except 'normal enlivened discussion'.

        Statement 7. Any difficulties.

Q.30   Introduction is to help interviewers: use at your discretion.

Q.33   May help respondent if you introduce the question. 'There are six possible answers to this question. Could you pick one of them which describes your feeling about each of the statements? I am going to read them to you.' Give respondent card with response categories listed.

Q.33   Statement 3. Ask father — drink alcohol in a pub with your wife. Ask mother — drink alcohol in a pub with your husband.

Q.34   General, not just for your people. May be helpful to preface questions with 'how do you feel about this?'

Q.37   Open-ended, e.g. categories not read out. But must be asked in exact words; no definition of alcoholism should be given.

Q.38   In general . . . .

Q.39   Long illness is defined as being sick at home or in hospital for six weeks or more.

Q.40   This question is designed to find out if the person being interviewed has ever taken the four items mentioned. Whether she or he has taken tablets on doctor's orders, in hospital or anywhere else is not relevant; what I want to know is — has he/she *ever taken* the items mentioned.

Q.42   If answer is 3,4,5,6 ask for examples of difficulties.

Q.44   This is to find out if respondents feel things are important in family life.

Who was PRESENT AT INTERVIEW

Respondent only 1   Both parents 2

Mother 3   Father 4

Daughters or sons 5   Friends 6

Other (please specify) ....

Where INTERVIEW TOOK PLACE

Living room 1   Kitchen 1   Hallway 3

Doorstep 4   Other (please specify) ....

RECEPTION

Excellent 1   Very good 1   Good 3

Fair 4   Fair, improving later.. 5   Cool 6

Hostile 7   Fair, not improving later 8

Amount of EXPLANATION NEEDED

General introduction only   1

General introduction and further explanation at beginning   2

General introduction and further explanation at the end   3

ACQUAINTANCE WITH SURVEY

Had heard of survey from person previously interviewed   1

Had heard of survey from other sources (specify)   2

Had not heard of survey   3

CALL ON WHICH INTERVIEW WAS OBTAINED: CIRCLE NO.

1 2 3 4 5 6 7 8 9 10 11 12 13 over 13

Additional notes

Appendix 3
List of scales and indexes

The aim of this appendix is to provide a brief description of the scales and indexes which were used in the study. This description supplements and overlaps, but does not substitute Appendix 2 — the Questionnaire design, Questionnaire, and Notes to interviewers. The scales and indexes are described as they appear in each chapter.

Chapter 5

Type of drinker index

This index is designed to measure both 18-21 year olds' and their parents' levels of drinking. Appendix 6 gives details of the formation of the type of drinker index.

Chapter 6

Reasons for drinking (Q.51§, Q.54§)

Explanations as to why respondents drink were explored by asking two pre-coded questions each with several items. A prompt card was used when the questions were asked. From these questions four Guttman type scales were devised to measure reasons for drinking:

1 Festive and social pleasure
2 Social conforming: drinking from a sense of obligation to meet group pressures
3 Personal effects: drinking to resolve problems or inadequacies
4 Mood changing: drinking to effect a change of mood

1. *Drinking for festive and social pleasure* (Q.51§, 1,2,8). Three items were selected (*Table A.1.45*), stated in increasing order of 'difficulty' of reasons for drinking, from the one most frequently found to the least frequently found, or the most 'difficult' of reasons for taking a drink. The cutting point for the items were as follows:

> 'Errors were randomly scattered and the cutting points evenly distributed. Exactly equivalent scales were constructed for both males and females, using the same items in the same order. In some cases different 'cutting points' for dichotomising responses were used for the different Irish, Anglo-Irish and English 18-21 year olds under study. In these cases, use of the same cutting points would have resulted in unacceptable levels of error.'
>
> (Nie, Bent, and Hull 1970)

Drink to celebrate special occasions:	Very important/ Pretty important
	Not too important/ Not at all important
Drink to be sociable:	Very important/ Pretty important
	Not too important/ Not at all important
Helps me to relax:	Very important/ Pretty important
	Not too important/ Not at all important

2. *Social conforming, drinking from a sense of obligation to meet group pressures* (Q.51§, 9, 6, 5). Three items were selected (*Table A.1.46*), stated in increasing order of 'difficulty' of reasons for drinking, from the one most frequently found to the least frequently found, or the most 'difficult' of reasons for taking a drink. The cutting point for the items were as follows:

Because the people I know drink:	Very important/ Pretty important
	Not too important/ Not at all important
A man/woman is expected to:	Very important/ Pretty important
	Not too important Not at all important
One way of being part of a group:	Very important/ Pretty important
	Not too important/ Not at all important

3. *Personal effects, drinking to resolve problems or inadequacies* (Q.51§, 7; Q.54§, 1,2,4,10).   Five items were selected (*Table A.1.47*), stated in increasing order of 'difficulty' of reasons for drinking, from the one most frequently found, to the least frequently found, or the most 'difficult' of reasons for taking a drink. The cutting point for the items were as follows:

When I want to forget anything:	Very important/ Pretty important
	Not too important/ Not at all important
When I am under pressure:	Very important/ Pretty important
	Not too important/ Not at all important
To forget my worries:	Very important/ Pretty important
	Not too important/ Not at all important
Drink because I need it when tense and nervous:	Very important/ Pretty important
	Not too important/ Not at all important
When I am feeling lonely:	Very important/ Pretty important
	Not too important/ Not at all important

4. *Mood changing, drinking to effect a change in mood* (Q.54§, 3, 9, 12).   Three items were selected (*Table A.1.48*), stated in increasing order of 'difficulty' of reasons for drinking, from the one most frequently found to the least frequently found, or the most 'difficult' of reasons for taking drink. The cutting points for the items were as follows:

To make me feel good:	Very important/ Pretty important
	Not too important/ Not at all important
A drink helps me cheer up when I am in a bad mood:	Very important/ Pretty important
	Not too important/ Not at all important
I drink to get some energy or pep:	Very important/ Pretty important
	Not too important/ Not at all important

Chapter 7

Norms for children as reported by parents*

In this study, parents' attitudes to their children's drinking behaviour were ascertained from reports given by parents and children separately, in terms of each of the following three considerations:

1 Drinking in a family and peer group context
2 Being drunk or visibly affected by drink
3 Mixing drinks and amount of alcohol consumed

Table A.3.1 shows the three way relationship between reported parental social norms (i.e. reported by parents themselves), children's perception of parental social norms, and children's classification on the type of drinker index. There was a low to moderate association between rules of drinking as reported by parents themselves and those reported by their children. In the detailed analysis it was shown that parents' social rules as reported by children emerged as better predictors of children's drinking behaviour, than did the social rules of drinking as reported by parents themselves. The measure used for examining the influence of parents' attitudes to their children's drinking behaviour was children's perception of their parents' social rules in relation to drinking.

Parents' questionnaire (Q.33§)

Both parents were asked to define the social rules for their 18-21 year olds drinking. A series of statements were read to each parent and they were asked if they: strongly approve, moderately approve, neither approve nor disapprove, (are) uncertain, or moderately disapprove each statement. From these statements three Guttman type scales were devised:

1 Attitudes towards their 18-21 year-old children drinking in a peer group and family context
2 Attitudes towards the effects of excessive drinking on their 18-21 year-olds i.e. being drunk at home, being drunk in a mixed group of friends, visibly affected by drink without being drunk
3 Attitudes towards their 18-21 year-old children mixing their drinks and drinking three or more drinks on one occasion

1. *Drinking in a peer group and family context* Five items were selected (*Tables A.3.2 and A.3.3*), in increasing order of 'difficulty' of attitudes of parents to their 18-21 year olds drinking, from the one most frequently found to the least frequently found, or the most 'difficult' of positive attitudes to hold.
    The cutting point for the items were as follows:

Drink in a mixed group in a pub:	Strongly approve
	Moderately approve
Neutral ⎫	Neither approve nor
Category ⎬	disapprove
⎭	Uncertain
	Strongly disapprove
	Moderately disapprove

*The scales were the same for parental social rules as perceived by their children. (See *Tables A.3.2—A.3.7.*)

Table A.3.1 Kendalls Tau C correlations between parental social rules of drinking for children and children's drinking behaviour using children's perceptions and parents' own report

	Fathers' social rules		Mothers' social rules	
	Males	Females	Males	Females
Drinking in a family and peer group context				
(1) Reported and perceived attitudes				
Irish	0.3241	0.3412	0.3208	0.4223
Anglo-Irish	N.S.	N.S.	N.S.	0.3317
English	0.2453	N.S.	0.2234	N.S.
(2) Parents' reported attitudes and children's drinking behaviour				
Irish	0.2252	N.S.	N.S.	0.3014
Anglo-Irish	N.S.	0.2626	0.2201	0.4041
English	N.S.	0.2524	N.S.	0.1969
(3) Perceived parents' attitudes and children's drinking behaviour				
Irish	0.2326	0.3553	0.1974	0.3926
Anglo-Irish	N.S.	0.2619	N.S.	0.2311
English	N.S.	N.S.	N.S.	N.S.
Being drunk and visibly affected by drink				
(1) Reported and perceived attitudes				
Irish	N.S.	0.1116	0.2708	N.S.
Anglo-Irish	N.S.	N.S.	N.S.	N.S.
English	0.3524	0.2806	0.4456	0.2413
(2) Parents' reported attitudes and children's drinking behaviour				
Irish	0.1425	N.S.	0.1318	N.S.
Anglo-Irish	N.S.	N.S.	N.S.	0.2892
English	0.2089	0.2009	N.S.	N.S.
(3) Perceived parents' attitudes and children's drinking behaviour				
Irish	0.1166	N.S.	N.S.	N.S.
Anglo-Irish	0.2532	0.2616	N.S.	N.S.
English	0.1705	0.2012	0.1925	N.S.
Mixing drinks and amount of alcohol consumed				
(1) Reported and perceived attitudes				
Irish	0.2259	N.S.	0.6665	0.1718
Anglo-Irish	N.S.	N.S.	0.1904	N.S.
English	N.S.	0.4176	N.S.	0.3281
(2) Parents' reported attitudes and children's drinking behaviour				
Irish	0.2721	N.S.	0.1266	N.S.
Anglo-Irish	N.S.	0.2906	N.S.	N.S.
English	0.1715	0.4333	0.1846	0.4269
(3) Perceived parents' attitudes and children's drinking behaviour				
Irish	0.2405	0.2508	0.2557	0.2410
Anglo-Irish	0.3536	0.3938	0.2549	0.3023
English	0.2563	0.3581	0.2700	0.2624

Table A.3.2 Respondents' perception of fathers' attitudes to respondent drinking in a family and peer group context as measured by repondents' responses and scaled by Guttman techniques (Q.39a§, 1, 2, 3, 4, 5)

Scale type cumulative	Males			Females		
	Irish 177	*Anglo-Irish* 89	*English* 114	*Irish* 179	*Anglo-Irish* 85	*English* 94
1. Negative to all statements	100% 59 (33.3)	100% 26 (29.2)	100% 29 (25.5)	100% 74 (4-.3)	100% 26 (30.6)	100% 26 (27.7)
2. Drink alcohol in a pub with parents	66.6 19 (10.7)	70.7 8 (8.9)	74.5 8 (7.0)	58.6 21 (1-.7)	69.4 4 (4.7)	72.3 6 (6.3)
3. Drink with your girl/boy friend in a pub	55.9 19 (10.7)	61.7 7 (7.8)	67.5 6 (5.2)	46.9 19 (10.6)	64.7 4 (4.7)	65.9 5 (5.3)
4. Drink in a mixed group in a pub	45.1 15 (8.4)	53.9 5 (5.6)	62.2 8 (7.0)	36.2 21 (11.7)	60.0 12 (14.11)	60.6 3 (3.1)
5. Drink in a pub with friends all the same sex	36.7 23 (12.9)	48.3 9 (10.1)	55.2 8 (7.0)	24.5 13 (7.2)	45.9 16 (18.8)	57.4 10 (10.6)
6. Taking a drink at home	23.7 42 (23.7)	38.2 34 (38.2)	48.2 55 (48.2)	7.3 31 (17.3)	27.0 23 (27.0)	46.8 44 (46.8)
N =	177	89	114	179	85	94
Coefficient of reproducibility	0.8531	0.9146	0.9333	0.8793	0.9106	0.9447
Minimum marginal reproducibility	0.5559	0.5528	0.6158	0.6324	0.5953	0.6064
Percentage improvement	0.2972	0.3618	0.3175	0.2469	0.3153	0.3383
Coefficient of scalability	0.6692	0.8090	0.8265	0.6717	0.7791	0.8595

Table A.3.3 Respondents' perception of mothers' attitudes to respondent drinking in a family and peer group context as measured by respondents' responses and scaled by Guttman techniques (Q.39b§, 1, 2, 3, 4, 5)

Scale type cumulative	Males			Females		
	Irish 184	Anglo-Irish 92	English 119	Irish 181	Anglo-Irish 84	English 98
1. Negative to all statements	100% 69 (37.5)	100% 32 (34.7)	100% 36 (30.3)	100% 81 (44.8)	100% 30 (35.7)	100% 27 (27.6)
2. Drink alcohol in a pub with parents	62.5 13 (7.0)	65.2 8 (8.6)	69.7 9 (7.5)	55.2 9 (4.9)	64.3 1 (1.1)	72.4 3 (3.0)
3. Drink with your girl/boy friend in a pub	55.4 21 (11.4)	56.5 3 (3.2)	62.1 1 (0.8)	50.2 20 (11.0)	63.0 5 (5.9)	69.3 4 (4.0)
4. Drink in a mixed group in a pub	44.0 12 (6.5)	53.2 8 (8.6)	61.3 7 (5.8)	39.2 15 (8.2)	57.1 9 (10.7)	65.29 7 (7.1)
5. Drink in a pub with friends all the same sex	37.4 18 (9.7)	44.5 10 (10.8)	55.4 13 (10.9)	30.9 12 (6.6)	46.4 12 (14.2)	58.1 12 (12.2)
6. Taking a drink at home	27.7 51 (27.7)	33.6 31 (33.6)	44.5 53 (44.5)	24.3 44 (24.3)	32.1 27 (32.1)	45.9 45 (45.9)
N =	184	92	119	181	84	98
Coefficient of reproducibility	0.8891	0.9217	0.9529	0.9072	0.9238	0.9388
Minimum marginal reproducibility	0.5522	0.5283	0.5866	0.6000	0.5643	0.6224
Percentage improvement	0.3370	0.3935	0.3664	0.3072	0.3595	0.3163
Coefficient of scalability	0.7522	0.8341	0.8862	0.7680	0.8251	0.8378

Take a drink at home:

Strongly approve
Moderately approve

Neutral Category } Neither approve nor disapprove
Uncertain

Strongly disapprove
Moderately disapprove

Drink in a pub with your husband/wife:

Strongly approve
Moderately approve

Neutral Category } Neither approve nor disapprove
Uncertain

Strongly disapprove
Moderately disapprove

Drink with girl/boy-friend in a pub:

Strongly approve
Moderately approve

Neutral Category } Neither approve nor disapprove
Uncertain

Strongly disapprove
Moderately disapprove

Drink in a pub with friends all the same sex:

Strongly approve
Moderately approve

Neutral Category } Neither approve nor disapprove
Uncertain

Strongly disapprove
Moderately disapprove

2. *Being drunk at home, being drunk in a mixed group of friends, visibly affected by drink without being drunk* Three items were selected (*Tables A.3.4 and A.3.5*) in increasing order of 'difficulty' of attitudes to their 18-21 year olds drinking, from the one most frequently found to the least frequently found, or the most 'difficult' of positive attitudes to hold.

The cutting point for the items were as follows:

Be visibly affected by drink without being drunk:

Strongly approve
Moderately approve

Neutral Category } Neither approve nor disapprove

Strongly disapprove
Moderately disapprove

Be what you describe as drunk at home:

Strongly approve
Moderately approve

Neutral Category } Neither approve nor disapprove

Strongly disapprove
Moderately disapprove

Table A.3.4 Respondents' perception of fathers' attitudes towards the effect of excessive drinking on respondents as measured by 18-21 year olds' responses and scaled by Guttman techniques (Q.39a§, 8, 9, 10)

Scale type cumulative	Males			Females		
	Irish 181	Anglo-Irish 89	English 114	Irish 181	Anglo-Irish 85	English 94
1. Negative to all statements	100% 134 (74.1)	100% 43 (48.3)	100% 56 (49.1)	100% 148 (81.8)	100% 55 (64.7)	100% 66 (70.2)
2. Be visibly affected by drink without being drunk	25.9 28 (15.4)	51.7 25 (28.0)	50.9 26 (22.8)	18.2 27 (14.9)	35.3 22 (25.8)	29.8 14 (14.8)
3. Be what you describe as drunk in mixed company	10.4 14 (7.7)	23.5 12 (13.4)	28.0 12 (10.5)	3.3 4 (2.2)	9.4 3 (3.5)	14.8 4 (4.2)
4. Be what you describe as drunk at home	2.7 5 (2.7)	10.1 9 (10.1)	17.5 20 (17.5)	1.1 2 (1.1)	5.8 5 (5.8)	10.6 10 (10.6)
N =	181	89	114	181	85	94
Coefficient of reproducibility	0.9448	0.8801	0.9415	0.9963	0.9529	0.9645
Minimum marginal reproducibility	0.8692	0.7154	0.6784	0.9245	0.8314	0.8156
Percentage improvement	0.0755	0.1648	0.2632	0.0718	0.1216	0.1489
Coefficient of scalability	0.7575	0.7589	0.8182	0.9512	0.7209	0.8077

Table A.3.5 Respondents' perception of mothers' attitudes towards the effect of excessive drinking on respondents as measured by 18-21 year olds' responses and scaled by Guttman techniques (Q.39b§, 8, 9, 10)

Scale type cumulative	Males						Females					
	Irish 187		Anglo-Irish 92		English 119		Irish 183		Anglo-Irish 84		English 98	
1. Negative to all statements	100%	158 (84.5)	100%	63 (68.5)	100%	72 (60.5)	100%	157 (85.8)	100%	64 (76.2)	100%	78 (79.6)
2. Be visibly affected by drink without being drunk	15.4	20 (10.6)	31.5	16 (17.3)	39.5	28 (23.5)	14.2	18 (9.8)	23.8	13 (15.4)	20.4	8 (8.1)
3. Be what you describe as drunk at home	4.8	4 (2.1)	14.1	7 (7.6)	15.9	9 (7.5)	4.3	6 (3.2)	8.3	4 (4.7)	12.2	4 (4.0)
4. Be what you describe as drunk in mixed company	2.6	5 (2.6)	6.5	6 (6.5)	8.4	10 (8.4)	1.1	2 (1.1)	3.5	3 (3.5)	8.1	8 (8.1)
N =	187		92		119		183		84		98	
Coefficient of reproducibility	0.9893		0.9203		0.9552		0.9709		0.9603		0.9728	
Minimum marginal reproducibility	0.9234		0.8261		0.7871		0.9344		0.8810		0.8639	
Percentage improvement	0.0660		0.0942		0.1681		0.0364		0.0794		0.1088	
Coefficient of scalability	0.8605		0.5417		0.7895		0.5556		0.6667		0.8000	

Be what you describe as
drunk in mixed company:

Neutral }
Category }

Strongly approve
Moderately approve
Neither approve nor
   disapprove
Uncertain
Strongly disapprove
Moderately disapprove

3. *Mixing drinks and drinking three or more drinks on one occasion*   Three
items were selected (*Tables A.3.6* and *A.3.7*) in increasing order of 'difficulty' of
attitudes to their 18-21 year olds drinking, from the one most frequently found to
the least frequently found, or the most 'difficult' of positive attitudes to hold.
   The cutting point for these items were as follows:

Drink three or four drinks
on one occasion:

Neutral }
Category }

Strongly approve
Moderately approve
Neither approve nor
   disapprove
Uncertain
Strongly disapprove
Moderately disapprove

Drink six or more drinks
on one occasion:

Neutral }
Category }

Strongly approve
Moderately approve
Neither approve nor
   disapprove
Uncertain
Strongly disapprove
Moderately disapprove

Mix their drinks·

Neutral }
Category }

Strongly approve
Moderately approve
Neither approve nor
   disapprove
Uncertain
Strongly disapprove
Moderately disapprove

Using Guttman's scalogram technique six scales were devised, three from
fathers' responses, three from mothers' responses. Errors were randomly scattered and the cutting points evenly distributed (Nie *et al.* 1970). An exact
equivalent scale was constructed for both father and mother, using the same
items in the order. Exactly equivalent scales were also constructed for the males
and females, using the same items. As will be seen in some of the scales the order
was not the same. Different 'cutting points' for dichotomizing responses were
used for the different groups — the Irish, Anglo-Irish, English, both parents and
young people — because use of the same cutting points would have resulted in
unacceptable levels of error.

Table A.3.6   Respondents' perception of fathers' attitudes towards respondents' mixing drinks and the amount of alcohol consumed as measured by respondents' responses and scaled by Guttman techniques (Q. 39a§, 6, 7, 11)

Scale type cumulative	Males			Females		
	Irish 180	Anglo-Irish 89	English 114	Irish 180	Anglo-Irish 85	English 94
1. Negative to all statements	100% 57 (31.7)	100% 17 (19.1)	100% 22 (19.3)	100% 126 (70.0)	100% 37 (43.5)	100% 34 (36.2)
2. Drink six or more drinks on one occasion	68.3 60 (33.3)	80.9 34 (38.2)	80.7 33 (28.9)	30.0 43 (23.8)	56.5 26 (30.5)	63.8 36 (38.2)
3. Drink four or more drinks on one occasion	35.0 43 (23.8)	42.6 25 (28.0)	51.7 42 (36.8)	6.1 6 (3.3)	25.9 16 (18.8)	25.5 18 (19.1)
4. Mix your drinks	11.1 20 (11.1)	14.6 13 (14.6)	14.9 17 (14.9)	2.7 5 (2.7)	7.9 6 (7.0)	6.3 6 (6.3)
N =	180	89	114	180	85	94
Coefficient of reproducibility	0.7148	0.7303	0.7427	0.8593	0.8353	0.7730
Minimum marginal reproducibility	0.7000	0.5730	0.5614	0.8704	0.7020	0.6809
Percentage improvement	0.0148	0.1573	0.1813	0.0111	0.1333	0.0922
Coefficient of scalability	0.0494	0.3684	0.4133	0.0857	0.4474	0.2889

Table A.3.7 Respondents' perception of mothers' attitudes towards respondents' mixing drinks and the amount of alcohol consumed as measured by respondents' responses are scaled by Guttman techniques (Q.39b§, 6, 7, 11)

Scale type cumulative	Males			Females		
	Irish 187	Anglo-Irish 92	English 119	Irish 183	Anglo-Irish 84	English 98
1. Negative to all statements	100% 72 (38.5)	100% 27 (29.4)	100% 34 (28.6)	100% 136 (74.3)	100% 40 (47.6)	100% 50 (51.0)
2. Drink four or more drinks on one occasion	61.4 52 (27.8)	70.6 36 (39.1)	71.4 44 (36.9)	25.7 40 (21.8)	52.4 25 (29.7)	48.9 24 (24.4)
3. Mix your drinks	33.6 45 (24.0)	31.5 23 (25.0)	34.4 33 (27.7)	3.8 3 (1.6)	22.6 15 (17.8)	24.4 14 (14.2)
4. Drink six or more drinks on one occasion	9.6 18 (9.6)	6.5 6 (6.5)	6.7 8 (6.7)	2.1 4 (2.1)	4.7 4 (4.7)	10.2 10 (10.2)
N =	187	92	119	183	84	98
Coefficient of reproducibility	0.8966	0.7101	0.7423	0.9454	0.8413	0.8435
Minimum marginal reproducibility	0.6952	0.6377	0.6246	0.8944	0.7341	0.7211
Percentage improvement	0.2014	0.0725	0.1176	0.0510	0.1071	0.1224
Coefficient of scalability	0.6608	0.2000	0.3134	0.4828	0.4030	0.4390

Problems related to 18-21 year olds drinking (Q.56)

Young people were asked to answer six statements about problems related to their drinking over the year prior to interview. They were asked to answer yes, no, or partly, to each statement. A cumulative index was created from these statements from the one most frequently found, to the least frequently found.

The cutting point for the items were as follows:

In the past year or so, have you ever had arguments with friends because of drinking:	Yes, Partly,* No
In the past year or so, have you ever had money problems because of drinking:	Yes, Partly, No
In the past year or so, have you ever had trouble with police either in connection with drunken driving or other behaviour resulting from drinking:	Yes, Partly, No
In the past year or so have you ever had health problems because of drinking:	Yes, Partly, No
In the past year or so, have you ever had difficulty with your job because of drinking:	Yes, Partly, No

Chapter 8

Perceived parental support (Q.79, Q.80)

Three items were selected to ascertain perceived parental support (*Table A.1.60*). These formed a Guttman type scale and are presented in increasing order of 'difficulty' of support, from the one most frequently obtained to the least frequently obtained, or the most 'difficult' of parental support to obtain.

The cutting point for these items were as follows:

Are/were they interested in your school/college work or work plans:	Always/Often/ Sometimes Hardly ever/ Never
Would you say that your parents generally encourage you to do things you are interested in doing:	Almost always/ Very often/ Sometimes Hardly ever/ Not too often
Do you parents help you when you are worried about some problem:	Always/Often/ Sometimes Hardly ever/ Never

Children's perception of parents' social rules for drinking
See *Tables A.3.2. — A.3.7.*

*Partly: very few people gave partly as an answer to any of the items.

Chapter 9

General social support from friends (Q.80)

Do you feel free to talk to your friends about personal problems when you want to:

> High level:
> Almost always
> Very often
> Medium level:
> Sometimes
> Low level:
> Not too often
> Hardly ever

Overall peer group support for drinking (Q.2§, Q.41ab, Q.42§)

Overall peer group support for drinking was devised from a number of questions as is seen in *Table 14* (see p.119). It was a cumulative index based on the replies of those who took a drink at the time of interview. Eight items were selected, stated in increasing order of 'difficulty' of support, from the one most frequently found to the one that was least frequently found, or the most 'difficult' support to obtain from peers. This was a measure indicating a young person's immersion in a context of regular and frequent drinking located exclusively in a peer group context.

The cutting point for the items were as follows:

Friends drink regularly:	All or most friends	No friends
Usual place to meet friends:	Pub	Other place
Drinks with a group of boys/girls, once a month or more:	Yes	No
Goes out for a drink with the lads/girls:	Very frequently Frequently	Occasionally Rarely Never
Drinks on a date:	Very frequently Frequently	Occasionally Rarely Never
Drinks with lads or girls before dancing:	Very frequently Frequently	Occasionally Rarely Never

Attitudes to young people of own age drinking, and single sex drinking among young people (Q.59a§)

To obtain two single measures (for use in the detailed analysis) of young people's attitudes to peers drinking, two Guttman type scales were established based on Q.59a§:

1 Attitude to young people of their own age drinking
2 Attitude to single sex drinking

1. *Attitude to young people of own age drinking*   Three items were selected (*Table A.1.67*), stated in increasing order of 'difficulty' of attitudes to peers drinking, from the one most frequently found to the least frequently found, or the most 'difficult' of positive attitudes to hold.

The cutting point for these items were as follows:

Lads of your age taking a drink:

Very good/
Good
Fair/undesirable

Girl-friend/boy-friend taking a drink:

Very good/
Good
Fair/undesirable

Girls of your age taking a drink:

Very good/
Good
Fair/undesirable

2. *Attitude to single sex drinking*   Three items were selected (*Table A.1.68*), stated in increasing order of 'difficulty' of attitudes to peers drinking, from the one most frequently found to the least frequently found or the most 'difficult' of positive attitudes to hold.

The cutting point for these items were as follows:

Drinking in all female group:

Very good/Good
Fair/undesirable

Drinking in all male group:

Very good/Good
Fair/undesirable

Girls in a pub on their own taking a drink:

Very good/Good
Fair/undesirable

Level of acceptable and tolerable behaviour while drinking in a mixed peer group (Q.63)

Two cumulative indexes (see *Tables A.1.69, A.1.70*) were formed to measure the level of acceptable and tolerable behaviour while drinking in a mixed peer group. In each index there are six items, and respondents were asked to answer yes or no to each item, in terms of whether they were acceptable or tolerable. The items are given in increasing order of 'difficulty' of levels of acceptance and tolerance, from the one most frequently found or the most 'difficult' to accept or tolerate.

The cutting point for these items on both indexes were as follows:

	Acceptable		*Tolerable*	
To be happy	Yes	No	Yes	No
To feel merry	Yes	No	Yes	No
To be very talkative	Yes	No	Yes	No
To be jarred	Yes	No	Yes	No
To be amorous	Yes	No	Yes	No
To be drunk	Yes	No	Yes	No

Chapter 10

The anomy scale as designed by McCloskey and Schaar (1965: 14) contained the following nine items:

1 With everything so uncertain these days it almost seems as though anything could happen.
2 What is lacking in the world today is the old kind of friendship that lasted for a lifetime.
3 With everything in such a state of disorder it is hard for a person to know where he stands from one day to the next.
4 Everything changes so quickly these days that I often have trouble deciding what are the right rules to follow.
5 I often feel that many things our parents stood for are just going to ruin before our very eyes.
6 The trouble with the world today is that most people really don't believe in anything.
7 I often feel awkward and out of place.
8 People were better off in the old days when everyone knew just how he was expected to act.
9 It seems to me that other people find it easier to decide what is right than I do.

The analytic procedure used by McCloskey and Schaar was as follows. For each of the statements that respondents agreed with, they got a score of one. The scores were then totalled for each of the statements. The maximum score that could be obtained was nine and the minimum zero. Those who scored between six and nine were considered highly anomic, a middle group scored between three and five, and those who scored between zero and two were considered to be non-anomic.

The scale was modified for the present study and only six items were used. The items omitted were items 2, 7, and 9, as it was felt after piloting the questionnaire, that they were not applicable to the present study. To counteract any possible patterning of responses, the six items from the McCloskey and Schaar anomy scale were interspersed with six very different items, some of which were used to form a separate Guttman type scale to measure perceived opportunity in and attitude towards the country in which the young people lived. These items were as follows:

2* Ireland/England is a good place to live in.
4 Having a religion is a great help in coping with life's problems.
6 Ireland/England as it is now is the place I'd prefer to bring up my children.
8 Anyone who is willing to work hard can make a good career in Ireland/England today.
10 The changes in the Catholic Church since the Vatican Council have done more good than harm.
12 The values people hold nowadays are more real than those held previously.

Each of the six items and these other items were read out to respondents who then said if they agreed, disagreed, or did not know. In the analysis the six items taken

*Indicates position in list of statements read out with aid of prompt card. See Appendix 2; 18-21 year olds' questionnaire (Q.82§).

from McCloskey and Schaar were rated as they had been by the authors. Those who obtained scores of four to six were rated as highly anomic, those getting two to three were in the middle, and those between zero and one were low-anomic.

Perceived opportunity in and attitude to country of origin (Q.82§, Q.85a,b)

An index was devised that was concerned mainly with the various aspects of perceived opportunities available in, as well as general feelings about the country in which those interviewed lived (*Table A.1.71*). This index formed a Guttman type scale, and comprised four items, three of which were pre-coded and read to each respondent, who answered either agree, disagree, or don't know, and one open-ended question on their image of Ireland/England. These items were stated in increasing order of 'difficulty' of attitudes held, from the one most frequently found, to the least frequently found, or the most 'difficult' of attitudes to hold.

The cutting point for the items were as follows:

Ireland/England is a good place to live in:	Agree Disagree Don't know
Anyone who is willing to work hard can make a good career in Ireland/England:	Agree Disagree, Don't know
Ireland/England as it is now is the place I would prefer to bring up children:	Agree Disagree Don't know
Image of Ireland/England:	Favourable Unfavourable

Values perceived to be important in family life (Q.78)

The young people were asked if the values of affection, dependence, independence and recognition were important in family life. A cumulative index was devised which placed those values in order of 'difficulty', those which respondents found the least important to those they designated as the most important.

The cutting points for the items were as follows:

Affection:	The love and affection you get in the family	Very important/ Pretty important Not too important/ Not important at all
Dependence:	Having somebody in the family you can count on to help out	Very important/ Pretty important Not too important/ Not important at all
Independence:	Being able to do things in the family your own way	Very important/ Pretty important Not too important/ Not important at all

| Recognition: | The good opinion in the family for the things you do well | Very important/ Pretty important Not too important/ Not important at all |

Religiosity Guttman type scale (Q.74)

This is a four-item Guttman type scale modified from Richard Jessors' (1969) scale of religiosity. The items shown in *Table 17* (see p.132) are presented in order of difficulty. This scale aimed at seeing whether prayer, belief in God, religious advice, and going to church were important in the young people's lives.

The cutting points for the items were as follows:

Prayer important:	To be able to turn to prayer when you are facing a personal problem	Very important/ Important Slightly important/ Not important
Believing in God:	To believe in God	Very important/ Important Slightly important/ Not important
Reliance on religious advice, counsel or teaching when he has a problem:	To be able to rely on religious advice, counsel or teachings when you have a problem	Very important/ Important Slightly important/ Not important
Going to church regularly:	To go to church regularly	Very important/ Important Slightly important/ Not important

Sensation excitement seeking (Q.72§)

An index was devised to measure young people's experience of sensation excitement seeking type behaviour. The following items comprised the index, with their cutting points:

1 Crashed a party:	Never Once or twice Several times/Often/Very often
2 Sneaked/got into a place of entertainment without paying:	Never Once or twice Several times/Often/Very often
3 Gone speeding or driving recklessly	Never Once or twice Several times/Often/Very often
4 Driven a car without a driver's license	Never Once or twice Several times/Often/Very often

Appendix 4
Methodology

Sampling frame and sample

There were different problems in drawing up sampling frames in Ireland and in England.

Dublin

In the Dublin area, a complete census of the community prior to the inception of the study was undertaken. This listed all households with children between 16 and 22 years of age. The census had been carried out by first mapping every household within the defined limits of the parish boundary line. This census was checked for reliability and proved perfectly adequate. The census list included 1,272 households with 2,207 people between 16 and 22 years of age — 1,059 females, and 1,148 males. Households selected at random from this list were then visited and interviewers ascertained the following information, by using a brief standardized census form:

1 The composition of the household, i.e. number of children
2 Place of birth of parents
3 Number of 18-21 year olds living at home
4 Place of birth of 18-21 year olds
5 Date of birth of 18-21 year olds born in Ireland

If the household fulfilled the sampling requirements, it was included in the survey.

Some 650 households were visited before the sample of 200 households with at least one applicable male between 18-21, and 200 different households with at least one applicable female between 18-21, was completed. Since the range of 16-22 is 1.75 that of the applicable range, the figure of 650 was not unacceptably large. However, there are some limitations to this method of sampling. First of all, the total number of applicable households in the area is not known, and can only be estimated. Further, the number of applicable households with one, two, three, or more applicable children is not known. Further discussion of these points will arise during consideration of the sampling error.

London

In general, the problem in the London areas was the absence of an easily accessible listing of (1) households with children between 18-21 years of age, and (2) the other criteria which were necessary to characterize the households into what have been called the Anglo-Irish and the English groups.

The Anglo-Irish in England　Since the highest percentage of Irish born seemed to be in certain areas of London (Markham 1971; Fitzpatrick 1971b), the least difficult place to get a sufficiently large sample subject to the fairly stringent conditions imposed by the study — i.e. households with 18-21 year olds living at home at least four nights a week for five months a year, parents born and reared in the Republic of Ireland and the 18-21 year olds born and reared in England — was in the London boroughs of Brent, Camden and Westminster.

After considerable discussion with Irish community leaders in London, and a pilot study to ascertain the composition of households in terms of age, sex, and ethnic background, the area selected was five miles square situated in the London Boroughs of Brent, Camden, and Westminster. Since the voting age in England is 18, it seemed sensible, in the absence of other information, to build up the sampling frame from the register of electors. The following procedure was followed:

1　Where three or more individuals of the same surname on the Register of Electors were residing at the same address, this was taken as indicating that they belonged to the same household.
2　All such addresses were visited to see if this was correct, and if correct, whether such a household satisfied the other requirements.
3　If the household was applicable, then an effort was made to interview the father and mother and one child between 18-21 years of age.

Experience of researchers with the English Electoral Register indicated the necessity of checking the roll for reliability. A house to house visit was completed on 1,200 houses, and only five households contacted were not on the register. This seemed perfectly satisfactory.

A further problem was the possibility that two-surnamed households might be applicable; the father and/or mother could be dead, or separated. In the 1,200 houses, three such two-surnamed households were discovered; this is discussed further below.

Unlike the Dublin area, total coverage was aimed at, i.e. all applicable households (under the three-or-more surname criteria) were interviewed. The total number of households covered was 4,718, of which 210 were applicable, somewhat under 5 per cent.

The English in England　Another London area similar in socio-economic characteristics to the area chosen for the high concentration of Irish-born, and to the Dublin area, was selected to find the third part of the sample, the English household. The sampling frame was derived in the same way, and total coverage was aimed at, as in the Anglo-Irish area. Here 1,777 households were contacted, of whom 273 were applicable, some 16 per cent. (For more details see O'Connor 1976a and b: 576-605).

Appendix 5
Statistical
procedures for analysis

Sampling error:
standard error of group differences

In order to decide whether differences in the percentages between groups are really different, or whether they may have arisen from chance alone, an estimate of the standard error of the percentages in each of the groups is needed (*Table A.5.2*).

The size of this error depends on the following factors:
1 The sampling error proper arises because it is a sample. Not all members of each group willing to be interviewed were selected to be interviewed.
2 Errors arise because it has not been possible to contact each person selected in the sample.
3 Errors arise because of the refusal of some people to answer.

The population which is being sampled can be considered to be made up of three corresponding strata consisting of:

Stratum 1: Those who will answer if asked.
Stratum 2: Those who cannot be contacted.
Stratum 3: Those who will refuse to answer if asked.

The error in Stratum 1 can be calculated from ordinary sampling techniques. To estimate the error for the other two strata, other methods must be used.

The overall sampling error, if results were used for area as a whole, is based on the following assumptions:

1 Non-contacts (Stratum 2) are not systematically different from those who respond (Stratum 1).
2 Refusals (Stratum 3) are not:
   (i)   more than 20 per cent different on either side of those who respond, or alternatively
   (ii) more than 10 per cent different on either side of those who respond.

Table A.5.1   Stratum sizes for various groups, based on the estimates of total population size*

		Irish	Anglo-Irish	English
Fathers:	Stratum 1	716	166	108
	Stratum 2	88	11	16
	Stratum 3	40	66	92
Mothers:	Stratum 1	845	218	256
	Stratum 2	26	5	3
	Stratum 3	36	32	66
Males:	Stratum 1	593	159	181
	Stratum 2	18	15	6
	Stratum 3	9	21	49
Females:	Stratum 1	601	157	153
	Stratum 2	10	9	4
	Stratum 3	30	9	37

*Deceased parents are not included in calculations. (Details of estimates in O'Connor 1976a and b: 579-93.)

Analysis

Analysis of the data is in the following pattern:

1 In Chapters 5, 6, and 7 the data are mainly descriptive, straightforward frequency counts, cross tabulations, and formation of indexes; Guttman type scales (Goodenough 1944: 179; Edwards 1948: 313) are also presented.
2 In the first part of Chapters 7, 8, and 9 the analysis follows the same pattern, and an assessment of a more analytic nature is then undertaken. The test employed, namely the Kolmogorov-Smirnov test (Siegel 1956: 47), helped simplify the data by identifying statistically significant correlates.
3 To provide more adequate measures of the effects of different variables taking into account their interrelations, Goodman's modified multiple regression method was used in Chapters 8, 9, 10, and 11 (Goodman 1972a and b, 1973).

Kolmogorov-Smirnov two-sample test

This test is concerned in the one sample case with the degree of agreement between the distribution of a set of sample values (observed scores) and some specified theoretical distribution. It does not provide estimates of the size of effects between variables nor allow account to be taken of more than one variable at a time. It determines whether the scores obtained in the sample could have come from a population having the theoretical distribution. The test involves the calculation of the maximum difference D, based on the cumulative frequency distribution which would occur under the theoretical distribution, and its comparison with the observed cumulative frequency distribution.

The point at which these two distributions, theoretical and observed, show the greatest divergence is the maximum difference. The sampling distribution indicates whether a divergence of the observed magnitude would occur if the observed scores were really a random sample from the theoretical distribution (Goodman 1954: 160; Siegel 1956: 47).

Table A.5.2   Standard error for different groups under:
Assumption (i) Refusals do not differ by more than 20 per cent from those who respond.
Assumption (ii) Refusals do not differ by more than 10 per cent from those who respond.

Observed	Assumption (i)					Assumption (ii)				
	10%	*20%*	*30%*	*40%*	*50%*	*10%*	*20%*	*30%*	*40%*	*50%*
Irish										
Fathers	1.8	2.2	2.5	2.6	2.7	1.5	2.0	2.2	2.4	2.4
Mothers	1.6	2.0	2.2	2.4	2.4	1.4	1.8	2.1	2.2	2.2
Males	1.9	2.5	2.9	3.1	3.1	1.8	2.4	2.8	3.0	3.0
Females	2.3	2.9	3.2	3.5	3.5	2.1	2.7	3.0	3.2	3.3
Anglo-Irish										
Fathers	3.9	4.2	4.5	4.6	4.7	2.5	2.9	3.1	3.2	3.3
Mothers	2.5	2.8	3.0	3.1	3.1	1.7	2.0	2.2	2.3	2.4
Males	3.0	3.7	4.1	4.3	4.3	2.5	3.2	3.6	3.8	3.8
Females	2.7	3.4	3.9	4.1	4.2	2.4	3.1	3.6	3.8	3.9
English										
Fathers	3.7	4.0	4.2	4.3	4.4	2.3	2.6	2.8	2.9	3.0
Mothers	2.5	2.8	2.9	3.0	3.1	1.7	2.0	2.1	2.2	2.3
Males	2.8	3.4	3.7	3.9	4.0	2.2	2.8	3.1	3.3	3.4
Females	3.9	4.5	4.9	5.1	5.1	2.8	3.4	3.8	4.0	4.0

Goodman's modified multiple regression method

This method was used for the analysis of dichotomous variables undertaken with the use of Goodman's Computer Program for modified multiple regression analysis. It enabled an assessment to be made of the relative amount of variation in young people's drinking behaviour that was accounted for by the main effects of parental, peer, social and personal, and ethnic and cultural factors.

Goodman's method was designed for multivariate causal analysis of survey data which does not meet assumptions of continuity, additivity, homoscedasticity, and independence of error terms required in conventional regression analysis. The Goodman method analyzes the relationships among cell frequencies of multi-level factorial designs, and provides effect parameters analogous to partial slopes in path analysis and measures of association analogous to the squares of zero — order, partial, multiple and multiple partial correlation coefficients. The method also provides estimates of the magnitude of all interaction effects and their levels of statistical significance. Effect parameters computed by the Goodman method are easiest to interpret when variables are dichotomized.

An assessment of the relative amount of variation accounted for by the main effects of the independent variables on the dependent variables is also made.

In more detail, the Goodman method first computes maximum-likelihood estimates of cell frequencies under different models (structural equations), using an iterative procedure described in Goodman. The estimated cell frequencies generated by the different models are then compared with the observed cell frequencies by computing chi-square based on either the conventional goodness-of fit statistic or the likelihood-ratio statistic. In the Goodman method, the chi-square values serve as measures of unexplained variation. Thus, the smaller the chi-square value (i.e. the better the estimated frequencies correspond to the observed frequencies) under a given model, the stronger is the explanatory power of the independent variable or variables in the model. By computing the relative reduction in chi-square values from various models containing different combinations of independent variables, the strongest model can be arrived at. With the dependent variable a measurement is obtained, roughly analogous to coefficients of determination, multiple determination, and partial determination in conventional regression analysis.

For a detailed example of Goodman's modified multiple regression for the analysis of dichotomous variables see Goodman (1972a: 28, 1972b: 1035). A more mathematical discussion is to be found in Goodman (1970: 226). For a detailed discussion of how the method was used in this study and for the tables relating to the analysis see O'Connor (1976a and b).

Appendix 6

Measurement
of levels of drinking

Type of drinker index

A study that deals with the drinking behaviour of a particular group, must cope with the problem of obtaining accurate measures of alcohol consumed by the people interviewed. The following gives details of the measure used in this study, the type of drinker index. For a detailed discussion of the literature and research findings relevant to the measurement of levels of drinking and the technical aspects of measurement see O'Connor (1973a; 1967a and b: 613-59) and Pernanen (1974).

Formation of the type of drinker index

There are two basic considerations in the operation of this index:

1 The Cahalann-Cisin volume-variability index (1968: 642) and the modified absolute alcohol content index (Fitzpatrick 1970a and b) were employed in measuring the levels of drinking in the three groups under study. The figures used in computing the type of drinker index must therefore be viewed as estimates.

2 The use of the type of drinker index enables parents and young people to be ordered in terms of their alcohol consumption. The index is not a guide to actual measures of quantities of alcohol consumed.

Using the volume-variability index, there was a significant positive correlation (.65) between volume and maximum amounts of drinking in all groups under study. Further analysis showed that the volume measures on the volume-variability index did not adequately discriminate between the groups under study. It concealed the range of drinking as measured by volume within and between the groups. The variability of drinking as measured by Cahalann and Cisin's index (1968) was a more discriminating measure, especially if used in combination with the modified absolute alcohol content index (Fitzpatrick 1970a and b). The modified absolute alcohol content index translated respondents' drinking patterns into the estimated average amount consumed per month, per week, or per day. The new index was therefore based on a modification of the volume variability index and the modified absolute alcohol content index.

Individuals were placed in one of five types, depending on their score on the combined new index.

Type 0   :   Abstainers/virtual abstainers (infrequent drinkers)

Type I   :   Low maximum, volume as measured by the overall modified absolute alcohol content index

Type II   :   Medium maximum, volume as measured by the overall modified absolute alcohol content index

Type III   :   High maximum, volume as measured by the overall modified absolute alcohol content index

Type IV   :   High maximum, volume as measured by the overall modified absolute alcohol content index

The resultant index was a variability-absolute alcohol content index, incorporating the quantity frequency ideal. The first type, Type 0, comprised all 'did not drink', 'never took a drink', members of the temperance organizations, and ex-drinkers. (Virtual abstainers were people who drank less than once a month, more than once a year, and those who drank less than once a year.) For the other types maximum amount of drinking (i.e. variability of drinking) was designated as the discriminating variable. Respondents were assigned to types depending on their 'maximum' rating of (1) low, (2) medium, and (3) high maximum variability in relation to drinking. The high maximum type was further subdivided into two groups. The rationale for this was that in the other maximum groups, the volume range as measured by the absolute alcohol content index was small, and on the whole more evenly distributed than in the high maximum group. The volume range was from 1 to 9, i.e. from 0 fluid ounces up to 250 + fluid ounces of absolute alcohol. Also it was felt that to include all volume in combination with high maximum levels of drinking, would conceal different types of drinkers.

Once created, this index was tested to ensure that it discriminated adequately between different types of drinkers. The basis of the procedure was on the achievement of good discrimination between the independent variables and the respondents assigned to the different type of drinker group defined above. The mechanism of the discrimination was based on the means and standard deviation of each individual on particular variables, and the variation from the group or index type.

The steps taken were as follows:

1 The drinking index type was divided as shown above, and cut off points were based on the correlations between the variables, reasons for drinking, attitudes to peers drinking, and frequency of drinking in different situations.

2 The means and standard deviation of each such variable were obtained for each drinking index type.

3 Each individual score on each variable was then compared with its own group mean or index type mean.

4 Individuals who did not follow the group pattern were assigned to an adjacent type of drinker on the type of drinker index, until the overall homogeneity and the discrimination of the index type was maximized.

The resultant index based on this procedure is shown in *Table 9* (see p.79).

References

Ahammer, I. and Baltes, P. (1972) Objective Versus Perceived Age Differences, in Personality: How Do Adolescents, Adults and Older People View Themselves in Each Other? *Journal of Gerontology* 27: 46-51.

Aiken, M. and Hage, J. (1966) Organisational Alienation: a Comparative Analysis. *American Sociological Review* 31: 497-507.

Albert, W. (1973) *The Turnpike Road System in England 1663-1840*. London: Cambridge University Press.

Alcoholism and Drug Addiction Research Foundation (1966) *Alcohol Studies Guide*, Toronto.

Alexander, C. and Campbell, E. (1964) Peer Influences on Adolescent Educational Aspirations and Attainments. *American Sociological Review* 29: 93-96.

Allardt, E. (1957) Drinking Norms and Drinking Habits. In E. Allardt, T. Markkanen, and M. Takala, *Drinking and Drinkers*. Helsinki: Finnish Foundation for Alcohol Studies.

Allardt, E., Markkanen, T., and Takala, M. (1957) *Drinking and Drinkers*. Helsinki: Finish Foundation for Alcohol Studies.

Archard, P. (1973) Sad, Bad or Mad: Society's Confused Response to Skid Row Alcoholics. In R. Bailey and J. Young (eds) *Contemporary Social Problems in Britain*. Farnborough: Saxon House.

Archard, P. (1975) The Bottle Won't Leave You: a Study of Homeless Alcoholics and Their Guardians. *Alcohol Recovery Project*, London.

Arensberg, C. and Kimball, S. (1940) *Family and Community in Ireland*. Cambridge, Mass.: Harvard University Press.

Argyle, M. (1958) *Religious Behaviour*. London: Routledge & Kegan Paul.

Askwith, G.R. (1928) *British Taverns: Their History and Laws*. London: G. Routledge & Sons.

Ayles, D. (1976) Fresh Thames Water: None of Your Piped Sludge. *Alliance News, CXVI*: 14-15.

Bacon, M. and Jones, M. (1968) *Teen-Age Drinking*. New York: Thomas Y. Crowell.

Bacon, S. (1943) Sociology and the Problems of Alcohol: Foundation for a

Sociological Study of Drinking Behaviour. *Quarterly Journal of Studies on Alcohol* 3: 445-62.

Bacon, S. (1944) Inebriety, Social Integration and Marriage. *Quarterly Journal of Studies on Alcohol* 5: 86-125.

Bagley, C. (1967) Anomie, Alienation, and Evaluation of Social Structure. *Kansas Journal of Sociology* 3: 110-23.

Bailey, M., Haberman, P., and Alksne, H. (1965) The Epidemiology of Alcoholism in an Urban Residential Area. *Quarterly Journal of Studies on Alcohol* 26: 19-40.

Bales, R. (1946) Cultural Differences in Rates of Alcoholism. *Quarterly Journal of Studies on Alcohol* 6: 480-99.

Bales, R. (1962) Attitudes toward Drinking in the Irish Culture. In D. Pitman and C. Snyder (eds) *Society, Culture and Drinking Patterns*. New York: John Wiley & Sons.

Barnett, M. (1955) Alcoholism in the Cantonese of New York City. In O. Diethelm (ed.) *Etiology of Chronic Alcoholism*. Springfield, Illinois: Thomas.

Bealer, R. and Willits, F. (1961) Rural Youth: a Case of the Rebelliousness of Adolescents. *Annals of the American Academy of Political Social Science* 338: 63-69.

Bengtson, V. (1970) The Generation Gap: a Review of Typology of Social-Psychological Perspectives. *Youth and Society* 2: 22-25.

Bengston, V. (1970) Interage Perceptions and the Generation Gap. *Gerontologist* II: 85-89.

Bengston, V., Furlong, M., and Laufer, R. (1974) Time, Ageing and the Continuity of Social Structure: Themes and Issues in Generational Analysis. *Journal of Social Issues* 30 (2): 1-30.

Bernstein, S. (1967) *Alternatives to Violence : Alienated Youth and Riots, Race and Poverty*. New York: Association Press.

Birmingham, J. (1840) *A Memoir of the Very Rev. Theobald Mathew*, Dublin.

Blacker, E. and Demone, H. (1965) Drinking Behaviour of Delinquent Boys. *Quarterly Journal of Studies on Alcohol* 26: 223-37.

Blanc, H., Hill, M., and Brown, E. (1968) Alienation, Self-Esteem and Attitudes toward Drinking in High School Students. *Quarterly Journal of Studies on Alcohol* 29: 350-64.

Blauner, R. (1964) *Alienation and Freedom*. Chicago: University of Chicago Press.

Bogue, D. (1963) *Skid Row in American Cities*. University of Chicago: Community and Family Study Centre.

Bonjean, C. and Grimes, M. (1970) Bureaucracy and Alienation: a Dimensional Approach. *Social Forces* 48: 365-73.

Booth, C. (ed.) (1889-1903) *Labour and Life of the People of London* (17 Vols). London: Macmillan.

Bossard, J. and Boll, E. (1960) *The Sociology of Child Development*. New York: Harper & Row.

Bottoms, A. (1967) Delinquency among Immigrants. *Race* 8: 359-83.

Boyd, R. (1969) *Health Education and Alcohol Report, HESC* 17. Edinburgh: Scottish Health Education Unit.

Bretherton, R. (1931) Country Inns and Alehouses. In R. Lennard (ed.) *English-men at Rest and Play: Some Phases of English Leisure, 1558-1714*. Oxford: Clarendon Press.

Briggs, A. (1974) *The Age of Improvement*. London: Longman.

Brittain, C. (1963) Adolescent Choices and Parent-Peer Cross Pressures. *American Sociological Review* 28: 385-90.

Brody, H. (1973) *Inishkillane: Change and Decline in the West of Ireland*.
    London: Allan Lane.
Brothers, J. (1971) *Religious Institutions*. London: Longman.
Brunn, K. (1969) The Actual and the Registered Frequency of Drunkenness in
    Helsinki. *British Journal of Addiction* 64: 3-8.
Brunn, K. and Hauge, R. (1963) *Drinking Habits among Northern Youth*.
    Helsinki: Finnish Foundation for Alcohol Studies.
Budd, S. (1973) *Sociologists and Religion*. London: Collier-Macmillan.
Bullough, B. (1967) Alienation in the Ghetto. *American Journal of Sociology* 72:
    469-78.
Bunzel, R. (1940) The Role of Alcohol in Two Central American Cultures.
    Psychiatry 3: 361-87.
Burns, D. (1881) *A Consecutive Narrative of the Real Development, and
    Extension of the Temperance Reform*, London.

Cahalann, D. (1970) *Problem Drinkers*. San Francisco: Jossey-Bass.
Cahalann, D. and Cisin, I. (1968) American Drinking Practices: Summary of
    Findings from a National Probability Sample. (1) Extent of Drinking by
    Population in Subgroups. *Quarterly Journal of Studies on Alcohol* 29:
    130-51.
Cahalann, D. and Cisin, I. (1968) American Drinking Practices: Summary of
    Findings from a National Probability Sample. (2) Measurement of Massed
    Versus Spaced Drinking. *Quarterly Journal of Studies on Alcohol* 29: 642-56.
Cahalann, D., Cisin, J., and Crossley, H. (1969) *American Drinking Practices*.
    New Haven, Conn.: Rutgers Center of Alcohol Studies.
Cahalann, D. and Room, R. (1974) *Problem Drinking Among American Men*.
    New Jersey: Rutgers University Press.
Campbell, W. and McSweeney, R. (1970) The Peer Group Context. In W.
    Campbell (ed.) *Scholars in Coontext*. London: John Wiley & Sons.
Carleton, W. (1846) *Tales and Stories of the Irish Peasants*, Dublin.
Carter, H. (1932) *The English Temperance Movement: A Study in Objectives*.
    London: Epworth.
Chand, I., Crider, D., and Willits, F. (1975) Parent-Youth Disagreement as
    Perceived by Youth: a Longitudinal Study. *Youth and Society* 6: 365-75.
Chart, D. (1910) *Ireland from the Union to Catholic Emancipation*. London:
    J.M. Dent & Sons.
Cisin, I. (1963) Community Studies of Drinking Behavior. *Annals of the New
    York Academy of Sciences* 107: 607-12.
Cloward, R. and Ohlin, L. (1960) *Delinquency and Opportunity*. Chicago: Free
    Press.
Cochran, W. (1963) *Sampling Techniques*. New York: John Wiley & Sons.
Cohen, A. (1955) *Delinquent Boys*. Chicago: Free Press.
Cohen, A. (1966) *Deviance and Control*. New Jersey: Prentice-Hall.
Cohen, S. (ed.) (1972) *Images of Deviance*. Harmondsworth, Middlesex:
    Penguin.
Coleman, J. (1961) *The Adolescent Society*. New York: Free Press of Glencoe.
Commission on Driving While Under the Influence of Drink or a Drug (1963).
    Dublin: Government Publications.
Commission of Inquiry on Mental Illness (1966). Dublin: Government
    Publications.
Connell, K. (1965) Ether Drinking in Ulster. *Quarterly Journal of Studies on
    Alcohol* 26: 629-53.

Connell, K. (1968) *Irish Peasant Society*. London: Oxford University Press.

Connor, R. (1962) The Self Concepts of Alcoholism. In D. Pittman and C. Snyder (eds) *Society, Culture and Drinking Patterns*. New York: John Wiley & Sons.

Cook, T. (1975) *Vagrant Alcoholics*. London: Routledge & Kegan Paul.

Cosper, R. (1969) Interviewer Bias in a Study of Drinking Patterns. *Quarterly Journal of Studies on Alcohol* 30: 257-58.

Couling, S. (1862) *History of the Temperance Movement in Great Britain and Ireland*, London.

Coulton, C. (1907) Parish Life in Mediaeval England. *The Churchman*.

Cousins, S. (1964-67) Population Trends in Ireland at the Beginning of the Twentieth Century. *Irish Geography* V: 387-401.

Cousins, S. (1965) The Regional Variation in Emigration from Ireland in 1821 and 1841. *Translations of the Institute of Geographers* 37: 15-30.

Cullen, J. (1911) The Pioneer Movement: Its Story and Origin. Address, City Hall, Cork.

Cullen, L. (1968) *Life in Ireland*. London: Batsford.

Curtis, R. (1974) Parents and Teens: Serendipity in a Study of Shifting Reference Groups. *Social Forces* 53: 368-75.

Dahrendorf, R. (1958) Out of Utopia: Towards a Pre-orientation of Sociological Analysis. *American Journal of Sociology* 64: 115-17.

Dargan, D. (1969) The Pioneer Commitment. *Pioneer* (February).

Davies, D. (1977) Alcoholism — the Preventable Condition. Paper presented at the World Psychiatric Association, Dublin.

Davies, J. and Stacey, B. (1972) *Teenagers and Alcohol* (Vol. II). London: HMSO.

Dean, D. (1960) Alienation and Political Apathy. *Social Forces* 38: 185-90.

Dean, D. (1961) Alienation: Its Meaning and Measurement. *American Sociological Review* 26: 753-58.

De Lint, J. and Schmidt, W. (1968) The Distribution of Alcohol Consumption in Ontario. *Quarterly Journal of Studies on Alcohol* 29: 968-73.

De Lint, J. and Schmidt, W. (1971) Consumption Averages and Alcoholism Prevalence: a Brief Review of Epidemiological Investigations. *British Journal of Addiction* 66: 97-107.

Demone, H. and Wechsler, H. (1976) Changing Drinking Patterns of Adolescents during the Last Decade. In M. Greenbelt and M. Schuckit *Alcoholism Problems in Women and Children. Seminars in Psychiatry*, New York.

Dight, S. (1976) *Scottish Drinking Habits*. London: HMSO.

Dingle, A. (1972) Drink and Working Class Living Standards in Britain, 1870-1914. *Economic History Review* 25: 608-22.

Dollard, J. (1945) Drinking Mores of the Social Classes. In *Alcohol, Science and Society*. New Havan Journal of Studies and Alcohol: 95-104.

Douvan, E. and Adelson, J. (1966) *The Adolescent Experience*. New York: John Wiley & Sons.

Dubey, S. (1971) Powerlessness and Mobility Orientations among Disadvantaged Blacks. *Public Opinion Quarterly* 35: 183-88.

Duffy, G. and Dean, G. (1971) The Reliability of Death Certification of Cirrhosis. *Journal of the Irish Medical Association* 64: 393-97.

Dunlop, J. (1839) *A Philosophy of Artificial and Compulsory Drinking in Great Britain and Ireland*, London.
Durkheim, E. (1951) *Suicide*. Chicago: Free Press.
Durkheim, E. (1965) *The Division of Labour*. New York: Free Press of Glencoe.

Edwards, A. (1948) On Guttman Scale Analysis. *Educational Psychological Measurement* 8: 313-18.
Edwards, A. (1957) *Techniques of Attitude Scale Construction*. New York: Appleton-Century-Crofts.
Edwards, G., Chandler, J., and Hensmen, C. (1972a) Drinking in a London Suburb (1). *Quarterly Journal of Studies on Alcohol*, Supplement No.6: 69-93.
Edwards, G., Chandler, J., Hensman, C., and Peto, S. (1972b) Drinking in a London Suburb. (2) Correlates of Trouble with Drinking among Men. *Quarterly Journal of Studies on Alcohol*, Supplement No.6: 94-119.
Edwards, G., Hensman, C., and Peto, S. (1972c) Drinking in a London Suburb. (3) Comparisons of Drinking Troubles among Men and Women. *Quarterly Journal of Studies on Alcohol*, Supplement No.6: 120-28.
Edwards, J. (1971) *Social Patterns in Birmingham 1966-1970*. Birmingham: University of Birmingham Centre for Urban and Regional Studies.
Eisenstadt, S. (1956) *From Generation to Generation*. London: Routledge & Kegan Paul.
Eisenstadt, S. (1963) Archetypal Patterns of Youth. In E. Erikson (ed.) *Youth: Change and Challenge*. New York: Basic Books.
Ekholm, A. (1968) A Study of the Drinking Rhythm of Finnish Males, 28th International Congress on Alcohol and Alcoholism, Washington D.C.
Elder, G. (1972) The Social Context of Youth Groups. *International Social Science Journal* XXIV: 271-89.
Elkin, F. and Westley, W. (1955) The Myth of Adolescent Culture. *American Sociological Review* 20: 680-84.
Engels, F. (1958) *Condition of the Working Class in England* (1844). London: Basil Blackwell.
Epperson, D. (1964) A Reassessment of Indices of Parental Influence in the Adolescent Society. *American Sociological Review* 29: 93-96.
Ewing, J. (1970) Notes on Quantity Frequency Studies on Alcohol Intake. *The Drinking and Drug Practices Surveyor* I: 8-11.
Ewing, J. (1972) Measuring Alcohol Consumption by the Alcohol Quotient. Paper delivered at the 30th International Congress on Alcoholism and Drug Dependence, Amsterdam.

Falding, H. (1964) The Source and Burden of Civilisation: Illustrated in the Use of Alcohol. *Quarterly Journal of Studies on Alcohol* 25: 714-24.
Ferguson, S. (1975) *Drink*. London: Batsford.
Feuer, L. (1969) *The Conflict of Generations*. London: Heinemann Educational.
Field, P. (1962) A New Cross-Cultural Study of Drunkenness. In D. Pittman and C. Snyder (eds) *Society, Culture and Drinking Patterns*. New York: John Wiley & Sons.
Fischer, C. (1976) Alienation: Trying to Bridge the Chasm. *British Journal of Sociology* XXVII: 35-49.
Fitzgerald, G. (1968) Economic Comment. *Irish Times* (April 3rd).

Fitzpatrick, J. (1970a) Drinking and Young People: A Sociological Study. Unpublished M.Soc.Sc. thesis, National University of Ireland.

Fitzpatrick, J. (1970b) Drinking and Young People: A Sociological Study. Report to the Irish National Council on Alcoholism, Dublin.

Fitzpatrick, J. (1971a) Drinking and Young People. In B. McCarthy (ed.) *Alcoholism*. Dublin: Impact.

Fitzpatrick, J. (1971b) Considerations in Relation to Choice of Area. Report to Anglo-Irish Research Committee (April).

Fitzpatrick, J. (1971c) Drinking and Young People. *Journal on Alcoholism* 6: 90-94.

Fitzpatrick, J. (1972) Drinking among Young People in Ireland. *Social Studies, Irish Journal of Sociology* I: 51-60.

French, R. (1891) *Nineteen Centuries of Drink in England* (2nd ed.), London.

Fryer, P. (1963) *Mrs. Grundy Studies in English Prudery*. London: Corgi Books.

George, M. (1966) *London Life in the 18th Century*. Harmondsworth Middlesex: Penguin.

Ghaem-Maghami, F. (1973) Alienation and Political Knowledge: Some Research Findings. *Human Relations* 26: 497-516.

Gibbens, T. and Ahrenfeldt, A. (eds) (1966) *Cultural Factors in Delinquency*. London: Tavistock.

Gillis, J. (1974) Youth in History: Progress and Prospects. *Journal of Social History* 7: 201-7.

Glad, D. (1947-48) Attitudes and Experience of American Jewish and American-Irish Male Youth as Related to Differences of Adult Rates of Inebriety. *Quarterly Journal of Studies on Alcohol* 8: 406-72.

Glatt, M. and Hills, D. (1968) Alcohol Abuse and Alcoholism in the Young. *British Journal of Addiction* 63: 183-91.

Glazer, N. and Moynihan, D. (1963) *Beyond the Melting Pot*. Cambridge, Mass.: MIT Press and Harvard University Press.

Globetti, G. (1964) A Survey of Teenage Drinking in Two Mississippi Communities. Preliminary Report No.3, Social Science Research Center, Mississippi State University.

Globetti, G. (1967) A Comparative Study of White and Negro Teenage Drinking in Two Mississippi Communities. *Phylon* 28: 131-38.

Globetti, G. (1969) The Use of Beverage Alcohol by Youth in an Abstinence Setting. *The Journal of School Health* 39: 179-83.

Globetti, G. (1970) The Drinking Patterns of Negro and White High School Students in Two Mississippi Communities. *The Journal of Negro Education* (Winter): 60-69.

Globetti, G. and McReynolds, M. (1964) A Comparative Study of the White and and Negro High School Students' Use of Alcohol in Two Mississippi Communities. Preliminary Report No.4, Social Science Research Center, Mississippi State University.

Globetti, G. and Windlaws, G. (1967) The Social Adjustment of High School Students and the Use of Beverage Alcohol. *Sociology and Social Research* 51: 148-57.

Glock, C. and Stark, R. (1965) *Religion and Society in Tension*. Chicago: Rand McNally.

Glover, J. (1960) *The Story of Scotland*. London: Faber.

Goodenough, W. (1944) A Technique for Scale Analysis. *Educational Psychological Measurements:* 179-90.

Goodman, L. (1954) Kolmogorov-Smirnov Tests for Psychological Research. *Psychological Bulletin* 51: 160-68.

Goodman, L. (1970) The Multivariate Analysis of Qualitative Data: Interactions among Multiple Classifications. *Journal of the American Statistical Association* 65: 226-56.

Goodman, L. (1972a) A Modified Multiple Regression Approach to the Analysis of Dichotomous Variables. *American Sociological Review* 37: 28-46.

Goodman, L. (1972b) A General Model for the Analysis of Surveys. *American Journal of Sociology* 77: 1035-86.

Goodman, L. (1973) Causal Analysis of Data from Panel Studies and Other Kinds of Surveys. *American Journal of Sociology* 78: 1135-91.

Goudy, W. (1973) The Magical Mystery Tour: An Encounter with the Generation Gap. *Youth and Society* 5: 212-24.

Gottlieb, D. (ed.) (1972) *Youth in Contemporary Society*. New York: Sage Publications.

Graham, G. and Pride, R. (1972) Styles of Political Participation, Conversion and Political Support among Adults and Students in a Metropolitan Community. *Youth and Society* 3: 277-310.

Greeley, A. (1971) The Strange Case of the American Irish. *Social Studies, Irish Journal of Sociology* 1: 38-50.

Greeley, A. (1973) *The Persistence of Religion* London: SCM Press.

Gusfield, J. (1969) *Symbolic Crusade*. Urbana: University of Illinois Press.

Habitual Drunken Offenders: Report of the Working Party (1971). London: HMSO.

Hackwood, F. (1909) *Inns, Ale, and Drinking Customs of England*, London.

Hajda, J. (1961) Alienation and Integration of Student Intellectuals. *American Sociological Review* 34: 758:79.

Haller, A., and Butterworth, C. (1960) Peer Influences on Levels of Occupational and Educational Aspiration. *Social Forces* 38: 289-95.

Hammond, J. and Hammond, B. (1964) *The Age of the Chartists: 1832-1854*. New York: The Shoe String Press.

Hannan, D. and Katsiaonni, L. (1977) *Traditional Families?* Dublin: Economic and Social Research Institute.

Harrison, B. (1967) Drink and Sobriety in England, 1815-1872: A Critical Bibliography. *International Review of Social History*, Part 2: 204-76.

Harrison, B. (1968) Two Roads to Social Reform: Francis Place and the Drunken Committee of 1834. *Historical Journal* XI: 272-300.

Harrison, B. (1969a) The Power of Drink. *The Listener* (13th February): 204-6.

Harrison, B. (1969b) A World of Which We Had No Conception: Liberalism and The English Temperance Press 1830-1872. *Victorian Studies* (December): 125-56.

Harrison, B. (1971) *Drink and the Victorians*. London: Faber.

Harrison, B. (1973) Drunkards and Reformers: Early-Victorian Temperance Tracts. *History To-day* 13: 178-86.

Harrison, J. (1971) *The Early Victorians*. New York: Praeger.

Hartley, D. (1964) *Water in England*. London: Macdonald.

Hawker, A. (1977) Drinking Patterns of Young People. Proceedings of the Third

Institute on *Alcoholism and Drug Addiction*, Liverpool, April, 1976, New York: Plenum.

Hayler, M. (1953) *The Vision of a Century 1853-1953*. London: United Kingdom Alliance.

Heath, D. (1975) A Critical Review of Ethnographic Studies of Alcohol Use. In R. Gibbons, Y. Israel, H. Kalant, R. Popham, W. Schmidt, and R. Smart (eds) *Research Advances in Alcohol and Drug Problems* (Vol. 2). London: Wiley.

Hess, R. and Torney, J. (1967) *The Development of Political Attitudes in Children*. Chicago: Irvington.

Heyneman, S. (1976) Continuing Issues in Adolescence: a Summary of Current Transition to Adulthood Debates. *Journal of Youth and Adolescence* 5: 309-24.

Hickey, J. (1960) The Irish Rural Immigrant and British Urban Society. *Newman Demographic Survey*.

Hiller, H. (1975) A Reconceptualisation of the Dynamics of Social Movement Development. *Pacific Sociological Review* 18: 342-60.

Hilton, G. (1960) *The Truck System*, Cambridge: W. Heffer & Sons.

Hiro, D. (1973) *Black British, White British*. Harmondsworth, Middlesex: Penguin.

Holmes, W. (1976) The Theory of Alienation as a Sociological Explanation: Its Advantages and Limitations. *Sociology* 10: 207-24.

Houghton, W. (1975) *The Victorian Frame of Mind 1830-1870*. London: Yale University Press.

Horton, J. and Thompson, W. (1962) Powerlessness and Political Negativism: a Study of Defeated Local Referendums. *American Journal of Sociology* 67: 485-93.

Hoy, W. (1972) Dimensions of Student Alienation and Characteristics of Public High Schools. *Interchange* 3: 38-52.

Hyndman, F. (1911) *Records of an Adventurous Life*, London.

Jackson, J. (1963) *The Irish in Britain*. London: Routledge & Kegan Paul.

Jackson, J. (1967) Report on the Skibbereen Social Survey, Human Sciences Committee, Dublin.

Jackson, J. and Connor, R. (1953) The Skid Row Alcoholic. *Quarterly Journal of Studies on Alcohol* 14. 199-320.

Jahoda, G. (1972) *Children and Alcohol*. London: HMSO.

Jennings, K. and Niemi, R. (1968) Patterns of Political Learning. *Harvard Educational Review* 36: 443-69.

Jennings, K. and Niemi, R. (1968) The Transmission of Political Values from Parent to Child. *American Political Science Review* 62: 169-84.

Jennings, K. and Niemi, R. (1974) *The Political Character of Adolescence*. Princeton: Princeton University Press.

Jensen, G. (1972) Parents, Peers and Delinquent Action: a Test of the Differential Association Perspective. *American Journal of Sociology* 78: 562-75.

Jessor, R., Carmen, R., and Grossman, P. (1968) Expectation of Need Satisfaction and Drinking Patterns of College Students. *Quarterly Journal of Studies on Alcohol* 29: 101-16.

Jessor, R., Graves, T., Hanson, R., and Jessor, S. (1969) *Society, Personality and Deviant Behaviour: A Study of a Tri-Ethnic Community*. New York: Holt, Rinehart & Winston.

Jessor, R., Young, H., Young, T., and Tesi, G. (1970) Perceived Opportunity, Alienation and Drinking Behaviour among Italian and American Youth. *Journal of Personality and Social Psychology*, 15: 215-22.

Jessor, R., Collins, M., and Jessor, S. (1972) On Becoming a Drinker: Social Psychological Aspects of an Adolescent Transition. *Annals of the New York Academy of Sciences* 197: 199-213.

Jessor, R. and Jessor, S. (1975) Adolescent Development and the Onset of Drinking. *Journal of Studies on Alcohol* 36: 27-51.

Johnston, L. (1973) *Drugs and American Youth*. Ann Arbor, Michigan: University of Michigan Social Research.

Josephson, E. and Josephson, M. (1962) *Man Alone: Alienation in Modern Society*. New York: Dell.

Kalish, R. and Johnson, A. (1972) Value Similarities and Differences in Three Generations of Women. *Journal of Marriage and the Family* 34: 49-54.

Kandel, D. and Lesser, G. (1972) *Youth in Two Worlds*. San Francisco: Jossey-Bass.

Kasschen, P., Ransford, E., and Bengston, V. (1974) Generational Consciousness and Youth Movement Participation: Contrasts in Blue Collar and White Collar Youth. *Journal of Social Issues* 30: 69-94.

Kearney, N., Lawler, M., and Walsh, D. (1969) Alcoholic Drinking in a Dublin Corporation Housing Estate. *Journal of the Irish Medical Association* 62: 1-3.

Keniston, K. (1968) *Young Radicals*. New York: Harcourt Brace Jovanovich.

Kerr, N. (1894) *Inebriety or Narcomania*, London.

Kessel, N. and Walton, H. (1965) *Alcoholism*. Harmondsworth, Middlesex: Penguin.

Killian, L. and Grigg, G. (1962) Urbanism, Race, and Anomia. *American Journal of Sociology* 67: 661-65.

Kinsey, B. and Phillips, L. (1968) Evaluation of Anomy as a Predisposing or Developmental Factor in Alcohol Addiction. *Quarterly Journal of Studies on Alcohol* 29: 892-98.

Kirsh, A., Newcomb, C., and Cisin, I. (1965) An Experimental Study of Sensitivity Survey Techniques in Measuring Drinking Practices. Social Research Group, George Washington University, Report No. 1, Washington D.C.

Knupfer, G. (1963) Factors Related to Amount of Drinking in an Urban Community. California Drinking Practices Study Report No.6 Berkley: 52-57.

Knupfer, G. (1966) Some Methodological Problems in the Epidemiology of Alcoholic Beverage Usage: Definition of Amount of Intake. *American Journal of Public Health* 56: 237-42.

Knupfer, G. (1967) Epidemiologic Studies and Control Programs in Alcoholism. (V) The Epidemiology of Problem Drinking. *American Journal of Public Health* 57: 973-86.

Knupfer, G. and Lurie, E. (1961) California Drinking Practices Study. Report No.3 (revised), Mental Research Institute, California.

Knupfer, G. and Room, R. (1967) Drinking Patterns and Attitudes of Irish, Jewish and White Protestant America. *Quarterly Journal of Studies on Alcohol* 28: 676-99.

Lambert, J. (1970) *Crime, Police and Race Relations: A Study in Birmingham.* London: Oxford University Press.

Lane, R. (1969) *Political Thinking and Consciousness.* Chicago: Markham.

Larkin, E. (1968) *James Larkin: Irish Labour Leader 1876-1947* (2nd edn). London: Routledge & Kegan Paul.

Larson, L. (1972) The Relative Influence of Parent Adolescent Affect in Predicting the Saliance Hierarchy among Youth. *Pacific Sociological Review* 15: 83-102.

Lauer, R. (1973) The Generation Gap as Sociometric Choice. *Youth and Society* 2: 227-41.

Leake, C. and Silverman, M. (1966) *Alcoholic Beverages in Clinical Medicine,* Chicago.

Lecky, W. (1896) *Democracy and Liberty* (Vol.II), London.

Ledermann, S. (1956) *Alcool, Alcoolisme, Alcoolisation: donnés scientifiques de caractère physiologique économique et social* (2 Vols), Paris.

Le Fanu, W. (1893) *Seventy Years of Irish Life, Anecdotes and Reminiscences,* New York.

Lemert, E. (1954) Alcohol and the Northwest Coast Indians. *Culture and Society* 2: 303-406.

Lemert, E. (1962) Alcohol, Values and Social Control. In D. Pittman and C. Snyder (eds) *Society, Culture and Drinking Patterns.* New York: John Wiley & Sons.

Lemert, E. (1964) Forms and Pathology of Drinking in Three Polynesian Societies. *American Anthropology* 66: 361-74.

Lenski, G. (1961) *The Religious Factor.* New York: Doubleday.

Lerner, R. and Knapp, J. (1975) Actual and Perceived Intrafamilial Attitudes of Late Adolescents and their Parents. *Journal of Youth and Adolescence* 14: 17-36.

Levy, H. (1951) *Drink: An Economic and Social History.* London: Routledge & Kegan Paul.

Lolli, G., Serianni, E., Golder, G., and Luzzatto-Fegiz, P. (1957) *Alcohol in Italian Culture.* Glencoe, Illinois: Free Press. *Alcohol* 13: 27-48.

Lolli, G., Serianni, E., Golder, G. and Luzzatto-Fegiz, P. (1957) *Alcohol in Italian Culture,* Glencoe, Illinois: Free Press.

Longmate, N. (1968) *The Waterdrinkers.* London: Hamish Hamilton.

Lowenthal, M. (1964) Social Isolation and Mental Illness in Old Age. *American Sociological Review* 29: 54-70.

Lynn, R. and Hampson S. (1970) Alcoholism and Alcohol Consumption in Ireland. *Journal of the Irish Medical Association* 63: 39-42.

MacAndrew, C. and Edgerton, R. (1970) *Drunken Comportment: a Social Explanation.* London: Nelson.

McCarron, S. (1951) *A Short Temperance Catechism.* Dublin: Pioneer Association.

McCarthy, M. (1911) *Irish Land and Irish Liberty.* London: Robert Scott.

McCarthy, R. (ed.) (1964) *Alcohol Education for Classroom and Community.* London: McGraw-Hill.

McClintock, F. and Avison, H. (1968) *Crime in England and Wales.* London: Heinemann Educational.

McClintock, F. and Gibson, E. (1967) *Robbery in London*. London: Macmillan.

McCloskey, M. and Schaar, J. (1965) Psychological Dimensions of Anomy. *American Sociological Review* 30: 14-40.

McCluggage, M. (1956) *Attitude towards the Use of Alcoholic Beverages; A Survey Among High School Students in the Wichita Metropolitan Area and in the Non-Metropolitan Countries of Eastern Kansas*. New York: Mrs J.S. Sheppard Foundation.

McCord, W. and McCord, J. (1960) *Origins of Alcoholism*. London: Tavistock.

McDill, E. and Coleman, J. (1965) Family and Peer Influences in College Plans of High School Students. *Sociology of Education* 38: 112-26.

McGuire, E. (1973) *Irish Whiskey: a History of Distilling in Ireland*. Dublin: Gill & Macmillan.

McKenna, L. (1924) *Life and Work of Rev. James Aloysius Cullen S.J.* London: Longman.

McLysaght, E. (1939) *Irish Life in the Seventeenth Century After Cromwell*. London: Longman.

McManus, M. (1939) *Irish Cavalcade 1550-1850*. London: Macmillan.

McNabb, P. (1967) Social structure. Part IV in J. Newman (ed.) *The Limerick Rural Survey, 1958-1964*. Tipperary: Muintior Na Tire.

McPherson, K. and Gaitskell, J. (1967) *Immigrants and Employment: Two Case Studies in East London and in Croydon*. London: Race Relations Institute.

Maddox, G. (1964a) High School Student Drinking Behaviour: Incidental Information from Two National Surveys. *Quarterly Journal of Studies on Alcohol* 25: 339-47.

Maddox, G. (1964b) Adolescence and Alcohol. In R. McCarthy (ed.) *Alcohol Education for Classroom and Community*. London: McGraw-Hill.

Maddox, G. (1966) Teenagers and Alcohol: Recent Research. *Annals of the New York Academy of Sciences* 133: 856-65.

Maddox, G. (1968) Role-Making: Negotiations in Emergent Drinking Careers. *Social Science Quarterly* 49: 331-49.

Maddox, G. (1970) Drinking Prior to College. In G. Maddox (ed.) *The Domesticated Drug: Drinking Among Collegians*. New Haven, Conn.: College and University Press.

Maddox, G. and Borinski, E. (1964) Drinking Behavior of Negro Collegians: A Study of Selected Men. *Quarterly Journal of Studies on Alcohol* 25: 651-68.

Maddox, G. and McCall, B. (1964) *Drinking Among Teenagers*. New Hayen, Conn.: Rutgers Center for Alcohol Studies.

Maddox, G. and Williams, J. (1968) Drinking Behavior of Negro Collegians. *Quarterly Journal of Studies on Alcohol* 29: 117-29.

Maguire, J. (1865) *Father Mathew: A Biography*, London.

Makela, K. (1971) Concentration of Alcohol Consumption. *Scandinavian Studies in Criminology* 3: 77-88.

Malcolmson, R. (1973) *Popular Recreations in English Society 1700-1850*. Cambridge: Cambridge University Press.

Mandell, W. (1962) *Youthful Drinking*. New York State: Wakoff Research Centre.

Mangin, W. (1957) Drinking among Andean Indians. *Quarterly Journal of Studies on Alcohol* 18: 55-66.

Mannheim, K. (1952) *Essays on the Sociology of Knowledge*. London: Routledge & Kegan Paul.

Manning, P. and Truzzi, M. (eds) (1972) *Youth and Sociology*. London: Prentice-Hall.

Markham, S. (1971) What about the Irish? Runnymede Trust Publications Information Paper, B5 (February).

Mathais, P. (1958) The Brewing Industry, Temperance and Politics. *Historical Journal* I: 97-114.

Mathew, F. (1890) *Father Mathew: His Life and Times*, London.

Matza, D. (1961) Juvenile Delinquency and Subterranean Values. *American Sociological Review* 28: 102-18.

Matza, D. (1964) *Delinquency and Drift*. New York: John Wiley & Sons.

Matza, D. (1969) *Becoming Deviant*. New Jersey: Prentice-Hall.

Maxwell, C. (1956) *Dublin under the Georges 1714-1830*. London: Faber.

Maxwell, C. (1949) *Country and Town in Ireland Under the Georges*. Dundalk: W. Tempest.

Maxwell, M. (1958) A Quantity-Frequency Analysis of Drinking Behaviour in the State of Washington. *Northwest Science* 32: 57-67.

Mayhew, H. (1968) *London Labour and the London Poor 1812-1887* (Vols I-IV). London: Frank Cass.

Mead, M. (1947) Adolescence in Primitive and Modern Society. In E. MacCoby *et al. Readings in Social Psychology*. New York: Society for the Psychological Study of Social Issues.

Mead, M. (1970) *Culture and Commitment: A Study of the Generation Gap*. New York: Doubleday.

Medical Council on Alcoholism (1970) *Report on Alcoholism*, London.

Meier, D. and Bell, W. (1959) Anomia and Differential Access to the Achievement of Life Goals. *American Sociological Review* 24: 189-202.

Merton, R. (1963) *Social Theory and Social Structure*. New York: Free Press of Glencoe.

Middleton, R. (1963) Alienation, Race and Education. *American Sociological Review* 28: 973-77.

Miller, G. (1967) Professionals in Bureaucracy: Alienation among Industrial Scientists and Engineers. *American Sociological Review* 32: 755-67.

Miller, J. and Wahl, J. (1956) *Attitudes of High School Students toward Alcoholic Beverages*. New York: Mrs J.S. Sheppard Foundation.

Mills, C. (1940) Situated Action and Vocabularies of Motives. *American Sociological Review* 5: 704-993.

Mills, C. (1951) *White Collar: The American Middle Classes*. New York: Oxford University Press.

Mizruchi, E. (1960) Social Structure and Anomia in a Small City. *American Sociological Review* 25: 645-54.

Moeller, G. and Charters, W. (1966) Relation of Bureaucratisation to Sense of Power among Teachers. *Administrative Science Quarterly* 10: 444-65.

Monckton, H. (1969) *A History of the English Public House*. London: Bodley Head.

Mooney, T. (1850) *Nine Years in America: A Series of Letters to His Cousin, Patrick Mooney, A Farmer in Ireland*, Dublin.

Moos, R., Moos, B., and Kulik, J. (1976) College Student Abstainers, Moderate Drinkers, and Heavy Drinkers: A Comparative Analysis. *Journal of Youth and Adolescence* 5: 309-24.

Morton, R. (1973) *Come Day, Go Day, God Send Sunday*. London: Routledge & Kegan Paul.

Morris, T. (1964) Review of: 'Crimes of Violence'. IRR Newsletter (February).

Morrison, S. (1969) Alcoholism in Scotland. *Health Bulletin* 22: 1-8.

Moser, C. and Kalton, G. (1971) *Survey Methods in Social Investigation.*
London: Heinemann Educational.

Moser, G. (1974) *Problems and Programmes Related to Alcohol and Drug
Dependence in 33 Countries.* Geneva : WHO.

Mulford, H. (1964) Drinking and Deviant Drinking, USA 1963. *Quarterly
Journal of Studies on Alcohol* 25: 634-50.

Mulford, H. (1966) Identifying Problem Drinkers in a Household Survey. A
Description of Field Procedures and Analytical Procedures to Measure the
Prevalence of Alcoholism. Public Health Service Publication No.1000,
Service 2, Washington D.C.

Mulford, H. and Miller, D. (1959) Drinking in Iowa I. Sociocultural Distribution
of Drinkers with a Methodological Model for Sampling Evaluation and Inter-
pretations of Findings. *Quarterly Journal of Studies on Alcohol* 20: 704-26.

Mulford, H. and Miller D. (1960) Drinking in Iowa II. The Extent of Drinking
and Selected Sociocultural Categories. *Quarterly Journal of Studies on
Alcohol* 21: 26-39.

Mulford, H. and Miller, D. (1963) The Prevalence and Extent of Drinking in
Iowa 1961: a Replication and an Evaluation of Methods. *Quarterly Journal
of Studies on Alcohol* 24: 36-53.

Murray, J. (1971) The Generation Gap. *Journal of Genetic Psychology* 114:
71-80.

Neter, K. and Waksberg, C. (1965) Response Errors in Collection of
Expenditures Data of Household Interviews. US Bureau of the Census-
Technical Paper II.

Nettler, G. (1957) A Measure of Alienation. *American Sociological Review* 22:
670-77.

Nie, H., Bent, D., and Hull, C. (1970) *Statistical Package for the Social Sciences.*
London: McGraw-Hill.

Offences of Drunkenness 1973 (1974) London: HMSO.

Offences of Drunkenness 1975 (1976) London: HMSO.

Office of Health Economics (1970) Alcohol Abuse. London: OHE Publications
34.

O'Connor, J. (1973a) Measurement of Levels of Drinking. *Economic and Social
Review* 4: 245-65.

O'Connor, J. (1973b) Methodology of a Cross Cultural Study: Social Studies.
Irish Journal of Sociology 2: 147-57.

O'Connor, J. (1974) The Temperance Movement in Ireland and England: A
Sociological Study of a Norm-Oriented Movement Influencing Social
Change. Inaugural Meeting of Irish Sociological Association (April 19th).

O'Connor, J. (1975) Cultural Influences and Drinking Behaviour. Drinking in
Ireland and England: A Tri-Ethnic Study of Drinking among Young People
and Their Parents. *Journal of Alcoholism* 10: 94-121.

O'Connor, J. (1976a) Social and Cultural Factors Influencing Behaviour Among
Young People: a Cross National Study of the Drinking Behaviour and
Attitudes Towards Drinking of Young People and Their Parents (Vols I,
II). Ph.d. thesis, National University of Ireland, (February).

O'Connor, J. (1976b) Social and Cultural Factors Influencing Behaviour Among
Young People: A Cross National Study of the Drinking Behaviour and
Attitudes Towards Drinking of Young People and Their Parents (Vols I, II).
Report to the British Medical Council on Alcoholism, (Spring).

O'Connor, J. (1976c) Social and Cultural Factors Influencing Drinking Behaviour. In D.L. Davies (ed.) *Aspects of Alcoholism*. London: Alcohol Education Centre.

O'Connor, J. (1976d) Parental Influences: A Tri-Ethnic Study of the Transmission of Drinking Behaviour from Parent to Child — Preliminary Communication. *Journal of the Irish Medical Association* 69: 152-58.

O'Connor, J. (1977) Normal and Problem Drinking Among Children: A Review. *Journal of Child Psychology and Psychiatry* 18: 279-84.

O'Connor, K. (1972) *The Irish in Britain*. London: Sidgwick and Jackson.

O'Hanlon, T. (1976) *The Irish: Portrait of a People*. London: André Deutsch.

O'Hare, A. and Walsh, D. (1972) First Admissions to Irish Psychiatric Hospitals 1965-1969. *Journal of the Irish Medical Association* 65: 189-92.

Oppenhcim, A. (1966) *Questionnaire Design and Attitude Measurement*. London: Heinemann.

Oppenheimer, M. (1968) The Student Movement as a Response to Alienation. *Journal of Human Relations* 16: 1-16.

Park, P. (1962) Problem Drinking and Role Deviation: a Study of Incipient Alcoholism. In D. Pittman and C. Snyder (eds) *Society, Culture and Drinking Behaviour*. New York: John Wiley & Sons.

Park, P. (1967) Dimensions of Drinking Among Male College Students. *Social Problems* 14: 473-82.

Parsons, T. (1954) Age and Sex in the Social Structure in the United States. In *Essays in Sociological Theory*, Glencoe, Illinois: Free Press.

Patmore, J. and Hodgkiss, A. (1970) *Merseyside in Maps*. London: Longman.

Patterson, S. (1969) *Immigration and Race Relations in Britain 1960-1967*. London: Oxford University Press.

Perceval, R. (1955) Alcohol and Alcoholism in the Republic of Ireland. *International Journal on Alcohol and Alcoholism*: 146-55.

Perceval, R. (1969) Alcoholism in Ireland. *Journal of Alcoholism* 4: 251-57.

Pernancn, K. (1974) Validity of Survey Data on Alcohol Use. In R. Gibbons, Y. Israel, H. Kalant, R. Popham, W. Schmidt, and R. Smart (eds) *Research Advances in Alcohol and Drug Problems* (Vol. I), London.

Pittman, D. (ed.) (1967) *Alcoholism*: New York: Harper & Row.

Pittman, D. and Gordon, C. (1958) *Revolving Door: A Study Of The Chronic Police Case: Inebriate*. Glencoe, Illinois: Free Press.

Pittman, D. and Snyder, C. (eds) (1962) *Society, Culture, and Drinking Patterns*. New York: John Wiley & Sons.

Plant, M. (1975) *Drugtakers in an English Town*. London: Tavistock.

Plant, M. (1977) Occupational Factors in Alcoholism. In Marcus Grant and W.H. Kenyon (eds) *Alcoholism and Industry*. Alcohol Education Centre; Merseyside, Lancashire and Cheshire Council on Alcoholism.

Plunkett, H. (1904) *Ireland in the New Century*. London: John Murray.

Popham, R. (1970) Validity in Survey Questions on Drinking. *The Drinking and Drug Practices Surveyor* 1: 6-7.

Preston, J. (1969) Religiosity and Adolescent Drinking Behaviour. *Sociological Quarterly* 10: 372-83.

Report of the Departmental Committee on Liquor Licensing (1972). London: HMSO.

Rex, J. and Moore, R. (1967) *Race, Community and Conflict*. London: Oxford University Press.

Riley, J. and Marden, C. (1947) The Social Pattern of Alcoholic Drinking. *Quarterly Journal of Studies on Alcohol* 8: 265:73.

Roberts, B. and Myers, J. (1954) Religion, National Origin, Immigration. *American Journal of Psychiatry* 110: 769-74.

Roberts, B. and Myers, J. (1968) Religion, National Origin, Immigration and Mental Illness. In S. Weinberg, (ed.) *Sociology of Mental Disorders*. London: Staples Press.

Robins, L., Murphy, G., and Breckenridge, M. (1968) Drinking Behavior of Young Urban Negro Men. *Quarterly Journal of Studies on Alcohol* 29: 657-84.

Robinson, D. (1976) *From Drinking to Alcoholism: A Sociological Commentary*. London: John Wiley & Sons.

Roebuck, J. and Kessler, R. (1972) *The Etiology of Alcoholism: Constitutional Psychological and Sociological Approaches*. Springfield, Illinois: Thomas.

Rogers, P. (1943) *Father Theobald Mathew, Apostle of Temperance*. Dublin: Browne and Nolan.

Rolleston, J. (1933) Alcoholism in Mediaeval England. *The British Journal of Inebriety* XXXI: 34-49.

Room, R. (1976) Ambivalence as a Sociological Explanation. The Case of Cultural Explanations of Alcohol Problems. *American Sociological Review* 41: 1047-64.

Rose, E. (1969) *Colour and Citizenship: a Report on British Race Relations*. London: Oxford University Press.

Rosen, B. (1955) Conflicting Group Membership: A Study of Parent-Peer Group Cross Pressures. *American Sociological Review* 20: 155-61.

Rosow, I. (1967) *Social Integration of the Aged*. New York: Free Press.

Roszak, T. (1969) *The Making of a Counter Culture*. New York: Doubleday.

Rotter, J. (1966) Generalised Expectations for Internal Versus External Control of Reinforcements. *Psychological Monographs* 80: 1-28.

Reich, C. (1972) *The Greening of America*. Harmondsworth, Middlesex: Penguin.

Rowntree, B. (1902) *Poverty: A Study of Town Life*. London: Macmillan.

Rowntree, B. and Lavers, B. (1951) *English Life and Leisure*. London: Longman.

Rowntree, J. and Sherwell, A. (1901) *The Temperance Problem and Social Reform,* London: Hodder & Stoughton.

Rubington, E. (1958) The Chronic Drunkenness Offender. *Annals of the American Academy of Political and Social Sciences* 315: 65-72.

Russell, M. (1964) The Irish Delinquent in England. *Studies* (June): 136-48.

Sadoun, R., Lolli, G., and Silverman, M. (1965) *Drinking in French Culture*. New Brunswick: Rutgers Center of Alcohol Studies.

Sariola, S. (1956) *Drinking Patterns in Finnish Lapland*. Helsinki: Finnish Foundation for Alcohol Studies.

Seidler, M. and Ravitz, M. (1955) A Jewish Peer Group. *American Journal of Sociology* 61: 11-15.

Schaefer, E. (1961) Converging Conceptual Models for Maternal Behaviour and for Child Behaviour. In J. Glidewell (ed.) Parental Attitudes and Child Behaviour. Proceedings of the Second Annual Conference on Community Mental Health Research, Social Science Institute, Washington, D.C.

Scott, G. (1967) *The R.C's*. London: Hutchinson.
Seeman, M. (1959) On the Meaning of Alienation. *American Sociological Review* 24: 783-91.
Select Committee on Drunkenness of the House of Commons (1834) *Evidence on Drunkenness presented to the House of Commons*, London.
Shaw, S. (1976) The Size of the Problem. In D.L. Davies (ed.) *Aspects of Alcoholism*. London: Alcohol Education Centre.
Sherif, M. and Sherif, W. (1964) *Reference Groups Exploration into Conformity and Deviation in Adolescents*. New York: Harper & Row.
Siegel, S. (1956) *Non-Parametric Statistics for the Behavioural Sciences*. New York: McGraw-Hill.
Simmons, L. (1971) The Real Generation Gap: a Speculation on the Meaning and Implications of the Generation Gap. *Youth and Society*: 119-35.
Simpson, R. (1962) Parental Influence, Anticipatory Socialisation and Social Mobility. *American Sociological Review* 27: 517-21.
Singer, K. (1974) The Choice of Intoxicant Among the Chinese. *British Journal of Addiction* 69: 257-68.
Skolnick, J. (1958) Religious Affiliation and Drinking Behaviour. *Quarterly Journal of Studies on Alcohol*: 452-70.
Slater, A. (1952) A Study of the Use of Alcoholic Beverages among High School Students in Utah. *Quarterly Journal of Studies on Alcohol* 13: 78-86.
Smart, R. (1976) *The New Drinkers*. Toronto: Addition Research Foundation.
Smart, R. (1970) *The Extent of Drug Use in Metropolitan Toronto Schools: A Study of Changes from 1968-1970*. Toronto: Addiction Research Foundation.
Smelser, N. (1970) *Theory of Collective Behaviour*. London: Routledge & Kegan Paul.
Smiles, S. (1875) *Thrift*, London.
Smith, T. (1976) Push versus Pull: Intra-Family Versus Peer Group Variables as Possible Determinants of Adolescent Orientations towards Parents. *Youth and Society* 8: 5.
Smollett, T. (1848) *History of England* (Vol. II), London.
Snyder, C. (1958) *Alcoholism and the Jews*, New Jersey.
Snyder, C. (1962) The In-Group Out-Group Factor. In D. Pittman and C. Snyder (eds) *Society, Culture and Drinking Patterns*. New York: John Wiley & Sons.
Snyder, C. (1964) Inebriety, Alcoholism, and Anomie. In M. Clinard, (ed.) *Anomie and Deviant Behaviour*. New York: Free Press.
Sower, C. (1959) Teenage Drinking as Group Behaviour: Implications for Research. *Quarterly Journal of Studies on Alcohol* 20: 655-68.
Spindler, G. (1963) *Education and Culture: Anthropological Approaches*. New York: Holt, Rinehart & Winston.
Srole, L. (1956) Social Integration and Certain Corollaries: An Exploratory Study. *American Sociological Review* 21: 709-16.
Stacey, B. and Davies, J. (1970) Drinking Behaviour in Childhood and Adolescence: An Evaluative Review. *British Journal of Addiction* 65: 203-12.
Stanton, H. (1849) *Sketches of Reforms and Reformers of Great Britain and Ireland*, New York.
Stivers, R. (1971) The Bachelor Group: Ethnic and Irish Drinking. Unpublished Ph.d. thesis, Southern Illinois University.

Straus, M. (1964) Power and Support Structure of the Family in Relation to Socialisation. *Journal of Marriage and the Family* 26: 318-26.

Straus, R. (1946) Alcohol and the Homeless Man. *Quarterly Journal of Studies on Alcohol* 7: 360-404.

Straus, R. and Bacon, S. (1953) *Drinking in College*. New Haven, Conn.: Yale University Press.

Stuening, E. and Richardson, A. (1965) A Factor Analytic Exploration of Anomia, Alienation and Authoritarianism Domain. *American Sociological Review* 30: 768-76.

Sutherland, E. and Cressey, D. (1970) *Criminology*. New York: Lippincott.

Swiecicki, A. (1970) Polish Studies. *The Drinking and Drug Practices Survey* 1: 7

Tackerary, W. (1843) *The Irish Sketch Book*, London.

Tayler, R. (1973) The Present Need of the Temperance Movement. *Alliance News* CXI: 15

Thale, M. (ed.) (1972) *The Autobiography of Francis Place 1771-1854*. London: Cambridge University Press.

Thomas, E. (1974) Generational Discontinuity in Beliefs: An Exploration of the Generation Gap. *Journal of Social Issues 30: 1-22.*

Thompson, E. (1963) *The Making of the English Working Class*. London: Victor Gollancz.

Thorner, I. (1953) Ascetic Protestantism and Alcoholism. *Psychiatry* 16: 167-76.

Trevelyan, G. (1942) *English Social History*. London: Longman.

Trice, H. and Pittman, D. (1958) Social Organisation and Alcoholism: A Review of Significant Research since 1940. *Social Problems* 5: 294-307.

Tynan, K. (1908) *Father Mathew*, London.

Ullman, A. (1968) Sociolcultural Background of Alcoholism. *The Annals of the American Academy of Political and Social Science* 135: 48-54.

Walsh, B. (1970) Migration to the United Kingdom from Ireland, 1961-1966. *ESRI Memorandum Series No. 70.*

Walsh, D. (1968) Alcoholism in Dublin. *Journal of the Irish Medical Association* 61: 153-56.

Walsh, D. (1969) Alcoholism in the Republic of Ireland. *The British Journal of Psychiatry* 115: 1021-25.

Walsh B. and Walsh, D. (1970) Economic Aspects of Alcohol Consumption in the Republic of Ireland. *Economic and Social Review* 2: 115-38.

Walsh, B. and Walsh, D. (1973) The Validity of Indices of Alcoholism: A Comment from Irish Experience. *British Journal of Preventive and Social Medicine* 27: 18-26.

Walters, J. and Stiwne, J.N. (1971) Parent Child Relationships: A Decade Review of Research. *Journal of Marriage and the Family.* 33: 70-111.

Ward, C. (1967) *Manpower in a Developing Community*. Dublin: An Roinn Saothair.

Webb, B. (1866) *My Apprenticeship*, London.

Webb, S. and Webb, B. (1903) *The History of Liquor Licensing in England Principally from 1700 to 1830* (Vol. II), London.

Wechsler, H., Demone, H., Thum, D., and Kasey, E. (1970) Religious-Ethnic Differences in Alcohol Consumption. *Journal of Health and Social Behaviour* 11: 21-29.

Wellman, W. (1955) Towards an Etiology of Alcoholism: Why Young Men Drink Too Much. *Canadian Medical Association Journal* 73: 717-25.

Whitehead, P. and Harvey, C. (1974) Explaining Alcoholism: An Empirical Test and Reformulation. *Journal of Health and Social Behaviour* 15: 57-65.

Wiener, R. (1970) *Drugs and Schoolchildren*. London: Longman.

Wilkinson, R. (1970) *The Prevention of Drinking Problems: Alcohol Control and Cultural Influences*. New York: Oxford University Press.

Wilson, G. (1940) *Alcohol and the Nation*. London: Nicholson & Watson.

Winskyll, P. (1891) *The Temperance Movement and its Workers* (4 Vols), London.

World Health Organization (WHO) (1952) World Health Organization Technical Report Series, No. 48. Alcoholism Sub-Committee Report, Geneva.

Wright, T. (1867) *Some Habits and Customs of the Working Classes by a Journeyman Engineer*, London.

Young, J. (1971) *The Drugtakers*. London: MacGibbon and Kee.

Young, J. and Brooke-Crutchley, J. (1972) Student Drug Use. *Drugs and Society* 1: 11-15.

Young, J., Taylor, L., and Walton, P. (1973) *The New Criminology: for a Social Theory of Deviance*. London: Routledge & Kegan Paul.

Zucker, R. (1968) Sex Role Identity Patterns and Drinking Behaviour of Adolescents. *Quarterly Journal of Studies on Alcohol* 29: 868-84.

Zucker, R. (1976) Parental Influences upon Drinking Patterns of their Children. In M. Greenbelt and M. Schuckit *Alcoholism Problems in Women and Children: Seminars in Psychiatry,* New York.

Zacune, J. and Hensman, C. (1971) *Drugs, Alcohol and Tobacco in Britain*. London: Heinemann.

Zweig, F. (1948) *Labour, Life and Poverty*. London: Victor Gollancz.

Name index

Subject index

BRYANT & MAY OFF THE RAILS

www.rbooks.co.uk

BRYANT & MAY OFF THE RAILS

CHRISTOPHER FOWLER

ANNESBURG

TRANSWORLD PUBLISHERS
61–63 Uxbridge Road, London W5 5SA
A Random House Group Company
www.rbooks.co.uk

First published in Great Britain
in 2010 by Doubleday
an imprint of Transworld Publishers

A CIP catalogue record for this book
is available from the British Library.

ISBN 9780385614665

Addresses for Random House Group Ltd companies outside the UK
can be found at: www.randomhouse.co.uk
The Random House Group Reg. No. 954009

The Random House Group Limited supports The Forest Stewardship Council (FSC),
the leading international forest-certification organization. All our titles that
are printed on Greenpeace-approved FSC-certified paper carry the FSC logo.
Our paper procurement policy can be found at
www.rbooks.co.uk/environment

Typeset in 11/13pt Sabon by
Kestrel Data, Exeter, Devon
Printed and bound in Great Britain by
Clays Ltd, Bungay, Suffolk

2 4 6 8 10 9 7 5 3 1

Mixed Sources
Product group from well-managed
forests and other controlled sources
www.fsc.org   Cert no. TT-COC-2139
© 1996 Forest Stewardship Council

For Peter Chapman

ACKNOWLEDGEMENTS

Every Bryant & May novel is self-contained, and each a separate pleasure to write. This latest volume reflects my crowded city life and the happiness of chance meetings. I'd like to thank the London Underground staff who found the time to answer my dumb questions while patiently helping the millions of commuters who use the system every day. I don't know how you remain so calm and clear-headed. My Transworld editor Simon Taylor clearly knows the secret, because he maintains the same kind of grace under pressure, which entirely eludes me.

In life everyone needs a good teacher, a good doctor and a good lawyer. To that I would add a great agent, and would like to thank Mandy Little once again for her practically perfect patience and positivity. Kate Samano has a talent for making these books better, so my respect goes out to her, and to Lynsey Dalladay and the rest of the Transworld team.

A thumbs-up too to everyone who has posted suggestions on my website about Bryant & May (and all my other books), a number of which eventually find their way into print. Join us on my blog at www.christopherfowler. co.uk, which is somewhat different to usual author sites in that you can add entirely irrelevent thoughts or simply get into a fight with strangers.

'Youths green and happy in first love,
So thankful for illusion;
And men caught out in what the world
Calls guilt, in first confusion;
And almost everyone when age,
Disease or sorrows strike him,
Inclines to think there is a god,
Or something very like him.'

Arthur Hugh Clough

The Old Warehouse
231 Caledonian Road
London N1 9RB

THIS BUILDING IS NOW OCCUPIED BY THE PECULIAR
CRIMES UNIT UNTIL FURTHER NOTIFICATION FROM
THE HOME OFFICE

STAFF ROSTER: MONDAY

Raymond Land, Acting Temporary Unit Chief
Arthur Bryant, Senior Detective
John May, Senior Detective
Janice Longbright, Detective Sergeant
Dan Banbury, Crime Scene Manager/ InfoTech
Jack Renfield, Desk Sergeant
Meera Mangeshkar, Detective Constable
Colin Bimsley, Detective Constable
Giles Kershaw, Forensic Pathology
Crippen, staff cat

STAFF BULLETIN BOARD

Clipping from the Police Review:
'King's Cross Executioner' kills PC, escapes custody

A hired killer who left his beheaded victims on building sites in the
King's Cross area would have fatally undermined public confidence
in the multi-million-pound project to reinvigorate the former

red-light area if he had not been identified, said an official Home Office report last week.

However, the report went on to castigate the unit bosses for failing to provide adequate security checks at its temporary head-quarters, an oversight which resulted in the escape of the suspect.

The investigation had been conducted by London's Peculiar Crimes Unit, a little-known police division created by academics in 1940 to handle serious crimes that could be considered a threat to public order and confidence. As a secret wartime department, the PCU was allowed to develop many innovative (and question-able) investigative techniques. In the 1950s the unit fell under the jurisdiction of the Metropolitan Police, and was later absorbed into the British Military Intelligence department MI7 to handle cases involving domestic and foreign propaganda. In the last few months, the PCU has found itself increasingly mired in controversy after being placed under Home Office jurisdiction, and the principles upon which it was founded have been called into question.

Ministers accused the management team of failing to follow accepted procedural guidelines. But its senior detectives, Arthur Bryant and John May, remained determined to operate on the London streets using investigation methods unauthorized by present-day government officials. As a result, they successfully brought in a suspect known only as Mr Fox, who admitted carrying out the King's Cross murders for financial gain.

However, what should have been a cause for celebration turned to tragedy after Mr Fox succeeded in breaking out of the unit's holding cell and stabbing the officer on duty to death. PC Liberty DuCaine lost his life after being attacked by the accused, who then found his way back to the street. To date, the killer has not been recaptured.

Despite their ultimate exoneration by an independent judicial body, the PCU's future is looking less secure than ever before in its contentious history.

From the Desk of Raymond Land:

Is it necessary to remind staff NOT to provide the press with information about the escape of the so-called 'King's Cross Executioner'? We don't want to give tabloid hacks a reason to go through our dustbins for the next six months. DON'T SPEAK TO ANYONE. If you're in any doubt, talk to me first.

A word of warning about PC Liberty DuCaine's funeral: his family don't want any of you lot going anywhere near them this morning. They already had the Mayor creeping round for a photo op, and sent him away with a flea in his ear. Send flowers if you want, but stay away from the service.

I have to acknowledge the resignation of our Liaison Officer April May from the unit, effective immediately, for health reasons. April is planning to spend some time with her uncle in Toronto, following the recurrence of her agoraphobia. I'm sure you all join me in wishing her well for the future. I thought we should have a whip-round to get her something nice. By the way, when April said she'd like a gift voucher for a couple of hours in a flotation tank she was, in fact, joking.

As of this morning we now have fully functional computers and phones. You have John May to thank for this. I don't know how he did it. No one tells me anything.

Older members of the PCU will recall a pair of utterly useless workmen who sat in our former offices at Morning Crescent for months, brewing endless pots of tea instead of getting on with their work. You'll be thrilled to know that another pair of layabouts, two Turkish gentlemen both called Dave, will be arriving today to restore the electrics and plumbing, while no doubt offering unsought for advice on the policing of the capital. Don't complain, their quote came in a lot lower than anyone else's. I daresay we'll find out why in due course.

By the way, there's a hole in the floor in Mr Bryant's office. Don't go near it.

If anyone sees Crippen, can they please butter his paws before letting him out? We don't want him getting lost in this neighbourhood. He's put on a bit of weight lately, and there are a couple of dodgy takeaways on the Caledonian Road that look like they could use the meat.

I

A PRIVATE FEUD

FROM: LESLIE FARADAY, HOME OFFICE SENIOR POLICE LIAISON

TO: RAYMOND LAND, ACTING TEMPORARY HEAD, PECULIAR CRIMES UNIT

CONFIDENTIAL

Dear Raymond,

With regard to your apprehension of the hired assassin operating in the King's Cross area, this so-called 'King's Cross Executioner' chap, thank you for acting so quickly on the matter, although it's a pity he subsequently managed to give you the slip. I had a bit of trouble opening your report because, frankly, computers have never been my strong point, but the new girl in our office seems to understand these things and printed out a copy for me.

Following the judicial review we decided to scrap the idea of holding a press conference, but we're speaking to our key contacts today, so we'll have some idea of the coverage that's likely to run in tomorrow's papers. Always talk to the press, I say, even when you've got nothing to tell them. We're hoping that a bit of publicity might flush him out. I'm trying to discourage sensational references to his nickname, without much luck, I'm afraid, but when a little boy finds a human head while fishing for eels in a canal, you can expect the press to react strongly.

I have passed your amendments and conclusions on to my superior and other concerned department heads, and will return with their reactions in due course. I also have to acknowledge the receipt of an additional report on the case from one of your senior detectives, Arthur Bryant, although I must admit I was only able to read portions of this document as his handwriting was extremely small and barely legible, and pages 23 to 31 had some kind of curry sauce spilled over them. Furthermore his account is opinionated and anecdotal in the extreme, and on several occasions positively offensive. Could you have a word with him about this?

Naturally we are all sorry to hear about what happened. It is always with great sadness that one hears of a police officer's demise in the course of his duty, especially in this case when the officer in question was so highly regarded, with such a bright future ahead of him.

Although the tribunal was reasonably satisfied that no member of the PCU could be held responsible for the unforeseen events occurring on your premises, we do not feel that full autonomy can be returned to the unit until a series of regulatory safeguards have been put in place to ensure that the impossibility of such an incident—'

'Oh, for God's sake get on with it,' Arthur Bryant complained at the page, balling it up and disdainfully throwing it over his shoulder as he skipped to the concluding sheet. He had filched the report from Raymond Land's mailbox and was vetting it before the acting chief arrived for work. 'Let's see – "inadequate safeguards", *yadda yadda yadda*, "irregular procedures", *yadda yadda*, "unnecessary risk factors" – all predictable stuff. Ah, here's the bit I was expecting – "because the perpetrator of these crimes was allowed to escape and is still at large, he remains a potential menace to society, therefore we cannot consider fully reinstating the PCU until he is apprehended." In other words, catch him but don't expect us to help you with additional resources. Bloody typical. Oh, listen, you'll like this bit. "Due to the financial reorganization of the Home Office's outsourced operations units, you have until the end of the week (Saturday at 6:00 p.m.) to conclude this and any other unfinished investigations in order to qualify for annual funding." So he wants us to achieve the impossible in one week or he and his ghastly boss Oskar Kasavian will cut us off without a penny. "Your Obedient Servant, Leslie Faraday." Who signs their letters like that any more? Anyway, he's not our Obedient Servant, but I suppose he couldn't sign it Sad Porky Timeserver or Snivelling Little Rodent.'

With increasing age the grace notes of temperance, balance, harmony and gentility are supposed to appear in the human heart. This was not entirely true, however, in Arthur Bryant's case. He remained acidulous, stubborn, insensitive and opinionated, and was getting ruder by the day, as the byzantine workings of the British Home Office sucked away his enthusiasm for collaring killers.

Bryant started to screw up the rest of the memo, then remembered he wasn't supposed to have seen it, and flattened it out imperfectly. He fished the other pages out of the bin, but now they were smeared with the remains of last night's takeaway.

'I don't know why you get so het up, Arthur. What did you honestly expect?' John May carefully pinched his smart pinstriped trousers at the knee and bent to give him a hand picking up the pages. 'A man kills three times, is arrested by us, breaks out of a locked cell, stabs a police officer in the neck and vanishes. We were hardly going to be rewarded for our efforts.'

'What about the innocent people we protected, the deaths we prevented?' Bryant asked, appalled.

'I think they're happier counting the millions of pounds we saved them.' May rose, twisted his chair and flopped down, stretching himself into a six-foot line. 'Just think of all the companies that would have pulled out if we hadn't been able to secure the area.'

'What a case for my memoirs,' Bryant muttered. 'Three mutilated bodies found on the mean streets of King's Cross. Murders committed solely for financial gain, by a slippery, adaptable thief who's grown up in the area around the terminus, a small-time crook propelled to the status of murderer when a robbery went wrong. You know what's happened, don't you? For the first time in his life this Mr Fox has been made to feel important, and the escalation of his criminal status from burglar to hired killer has increased his determination to stay free.'

There was a darkness at the heart of this chameleon-like killer that the members of the Peculiar Crimes Unit had underestimated. For a while it had felt as if gang war was breaking out in the area, but by getting to the root of the crimes, the detectives had managed to allay public fears and reassure investors that the newly developing region was still open for business. In the process they had lost an officer, and had been unable to stop their quarry from escaping back into the faceless crowds.

Bryant pottered over to the sooty, rain-streaked window and tapped it. 'He's still out there somewhere,' he warned, 'and now he'll do one of two things. Having had his fingers so badly burned he'll either vanish completely, never to be seen again, or he'll returneth like a dog to vomit, just to taunt me further. Proverbs 26:11.'

'I don't understand,' said May. 'Why are you taking this so personally?'

'Because I'm the one he's after. DuCaine just got in the way.' Bryant had never exhibited much empathy towards his co-workers, but this struck May as callous even by his standards.

'Liberty DuCaine's parents have just lost a son, Arthur, so perhaps you could keep such thoughts to yourself. Don't turn this into a private feud. It concerns all of us.' May rose and left the room in annoyance.

Bryant was sorry that the lad had died – of course he was upset – but nothing could bring him back now, and the only way they could truly restore order was by catching the man responsible. With a sigh he popped open his tobacco tin and stuffed a pipe with Old Arabia Navy Rough Cut Aromatic Shag. His gut told him that Mr Fox would quickly resurface, not because the killer had any romantic notion of longing to be stopped, but because his anger would make him careless. His sense of respect had been compromised, and he was determined to make the police pay for cornering him.

I'll get you, sonny, Bryant thought, *not just because I owe it to DuCaine, but to every innocent man, woman and child out there who could become another of your statistics. You'll turn up again, soon enough. You've tasted blood now, and the need to let others see how big you've grown will drive you back out into the light. When that happens, I'll have you.*

Unfortunately, Bryant tried to avoid reminding himself, it would need to happen this week.

2

CHOREOGRAPHY

DC Colin Bimsley and DC Meera Mangeshkar were watching the station. They had no idea what their suspect might look like, or any reason to assume he would suddenly appear before them on the concourse. But Mr Fox knew his terrain well and rarely left it, so there was a chance that even now he might be wandering through the Monday-morning commuters. And as the St Pancras International surveillance team was more concerned with watching for terrorist suspects following a weekend of worrying intelligence, it fell to the two detective constables to keep an eye out for their man. At least it was warm and dry under the great glass canopy.

Each circuit of the huge double-tiered terminus took between twenty minutes and half an hour. Bimsley and Mangeshkar wore jeans and matching black nylon jackets, the closest anyone at the PCU could come up with to an official uniform, but Bimsley was a foot taller than his partner, and they made an incongruous pair.

'Down there,' Meera pointed, leaning over the

balustrade, 'that's the third time he's crossed between the bookshop and the florist.'

'You can't arrest someone for browsing,' Bimsley replied. 'Do you want to go and look?'

'It's worth checking out.' She led the way to the stairs. Colin checked his watch. Eight fifty-five a.m. The Eurostar was offloading passengers from Brussels and Paris, the national rail services brought commuters from the Midlands and the North, trains were disgorging suburbanites and reconnecting them to the Tube. Charity workers were stopping passers-by, others were handing out free newspapers, packets of tissues and bottles of water, a sales team was attempting to sell credit services, the shops on the ground-floor concourse were all open for business – and there was a French cheese fair; tricolour stalls had been set out down the centre of the covered walkway. Travellers seemed adept at negotiating these obstacles while furling their wet umbrellas and manhandling their cases through the crowds. But was a murderer moving among them?

'There he goes again,' said Meera.

'You're right, he just bought a newspaper and a dough-nut, let's nick him. Uh-oh, look out, he's stopped by the florist. I'll make a note of that; considering the purchase of carnations. Well dodgy.'

'Suppose it's Mr Fox and you just let him walk away?'

'You want to call it? I mean, if we're going to start stop-and-search procedures down here, we'd better have some clearly defined criteria.'

'You can come up with something later – let's take him.' Meera paced up through the crowd, then stopped by the French market, puzzled, looking back. 'Colin?'

'What's the matter?'

'Something weird.' She pointed to the far side of the concourse, where half a dozen teenagers had suddenly stopped and spaced themselves six feet apart from each other. Bimsley shrugged and pointed to the other wall, where the same thing was happening. 'What's going on?'

All around them, people were freezing in their tracks and slowly turning.

'They're all wearing phone earpieces,' Meera pointed out.

Now almost everyone in the centre of the station was standing still and facing forwards. Beneath the station clock, two young men in grey sweatshirts and hoods set an old-fashioned ghetto blaster on a café table and hit 'Play'.

As the first notes of 'Rehab' by Amy Winehouse blasted out, they raised their right arms and span in tight circles. Everyone on the concourse copied them. The choreography had been rehearsed online until it was perfect. The station had suddenly become a ballroom.

'It's a flash mob,' Meera called wearily. The internet phenomenon had popularized the craze for virally organized mass dancing in public places, but she had assumed it had passed from fashion a couple of years ago.

'I took part in a freeze in Victoria Station once,' said Bimsley, watching happily. 'Four hundred of us pretending to be statues. It's just a bit of harmless fun.'

'Well, our man's using it to cover his escape.'

'Meera, he's not *our man*, he's just a guy catching a train.'

The diminutive DC did not hear. She was already haring across the concourse, weaving a path between the performers. The song could be heard bleeding from hundreds of earpieces as the entire station danced. The song hit its chorus and the choreography grew more complex. Colin could no longer see who Meera was chasing. Even the transport police were standing back and watching the dancers with smiles on their faces.

As the song reached its conclusion there was a concerted burst of leaping and twirling. Then, just as if the song had never played, everyone went back to the business of the day, catching trains and heading to the office. Meera was looking through the crowds, furious to find that her target had disappeared. But just as Bimsley started walking towards her, someone grabbed at his shoulder.

Colin turned to find himself facing a portly, florid-faced businessman who was slapping the pockets of his jacket and shouting to anyone who would listen. 'Hey, calm down, tell me the problem,' Bimsley advised.

'You are police, yes?' shouted the man. 'You look like police. I have been robbed. Just now, I am crossing station and this stupid dancing begins, and I stop to watch because I cannot cross, you know, and my bag is taken from my hand.'

'Did you see who took it? What was the bag like?'

'Of course I did not see, you think I talk to you if I see? I would stop him! Is bag, black leather bag, is all. I am Turkish Cypriot, on my way to Paris. The takings are in my bag.'

'What takings?'

'My restaurants, six restaurants, all the money is in cash.'

'How much?'

'You think I have time to count it? This is not my job. Maybe sixty thousand, maybe seventy thousand pounds.'

'Wait a minute,' said Bimsley. 'You're telling me you were carrying over sixty thousand on you – in notes?'

'Of course is notes. I always do this on same Monday every month.'

'Always the same day?' Bimsley was incredulous. How could anyone be so stupid?

'Yes, and is perfectly safe because no one knows I carry this money. How could they?'

'Well, what about somebody from one of your restaurants?'

'You tell me I should not trust my own countrymen? My own flesh and blood? Is always safe and I have no trouble, is routine, is what I always do. But today the music start up and everybody dance and someone snatch the bag from me. Look.' The irate businessman held up his left wrist, dangling from which was a length of plastic cable, neatly snipped through. 'I want to know what you will do about this,' the man shouted, waving his hairy wrist in Bimsley's perplexed face. 'You must get me back my money!'

Meera came back to his side. 'What's going on?' she asked.

'Nothing,' Colin sighed. 'Another bloody Monday morning in King's Cross.'

3

PARASITICAL

Bryant stared down into the sodden streets. It was hard to detect any sign of spring on such a shabby day. At least the doxies and dealers had been swept out of the area as the fashionable bars moved in. Eventually the raucous beckoning of hookers would only be recalled by the few remaining long-term residents. Such was life in London, where a year of fads and fancies could race past in a week. Who had time to remind themselves of the past any more?

Maybe it's just me, thought Bryant, *but I can see everything, stretching back through time like stepping stones, just as if I'd been there.*

No one now remembered Handel playing above the coal-shop in Clerkenwell's Jerusalem Passage, or Captain Kidd being hanged from the gibbet in Wapping until the Thames had immersed him three times. Thousands of histories were scrubbed from the city's face each year. Once you could feel entire buildings lurch when the printing presses of Fleet Street began to roll. Once the wet cobbles of Snow Hill impeded funeral cortèges with such frequency that it became a London tradition for servicemen to haul hearses with ropes. For every riot there was a romance, for every slaying, a birth; the city had a way of smoothing out the rumples of the passing years.

The elderly detective tossed the remains of his tea over the filthy window and cleared a clean spot with his sleeve. He saw coffee shops and tofu bars where once prophets and anarchists had held court.

The recent change in King's Cross had been startling, but even with buildings scrubbed and whores dispatched, it had retained enough of its ruffian character not to feel like everywhere else. Bryant belonged here. He basked in the neighbourhood's sublime indifference to the passing of time and people.

A week to solve a case. Well, they had risen to such challenges before. Carefully skirting the alarming hole in his office floor, Bryant donned his brown trilby, his serpentine green scarf and his frayed gabardine mackintosh, and headed out into the morning murk. At least it felt good to be back in harness. As he left the warehouse which currently housed the Peculiar Crimes Unit he almost skipped across the road, although to be fair he had to, as a bus was bearing down on him.

Arthur Bryant: have you met him before? If not, imagine a tortoise minus its shell, thrust upright and stuffed into a dreadful suit. Give it glasses, false teeth and a hearing aid, and a wispy band of white hair arranged in a straggling tonsure. Fill its pockets with rubbish: old pennies and scribbled notes, boiled sweets and leaky pens, a glass model of a Ford Prefect filled with Isle of Wight sand, yards of string, a stuffed mouse, some dried peas. And fill its head with a mad scramble of ideas: the height of the steeple at St Clement Danes, the tide tables of the Thames, the dimensions of Waterloo Station, and the methods of murderers. On top of all this, add the enquiring wonder of a ten-year-old boy. Now you have some measure of the man.

Bryant jammed the ancient trilby harder on his bald pate and fought the rain on the Caledonian Road. Typically, he was moving in the wrong direction against the elements. He seemed to spend his life on an opposite path, a disreputable old salmon always determined to head upstream.

As he marched, he tabulated life's annoyances in escalating order of gravity. He was sleeping badly again. He had forgotten to take his blue pills. His left leg hurt like hell. He had six days in which to close the unit's cases, and no money to pay his staff. He was likely to be thrown out of his home any day now. A good officer had died in the line of duty. And he had a murderer on the loose who was likely to return and commit further acts of violence. Not bad for a Monday morning. With a gargoyle grimace, he looked up at the rain-stained clouds above and muttered a very old and entirely unprintable curse.

Everyone talks about the unpredictable weather in London, but it has a faintly discernable pattern. At this time of the year, the second week in May, caught between the dissipation of winter and the failed nerve of spring, the days were drab, damp and undecided, the evenings clear and graceful, swimming-pool blue melting to heliotrope, banded altostratus clouds forming with the setting of the sun. You can forgive a lot when a dim day has a happy ending.

On this Monday morning, though, there was no sign of the fine finish to come. Bryant made his way to the threadbare ground-floor flat in Margery Street where their escaped assassin, Mr Fox, had been living.

The building was a pebble-dashed two-storey block set at an angle to the road, possessing all the glamour of an abandoned army barracks. Dan Banbury, the unit's Crime Scene Manager, had already been at work here over the weekend, tying off the apartment into squares for forensic analysis. Bryant stepped over the red cords in his disposable shoe covers, but managed to lose one and dislodge a stack of magazines on the way.

'Just sit over there on the sofa, can you?' Banbury demanded irritably. 'Stay somewhere I can see you. You're supposed to wear a disposable suit.'

'I am. Got it from a secondhand stall on Brick Lane.'

'At least put your hands in your pockets. There's meant to be a constable on guard to log visits but Islington wouldn't provide one. Dispute over jurisdiction.'

'You're an SCO, you can let in who you want. Have you had your ears lowered?'

'Oh, my nipper came back from school with nits and wanted his hair cut off, but he wouldn't let me do it until I'd tested the electric shaver on myself. I went a bit too short.'

'Wise lad.' Bryant stuck his hands in his coat and found a boiled sweet that was probably a barley twist under the pocket fluff. He sucked it ruminatively, looking around. 'Still using pins and bits of string? I thought you could do it with a special camera now.'

'That's right. Buy me the equipment and I'll mark out the grid electronically. I think it's about seven grand.'

'Point taken. Bagged much up?'

Banbury sat on his heels and massaged his back. He had been staring at biscuit crumbs and dead flies for the last half hour. 'There's no physical evidence to take.'

'Don't be daft. There's always evidence.' Bryant picked a bit of fluff off his barley sugar and flicked it on to the floor.

'Not in this case.'

'Have you started on the bedroom?'

'Not yet. But if you're going to poke around in there, please don't – you know – just don't.'

Bryant was infamous for his habit of traipsing through crime scenes and fingering the evidence. He had begun his career at a time when detectives had been trained simply to observe with their eyes rather than to illuminate body fluids with blue lights and Luminol reagents. These days, specialist equipment came with specialists who charged by the hour. Many routine cases of criminal damage and assault were dumped simply because it was too slow and expensive to send off samples.

Bryant stood at the head of Mr Fox's single bed and studied the room. No books on display. Hardly any furniture. A framed photograph of a blue-eyed girl with long blonde hair, vacuous to the point of derangement. It was the photograph that had come with the frame. Mr Fox was a human sponge, a magnet for the knowledge of others, but he had no interest in real human beings and therefore possessed no real friends. He couldn't trust himself in any relationship that demanded honesty.

According to the Council's rental records, their murderer had lived here for almost ten years under the name of Mr Fox. Yet there was no character to be found in the rooms, nothing that would reveal his personality traits or give any clue to his real identity. Most people's hotel suites offered up more than this. To Mr Fox the flat was a place to sleep and visit periodically for a change of clothes, but even here he had been careful not to leave spoor.

'Fox,' said Bryant aloud. 'Dictionary definition: a wary, solitary, opportunistic feeder that hunts live prey. Good choice of a name. No real sign of who he is, I suppose.'

'Nothing,' Banbury called back. 'It's really odd. You and John met the man. You interviewed him at length. You didn't get anything at all?'

'We did, but it was all lies. Our mistake was taking

27

what we saw at face value. He played us beautifully. I don't understand how he disarmed me. I'm usually so suspicious.'

Bryant felt that he understood very little about serial killers. Demonstrable motivation was the keystone of criminology, and just as altruists made the best benefactors, murderers were at their most comprehensible when it was possible to see what they gained from their actions. This chap was a total cipher.

Mr Fox should have been easy to find. After all, he had initially killed for gain, not because he derived pleasure from it. But, Bryant wondered, would he *have* to continue killing, now that he had discovered the taste?

A parasite, he thought. *He takes and takes without giving anything back, and remains in place until the host is dead.* He studied the lair of his quarry, and felt an ominous settling in his stomach that warned him of imminent danger – although it might have been germs on the barley twist.

4

THE VOID

'A serial killer,' said Banbury, standing up to stretch his aching calves. 'That's what I reckon we've got here. We've not had many of them at the PCU, have we?'

'Not proper saw-off-the-arms-and-legs-boil-the-innards-put-the-head-in-a-handbag-and-throw-it-from-a-bridge jobs, no.' When it came to fathoming the private passions of serial killers, Bryant felt lost. What were their most notable attributes? Solitude and self-interest. The rest must surely be conjecture. Novels and films were filled with the abstruse motivations of intellectual murderers – they carved designs into corpses according to biblical prophecies and hid body parts in patterns that corresponded to Flemish paintings – but the reality was that the act of murder remained as squalid and desperate as it had always been, the province of the spiritually impoverished.

Bryant dug out a none-too-clean handkerchief and noisily blew his nose. 'Why do you think he's a serial killer?'

'Well, here's the thing, Mr Bryant. It's very hard to

completely hide your personality. I know when my boy's been in my room, no matter how hard he tries to cover his tracks.'

'The poor little bugger's got a forensic scientist for a father. How can he ever hope to pull the wool over your eyes?'

'And we always know where you've been – we follow the smell of your pipe, the mud and the sweet wrappers. It's easier if you've no personality there to begin with. And serial killers suffer from a sort of moral blankness. There was a case in America, a young couple, Karla Homolka and Paul Bernardo. They were known as the Ken and Barbie killers because they were middle-class WASPs. In the trial notes, the prosecution asked Karla how she could take breaks to sit downstairs in the lounge reading, while her husband murdered a young girl upstairs. Do you know what she replied? "I'm quite capable of doing two things at once." Blankness, see? And they go about things in the wrong way. Karla was worried that she'd leave behind evidence, so she shaved a victim's head. It really confused the profilers, who thought it must be a psychosexual signature, but she'd done it so she wouldn't have to throw away the rug that the corpse was lying on. She was more concerned about the rug than the murdered girl.'

'And you can see something like that here, can you?' Bryant could not appreciate the silence of empty souls; his passions were too rich and various. They included Arthurian history, anthropology, architecture, alchemy and abstract art, and those were just the As. He let his partner handle the messy human stuff. While he appreciated the biological intricacies of the heart, its spirit remained forever encrypted.

An absence of personality. Banbury's right. Mr Fox takes alienation to a new level. He examines others as if they're circuitry diagrams. Bryant studied the murderer's cold, bare little bedroom in wonder. *He sees this weakness as a skill, but we have to make it the cause of his downfall.*

The room was as dead as an unlit stage set. *Ten years,* he thought. *That's how long you've been hiding your true nature. When did you come to realize you were different? What happened to make you like this? Do you even remember who you once were?*

Bryant knew that the man they were looking for had befriended several local residents. They had visited him, and Mr Fox had socialized with them in order to use their knowledge of the area. Had he let them inside the flat? Why not – he had nothing to hide here. He was an actor who adopted personalities and characteristics that he thought might prove useful. Actors were good at doing that. How many books had been written about Sir Alec Guinness without ever revealing what he was truly like?

'When you report in to Janice, get her to circulate Mr Fox's description to acting schools, would you? There are several in the immediate area,' said Bryant. Banbury threw him an intrigued look as he repacked his kit. 'This ability to deceive might be rooted in some kind of formal training.'

Bryant could only sense his quarry in the broadest of sweeps. There were people out there who were touched by nothing. The damaged ones were the most dangerous of all. He needed concrete facts about his quarry. But even the people who had been befriended by Mr Fox seemed to recall nothing about him. In a world of streaming data, how could one man leave behind so little?

'Dan, can I borrow your brains for a minute?' Banbury was good at repopulating empty rooms; he could put flesh back on the faintest ghosts. Everyone at the unit knew that Banbury had been a lonely child, overweight and socially lost, locked in his bedroom with his flickering computer screens. Perfect PCU material in training, as it turned out.

Banbury dusted powder from his plastic gloves with an air of expectation. Bryant had a habit of asking questions that weren't easily answered.

'What can you tell me about Mr Fox from this room? I don't mean on a microscopic level, just in general. There must be something. I can't read much at all.' Bryant looked around at the IKEA shelves, the cheaply built bed, the bare cupboards.

'You met him, Mr Bryant, you know what he looks like.'

'That didn't tell me a lot. He stuck to answering questions, gave us facts without opinions, avoided bringing himself into the conversation. He's very clever at not sticking in the memory, especially a memory like mine.'

'Well, give me your impression.'

'I don't do impressions. Let me think. Slight but muscular. About five ten. Smooth, unmemorable face, like a young actor without make-up. Fair complexion. Grey eyes. Not much hair, although I have a feeling he shaved his hairline. I wish we'd had a chance to photograph him. I got one interrogation in before going to brief the others – entirely my fault; I was anxious to get down the details of the case. We should photograph them on arrest, the way they do in America. John took a picture on his mobile, but the room was dark and it didn't come out very well.'

'OK, so we don't have an ID for him, but there's a piece of face-recognition software that might pick up his main features from your shot and find a match. That's assuming he has a record.' Banbury took a few steps forward, pinched his nose, leaned, peered, scratched at his stubbly head. 'I've already had a good look around, of course – '

Of course you have, thought Bryant. *Natural curiosity got the better of you. We all want to know about the kind of man who can kill without thinking twice.*

'I think he's probably lived here since his late teens, which makes him just under thirty. A loner from a broken home. Very closed off about the past. Something bad happened there that he doesn't go into very often – there's usually some kind of family trouble in the background. We know that his friendships are cultivated for their usefulness, and any emotions he expresses are meticulously faked. The habit of never presenting his true self to anyone is probably so ingrained that he wouldn't be able to reveal himself now if he tried. A classic user, unemotional and unrepentant. You tell 'em they've done wrong and they look at you as if you're speaking French. This really does place him in the serial-killer category. Clever planning, no witnesses, no evidence; it's a pattern. I bet he hasn't used his real name for so long that he's almost forgotten it. Probably has OCD. A fantasist, a reinventor, but it has all come out of necessity.'

'Where are you getting all this?'

'Oh, the belongings, mainly.' Banbury waved a hand across the shelves. 'A few other points of interest. The picture on the wall there.' He indicated an evenly lit photograph of an empty red metal bench against a white tiled wall. 'You couldn't get much more sterile than that, could you? He doesn't do people. Except his grandparents – there's an unframed photo of an old couple on the bedside table. We'll see if we can get anything from it. There are only two types of items here: the stuff he owned as a child, and recent acquisitions. In the former group you've got the alarm clock with the chicken on it beside the bed, and that little grey metal animal – an armadillo, I think. The clock's from the early 1950s so I'm guessing it was purchased by the grandparents. Anything that ugly would

33

have to have sentimental value. The armadillo figurines
were popular in Texas in the mid 1970s, but were available
here. Maybe it reminds him to keep a tough shell. Might
have been a gift from his father.'

'That's a bit of a leap.'

'The trick is not to look at anything in isolation.
Whether they mean to or not, most people continually
reassess their belongings, adding and subtracting all the
time to keep everything in balance. So I add the picture,
the clock and the armadillo to that book over there.' He
pointed to a single hardback in an alcove beside the bed.
Founders of the Empire was a volume on great British
explorers. 'It's signed with a message from his father. No
names, unfortunately.'

Banbury picked up the book and showed Bryant. He
wasn't about to let the detective touch it without gloves.
'See, he's written on the flyleaf. "An independent man
makes his own way in the world – Dad." Hard to imagine
a more impersonal note. I guess he wanted his kid to
grow up self-reliant and disciplined. No sign of a mother
anywhere. Kid's stuff here, near the bed – adult stuff over
there. The teenage years are missing. Then we jump to
a few recent purchases in the cupboard: the paperback
copy of Machiavelli, psychology manuals, the fiction
choice suggesting that he likes reading about villains
more than heroes – *American Psycho*, *The Killer Inside
Me*, damaged people. He's interested in learning how to
control others. He's probably disdainful of ordinary folk,
despises their weakness, thinks of them as lower life forms.
The books and magazines are arranged thematically
and alphabetically. Four separate volumes on the great
disasters of London; maybe he enjoys reading about other
people's tragedies. He's obsessive-compulsive because at
first it was the only way to protect himself and keep his
real feelings hidden, and now it's an unbreakable habit.'

Banbury walked around the bed. 'Check out the wardrobe drawers. His clothes are neatly grouped into different outfits for the personalities he wants to project. Grey suit, white shirt, blue tie; jeans and grey T-shirt. Grey, white, blue, the colours of sorrow, austerity, emptiness. The brands are H & M, Gap, M & S. No choices that reveal any sign of individuality. The bed linen's been washed so there aren't even any fabric prints to lift. One plate and one mug – he certainly wasn't planning to have anyone over to stay. He lives here and yet he doesn't.'

'What do you mean?'

Banbury scratched his nose and thought for a minute. 'Some people have no sense of belonging, because they live inside their heads. They carry themselves wherever they go. They're complete from one moment to the next. Most of us, if we were told we had to board a plane in the next couple of hours, would need to head home first. We like to tell others what we're doing, where we're going. We go online, make calls, form connections. He doesn't. No phone, no mail, no laptop, no keys, wallet, money, bills or passport. He always makes sure he's got every-thing he needs on him.'

'But he had nothing on him when he was arrested.'

'Then he has a place to stash stuff. Obviously he'd be tagged at any airport.'

'I don't think he wants to leave the country,' said Bryant, 'or even leave the area. Something is keeping him right here.'

'Then what are we missing? Don't touch that, it's not been dusted yet.' Banbury pulled out a camel-hair brush and twirled it between his fingers. 'It's complicated. He's living off the grid, old-school fashion, face contact only. He stays in this block because it's Council-owned but cared for by the residents, which means the cops aren't as familiar with it as they are with the Evil Poor Estate up the road.' The so-called Evil Poor Estate was home to multi-generational criminal families whose recourse to violence and destruction was as natural to them as going to the office was for others. Such estates formed modern-day rookeries around London.

'Have a look at this,' said Banbury. 'There are stacks of local newspapers in the cupboards, articles starred in felt tip – he's fascinated by London, particularly the area in which he lives. Plenty of neatly transcribed notes about the surrounding streets and Tube stations. He has abnormally strong ties to his home. This is interesting because it contradicts all the other signifiers. To me, it's the only part of his behaviour that's outwardly irrational.'

'An emotional attachment to the neighbourhood. Why would you stick around if you'd killed someone?'

'Killers do. But it's usually the disorganized, mentally subnormal ones who stay on at the location. The organized ones use three separate sites: where the victims are confronted, where they're killed and where they're disposed of. Then the killer leaves the area. So we have a contradiction.'

'Hmm. Anything more from the newspapers?'

'He's earmarked the obituaries of people who live around here. Maybe he was planning identity theft.'

'Think he'll come back to the flat? Is it worth keeping someone on site?'

'He's got no reason to return. There's nothing worth taking.'

'Come on, Dan, give me something I can use.' Bryant impatiently rattled the boiled sweet around his false teeth.

'OK. His name. I've bagged one of the notes you might find interesting, some research about a dodgy pub that used to exist nearby called The Fox At Bay. He's clearly a local lad, born in one of the surrounding streets. Maybe he took his name from the pub. He won't have become friendly with anyone else in the building, but maybe someone knew his old man. I think at some point Mr Fox lost contact with his family, maybe when his folks split up. He cuts his own hair, is capable of changing his appearance quickly. But he's cleaned his electric clippers so that there's not so much as a single hair left behind. He's bleached everything. He left home fully prepared to travel, because there's nothing of value here, only the two changes of clothes and one pair of knackered old shoes. No one else's fingerprints but his own, and he hasn't got a record so we can't match them. No foreign fibres so far, nothing to link him to the murders beyond what we already have. We could try the National DNA Database, but less than 8 per cent of the population is recorded on it, so if he's managed to keep himself out of trouble and away from hospitals it's of no use. He keeps his dirty work off the premises. Hair dye in the bathroom cabinet, and a pair of steel-rimmed spectacles with plain glass in them. Not exactly a master of disguise, but you do feel he enjoys the power that accompanies deception. No sign of a woman anywhere. He's the kind of man who visits prostitutes. He can't risk getting close to anyone. He wouldn't trust them.'

'Well, I'm disappointed,' Bryant complained. 'I thought you were going to provide me with some genuine revelations instead of a load of old guesswork.'

Banbury blew out his cheeks in dismay. 'Blimey, Mr Bryant, I thought I was doing quite well.'

'Let me tell you something about this man. He doesn't see himself as damaged. The cities are our new frontiers; it's here that the battles of the future will be fought, and he's already preparing himself for them. He knows that the first thing you have to do is chuck out conventional notions of sentiment, nostalgia, spirituality, morality.

There's no point in believing that faith, hope and charity can help you in a society that only wants to sell you as much as it can before you die. Mr Fox has divested himself of his family and friends, and he's taking his first steps into uncharted territory. He considers himself as much of a pioneer as, oh, Beddoes or Edison.'

Banbury stared in bewildered discomfort at Bryant, who was cheerfully sucking his sweet as he considered the prospect.

'You think he's some kind of genius, then? Sounds like you admire him.'

'No, I'm just interested in the way people protect themselves in order to survive. It's an instinct, but he's turned it into an art. And this solipsism ultimately blinds him. Ever had dinner with an actor?'

'No.'

'Don't. All they ever talk about is themselves. They never ask questions, never bother to find out who you are. They're not interested in anything but getting to the truth of their characters. And in most cases there isn't any truth, just an empty, dark, faintly whistling void. The serial killer Dennis Nilsen was so incredibly boring that he actually sent his victims to sleep.'

'Blimey.'

Bryant broke the unsettling silence. 'I had an aunt once who appeared in drawing-room comedies. She was doing a Noel Coward at Richmond Theatre – *Hay Fever*, I think – when a man in the front row dropped dead. She was very put out, because there was a practical meal in the second act and they had to halt the show while the St John's Ambulance Brigade carried the body out, so her food got cold. Heartless and selfish, you see. Do you want a gummy bear? They're a bit past their sell-by date but that just improves the flavour.' He seductively waved a paper packet at Banbury.

'No thanks. I'm going to close up here, then.' He stopped in the doorway and looked back. 'It's incredible that someone can operate as a lone agent in a city this size. You wouldn't think it possible. We've got four million CCTVs beaming down on us, rampant personal-data encryption and local-authority surveillance, and he can still make himself invisible.'

'Urban life has an alienating effect on all of us, Dan. When was the last time you got a smile in a shop or talked to someone on the Tube? Mr Fox has learned to adapt and embrace the new darkness. He has the tools to control it. His life unfolds inside his head. I need to know what he's planning next.'

'I don't know how you can find that out. He's a murderer, Mr Bryant. He's separated from everybody else.'

'Maybe he always has been. What happened to create the void in him? There's a danger that when you pack up from here, tape the front door shut and leave, we may never see or hear from him again, do you understand? I can't let that happen.'

'I've done my best, but I can't work with what isn't there.' Banbury shrugged.

'We're supposed to specialize in finding out what isn't there. Find me something.'

'Some people – ' Banbury sought the right phrase, ' – don't have a key that unlocks them. But if Mr Fox does, I'm willing to bet it'll be in his formative years, between the ages of, say, seven and twelve. It won't tell us where he is now, of course – '

'Maybe not, but it's a place to start,' said Bryant. 'Keep looking, and leave everything exactly where it is, just in case he decides to come back. I'll see if we can run surveillance for a few days at least.'

Bryant was about to leave, then stopped. Inside the open bathroom cabinet he could see a small white plastic pot.

Removing it, he checked inside. 'He wears contacts. The case is still wet, and there's what looks like an eyelash. Can you run this through your DNA Database?'

'Depends on whether the saline solution has corrupted the sample, but I'll give it my best shot.'

'You'll need to. We don't have anything else.'

'Do you think he's insane?'

'We're all mad,' Bryant replied unhelpfully. 'That chap Ted Bundy was working as a suicide-prevention officer while he was murdering women. In 1581, the test of legal insanity was based upon an understanding of good and evil. A defendant needed to prove that he couldn't distinguish between right and wrong. But what if he could, and still committed atrocities? The insanity ruling was amended to allow for those who couldn't resist the impulse to kill. Nowadays, that clause has been removed because serial killers don't fit the legal definition of insanity. They accumulate weapons, plan their attacks, hide evidence and avoid detection for years, so it's clear they should know right from wrong. They certainly appear to be making informed choices. Voices in the brain? Perhaps. Something in the darkness speaks to them.'

'I thought you didn't know anything about serial killers,' said Banbury.

'I don't,' Bryant replied. 'But I've seen the things that make men mad.'

5

TROUBLE

Detective Sergeant Janice Longbright was not exactly the tearful type. She had been around police stations all her life, and it took a lot to upset her.

When she was seven years old she had been sitting in the public area of the old cop shop in Bow Street, waiting for her mother to come off duty, when a distressed young man walked in and cut his wrists with a straight razor, right in front of her. The scarlet ribbons that unfurled from his scraggy white arms were shocking, certainly, but she was fascinated by the trail of blood splashes he left as he walked on through the hall, because she had been seeing their pattern for the previous two weeks whenever she shut her eyes. His death seemed to clear the problem, and her sleep that night was deep and dreamless.

Longbright's mother had often brought copies of case notes home with her at night. Gladys was always careful not to leave them lying around the flat, but her daughter knew exactly where to find them. Shootings, stabbings, men 'going a bit mental' – political correctness had been thin on the ground back then. No diversity training, no child-trauma services, nothing much to comfort the beaten and bereaved beyond a cup of strong tea and a comforting chat. And somehow, perhaps because she was used to the subject of death being introduced at the meal table or between Saturday-night TV shows, young Janice had remained a well-balanced child.

Gladys had discussed the mysteries of human behaviour with her daughter in a kindly, dispassionate manner, as if they were stories that could only damage the sensibilities of other, less robust families. Janice had grown up tough enough to survive the defection of her father and the loss of her beloved mother. She had spent eleven years with a partner whose nerve had ultimately failed him when faced with commitment. There was a core inside her as firm as oak, inherited from a long line of strong women, and nothing could chip it away.

But by God, she was sorry to lose Liberty DuCaine.

Friends for four years, lovers for one night, they would probably have proved too similar to grow their relationship further, but the chance to try had been snatched away from her. So she sealed his death inside her head, somewhere at the back with the other sad things, and told herself she might look back one day in the future, but not yet. There was too much to do. Her colleagues probably all thought she was a hard cow, but it couldn't be helped. There was a time to cry, and it was not now.

First things first; if they were really going to clear up all outstanding work by the end of the week, they needed to get organized. The offices were a dirty, dangerous disgrace. The unit hadn't had a chance to catch its breath since it moved in. Crates were piled in the hall, taps leaked, light fittings buzzed and smouldered, the floors were strewn with badly connected cables, doors jammed shut or opened by themselves. The detectives' files were a hopeless mess. Bryant kept hard copies in cardboard folders, May kept his on hard drives, and neither knew what the other was doing.

She had hoped April would help her sort everything out, but the poor girl had declined into her former agoraphobic state after DuCaine's death, and could not be persuaded to return to the unit. Janice was annoyed with her for giving in to her demons. Her departure had handed another small victory to Mr Fox. *She's gone and it's a shame, but there's work to do*, she thought, rolling up her sleeves and filling a bucket.

The PCU's new home was situated on the first and second floors of an unrenovated warehouse on the corner of Balfe Street and Caledonian Road, sandwiched between a scruffy Edwardian residential terrace and a traffic-clogged arterial road. The detectives' room overlooked the latter, and despite the detective sergeant's best efforts, they had so far resisted rehabilitation.

A little chaos had always suited the elderly detectives. The world was an untidy place, Bryant always told her, and he had an innate suspicion of those who tried to keep it too neat. John May was, of course, the exact opposite. His white apartment in Shad Thames was eerily immaculate, and only the burbling presence of a small television, left on a rolling news channel whenever he was at home, disturbed the sense of orderly calm. But here in King's Cross, their chaotic offices defied order.

Longbright looked over at the two Turkish Daves. One was drinking tea and the other was reading Thackeray's *Vanity Fair*. 'Are you two going to do any work?' she asked.

'We're waiting for the wood,' said one.

'Can't do anything without the wood,' said the other.

She snatched away the mug of tea and the novel. 'If you're reading this for tips on British society, it's out of date. These days, pushy little bitches like Becky Sharp end

up working in the media.' They looked blankly at her.
'It doesn't matter. Go and get the wood or you'll get the
boot.'

'No good,' said one. 'We got no cash.'

Longbright dug a roll of notes from her pocket and
tossed it over. 'Buy the wood, bring me the change and
get a receipt or I'll break your nose.'

The workmen left, muttering under their breath.

Longbright wondered if she could get away with
throwing out some of Bryant's rubbish. He would notice
if the bear's head table-lamp went missing, but perhaps
his collection of Great Western railway timetables 1902–
1911 could be quietly dumped in the skip at the back of
the building. She hoisted up a mouldy carton.

'I'll kindly thank you to return my railway timetables
to where you found them,' said Arthur Bryant, poking her
in the back with his walking stick.

'You can't possibly need all this stuff, Arthur.' She
dropped the carton back on his desk with a cloudy
thump.

'It's not all timetables, you know,' said Bryant, pulling
off his overcoat. 'Remove the top volume.'

Longbright did as she was told. Underneath was a dog-
eared copy of *Greek Mausoleums: Their History and
Meaning*.

'You see?' Bryant declared triumphantly. 'You'd have
felt a bit silly throwing that away.'

Longbright wrinkled her nose. 'It's even less useful than
the timetables.'

'Wrong. The sculptor Scopas carved mythical figures
with the features of humans, not gods. He was the first
artist to notice that hidden muscles shaped the face, which
was square rather than oval. He taught us to see what was
hidden. In that sense, he was the first detective.'

'All right, but we've moved on a bit since then.

We've got forensic psychology and seriology, DNA testing – '

'You're missing the point, enchantress. A body is more
than mere meat and fluids. Its humours are ultimately un-
knowable. Why do people behave as they do? Every book
I own adds a tiny piece to the puzzle.'

'But books don't hold the key to people.'

'They hold the key to society, and if we ignore that,
we know nothing. Now put everything back in the same
order.'

'There was no order.'

'*Exactly*,' said Bryant mysteriously.

'What about these then?' Longbright held up a set of
tattered blue volumes. '*Conjuring & Tricks with Cards*,
volumes one to six. What are they going to teach you?'

'I'll show you. Over there in the corner you'll find a
small blackboard.'

Longbright picked up the board, which was divided
into nine panels.

'Stand it on the shelf behind John's desk,' Bryant instructed, pulling out a pack of cards. 'Now pick one of
these. Look at it, then pick eight more.' Longbright drew
the three of spades, and added eight further cards. Bryant
gave her a handful of drawing pins. 'Shuffle your cards
and pin them face down on the squares of the board.'

'I've got better things to do with my time,' the DS complained. She completed her task and turned to find Bryant
pointing a gun at her. It looked like a Colt Single Action
Army revolver. 'Where did you get that?'

'Evidence room. Get out of the way. You don't know
which square holds the card you picked, do you?'

'No. Are you sure this is safe?'

'Of course. It's a Victorian parlour trick.' Bryant aimed
randomly, squeezed his eyes shut and fired the gun. The
explosion made their ears ring. 'Check the board,' he

instructed. Longbright found a bullet hole in the centre of one card. She unpinned it and turned it over.

'Is that the card you chose?'

'No. I picked the three of spades. This is the nine of clubs. What did you do?'

'You were meant to pick the nine of clubs. An identical card with a bullet hole was pinned to the back of one of the board's squares. The square is on a pivot. When you pressed the card on to it, you activated a timer that flicked the square over. Persistence of vision covered the switch. The gun was loaded with a blank, obviously.'

'Well, if you'd forced the right card it would have worked,' said Longbright encouragingly.

Just then, Raymond Land came storming into the office. 'What the bloody hell is going on?' he demanded. 'Someone just fired a gun!'

'That was just a blank,' Longbright explained. 'Mr Bryant was showing me a trick.'

'Blank my arse. The bullet came straight through my wall. You could have killed me! It missed my ear by about two inches and exploded Crippen's litter tray. Gave him the fright of his life. Look.' He held up a squashed slug.

'My mistake,' Bryant apologized absently. 'I'm sure I gave you the nine of clubs. I think I'll just step out to my verandah for a smoke and a ponder. Behave appropriately while I'm gone.'

'Wait, come back, you've got no right – ' Land began, but Bryant had slipped out.

After all this time he's still trouble, thought Longbright. *I like that in a man.*

Land was looking for someone to blame. 'And you, the way you encourage him,' he said, shaking a finger at her.

'Don't look at me, boss. Mr Bryant's teaching himself magic.'

'Well I'll teach him how to disappear if he's not careful,' Land concluded ineffectually, returning to his room.

Longbright replaced the books in their rightful places, but the dust was setting off her hay fever. Checking her watch, she noted that Liberty DuCaine's funeral would soon be starting. Although the unit had been warned to stay away, she felt that someone should be there. Reaching a decision, she donned her jacket and set off.

6

BEST BOY

At first glance, the City of London crematorium appeared to be nothing more than a pleasant London park. There were a great many rose beds neatly arranged like ledgers, and a variety of clipped English trees: elm, walnut, chestnut, beech. On closer inspection, Longbright noticed the small rectangular plaques set at ground level in the grass. An aquamarine sky released soft patters of rain, accentuating the landscape's greenness, releasing the fresh smell of spring leaves.

Feeling guilty because she had forgotten to change from her PCU staff jacket, Longbright turned up her collar and headed for the chapel's ante-room. She could hear an organ recording of 'From Every Stormy Wind That Blows' coming to an end.

The doctor at University College Hospital had told her that if Liberty DuCaine's neck wound had been a centimetre lower, it would have been over his jawbone. The tip of the weapon would have been deflected and prevented from going into his brain. Instead it had slid straight up, tearing into his temporal lobe. Longbright had spent the weekend trying to imagine what she could have done differently. But there was no use wondering, because they were all at fault; they had fatally underestimated the capabilities of their suspect.

'What do you think you're doing?' asked a large Caribbean woman, watching her from the damp archway.

'I was just reading the tributes on the flowers,' said Longbright, straightening up.

'We don't want the police here. Did you even know my son?'

'I worked with him for a while.'

The woman examined the badge on Longbright's jacket. 'He wasn't at your unit for very long.'

'No, but we brought him in on a number of special investigations before he joined full-time.' Longbright held her ground. She had heard about Liberty's mother, and knew what to expect. 'I'm sure you'd rather not have anyone from the PCU here, Mrs DuCaine, but I counted myself a close friend.'

'How close?' Mrs DuCaine gave her a hard stare before approaching the floral display with a weary sigh. She bent with difficulty and tidied the tributes with the air of a woman who needed something useful to do. 'If you want to be here, I suppose I should accept with grace. There's too much bad blood in the world.'

'Thank you.'

She stood with a grimace, sizing Longbright up. 'I'm as much to blame as anyone. I encouraged Liberty to enter the force. We all did. But I didn't want him joining that crazy unit of yours. Most of his friends were against it. They said it would damage his career, that it wasn't even part of the real police.'

'There's a lot of prejudice against us, Mrs DuCaine. We don't operate along traditional lines.'

'Then what *do* you do?'

'We look after cases of special interest. Sometimes people commit crimes that can cause . . . unrest . . . in society.'

Mrs DuCaine waved the thought aside with impatience. 'I don't know what you mean by that.'

Longbright tried to think of a good example. 'Suppose two people were killed in your street in one week. People would think it was a bad neighbourhood.'

'We already live in a bad neighbourhood.'

'Well, in such a situation our unit would be called in to find out if the deaths were connected, or if it was just coincidence. We would try to lay public fears to rest. A lot of people live and work in this city. Someone has to look after its reputation. Your son was invited to help us do that. Not many people are good enough to be asked.'

'Is that supposed to make me feel better? He ended up getting stabbed in the neck.'

'It could have happened to him anywhere, Mrs DuCaine.'

'As soon as I heard the doorbell, I knew.' She reached past Longbright and delicately replaced a card on top of a spray of yellow roses. 'It was the stupidest thing. My mother had a plate, a big Victorian serving plate with scalloped edges, covered in big red roses. I dropped it. We never use that plate, it stays in the dresser and nobody touches it. But that day I used it. I remember looking at the pieces of china on the floor and thinking something must have happened.'

'We're going to catch this man. I don't know how long it will take, but we will. He's dangerous. He hurts people for money, and has no feelings for anyone except himself. But we're going to take him off the street.'

Mrs DuCaine studied the array of flowers. 'When someone in the police force dies, his friends are supposed to rally around him, aren't they? No one from Camden even called. His workmates deserted him because he told them he was moving to your unit.'

'I know.'

'Well then.' Mrs DuCaine studied the flowers with dry eyes. 'There's nothing more to say.'

Longbright knew she was being dismissed. She turned to leave.

'Take one of the yellow roses,' said Mrs DuCaine. 'It was his favourite colour.'

Longbright selected a rose and turned to see two horribly familiar figures looming out of the misty rain. With the arrival of Bryant and May, it became obvious that a police presence at the crematorium was not a good idea. One officer was acceptable, but three looked defensive. The rest of DuCaine's friends and relatives were emerging from the chapel into the cramped ante-room and a demarcation line quickly developed. DuCaine's father fired a baleful stare towards the detectives, who retreated on to the porch.

'I thought you weren't going to come today,' said Longbright, displeased to see them.

'We knew him for years,' May reminded her. 'We couldn't just stay away.'

'And I thought there was a chance *you know who* might turn up to gloat,' Bryant added, 'so I made John come with me.'

'All right, but please don't say anything to the family.' She knew only too well how Bryant's condolences had a habit of turning out.

Bryant thrust his hands deep into his pockets and watched as DuCaine's relatives moved slowly between the wreaths, reading the cards, rearranging flowers, conferring in low tones. 'You know as well as I do that every arrest contains an element of risk,' he told his partner.

'We should have covered all eventualities,' said May.
'You know that's impossible, John. The lock on that
door should have been strong enough to hold him.'
'But it wasn't, and that's an oversight on our part.'
Mr Fox's weapon of choice had been a slender sharpened rod that left virtually no trace of use. Using a skewer
to pick the lock of the holding room and attack DuCaine
had seemed bizarre at first, but the more Bryant thought
about it, the more expedient the method became. Their
killer had been raised on the streets of King's Cross, where
carrying a knife was still considered a necessity for many.
But knives were carried to provide a display of defence,
not for efficiency of attack. Mr Fox had streamlined the
concept, making his weapon easy to hide. The effect of
punching the skewer through the neck into the brain was
swift and lethal, like causing a stroke. In this case it had
worked despite the fact that their officer's sharp reflexes
made him a difficult target.

May watched as DuCaine's mother leaned heavily on
her husband's shoulder, staring down at a wreath from
the PCU. 'They'll come over if we stay any longer,' he
whispered to his partner, leading him away. 'We have to
go. The rest of the family's coming out.'

Emerging from the chapel were Liberty DuCaine's
grandparents, several aunts and uncles, his brother
Fraternity, and his attractive young sister, named, with a
certain amount of grim inevitability, Equality.

'Presumably she doesn't actually call herself that,'
Bryant mused.

'They call her Betty – apparently it was her grandmother's name.' The pair could replicate Holmes and
Watson's old trick of picking up each other's unspoken
thoughts. After so many decades together, it was second
nature.

'Look out, the family's finished, let's get out of here,'

said Bryant, heading for the crematorium car park. 'One tough old Caribbean bird in my life is more than enough, thank you.'

'You'd be lost without Alma and you know it,' said May. Bryant's former landlady was currently spending her days at the town hall, where she was defending the pair's right to stay in their Chalk Farm home. The building was scheduled for demolition. Bryant was meant to have gone with her, but he'd had his hands full for the last few days. The unit's investigations were rarely finite; many had loose ends that dragged on long after the cases had been officially closed. As a consequence, Bryant had been staying late through his weekends. There were times, May knew, when his partner used work to avoid his other responsibilities.

As they stepped back on to the rain-swept tarmac, DuCaine's mother appeared around the corner and waved an enormous rainbow-striped umbrella at them. Bryant tugged his trilby down over his eyes in an attempt to render himself invisible.

'Mr Bryant,' she called. 'Do you have a minute?'

'Oh Lord, she's going to beat me with that umbrella,' he warned, forcing a smile. 'Ah, Mrs DuCaine.'

She planted herself squarely in front of him, blocking the route to May's car. 'I need the answer to a question, and no one has been able to give me a satisfactory explanation. Can you tell me why my son was left alone to guard a dangerous criminal?'

'The criminal was locked in a holding room,' Bryant replied. 'We've already been through this.'

'A holding room – not a proper cell.'

'We'd been forced out of our old offices, Mrs DuCaine, and were short-staffed. We were having to make do. We'd taken every precaution—'

'No, you had not. If you had, my boy would still be

alive.' Her tone was firm and fair, but there was no simple answer to her complaint. 'I could take this much further, you know that. But Liberty thought the world of you both. He never stopped talking about you and the unit. And all the complaining and compensation in the world isn't going to bring back my boy.' She peered out at them from under the great umbrella, seeking a kind of closure the detectives were not equipped to provide. 'I lost my best boy,' she said simply. Bryant saw a tremble in her features, a brief ripple that, if it was allowed to stay, would shatter into public grief.

'If you need any help,' he offered, 'we have a system in place that can—'

'We can provide for ourselves, we don't need your money or your sympathy,' Mrs DuCaine snapped. 'Every policeman knows about the dangers involved, isn't that right?' Her tone softened a touch. 'We were just so proud of him. And the move made him happy. But I want the pair of you to promise me something.'

'We'll do whatever we can,' May promised.

'You have to find this man and bring him to justice. None of us can rest easy until we're sure that everything possible has been done to catch him. You know you owe it to Liberty.'

'I'm very aware of that,' Bryant replied. 'I won't be able to rest until he's been made to pay for his crimes.'

'That's all I ask.' She turned to go, then stopped. 'There is one other thing you could do.'

'Name it, Mrs DuCaine.'

'His brother, Fraternity, wants to follow in Liberty's footsteps. I said no, but he won't be talked out of it. He did his officer training at Henley last year and got good grades, but they still failed him. We don't know what happened. He won't tell me, and nobody ever explained anything to us. I want you to find out what went on up there. If he wasn't good enough, that's fine – but my boy is convinced he should have passed, and was still turned down. I don't want this to have been about the colour of his skin.'

Bryant scratched at his neck, thinking. 'I'll have a poke around in his files and see what I can find out, but I can't guarantee it will make any difference.'

May cut across his partner. 'Don't worry, Mrs DuCaine, we'll get to the root of the matter.'

They watched Liberty's mother as she rejoined the family, leading them to the limousines. 'A good woman,' sighed Bryant. 'No one should lose a child.'

'If we're going to honour her wishes, we need a plan of attack.'

'I don't think anyone at the Met or the Home Office will be able to give us any help,' replied Bryant, tugging at his hat. 'Come on, let's get out of here before the brother comes over. Head down, don't look back. He's a big bugger.'

7

FALLING ANGEL

She was wearing a poppy-red dress. You didn't see too many women on the Tube wearing bright-red dresses. Even better, it had white polka dots on it. If the dots had been black she'd have looked like a flamenco dancer, but they matched her white patent-leather heels and her red cardigan. She was glossy-haired and pretty, and maybe she'd been ballroom dancing, except it was early afternoon and she was reading a copy of the *Evening Standard*, or at least trying to, for she was jammed between two arguing Italian teenagers with ridiculous amounts of luggage.

Time to bump into her lightly, nudging a spot between her shoulder blades.

Make sure you're quick to apologize.

She did not bother to look up.

Check your watch. 15:40 p.m.

A flooding feeling of elation. Of rising triumph.

Is it possible to dare think that this could be the end of the problem? The best chance to get rid of the ever-present fear, the terrible nagging terror that keeps me awake all night, that's been haunting my every waking hour?

Push it out of your mind, it's making you sweaty and creepy. You know you can't allow that. Concentrate on something. Study her carefully.

From the tips of her shiny white shoes to the white plastic slide in her neatly combed hair, nothing was out of place. It took a minute or two to figure out her job, but suddenly it was obvious. The scent was the first clue; they always smelled like candy. The yellow plastic bag at her feet confirmed it.

If you lean forward on the tips of your trainers, you can take a peek inside and see the free sample tubes.

She worked on a cosmetics counter at Selfridges department store.

It was all too perfect. Everything fitted. Time to move a little closer without arousing suspicion. At Warren Street the Italians got off, dragging their huge suitcases with them, and suddenly there was space. But danger, too, because now she could get a clear view.

Move to one side, but be careful not to catch her eye.

She was skimming the pages, not really reading, just involving herself in an activity that stopped her from having to look at other passengers. As the train slowed on its way into Euston, she folded the paper shut and looked for somewhere to put it.

You can't get off now. If you leave now, everything will be ruined.

The platform appeared. The train came to a halt and the doors opened. She moved a little nearer and looked out.

No, don't do it.

Was there such a thing as telepathy? Because moments later she changed her mind and reclaimed her ground in the middle of the carriage.

As the doors slid shut and the train lurched away, it was time for the next phase.

Remove the mobile phone from the pocket of your jeans and slip it into the palm of your hand, deftly operating the buttons without needing to look.

One shot, two, three. A manoeuvre practised in the bedroom mirror for hours. No need for a flash in the bright compartment. Together the pictures scanned her entire body. Perfect.

Hands so slick that you almost dropped the mobile putting it away. For Christ's sake be more careful. She could have seen you.

Her eyes flickered over, attracted by the sharpness of the movement, but there was no thought behind her glance. A very faint smile appeared and faded.

Jesus, is that really sweat dripping from my forehead? Stay calm, you're nearly there. One more stop. She is so artificial, the make-up's so perfect, and yet she's beautiful. How long does it take to get her eyebrows like that? And her shapely figure, every girl on this train in drab jeans and a shapeless sweatshirt should be shaking with envy. Does she understand how her perfection shines through? Does she have any idea of the power she holds? She radiates so brightly that she's lighting the entire carriage, giving it purpose.

She is saving my life.

With each passing second, she restores me more and more. Maybe I'll talk to her afterwards, tell her how she came to be so important. She'd be like a sister, full of private confidences.

The announcement that the train was approaching King's Cross St Pancras brought passengers to their feet. Bags were gathered, newspapers dumped. The casual orderliness had a strange grace, each movement choreographed for efficiency without connection. No two strangers ever touched. Accidentally brushing someone's sleeve required the issue of an immediate apology. The doors opened, the carriage disgorged itself.

It was important to follow tightly behind her, right along the platform to the tiled hall and its bank of escalators. And to stand immediately behind, because it was time to take another photograph.

She never looked back, never noticed anything, her thoughts somewhere else. She stepped lightly on to the moving stairs and was borne aloft like a rising angel. She stood to the right with the middle two fingers of her hand brushing the black rubber rail, just enough to stabilize herself. Everything about her had a lightness of touch.

The banks of illuminated ad panels showed a bouncing cartoon orange. It might have been advertising a fruit drink, insurance or mobile phones. Who knew any more? Mobiles.

Fire off two more discreet shots and palm the thing back in your pocket. Remember to keep the flash off this time – you nearly wrecked everything the other day. One mistake and it's all over.

They reached the top of the escalator and she stepped off. It was a walk of less than twenty metres to the exit barriers. Her patent-leather heels were surprisingly high, and gave her an over-emphatic sashay, as if she was seeking to impress the men behind her. Women in those kind of heels learned to glide with one foot carefully placed in front of the other, if they wanted to avoid walking like farmers.

Her purse was already in her right hand, flipped open to her Oyster Card. She was ready to release herself through the barrier and climb the first bank of steps. Beyond was the semicircle of the station foyer, a great snaking queue of tourists buying exorbitantly priced tickets. She deftly avoided oncoming fleets of commuters as she got ready to swipe her card across the yellow panel. After that there would be twenty steps to the first sign of daylight, and the concourse of the mainline station. As she stepped into the light, she would unconsciously trigger the pathway to salvation. The urge to stop her and thank her for saving a pitiful human life was strong, but that would have spoiled everything.

But she didn't step into the light. Suddenly, right in front of the ticket barrier, no more than a few metres from the outside world, she stopped dead in her tracks.

Look out – you nearly piled right into her, step around! Stop beside the electronic gate and look back.

Behind, commuters were stacking up, impatiently trying to get through the barrier. What the hell was she doing?

You can't stop now. Everything's fine, keep going.

She seemed to be thinking about something. She pulled open her bag and stared into it, not seeing the contents. Then, with a smart turn, she headed back towards the escalators.

You stupid bitch! You can't do this, you're destroying everything, you're destroying me! There will never be another chance like this, you can't take it away now! I almost had you!

Surely she wouldn't go right back down into the station? The Oyster Card had to be put away again; it was necessary to see what she would do.

Sure enough, she walked back across the concourse and headed for the Piccadilly Line, but one escalator was out of order and the other had a queue of passengers, so she made for the central stairs, the static concrete ones that ran between the moving staircases, and began carefully walking down in spite of her heels, descending and wrecking everything.

There were few people on the middle stairs. Nobody liked using them.

Get further forward, come in as close as you dare behind her.

She knew what she was doing, that was obvious now. She had done it deliberately, building up so many hopes just to smash them down at the last minute. A torrent of furious filth rolled forth, silently.

I wish to God she was dead, the selfish bitch.

An anger rose up that could set fire to the world, reddening the tunnel, washing the walls in crimson flames.

She deserved to be punished, to have the life knocked from her body. It was odd to look down and see a disembodied right hand sharply rising to plant itself at the base of her spine. Suddenly she was propelled forward, just enough to throw the balance from those carefully planted high heels. She gave the smallest of gasps as she lurched forward at a startling angle, falling with surprising force and weight. She brushed against one, two other passengers on the staircase, but it wasn't enough to break her fall.

The steps were steep and the drop was long. Several times it seemed as if her descent might be stopped by the human obstacles in her way, but on she fell. She hit the bottom step face down, and by the time her body had settled to a stop, she was dead.

The yellow Selfridges bag landed beside her and burst open, rolling smashed cosmetic samples in an erratic rainbow of paint and powder around her, like a pair of iridescent wings.

8

BORN IN HELL

'I like my tea strong but this stuff's musclebound.' Bryant sat beside his partner in the Paris Café, St Pancras International Station, their elbows on the brushed-steel counter, steaming mugs folded in their mitts, listening to the rain hammering at the great arched roof. Bryant refused to go to the Starbucks down the road because he was allergic to any place that attracted children, and was bothered by the little trays of glued-down coffee beans that surrounded their counter.

John May perched straight-backed in his smart navy-blue suit and overcoat, his silver mane just touching the collar of his Gieves & Hawkes shirt. Bryant had receded so far into his moth-eaten raincoat that only his broad nose and bifocals showed above his equally threadbare green scarf. White seedlings of hair poked up around his ears like pond-grass, and there was cake on his chin. Even after all this time, they still made an oddly incongruous pair.

'There has to be a way of drawing him out,' Bryant muttered. 'He knows we have no way of finding him. But his pathological desire to stay hidden means he's forced to keep covering his tracks. He'll get rid of anyone who comes too close. His informants unwittingly provided him with knowledge of his victims, so he'll have to surface if he wants to guarantee their silence. And that means he'll reappear in King's Cross.'

'You're saying we should just sit back and wait for him to attack?'

'No, but we know where he operates. He's tied to the area around the stations. We need to intensify surveillance. Never our strong point.'

May drained his mug. 'Well, we don't have the facilities to do it well, and we can't get help from anyone else. Come on, let's get back. I've a lot of work to get through, and I'd like to leave on time tonight.'

'That must mean you're still seeing this French woman.' Bryant refused to be hurried. He dunked his cake, but half of it fell in his mug. 'Your grand-daughter told me she's very nice, for a divorced, bottle-blonde alcoholic.'

'Brigitte has gone back to Paris to see her children,' May explained as he watched Bryant fishing around for soggy icing. 'She loves red wine and tints the grey out of her hair.'

'But she *is* divorced.'

'Why is it de rigueur to have a pop at anyone who tries to have a life outside of the unit?'

'I suppose you'll be slipping more and more French phrases into your conversation from now on. Is that why you agreed to move the unit to King's Cross? So you'd be near the Eurostar?' Bryant enjoyed teasing his partner because May took so much at face value.

Bryant was the wilier of the two, but May knew how to deal with him. 'I'll bring Brigitte around to meet you next week,' he suggested. 'She works for the Paris tourist office.

I'm sure she'd love to tell you all about her wonderful city, and how much nicer it is than London.'

Bryant made a face and set the last of his tea aside. 'I remember Paris, thank you, all garlic and accordions and waiters refusing to cook your meat properly. Parisians are the most argumentative people I've ever met.' He unglued errant crumbs from his dentures with a fingernail. 'The last time I was in Paris some ghastly woman threw soup over me just because I accidentally sat on her dog. They carry them around fully loaded like hairy shotguns and feed them chocolates. I don't hold with animals in restaurants unless they're being eaten. Why can't you date a London woman for a change?'

'They have a different mindset. French women argue, but English women complain. French women are thin and think they're fat, but English women are fat and pretend they're thin. French women—'

'All right, you've made your point. Come on, Casanova, I've done with my tea, let's get back.'

They were just rising to leave when a skinny boy began moving towards them through the café tables. He looked as if he was on a Methadone programme. There were scarlet spots around his thin lips, and his skin was the colour of fish meat. When he spotted the detectives at the window, he made his way through the tangle of chair legs.

'Is one of you Arthur Bryant?'

'That's him,' May pointed.

The boy dug in the back pocket of his jeans, produced a crumpled white envelope and handed it across.

'Who gave you this?' Bryant asked.

'Some bloke outside.'

'What bloke?'

'Dunno. He's gone now.'

The boy was already heading off. 'Wait, come back here,' May called.

'No,' said Bryant, 'let him go. Look out of the window. There are about a thousand people out there.' He tore open the envelope and pulled out a slip of paper. He read it, then looked up with a grunt of annoyance. 'The boy won't be able to tell us anything.'

'Let me see.' May took the slip and read.

Mr Fox was born below in Hell and now there will be Kaos.

Beneath this was a small hand-drawn symbol: long red ears, a white snout. A fox's head.

'What is that supposed to mean?' asked May. 'Chaos with a K? Born in Hell? It's like something Jack the Ripper might have come out with. There was no sign that he was religious, was there?'

'None at all. This is all we need.' Bryant's frown settled more deeply. 'I humiliated him, so now we have to play cat and mouse. This is about respect. He has to re-establish his power over me.'

'You can't be sure it's from him, Arthur. The press know about this now. It might be anyone.'

'It's his method. He uses other people, and always seems to know exactly where we are.'

May rose and went to the window. 'That means he's within sight of us. It gives us a chance of catching him.'

'No it doesn't, John, any more than you could run after a real fox and seize it. They say criminals who do this sort of thing want to be caught, but I'm not so sure. I think he's arrogant enough to assume he'll always be one step ahead of us. And coming right back here, into the station! The nerve of him.'

'The message is a bit vague.'

'Is it?' Bryant studied the letters, thinking. 'I wonder. Hell in St Pancras Station? Torment and brimstone, down below – underground . . . Underground? You don't think he's talking about the Tube, do you?'

'How can you tell? There's not enough here to go on.'

Bryant tightened the threadbare scarf around his neck. 'I haven't got any better ideas.' He pointed towards the entrance to the Underground. 'Perhaps that's where we should start looking.'

9

PUSH

'One bleeding, sodding week,' said Renfield, watching the Daves as they attempted to thread electric cable through a skirting board with a bent coat hanger. 'They're having a laugh over at the Home Office.'

'They won't be if we pull it off,' Longbright replied.

'Oi, you're doing that wrong,' Renfield told one of the Daves. 'You'll need to earth it.'

'You leave the wiring to us,' Dave answered, 'and you can get on with what you're good at – setting up innocent bystanders and knocking protestors unconscious.'

Renfield's bull-like head sank between his shoulders as he strode over and snatched away the Daves' nailgun.

'Blimey, look at this.' Longbright pulled a water-stained book from beneath Bryant's desk. 'Put him down, Jack.'

Renfield finished nailing the Dave to the wall and came over. 'What have you got?'

She turned the page around to show him a photograph of a sooty old building surrounded by a howling mob waving burning sticks. 'This place, taken in 1908. The locals were trying to burn it down. Listen to the caption:

"Police were called in to disperse an angry crowd of residents attempting to incinerate the home of the Occult Revivalists' Society. According to unconfirmed reports, society members had succeeded in their attempt to invoke the Devil. Evidence of Satanic worship was found on the building's first floor (third window from right)." That's Raymond's office.'

'Can you get me down?' Dave called plaintively. 'You've ruined my jumper.'

Renfield ignored him and moved in for a better look at the photograph, although he was also enjoying standing close to Longbright. 'They summoned the Devil from Land's office?'

'That's what it says here.'

'That would explain a lot. The pentagram on the floor, for a start.'

'Maybe they succeeded,' said Longbright. 'Maybe that's where Mr Fox came from.'

A fine rain was falling with the kind of wet sootiness that stained the colours from the cityscape. Looking along Euston Road was like watching old black-and-white television, thought Bryant, like the original opening credits of *Coronation Street*, grey and grainy and out of focus.

He and May were taking the note back to the unit so that Banbury could analyse it, but Bryant was already convinced of its sender's identity. The few civilians who knew about Mr Fox had been interviewed, but their knowledge added nothing. Despite the vigilance of the anti-terrorist police and the ubiquity of the capital's camera network, it seemed he could appear and vanish at will.

'But he's shown us his greatest personality flaw,' Bryant shouted to his partner across traffic, wind and rain. 'An anger so intense that it uncouples his senses and wrecks his plans. And we know exactly where he operates.'

'Look where you're walking, Arthur, you nearly got hit by that van.'

'I have to be patient. I've stung his pride. He'll nurse the grudge until it forces him to show himself.'

'Then don't turn it into something personal, not while we need to lock down our unit status. Let's get the note examined first.'

Bryant almost got squashed between two buses, and was about to bellow a reply when the call came in and changed everything.

The new King's Cross Surveillance Centre was one of London's best-kept secrets. The underground room was accessed by an inconspicuous grey metal door, and its personnel monitored all activity above and below the surrounding streets. The local coppers referred to it colloquially as the North One Watch. Over eighty CCTV screens filled the dimly lit control room, and most of the monitors could be manually operated to provide other views in the event of an emergency. The afternoon's surveillance team was headed by Anjam Dutta, a security expert with almost twenty years' experience of studying the streets. He welcomed the detectives and led them into the monitor hub.

'One of my boys spotted something on Cam 16 at 15:47 p.m. That's the down escalator you can see here.' He swung out a chair and tapped a biro on his desk screen. From this monitor he could flip to any camera in the station complex. 'A young black woman fell down the entire flight of stairs. She died instantly. The steps are very steep, but we rarely have accidents because there's a crowd-management system in place here. Problems usually only occur late at night after lads have had a few. Most people are pretty careful.'

Dutta adjusted his glasses and peered at the monitors, pointing to each in turn. The detectives watched as passengers pulsed through the station, passing from one screen to the next.

'We switch the escalator directions according to traffic flow. At this time of the day we have more passengers coming up than going down, so there are four platform-to-surface escalators for every two descending, and over the next three hours they operate at their highest speed. If one of the escalators is out of order, customers spill over to the central fixed staircase. When that becomes heavily trafficked, we position a member of station staff at the base, where any accidents are most likely to happen.'

'What went wrong?' asked May. 'She didn't just miss her footing?'

'I don't think so. Watch this.' Dutta began playback on the disk that had recorded the event from the top of the concourse looking down. 'She's there on the right of the screen.' The detectives hunched forward and stared at the monitor, but the image was not sharp. 'What you can't see on a monochrome monitor is that she's wearing an outfit in a startling colour.'

'So plenty of people noticed her.'

'My lads certainly did. They can recognize strong tones just from the greys. The monitors are supposed to be in colour, but there's still another two months' work to do on the Victoria Line.'

'Meaning?'

'The Victoria tunnel crosses one of the station's main electrical conduits, and the power outages kick the monitors into black and white. We've completely lost some of the non-essential cameras.'

Dutta twisted a dial and forwarded the picture until it matched his disc reference. 'We can follow a single character through the thickest crowd without losing sight of them. There she goes.'

They watched as the woman tumbled, vanished, reappeared and was lost. 'I can't tell what's going on from that,' Bryant admitted. 'Who's standing immediately behind her?'

'We don't know. There's a focal problem. The system isn't perfect,' said Dutta. 'The best cameras are stationed in all the busiest key areas. Resolution remains lower in the connecting tunnels, basically the non-essential spots. This is a good camera, but it's due for an upgrade. Plus, you still get lens smears, dust build-up, focus shifts. Escalator cameras are key anti-terrorist tools because it's easier to identify someone when they're standing still on a step. The problem with the central fixed staircase is that it's not as well covered as the main escalators. There's another issue, which is the recording speed. We primarily use the system to control flow and identify passengers, but sudden movements can be problematic. We're trained to read images and interpret what we can't make out, so I knew at once it was a fall, but here's the interesting bit.' He re-ran the footage to the moment before the woman lost her balance. The detectives saw her shoulders drop and rise. Dutta ran it again, frame by frame. A ghost image fluttered by, little more than a dark blur at her back.

'There's the push,' said Dutta. 'Right there.'

'You can tell that?' May was surprised.

'I know a stumble, and I don't think that's one.'

'But we can't see who's moving behind her.' The screen showed a soft dark shape with the head cut off.

'It's unfortunate. A few feet further down, and we'd have got everything. The image was blocked by the people walking past to the left. By the time we get to the bottom and the rest of the commuters have bunched around the fallen woman, the suspect's already gone.'

'But you have witnesses?'

'Not really.'

'How could you not?'

'Commuting is a chore, something most people do without really engaging their faculties. When something unusual happens they only start noticing after the commencement of the event. Their attention and concern was focussed on the injured woman. And there was a train arriving. Most commuters were more worried about getting home than waiting around to help us. We've put up information-request boards.'

'Was she travelling alone?'

'Looks like it. We got a name and address from the contents of her bag. They're sending someone to her flat right now.'

'So do you have more footage taken from the bottom? Can you get any sort of a fix on who was directly behind her, anything at all?'

'No. As she fell she knocked against two other passengers, and by the time she reached the base there was chaos. It's impossible to see clearly who was walking at the back.'

'Presumably you don't evacuate the station for something like this?'

'No, that would take the setting-off of two or more alarms at the same time. A single accident can be easily dealt with. Fatalities only take about an hour to clear away, so long as they're handled by LU staff and not the Fire Brigade – firefighters like to play trains. We only call them in when we've got an Inspector Sands.'

"What's that?'

'Tannoy code for a fire alert. It's an old theatrical term,

a call for the sand buckets they always kept in theatres to put out fires.'

'But I don't understand why you rang us,' Bryant admitted.

'We called Camden but they didn't seem too interested. They've got a lot on their hands at the moment, with the pub.' One of Camden's best-known public houses had burned down at the weekend, forcing the closure of a major road to the North, and the re-routing of all traffic. Camden police were being blamed for overreaction by angry shopkeepers, who were staging a protest. 'One of your former staff members is the new St Pancras coroner, and he suggested giving you a call. It sounded like your kind of thing – a problem of social disorder.'

'Do you get many actual attacks in the system?' May asked.

'Hardly ever. If gang members want to pick fights with each other they generally do it away from bright lights and other people. Besides, this lady doesn't fit the victim pattern, which is usually male and teenaged. But if she was shoved down that flight of stairs by a complete stranger, it's a pretty nasty thing to do. And if he's done it once, he could do it again, couldn't he?'

Bryant looked back at the suspended image of the flailing woman, and wondered if Mr Fox's anger had risen to the surface once more. A murderer in the Tube. He had to be dragged away from the screens when Anjam Dutta finished his report.

10

DESCENDING

'What do you know about the London Underground?' asked Bryant, who loved the Tube as much as May loathed it. He felt entirely at home in the musty sunless air beneath the streets. He could scurry through the system like a rat in a sewer, connecting between lines and locating exits with an ease that defeated his partner. If Mr Fox had gone to ground here, he had found himself a worthy adversary.

'It's the oldest in the world, the Northern Line is crap and I hate the way it makes my clothes dirty,' May replied. 'I know you seem to find it romantic.'

'You have to think of it as a mesh of steel capillaries spreading across more than 630 square miles,' said Bryant, shaking his head in boyish wonder. 'Of course, it was built to alleviate London's hellish traffic problem. Imagine the streets back then: a rowdy, smelly collision of horses, carriages, carts, buses and people. But they only dug beneath the city streets when every other method of surface control had failed. They'd tried roadside semaphore, flashing lights and warning bells, but the horses still kept crashing into each other and trampling pedestrians to death. It was a frightful mess. Thank God for Charles Pearson.'

'Who's he?'

'The creator of the Metropolitan Railway Line. He dedicated his entire life to its construction, and turned down every reward he was offered. He dreamed of replacing grey slums with green gardens, linking all the main-line stations from Paddington to Euston, and on to the City. In the process he wiped out most of London's worst slums, but he also had to move every underground river, gas pipe, water main and sewer that stood in the way. And London is built on shifting marshlands of sand and gravel. An engineering nightmare. Can you imagine?'

'No, not really.'

'An engineer called Fowler came up with the cut-and-cover system that allowed tunnels to be built under busy streets.'

'Fowler, eh? Sounds dodgy.'

'The Tube displaced a huge number of the city's poorest citizens. Naturally, the rich successfully convinced the railway to pass around them. In the three years it took to build, there were endless floods and explosions. Steel split, scaffolds were smashed to matchwood, suffocating mud poured in. At one point the Fleet Sewer burst open, drowning the diggings and burying everyone alive. The line finally opened in 1863, a year after Pearson's death. They tried a pneumatic train driven on pipes filled with pressurized air, but the pipes leaked and rats made nests inside them, so they built steam locomotives instead.'

When May stopped to buy some chewing gum and a newspaper, Bryant began to sense that he was losing his audience.

The Tube's history fascinated him because of the way it transformed the city. The directors of the world's first Tube lines were old enemies with an abiding hatred of one another, and when the captains of industry clashed, all London felt the fallout. Streets were dug in and houses ripped out like rotten teeth, without the approval of parliament or public. The despoliation of the city provided visible proof of the monstrous capitalism that was consuming the streets. While ruthless tycoons fought over land and lines, the project caught the national imagination and threw up moments of peculiar charm; when a baby girl was born in a carriage on the Bakerloo Line, she was supposedly christened Thelma Ursula Beatrice Eleanor, so that her initials would always serve as a reminder of her birthplace. Typically for London, the story turned out to be untrue.

The Underground was Bryant's second home. He had always felt warm and safe in its sooty embrace, and loved the strange separateness of this sealed and secret world. A century of exhaust fans, ozonizers and asbestos sweepers had improved the air quality below, but the atmosphere was still as dry as Africa on the platforms for reasons that no one was quite able to fathom. Strange whorls of turbulence appeared before the arrival of a train, and tangles of tunnels could lead you back to where you started, or simply came to a dead end. The system's idiosyncrasies arose from its convoluted construction.

'You know, there are all sorts of intriguing stories about the Tube, or "the train in the drain" as I believe it was once called,' said Bryant, swinging his stick with a jauntiness that came from sensing that murder was once more on the agenda. 'There's a story that an Egyptian sarcophagus in the British Museum opened into a secret passage leading to the disused station at Bloomsbury. I don't give it much credence myself.'

'Really? You surprise me,' said May, steering his partner away from the station. They headed along York Way in the direction of the St Pancras coroner's office.

'Oh yes. The straightening of the Northern Line almost caused the demolition of a Hawksmoor church, St Mary Woolnoth, but the public outcry was so great that the railway company had to underpin it while they built Bank Station underneath. That's why the station entrance is marked by the head of an angel.'

'Well, I'm sure this is all very fascinating,' said May, 'but we've a young dead woman who's being taken to Giles Kershaw's morgue right now, and it would be a good idea if you could help me find out what happened to her.'

'You see, that's your trouble right there. You can't do two things at once. I've got a dozen different things going on in my mind.'

'Yes, and none of them make any sense.' Cutting away from the crowded thoroughfare of Euston Road, the detectives found themselves alone in Camley Street, which angled north beside the railway line. 'Do you honestly think Faraday will allow us to remain operational? We allowed a suspect to escape.'

'He's not a suspect, John, he's a murderer, and his continued freedom provides us with a reason for staying open. We're the only team likely to catch him. If anything, his arrest will trigger our closure. A cruel paradox. Let's see what Giles has got for us.'

The desolate redbrick building behind the graveyard of St Pancras Old Church was situated in one of central London's emptiest spots. It might have been built on the edge of Dartmoor for the number of guests it received.

'I wonder what the staff do for lunch,' Bryant said, looking around. 'I suppose they must bring sandwiches and sit among the gravestones.'

'You realize that every time we've been here in the last month, Mr Fox was probably watching us?' May pointed to the rowan tree where the murderer had waited for them. Mr Fox had been employed as a caretaker by the church.

He had befriended both the vicar and Dr Marshall, the previous coroner of St Pancras, in order to steal secret knowledge from them.

'I know, and it gives me the creeps. You can never be quite sure what's lurking below the waterline around here.' Bryant rang the bell and stepped back. 'Look out, here comes old Miseryguts.' He waited while Rosa Lysandrou, the coroner's daunting assistant, came to the door.

'Mr Bryant. Mr May. He's expecting you.' Rosa stepped back and held the door wide, her face as grim as a gargoyle. Dressed in her customary uniform of black knitwear, she never expressed any emotion beyond vague disapproval. Bryant wondered what Sergeant Renfield had seen in her. He couldn't imagine them dating. She looked like a Greek widow with an upset stomach.

'How very lovely to see you again, Rosa,' he effused. 'You're looking particularly fetching in that – smock thing.'

Rosa's lips grew thinner as she allowed them to pass. 'She has hairy moles,' Bryant whispered a trifle too loudly.

'Dear fellows! So remiss of me not to have swung by.' Coat-tails flapping, Giles zoomed at them with his hands outstretched. Although he had achieved his ambition to become the new St Pancras coroner, he missed his old friends at the PCU more than he dared to admit. 'Come in, we hardly ever seem to get visitors who are still breathing, there's just me and Rosa here.'

The energetic, foppish young forensic scientist had brought life and urgency into the still air of the Victorian mortuary. The building's gloomy chapel of rest and green-tiled walls encouraged reflection and repentance, but Kershaw's lanky presence lifted the spirits.

'I heard about Liberty DuCaine, poor fellow. I thought

it best to stay away from the funeral. There was something grand about that man; what an utterly rubbish way to die. Have you got any leads?'

'We're running lab tests on his flat and re-interviewing witnesses, but no, we've nothing new apart from a cryptic little warning note,' May admitted.

'He grew up in these streets, didn't he? I'm keeping an eye out for him and will bring him down with a well-timed rugby tackle if spotted, rest assured.'

'You're very cheerful,' said Bryant with vague disapproval. 'What's wrong?'

'What's right, more like.' Grinning broadly, Kershaw dug his fist into his lab coat and pulled out a letter, passing it over. 'Have a read of that, chummy.'

May snatched the envelope away from his partner. He couldn't bear having to wait for the protracted disentangling of spectacles that preceded any study of writing less than two feet high. Home Office letterhead, two handwritten paragraphs and a familiar signature. 'I don't believe it,' he muttered, genuinely awed.

'What? Show me,' barked Bryant, who hated not knowing things first.

'Giles, you are a genius. He's pulled it off, Arthur. He's done something neither you nor I could achieve.'

'Let me guess. He's worked out why people who don't drive always slam car doors.'

'No, he's got the unit reinstated.' May waved the paper excitedly.

'How did he do that? Give me that.' Bryant swiped at the page.

'You're not the only one with friends in high places,' said Kershaw, pleased with himself. 'But I did owe you a favour. It cost me a couple of expensive lunches at the Ivy.'

Although he had been told often enough, Bryant had

forgotten that Kershaw had once dated the former Home Secretary's sister-in-law. 'So you pulled a few strings for us.'

'Less string-pulling than back-scratching,' Kershaw replied. 'He's pleased that you recommended me for the position. The old St Pancras coroner, Dr Marshall, was a scandalous old Tory of the more-than-slightly-mad school. Got caught charging the construction of a duck pond on his expenses. They'd wanted him out for years.'

'We recommended you because you were the best person for the job, Giles. You deserved the chance of advancement.'

'Well, you're to be officially recognized once more, effective from next Monday. And you're to be allocated an annual budget. It's conditional on you clearing up this business with Mr Fox by then, but I'm sure you'll be able to do it, won't you? You might even get some new equipment out of it.'

'That's wonderful news,' said May. 'Giles, you're a star.'

Bryant slapped his hands together gleefully. 'Don't tell Raymond Land, I'll do it. I want to watch his face drop. All we have to do now is recapture London's most elusive killer by Saturday.' His irony fell on deaf ears.

'I know why you're here today. Come and meet Gloria Taylor.' Kershaw ushered them through to the morgue's autopsy tables.

Gently unfolding the Mylar wrapping around the badly bruised face of a black woman in her mid-twenties, he pulled out the retractable car antenna Bryant had given him as a leaving present and tapped the corpse with it. 'Identifying marks – well, the teeth would have given us her name if the contents of her bag hadn't. Unusual bridgework. Ms Taylor is single, lives in Boleyn Road, Islington, has a kid, a little girl of five, no current partner, that's all I know about her life so far, but I can tell you a little more about her body.'

'Why do coroners always refer to their clients as if they were still alive?' Bryant wondered.

'Well, they are alive to us, just not functioning. Her hair and nails are still growing. There's all kinds of activity in her gut—'

'Thank you, you can stop there. You'll end up giving everyone the creeps, just like your predecessor.'

'She was in pretty good shape, but she'd had an operation on her right leg below the knee. It had left this muscle, the tibialis anterior, severely weakened. It's why she wasn't able to stop herself when she fell; she knew it would hurt to throw sudden weight on it. Instinctively, she tried to protect her head but still fell badly, breaking her neck. It was all over in seconds. It didn't help that she was wearing ridiculously high heels. A terribly dangerous fashion, but women won't be told. There are the usual surface injuries you'd expect from this kind of fall, damage to the knees, hips and wrists. She slipped, went head-first, velocity kept her going all the way to the bottom. It's a pity nobody thought to grab her dress as she passed. The English stand on the right and walk down on the left. In the case of a fixed staircase like this, there are still unspoken right-and-left rules. Those on the right walk slowly, the ones on the left walk faster.'

'I imagine the weight imbalance on the treads of moving escalators is the reason why they're constantly being replaced,' Bryant remarked, inadvertently reminding the others that he was more concerned with the mechanics of death than the tragedy of its victims.

'The slow-walking people probably thought she was being rude, trying to barge past, and got out of the way. Certainly no one stopped her. I understand there weren't many on the staircase – the rush-hour hadn't started. In any event there was nothing to impede her fall and she hit the ground with a wallop. The impact was enough to tear her dress, which according to Janice is an original Balenciaga outfit from the 1950s.'

'Trust her to know. So you think it was an accident?'

'From a forensic point of view, yes. If you fall off a tall building, you reach terminal velocity at around 200 kilometres an hour and death is most likely to be instantaneous. Fallers instinctively try to land the right way up, so they fracture the pelvis, lower spine and feet. The impact travels through the body, and can burst the valves and chambers of the heart. Survivors say that time passes more slowly during a fall. This is because the brain is speeding up, trying to find ways of correcting the balance. Gloria didn't actually travel that far, but she went head-first. You can survive a considerable fall if you've got something soft to land on, or if you're drunk, because your limbs are relaxed. You're more likely to land on your head in a short, angled fall from, say, under ten metres, which is the case here.' Kershaw scratched the tip of his nose with the antenna. 'Now ask me what I think from a personal perspective.'

'What do you mean?'

'Well, say you stumble and try to right yourself. It's harder to fall downstairs – I mean properly fall – than most people think. It feels like she was launched. It's a matter of momentum. She didn't land on her knees and slide the rest of the way, as most people would – she went out and down, like a high diver.'

'How do you know? It's not on the CCTV.'

Giles ran a hand through his blond hair. 'Well, the heaviness with which she landed. The angle of injuries. I'm not sure the evidence would stand up in court. There's nothing I can directly point to. Something just feels wrong about it. Then there's this. Her doctor's records show she suffered from Ménière's Disease. She was deaf in her right ear and was supposed to wear a small hearing aid, but her colleagues say she hated having to use it. So if somebody stumbled behind her or made a warning noise, she may not have heard it.' He opened a drawer beneath his examination table and produced a plastic packet of clothes. 'Her outfit was very distinctive. Where is it? Ah, here. She was wearing this over her dress.' He held up a small red cardigan. In the middle of the back panel was a plastic sticker.

'Wait, I need my glasses.' Bryant dug out one of several pairs of spectacles that had become interlaced in his pocket. The lenses were so scratched that it was a miracle he could see anything through them at all. He examined the orange sticker. A line drawing showed the right half of a shaggy-haired male, standing with his arm raised and his legs apart. 'It's da Vinci's figure of a man, surely, seen from the back?'

'Either somebody stuck it there or it came from the Tube seat,' said Kershaw.

'Seems a bit unlikely, doesn't it?'

'I don't know, all sorts of odd things happen on Tube trains. I've been going through my predecessor's online log book. Fascinating reading. Dr Marshall had a fellow in here, found dead on a Victoria Line Tube. His trousers were burned, and there were blisters on the backs of his thighs. Turned out a workman had stood a plastic canister filled with a corrosive chemical on the seat before him, and it had leaked into the cushion. This chap sat down, the caustic fluid went through his trousers and gave him the skin rash. The reaction raised his body temperature and caused a seizure.' He peered at the roundel, flicking his hair from his eyes. 'I don't know, maybe it was put there by the person who pushed her. But I'm pretty sure she was pushed.'

'It's not much of a starting point, Giles, but I don't think we're going to get anything more from the CCTV. Can I take this?'

'Of course. I got a partial thumbprint from it. I ran it through IDENT1's online database but drew a blank.' Kershaw carefully divorced the sticker from the cardigan and slipped it into a sample bag.

'It looks to me like a sticky-backed advert that got transferred from someone else during her journey,' said May.

'I don't think so. The only fibres on the glue are from her coat and the train seat.'

'Then we concentrate on the logo itself,' said Bryant, squinting at the symbol. 'It might stand for something.'

'What do you mean?'

'Well,' he replied, adjusting his spectacles, 'if it's Leonardo da Vinci, perhaps she'd visited a place where you might be likely to find such a sticker. A museum shop, perhaps.'

'The figure's cut in half,' May pointed out. 'You look at this and see da Vinci. I just see the letter K. As in Kaos.'

II

VISIBILITY

Mac was jittery. His old employer, Mr Fox, was out there somewhere, and was probably looking for him. He regretted ever having met the guy. He should have known from the start that it would end in trouble.

Mac had allowed himself to be picked up in St Pancras Station, and had agreed to perform a few simple, legal services – driving a van, acting as a contact for a client, nothing that would undermine his probation record. He had fulfilled his tasks and been paid well for them, but then something had gone wrong. The deal had ended in disaster. Mr Fox had screwed up, and Mac knew about it.

He chose not to look too deeply into what had happened; he suspected there had been a beating, possibly even a death. It was nothing to do with him. He didn't want to know.

He had assumed that Mr Fox was a small-time crook just like the ones you could find all over King's Cross, the ones studying their phones in snack bars and stations, who made themselves available at short notice whenever middle-class urbanites decided their dinner parties should end with a few lines of coke. But there was more to Mr Fox than that. There were shadows in him that made Mac deathly afraid. The job had ended badly, as these things sometimes did, but Mac was fearful that Mr Fox would somehow blame him and come looking to take his pound of flesh. There was a terrifying irrationality about the man, and now Mac was peering around every corner with trepidation.

But Mac couldn't get out of town, because he was working right outside the station. He'd needed to make some money fast, so he'd borrowed a monkey from a dealer in Farringdon and put it on an outsider running at Aintree because the tip was sweet as a nut, only somehow he'd got the wrong horse and it had run like a fat girl, coming in last. And now he needed to make some downpayments before he got his head kicked off his shoulders. So he had taken a couple of legit jobs, one of which was handing out copies of a daily freesheet to commuters. It meant making himself visible to as many people as possible. He knew it was the last thing he should be doing right now, but the need for cash had made him desperate.

On Monday evening, in what was already shaping up to be the wettest spring on record, he was standing on the pavement thrusting copies of the paper at pedestrians, who would take three minutes to skim it before abandoning it on the Tube, adding to the tons of rubbish and clutter no one really wanted or needed.

As he handed them out, he flinched whenever anyone brushed against him, fearing an unseen tap on his shoulder. Then, by the station entrance, he thought he saw Mr Fox watching him from beneath the brim of a red Nike baseball cap.

But he looked different. A tanned face, a black soul

patch, trendy glasses, thick upper-arm mass in his short sleeves – and now Mac had doubts, because if it really was him, Mr Fox had radically changed his appearance in a matter of days. When the shades came off, though, there was no hiding from those dead eyes. Mac would have known them anywhere.

He tried to ignore the motionless figure and carried on handing out papers. He wanted to run, but couldn't move far because two other vendors were staking out the other Tube entrances, and his team leader would send him back if he tried to leave.

He stared at the great stack of freesheets on his cart, panic dancing in his brain. When he glanced back the figure had vanished, and he wondered if his fearful mind was playing tricks. He needed to get away right now.

Mac dropped the papers in his cart and took off. He was thinking fast – or at least, as fast as he could – about how to escape into the crowds.

He sent himself bouncing down the stairs into the station. Northern, Victoria and Piccadilly lines to the right, Metropolitan, Hammersmith & City lines straight ahead. Office workers, tourists and students were milling about with bags and cases. People were walking so slowly, stopping to examine maps, just getting in the way. He pushed through the ascending travellers, down the next flight of steps, and was quickly caught up in a contraflow of commuters heading for the escalator.

So many people. A distressed woman trying to man-oeuvre a double-width baby buggy, a crowd of arguing Spanish teenagers, a smiling old man carrying a cocker spaniel, a couple just standing there in the busiest section of the tunnel, bewildered and lost. Mac looked around, trying to sort through the oncoming faces. Some part of him had known all along that Mr Fox was a killer. Mr Fox knew that Mac knew, and perhaps nobody else at all knew because the man pushing through the ticket barrier towards him had taken care of them all.

He was coming up behind Mac on the descending escalator.

Now he stopped and was standing on the right, in no hurry, looking straight ahead. When Mac looked back, Mr Fox failed to catch his eye. There was nothing to guarantee it was the same person, but Mac was surer than he'd ever been in his life, just as he knew that Mr Fox would somehow manage to kill him in public view and get away with it.

At the bottom of the escalator he swung right and headed to another, lower escalator. At the base he stepped beneath a cream-tiled arch that opened out on to the platform. A train was in, and the crowds were pushing forward to board it. He skirted the passengers and continued along the platform, turning off and running up the stairs towards the Piccadilly Line.

Mac's stomach was an acid bath. He glanced back and saw Mr Fox closing in, and felt sure he was being forced in the wrong direction. He knew the station as well as anyone and remembered that the foot tunnel they had entered was now out of use. It led to the long uphill subway connecting the station to the former Thameslink line, which had been closed down. *Christ, I'm going into a dead end*, he thought. He tried to keep calm, but knew that Mr Fox meant to kill him.

There was one hope; the tunnel had a cross-branch from the Piccadilly Line which was still in use. Maybe he could turn off into the crowds once more.

He sensed Mr Fox tacking closer, seeking ways to move ahead, from left to right and back. He didn't know how it happened, but when they reached the junction the crowd was too dense and Mac was forced to continue straight across. Into the section where the tiles were already crusting with grey dust, and the CCTV cameras had been dismantled, and litter had blown in from the other tunnels; into the corridor that no longer led anywhere.

On, towards his death.

12

IN THE TUNNEL

On top of everything else, Arthur Bryant was meant to be conducting a walking tour around the King's Cross Underground system at seven p.m.

He had all but given up his little sideline lately. The anglophile tourists irrationally annoyed him with their endless questions, and were always trying to trip him up. If they knew so much about the subject, why did they bother coming along? The only other people who attended Bryant's admittedly esoteric tours were retired archivists, bored housewives or socially awkward loners filling their days with museum trips and cookery courses. His pastime required him to talk to strangers, something he had little interest in doing if it didn't involve arresting them.

When the tour company called Bryant to remind him of his obligation, he tried to wriggle out of it, but it was too late to cancel. Now he looked around at the group assembled before him and conducted a head-count, studying them for the first time, and found the usual suspects.

A pair of charming Canadians in matching fawn

raincoats and pristine white trainers who were looking as English as possible, and consequently stood out from the surrounding grubbiness like clowns at a wake. A Japanese couple, neat and insular, in straight-from-the-suitcase walking outfits, who oozed such attentiveness and respect that Bryant avoided catching their eye in case they started bowing. A handsome young man of indeterminate Arabic extraction, the kind who could freeze an entire railway carriage just by reaching into his backpack. A handful of sturdy older ladies squeezing the walk in between a Whistler exhibition and a display of traditional dancing at the English Folk Society. A sour-faced man with an annoying sniff and a hiking stick who looked as if he harboured thoughts of attacking kittens with a hammer. And a smattering of invisibles, attending either because they wished to get out of the rain, or by accident.

'We now find ourselves standing in a passage that passes beneath Pentonville Road,' Bryant told the group, not all of whom appeared to be following his words. 'During the War, anti-blast walls were placed over station entrances, flood gates were erected in tunnels and trains had nets fixed over their windows to reduce injury from flying glass.'

'How could passengers tell where to get off?' asked the kitten-hammerer.

'The nets had little holes cut in them so they could still read the station names,' Bryant explained. 'The service ran normally despite the fact that many of the stations were modified to provide shelter. They had libraries and bunk beds, medical posts, play centres and even classrooms.'

'And racketeers,' said the Canadian lady. 'I heard ticket touts illegally sold sleeping spaces on the platforms.'

'The unscrupulous are always ready to profit from war, Madam,' said Bryant patiently. 'When the fighting ended, the Tube's defences were dismantled at an astonishing speed, and life returned to normal very quickly.' He had one eye on a Chinese man who was more interested in the wall tiles. Perhaps he had been expecting a ceramics tour.

'What about the flood gates?' asked the Canadian lady. 'They weren't dismantled after the War.'

'No, you're right. There was a worry that an un-exploded bomb might breach one of the tunnels under the Thames, so they stayed in place.'

'But didn't they also—'

'Perhaps you'd like to take over the tour while I go and get some shopping in,' Bryant snapped. 'I'm out of milk and you obviously know more than me.'

'You've no need to be rude.'

'No, but it helps to pass the time.'

Bryant struggled on for several minutes before noticing that some members of the group had lagged behind. Now one of them came running back.

'Mr Bryant, I think you'd better come, someone's been hurt.' A young man, one of the group's more invisible members, was pointing back into a closed-off branch of the tunnel. Bryant pushed through the gathering and followed the speaker into the disused passageway. He could see the boy sprawled on the ground, face-down, a dark pool forming around his neck.

He knew at once what he was seeing; the aftermath of a stabbing, without question. The boy reminded him of the one who had come into the café with the note; he had the facial wasting of a long-term heroin addict. Blood circled his throat like a red silk bandanna. Bryant pulled back his collar, releasing an abundance of gore. His fingers could not undo the shirt buttons. Remembering that his Swiss Army knife was in his top pocket, he pulled open a blade and sawed through the buttons. The boy's carotid artery had been pierced at two points just centimetres apart. It looked as if a vampire had attacked him.

Blood was running across the sloping tunnel floor in a thin, persistent stream. Bryant tore off his scarf and applied pressure to the boy's neck. 'Did you see who he was with?' he asked.

'I heard a noise behind me. I turned around and saw this guy arguing with someone. There was a scuffle – I don't know – this one fell and the other ran off.'

'Get a good look at him?'

'No, man. It's dark down there. Look at it.' Bryant took the point. The end of the tunnel was lost in shadow. The ceiling lights were out.

'Wait here,' he called to the rest of the group. 'I just need one of you. You, Ma'am? Could you come over here?' He led the Canadian lady to the victim. 'I want you to take over from me, just press on his neck if you'd be so kind.'

'I know what to do. I trained as a nurse.'

'Excellent. The rest of you, stay exactly where you are.' He flicked open his mobile but it had no reception. 'Has anybody got a signal?' He raised his mobile, pointing, but saw only a sea of shaking heads. 'Nobody is to move, understand?'

Bryant headed for the nearest CCTV point, a dusty camera wall-mounted at the junction to the Piccadilly Line. He raised his arms in front of it, hoping that Dutta's crew was paying attention. The stairs would take him to ground level, where he could call an ambulance.

Pinpoints of sound sparkled in Mac's brain. His senses seemed to be shorting out. He was lying on his back, with something warm and wet around his neck. The dirt-streaked tiles of the Tube tunnel drifted into his vision. *Dumped out with the rubbish*, he thought without rancour. *Well, this is pretty much how I expected to die.*

Bryant got through to the London Ambulance Service. The emergency crews were always stretched on Mondays. Fewer patients were discharged by hospitals at weekends because it was harder to find staff who could assess them, so they stacked up in the wards, meaning that A & E trolleys could not be found for incoming patients, and medics were forced to slow down. Luckily, University College Hospital was close by, and their EMTs came charging down the stairs in under six minutes.

Years of heroin addiction had damaged Mac's lungs. He developed breathing difficulties in the ambulance, and started to undergo respiratory collapse just as the vehicle was pulling into the A & E bay at the hospital.

When Bryant arrived to give his report, the staff nurse told him they weren't sure whether their patient would survive the night.

13

MEMENTO

'I don't understand.' Raymond Land stalked back and forth past Bryant's desk. The floorboards nearest the metre-wide hole creaked dangerously as he did so. 'How did you manage to lose the witness?'

'I was forced to leave him with the others while I called the ambulance.' The detective had a conjuring manual open on his desk, and was attempting to shuffle a pack of cards.

'Couldn't someone else have gone?'

'I knew the EMT codes, I knew the equipment we needed, it was faster for me to go. Time was of the essence.'

'This late display of efficiency isn't like you, Bryant, but I'd be more impressed if you hadn't lost him. Any of the others in your group know this bloke?'

'They'd all just met for the first time. Most of them pay in advance, so the company has their booking details. Don't worry, Janice will find him. She's on his case right now.'

'What about an ID on the victim? Can you put those things down for a minute?'

'We're working on it, but there was nothing in his jacket or jeans.' Bryant attempted to shake out the nine of clubs. 'By the way, there was a journalist in the station when it happened. Followed the ambulance to the hospital. Got a good look at the victim, I'm afraid.'

'So what? Stabbings aren't news any more.'

'There was something unusual about the attack. The boy was hit twice in the neck. The attacker knew exactly what he was doing and punctured the carotid artery, but unfortunately the wound looked a bit like a bite mark.'

Land was even more confused than usual. 'You've lost me.'

'You do remember, I suppose, that we investigated the Leicester Square Vampire?'

'Oh no.' Land rubbed a hand over his sagging features. 'Don't tell me this hack's going to try and syndicate a "vampire running amuck on the London Underground" story. He's not, is he?'

'It's not a he,' Bryant replied. 'It's our old friend Janet Ramsey, the editor of *Hard News*. That awful Botox-faced woman who could put a frost on a cappuccino from twenty paces.' He lost control of the shuffle. One card pinged off the vase on his mantelpiece. Crippen ran for cover.

'She's on the story? What was she doing at the station?'

'Catching a train, I imagine.'

'You'll have to stop her. Wait, I'll do it.' Land punched Ramsey's number into his mobile.

'I can't prevent her from reporting the facts, Raymond, you know that. I've warned her that if she tries to foster an atmosphere of panic, we'll have her under the Public Order Act. Where's John?'

'He's gone to St Pancras Station, said you'd understand what he was up to. Really, I don't know why there always has to be an air of mystery about everything you two do. I'm surprised you don't leave each other messages in code.'

'We do sometimes. Well, I do, just to annoy you.'

'Hello? Janet Ramsey, please.' Land covered the phone. 'Could you put down those bloody cards for a second?'

Bryant set the pack aside and dug in his pocket for the parts of his pipe. Land was about to protest, but thought better of it. 'All right, you can have a smoke just this once. After all, we've got the unit back and a chance to put things right. I suppose that's something for you to celebrate.' He turned back to the phone. 'Well, when will she be out of the meeting?'

'Oh, for God's sake give me that,' said Bryant, waggling his fingers at the phone until Land reluctantly handed it over. 'Put Miss Ramsey on right now,' he bellowed into the receiver. 'Tell her it's Arthur Bryant and if she doesn't pick up at once I'll send someone around to have her arrested for obstruction. And you too. Janet, hello. Next time you get your PA to lie for you, try not to be heard in the background. You think you're speaking softly but it sounds like someone mooing through a traffic cone. Perhaps you're going deaf. Listen, if you publish a single reference to vampires or madmen running loose in the Underground I'll bring you in for questioning and keep you here for so long that by the time you get home all your house plants will be dead. Yes, I know I'm a horrible old man, but at least I'm attractive on the inside, which is more than you'll ever be, unless you become a nun.' He threw the phone back to Land. 'So, they've officially given us Gloria Taylor, the woman who was pushed down the escalator?'

'The Camden team has nothing to go on so they've turned the case over to us. It clearly falls under our jurisdiction. Risk of causing panic at London Tube stations.'

'Good news for once. You could break open that bottle of Greek brandy you keep under your desk.'

'I haven't got a desk. I have two packing crates held together with bits of duct tape. But all right, yes.'

'Excellent, it will kill some time while I'm waiting for Meera to come back with the X-rays.'

'What X-rays?'

'Sorry, *vieille chaussette*, I forgot to mention. The stab-victim, we're getting X-rays ahead of the post-mortem – not that he's quite dead yet, but he's on a respirator, and I don't suppose he's long for this world. The entry wound suggests he was stabbed with a skewer, and they should tell us if he was, which would mean that Mr Fox has resurfaced, just as he said he would.' Bryant lit his pipe and sucked pensively. On the desk before him lay the note. 'Take a look at that.'

'So this is the famous warning? Not very informative, is it?'

'It's suggestive. Foxes live underground. Hell is underground. And the misspelling of chaos, there's a sense of timeless tragedy.'

'A sense of illiteracy, more like.' Land gave a harrumph. 'Wishful thinking on your part.'

'Not at all. He's growing in confidence, but perhaps he also wants to be stopped. Something torments him. Why else would he bother to send a message like that? There's another thing. Giles thinks the sticker on Gloria Taylor's back is a letter K. Suppose it stands for Kaos?'

'Are you seriously suggesting he attacked two different people in the same Tube station a little more than two hours apart? Why didn't he use the same method for both?'

'I don't know. Do me a favour, will you, and pick a card.'

Land was so used to Bryant's odd behaviour that he

accepted the card, looked at it and put it back in the pack. 'Why would he leave a sticker on one victim but not the other? It doesn't make any sense.'

'For once I agree with you. Nine of clubs.'

Raymond smoothed his straggling hair across his bald patch, a sure sign that he was attempting to think. 'I mean, what possible connection could exist between a single mum working at a cosmetics counter and a King's Cross junkie?' He gave a weary sigh. 'It was the four of diamonds. Let's hope you're a better detective than you are a magician.'

'I don't know how you can eat that,' said Meera Mangeshkar. She watched as Colin Bimsley stuffed a forkful of dripping orange noodles into his mouth. He was sitting on top of a green plastic recycling bin, grazing from a yellow polystyrene box, and didn't seem to mind the smell of rotting garbage that permeated the brick yard.

The pair were staking out the Margery Street flat from the rubbish-disposal area. It was the only place on the ground floor of the estate that could not be seen from the windows of the apartment. Half past nine on a murky, saturated Monday night. Meera was wet, cold and impatient for results. She was also annoyed that Bimsley appeared to be enjoying himself.

'I can eat anything if I'm hungry,' he told her, thrusting his plastic fork into the glutinous contents of the box. 'Chicken korma, pad thai, shawarma, fishcakes, spag bog, whelks.' He chewed ruminatively on a piece of stir-fried pork. 'Sushi, cod and chips, saveloy, doner kebab, pasties.' A tiny old woman came to throw some leaking binbags into a container and pretended not to notice him. 'Sauerkraut, pickled eggs, curried goat, fried bananas.' He air-ticked the items with his fork.

Meera grimaced. 'You're a genuinely disgusting person, do you know that?'

'No, I just come from a big family of coppers, that's all. None of them ever went home and cooked after being on duty, they were all too knackered, we lived on takeaways. The difference between you and me is that you saw the career as a way out, whereas it never occurred to me to do anything else.'

'So you want to spend your life sifting through rotting crap and doing surveillance? You don't want to better yourself?'

Bimsley spat a piece of gristle back into the box and looked at her with blank blue eyes.

'I give up with you,' she said. 'We've got nothing in common.'

'That's why it'd be a good idea for you to go out with me. I never trust those online dating questionnaires where you list all the things you like and find someone who likes exactly the same stuff. I mean, what's the point of having someone who agrees with you all the time?'

'And that's your entire philosophy for dating, is it?'

'Yeah, I ask out the least likely women. It worked until I met you.'

'If you know we've got nothing in common, why do you keep asking?'

'I figured you'd eventually crack. I thought one day I'd be talking to you and there would be this tiny noise, like – ' There was a tinkle of breaking glass. 'Yeah, like that.'

'No. Someone's got in,' said Meera.

Bimsley threw his dinner carton behind him and jumped to his feet. The pair ran around the corner in time to see a leg vanishing through Mr Fox's kitchen window.

'There's a back way,' said Mangeshkar. 'You take it. I can get through the front.' They splattered through the flooded forecourt to the flat. Meera reached the kitchen window, lifted herself to the sill and carefully climbed through. The apartment was in darkness, but she could hear footsteps in the room beyond. After dropping to the floor, she entered the hall and saw a far door closing. She padded along the hall and cautiously pushed it open.

A familiar figure was framed outside the window. 'He's already gone,' Bimsley called. 'Go back out the front.'

They met outside the block, but there was no sign of anyone. A small park backed on to the estate. Beyond that was a maze of misted sidestreets. 'How could he have gone through the flat so quickly?' Meera asked.

'He came back for something and knew exactly where to look,' said Colin. 'Call it in.'

Dan Banbury was halfway home when the message came through. Bryant wanted him to return to Margery Street and see if anything was missing. Banbury had taken photographs, but did not need to rely on them. He could always tell when something had been moved at a crime scene. As a kid he had conducted memory tests for bets. A favourite party trick had been to divine the contents of other kids' pockets, a pastime he was now teaching to his own son.

He arrived back on the estate half an hour later, and found Bimsley waiting for him. It only took a few seconds of looking around the lounge to spot what had been removed.

'A framed photograph – there.' Banbury pointed to a small space on the wall. 'It doesn't make sense.'

'What do you mean?' Bimsley cocked his head at the rectangle of pale wallpaper.

'It was a photograph of a metal bench,' Banbury replied.

'And that's all he's taken?'

'Nothing else has been touched.'

'What kind of frame?'

'Aluminium, with a cardboard back.'

'Blimey,' said Bimsley. 'There must have been something pretty valuable hidden inside it to risk getting caught like that.'

14

THE LETTER K

John May checked his vintage Rolex for the fifth time. He was seated at the bar of the St Pancras Grand, a restaurant on the upper level of the vast, airy St Pancras Station. He was waiting for Rufus Abu. Like a pixilated image on a TV screen, Rufus was infernally difficult to keep in focus. He left a ghost-track across the city's security network, and never stayed longer than a few minutes in any public place. May had tried contacting him on every electronic device he owned, but there had been no answer. All he could ever do was send a call into the ether and wait for him to appear at a pre-arranged spot.

The police remained unconvinced that the diminutive teenaged hacker was on their side. He was still wanted for extradition by an American intelligence agency operating in London, because he had slipped under the tracking defences of a US insurance company and exposed their vulnerability to cyber-attack. The fact that Rufus had merely intended to highlight the firm's security issues revealed his greatest weakness: he was driven to try and change the world for the better, without realizing that he would always make the wrong people angry.

'Don't make me eat here.'

May turned and found Rufus standing beside him at the counter.

'Just get me an OJ. I have my own gin.'

'I knew you wouldn't stay long enough to have dinner,' May replied. He had picked the venue because there was only one surveillance camera in operation, by the door, and he was blocking its view. 'How are you doing?'

'Copacetic, John, staying fly and dry. Cotchin' down in the South Bank until the fudges pass. Buncha drag-ass cholos in old-school Pumas looking for a face-up.'

May had trouble deciphering Rufus's retro-slang, but vaguely recalled that a *fudge* was an idiot because the initials stood for low examination grades. For once the hacker was dressed like a regular teenager, in jeans and a black sweatshirt, instead of looking like a miniature version of a suburban nightclub manager.

'Sorry your 187 'scaped.'

May gave him a blank look.

'Your killer, man. He'll pop again. Listen, I need your help. Can you get me off the grill?'

'You're wanted by American intelligence, Rufus, what do you expect me to do? Maybe I could talk to someone, but you'll have to do something for me.'

'Spell it, I'm listening.'

May waited while Rufus added homemade gin to his orange juice, then took the plastic sticker from his pocket. 'Have you seen anything like this around town?'

Rufus studied the label. 'Where'd you catch it?'

'From the coat of a dead woman. There's a chance the killer might have marked her with it for some reason. We're running checks on her friends and family, going through her apartment, the usual stuff, but I don't think we'll get much. If you have a fight at home with someone, you don't wait until they're boarding a train to take a pop at them.'

'Wait, I have an IRC CyberScript giz for this.' Rufus pulled out a white plastic stick no thicker than a ballpoint pen, and extended an antenna the width of paperclip wire. He ran it over the sticker and jacked the other end into a slender white credit card. 'We 'steined this from some military defence pattern recog software – simple stuff, just creates a rolling design database.'

'"We"?' said May. 'There's more than one of you?' His question went unanswered.

'Man, this station's wi-fi is dragging. Give me a minute.' He shook the box impatiently. 'One ID traceover. It's a bar.'

'A bar? What does that mean?'

'No man, a *bar* – a drinking establishment.' He turned the screen around and showed May the logo of the Karma Bar. 'Corner of Judd Street and Tavistock Place – it's the nearest bar to UCL, apart from the college union lounge. Either your vic chilled there, or you're looking for some-one who hung with her. UCL suggests a student.'

'Rufus, you're a genius, I owe you one.'

'So pay the debt. Call off the intel before they cap me.'

'I'll try, Rufus, but you know I can't promise. I'll do what I can. Don't worry, they're not going to shoot you.'

'I can't keep running, John. I'm getting too old. There are faster guys comin' up under me.'

May looked at the small-boned West Indian boy, noting that his oversized trainers barely reached the lower rung of the stool. He tried to imagine what a faster, younger generation of computer hackers would be like, but the idea was quite beyond his grasp.

He could easily have arranged for someone else to cover it, but May headed for the bar because he had nothing better to do. He felt bad about April. His grand-daughter had been doing well at the unit until the traumatic events surrounding DuCaine's death had unseated her. Refusing to talk to her grandfather, she had folded a few clothes into a suitcase and used the ticket her uncle Alex had emailed. For a girl who claimed to suffer from phobias whenever she became stressed, he thought it odd that she had no qualms about getting on a plane. *All that hard work with her*, he thought, *and I'm back where I started.*

The newly divorced Brigitte was back in Paris for the week, visiting her two sons. May wanted to stay in her rented apartment in Bloomsbury, to slouch on her ridiculous beaded floor cushions drinking fierce red wine and talking until all the street traffic had died away. He couldn't survive as Bryant did, with only his books and his disapproving landlady for company. He had long been considered a ladies' man, but now the advancing years made the idea unseemly. *There's nothing less attractive than an ageing gigolo*, he thought. *Brigitte might be the one I could settle down with, but she doesn't seem that interested. She only calls me late at night, when she's been drinking.*

So he defaulted back to work. The Karma Bar was marked by a small steel sign featuring the same logo that was found on Gloria Taylor's back. Beside the entrance, a bouncer with a head shaped like a stack of bricks stopped him and searched his bag. 'Give me a description of your grand-daughter,' he suggested, 'and I'll go and see if she's inside.'

'Very funny. Let me in or I'll arrest you.' May flashed his badge.

'Right-ho.' The bouncer swung aside.

Inside the doorway, stacked with various club flyers and student special offers, were pages of the same plastic labels, eight to a sheet. May was assailed with doubt. If the design was that familiar, it was likely to be stuck on posters all over town. Taylor had probably leaned against one and inadvertently transferred it to her jacket.

May found himself in a pleasant, dark-wood bar-room surrounded by counters of illuminated white glass. When the barman set his beer bottle down, digitized silver ripples pulsed out around its base. The sound system was playing 'Jazz Music' by the German funk band De-Phazz, a personal favourite, but surely an old-fashioned choice for a student bar. *We had nowhere like this to hang out when I was a kid*, he thought with a twinge of jealousy. *Mind you, we didn't have to borrow money for our education, either, so it's swings and roundabouts.*

Once his eyes had fully adjusted, he could see that the place was full of students sprawled across low brown-leather seats. Except that they didn't look like his idea of students. Monochromatically attired, calm and quiet and faintly dull-looking, they could have passed for trainee accountants. Did they still march, squat, riot, rally, fight? Or did they only communicate through screens and share their opinions with strangers? It was hard to know what the young honestly thought, because the barrier of years increasingly barred his way.

'This symbol, do you know what it means?' he asked the barman, pointing to the logo.

'I don't know, it's just a design for the bar. I don't think it means anything.'

'You get mostly students from UCL in here?'

'They get a discount.'

'Any trouble?'

The barman realized he was talking to a policeman, and imperceptibly stiffened. 'It's not that kind of bar.'

'What kind is it?'

'What is it you want?'

'One of these stickers was found at a crime scene. I'm just checking it out. Hang on.' He pulled out a photograph of Gloria Taylor. 'Ever seen this woman in here?'

'No, no one like her, and I'm on most nights. You can talk to the girl who designed the sticker, though – she's over there. The one with the hair.'

The first thing May noticed about the girl was her height. She was folded over a sofa that didn't seem long enough to contain her. Her head was close-cropped, except for an immaculate blonde centre braid that made her look like a virtual-reality version of herself. She was talking with two Asian boys who, from May's attenuated viewpoint, looked about fifteen years old. When May introduced himself, she shook his hand in a curiously genteel fashion, which made him warm to her.

'I'm Cassie Field. Can I help you?'

'I understand you designed this logo.'

'Yeah, though the brewery never paid me for the job.'

'So you're an art director, a designer, what?'

'Visual artist. If you can work in the media these days everyone assumes that you have rich parents and tries to avoid paying you, like designing isn't real work. I ended up covering the print bill myself. And I don't have rich parents.' She gave a throaty laugh. 'I run this place – well, four nights a week. I split-shift with another manager. It's paying for my tuition.'

'What are you studying?'

'English Civil War documents at the British Library, they're for an educational video-game project. I can give my eyes and brain a rest here after I've been working on my laptop all day.'

'So you must know most of the regulars.'

'Yeah, it's a pretty familiar crowd.'

'I'm interested in these stickers.' May held up the one

removed from Taylor's body. 'The K is for Karma, right? Not Kaos.'

She looked at him properly now, intrigued. 'Not necessarily. Show me.' She took the bagged sticker from him and examined it. 'This one's been coloured in. The man's body, see? Day-Glo orange marker. The originals are lighter.' Bryant had not noticed in the dim light of the bar. 'I've seen a few around like this.'

'In here?'

'I suppose so. I can't think where else. A lot of different tribes come in. Emos in that corner, bless 'em, Goths over there. The rest are mostly – to tell the truth, I don't know what they are any more. It evolves, you know? Mostly they're just students. Quite a few Japanese kids. All they do is talk about work. The idea was to get people to customize the stickers and put them on their bags. The bar owners told me to make sure they didn't end up on walls. It's illegal to flypost around here.'

'Since when were students worried about legalities?' May asked.

'Since their education could be cancelled,' Cassie replied tartly.

'Could you do me a favour? Keep a lookout for any stickers shaded in this fashion? I have a number you can ring if you see anything.' He handed her his PCU card, then thought for a moment. 'Actually, don't just call if you see the sticker. Call if you see anything unusual – anything at all. It might seem insignificant to you at the time, but make a note and ring me.'

'There's a group that comes in . . .' She tapped a frosted white nail against her teeth. 'They're here most nights of the week. Something funny about them. I don't know . . .'

'Funny in what way?'

'I guess they're just really focussed. They don't like to

mix with anyone else. I think I've seen the orange-coloured stickers on their bags. They huddle together in the corner at night, working on their PDAs.'

'So what makes them funny?'

'I guess it's just that they're too intense, working as if . . .'

'What?'

She gave a shrug. 'I don't know, as if their lives depended on it. Hang on – there's someone here who knows them.' A tall, smartly suited young man stood at the bar rummaging in a black leather briefcase. 'Theo!' Cassie called out. 'Over here.'

'Hey, Cassie.'

'Don't you ever pick up your voicemail?'

'I was in Devon visiting my folks. What's up?'

'Mr May, this is Theo. He may be able to help you.'

John May shook Theo's hand, taking note of a tanned wrist and an expensive-looking Cartier watch.

'Theo, those guys with the red sports bags are your flat-mates, aren't they?'

'Geek Central, yeah. The loser patrol. Have they been causing you any trouble?'

'No, but Mr May is trying to track down these.' She showed him the sticker. 'They have them on their bags, don't they?'

'Yeah, I think so. Cassie gives them out here in the bar.'

'Not coloured in, like this.' She turned to May. 'Can I say who you are?'

'I'm a detective,' said May. 'Maybe I could talk to these friends of yours?'

'I think "friends" is overdoing it. We share a house. Actually, it's my house and they pay me rent. I can give you the phone number there.' He flipped out a pen – another

Cartier – and scribbled on a card. 'I don't think they'll be too thrilled to hear from the police.'

'It's a long shot,' May confided. 'Right now I'm ready to try anything.'

Cassie had a killer smile. 'I'd get you a drink,' she suggested, 'if you weren't on duty.'

'I'm not,' May replied, 'and I'll have a whisky.' He wondered how much he should tell her, but figured it wouldn't do any harm to mention the case. The PCU had fewer restrictions on information than the CID. 'We have a woman who died on the Underground with one of these stickers on her back.'

'And you suspect my flatmates?' asked Theo, incredulous. 'That's brilliant. Oh, that's genius.' He started to laugh.

'What's so funny?' May asked.

Theo's smile broadened to match Cassie's. 'You'll find out when you meet them,' he said.

15

TUBE TALES

'North End.'
  'City Road.'
  'Down Street.'
  'British Museum.'
  'Lords.'
  'Trafalgar Square.'
  'Strand.'
  'That became the Aldwych.'

It was, Arthur Bryant conceded, an unusual way to end a Monday.

Seated in the gloomy, cluttered staffroom of King's Cross Underground Station at midnight, sharing bottles of warm beer and listening to the guards who had just come off duty, he wondered about the kind of person who would be attracted by such a lightless, closed-off world. He looked around at Rasheed, Sandwich, Marianne, Bitter and Stone, who were naming stations that had been closed down over the years.

Rasheed was so impossibly thin that his uniform seemed virtually uninhabited, although he had just eaten an enormous curried beef pie in under five minutes. 'I never heard of no station at Trafalgar Square,' he told the assembly, unwrapping a KitKat for dessert.

'It was on the Bakerloo Line,' said Sandwich, who was as broad as Rasheed was slender. When he tipped back on his plastic bendy chair, Bryant half-expected the legs to buckle. Sandwich's real name was Lando – he had been named after a character in a Star Wars film, and hated it – and now he was called Sandwich, because no one had ever seen him eat. 'They got rid of it 'cause it wasn't used enough, and anyway, it's only a two-minute train ride from Leicester Square to Charing Cross.'

'Covent Garden to Leicester Square is only 250 metres,' added Rasheed. Stone nodded in agreement; he rarely spoke. Small and nondescript, he looked like an exhausted lifer who had spent too many years underground, away from sun and fresh air. Bitter – so called because that was all she drank – was heavier and healthier-looking, but didn't like joining in with the others. Everyone agreed that she had communication issues. Apparently she liked working alone at nights, coordinating tunnel maintenance work.

'Most of the central London stations are only a couple of minutes apart,' said Sandwich. 'A strange line, though, the Bakerloo. Brown and gloomy, and all them twisting tunnels, loads of them derelict and closed off. The Bakerloo stations all seem underlit to me, even Piccadilly Circus. Sort of yellowy at night, but friendly.'

'I was posted at Camden Town for a while,' said Marianne, a West Indian ticket clerk, the only one who was dressed for the surface. 'They used to change the listing on the central destination board from Bank to Charing Cross branch, just to make the commuters run backwards and forwards between the platforms.'

'I don't believe that,' said Rasheed, finishing his KitKat.

'No lie,' Marianne told him. 'And we used to get them commuter pigeons.'

'I beg your pardon?' asked Bryant, intrigued.

'Yeah, they live outside the West End and come in for the food. We used to see 'em all the time on the Northern Line, but we couldn't work out how they knew which station to get off at.'

'You're having a laugh, man,' said Sandwich. 'All right, then, here's a good one. Which is the only Tube station with a "Z" in its name?'

'Belsize Park,' said Marianne. 'Easy. Which station is the only one that doesn't have any letters in the word "Mackerel"?'

'St John's Wood,' said Stone.

'I suppose there are a lot of games you can play with the Tube map,' said Bryant.

'Oh yeah, loads. Like the one where you have to make a journey that passes through one station on each of the thirteen lines. I can tell you something weird about the District Line,' said Stone, who looked as if he hadn't visited the city's surface since the death of Winston Churchill. 'I know why the trains run quieter when they pass under the Inns of Court and the Houses of Parliament.'

'What do you mean?' asked Bryant.

'When the District Line was being built, the MPs and the lawyers all complained. Said the noise of the trains would ruin their concentration. So the railway company chopped up the bark of hundreds of trees and laid it below the tracks to cushion the carriages, just for them. Money talks, see.'

'Tell him about Bumper Harris,' said Sandwich.

'Oh, everyone knows that one,' Stone replied dismissively.

'I don't,' said Bryant, who did, of course, but wanted to hear their version.

'When they opened the first escalator at Earl's Court in 1910, everyone was too scared to use it. So they hired a bloke called Bumper Harris who had a wooden leg, just to go up and down on it all day. Passengers figured that if a one-legged man could use it safely, they could too.'

'Why was he called Bumper?'

'Apparently he lost his leg when two railway carriages bumped together.'

'When they dug out the tunnel at Earl's Court they found a seam of prehistoric oak, and six walking sticks were made out of it, with silver handles,' Sandwich added.

'Yeah, pull the other one, it's got bells on,' said Rasheed.

'It's true. My grandad had one of 'em. His missus was a Confetti Girl at Chiswick Works. She counted the bits cut out of tickets to tally the change.'

Bryant had come down here to question the staff about unusual events occurring on the Tube system, but had been sidetracked. He had not fully realized what he was letting himself in for; everyone, it seemed, had tales of drunks and madmen, gropers, flashers, con artists, thieves, buskers, fights and suicides. Yet, for the most part, it seemed that the system ran with astonishing efficiency. Nearly eighty million passengers passed through King's Cross Station every year. Sometimes, over three million journeys were made through the Tube system in a day. Bryant was surprised just how few deaths there were.

'My cousin Benny, right, he was in charge of the track-mounted flange greasers at Rayners Lane,' said Sandwich, whose whole family worked down the Tubes, 'and one morning he got the grease dosage wrong, and every train on the Victoria Line ended up skidding straight past its stations. There was a right ruckus about that.'

'So what happens if you spot something suspicious in the foot tunnels or on the platform?' asked Bryant.

'I can get the LT police there in seconds, but if there's a problem, like it's rush hour on a Saturday night or Arsenal's playing at home and the LTP are busy dealing with something else, I can issue a station code and we send our nearest team down there. Other passengers used to help out more, but they're scared to now, what with knife crime.'

'But I've heard about weird stuff at this station,' said Rasheed, hunching forward on his chair. 'Always late at night. You follow someone on one camera, you know instinctively they'll appear on the next one – only, according to some of the guards, they don't. They just vanish into thin air. There's this one bloke, I've heard about him a few times from a guard at Canonbury Station, one moment he's heading down the escalator, then he's running in the tunnel and the guard's thinking why's he running? He can't hear a train coming 'cause there's not another due for three or four minutes, then he watches the platform monitor, expecting him to appear – only he doesn't. The way this bloke tells it, he's the ghost of a dead passenger, a bloke with a broken heart who threw himself under a Piccadilly Line train a few years back.'

'I've heard about him too,' said Marianne. 'After the last Victoria Line train had gone, creeping along one of the empty tunnels, close to the floor, in a shiny black raincoat, like a giant bat. Gave my friend Shirley the willies. She saw him again a few days later, standing on the concourse at Highbury & Islington in the same outfit, surrounded by people, but nobody else noticed him. She thought she was going mad. A giant bat, just crawling through the empty tunnels . . .' She let the thought hang in the air.

'They reckon that passengers saw ghosts after the Moorgate disaster in 1975—'

'A real mystery, that was,' Sandwich interrupted. 'Forty-three dead – train overshot the platform and ploughed into the dead-end tunnel. There was nothing wrong with the train, the track or the signalling equipment. The driver was a good bloke, careful, conscientious, he just didn't apply the brakes. Hadn't even raised his hands to cover his face before the impact. He was sitting bolt upright at his post before the collision, holding the dead man's handle.'

'Must have been suicide, then,' said Stone, opening a beer. 'Bitter, do you want a bitter?' Bitter accepted the can.

'The driver had three hundred quid in his pocket when he died – he was going to put a deposit on a car for his daughter after his shift. That's not the action of a suicide. I suppose some good came out of it, with TETS.'

'What's that?'

'"Trains Entering Terminal Stations", also known as the Moorgate Control. Special stop units put in place to release the air from the train's braking system.'

'And what about the blood thrower?' added Rasheed. 'About once every couple of months, someone on the last Piccadilly Line southbound gets sprayed with blood. They're not hurt or nothing – it's just this nutter who goes around chucking blood over people. We don't know where he gets it, and we can't catch him. 'Course, the tunnel power goes off after the last train, for the incoming workers from Tube Lines, the company in charge of the infrastructure, so maybe he escapes to the next station.'

'Can we stop now?' asked Marianne. 'All this talk's starting to give me the willies too.'

'Yeah, I'll give you the willies,' laughed Sandwich,

cracking up the others. Even Bitter managed a lipless smile.
'Here, you know Upminster Bridge Station in Havering?'
'Yeah, end of the District Line,' said Rasheed.

'There's a swastika on the ticket-office floor – can't
tell if it's a Nazi-type swastika or like Hindus have, you
know – the reversed swastika for good luck. I used to be a
homebeat officer on a council estate in West London, and
when Indian families got a flat, the first thing they did
was create one out of dried beans on the floor.'

Bryant studied his new friends with interest. Perhaps
the London Underground system was a place where men
and women could come to forget the outside world, like
the Foreign Legion. Was it really only a job, or did some
of them feel uncomfortable when they finally ventured
out, blinking, into the sharp blue light of day?

'Come on, just one more,' said Rasheed.

Everyone groaned in protest, but he continued. 'I heard
about a man who got off the train when it opened its doors
by mistake at South Kentish Town. This was in 1951, and
the station had been shut for years, but the train doors
closed before he could get back on, right. His name was
either Brackett or Green – there's different versions of
the story. He used his lighter to find his way along the
platform, and burned bits of old posters to provide light.
The lifts were turned off so he tried to get out by climbing
all 294 steps up the spiral staircase, but when he got to
the top he banged his head on the boarded-over floor of
the shop above, and had to go back down. He tried to
flag down trains for days afterwards, but none of the
drivers would stop, and eventually he became too weak
to move. He was found by a bunch of gangers coming up
the tunnel, but they were too late to save him.'

'There are so many things wrong with that bloody story
I don't know where to start.' Marianne had a throaty,
dirty laugh. 'How could he get out at an unlit station?

And if he died, how does anyone know he banged his head? What do you think, Mr Bryant?'

Arthur was miles away. He was trying to understand why Mr Fox might have moved his operations underground. The Tube system was vast, and connected every part of London. But more importantly, its axis was now King's Cross, where the Eurostar linked it to the rest of Europe. Almost overnight, Mr Fox's lair had become the gateway to forty-eight countries.

But what he was doing here, and what he might be planning to do, remained a disturbing mystery.

16

CRUELTIES

'What a day. New funding for the unit and a case properly sanctioned by the Home Office. Welcome back.' John May raised his beer in salute. The two detectives had dug down into a musty sofa at the rear of the Charles I, an oaky little pub tucked away behind King's Cross railway terminal that had a fireplace, stag heads, bookshelves and an occasional willingness to continue serving behind closed shutters. It was very late, but neither of them slept much when they were on a case. May had wanted to share his discovery about the Karma Bar sticker, and had caught Bryant leaving the Underground station. He studied his pensive partner. 'What's the matter?'

'I don't like being made a fool of,' Bryant complained. 'The case would have been closed by now.'

'There's no point in dwelling on what might have been, Arthur.'

'I suppose Mr Fox picked his name because he thinks of himself as feral and adaptable. But he's a small-time conman who accidentally became a killer. The act has strengthened him, John, that's the awful thing.'

'Why do you say that?'

'He leaves bodies scattered around the neighbourhood and gets us to clear up the mess. We nail him, he kills again as he escapes – he didn't need to do that – and he immediately returns to his old stamping ground to continue. He's humiliating us. He thinks he's above the law, and that can't be allowed to happen.'

'We badly need the link between the beautician and the junkie.'

'Maybe she's a former girlfriend.'

'No. Janice interviewed Gloria Taylor's work colleagues. They say she was very strict about her partners, happy on her own, wasn't currently involved with anyone. Meera spoke to her ex and he says the same thing. They were still close; she called him two or three times a week. Never mentioned anything out of the ordinary. Had her hands full just keeping her job and looking after her little girl. The junkie, well, that's a different matter. Maybe their paths crossed on the streets around here. You can imagine Mr Fox and his victim starting out as thieves together.'

'If Mr Fox is getting rid of anyone who knows who he was,' said Bryant, 'it's because he means to go on.'

'That might explain the junkie, but not why he would shove an innocent woman down an escalator.'

'And in front of witnesses. Can they be traced?'

'We can trawl through the tags on their travel cards. If we start checking records from, say, thirty seconds before Gloria Taylor passed through the barrier, we'll be able to get all the registered user addresses. But it's a lengthy process tracking them all down. The fact that St Pancras is an international station means many of them could now be abroad.'

'Well, I'll leave the gadgetry to you and Dan. You know what happens when I touch anything electronic. I rewired one plug in the new building, that's all.'

'Janice told me you melted it to the floor.'

'Not intentionally. I've been thinking about the sticker. If that's some new part of the MO, why not do the same to the junkie?'

'Maybe he killed the woman for the sheer pleasure of being cruel.'

'But why kill both at the same Tube station?'

'It's the most crowded crossing-point in England, so that's not much of a surprise.'

'The station staff are a lovely bunch of people, they were telling me ghost stories about the London Underground. Apparently, the developers tore down an old theatre, the Royal Strand, to make way for the Aldwych station. Before the 1970s, there was an army of women who used to enter the system after the last train had run. They were called Fluffers, and their job was to remove all the dust-balls, flakes of skin and human hair that had gathered in the tunnels. They were frightened by the spectre of an actress from the Royal Strand who had committed suicide on the spot where her old dressing room had been, and refused to clean the Aldwych tracks any more.'

'Collective hysteria.' May took a swig of his beer. 'Mind you, I imagine you'd be spooked too, if you had to walk through pitch-black tunnels every night. It must have made people very jumpy in the days before they improved the lighting.'

'Did you get to meet up with that funny little boy?'

'You mustn't call Rufus a boy, he gets terribly upset,' May admonished. 'He has the IQ of an Oxford lecturer, and considers it a grave misfortune to be trapped in a child's body. The roundel with the 'K' is the logo of a bar in Judd Street. I've got a lead out of it, if you can call it that. A bunch of students – I'll go and see them tomorrow.'

Bryant gave a weary sigh. 'I miss the old cases. Things

were more clear-cut when we started. Generations of robbers and professional thieves, you saw the same people year in and year out, and you could always get a lead by talking to the families. All those mothers, brothers and uncles who couldn't keep their mouths shut. It's not like that now. Death has become so random. Angry children attacking one another over issues of respect – such a terrible waste of life. And I can't categorize Mr Fox, he doesn't fit anywhere. Half a dozen people have seen and spoken to him. We've actually interviewed him, for God's sake. And what have we got between us? A pencil sketch of a nondescript man, nothing more.'

'There must be someone out there who knows what he's like. I mean, what he's *really* like, when he lets his guard down.'

'Janice is having trouble finding the witness in my tour group. She got hold of the Canadians, but they didn't remember anything significant about him.'

'Wait, you've got witnesses trying to remember another witness?'

'Well done for keeping up. I suppose we could have them hypnotized.'

'That's illegal, Arthur. Let's try and keep our noses clean this week, eh?'

Bryant was taken with the idea. 'Actually, I know someone who would do it. Old Albert Purberry, he's legitimate now, almost, and he'd be cheap.'

'What do you mean, *almost*?'

'He had some problems a couple of years back – it was nothing. A trick that went wrong, that's all.'

'What happened?'

'He was booked for a stag night and hypnotized the groom-to-be, told him he would fall in love with the first person he saw on his wedding day. Unfortunately, the first person he saw the next day wasn't his wife.'

'Who was it?'

'Barry Manilow. On the television. He drove to Birmingham, where Manilow was performing, broke into his dressing room and proposed, but Manilow turned him down. Then Manilow had to get a restraining order, and the wedding was called off and the fiancée's mother burned Albert's house down. But he's better now. I'll give him a call.'

'I'd hold off for a day or two,' May cautioned. 'If we don't find a link between the deaths tomorrow, we treat them separately. Do we have a deal?'

'Do I have a choice?' asked Bryant.

Janice Longbright was on all fours under her desk. There was something wrong with the electric socket on the floor that Dave and Dave, the two builders, had connected up. It was crackling and popping, but as Bryant had blown up the other circuit, she needed it to work. She was tired and wanted to go home, but staying in the office stopped her from thinking about Liberty DuCaine.

'Need any help?' asked Renfield, bending low.

'There's some kind of intermittent fault, the power keeps shorting out.' She refused his offer of a hand and clambered up. 'Don't worry, I can fix it.'

Renfield folded his thick arms and regarded her sternly. 'You don't always have to be so independent, you know.'

'It comes naturally to me.' She dusted herself down. 'Was there something you wanted?'

'I'm sorry about DuCaine.' He looked awkward. 'I know you and he got . . . close.'

'We slept together once, Jack. There's no need to be coy about it. I'd be sorry for anyone I knew who got killed in the line of duty. So I'm sorry he died, nothing more.'

'Bit of a harsh way of looking at it.'

'Well, small cruelties are what get us through.'

Renfield looked uncomfortable. 'I was going to say that I'm here if you get fed up, or need to talk to someone.'

'Thanks for the offer, but I've been around the block, it's happened before. If I think too hard about it I won't come in tomorrow morning. So let's just draw a line under the matter.'

'OK. I just wanted to say . . . you know . . .'

'Can we talk about this some other time? Go home and get some rest.'

Renfield looked dejected.

She touched his arm. 'But it's good of you to think of me.'

She dropped back into her chair and pinned a stray auburn curl behind her ear. Releasing a long, slow breath, she looked around the room. *This is it*, she thought, *the other end of my rat run. It starts at my empty flat in Highgate, and descends to a derelict warehouse in King's Cross. There and back. My life in the service of the public. I wanted to be a burlesque dancer and ended up being a copper like my Ma.*

Liberty DuCaine had given her a glimpse of the outside world. Most men seemed to smile on her in the way that they might admire an old Land Army poster, for vigour and colouring. Liberty had found more within her, and liked the very qualities other men found unappealing. She had no desire to change. She was big-boned, strong-willed, blunt, outspoken, womanly, as glamorous as a lipstick lesbian and as kind as a man's memory of his mother. In the catalogue of desirable female attributes, it felt as though she had managed to tick all the wrong boxes.

She caught sight of herself in a huge gilt mirror that stood propped against the opposite wall and knew this was who she would always be, a Diana Dors lookalike who wore a corset under her uniform and made weak men afraid. *To hell with them*, she thought with sharp finality. *If they can't handle me, that's their problem, not mine. I'm not going to change who I am now. Tomorrow I'm going to bleach the hell out of my hair and go back to being big, blonde and buxom. I reined it in for you, Liberty, because I wanted you to want me. I won't do that again for anyone.*

She stayed for want of something better to do. Paperwork smothered her desk; there were dozens of King's Cross passenger statements still to sort through. With any luck, it would keep her busy for the rest of the night. She could sleep on Bryant's motheaten sofa and start again first thing in the morning.

17

IN PLAIN SIGHT

At 11:47 a.m. on Tuesday morning, John May received a phone call from Cassie Field. 'You said to call if I saw any of the stickers,' she explained. 'Well, I saw some last night.'

'In the bar?'

'Yeah, on the backpacks of that group I told you about, the ones who spend all evening on their PDAs. They came in just after Theo left. I got talking to one of them, and got his mobile number for you.'

'Thanks. I've been trying the house phone, but nobody answers. That was thoughtful of you.'

'Not really. I fancied one of his mates and was trying to pick him up. He wasn't interested, so I thought I'd turn them all over to the police. Have you got a pen?'

'Fire away.'

'His name's Nikos Nicolau. He's taking some kind of pharmaceutical course at UCL. He started to tell me about it but he's got a bit of a speech impediment, and the music was too loud for me to hear him properly, plus he was boring. I asked him about the stickers, but he was

evasive. He's kind of creepy. I thought I'd better call you.'
She gave him Nicolau's mobile number.

'I'm on it,' said May, thanking her. He rang off and
called Nicolau, who sounded uncomfortable about being
contacted by a police officer. May arranged an appointment for 2:00 p.m. at the college and was heading out of
the room when he collided with Bryant coming in.

'You will not believe this,' said Arthur, out of breath.
'He doesn't exist!'

The two Daves, who had been attempting to fit an
inadequate piece of hardboard across the hole in the
detectives' office, stopped work and turned their attention
to Bryant. He seemed to fascinate them.

'Who doesn't exist?'

'My blithering, blasted, bloody witness. Inattentional
blindness, the oldest trick in the book.'

'I have no idea what you're on about.'

'He's playing psychological games with me. Do you remember there was this perception experiment, conducted
in the 1990s?'

'Strangely enough, no.'

'A researcher pretended to have lost his way and
stopped people to ask for help. Each time he did so, two
workmen carrying a door barged between them. One of
the workmen switched places with the researcher. Over
half the subjects failed to notice they were now talking
to someone else, because they were concentrating on the
problem at hand, not on the researcher's face.'

'Who are we talking about?' May threw up his hands
helplessly. 'I'm lost.'

'I'm sorry, I forgot you exist in an alternate universe
where everything has to be slowly explained to you. The
man who was on my walking tour, the one who saw Mr
Fox attacking the addict? We got his ID from the tour
company, but he's not the man I remember meeting.'

'Maybe I'm being dense – '

'You most certainly are and it's very simple. I did a head-count when we set off – I always do to make sure we don't lose anyone. Sometimes when I get too interesting they try to slip away. We had the same number at the end as we had at the start. Mr Fox followed his victim, forcing him into a dead-end tunnel. After stabbing him, he knew he couldn't get out of the other end, so he had to double back. It meant having to pass through my group, so rather than draw attention to himself he dismissed the person who most looked like him and replaced him. Obvious, really, just what I would have done.'

'What do you mean? How do you "dismiss" someone?'

'Who knows, maybe he gave him money or just threatened to duff him up. Took his jacket, changed his hair – I don't know exactly how he does it, but he does. To be honest, he could have switched with almost any of the invisibles in my group because I barely noticed them.'

'Invisibles?'

'It doesn't matter. Then he drew my attention to the attack, which allowed him to manipulate the situation and slip away.'

'What are you going to do now?'

'I think I have a vague idea of what he looks like at the moment. He's shortened his hair and smartened up. He's been to a tanning salon and done something to his face that makes it look different, but I can't put my finger on it. I can get out a basic description.'

'He'll change his appearance again, you know that. Keeping one step ahead is a matter of pride with him.'

'But he's tied to the area, John. I don't know what keeps him here, but that's how we're going to get him.'

'So what have we actually got? He doesn't mind being seen because he's never the same person for long. He absorbs others and uses their knowledge until it's time to change once more. The danger is knowing something about him in return. What did the victim know that placed him at risk? Get Janice to dig into the boy's background, we might get lucky and turn up something. Has anyone spoken to UCH this morning?'

'He's alive and stabilized, but not conscious. Janice is talking to his doctor right now.'

'The Taylor case gets priority treatment. You know how this goes, Arthur; a junkie's death matters less than a young mother shoved down the stairs, because if it turns out she's done nothing wrong and was pushed by a stranger, everyone is at risk, and then it's a matter of public safety – '

' – and a case for the PCU,' said Bryant impatiently. 'Yes, I appreciate that. But if we keep a watch on the Tube station, we can tackle both problems at once.'

'It's a big place, I don't see how we can cover it with only a handful of staff. Dan, wait.' May collared Banbury as he passed the doorway. 'I heard you applied for a priority DNA check – anything from the contact lens case in the apartment?'

'Nothing from the eyelash,' said Dan. 'The saline had corrupted it. But there were fingerprints on the exterior of the case, and they match Janice's ID of the victim lying in UCH.'

'She's got an ID? Why didn't I know this?'

'Only just happened. Tony McCarthy, aka Mac, small-time crook, recovering heroin addict, a known face in the dodgier King's Cross pubs. He's got an impressive string of convictions. He pulled down a couple of years in Pentonville for dealing.'

'Looks like Mr Fox slipped up,' said May.

'It's not like him,' Bryant insisted. 'He's too careful for that.'

'If he's addicted to changing his appearance, he probably wears coloured contacts. And Mac was a junkie. If Mr Fox invited him over and left him alone for even a minute, it's likely he'd go through his host's bathroom cabinet looking for something to steal or swallow. He picked up the lens case, checked it out, put it back somewhere different, and Mr Fox failed to wipe it clean.'

'OK, we've been handed McCarthy, but if there's something in his past that connects the pair of them, Mr Fox must know we'll find it. He wants me to try and stop him. Wouldn't you want to measure your opponent's strength? See how close he's likely to get?'

'What kind of man thinks like that?' asked Long-bright.

'It's about power, Janice. There are some men who use everything as an opportunity to prove their superiority. Life is a perpetual dare for them. This is his work, and rather than shift from his location he'll hide in plain sight until one of us is forced to make a move.'

'Killing people is not normal work, Arthur,' May pointed out. 'I don't think it's a good idea for you to act as if you admire him.'

'Of course I don't.' Bryant's watery blue eyes rolled behind his bifocals. 'I think he's horrible. But if something wriggles under a rock, don't you want to pick the rock up and take a look? I wouldn't be much of a criminologist if I wasn't intrigued.'

'Then I shall leave you to your intrigues.' May searched around for his coat. The two Daves were standing by with screwdrivers raised, listening with interest. 'I'm going to try and throw some light on why an innocent woman died. Perhaps you'll give us the benefit of your intelligence by doing the same.'

'I have my suspicions about her death,' Bryant told his

partner's retreating back, 'but you're not going to like it. You never do.'

'You're not going to win this one by ploughing through a bunch of old books, Arthur,' May called back. 'It'll come down to modern detection techniques. I'm willing to put money on it.'

'So am I,' said one of the Daves. 'Twenty quid says he proves the old codger wrong.'

'Make it fifty,' said the other, 'and you've got yourself a bet.'

18

LUNACY

Rain was sifting through the office ceiling. Everyone looked up as a piece of plaster divorced itself and fell into a bucket with a plonk. They dragged their attention back to the acting head of the unit.

'Words fail me,' Raymond Land continued, despite the fact that they clearly did no such thing. 'What more am I supposed to do, for God's sake? You get your old positions back, we might finally be allocated a decent budget, thanks to Giles Kershaw's old school network, our enemies at the Home Office have heard the news and are wandering around with faces like slapped arses, we even get a case that fits our public remit, and what happens? I ask you, what happens?'

Ask he might, but there was no response. The assembled staff of the PCU looked at one another in puzzlement. Outside the door, one of the Daves was using a spanner to hit a pipe with the desultory air of a Victorian nanny beating a child. Land pressed his eyelids together and waited for the workman to finish.

'Exactly. Nothing. Twenty-four hours is a bloody long

time in this area, and the trail has wiped itself clean. I walk around the office – if that's what you can call this dosshouse – hoping to see someone in the throes of a revelation, or at least bothering to fill in their paperwork, and what do I see?'

'Is this going to take very long, sir?' asked Meera.

'You'll stay here until I've finished, young lady.' He tried to take his eyes from her and failed. 'What . . . what is all that stuff on your face?'

'Lip gloss and blusher, sir. Janice gave me some make-up tips. I had a makeover.'

'During your duty hours? What the hell is going on here?'

'Not here, at Selfridges, in the cosmetics department where Gloria Taylor worked. I got more out of her colleagues that way, catching them while they were working. Taylor caught the same train home every night. She was in perfectly normal spirits when she left, looking forward to seeing her daughter because she was going to take her to the cinema for the first time, to see an old Disney film they had just reissued at the Imax, *The Lion King*. She'd bought the kid a stuffed lion from the Disney Store, but hadn't taken it home with her. It was still in her locker. I filed my report and emailed it to you.'

'Oh, well, I suppose that's all right. But the rest of you . . .' His attention fell upon Colin Bimsley, who was reading a cookery book. 'I assume that's not a police manual in your hand?'

'No sir, it's aubergine and mozzarella parcels. I'm thinking of taking a course in Italian cuisine.' He had found the book in one of the bins while he was staking out Mr Fox's apartment, and had decided it was about time to learn a new skill. John May encouraged them all to do so whenever they were inundated with paperwork, to keep their brains sharp. Besides, Longbright had tipped him off that Meera liked Italian food.

'What about the requisition forms I asked you to handle? You can't have finished those already.'

'They've all gone off. John created online spreadsheets for us so we wouldn't have to print hard copies any more. But I ran out some sets for you and Mr Bryant because I knew you'd prefer paper. They're on your desk.'

Land wasn't keen about being yoked with Bryant. 'I know how to open a spreadsheet, thank you, I can do that. I do know about computers, Bimsley, you don't have to patronize me.'

'Good, because I didn't fix your printer utilities, so I guess I can leave you to upgrade the file manager for—'

'Fine, fine, whatever, and I suppose the rest of you have completed your duties for the day?'

'No, sir,' said Banbury. 'Obviously, we won't have done that until we find out who was standing behind Gloria Taylor. I've been through every second of the CCTV footage covering the escalator, but we have no clear shots of her falling. The movement is just too fast. I've sent some frame grabs out for enhancement. I'm just waiting for them to come back.'

Land was starting to suspect that he had been set up. 'Then where has John got to? I'm supposed to be informed whenever anyone goes out.'

'He's interviewing a student at UCL,' Longbright told him. 'Following up a lead on Taylor.'

'Well, somebody should have told me. What about you?' Land pleaded. He turned to Bryant in desperation. 'What do you expect to find in that huge filthy-looking book?' He pointed at the leather-bound volume wedged under the arm of London's most senior detective.

'This? Glad you asked. It's a copy of the asylum records from Bedlam, after it moved to St George's Fields,

Southwark,' said Bryant, happily holding the book up for Land's perusal.

'You can't tell me that this has something to do with the case.'

'Actually I can. The sticker found on Taylor's body is a reinterpretation of a design used by the hospital. As you can see here, the patient's arms and legs are held apart by iron rods which are then chained to the walls.' He pointed to the inked symbol within the pages. 'At first I thought the drawing was taken from Leonardo Da Vinci, but then I noticed the thin black bands on the wrist and the ankle, see? The illustration here is described as "an unspecified method of coercion for violent lunatics and proponents of unwarranted anarchy, 1826". Gloria Taylor told everyone she was twenty-three, but she was younger. She became pregnant at the age of sixteen and suffered a nervous breakdown two years later. Her parents tried to have her sectioned. It's probably just a coincidence that the symbol somehow became attached to her, but I thought you'd want us to investigate all avenues.'

'I suppose you all think you're very clever,' Land ended lamely. 'I'm sure you imagine you can run this place without me, but I'm here to make sure you can't. Because you don't think of everything, you know. There are two workmen brewing up tea on a primus stove in the hall, both apparently called Dave, and they don't seem to have been given any instructions about what to do.'

'That's because they're your responsibility, old sausage,' Bryant reminded him. 'You specifically said you wanted to take care of them, remember? I imagine you don't, otherwise you'd have arranged a work schedule for them. OK, someone deal with the Daves for poor old Raymondo here, I'll put the kettle on and let's all get back to work.'

Having returned the acting temporary chief to his usual

state of incandescent frustration, Bryant strolled out to the balcony for a smoke, but Land followed him.

'And there's another thing I've been meaning to talk to you about,' he hissed. 'Your memoirs. You can't be serious.'

'I have no idea to what you are referring, *mon vieux tête-de-navet*.'

'You should do. I found a manuscript of the first completed volume when I was unpacking one of your boxes yesterday morning. What the bloody hell do you think you're playing at?'

Bryant regarded him innocently. 'I'm writing down histories of our cases at the unit precisely as I remember them.'

'That's the problem – you don't remember anything precisely.'

'Oh, I have a system for that.' Bryant screwed up an eye and peered into his pipe-stem. 'When I remember two facts but can't recall the event that connects them, I use the bridge of my imagination.'

'All I can say is it's a bloody long bridge. You wrote up a full account of your first case—'

'The business at the Palace Theatre, the crazed killer who struck during a rather saucy production of *Orpheus in the Underworld*. You read it?'

'Yes I did, and I've never read such a pile of old rubbish in my life.'

'Obviously I had to make a few changes to protect the innocent.'

'A few changes? You say it took place during the Blitz, for God's sake! I know for a fact that you didn't meet John until the 1950s.'

'Yes I did.'

'No you didn't. You met when you were working out of Bow Street Station.'

'No we didn't.'

'Yes you did. Apart from anything else, if your account was true you'd be in your late eighties by now, whereas you're clearly not.'

'Yes I am.'

'No you're not. Don't be ridiculous. I'm not denying the basic facts – I've seen the official case notes – but you've moved the whole investigation back by about fifteen years.'

'No I haven't.'

'Yes you have. Stop contradicting me!'

'I'm not. You only think I am.'

'I don't.'

'You do.'

'Just stop it! I know what I'm talking about. The unit was founded in September 1940, but you weren't in it then. I've read the Home Office file on the place. It was called the Particular Crimes Unit at that point. It didn't become Peculiar until you came along.'

'That's not how I remember it. And if that's not how it happened, it's how it *should* have happened. Far more colourful background material.'

'What, so the Palace Theatre murderer was killed by a bomb while escaping, instead of getting banged up in Colney Hatch Asylum until finally being carried out in a box?'

'Poetic licence. If I wrote down your days exactly as they happened, my readers would be asleep in minutes.'

'Well, I hope we're not going to be treated to revised versions of all our cases.' Land had a sudden frightening thought. 'And I hope I'm not featuring in any of these lurid fabrications?'

'Oh, I'm weaving you in all the way through, dear chap.' Bryant patted him consolingly on the shoulder. 'My publisher said I should make it as amusing as possible, so I shall be popping you in whenever my readers are in need of a cheap laugh.'

He closed the balcony doors behind him and lit up a satisfying pipe.

19

NIKOS

As John May descended the basement steps and entered the University College Cruciform Library on Gower Street, he realized he had no description of the man he was there to meet. He needn't have been concerned, as Nikos Nicolau was waiting for him.

May knew it was wrong to judge by appearances, but it seemed that Nicolau had gone out of his way to appear unprepossessing. He had been put together wrongly: his head was too large, his back slightly hunched, his eyes protuberant. Thinning hair was slicked across a broad expanse of skullbone, although he couldn't have been more than twenty-one. He was wearing a crumpled baggy T-shirt bearing the slogan *A Joy To Have In Class*, which seemed unlikely as he didn't smell very fresh. The senior detective was fastidious about personal grooming, and it bothered him to admit that he was adversely influenced by its lack in others.

'Mr May? There's a corner over here where we can talk.' Nicolau led the way to a pair of red sofas screened off from the central part of the library. 'I have trouble working down here because there's no natural light. I have a melatonin imbalance, and get very claustrophobic, but it's necessary for me to be here because they have good pharmacological reference tools, and that's my study area.' He spoke with the clipped North London accent of a transported Greek, but sounded as if he had trouble with his sinuses.

'I appreciate you making the time to see me.' May seated himself and extracted a notebook. 'Cassie Field gave me your details. She works for the Karma Bar just behind here?'

'Oh, the *babe*.' Nikos gave a snort of delight and was forced to wipe his nose. 'She knows who I am?'

'Well, she must do, because she gave me your number.'

'I give out my number all the time, but people don't usually . . . especially . . .' He could see how that was starting to sound, and killed the rest of the sentence. 'How can I help you?'

May produced the sticker in its clear plastic slipcase. 'Seen one of these before?'

'Yeah. They're from the bar.'

'Were you aware that it's an early Victorian symbol denoting lunacy?' He had promised Bryant he would ask.

'No, I had no idea. Interesting.'

'This one's hand-coloured. Like the one on your bag.' May pointed at the satchel between Nicolau's boots.

'Yeah, I coloured it in.'

'Any others like that?'

'A few of us have them, I guess.'

'Are you some kind of a group – a club?'

'Just friends, some of us started on the same day. Three guys are doing urban planning, I'm in biochemical engineering, ah – ' he scrunched his eyes shut, thinking, ' – someone's doing computational statistics. A bunch of us share the same house.'

'I can't imagine you would have that much in common, all doing different courses.'

'The bar. We have the Karma Bar in common. It's a good place to meet girls and just hang out. There are a few pubs nearby but they get too crowded with suits in the evening, and they screen football. None of us are very interested in sport.'

'So – what? Miss Field gave each of you a sticker, or did one of you hand them out to the others?'

'I don't remember, but I can tell you why we put them on our stuff. Nearly everyone who goes in there is carrying a laptop bag. They get piled in a heap by the bar, and many of them look the same, so one evening Ruby coloured the stickers, so that we'd be able to find our gear when we were leaving.'

'Ruby?'

'She's Matt's girlfriend. He's in the house as well. I don't really know her well, she just came along one evening. It may even have been her idea.' He settled his glasses further back on the bridge of his nose. He was sweating heavily. 'Can I ask why you're so interested?'

'One of these was found on a dead body.' May waited for the idea to sink in. 'In an investigation of this kind you check anything that's unusual, or even just a little bit different.'

'If I can give you a suggestion? People often chuck their coats on top of the bags – maybe it got transferred.'

'You're probably right.' There didn't seem to be anything more May could glean which might be of use. 'Well, it was a point worth covering. Thanks for your time.' He rose to leave. 'Tell you what, though. In case I need to check any further, I don't want to disturb you. Perhaps you'd give me contact details for this girl – Ruby?'

'Sure.' Nicolau seemed relieved. He scribbled something

on a scrap of paper. 'Ruby Cates. Here's her email address.'

May left, but somewhere an alarm had been triggered. The harder he tried to focus on what was wrong, the less sure he became. *Leave the thought*, he told himself, *it will surface when it's ready.* The uneasy feeling stayed with him all the way back to the unit.

Then he remembered. It was something Cassie Field had said. *Too intense.* Nicolau had been trying hard to convince. The look of relief on his face when May had switched his attention to the girl had been palpable.

20

FALLING IDOL

Panic was setting in now. What if it was too late? But there was no point in thinking about what might already have happened, and anyway, here was Matt in his crazy old rainbow-striped coat and brown woolly hat, raising a hand in greeting from the other side of the bar.

'I'm really sorry I'm so late, I don't know where the time went.'

'That's OK.'

'I bumped into an old pal from Nottingham, and we had some catching up to do. Hit a few bars together, I'd forgotten how much he could drink. Then I spent ages on the phone, and you know how that goes, right? It's like I can't do anything to please her. I'm like "If you don't want to go out with me, just say so," right? Can I get you a drink?'

'No, let me get you one.' The smile must have looked painfully forced. The barman was summoned and a drink was poured. 'Did you have a lecture this afternoon?'

'Yeah, the architect from Bartlett, the one with the stoop, it was meant to be about traffic restructuring in the late 1960s, but it was so data-driven that he lost most of us about halfway through. And I still have a hangover from last night. Then I got the nagging phone call and wasn't allowed off the hook until she'd described everything that's wrong with me in huge detail.'

'Did you tell her you were coming to meet me?' The obviousness of the question caused an inward cringe.

'No, you know I didn't, you told me not to. Anyway, if she thought I was meeting up with you she'd accuse us of conspiring against her. A toast to my good fortune.'

'To winners.'

'Damn right. We've got the skills that pay the bills. Just in time, because I'm seriously broke. Here's to money, the root of all evil.' Matt downed his vodka cocktail in one. He was drinking something that was a spin on a Smith & Wesson – vodka and coffee liqueur with a dash of soda. His version added an oily sambuca to the mix.

Matt looked even messier than usual. His tumbleweed hair needed a wash and there were violet crescents beneath his eyes. Everybody knew he was on his way to becoming a serious alcoholic, but tonight it was important that Matt drank at least another two or three doubles, otherwise the plan wouldn't work.

'You're always good with advice. I don't know what I'm going to do about her. I just think I'm a little too wild for her, right? She always wants to do the kind of things her parents do – go to Suffolk and see the rest of her family, go hiking, stuff like that. I don't know what she's going to do with a degree in urban planning. I don't think she knows, either. She says she wants to become a member of the Royal Town Planning Institute, like her old man, but she's doing it for his sake.'

'You have to stop worrying about it so much, Matt. Take things as they come.'

'I can't this week, you know that. There's too much at stake now. Look at me, I'm shaking.'

'Let me get you another cocktail.'

They drank until the bar became too noisy and crowded. When Matt slithered down from his stool to weave his way towards the bathroom, it was obvious that he was trashed. The rising temperature and the accelerating beats had conspired to increase the pace of their drinking.

OK, while Matt's gone you've got less than a minute to dig into his backpack and see what's there. Evidence, evidence – mobile, laptop, what else has he got? Now put everything back before he reappears. Done it – did he notice anything? No, he looks out of it.

'It's getting late, let's get out of here.' Matt jammed his hat back on his head.

The cold air outside was a sobering shock. It was important to get Matt into the warmth of the station before he became too sharp. They tumbled down the steps into Liverpool Street Tube and made their way to the Circle Line.

There were no empty seats, so they sat on the platform floor to wait for the train.

Matt tried to focus. 'I've got to stop drinking Smith & Wessons, nobody knows how to mix them properly. They're meant to taste like a liquidized Cuban cigar.'

'Yes, you told me that before.'

Matt massaged his forehead. 'My brain's banging against the sides of my skull. If I still feel like this in the morning I'm going to cut my first lecture.'

'It's your call, I suppose, but you seem to be missing an awful lot of them lately.'

The train arrived and they lurched to their feet. Inside, unable to sit, they stood jammed against the curving doors of the carriage. Racing through the uphill tunnels towards the King's Cross interchange, it was necessary to keep a surreptitious eye on Matt. The thought came unbidden: *why did you ever put up with him?* The amazing thing was that everyone seemed to idolize the guy. He was a walking disaster, yet the scruffier he looked and the more chaotic his life became, the more they hung on his every word. Especially other girls, the ones from outside the group, they couldn't get enough—

A buzz emanated from Matt's backpack.

'Damn, that's my phone.' Matt swung the bag from his shoulder and started rooting about inside it.

'You've got reception down here?'

'God, where have you been for the last two years? There's mobile reception everywhere west and south of here now. Hampstead and . . .' a long pause while he tried to frame the thought, 'Old Street, still a problem because of the tunnel depth or something. I dunno. Where the hell . . .' The contents of his bag were tumbling over people's feet: a dirty ball of stained T-shirts, some books with loose pages, half a dozen plastic pens, his mobile –

'Here, let me give you a hand.' Together they started shovelling everything back into the bag. Matt helplessly attempted to pick up the fluttering pages. Then the train was slowing and they were arriving at King's Cross.

'Come on, you have to change here. Zip up your bag.'

Matt followed, lurching from the carriage and along the platform.

The scabrous, half-retiled tunnel led to stairs, but Matt baulked before climbing them. 'Give me a minute,' he protested, holding back in an attempt to steady himself, like a sailor in a storm. His chest was wheezing. Three teenaged girls passed them, heading towards the exit. A few tourists were dragging cases; a smartly dressed young couple and a drunk middle-aged man passed; after a few more seconds, there was no one else.

'Hang on, I have to tell Ruby—'

'You don't, you're fine.'

'No, have to do it . . . always letting her down . . . promised to say when I was on my way.' He rummaged in his bag for his mobile and still managed to fire off a text in record time. The effort of concentrating so hard nearly made him fall over.

'It's OK, I've got you. Wait, wait.' It was time to produce the inhaler. 'Here, you left it in the bar. You should be more careful. You know how Ruby gets when you've been smoking and drinking.'

'Yeah, she can be a pain,' said Matt, compliantly opening his mouth and sticking out a furry tongue.

'Put your tongue in. Come on, Matt, you know how to do this.'

'OK.' He was finally ready. 'God, it tastes like—'

'That's because you've been hammering the cocktails tonight.' Anyone coming? No, the coast was clear. 'Look, I have to get you home.'

'I'm meeting—'

'I know, I heard. Don't worry, I can fix that.'

'The train—'

'Come on, concentrate on the stairs, you can do it.'

There was the depth-charge rumble of a train arriving, the last southbound Piccadilly Line trip of the night. A plug of warm air pulsed in the tunnel and lifted a newspaper. Pages drifted past as if brought to life.

Something was happening to Matthew Hillingdon. He felt himself rising, moving. *Everyone likes me*, thought Matt. *It's so great that everyone wants me to succeed, but they don't know my secret. The secret is that I can't help myself.* Everything he ever did was because others told him to. Even when he could sense that their advice was hopelessly misguided, he followed it. He was like a stick in a drain, swirling around and heading for the gutter, but someone was always there to pull him out in time. *She's always there for me*, he thought. *Girls are great, they'll give you, like, six or seven chances at least, if they really like you.* Lately, though, events had been shifting beyond his comprehension. You had to trust your friends, though, didn't you? Otherwise you had nothing.

He was having trouble lifting his legs. Now his right arm was tingling. He'd drunk more than this before without losing control of his limbs. Weird.

The feeling got worse. Was this what dying felt like? *My neurons are being deprived of oxygen*, he thought. *It just feels like I'm falling very gently. Swirling around and around, towards the gutter.*

I'm one of life's naturally lucky guys, he told himself. *What a charmed life I lead, there's always someone there to catch me when I fall. I think I'm falling faster now. And there's someone right here to catch me again. How perfect is that?*

21

ALPHA MALES

Wednesday's dawn was fierce and raw, low crimson light splashing the sides of the glass offices in Canary Wharf. A turbulent sky of sharp blue cloud unfurled over the frothing reaches of the river. John May leaned against the railing of his steel balcony on the fourth floor of Shad Thames, and drew in the brackish smell of the tide. As a child, he had played on the shore below these windows. *I haven't strayed very far from home in my life*, he thought. *How we love to tether ourselves.*

Leaning over the rail, he looked down at the pebbles stained with patches of verdigris, wondering if the sand beneath held the memory of his footprints. His mother had once lost a bracelet while chasing him along the shore. Was it still buried in the mud, another layer of London's history? Although the embankments had been transformed, the cranes and wharves giving way to boxy riverview apartments, the shoreline had hardly changed at all. It seemed strange that he and the other kids had once swum here. Surely the water was cleaner now, free of tyres and trolleys and iridescent lumps of tar? His sister

Gwen had never joined them. Fastidious and superior, she had always sat on the river wall to wait, smoothing her patterned dress, ignoring their yells, biding her time.

He smiled sadly at the thought. Gwen, happily living in Brighton with her extended family, was the only one to have survived unscarred. A strong sense of self-preservation had protected her, but the rest had all suffered in some way. His wife Jane, fragile and disturbed, in Broadhampton Hospital; his daughter Elizabeth, dead; his grandchildren at war with their own devils; and now a new woman in his world, the beautiful, haunted Brigitte, who had called him a few hours ago, drunk again. If he had not been able to help his own family, how would he ever be able to help her?

He listened to the city. A few minutes earlier it had been virtually silent, but almost on the stroke of seven a low, steady roar began and grew, like the sound of factory machinery starting up. It was the hum of engines, the turning of pistons, of voices and vans and coffee machines, of peristaltic traffic and disgorging trains. The sound of London coming to life.

He used the last of his cold coffee to wash down a statin designed to tackle his high cholesterol. As he stood above the water, his thoughts turned to Gloria Taylor's uncomprehending daughter, and his fingers brushed the cotton of his shirt, over the ridged scar on his heart. A five-year-old girl left without a mother. The wound opened by the loss of a life could never be fully healed, but it was the PCU's duty to find a way of restoring balance. He had not been able to save those closest to him, but perhaps he could make a difference in the life of a stranger.

He knew it was what his partner would be trying to do, in his own mad way. Tonight, long after the others had gone home, the top-floor lights in their King's Cross warehouse would be burning as Arthur worked on, driven less by a sense of injustice than the need to solve a puzzle. At least they would work towards the same end. The city was a blind, uneven place where injustices could never be fully righted, just smoothed out a little. With its funding returned, the unit stood a chance of making a difference. If it failed in its first case, the fragile faith it had newly engendered would be destroyed.

He took the circular sticker from his pocket and traced the outline of the figure with his forefinger. It wasn't much to go on, but anything with a connection to the case, no matter how tangential, was worth exploring.

Ruby Cates rented an apartment on the second floor of a house in Mecklenburgh Square, in the back of Bloomsbury. The square, built on the grounds of the Foundling Hospital, had been named in honour of Queen Charlotte. The damage it had sustained in World War Two had been tidily repaired, but the grand square and its spacious roads were little-used and overlooked. At the centre was a high-railed garden filled with mature elms and plane trees, shadowy and vaguely mournful, in the way that empty London squares could feel damp even in high summer.

Ruby answered the door in a sweat-stained red Mets T-shirt, with a white towel knotted around her neck. She was pleasant-faced, but too thin and fiercely blonde, with an intensity in her deep-set eyes that put May on his guard. Having emailed her first thing, he had received an instant reply providing her address and the time she would be at home. She held open the door and started explaining the moment he stepped inside. May saw that the lower half of her left leg was locked in a grey plastic cast.

'I went up to Camden police station but they said I have to wait until tomorrow. I told them there couldn't be any mistake but they weren't interested in listening to me, so I went down to the Tube to check for myself.' Her voice had a soft country burr, Dorset perhaps.

'Come through. This is my kitchen, but the others tend to turn up here for coffee. It's not really fair because they have bigger bedrooms. There's another kitchen upstairs but they use it as a storeroom. There's a mountain bike in it no one's ever ridden. I've learned one thing: never be the only woman in a household of men.' Ruby's kitchen was overflowing with dirty crockery, newspapers, magazines and books. A heavy blue glass ashtray pinned down wayward paperwork. There was a faint smell of tobacco, as if someone had been rolling it from a pouch.

'Under normal circumstances I would have run back up here. I run everywhere. I finished the marathon last year. Not going to do it this time, though.' She knocked on the plastic cast.

'What happened?'

'I was training. Really stupid of me, I slipped off the kerb outside the house and fell badly. I didn't even feel the bone break. I'm working out every day, trying to keep the muscles strong. It should be off soon. I didn't leave details about Matt at the station, so I suppose you're going to take a statement now?'

'I'm sorry, I think we're at cross purposes. This is a routine inquiry about an accident.'

'You're not here about Matthew Hillingdon?'

'No, a chap called Nikos Nicolau gave me your email address.'

'So you haven't spoken to the police at Camden? That's really weird.' Ruby shook the idea around in her head. 'Well, it's good you're here.'

'Why?'

'Because Matt is missing – I reported him missing.'

'Ah – no, I'm not connected with that. I'm tracing a set of these things a girl called Cassie handed out at her bar.' He passed over the plastic sachet containing the sticker.

'But you must have known something. Matt has one of these things on his computer bag.'

'I think you'd better start from the beginning,' said May, sitting down.

'Matthew Hillingdon is a friend of mine. Well, maybe a bit more than a friend – I've been seeing him. He lives here.' She paced awkwardly to the window and back, unable to settle. 'We study together at UCL. We were supposed to be meeting up last night, but he never showed.'

'And you went to the police?'

'As soon as he failed to appear. I know, I know, you're going to say I was overreacting – that's what they said – but I had my reasons. I haven't heard from him since.'

'But if it was only last night . . .'

'He texted me just as he was entering King's Cross Station and said he'd be on the last train, OK? He'd been out drinking at some bar in Spitalfields.' She dug her mobile from her pocket and showed him the message. *At KX just made last train C U 2mins*. The call register showed that the text was sent at 12:20 a.m. 'He was probably pretty pissed.'

'What makes you say that?'

'He has a habit of texting me when he's had too many, because if he calls I'll hear him slurring his words, and he knows I don't approve of him getting wasted when he's got a lecture the next morning.'

'Does he get drunk a lot?'

'Yes, lately. He's under a lot of pressure. He's got money worries. And he's finding the course difficult.'

'Did he tell you who he was drinking with?'

'No, one of his classmates, probably. But look at the time of the call. He always catches the Tube, so he'd have come on the Circle, Metropolitan or Hammersmith

& City Line, and changed on to the Piccadilly at King's Cross. We both know that the last train goes at 12:24 a.m. I was waiting by the exit at the next stop, Russell Square. The train only takes two minutes, and came in at 12:26, but he wasn't on it.'

'Maybe there's another way out of the station.'

'No, I've waited there often enough, there's only one exit and I was there, right at the barrier, as always.'

'Then he must have missed it.'

'He'd have walked down to me. It doesn't take long.'

'He could have chosen not to catch the train for some reason.'

'In that case, why would he bother to call and tell me he'd be on it?'

'The London Underground is the most heavily monitored system in the world,' May said. 'There are some things we can do to establish where your friend went. But before I start that process, I need you to be absolutely sure about the facts.'

'If you knew me, Mr May, you'd know I'm sure.'

'One thing at a time. Tell me about the sticker.'

'I don't know anything more. It was on his bag, that's all. They're from the Karma Bar. All the geeks have them. I said I wouldn't call them geeks, but it's just that they hang out together so much and they never stop working.'

'And you also have one.' May pointed at the label on Ruby's backpack.

Below them, the doorbell rang. 'Excuse me for a moment,' said Ruby.

'Do you want me to get it? Your leg . . .'

'I can manage.'

May walked over to the kitchen table and thumbed through a paperback. He heard the slam of the front door, followed by thumping footsteps on the stairs.

The wild-haired Indian student who appeared in the

doorway did not bother introducing himself. He was trying to prevent a fat stack of papers from sliding out of a plastic wallet, which was splitting under several loose items of shopping. 'Have you seen Theo?' he asked Ruby.

'I think he had a meeting with one of his tutors. Why on earth didn't you get a bag?'

'I forgot. Don't start. I don't know what he's bloody playing at. Did Matt leave me any money?'

'He didn't turn up last night. I'm really upset, actually. Are you making toasted sandwiches?'

'You know I am, I don't know why you always have to ask.' The boy stamped off up the stairs.

'That was Rajan,' Ruby explained, 'he has the room above this one.' She did not seem pleased to see him.

'Who else lives here?' May asked. He had forgotten the peculiar atmosphere of urgency, languor and confusion that could be detected in student digs.

'Apart from Matt, there's a guy called Toby Brooke, then there's Nikos Nicolau and the guy you just saw, Rajan Sangeeta. Theo Fontvieille has the top floor because his rich parents own the building, and we pay his family the rent direct, so it gets kind of feudal around here just before rent day.'

'And you,' May reminded.

'They gave me the attic at first. I wanted to change rooms so I wouldn't have to go up and down the stairs all the time, but of course I'm a mere girl, so my vote didn't count until Theo stepped in and supported me. We have too many alpha males living under one roof. The competitiveness drives me crazy sometimes.'

'Are you in the same field of studies?'

'Toby, Theo, Matt and Rajan are all taking social engineering together.'

'That sounds rather Nietzschean.'

'It's a branch of urban planning, they're happy to explain

it to anyone who listens. Nikos's aiming for a degree in biochemistry. The rest of his family owns restaurants, and they're very anxious to ensure that he passes. Theo's in line to inherit his parents' fortune and doesn't have to study, so he's just doing it for fun.'

'Why were you meeting Matthew Hillingdon at Russell Square Tube?'

'We were going to go to the Horse Hospital. I mean, it's not a horse hospital any more, although it's still got cobblestones and there are horse ramps inside. It's a club, stays open until two. My leg was hurting like hell, but I wanted to spend some time with Matt. Have you got a cigarette?'

'I don't smoke. So you're at the same college?'

'I'm a second-year research student, doing bio-informatics.'

'I'm afraid I have no idea what that is.'

'It's mostly about searching databases for protein modelling and sequence alignment.'

'How long have you been seeing Mr Hillingdon?'

'He's missing – you don't need to know about our private lives, do you?'

'No, but I might find something you haven't thought of. Please.'

'Well, we've been dating about four months. He's very sweet, a bit helpless. Probably needs a mother more than a girlfriend. I met him at the Karma Bar. Some of the stuff he's studying crosses over with the others, which is how they met. He specializes in the analysis of pedestrian traffic flow in urban areas. He's very goal-oriented, works long hours.'

'And sometimes forgets about meeting you?' added May.

'It's happened before. But not this time, I'm sure of it. When I spoke to him, he was definitely catching that train.' She checked her watch. 'I'm due at a class.'

'I'll walk down with you.'

The sound of The Avalanches playing over the roar of an engine outside sent Ruby to the landing window. 'Here's another one,' she told May. 'Theo's probably the richest guy in the whole of UCL. His father owns, like, half of Hertfordshire or something.'

'That would explain the car,' said May, impressed. Fontvieille was driving a new red Porsche Carrera, a beacon of conspicuous consumption branded with the numberplate THEO 1. He was unfolding himself from the driver's seat as May arrived back on the street.

'Theo, this is John May. He's from—'

'The Peculiar Crimes Unit,' May explained, holding out his hand. 'We've met.'

'I thought you were a little too old to be a foot soldier. Peculiar Crimes Unit? What's that?' The surname might have been French, but he had no trace of an accent. Although he shook hands, Fontvieille was clearly keen to get inside.

'It's a specialist detection unit.'

'I don't understand, why are you here? Ruby, what have you been up to?' Although he could have been no older than twenty-one, Fontvieille had the patrician air of someone mature, confident and secure in his wealth. Tanned and moisturized, his long black hair sleekly groomed, he was dressed in a grey hooded top and jeans too well cut to be confused with the kind generally worn on the street. His clothes were bookended with a red silk scarf and red leather trainers that perfectly matched his car. He might have been a model or a city executive, except that there was a discordant note in his appearance that May couldn't nail down.

'This young lady has lost a friend,' he said.

'What's he talking about? Ruby, who have you lost?'

'Matt's been missing since last night.'

'You know he doesn't always come home.'

'He was supposed to be with me.' She was clearly uncomfortable arguing about a mutual friend in front of May.

'You've got to give the guy a bit of room to manoeuvre, he's really stressed out at the moment.'

'That's easy for you to say, Theo, you never get worried about anything. You don't have to worry.' It sounded like a put-down. *She's wrong*, thought May, who had pinpointed what was bothering him. Theo Fontvieille looked as if he had not enjoyed a good night's sleep in a week. Beneath his smooth tan were fault-lines and shadows.

'I've got to get going,' said Theo. 'I'm meeting Rajan, running late. Is he up in his room?'

'God, you guys hang out together every night – don't you ever get tired of each other's company?' She sounded jealous.

'Ask me in five years' time, when we're running the country. Nice to meet you again, Mr May – and Ruby, when you find Matt tell him he owes me fifty quid.' Theo swung a smart red leather case on to his shoulder and bounded up the stairs.

'Not the bookish type?' May suggested.

'I'm sure he only attends UCL to annoy the rest of us, he makes it all seem so easy. He'll go to an all-night party, then come back and knock out a paper that will have his lecturers mooning over him for weeks.'

'No Karma Bar logo,' May noted.

'Theo wouldn't be seen dead sticking a cheap club advert on his fine Italian leather. I fear our common ways don't appeal to him.' *She hates him*, thought May. *Just because of his money, or is there something else? Perhaps that's not hatred in her eyes but something quite the opposite.*

'All right,' he said, 'I'll cut a deal with you. Keep your eyes open for any more of these stickers, and I'll see if I

can get you some information on Mr Hillingdon's whereabouts today, to save you waiting for the regular police.'

'You could do that? I'd be really grateful. I wouldn't
have gone to the police if I wasn't worried.' She shook his
hand. 'He has . . . a history . . . of being found in unlikely
places, rather the worse for wear.'

Strange, thought May as he walked away along the
rainy street, *she showed little interest in why I had come
to see her. She didn't ask me anything. Presumably too
preoccupied with the missing boyfriend. But then there's
the book.*

He had seen a bright-yellow paperback on her kitchen
table, packed with bookmarks and Post-it notes. It had
set him wondering if she had deliberately chosen to tell
him lies.

May looked back up at the house, and thought he saw
Ruby's face at the rain-streaked second-floor window,
staring blankly down at him. A moment later, it was
gone.

22

THE GHOST SYSTEM

Late on Wednesday morning, the two detectives stood in their usual positions, side by side, leaning on the balustrade of Waterloo Bridge, looking into the heart of the city. The clouds moved like freighters, flat-bottomed and dark, laden with incoming cargoes of rain. Bryant had ill-advisedly washed his favourite trilby after venturing into snowdrifts in an earlier case, and its brim had lost all shape. With his hands stuffed in the voluminous pockets of his ratty tweed overcoat and the backs of his trouser bottoms touching the pavement, he appeared to be vanishing entirely inside his clothes. It seemed that a breeze might come along and blow what was left of this bag of rags into the river.

May, on the other hand, stood with his back erect in a smart navy-blue Savile Row suit, his blue silk tie knotted over a freshly pressed shirt, his white cuffs studded with silver links. As rain began to fall, he unfurled a perfect black umbrella and held it over them. Whenever May felt that his life lacked order, he redressed the balance by sprucing up.

It had commonly been noted that anyone becoming involved with one had to accept the priority of the other. This fact had resulted in two lifetimes of dissatisfying romantic attachments, but could not be helped. To remove either would have been like cutting away a supporting vine, and would have created a sense of misfortune in both that no woman would have been able to forgive herself for.

'Sorry to drag you down here,' said Bryant. 'Old habits die hard. I needed to come and do some thinking. I was going to try the Millennium Bridge, but there are too many tourists.'

'That's OK.' May leaned forward to watch a police launch chug under an arch. 'Brigitte called late last night. She wants me to come and visit her in Paris.'

'I bet she was drunk.'

'She was, a bit.'

'I hope you told her you're in the middle of an important investigation.'

'I said I'd go if we could close the case and stabilize the unit. But we're not getting anywhere fast, are we, and unless something breaks . . .'

'It will. If we fail the Taylor woman, we'll have struck out twice in a row. There won't be a third chance. How did you get on with your student?'

'She thought I'd come to visit her because she'd reported her boyfriend missing,' May explained. 'Reckons he disappeared at King's Cross Station early this morning.'

Bryant's ears pricked up. 'Strange coincidence.'

'Most of the other students in the house had the same altered sticker on their bags. And I saw something in her flat that bothered me.'

'Oh, snooping around, were you?'

'Hardly. It was on the kitchen table, in plain sight. A pocket guide to the haunted stations of the London Underground called *Mind the Ghosts*, with her name pencilled inside. It resonated a little too much with what she was saying. I swiped it. Here.' He pulled the dog-eared paperback from his pocket and passed it to Bryant. 'Take a look at Chapter Six. She's bookmarked a section about the ghost of a girl called Annie Evans.'

'This is more my territory than yours. I'm impressed you'd think of it.' Bryant dug out his reading glasses, wound them around his ears and found the passage. 'Says here "a sickly child, imprisoned, starved and beaten to death by the woman who employed her, in 1758". I'm not entirely with you.'

'If you look at the next page, it explains that her ghost is supposed to haunt Russell Square Tube Station between midnight and one a.m. The guards hear her running along the platform, but as soon as she boards a carriage she vanishes. The girl I saw, Ruby Cates, said she had been waiting at Russell Square for her boyfriend under identical circumstances.'

'So you think she read this and concocted the story?'

'I really don't know what to think. I mean, what would she have to gain by doing so? And why bother to report him missing at all?'

'You know, you're finally starting to think like me. Leave me the book and I'll see if there's anything you missed.'

'Be my guest.'

'Students,' Bryant sighed. 'They're all so impatient to get on with their careers now. Why can't they go back to smoking pot and talking rubbish like in the good old days?'

'At least they're not scruffy any more.'

'Oh, you think anyone who doesn't wear a tie is scruffy. Your mother started your toilet training too early. I've watched you in restaurants, lining up your knife and fork with the edges of your napkin. And that new flat of yours, so bare that it looks like the furniture delivery van took a wrong turn and never found the place.'

'I can't abide clutter, you know that. Rooms reveal the inner workings of the mind. I just thought it was odd that she had left the book out, that's all.'

Bryant perused the chapter. 'I say, listen to this – the section has been underlined. "Thirteen-year-old Annie Evans, a child of sickly nature, locked in a cupboard for three years, left unfed and repeatedly beaten by her employer with a broom handle. She escaped twice but was sent back to the house both times. Died from infection and multiple fractures, compounded by malnourishment. Her maggot-filled body remained in the attic for two months, because her employer feared it would provide clear evidence that she had been brutalized. The property stood on the site of Russell Square Tube. Parts of her burned body were found in Chick Lane gully-hole by the nightwatchman, and were taken to the coroner. Her employer was brought to trial at the Old Bailey and was found guilty, after being turned in by her own daughter. On certain nights, just past the hour of midnight, the ghost of Annie Evans still appears in the last train at Russell Square Station, only to vanish just as suddenly."'

'The house where Ruby's boyfriend lives is full of students studying public-transport systems and traffic control,' said May. 'Funny how everything keeps coming back to the London Underground.'

'Not really,' Bryant argued. 'This guide has a UCL library tag. It's a bit of light reading for anyone studying transport systems. Besides, you can't help but be aware of the tunnels beneath your feet when you walk around the city.' He thumped his walking stick on the pavement. 'I always think that the system operates as a kind of ghost London, just below street level. Its routes mirror the streets, which in turn follow the hedgerows marking out the city's ancient boundaries. So you could say that the Underground provides us with a kind of spiritual blueprint for the passage of London's residents.'

'No, I'm not buying that,' May declared. 'There's nothing at all spiritual about the Underground railway, just tunnels full of mice and dust.'

'But it's also a closed system filled with dead ends and unrealized plans, and that makes it fascinating. All the stations that were excavated and never opened, the platforms that were used to hide art masterpieces in the war, follies like the theatre train that only ran in one direction. And of course there's a lot more Underground than just the Tube network. I heard tell of a huge shelter beneath Clapham where the authorities chose to leave all the *Windrush* passengers.' The *Empire Windrush* ship had docked in June 1948, carrying nearly five hundred West Indian immigrants, ready to start new lives in the UK. Their arrival sparked a national debate about identity, and exposed deep prejudices. 'Supposedly, the families were fed up with being forced to live in the shelter, and came above ground to make Brixton the strong ethnic enclave it is today. You can't hide people away; they find ways to blossom.'

'You know your trouble?' said May. 'You're a hopeless romantic. You see a bit of old tunnel and imagine it's a secret passage to another world. Nothing's ever straight-forward with you, it always has to have a hidden meaning. You have too much imagination. You don't believe in filling out a tax form, but you believe in ghosts.'

'Of course. What about all the lives lost and changed below ground?' Bryant's rising passion changed the colour of his nose in the cold air. 'I honestly believe that the rules are different down there. The suicides, the crash victims, the missed liaisons, the romances and betrayals, the lovers parting or rushing to meet each other. Don't you think something of them has been left behind within those curving tiled walls?'

'The only things they leave behind are bits of dead skin and the odd newspaper,' said May. 'You know how many deaths there are on the Underground every year?'

Bryant peered out from beneath the ridiculous brim of his hat. 'I've no idea.'

'Well neither do I, but I bet it's a lot, and no reasons ever come to light about why these things happen – they just happen, and that's all there is to it. Now you've had me standing here in the freezing rain for ages – let's head back to the Tube.'

'The station guards I went to see might be able to help us,' said Bryant, clattering his stick against the railings like a schoolboy as they walked. 'They can pull up camera footage of the entrance hall, the escalators and the platform, and form a sort of visual mosaic that shows the boy's movements.'

'Fine, give me your contact there and I'll call them now, get them ready for our arrival.'

'This lad Matthew, he's not been missing for very long.' Bryant pushed up his hat and fixed his partner with an aqueous blue eye. 'He'll turn up at a friend's flat with a flaming hangover. We have to concentrate on closing up the Taylor case.'

'Giles Kershaw isn't prepared to write it off as misadventure. He's convinced she was pushed.'

'He has no hard evidence for that.'

'Well, it must have been a complete stranger, because it's not someone from her past. Taylor was ostracized by her family because of the pregnancy, but was on good terms with the father. She overcame the problems caused by her breakdown. Everyone at work liked her. There's no one else. All we can do is keep on tracking witnesses.'

'Gloria Taylor couldn't see her attacker, but the killer

was also denied the satisfaction of eye contact with his victim. It was the act of an angry coward who simply wanted to maim someone.'

'I imagine it's a bit too mundane for you,' said May. 'Not weird enough, a woman falling down some stairs. The sticker on her back was the only mark of interest. You were secretly hoping it was a sign that she belonged to some kind of secret society.'

Bryant pursed his lips, annoyed. 'No,' he said, 'I was hoping it was a sign that her killer does.' He gave his partner an affectionate pat on the back. 'Come on, a quick cup of tea first, then we'll see if we can find your student. You're right, of course. We should concentrate on clearing up one mystery at a time. But the missing boy and the book of ghosts, they're – well, suggestive.'

May could not resist asking, 'Of what?'

'Oh, of an entirely different direction,' said Bryant, and he would not be further drawn.

23

LAST TRAIN

'I didn't think we'd get you back so soon,' said Anjam Dutta, the security expert at North One Watch, the King's Cross Surveillance Centre. The luminescent monitors surrounding him showed such long queues building up at the ticket windows that temporary barriers had been installed to filter passengers. Dutta saw them watching the screens.

'We've got a new office building just opened this month and two new blocks of student accommodation, totalling an extra 2,200 potential passengers, and they're nearly all Tube users. Usually it wouldn't make a difference but a couple of trade fairs just opened on Monday, one at the Excel Centre, the other at Earl's Court, and there are a lot of visitors staying in the nearby hotels. We can regulate the number of people entering the station by reducing surface access, but we've already had to shut off the escalators several times this week because of passenger overload. The system works on the probability ratio of a certain number of travellers per day, and has trouble coping with unexpected demand.'

'I noticed you're renovating some of the platform and tunnel walls as well,' said May. 'How do you cope with that?'

'The equipment is stowed during Tube working hours, but it means a couple of the monitors are disengaged. When you've only got four hours a night to find an electrical fault, it can take several days to sort out. What can I do for you gentlemen today? Is this about the escalator footage?'

'No, it's a new problem that may be related. We've lost someone. He was supposed to catch the last southbound Piccadilly Line train last night. A student called Matthew Hillingdon.'

'It would have passed through here at 12:24 a.m. The service was good last night. There's a Northern Line train three minutes later and then that's your lot until the next morning.'

'Ridiculous that we don't have a twenty-four-hour system,' Bryant complained. 'We know he called his girlfriend from – what's the nearest point to the trains that still has mobile reception?'

'That would be the lower hall.'

'Below the escalators?'

'He'd get general coverage until about halfway down the final flight of stairs, but some networks have transmitter points on the Piccadilly. Who was he with?'

'Virgin,' May remembered.

'He would have been able to transmit as far as the interchange, but not on the platform.'

'He texted her from King's Cross at 12:20 a.m., a bit the worse for wear. He'd been out with a mate and was heading for Russell Square Tube.'

'It's only a two-minute journey.'

'I know, but he never made it. I need to find out whether he got on the train. If he didn't, perhaps we can see which exit he used from the station and collect witnesses from that point.'

'OK, give us a couple of minutes. Everything's digitally backed up 24/7, so it shouldn't be hard to nail. Most of the cameras are recording constantly. As you pointed out, a couple of tunnels are being retiled, so they're not fully covered, but we can pick up action on the platform overheads.'

The detectives seated themselves in the darkened room and watched the screens around them. 'Look at all these passengers. Why do people have to move about so much?' asked Bryant irritably. 'Everyone would get a lot more done if they just stayed in one place.'

'You're a fine one to talk,' May replied. 'You can't sit still for a minute.' He looked back at the screens. 'They're like blood cells pulsing through an artery.'

'That's what they are. They're feeding the city with energy. There's no pushing or shoving; it's so orderly and purposeful. Rather beautiful to watch.'

'OK, we have this now.' Dutta punched a series of illuminated keys on what looked like a studio mixing board, and footage speckled through one of the monitors. 'I'm starting it from 12:17 a.m. The left screen is the camera footage covering the interchange tunnels from the Circle to the Piccadilly Line. I've got another one covering the main entrance, but from what you're saying there was no reason for him to leave the station. There are two ways of switching lines, depending on which end of the platform you're coming from. The main problem is that one of the tunnel cameras was out, and one currently has restricted vision.'

'That's not very efficient, is it?'

'Not our fault. Health & Safety carried out a junction install that's affected some of the camera sightlines. We're waiting to get the mountings re-sited. That's not public knowledge, though, so we're pretty well covered. The cameras are still up there. As long as people think they're being watched, they behave themselves. What does your man look like?'

May passed over a photograph showing Matthew Hillingdon in a brown woollen hat and a long grey over-coat sewn with thin rainbow stripes. 'He was hardly ever seen wearing anything else,' he explained.

'Well, it's distinctive.' Dutta's nimble fingers tapped at the speed controls as he checked the images. 'The Tube is still busy up to the minutes just before the last train, then it empties fast. Most Londoners have a pretty good idea how late they can leave it to get home. Is that him?'

'Too short,' said May.

'How about this one?'

The images in front of them fractured into blurred squares, then slowed and restored themselves as a man in a dark raincoat entered from the right of the camera field.

'Similar – but no, I don't think so.'

Dutta tried again. 'How about this one?'

'That looks like him.' May tapped at the rainbow coat.

May checked the screen's time readout, which had ticked to 12:21 a.m. The boy wavered at the far side of the screen. He was putting his mobile away, but appeared to be having trouble finding his pocket. Now they could clearly see the top of his brown woollen cap. Hillingdon had trouble staying upright as he staggered towards the stairs. There was a brief dark blur to his left.

'Wait, is there somebody with him?'

Dutta dialled the speed down to single frames. The blur vanished. 'If there was, they knew how to stay out of the shot.'

'He's very drunk. Can you get him from another camera?'

'No, that's the one that's out.'

Hillingdon had passed beyond the camera's range now. The scene showed the shadowed empty arch of the half-tiled tunnel.

'There are two more cameras between the boy and the train,' Dutta explained. 'One is situated in the short stairway leading to the platform, the other is on the platform itself.'

The detectives watched the deserted staircase, waiting for Hillingdon to appear. The time readout said 12:23 a.m. Suddenly a drunken figure burst into the frame, striped coat-tails flying. He virtually fell down the steps in his rush to get to the platform.

'Hillingdon's got less than a minute before the train is due, so can we assume he heard it approaching through the tunnel?' asked May. 'Do your guards stop people boarding trains when they're plastered?'

'If they look like they're a danger to themselves,' said Dutta. 'Hillingdon's borderline. We get much worse. I don't think there was anyone in the immediate area. More crucially, it probably wasn't picked up on the monitors. It'll be easy to check and see who was on duty.'

The screen was empty now. The stairwell's fixed camera could only catch a figure passing through. Dutta switched screens, searching the tiled labyrinth.

'Now this last camera is moveable and has a large wide-angle lens. It's in the centre of the roof above the platform, and we can see everything that's going on. It slowly pans back and forth to build a picture of the level as a whole. Plus, we can zoom in and pull off detailed shots, but they're quite distorted. It's really for general surveillance. Our clearest ID shots all come from the barriers rather than the platforms.'

He twisted a dial back and forth, and the image of the platform shifted from one end to the other. The time readout was now at 12:24 a.m. There were four other passengers waiting for the train: a middle-aged Chinese couple and two young black girls.

'Would it be hard to get witness traces on them?'

'Not if they used Oyster cards. They can't be tracked if they just bought tickets, although we might get general descriptions from the counter staff. But only tourists use the windows.'

'Here it comes, right on schedule.'

They watched as the silvered carriages slid sleekly into the station. The camera had lost Hillingdon. The doors opened. Dutta panned the device back along the platform. At the last moment Matt Hillingdon's striped overcoat and woollen hat shot into view. He was moving with dangerous speed. It clearly required a superhuman effort to jump the gap into the carriage, but he made it just before the doors closed. In fact, the door shut on the tail of Hillingdon's coat, trapping it.

'I'm annoyed about this,' said Dutta. 'Somebody really should have cautioned him.'

They watched as the student pulled at the tail of his coat, which remained trapped in the door. A moment later, the carriage doors opened again while he was still pulling, so that he fell over, vanishing from view.

'If you ever see me that drunk,' said May, 'shoot me.'

'The train remained here a little longer than usual. The last one of the night often does that, to pick up the last few stragglers,' said Dutta, accelerating the footage. He slowed it down once more as the Tube doors opened and closed, and the train started to move out.

'If Hillingdon got on the 12:24 a.m. he could have fallen asleep and missed his stop,' May suggested.

'The stations are only a couple of minutes apart,' said

Bryant. 'If he knocked himself out when he fell, we'd have heard about it by now. I think it's more likely that your Miss Cates lied. She might be playing you for a fool.'

'She seemed sincere enough.' May frowned, puzzling. 'I don't see what she would have to gain by making up the episode.'

'To throw you off the track of something else?' Bryant suggested. 'You said she'd been reading about vanishing passengers. It looks to me like they're in it together.'

'Then where did he go?' asked May.

Bryant pulled his sagging trilby back on to the crown of his head. 'Next stop, Russell Square,' he replied.

24

PHANTOM PASSENGER

Shiny red arches, leaf-green corridors: the Tube stations of London had once sported a uniform look, just as the roads had been matched in neat black and white stripes. In the 1980s they received a disastrous cosmetic makeover. Ignoring the fact that the system was coming apart at the seams, lavish artworks were commissioned and left unfinished, stations were closed instead of being repaired, and only a handful of the oldest remained unspoiled. Russell Square was one of the few that survived. Similar in style to the Tube at Mornington Crescent, the frontage of crimson tiles, the blue glass canopy and the arched first-floor windows remained intact. The station was largely used by tourists and students staying in the nearby hotels and hostels, so the entrance was always crowded with visitors consulting maps.

Mr Gregory, the station-master, was a thin, peppery man with a face that, even in repose, made him look as if he was about to sneeze. He greeted the detectives with a decongestion stick wedged up his right nostril. 'I'm sorry,' he apologized, 'my passages get bunged up in dusty atmospheres.'

'You picked the wrong job, then, didn't you?' said Bryant with an unsympathetic laugh.

'It's not the station, it's pollen from over there.' Mr Gregory pointed to the tree-filled square that stood diagonally across from them. 'Too much bloody fresh air coming in.' He led the way behind the barriers, ushering them through. 'Can I get you anything?'

'A cup of tea and a Garibaldi biscuit would hit the spot.' Bryant looked around the monitoring station, a small bare room with just two monochrome monitors on a desk, one focussed on each of the platforms. 'You don't have a camera over the entrance door?'

'No, someone's always here keeping an eye out. It's an old-fashioned system, but I find it works well enough. LU Head Office wasn't happy, but I told them not everything has to be high-tech. That's an original Victorian canopy. I don't want dirty great holes drilled through it.'

'A man after my own heart,' Bryant agreed, finding a place to sit.

'A Mr Dutta from King's Cross called and told me you were on your way. He said you wanted to see the arrival of yesterday's 12:26 a.m. It'll take me a few minutes to cue up the footage. Our regular security bloke isn't here today, he's up before Haringey Magistrates' Court for gross indecency outside the headquarters of the Dagenham Girl Pipers.'

'So you're not fond of fresh air, then,' said May, changing the subject with less fluidity than he'd hoped.

'Not really, no.' Mr Gregory sniffed. 'My lungs can't cope.'

'Only people usually complain about the poor air quality down there.'

Mr Gregory looked aghast. 'That's rubbish. Travelling

on the Tube for forty minutes is the equivalent to smoking two cigarettes, so I save a bit on fags. Plus it's about ten degrees warmer on the platforms in winter. I've worked for London Transport for over twenty years, and I've got a lot of mates down the tunnels. There's the casual workers, your economic migrants who're just doing it for a job, like, and then there's your tubeheads. It's a place where you can forget the rest of the world.'

'So is the Foreign Legion, but that doesn't make it a good thing,' Bryant pointed out.

'I hold the world record for visiting all 287 stations in one go, you know,' Mr Gregory told them. As a conversational gambit it was chancey at best. 'I did the entire network in eighteen hours, twenty minutes.'

'Is that a popular sport?'

'Oh yes.'

'You do surprise me.' Bryant pantomimed stifling a yawn.

'People have been beating the time since 1960. There's a set of rules laid down by *The Guinness Book of Records*, but that's just the start – we also hold the annual Tube Olympics, and there are all sorts of challenges.'

'Really,' said Bryant flatly.

'Oh yes, like the ABC challenge – that's where we have to visit twenty six Tube stations in alphabetical order. The current record for that is five hours twenty minutes. And the Bottle challenge . . .'

'What's that?' asked May, trying to show an interest while they watched for the footage.

'Look at the centre of the Underground map,' Mr Gregory instructed him. 'The lines form the shape of a bottle on its side. That's the circuit. My aim is to beat the record of two hours thirteen minutes.'

'This is all very riveting,' said Bryant, 'but might we get back to the matter in hand?'

'Here we go. The train came in just under a minute late.' The station-master clicked off the lights, and the trio watched the screen.

The monitor revealed an angled shot of the silver carriages pulling into the platform. 'Can you home in on a specific carriage?' May asked.

'Which one do you want?'

'The third from the end.'

'Which end?'

May decided not to point out that there was only one end to a train arriving at a station, for fear of sounding pedantic. The station-master expertly panned along the train and settled the screen on the correct carriage. The shot was just wide enough to include all three exit doors, which now slid open. Inside, all was bright and bare.

'I don't believe it,' Bryant exclaimed. 'The damned thing's empty!'

'There must be some mistake,' May told the station-master. 'This can't be the right train.'

Mr Gregory tapped the numerals at the bottom of the screen with his forefinger. 'That's the time-code, 12:27 a.m., right there. There's no tampering with that.'

'You're sure this is yesterday?'

'Definitely. And it's the last train through. The journey took two minutes fifty seconds.'

'We saw him get on,' said Bryant. 'Could the train have stopped anywhere on the way?'

'No, there's no junction at Russell Square, it's a straight line without any branch-offs. Even if it halted for some reason, the doors wouldn't open. Nobody could have got out. You can interview the train driver if you want, but he'll tell you the same thing.'

'What about between the carriages? The connecting doors are kept unlocked, aren't they?'

'That's right, but they only open into other carriages,

so no one could get off. Let's see who alighted here.'
Mr Gregory panned along the entire length of the train.
'There you are, only two passengers.' He zoomed in on
them. One was a small elderly man laden with plastic
shopping bags, barely five feet tall, and the other was an
overweight, middle-aged Nigerian woman.

'I don't suppose he could have disguised himself?' asked
Bryant. 'In order to give his girlfriend the slip?'

Mr Gregory zoomed the camera in, first on the old
man, then on the Nigerian woman. Even a master of disguise would have been unable to transform himself into
either of these characters.

'Could he have let himself into the driver's cockpit
somehow?'

'Not a chance, it's dead-bolted.'

'Then he must simply have stayed on board the train.'

Mr Gregory reversed the footage and panned along each
of the carriages while the train stood with its doors open.
They zoomed in on all of the few remaining passengers,
but there was no one in a striped coat and woollen cap.
'See for yourself. I don't know where you think he could
have gone, unless he found a way of tearing the seats up
and hiding inside them.'

'You're telling me a six-foot-tall student vanished into
thin air on board a moving train?' Bryant complained.

'No,' said Mr Gregory, 'you're telling *me*.' He shoved
the inhaler back up his nose and snorted hard.

On their way back out of the station, the detectives passed
a neat row of 'K' stickers that had been stuck on the tiled
walls. 'Oh, those,' said Mr Gregory, when they were
pointed out. 'Bloody anarchists.'

'It's advertising a local bar, isn't it?'

'It might be now, but those stickers have been around
for donkey's years. They're a bugger to get off.'

Bryant picked at one with a fingernail. 'How do you know they're anarchists?'

Mr Gregory shook his head in puzzlement. 'Actually, now I come to think of it, I don't know. Somebody must have mentioned them before. It's a local symbol, like. Been up on the walls since I was a nipper. My old man used to bring me here. I'm sure it's something to do with wanting to bring down the government. Someone must have told me. Hang on.' He called across the station forecourt to a guard. 'Oi, Aram, them stickers along the wall, what are they for?'

'Anarchists, innit,' Aram confirmed. 'Bash the rich an' that.'

'Ah, a psychogeographical connection.' Bryant perked up. 'Leave this to me.'

'No,' May replied. 'There's no time left for your pottering.'

'I'll have you remember that my "pottering", as you call it, caught the Fulham Road Strangler.' Bryant had discovered that their suspect was a collector of Persian tapestries, and had matched a fibre left on one of his victims. Tracking him to an antique shop, May had wrestled him to the ground while Bryant crowned him with the nearest object to hand, which unfortunately proved to be a rare seventeenth-century ormolu clock. The killer's sister had sued the unit.

'It was a horrible clock anyway,' mused Bryant. 'Let me potter for a few hours and I might surprise you.'

May wearily pressed a thumb and forefinger on the bridge of his nose. 'We're already looking for an invisible passenger and an anarchist,' he said. 'Let's not have any more surprises today.'

25

LATE-NIGHT CONVERSATION

Bryant spent the next few hours in a dim basement library you could only access with the possession of a special pass and a private knock. For the other members of the PCU, Wednesday dragged past in a grim trudge of paperwork, legwork, statements and interviews. Colin Bimsley and Meera Mangeshkar were now resigned to being yoked together, but the paucity of leads made it feel as if there was barely a case to resolve. Meera felt guilty for thinking so, but it was certainly not the kind of investigation upon which reputations were built, not unless there was a racial or political motive for the attack. What did they really have to go on, other than a couple of hunches and the vague sensation that something was wrong?

Just after noon, one of the Daves took the curl out of his hair by cutting through a power cable, which darkened the offices and killed the computers.

At 2:15 p.m. Crippen managed to locate the packet of butter that had been used on its paws and ate the whole thing, regurgitating his lunch into Raymond Land's duffel bag.

At 4:45 p.m. the other Dave, now differentiated from his colleague by the lack of singeing in his extremities, removed some plaster from a wall in order to locate a pipe, and in doing so uncovered an amateurish but alarmingly provocative fresco of naked, overweight witches cavorting in a devil's circle. It was further proof, if any more was needed, that the warehouse had once been used for something damnably odd. Land had immediately demanded to know what the witches were doing there, and was not satisfied with Bryant's suggestion that it might be the foxtrot.

By 8:30 p.m., having exhausted all existing avenues of enquiry, the worn-out investigators reached a dead-end and were sent home, leaving only Bryant and his favourite Detective Sergeant at King's Cross head-quarters.

DS Janice Longbright pulled the cork from a bottle of Mexican Burgundy with her teeth and filled two tumblers. 'The trouble with you, Arthur,' she began, with the cork still in her mouth.

'Any sentence that starts like that is bound to end with something I don't want to hear,' Bryant interrupted. 'Take a card.' He held out the pack in a hopeful fan.

'The trouble with you is that once you get the bit between your teeth you can't be shifted. Two of diamonds. Like this thing with Mr Fox. Take a look.' She spat out the cork and threw a page across his desk. 'It's a screen grab from your security-wallah, Mr Dutta.'

'You weren't supposed to tell me what the card was.' Bryant fumbled for his spectacles and held the page an inch from his nose. The blurred photograph showed Mr Fox and his victim walking side by side outside King's Cross Station. 'Well, that's just what I told you. He followed McCarthy into the Tube and stabbed him.'

'Come on, even I noticed this.' She threw him another

sheet, the same scene a few frames later, as the pair moved into clearer view.

'Oh, I see what you mean,' said Bryant. 'That looks like Mr Fox in his earlier incarnation, before he shaved his hair closer to his head.'

'Because it was taken ten days ago. Concrete evidence that they knew each other. You were right, Mr Fox was taking care of business, getting rid of an unreliable junkie who had something on him.'

'Any news from the patient?'

'Nope, he's still unconscious. There's a staff nurse on duty outside his room, making sure nobody tries to get in. She'll call us if and when he comes around.'

'Has anyone tried to see him?'

'He's had no visitors at all.'

'I wonder if Mr Fox thinks he's dead. You'd better check and see if anyone's been talking to the ambulance crew. Take another card.'

'Do I have to?'

'Humour the meagre amusements of a frail old man.'

Janice threw him an old-fashioned look and withdrew a card.

'Remember it and put it back.' After she had done so, he threw the pack at the wall. One card stuck. Grunting, he reached across and turned it over. 'Nine of clubs.'

'No, it was the queen of spades.'

'Bugger. You know those television detectives who put themselves in the minds of killers? I've never been able to do that. I never have the faintest idea what killers might be thinking. But I would imagine Mr Fox would like to make sure Mac never opens his mouth again. He'll be watching the hospital, or asking around.' Bryant tasted his wine. 'This tastes like that bottle of Chateau Gumshrinker I meant to throw out when we moved.'

'There was nothing else in the kitchen. Try not to let it touch your teeth.'

'It doesn't matter, they're made of plastic. Did you get a chance to look into Mrs DuCaine's claim that her other son was turned down for the force?'

'I put in a couple of calls to Hendon, but Fraternity's file appears to have gone missing.'

'You think there's been some funny business?'

'Not sure,' said Longbright. 'I spoke to a guy called Nicholson, who'd been one of his examiners. He says Fraternity was a good bloke, fully expected him to pass with flying colours, doesn't know what happened.'

'A bit odd. Not like them to be evasive. Who was he under?'

'That's the funny thing – nobody could tell me. If I can find out the name of the team leader, I might get somewhere. Nicholson remembered that the regular officer had been taken sick, so they had a replacement for a few days.'

'Sounds like someone took a dislike to Fraternity and put the boot in. Keep trying, will you? It's the least we can do for his mother.'

Longbright sipped some wine and winced. 'I heard Raymond was upset about one of the Daves uncovering another creepy painting in his room.'

'The waltzing witches?' Bryant released a hoot of laughter. 'Poor old Raymondo is spooked because he thinks there was some kind of Satanic secret society operating out of this place. He says he keeps hearing strange noises at night. Doesn't fancy being left alone on the premises.'

'Was there really a secret society here?'

'Oh, absolutely. That's why the estate agent had trouble renting it. The Occult Society of Great Britain conducted a series of legendary experiments in this very building in the 1960s. The society was closed down after one of their rituals resulted in a death.'

'How do you know about this?'

'Maggie Armitage still has the press clippings. She never throws anything away.' Bryant's old friend was the white witch who ran the ailing North London branch of the Coven of St John the Elder. 'She reckons the occultists chose the property because it was built on one of London's strongest ley lines, which runs from the Pentonville Mound to Sadler's Wells, passing right through the centre of this building. Of course, John thinks I chose the premises just to wind Raymond up.'

'Do you think he's fully recovered from his operation? He seems a bit . . .'

'He's fine,' said Bryant, dismissing the idea that anything might be wrong with his partner. 'He's had heart problems before. His doctor has started bleating about retirement again, but we both know where that would lead. I've just finished reading John's notes on the Mr Fox investigation, and I'm starting to think he's right after all. The deaths can't be connected. Perhaps it's wrong of me to try and forge a link between them.'

'So our priority is still to find Gloria Taylor's attacker.'

'You'd better copy Mr Fox's updated file, the one with the new photos, get it over to Islington and Camden, and let's hope the plods at the Met manage to pick him up on their rounds. You know how they think: if he gets rid of a few thieving junkies, it might be better to let him continue clearing the streets.'

Longbright sat back and allowed herself to relax. 'I've reached a dead end with the witness statements. Nobody remembers who was walking behind Taylor on the stairs. If it had happened on the escalator they'd have been standing still, not concentrating on where to place their feet, and someone might have noticed who was there.'

'Maybe Giles is wrong and it was just an accident. But the man has good instincts. I keep asking myself, how could it have been murder? There are simply too many variables. First, there was the risk of being seen and blamed. Then, the chance that someone else would catch her or merely get in the way and break her fall. Even pushing an old lady down her stairs at home doesn't guarantee that she's going to die. It's best to test these things out with physical experiments. I tried it once before with a pig.'

'What happened?'

'It was very upset, jumped over the banisters and landed rather heavily on an occasional table. Alma was furious. I should have used a dead one, but I was minding it for a friend.'

'I notice Taylor's death didn't warrant a mention in the press today. It's been written off as an accident. And Janet Ramsey didn't pick up on Mac's vampire wound.'

'I'd probably be inclined to think it was accidental if I didn't share John's puzzlement over these students,' said Bryant. 'If you were going to attempt to take someone's life in such a damned awkward manner, you wouldn't risk drawing attention to yourself by whacking a label on your victim's back. Why leave a clue at all? And once you've pushed her, then what do you do? You can't fight your way up the staircase when everyone's coming down, so you have to carry on walking to the bottom. Too much of a risk.' Bryant wiped his lips and set down his tumbler. 'It's no good, I can't drink any more of that. Is there really nothing else?' He tipped the remains into Crippen's bullet-punctured litter tray.

Longbright poked about in one of the crates. 'There's half a bottle of Merlot here. You try it.' She unscrewed the top and tipped some in his glass.

The bouquet forced his eyes shut. 'Well, it's got a bit of a bite. It would probably burn quite well.' Bryant examined the label. 'Produce of Morocco. Why was it in the crate?'

'Old evidence.'

'Not the Lewisham Poisoner? Give me a top-up.'

'When you think about how crowded the Tubes get it's amazing there aren't more accidents.' Longbright kicked off her heels and put her feet up on Bryant's desk, crossing her nyloned ankles.

'The guards were telling me that drunks tend to fall down the stairs or on to the tracks further out of town, away from the West End stations, because the alcohol is kicking in just as they arrive at their destinations. There are very few deliberate assaults, though. I suppose it's the proximity of others, the lighting and the CCTV system. No, I think we have to assume the Taylor death is a one-off. Hillingdon's disappearance is bloody odd, though. You can't vanish on a moving Tube train in the two minutes it takes to travel between stops. He'll probably turn up with some silly-ass explanation.'

'I hope you're right.'

'As far as I know, there's never been a serial killer with such a random MO, even in the Forties, when entire neighbourhoods slept down on the platforms during the air-raids. Once you go down those stairs, it seems as if there's a separate unwritten code of manners in place.'

'The peer pressure of the crowd,' said Longbright. 'Everyone has a go at you if you do something wrong.'

'It's like all these freesheets they give out at the stations. There's an understanding that you can leave your paper folded on the back of the seat when you leave because someone else will read it – a form of recycling that's acceptable. And this thing with the litter bins.'

'What thing?'

'Well, there aren't any. Not around the station anyway, because of terrorist threats. So people tuck bottles and coffee cups in every little corner of the street. They can't be bothered to take stuff home, but they don't want to leave the place untidy either. What strange creatures the English are. We make up our own rules, despite the politicians trying to control us. Remember when the Mayor banned booze on the Tube and everyone had a huge party in the carriages the night before it came into effect? I love a bit of anarchy, so long as it doesn't harm the undeserving.'

'Absolutely. It's a bloody good idea to frighten Whitehall once in a while.'

'Funny about the stickers being a symbol for anarchy. The mad are often seen as being free instead of prisoners.'

'I had the same logo on an old Vivienne Westwood T-shirt, back in the 1980s.' Longbright emptied the last of the bottle into their glasses. 'This takes me back to the old days, when the three of us would take on lost causes, the cases no one else believed in, like your Deptford Demon, the Oxford Street Mannequin Murderer, and that business with those glamour models, the Belles of Westminster. You should put them in your memoirs.'

'I will if I ever find the energy,' Bryant promised. 'There are so many projects I'd like to embark on, I can't imagine finishing them all. I sense a gathering darkness, Janice, not just in me but in the world outside. Perhaps it's something everyone of my age feels. But I do wonder if anyone really cares about the same things any more. Who honestly wants to know about the history of pubs or hidden waterways, or mysterious goings-on underneath the streets? I have no conversation about diets and celebrities or the bad habits of television personalities. Just once I'd like some bottom-feeding media slug to be caught in a criminal situation more imaginative than one involving call-girls and drugs. Their world is too predictable and mundane for me, but it's what everyone else seems to be interested in.'

'You can't blame people for being fascinated by their own species,' said Longbright.

'That's where John comes in. He's the human half of the team. I think I'm more of an ideas man. But I do care.' He removed his glasses and smiled at Longbright with suddenly smaller eyes. 'I know it seems he and I disagree about everything, but we don't about the important things. He has very sound instincts. I believe in him. And in you. I remember when you used to come to Bow Street with your mother. She'd leave you to play with us while she was on duty, and I used to threaten to lock you up when you became annoying. Once I even marched you down to the cells. I had every intention of leaving you there because I've never been able to abide children. But even then you knew how to wind me around your little finger. I'm so sorry you lost him.'

'Oh, Liberty. I'm sorry for him, not me. I'm still here. Don't start getting sentimental in your old age.' She made a show of looking stern.

'I know everyone thinks I'm difficult. It's just that as I've got older I've become less gullible. And that makes me harder to control. I don't listen to my peers any more, but that's because most of them are either dead or have gone mad, so now I'm free to explore anything I want.'

'Then why not apply a bit of free thinking to this case?' Longbright suggested. 'What's the most unlikely thing you can come up with?'

Bryant studied the cracks in the ceiling for a minute. 'The most unlikely thing? That Gloria Taylor was deliberately targeted and attacked by someone who thought he could get away with it,' he said finally.

Longbright flourished her palms. 'Then that,' she announced, 'should be your starting point.'

Their conversation was interrupted by a crash from above. 'There's no one else in the building, is there?' Bryant asked.

'You stay here.' Longbright jumped up and headed for

the stairs. Bryant listened to the creaking floorboards over his head, and the chill memory of the attack on Liberty DuCaine crept up on him. He was sure they were the only ones left in the old warehouse, but it had sounded as if someone was walking directly above.

Longbright returned with a frown on her face. 'There's nobody,' she said, puzzled. 'I definitely heard someone, didn't you?'

'You don't think Raymond's ghost is putting in an appearance, do you?' he asked, lightening the moment, but it wasn't enough to remove her anxiety. Longbright was also remembering the murder of a police officer on the floor above.

26

ANARCHISTS

Thursday morning. With the arrival of bitter blasts from the north-east, the temperature plunged, and the office roofs of central London were pearlized with late frost. In the PCU's warehouse, Arthur Bryant had cleared away the evidence of last night's drinking session, and was buried within a tottering fortress of soot-encrusted ledgers.

'How are you getting on with the anarchists?' asked May, tossing his elegant overcoat on to the armchair that sat between their desks.

Bryant had enjoyed less than three hours' sleep. He peered over the printed parapet and rubbed at his unshaven face. 'I've found a link with the missing boy, but I don't think you're going to like it.' Reaching down to pull a bundle of straw from a crate, he unloaded another ledger and blew the dust from it.

'You'd better tell me while I'm still in a good mood. We can't keep all of those books in here. Where are you getting them from?'

'Don't worry, they're on loan from the London Metropolitan Archive. They're going back after I've done with them.' Bryant raised his watery blue eyes to his partner. 'I was having another look through the patient files for the Royal Bethlehem Hospital, Moorgate, 1723–33.'

'As you do.'

'Ah, well, yes. You see, back in the early 1700s some anarchists were arrested and labelled "incurables" because they wouldn't renounce their beliefs. These are the ones who were banged up in Bedlam and left to die, attached to the cell walls with rods and chains. You see where I'm going here.'

'The sticker.'

'Precisely. The London Anarchists was a society formed to avenge the Bedlam Martyrs. It survived for half a century, then died out.' He tapped the bright-red paperback in his hand. 'This is the *Time Out Guide to Alternative London, 1971*. Gosh, we did a lot of marching in those days, didn't we? There's an article in the Agitprop section here – imagine, political agitation had its own section! – all about the revival of the London Anarchists, one branch of which was a protest group called Bash the Rich.'

May maintained his patience with dignity. 'We had a few punch-ups with them at Bow Street, if I recall.'

'That's right, rather a sad little gang, not much of a threat to the established order. Their rallies rarely involved much more than some synchronized chanting, the odd scratched Mercedes and a few broken windows in a wealthy neighbourhood. I always felt we were instructed to come down too hard on them. But they used the same logo. So now we have an active symbol of anarchy with virtually a three-hundred-year history attached to it.'

'The bar designer probably found it in a copyright-free book, liked the look of it and adapted it for commercial use.'

'No. I took the liberty of calling Miss Field. The symbol

was suggested by someone in the bar who knew its meaning. She liked the anarchy connection and added it to the existing lettering. But she can't remember who suggested the idea.'

'This is really clutching at straws, even for you.'

'All right, but in turn the symbol gets used by a group of students who all live in the same Bloomsbury house, one of whom is now missing. Have I got it right so far?'

'Yes, but as is so often the case, I don't quite see the point you're trying to make.'

'Have you considered the idea that they might belong to a revived society of secret anarchists?'

May felt his tolerance level start to slip. 'What is it with you and secret societies? These young people hang out – along with hundreds of other students – in the same bar because it's the cheapest and nearest watering hole outside the university. There are no underground organizations, satanic sects or secret societies any more, OK?'

'That's where you're wrong. There are terrorist cells.'

'I met Theo Fontvieille, one of the flatmates, and I can tell you that the only private club he's likely to belong to is one that serves vodka martinis on a Soho roof terrace. The girl, Ruby Cates, is so focussed on her future career that the only way she can relax is by running marathons. Nikos Nicolau looks like he's been locked in a windowless library for the past ten years. Students have changed, Arthur. They're more focussed now, more concerned with personal growth.'

'I was never a student,' Bryant admitted. 'I was chucked out to work at fourteen, so perhaps I feel an affinity with London's rowdier residents. The city has an extraordinary history of anarchy, you know. In the eighteenth century it was virtually ruled by rioters. The mob was referred to as the fourth estate in the constitution, because it decided which laws would be enforced.'

'And I suppose you'd like to return to those times.'

'Heavens, no. The lower classes specialized in public disorder, perhaps because they lived so much of their lives on the streets. They expressed violent opinions at every level, kicking pregnant women in their stomachs for begetting illegitimate children, exposing the private parts of enemies. Attacking someone's nose in public was considered an act of defamation because you were suggesting they had a sexually transmitted disease – it was where syphilitic infections became most visible. And of course the city was filled with small businesses that existed on credit, so if you humiliated a merchant in front of his customers, you could ruin him. The crowd, the so-called King Mob, could destroy reputations. It must have been a fascinating time.'

'Well, Gloria Taylor worked for a shop.'

'She sold cosmetics. How angry would a woman have to be to shove her cosmetician down the stairs?'

'I don't know, Janice tells me she gets pretty annoyed when they don't have her eye-liner in stock.'

'Most of us tend to limit ourselves to verbal assaults these days. But in some ways, the cities of the past weren't much different from the present ones. The main thoroughfares were just as noisy. Imagine the processions and pageants, the duels, cockfights and boxing matches, crowds jeering at prison-carts, public hangings, floggings, and everyone having their say.'

'Hmm. I can see you at a public hanging.'

'The point I'm making is that they were there.'

'What? Who? Where?'

'Do try to stay in the game. The anarchists, they shared a house in Bloomsbury. And these students of yours . . .'

'You're not going to suggest they're living in the same building.'

'No, but they were in the same street. Right next door,

in fact. And back in 1725, the two buildings might have been one.'

'So you think a bunch of students are running an organization of secret anarchists just because they're living on the same spot? Everybody in central London is living where someone else lived. That doesn't make us adopt their habits.'

'I'm not saying they're all anarchists. Perhaps only one, for reasons of his – or her – own. And somehow it involves the taking of life.'

'I can guess where you're going with this, Arthur, but you're way off track. These students don't look like anarchists. I imagine they do a little ethical shopping and wear a badge or two, but they're more concerned about their future prospects. A fall down some stairs and a missing lad, that's everyday life in the city, not a criminal conspiracy. Don't you have any better ideas?'

The ringing of Bryant's old Bakelite phone made them both jump. May answered the call and listened for a minute. 'Tony McCarthy's off his respirator,' he announced.

'What, dead?'

'No, it sounds like he's going to be OK.'

'A witness. Hallelujah. Can he talk?'

'Nurse says we'll be able to see him late this after-noon.'

'Why not now?'

'He's just had a tube down his throat, Arthur, and he's heavily doped up. She doesn't want him seeing anyone before 5:00 p.m. at the earliest.'

'Book us in,' said Bryant. 'As long as he survives, he'll remain a threat to Mr Fox. I stayed up late last night think-ing about everything. I'm starting to see a way forward, but it will require diligence, nerve and a complete lack of scruples. Best not to tell Raymond what we're up to.'

'What are we up to?' May wondered.

'Let's see the boy first. Make sure nobody else goes near him. Meanwhile, perhaps Janice could arrange a little informal gathering of your students for me in about an hour. I want to meet them alone. I don't care where they are or what they're doing; have her find them, pull them out of class, but get them waiting for me at their house.' Bryant bared his false teeth in an approximation of a grin. 'You know how I always enjoy meeting young people.'

27

PERSONAL SPACE

'Some of you met my partner, John May,' said Bryant, fumbling in his voluminous coat for a toffee éclair and searching for somewhere to sit.

'Yes, he was very nice,' said Ruby, clearing an armchair for him.

'Well, I'm the other one.' Unable to locate the sweet, he pulled out one half of his pipe and waved it about. 'Mind if I smoke?'

'Yes, we do actually,' said Nikos, with a censorious look.

'Ah. Only I saw the ashtray . . .' He pointed to the side table.

'We use it as a paperweight,' said Ruby hastily.

'Odd that it has ash in it, then.'

'I'm the only smoker, but I use the balcony.' She indicated the others. 'This is Nikos – '

'I met your partner at the library,' said Nikos. 'He was asking me about some stickers. I couldn't help him.'

'You gave him my email address,' said Ruby with a trace of indignation.

'Theo Fontvieille,' said Theo, jumping forward to pump Bryant's hand.

'That must be your car outside,' said Bryant. 'You're very lucky to have such a beautiful motor.'

'Yes, it's funny,' said Theo, 'the harder my parents work, the luckier I seem to get.' He threw himself back in his armchair with an annoying laugh. 'It's a reward for getting good grades, Mr Bryant, it has nothing at all to do with luck.'

'I meant no offence. You'll know when I do.' He glanced at the slender Indian boy sitting beside Fontvieille. 'And you are?'

The student looked about himself theatrically. 'I am what?'

'Your name. It was simple enough English.'

'Well, that's not my nationality.'

'We seem to have got off on the wrong foot. Let's try again. My name is Arthur Bryant. What is yours?'

'You don't have to talk to me as if I were a child. My name is Rajan Sangeeta.'

'And you live here as well?'

'I pay my rent like everyone else in this room,' Sangeeta bristled.

'You seem very aggressive.'

'I don't like being questioned by the police when I've done nothing wrong.'

'Oh don't worry, the police can always find something wrong.'

'Mr Bryant is here to help us, Rajan,' said Ruby. 'He and his partner are trying to find Matt.'

'Which just leaves you,' said Bryant, pointing to the only person in the lounge who had not spoken. He had an impudent, friendly face, a stepped haircut and a broad baby nose. He had seemed keen not to draw attention to himself, but now he uncurled from the seat and held out his hand. He looked a year or two younger than the others. 'Toby Brooke.' He brushed Bryant's hand and drew back, casting his eyes downwards again, his dirty trainers drawn up beneath him.

'Tell me about Mr Hillingdon. Does anyone know anything that might be able to shed some light on his disappearance?'

The assembled students glanced at each other but remained silent.

'Let's keep it simple. Where is he from originally?'

'What does it matter where a person is from?' said Sangeeta. 'What relevance does that have?'

'He's from somewhere in Hertfordshire,' Ruby offered. 'He's got a sister and a step-brother. He doesn't get on with his parents.'

'And he's always broke,' added Theo. 'Entirely unambitious, finds his studies a struggle—'

'Theo.'

'Well he does, Ruby. Whereas the rest of us are concentrating on making our first million.'

'You've spoken to his tutors?'

'First thing I did,' said Ruby. 'They haven't seen him.'

'All right, let's find out a bit about you lot.'

'Why do you want to know about us?' Sangeeta complained. 'If something's happened to Matt, we're not automatically suspects. The burden of proof can only be fulfilled by the provision of evidence.'

'Ah, we have a budding lawyer in our midst,' said Bryant cheerily. 'You're going to love this part. I'm going to fingerprint you.' He pulled out Banbury's kit and set it up on the table to a chorus of complaint and disbelief.

'You can't do that!' stormed Sangeeta.

'That's the best part – I can. Because I may be about to transfer the burden of proof to one of you.'

'But for what?' asked Ruby.

'Murder, young lady. You see, one of the uniquely hand-coloured stickers you plaster over your bags was found on one of our corpses, and it contained a partial thumbprint.' Bryant was moving on to extremely shaky ground and knew it. But he was counting on peer pressure; everyone would be keen to clear themselves of blame. He looked around the room and waited for someone to turn him down. 'I'm being overdramatic,' he explained, opening the ink pad. 'We detectives are prone to that. We'll probably have to test everyone who uses the Karma Bar, but I thought you'd like to eliminate yourselves while we're all here. Especially as I have an inducement. I'll find Matthew Hillingdon for you, and I'll keep the prints out of the national database.'

'What if I refuse?' asked Sangeeta, suddenly less aggressive.

'I think you know the answer to that one. Get a lawyer.' *And risk looking suspicious to everyone else*, he thought, praying that no one would do it.

'I'll go first,' said Theo, breaking the deadlock.

'Excellent. And while he's doing that – Toby, why don't you tell me about yourself.' He needed to keep them talking, and to do that it made sense to start with the one who least wanted to join in the conversation.

'W-why me?' Toby stammered. 'There's nothing much to tell.'

Suddenly, Bryant realized, the subject of class had crept into the room. He had accidentally picked the working-class boy. Toby sounded as if he was from one of the rougher boroughs south of the river.

'Ah, a Londoner like myself.' Bryant deftly took the first prints, then passed Theo a tissue. 'Whereabouts?'

'Deptford.'

'I caught the Deptford Demon there, you know. There

was quite a hoo-ha at the time. Your parents probably told you about it.'

'No.'

Bryant was disappointed. He liked to think he'd achieved local fame, at least. The borough of Deptford had always been poor and troubled. The detective had spent many a night there as a kid, sitting on the steps of the Royal Albert pub, waiting for his father to finish drinking with his sister Nell. Most Saturday nights had ended with a fight.

Bryant studied each of them as they stepped up to the pad. One Indian, one Greek Cypriot, two from the Home Counties, one working-class Londoner – and one missing. Not exactly the dog-on-a-rope brigade.

'So, Toby, you're also in the same field as . . .' he glanced over at the piece of paper May had given him, 'Mr Hillingdon and Mr Sangeeta. Social engineering? It sounds rather sinister.'

'It's more like learning confidence tricks,' said Toby, examining his inky thumb nervously. 'It's as much about people as anything. They have cognitive biases you can expose and use. The term is used a lot by hackers, but we're studying it in conjunction with architectural urban planning.'

'How does that work?'

'At its most basic level, you know people have a habit of unconsciously walking on the left side of a pavement because we drive on the left? When you're designing entrances for a building you have to put them in places where everyone expects to find them.'

'As usual, Toby, you're being hopelessly over-simplistic.' Theo sighed and made a show of sitting down and slumping in boredom. Clearly, he was used to owning the conversation.

'Please,' said Bryant, 'go on.'

'Well, before you plan a building, you have to take into account the way people behave. A lot of our research is about pack mentality, leader establishment, group behaviour. For example, the distance you stand from someone is your way of establishing your relationship with them. There are several scientifically defined zones of proximity.'

'Such as?'

'Well, public space is an ideal measurement, placing you three metres from another person. It's what you see on architects' CAD plans of new buildings. Beneath that there's a social-consultative zone of between three metres and 1.2 metres. That's ideal for bars, restaurants, recreation areas. You can talk in comfort but you still own your space. Personal space is the half-metre to 1.2-metre zone that surrounds you, so when you're designing an office this is your minimum space between chairs. And private space is when you're less than half a metre from another person.'

Bryant pressed another thumb into his pad. 'But what about the London Underground? People are forced into much closer proximity during rush hour.'

'Which is why they get so uncomfortable,' Rajan cut in.

'The proximity thing is OK when the train is moving, because social convention dictates the necessity of this travel mode, but when it stops and everything goes silent we feel threatened. Our behaviour becomes more protective. That's why drivers now make frequent public announcements.'

'So, imagine you're walking down a public staircase, and somebody near you slips and falls. What's the reaction of the people standing nearby?'

'That would be dependent on a more practical problem,' said Toby. 'The people behind would see the accident but couldn't physically help, because it's taking place ahead of them, lower down, and those in front would have a similar problem because it's happening behind their backs, and they'd receive no warning.'

'Interesting.' Bryant made a show of looking at everyone in the room, but while Toby seemed interested in the practicality of the question, no one else showed any response.

'I suppose we'd better get to the subject in hand, your missing flatmate.' Bryant dug out a notepad and pen.

'I thought you said you weren't going to keep anything on file,' said Rajan.

'I won't, Mr Sangeeta, these will be purely for personal use. It seems Mr Hillingdon boarded the train he told you he'd catch, Miss Cates, but he never alighted from it.'

'He must have done,' said Ruby. 'Where else could he have gone?' She shifted the weight of her plastic cast, trying to find a comfortable place to rest it while she had her thumb inked.

'We checked the camera footage at the station and couldn't find him. I thought perhaps he'd slipped and fallen between the carriage and the line, but we've had Tube workers walk the entire length of the tunnel between King's Cross and Russell Square, and they've found nothing. So it appears we have a rather peculiar mystery on our hands. Perhaps it would help if you told me a little more about the poor lad. Now, how did you all meet each other?' Bryant hoped he wasn't laying the avuncular act on too thickly; he sounded fake even to himself. At least they had been distracted from worrying about the prints. He closed the lid of the pad and discreetly slipped it back into his pocket.

They were politely waiting for each other to speak. 'We met him when he moved in, about four months ago,' said Ruby finally.

'So when did you two start dating?'

'Around about that time.'

Theo snorted. 'She didn't even let him get his coat off. You know how desperate some girls get.'

Ruby shot him a glance that could have cracked a wine glass. 'I felt sorry for him. He didn't know anyone. He'd just arrived here from Nottingham.'

'And you all got on with him? No problems, nothing at all unusual in the way he behaved?'

Silence, shrugging, vague looks of embarrassment.

'We advertised the room on the UCL student site,' Rajan explained. 'We interviewed him, then put it to the vote, and it was carried three-to-one.'

'Who voted against?' asked Bryant, intrigued.

'I did.' Theo raised his hand. 'I thought we could do better. He was rather desperate to be accepted, although nowhere near as desperate as Toby, obviously.' He laughed alone. 'I know, Toby, you're doing better academically than any of us, but you must admit you've got more to prove.'

'Leave him alone,' said Rajan. 'Everyone's equal here.'

'Do you really think so?' Theo drummed his foot impatiently against the table, looking amused by the proceedings.

'Mr Hillingdon was out with friends on Tuesday night,' Bryant stated. 'Who exactly?' The group looked blankly at each other. 'Well, someone must know. It's important.'

'We don't check with each other before going out,' said Rajan hotly. 'This isn't a police state.'

'Where was he before he went missing?'

'I have no idea,' Ruby admitted. 'He didn't tell me. In a bar. I asked around at college but nobody knows.'

'Does he use drugs? Is he on any medication? Drink so heavily that he forgets what he's been doing? Was he upset about anything? Has he any particular habits you think I should know about?'

Ruby looked to the others for approval. 'Well, he's asthmatic. He carries an inhaler. He drinks way too much. Smokes – you know – but doesn't do *drug* drugs. Nothing else that we're aware of.'

'You've checked with his family?'

'I called his parents in Nottingham. They haven't spoken to him in weeks. He had tickets for a band playing at the Bloomsbury Theatre last night, but he never showed to collect them. I'm out of ideas.'

'Did he ever shop at Selfridges?'

Puzzlement showed around the room.

'OK, what about the rest of you? He hasn't called any-one here? Have you tried his mobile?'

'Of course, that was the first thing we did. It's switched off.'

Silence descended again. Theo was watching Bryant with interest. Nikos was rubbing ink from his thumb. Toby still stared anxiously at the floor. Rajan looked more irritated than ever. Only Ruby seemed comfortable.

'So, if none of you were out with him, what were you doing on Tuesday evening? Why don't you start, Mr Sangeeta?'

'Why me? It's typical that you picked the non-Caucasian to go first.'

'I'd rather talk to you than to the chip on your shoulder, Mr Sangeeta, if you don't mind. You happen to be sitting nearest.'

'I don't have to answer any more questions. I know my rights.'

'Fine. This inquiry's still informal, so I'll just make a note that you didn't wish to cooperate with the police. Then if it becomes necessary we'll place things on a more formal basis.'

Rajan saw that he had been outmanoeuvred; the others would cooperate, leaving him looking like the only one with something to hide.

'I was in the Cruciform Library until seven, then I went and had something to eat.'

'Where?'

'At Wagamama, in the Brunswick Centre.'

'By yourself?'

'Yes, alone, all right?'

Great, thought Bryant, *now I've made him look like Nobby No-Mates.* 'Then what did you do?'

'I came back here to work.'

'See anyone when you came in?'

'No, I went straight to my room and sent some emails. You can look at the log on my laptop if you don't believe me.'

'I'd rather not get all my information from a computer if I can avoid it, Mr Sangeeta. Technology doesn't provide all the answers.'

'That's what Luddites always say,' Rajan scoffed.

'I'm not a Luddite,' said Bryant. 'I don't smash up computers because I think they're stealing my job. Perhaps if you spent less time in front of a computer you wouldn't be so quick to make assumptions. Or be so out of shape. Mr Fontvieille, how about you?'

Theo stretched and yawned. 'I went to the Buddha Bar on the embankment with Cassie Field, the girl your pal met in the Karma Bar. The UK arm of the company's planning a design makeover. She wants to pitch for part of the work, and I'm helping her to draw up a business plan.'

Bryant noticed that Ruby was glaring at him.

'So you drove there?'

'The assistant manager let me leave the car right by the door. Stupidly, I managed to lock the keys inside.'

'How long did you stay?'

'We had the meeting, then Cassie went back to the Karma and I stayed on with some friends. Eventually the place filled up with suburban trash, so I left, came back here and got the spare keys. If you want to check, you'll find at least a dozen people who saw me. I drove back at about half one.'

'I can vouch for that,' said Ruby. 'I saw him come in.'

'OK. Mr Nicolau?'

Nikos looked around at the others. 'I looked in at the Karma Bar around eight to see if there was anyone I knew. Cassie hadn't arrived, but she'd texted one of the barmen to say she was on her way. After that I was up in my room, defragging my hard drive. It took all evening, and it still isn't working properly.'

'I hope you backed up your work,' said Theo.

'I think I got most of it, but there are a few—'

'If we could stick to the subject,' said Bryant sharply. 'Did anyone else see Mr Nicolau?'

'You'll be able to check from the log on my laptop's webcam. I was on Skype talking to some friends in Athens.'

The atmosphere in the lounge had changed. Bryant's questions were forcing the residents to justify their actions. He wondered how he could push them further.

'Which just leaves Miss Cates and Mr Brooke.'

Ruby spoke first. 'I went for a quick drink at the Karma Bar with two girlfriends. You can talk to them if you want, they'll vouch for my whereabouts.'

'You didn't see Mr Nicolau?'

'Maybe we were there after him. We didn't get there until nine, about the same time Cassie arrived.'

'And after that, Miss Cates?'

'I came back here for a while, then went off to meet Matt. As you know.'

Toby cleared his throat. 'I, uh, went to see a film in Leicester Square.'

'Which film?'

'A horror movie, *Buried Alive*.'

'Oh, how was that?' asked Nikos, perking up.

'It was pretty rubbish. I fell asleep, don't even remember what it was about.'

'The film would have finished at, what, ten fifteen, ten thirty? What did you do then?'

'Ten fifteen or thereabouts. I just came back here.'

'Toby, you didn't get here until just before two,' said Theo. 'I heard you come in.'

'What did you do in the meantime?' Bryant asked.

Toby shifted uncomfortably. 'It wasn't that late.'

'I wouldn't swear to it, mate, but I think you'll find it was,' said Nikos.

'I went for a beer, then walked back here. I wasn't in any rush.'

'Where did you go for a beer?'

'A pub on the way, I don't remember.'

'Nobody really hears who comes in when we've got our doors shut,' said Ruby, in an effort to ease the tension. 'Not unless someone's really drunk and noisy.' She shot Theo a look. 'Why don't we show you Matt's room?'

Bryant climbed the stairs to the second-floor landing. Ruby went ahead and pushed open the door in front of him. 'I haven't touched anything.'

'Give me a minute. I just need to look.'

'Sure.' Ruby looked uncertain, and remained on the landing chewing a nail. Bryant wished he had brought Dan Banbury with him. He saw a mess of a bedroom: towers of books on an unmade bed, three pizza boxes, old newspapers, clothes strewn across the floor. It was impossible to know where to start. In order to arrange a meeting with his mysterious friends, Hillingdon could have used his mobile, which he probably still had on him, his laptop, which was here, or half a dozen other food- and beer-stained communication devices. Then again, he might simply have bumped into an acquaintance at college. *London might be the surveillance capital of the world*, thought Bryant, *but running a trace can be just as tricky as it's always been*. He had a good rummage in Hillingdon's bedside table, then poked through the clothes in his wardrobe.

This year's student trends appeared to involve tiny grey cardigans and slim-fit check shirts that made the wearer look like a premature grandfather. *Perhaps my clothes are finally fashionable*, he thought without much conviction. There was nothing illegal or even vaguely interesting to be found here. He considered impounding the laptop, but needed to get Hillingdon officially registered as a missing person first. Disappointed, he was about to leave when he saw a Post-it note stuck on the back of a book entitled *Future Paths: Urban Development and Public Transport*. It read, 'Pay Toby back'.

'Is this Mr Hillingdon's handwriting?' asked Bryant. Ruby came back in and checked the note.

'I think so.'

They descended to the front room, where the group was breaking up. 'Just a moment,' cautioned Bryant. 'Mr Brooke, why did Matthew Hillingdon owe you money?'

Toby Brooke could not have looked more guilty if he'd been caught drowning a bag of puppies. 'I lent him some,' he said lamely.

'How much exactly?'

'I can't remember.'

'Try to hazard a wild guess.'

'Seventy-five quid.'

'Did he say what he needed it for?'

Brooke would not meet his eye. 'No.'

'Go on then, bugger off,' snapped Bryant. 'But I know you're lying, and I'll be watching you.'

28

OBSERVATIONS

'You did what?' said May, incredulous.

'I fingerprinted them,' said Bryant, pleased with himself.

'Why would you do that? They're not even suspects.'

'A student vanishes from the Underground system – more specifically, he vanishes in the same station where we suspect that a psychotic killer may be hiding out – and those closest to him can't come up with a single reason why this could have happened. Mr Fox doesn't select victims at random. I haven't been able to find any link between Gloria Taylor and Matthew Hillingdon, but if either of them had a connection with Mr Fox and was unfortunate enough to run into him in the Tube, we'd have cause and effect. And perhaps those students hold the key to his disappearance. Plus, we might get lucky from the partial. Dan's running it right now.'

'Hmm.' May was far from satisfied. 'How did they react to you?'

'Oh, the usual bluster, deflection, sarcasm and showing off. Underneath the displays of bravado they're just your average annoying college students. Their alibis aren't exactly watertight, either. Fontvieille's the only one I'll be able to verify. Sangeeta ate alone, Brooke was at the pictures, Nicolau swears he was in his room and Cates was waiting by herself at Russell Square Station. Oh, and I saw another book similar to the one you showed me, called *Haunted Underground*. It was lying on the table by the window, but nobody seemed to know who it belonged to. Ruby didn't recall seeing it before, but it has her name written on the flyleaf. There was something else, something I couldn't quite put my finger on . . . an atmosphere of tension. It felt as if somebody in that room was keen on keeping certain bits of information hidden from me.'

'Are you sure it wasn't just your natural suspicion of the young?'

'I delight in the young folk, as you well know.'

May tried not to show his amusement. Bryant would have more easily been able to describe and date the architectural details of their house than recall anything about the five students he had just spent an hour with.

'Well, come on then. I don't suppose you did any better. What did you spot that I missed?'

'Specifically? OK, here are some of the notes I made. It's just the group's emotional background.' May produced the little black leather notebook Bryant had given him for Christmas and opened it. 'Ruby Cates may well be dating Matt Hillingdon, but she's in love with the rich boy, Theo Fontvieille. Her pupils dilate every time she looks at him. She knows more than she's telling. Then, as you say, there are the highly suggestive books.

'There are other undercurrents. Rajan Sangeeta feels the same way about Ruby. She's the only one he's not defensive with, and he always backs her up. Perhaps he made his feelings known and she rebuffed him; it might explain his spiky attitude. The rich boy is also worshipped from another quarter: Toby Brooke lowers his eyes whenever he speaks to Theo, and meekly accepts his criticism. This is probably a class issue, because Toby is constantly being reminded that he's the only working-class member of the household, and looks up to Theo even when he's being insulted. He has a chip on his shoulder almost as large as Sangeeta's. Theo doesn't care about breaking hearts. He looks after number one. He used to date Cassie Field, but now they're just friends. He still uses the bar with the others, which hurts her.'

'Well, that's very impressive – ' Bryant began.

'I haven't finished yet. Nikos Nicolau is obviously besotted with Cassie Field, but she's repulsed by him. By the way, according to him, Ruby is so competitive with the other flatmates that it's making her bulimic. She gives herself away by making elaborate excuses for her disappearances after mealtimes. The household is in debt – there's a stack of unpaid final demands in the kitchen. Presumably Theo could help everyone out and lend them some cash, but he chooses not to, so everyone borrows from Toby, who appears to have suddenly come into money in the last few days. He's entirely dressed in new clothes, the price tags for which are in the kitchen wastepaper basket. He's also sporting a brand-new laptop that only went on sale at the Apple Store at the beginning of this week.'

'You got all that from one fifteen-minute visit to their flat?' Bryant was staggered.

'They interested me,' said May simply.

'Hmm,' harrumphed Bryant.

'Is that all you've got to say?'

'No. I suppose you were very thorough, in your own way.'

'What's that supposed to mean?'

'Nothing. You're like some kind of gossip columnist. I don't notice stuff like that. And you missed a very interesting piece of evidence.' Bryant enjoyed knowing something no one else had picked up.

'All right,' sighed May, 'out with it.'

'Well, there's the business of the Oyster cards. Travel passes are oddly personal things. If you're a student and keeping an eye on your money, I imagine you know exactly how much you have left on your card. I took a look around Matt's bedroom. In a household where there are six students sharing the same lounge and kitchen you might have your own shelf in the fridge, but you keep the important stuff somewhere close to your bed.'

'I can see that. What's your point?'

'Matthew Hillingdon was travelling back from Spitalfields to meet Ruby. So why was his Oyster card in Toby Brooke's bedroom?'

'How do you know it was his?'

'He'd written his initials, MSH, across the top in felt-tip.'

'I hope you didn't take it.'

Bryant opened his hand to reveal the card. 'Of course I did. Let's find out where he went.'

29

NIGHT CRAWLER

They seemed to be spending more and more time below ground, as if the labyrinthine network of Victorian tunnels was drawing them down from the surface, away from cold natural light, into musty foetal warmth.

The detectives found themselves back in King's Cross Station, in the dimly lit guards' staffroom with Rasheed, Sandwich, Marianne, Bitter and Stone. The station was between rush hours, but to the untrained eye the concourse traffic seemed just as populous as ever. Sandwich had taken a reading from Matthew Hillingdon's travel card and was now checking the codes. 'Here you go, he used it on Tuesday night at 6:25 p.m. to go from Euston Square to Old Street,' he told the detectives.

'He'd been researching at the UCL library, so his nearest Tube would have been Euston,' Bryant told his partner.

'It was used again at Liverpool Street, 11:57 p.m., but it wasn't swiped out.'

'He changed at King's Cross – that's where he texted Cates – and should have used the card again to exit from Russell Square. He has to be in the Tube system somewhere.'

'I told you, the night shift covered every foot of the tunnel between here and Russell Square, but found nothing.'

'What about the terminus – did someone examine the train at Uxbridge?'

'It was a Heathrow train, so it stopped at all five flight terminals. It'll be an expensive business checking all the logs.'

'We know he got on board, and disappeared some time before its next stop.'

'But it's imposs—'

'Don't.' Bryant pressed his eyes shut and held up a warning forefinger. 'Just don't say that.'

'He went drinking in the East End with someone,' May reminded them. 'We could search the station footage at Old Street and Liverpool Street, see who he was with.'

'There's no reason to assume he was accompanied on the train journey,' said Bryant. 'He came over to King's Cross, changed platforms and went down to the Piccadilly Line to go to Bloomsbury.'

'Then how did his travel card mysteriously reappear in his house? We've got enough to bring in Toby Brooke for questioning. You said yourself Brooke's alibi doesn't hang together. Suppose they went drinking, had a fight and Hillingdon got concussed, woke up with amnesia somewhere? Brooke could have lifted his pal's card to prevent his exit from the Tube system being registered.'

'Surely he would have thrown it away rather than hang on to incriminating evidence?'

'Maybe he didn't know something was going to happen to his friend. Maybe Hillingdon went off with another girl and Brooke was helping him to hide the indiscretion from Ruby Cates.'

'Matthew Hillingdon called his girlfriend moments before running for the train!' Bryant all but shouted.

Anjam Dutta attempted to defuse the situation. 'I sent Rasheed here to go over the footage again,' he said, 'and the platforms were all empty within moments of the last train going. But there's something – '

'Me and Marianne, we told you about the man in the tunnels who looks like a crawling leathery bat,' Rasheed gabbled, 'and I know it was just a story an' that, 'cause there's no such thing as giant bats in the Tube system . . .'

'Are you all right?' said Bryant, almost concerned. 'Perhaps you should eat less sugar.'

'It was a silly story about something the guards said they'd seen in the tunnels, Mr Bryant,' Marianne reminded him.

'Yeah, we got something that looks like proof now, from two nights ago, the night your bloke went missing.'

'Wherever there's darkness there are ghost stories,' Bryant conceded. 'So what are you saying, that you've actually seen this creature for yourself?'

'Better than that,' Rasheed told him. 'We have footage. Mr Dutta was going through the hard drive checking it again and he found this.' Rasheed searched beneath the burger wrappers on the desk. 'Where did you put it, Sandwich?'

'Sorry, mate, I was using it as a coaster.' Sandwich pulled the disc box out from beneath his tea mug. Rasheed wiped it down and inserted the disc in the optical drive beside his desk.

'The footage is very dark because half of the lights are out,' he apologized. 'When the old Thameslink station shut down and moved over to St Pancras, they left the tunnels open because the maintenance crews still need access to the trunking at night. Most of the CCTVs have been decommissioned because there's no one down there any more. A couple are still used for fire prevention, but they're pretty dirty and have no burned-in timecode. We know the footage was shot late on Tuesday night, though, because the cameras are still programmed to record at set times, and there's an electronic log. Here we go.'

Rasheed hit Play, and they all watched the screen. At first it was difficult to make out what they were seeing. 'That's the tunnel wall, on the right,' said Rasheed, tapping the screen. 'Now watch the floor.'

On the monitor, a white flap tumbled and fluttered. 'That's just a sheet of newspaper. You feel the wind in the tunnels more at night.' In the murky brown corner of the screen, something appeared to be crawling slowly along the floor.

'See it?' asked Rasheed. 'It's too big to be a dog or anything like that.'

A tingle ran across Bryant's skin. The thing was scuttling like a crab, trying to claw its way up the wall, only to fall back. It had a shiny black carapace like an enormous wrinkled beetle, but there was no way of making out any details. 'What on earth could it be?' he asked, leaning forward.

Bitter suddenly spoke up. She opened her mouth so rarely and spoke so softly that everyone found themselves listening intently. 'It's the Night Crawler,' she said. 'People say it's the ghost of a dead man, but it's not.'

'Then what do you think it is?' asked May.

'A tramp. When we turned off the electrical supply to the tunnels, we created an ideal hiding place for outcasts. There are people living down there, but you'll never find them. Not without a guide. We can't cap off the tunnels, see.'

'It makes no sense,' Bryant insisted. 'Why would a bright, successful student with a great future ahead of him stage a disappearing act to live in an unlit network of tunnels with a load of homeless people?'

'If that's what he did, he must have been very frightened of something,' said May. His finger traced the crawling creature on the screen as it twisted and evaporated. The pixels split into rainbow prisms and the screen crackled into darkness once more.

30

LOST TRIBE

The asymmetrical complex of towers, gables, dormers, chimneys, spires and angled arches that comprised the old redbrick Cruciform Building had been abutted by the vast white façade of the University College Hospital. Together, the two medical centres, one Victorian, one millennial, dominated the streets around Euston. Meera Mangeshkar and Colin Bimsley arrived on the hectic third floor just before 5:00 p.m. Naimh Connor, the duty nurse, took them to Tony McCarthy's bed.

'How's your arm, Meera?' asked Connor. 'Fully healed? Only you didn't come back to get signed off.'

'I took the sutures off myself,' said Mangeshkar. She had recently received a minor injury in the course of duty, and regarded anything less than twenty stitches as not worth mentioning. 'How's he doing?'

'He's on heavy medication for pain management. I'd be in favour of keeping him that way, to be honest. He's nothing but trouble when he comes off his methadone programme.'

'You've had him in before?'

'He's turned up on my A&E shift a few times.'

'Is he ever with anyone?'

'Gentlemen with anger-management issues like Mr McCarthy here don't have too many friends,' said Connor. 'No one's tried to see him. You can have a word. Hope you get more out of him than I do.'

Mac was propped on a stack of pillows with a white plastic oxymask fixed to his face. His right wrist was strapped to the bed-guard to prevent him from pulling out his saline drip. He yanked down the mask when he saw the officers. 'I need to get to a private ward,' he told them. 'One with a door.'

'Sure,' said Mangeshkar. 'Give me your credit card and I'll have you moved this evening.'

'I don't feel safe in an open ward, man.'

'You think he's going to come after you again?'

'You don't know what he's like.'

'Tell us. We may be able to help you.'

Mac leaned up on one yellow bony elbow. He'd been washed, but still looked grubby. 'He's a crazy man. He hired me to do a bit of work, right, nothing shifty, make a delivery, drive a van, only he goes and . . .' Even in his doped-up state, Mac realized he was about to incriminate himself.

'Kills someone,' said Mangeshkar. 'We know all about Mr Fox.'

Bimsley pulled his partner to one side. 'And if he admits he does too, it could make him an accessory to murder,' he whispered. 'We have to tread carefully.'

'We want to stop him before he gets to you, Mac,' said Mangeshkar. 'He tried once, he'll probably try again. You're safe and secure in here. But once you step out of those doors, we can't protect you. Why did he attack you?'

'Because I know what he did – I know who he killed. I saw it in the paper.'

'So did everyone else in London,' said Bimsley. 'So why'd he single you out? Just because you performed a few legals for him? Doesn't make sense, mate.'

'It's not that. Other stuff.' Conflict twisted Mac's face.

'What other stuff?'

'If you don't tell us, we can't protect you,' Mangeshkar repeated.

Mac's eyes flicked anxiously from one officer's face to the other. 'I know who he really is,' he said finally.

'This was an ordinary street crime until you interfered,' claimed Raymond Land, somewhat unfairly. 'Now it's turned into the pair of you chasing some kind of super-natural being through the London Underground. I simply cannot sanction this. I can't have you creeping through the tunnels of the subway system looking for a giant bat, placing yourself and everyone else in danger.'

'I knew we shouldn't have told him,' mouthed Bryant, rolling his eyes.

'Apart from anything else, it is not under your jurisdic-tion. The transport police have their own division for this sort of thing.'

'We've spoken to them,' May explained. 'They have no record of anyone living rough in the system. 'I quote: "They used to have this sort of problem in New York, but it's never happened here." But if the boy is in hiding and there really are people down there, don't you think they might have taken him in?'

'They could be holding him against his will,' Bryant added, more for dramatic effect than anything. 'All right, perhaps I shouldn't have mentioned the part about the Night Crawler, but we know this creature was in roughly the same area when the boy disappeared.'

Land folded his arms in what he hoped was a pose of determination. 'You might as well tell me the boy's been eaten by cannibals or strung up inside a giant web by aliens. I'm simply not going to buy it.'

'All right, but Hillingdon is missing and may already be dead. Somebody in that house knows something, because a travel card used by Hillingdon on the evening he went missing has mysteriously reappeared in one of the student's bedrooms.'

'How do you know that?' asked Land. 'You didn't search the place without a warrant, did you?'

'No need for a warrant, old sock. I used my legendary charm and discretion. And my light fingers. Hardly any of his friends can properly vouch for their movements on Tuesday night.'

Land massaged the centre of his brow. He was starting to get a migraine. 'You usually come to me with some kind of theory that makes a sort of distant, twisted sense, but this is the first time you haven't even bothered with that. First you let Mr Fox get away, then you take it upon yourselves to start questioning a bunch of innocent students who obviously have nothing to do with the case I've put you in charge of. I sometimes wonder what I'm here for.'

'Don't worry, old sausage, we all wonder about that. Look, we've got evidence pointing in at least two directions and we think someone in Hillingdon's group knows where he is, so why don't we keep a discreet eye on them?'

'And how are you going to do that?' asked Land suspiciously.

'Well, there are five students, so we send Janice, Meera, Colin, Dan and Jack out to log their movements, see where they go and what they get up to. Meanwhile, John and I can search the Tube system.'

'Don't you think you're a bit old to be climbing down into tunnels?' Land scoffed.

'At least I'll be able to move at my own rate. I can't be expected to trail a fit young student all over town, not with my legs.'

'Fair point.'

'So we'll do it and report back.'

Land suddenly realized he'd been tricked into letting London's most senior detective team go underground to look for some kind of lost tribe. He dreaded to think how this would look on the report to the Ministry.

'Don't be so glum, chum.' Bryant gave his acting superior a friendly tap. 'Detection is not an exact science. It's not like you see on the telly, all mitochondria samples, antibacterial suits and slash-resistant gloves. Most days we're lucky if I can manage to locate the murder site on my *A–Z*.'

'That's because it was printed in 1953,' said Land. 'You are not filling me with confidence.'

'Look, if we're wrong about the giant bat, I'll simply blame my medication.'

'I'm the one who has to carry the can for the unit's mistakes,' Land complained.

'Then we'll tell the Home Office you've been under a lot of stress. We'll say you had a nervous breakdown after you found out about Leanne.'

'My wife? What has she got to do with this?'

'Oh. Er, nothing.' Bryant offered up an unreassuring smile. 'Right, let's get cracking.'

31

INTO THE TUNNELS

May was sceptical about the idea, but Bryant would not be dissuaded. The pair would personally search the tunnels for any sign that Matthew Hillingdon had been abducted.

This time Raymond Land had insisted they do everything by the book. Before photo passes could be issued along with their Personal Protection Equipment, the detectives had been required to sign a liability register and read the health and safety regulations, which covered everything from the danger of discarded syringes to Weil's Disease in rats, and the risk of being bitten by the Tube system's unique breed of mosquito.

Now, dressed in lemon-yellow reflective vests, goggles and steel-capped workboots, the pair waited at the bottom of the King's Cross escalators for their guide. It was 1:00 a.m. and the Tube lines were closed for the night. An army of maintenance personnel had moved in to replace tiles, remove fire hazards, renovate paintwork, fix water damage and rewire cable boxes. They had just four hours to get everything done; all adhesive, paint and cement had to be touch-dry before they left, all equipment repacked and stored away.

'I'm Larry, your SPIC,' said the Site Person In Charge for the evening, Larry Hale. He solemnly shook each of their hands in turn. Their guide was a barrel-chested black man in his late forties with pugnacious features and gold ear studs. 'We've only got a couple of lads repairing some lights down here tonight, so you won't be in anyone's way. I say lads, but there's more women than you'd expect. Good workers.'

'How many are there on a team?' asked May as they walked towards the platform.

'Depends on the size of the job. We had nearly two hundred at Piccadilly Circus for the refit,' he told them. 'When we add electronics, the new systems run in tandem with the old ones for two weeks, to iron out bugs.'

'I've heard there's a second set of tunnels, too,' said Bryant, 'built for emergencies on sensitive sections of the line.'

'Don't know anything about that,' said Hale, and Bryant sensed he had stumbled upon an area of secure information. 'There's storage behind here, but that's not ours.' He indicated a rampart of blue-painted plywood. 'Licensed by the London Fire Brigade. There are other control and server rooms down here, as well as the giant vents. You're looking for a place a lad could hide, yes?'

'Or somewhere he might have fallen,' said Bryant.

'There are a lot of dead areas in the system,' said Hale. 'Whenever platforms get rebuilt, the old layouts get left behind. The dead tunnels are capped but not filled in. The old City and South London Line's still there, and parts of the Northern Line that fell out of use, plus there are all the connecting staircases. Many have got access doors, but we keep them locked, so he wouldn't have been able to get in. Mind you, even I don't know where all the accesses are, and I've been down here seventeen years. My missus says I spend more time here than at home. You'll have to keep your eyes peeled.'

'Does the air ever get to you?' asked Bryant.

'It's no worse than what's up on the surface,' Hale replied. 'There's a story going around that the air down here can cure anorexia, but I don't believe that. There used to be plants pumping ozone into the system, but it didn't seem to make much difference to the smell.'

Resculpted in scaffolding and blue plastic sheeting, the platform looked very different now. 'What's all the chicken wire for?' asked May, pointing to the metal mesh that ran along the platform roof.

'We can't take all the panels off every night when we're installing electrics, so some of these are ongoing repairs. Don't worry, nobody could get behind them. OK, the power's off now. It's safe to come down on to the tracks.' He dropped below the platform edge and helped Bryant down. 'Don't panic if you hear something that sounds like an approaching train. It's just the wind in the tunnels.'

'That's a relief.'

'Our biggest problems are caused by trespassers, idiots who've decided to do a bit of potholing through the system. They try to get in from the so-called 'ghost stations' like Aldwych, and leave litter on the line. There are a couple of dozen disused stations, and many more abandoned ones. Security's a big issue now, of course. Your lad, what was he doing down here?'

'Catching a train, so we thought,' said May.

'Well, he wasn't a jumper. We'd have found his remains by now. I've seen a few fried on the positive rail and it's a sight you don't forget. Keep your eyes on your feet – there are a few transverse cables here.'

They were moving out of the light now, into the gloom

of the tunnel. The smell was different here, both sharp and musty, with a hint of electrical ozone.

'The section to the south-east of the main station was closed off when the old Thameslink terminal shut,' Hale told them over his shoulder, 'but the disused platforms and the tunnel network can't be bricked up because we still need drainage access.'

It had grown surprisingly warm. May loosened his collar. 'Are you all right, Arthur?' he called. He had noticed that his partner was lagging behind.

'Don't worry about me, I'm fine. I was just watching a family of mice trying to drag a fried chicken leg home.' Bryant caught up with them, his overcoat flapping in a sudden rogue breeze from the tunnel.

'We're now entering the closed-off part,' said Hale. 'Not too many lights down here, I'm afraid. The power's off, so it's best to switch your torches on.'

May was carrying his Valiant, the old cinema torch he had used for years on investigations. The curving walls were crusted with necklaces of soot. Fibrous brown matter like carpet fluff coated the floor. 'Skin flakes,' said May. 'Dan would have a field day down here.'

They had passed beyond the territory of the cleaners. Hale led them between a set of flimsy red and white plastic barriers, into the connecting tunnel that linked the two stations.

'I haven't been along here since the station was shut,' Hale admitted. 'You can't cover everything.'

'When you think about it,' said Bryant, 'there's a strong link between the LU network and civil defence facilities. Didn't part of the Piccadilly Line become secure accommodation for the Electricity Board during the Sixties?'

'That's right. The old Brompton Road Station was the Royal Artillery's Anti-Aircraft Operations Room, and part of the Central Line was turned into a sterile production unit for aircraft during the War. Safe from the bombs, see. That's why the National Gallery stored its paintings on the Tube during the Blitz.'

The darkness was almost complete now, and oppressive. May was feeling distinctly uncomfortable. A smell of burned dust filled the air. Bryant seemed entirely in his element.

'Wait.' May's flashlight illuminated Hale's raised hand. 'I heard something.' They came to a halt and listened. Beneath the faint sussurance of the tunnel wind they heard a snuffling, shuffling sound. 'There.' Hale pointed. The detectives converged their light beams.

Ahead, at the point where the tunnel broadened out into the edge of the closed station, they saw a bundle of rags shift inside walls of dirty brown cardboard.

Hale moved in and knelt down. 'Come on out,' he said firmly. 'Let's have a look at you.'

A tousled head appeared above the box. The boy was in his late teens, wrapped in a blue nylon hooded jacket several sizes too large for him. He peered blearily at the trio, waiting to be given grief.

'It's OK, we're not here to turn you out,' said Bryant.

'We bloody are,' said Hale.

'I just want to ask you a question. Did you see a young man down here on Tuesday night, shortly after midnight?'

'No.'

'You were here then?'

'Yes.'

'Think hard. Are you sure there was no one else?'

'I don't know, we hear a noise.' The boy had a strong Eastern European accent.

'How many of you are there down here?' asked Hale. 'You know you're not supposed to be in this part of the station.'

'What did you hear?' Bryant asked.

'I don't know – somebody fall down. We hear him shout.'

'Can you tell us where?'

A second head appeared beside the boy's, a girl who was equally sleepy. 'Over there.' She pointed off into the dark.

'What's down there?' asked Bryant.

'It's a short service tunnel. We used to store cleaning equipment there until H & S made us move it,' Hale explained, turning back to the sleepers. 'I'm afraid you two can't stay here.'

'We only stay one week, no more,' pleaded the boy. 'We have job cleaning buildings in London, near . . .' He consulted the other. 'Where is it we must go?'

'Aberdeen,' said the girl hopefully.

'I'll leave you to sort this out,' Bryant suggested. 'John, come with me.'

'Don't go far,' Hale called after them. 'I'll be with you in a minute.'

The detectives carefully made their way along the track. 'Why would he have come along here?' asked May, not happy about wandering off into the darkness.

'We're still not far from the main Piccadilly Line platform,' Bryant answered. 'I bet it's not more than a few hundred yards. It just seems further because you're dawdling.'

'It's a wild goose chase. If he'd suffered some kind of *petit mal*, or was simply in a state of intoxicated confusion, he'd have gone up, not down.'

'Not if he was physically too weak to climb the stairs. What's that over there?' Bryant pointed ahead.

'You can barely see in daylight, I don't know how you can spot anything down here,' May complained, but he went to look. The green plastic bin was the size of a man and missing its lid. It lay on its side between the tracks. As he approached, Bryant shone his torch inside.

It was hardly surprising that no one had discovered the body. Matthew Hillingdon was curled up within, as if, in pain and desperation, he had sought the warmth and solace of an artificial womb.

32

IN MEMORIAM

The only way to avoid thinking about Liberty DuCaine was to keep busy. Janice Longbright finished unpacking the last of Bryant's crates and loaded May's computer with witness statements, then sat back to regard the chaotic room. No amount of organization would turn it into a decent centre of operations.

The Daves had nailed cables along the skirting boards to provide extra juice, but the walls were rotten, and there seemed to be a real danger that the hole in the floor might suddenly expand and send them all down to the basement. They were planning to lay new floorboards, but could not agree how to go about it. Everything was lopsided, as if a wartime bomb had shifted the building slightly off-kilter, jamming windows in their frames and causing doors to gouge grooves in the floorboards.

While the workmen argued, Longbright called in the detective constables and impatiently listened to their report. 'Tony McCarthy doesn't know if this is the real name of the man who employed him,' said Meera, 'but he's given us our first solid lead. Mr Fox taught English at Pentonville Prison two years ago. He was employed by the former head of educational services, but she died of cancer last year. Fox was registered in her files under the name of Lloyd Lutine, and McCarthy confirms this was the name he used.'

'That must be an alias,' said Longbright.

'Why?' asked Meera, puzzled.

'The Lutine Bell is in Lloyds Bank, in the city. It used to be rung once to signify bad news. Here it is.' Longbright walked around Bryant's cluttered desk and located a miniature brass copy of the original cracked ship's bell. 'A gift from a Lloyds client. Arthur used to ring it whenever a new murder case came in.'

'Couldn't the name just be a coincidence?' asked Colin.

'Come on, Lloyd *and* Lutine? I can't believe he got security clearance on a moniker like that.'

'He must have been confident that no one would get the connection.'

'Multiple killers have a kind of arrogance,' said Longbright grimly, thinking momentarily of her mother's death. 'Don't worry, when we get him this time, we'll put him on the national DNA database. I'd like to see him fake his genetic code. Got anything else?'

'Yeah. He made a friend at the prison. A history teacher. We've got her address.'

'Go home, I'll go and see her.'

'We could do it first thing in the morning,' Colin offered.

'No, let me see if she's up for a visit tonight. I'm not tired.'

It didn't take Longbright long to walk to the Finsbury address. Georgia Conroy had the evasive eyes of a gentle-woman living in humbled circumstances. Her pale, lined face was designed for disappointment. 'Please, come in,' she offered, drawing her dressing gown against the cold air and stepping back from the door. 'I'm afraid the place isn't very tidy. I was about to go to bed when you called.' The flat was perfectly neat, but smelled of damp and loneliness. Longbright accepted an offer of tea, knowing that interviewees were more relaxed when they had something to do. Kitchens were places for confidences.

'Of course, I knew the name was false the moment I heard it,' said Georgia, rinsing a teapot. 'Either that, or his father had been a sailor with a sense of humour. Our time at the prison overlapped by about eight months, but we were on different shifts. He took me out for a drink a couple of times, said I reminded him of his mother – not much of a compliment. I felt a bit sorry for him.'

'Why?'

'He didn't seem to have any friends.'

'Did he tell you much about himself?'

'Only bits and pieces. He was very guarded about his private life. Hated the job. Couldn't wait to leave. I thought we got on quite well, but one day I came in and they told me he'd resigned. He never even came back to clear out his locker.'

'Here's my problem – '

'Georgia, please.'

'Georgia. Mr Fox has killed a number of times since he left his job at Pentonville, but we're having a hard time getting any leads. If there's anything you can remember . . .'

'He was obsessed with graveyards,' she said without hesitation. 'Apart from the mother thing, that's what put me off him. When we went for a drink it was all he talked about.'

The information fitted with Longbright's knowledge that Mr Fox had worked as a gravedigger in St Pancras.

'Did he ever explain why he was so interested in them?' she asked.

'Not really. But I got the feeling it was connected with his family. Some damage in the past . . .' She dried the pot thoughtfully. 'That's it. He wanted me to go and visit his father's grave with him, but I thought it was a weird thing to do with someone you barely knew, so I said no.'

'Did he tell you where his father was buried?'

'Oh yes, Abney Park Cemetery, in Stoke Newington. I remember the family name, too – Ketch – because it made me think of Jack Ketch, the executioner employed by Charles II. I'm a history teacher,' she added apologetically.

'If Lloyd Lutine was a pseudonym, how did he explain that his father had a different name?'

'He told me he was adopted. When it came to answering questions he was pretty glib, almost as if he'd rehearsed the answers.'

It had gone midnight by the time Longbright reached Stoke Newington's neglected cemetery. The gravestones seemed incongruous in their setting, surrounded by the terraced houses of a shabby North London town. Once, Isaac Newton had sat here composing hymns. Now, the graveyard was wedged between betting shops and fried-chicken outlets.

Longbright knew she shouldn't have worn stockings and heels, but old habits died hard. The paths were muddy and half-buried in brambles. Sulphurous light fell from the distant streetlamps, but did not penetrate the knotted undergrowth to any depth. *I must be mad*, she thought. *I'm not going to find anything useful here.*

There had been one lucky break; the night caretaker had explained that only those who held plots bought before the cemetery company closed in 1978 could still be buried on the land. He directed her across the site, past the derelict non-denominational chapel that could have passed for a set in a Dracula film, to a neglected corner swamped by nettles and briars. The lights from a row of houses supplemented her torch-beam as she searched the overgrown plots.

The small plain memorial was notable for its newness; the remainder of the headstones in the area were more than a hundred years old. She leaned closer and scraped away some kind of parasitical weed that had clamped itself to the stone. Using her mobile, she took a shot of the inscription:

IN MEMORIAM
Albert Thomas Edward Ketch
Died 47 Years of Age
We Are Born in the Wilds of Darkness and Die
on the Pathway to Enlightenment.

The inclusion of his middle names meant that she should easily be able to track him through the electoral register.

She was just clipping her pen to her jacket pocket when she heard a scuffling noise behind her. Turning slowly, she found Mr Fox standing motionless with his legs set wide apart in the undergrowth, his hands at his sides. He was dressed in black jeans and a black hooded sweatshirt, and was staring back at her as if trying to make sense of a particularly abstract sculpture.

Longbright assessed her position. After dark in a secluded cemetery, less than ten feet from a man who had shown enough confidence to commit murder on a crowded thoroughfare. There was no point in playing dumb; they knew each other well enough. Mr Fox wore a black woollen hat that possessed more character than his face; if asked to re-create his image, she knew she would literally draw a blank, but still she tried to memorize the arrangement of his features.

She guessed he had continued to watch them all, tracking her from the unit to the teacher's flat to the cemetery, just as she knew that she was now in the greatest danger. Here was something he could not afford to have exposed, a piece of his past that would give them the key to his nature. He remained quite still, watching her and waiting, but a single sliver of streetlight flickered through the trees and caught the silver skewer as it slid gently down from the sleeve of his jacket, into his waiting fist.

Did he think she hadn't seen it? She had not taken her eyes from his; her peripheral vision had picked up the movement. Unit members were not licensed to carry weapons, but back in the days when she had carried a handbag, Longbright had always kept a housebrick in it. She wished she had it with her now.

She realized she was in a narrow corner where two high walls met. It was almost as if the grave had been designed to trap her. There was no way back, only forward past him. Absurdly, the warbling song of a thrush rose in the branches above her to end on a high, watery trill. She looked up and saw the boughs extending beyond her reach to the wall.

In the moment she glanced away he moved, passing through the brambles without making a sound. Did he reckon she was going to jump and somehow clear him? *He obviously doesn't know how much I weigh*, she thought, stepping back on to his father's grave, raising her heel on to the headstone and lifting herself straight over the wall behind as he suddenly grabbed at her left leg.

Too late, though – she was over, dropping into a back garden of sheds and ponds, stone swans, a heap of children's toys in circus colours. But he followed her over as she ran for the next garden, and suddenly they were performers in a bizarre suburban steeplechase, clambering over one garden fence after the next, stumbling, falling, rising again.

This should be the other way around, she thought, *me bloody chasing him*. But she had seen the damage the skewer could inflict, and had not been taught any manoeuvre that could beat its speed and dexterity.

He was at her heels, faster, lighter, and suddenly straight ahead was a garden fence that could not be climbed because it was buried within an immense juniper bush, and there was nowhere else to run.

She saw his arm lift and his fist arc towards her throat, and moved just enough for the skewer to stick in her padded jacket, slicing the kapok and stinging the flesh of her shoulder. But it was easily removed to use again, and as he did so she realized she was stuck, her heel wedged into the soft lawn, anchoring her to the spot. She felt sure she was about to die.

But Mr Fox had stopped too. Frozen, he was looking past her with something akin to horror in his eyes.

She turned to witness the same sight: a father surrounded by a rippling skirt of children, flooding out of the patio doors with murder in their eyes. And as the shout went up, 'What the bloody hell do you think you're playing at?', she realized his worst fears of attention and exposure had surfaced.

Even as she called back 'I'm a police officer,' she knew they would not catch him this time, because he had already spotted an escape route across the roof of a shed, into the alley beyond, and she was calling after him as she ran, the tables turned as she transmitted to any unit in the area, *Anyone come in, help.*

But he was fleet-footed and light – then gone.

Too late, she knew, *too damned late, even if someone*

picks up the call right now. He's away. This won't be over until he's tried to spill more blood.

She stopped and dropped her hands to her knees, fighting to regain her breath as the excited children appeared and swarmed around her.

33

ACCIDENTAL DEATH

Back in King's Cross, underneath the closed Thameslink station, Dan Banbury was wedged inside the green plastic bin, grunting and complaining while Bryant and Hale trained their torches on him.

'No signs of violence on the body from what I can see, not that I can see anything. They haven't got an extension lead long enough, can you believe it? We need to get him over to Camley Street. Giles is waiting for the delivery. He wasn't thrilled about being dragged back to work at this time of night. Don't come any closer if you're not suited up. I don't want your leavings all over my site.'

'Oh stop complaining,' grunted Bryant, flicking off his torch to leave Banbury floundering about in the dark. 'What the hell did Hillingdon think he was doing, playing silly buggers down here? John, where are you?'

'Over to your left,' May called. 'The dust's thick and undisturbed in this part. We've got a single set of footprints. Looks like he was alone.'

'So he boarded the last train by himself, somehow managed to pass through a number of solid walls, and wound up wandering about in a disused tunnel, whereupon he fell asleep and died for no reason.'

'That's about the size of it,' called Banbury. 'I've got his mouth open. There's a strong trace of alcohol, and something else on his skin that I can't place. Might be aftershave, I suppose. At least the mice haven't been at him. The body position is suggestive. I'm wondering if he crawled in here just to stop the room from spinning. Come on, give me a hand out.'

'What are you saying, the booze made him haemorrhage?'

'There's no blood or vomit that I can see. Perhaps he simply suffocated. Or suffered some kind of delayed allergic reaction to an ingredient in a cocktail. Anaphylactic shock. It happens. His hypostasis appears normal, which means he wasn't moved after death. I'll need to take samples and do the shots tonight, so I'll be a while.'

'Come on, is that all you've got?' Bryant complained. 'You're telling me he couldn't handle his drink? How am I supposed to fit that in with my theories?'

'You know the trouble with you, Mr Bryant?' Banbury called back.

'Why does everyone want to tell me what the trouble with me is?'

'You don't communicate with other people. You develop these so-called theories and keep them all to yourself. How do I know what to look for if you don't give me a clue about what's going on in your head?'

'I don't wish to make suggestions about what you should be finding,' said Bryant testily. 'If I do that, the investigation is compromised. I want you to make deductions I can corroborate without twisting the facts to fit.' He had been accused of forcing his theories on others in the past, and wasn't about to make the same mistake again.

'I'm just here to assess the crime scene, if that's what it

is. At the moment I'm looking at a verdict of accidental death, although maybe some decent lighting will reveal something I'm missing at the moment.'

'Any money on him?'

'Why?'

'He could have been mugged earlier, suffered some kind of a stroke and lost his bearings down here.'

'He's got a few loose coins. No mobile, no asthma inhaler.' Banbury passed a wallet out to them. 'Take a look at that, if you're wearing gloves. It was in his jeans. No money in it, no credit cards, so maybe it was a robbery. He's not wearing a jacket.'

Bryant flicked open the wallet and pulled out a handful of paper scraps, reminders to go to the bank and collect shopping, nothing of use. 'Matthew Hillingdon is supposed to be in Russell Square, not the arse-end of King's Cross.'

'Gloves,' Banbury reminded, 'are you wearing them?'

Bryant ignored him. 'I want this lad tested for drugs. Nice middle-class boy, he's bound to have dabbled. His medical records were clean, no fits or dizzy spells, no history of seizures, nothing. No enemies, everybody liked him. Something wrong with that, for a start.'

'You're a cynic, Mr Bryant.'

'If you live long enough, you will be too.' Bryant pulled his scarf over his squat nose. 'There's a bad smell down here. Standing water. And I speak as one who knows.'

'Ah yes, your little adventure through the city sewers,' said Banbury. 'I'm amazed you didn't get sick.'

'I've built up plenty of antibodies by eating Alma's cooking. Do you need a hand getting him out?'

'No, Mr Hale and I can bag him and move him as far as the platform. Then we'll need the med team to stretcher him. I'll get some of these fibres off to Portishead, and bung out the dabs off.'

'Can we afford it?'

'Only if it turns out to be murder, so we'll have to take a gamble. They should have finished running a match on your students by now. Why don't you go back up?'

'Come on, John, let's get out of here.' Bryant pulled at his partner's arm, but May remained in place, staring at the body that lay face-down in the bin. 'What's the matter?'

'He reminds me of Alex when he was a student,' said May quietly. 'I've lost them both, haven't I?'

'I know you and your son never saw eye to eye, but Alex moved to Toronto to follow his work. Staying with him will be a healthy change for April. She isn't taking sides against you. She'll come back when she's ready, you'll see.' Bryant was no diplomat, but he could recognize the problem from both sides. May's granddaughter had little chance of leading a normal life while she worked at the unit. She needed to be at peace with herself. 'Come on, let's see if we can find a pub that's still open.'

May lingered near the corpse of the student. 'We can go for them now,' he said at last. 'Hillingdon's misplaced travel card is just cause for a full property search. Let's come down hard on the students. Get their phone records subpoenaed and their emails opened. I'll want their laptops, mobiles, hard drives, PDAs, anything else they've got. If one of them is responsible, we'll find something that doesn't make sense.'

'If you're dealing with someone smart,' Banbury called back, 'he'll be using a pay-as-you-go phone and keeping his texts and emails clean of evidence.'

'They're college students,' May replied, nettled. 'One of them will slip up. They won't all manage to corroborate their stories. They're already under stress. We need to light a fire beneath them.'

As they walked towards the surface their mobile-phone reception returned and they received Longbright's message, informing them that she had encountered the sharp end of Mr Fox's silver skewer.

34

SURVEILLANCE

Early on Thursday morning, London was buffeted by storm-winds from the east bringing ever darker threats of rain. Three days now remained before the unit had to present its caseload closed and ready for audit.

Meera stood outside the Tottenham Court Road coffee shop and watched as, on the other side of the glass, Nikos Nicolau consumed yet another breakfast, this time a toasted cheese-and-tomato sandwich. So far he had searched three locations for discount computer software, purchased a new mobile and stopped at three different coffee shops. While he ate, he fired up the new phone and discarded its packaging on the floor. He seemed to shed litter wherever he went. At least he was totally absorbed by his tasks and took no notice of his surroundings. That made him easier to follow.

Meera was bored and cold. Usually she could find a way to enjoy surveillance, but Nicolau was an uninteresting subject, and she had not dressed warmly enough. In between snacks, the student wandered, mesmerized, around the software shelves. He seemed in no hurry to get to college, or anywhere else for that matter. The only other stop he'd made was at the Karma Bar, where he cupped his hands over the window and peered inside, looking for someone.

She huddled down in the doorway next to the Mac World store, and waited for him to finish stuffing himself. Nikos did not look as if he was capable of murdering anyone, but he was certainly on some kind of mission. Every now and again he extracted a pen from his top pocket and scribbled urgent notes on a scrap of paper. He had screwed the first pages up and shoved them in his jacket pocket.

Nicolau wiped his mouth and rose to leave, stepping out of the detritus he had created as if shucking off an old skin. Meera raised her collar and dropped back into the shadows as he passed. *Boring and obnoxious*, she thought, *but not a killer*. Even so, the intense look she caught on his face as he passed disturbed her.

Further up the road, Rajan Sangeeta threaded himself quickly and nervously through the morning crowds. He had attended an early lecture on 'Light Density Retail Building: Creating Urban Downtowns', before heading for the British Library. But he had then stopped dead in the middle of the deserted library square to take a phone call. Colin Bimsley, who had been following a few paces behind him, was brought up short and had to hastily divert behind a tree; being inconspicuous had never been his strong point. He tried to listen as he passed, but caught only a few words: '. . . it just feels wrong . . . more careful in future.' Taken out of context, the phrases sounded sinister. He strained to hear, but a refuse truck drawing up outside the library gates drowned out the rest of the conversation.

Sangeeta headed for the library coffee shop and worked

on his laptop, but there were flickers of anger within him. At one point he suddenly screwed up his eyes and pressed a palm across them, as if to try to relieve a pain he knew he could not control. Bimsley ordered a coffee and settled himself, knowing he was in for a long wait.

Longbright's shoulder was sore, but the dense padding of her jacket had prevented the skewer from penetrating more than a couple of centimetres. She had cleansed and swabbed the small wound, and was now staking out Theo Fontvieille. He, too, had attended the 'Urban Downtowns' lecture – Longbright had spotted Bimsley outside the college – but he had left and was standing on the corner of Gower Street and Torrington Place, obviously waiting to meet someone.

She wasn't surprised when Ruby Cates turned up. After all, the pair were sharing a house. But the lingering kiss that followed changed the nature of their relationship, and sent Longbright's thoughts in a new direction. Everyone assumed that the killer was a man, but suppose Ruby had told Matthew Hillingdon she was breaking up with him? What if he had taken it badly and threatened her? What if she had needed to get rid of his attentions?

Theo was smiling, holding her eyes with his. Ruby didn't exactly seem to be in mourning for her missing lover. They talked, and as Longbright watched from the doorway of the Japanese restaurant opposite, she sensed something else: anxiety darted across Theo's face. It seemed he had said something that Ruby felt strongly about, because now they were sniping at each other, and this quickly turned into a full-blown argument.

Suddenly, Ruby Cates didn't seem so friendly and helpful. She looked downright lethal.

It was raining hard, but neither of them seemed to notice. Ruby stabbed her finger at Theo, who tried to laugh off her anger, and now he was asking her to please come back as she stormed off along the pavement with damp shoulders and furiously dark eyes.

Longbright was about to go after Theo when she saw Dan Banbury in the next doorway, from where he had been watching Ruby. 'What was all that about?' he asked, coming over.

'I've no idea. Has she been seeing both of them? Quick, go after her, you'll lose her.'

Banbury chased after Ruby, and Longbright headed off into Bloomsbury behind Theo Fontvieille.

Meanwhile, Sergeant Jack Renfield was running surveillance on Toby Brooke. The problem was that Toby knew he was being followed. Renfield had no idea how he knew. He'd been careful, keeping well back as Brooke headed to the UCL canteen, drank tea, exited and searched the Gower Street Waterstones bookshop, emerging with a book in a plastic bag. But Brooke knew he was there all right. He caught sight of the sergeant in several store windows, and even seemed to be waiting for him.

When the rain started falling hard, Toby unfurled a rainbow-coloured golfing umbrella and continued on in the direction of the house in Mecklenburgh Square. But when the traffic lights changed between them and Renfield briefly lost him, Brooke waited for the sergeant to catch up. At the gates of Bloomsbury Square he seemed to be toying with the idea of actually coming back to talk.

I'll make it easier for him, thought Renfield, cutting off the corner of the square and beating Brooke to the fountain at the centre of the park. He stopped in Toby's path, bringing them both to a halt.

'Hi,' said Toby awkwardly. 'You've been following me for over an hour. Aren't you soaked?'

'Part of the job,' said Renfield. 'How did you know I was behind you?'

'I just had a feeling. So, what happens now?'

'Yeah, that's a bit of a problem, my cover being blown,' Renfield admitted. 'I used to be better when I was still on the beat. Desk copper, y'see, you lose the knack.'

'Matthew,' said Toby suddenly, his face changing oddly.

'Mr Hillingdon, yes.' Renfield knew the detectives had found the boy's body beneath the Thameslink station, but was aware that the other students had not yet been told. He wondered if he should break ranks and raise the subject. Better to let Toby speak first; he looked as if he had something to get off his chest. Renfield waited. The rain lashed at them both. Toby finally broke.

'I'm not . . . safe.'

'What do you mean?'

He looked up into the dark sky, and for a moment Renfield was sure he was fighting back tears. 'I've had to hide things. I can't control myself. I know it's nobody's fault but my own. I'll deal with it, OK – but it has nothing to do with any of you.'

He turned and ran off, dashing through the puddles on the path. Moments later he had turned a corner and there were only wet trees and veils of falling rain.

How the rain fell.

Looking out across the garden square, the dripping plane trees, the buckling plumes of the wind-battered fountain, the few passers-by fighting to control their umbrellas, it was easy to think *I hate this city and everything it's driven me to.* The fear had begun as a small but insistent pain, gnawing and nagging like an ulcer, but it had grown each day and now consumed every waking hour.

They're watching us, and if anything else breaks now

the game will be up. I have to be stronger than I've ever been before. This will soon be over.

It was like a cracked pipe that was leaking under pressure, and the more the crack grew, the more attention it drew to itself. You had to treat it like any other emergency: seal it off, mend it quietly and invisibly, then get as far away as possible. There was still a chance to do that, wasn't there?

The nightmare that had begun on Monday afternoon seemed as if it would never end. It made you want to screw up your eyes and scream with the pain of it all. How much could you age in a single week?

The cliché is true, money really is the root of all evil. If I hadn't been so broke and desperate for cash, if I hadn't needed status and respect so badly, none of this would ever have happened. It's my own fault, all of it, and now I have to grow some balls and see it through.

The thought of more violence to come was sickening, but it was too late to turn back.

One more day should do it. I can still get out of this in one piece. Stupid of me to give the game away like that. Sometimes I don't think clearly – that's when I behave like an idiot. I can cover the damage, but I have to stay ahead of the others and hold my nerve.

Some children splashed past on the path, shrieking and howling, without a care in the world. *This time next week I'll be like that,* said the voice inside. *I'll be laughing about what a nightmare it all seemed. I just have to get through the next twenty-four hours.*

Even though it means killing again.

35

CONSPIRACY TO MURDER

Kershaw welcomed Bryant and May into his autopsy room as if ushering a mistress into a box at the Royal Opera House. It was obvious that Giles was going the way of the unit's previous incumbent, who had begun as a normal medical student only to become a social outcast, reeking of body fluids and avoided by women. Enthusiasm for the job was all well and good, but too much gave people the creeps. Kershaw was virtually dancing around them in excitement, and that was how Bryant realized he knew how Matthew Hillingdon had died.

'Come on then, out with it,' he said wearily. 'I'm old and tired. I could die at any minute. I don't have time for pleasantries. If you know what killed him, just say so.'

'I might have an idea,' Kershaw teased. 'And it's all thanks to you and your filthy habits.'

When Bryant frowned, his forehead wrinkled alarmingly. Right now he frowned so hard that it looked as if his face might fall off. 'I don't have any filthy habits. Everyone else makes too big a fuss about cleanliness. We need a few germs to keep us healthy. Wipe that grin off your face, and show some respect for the dead while you're at it.'

'I'm sorry. Rosa keeps warning me about that. I examined the boy, Matthew Hillingdon. Do you want to see?'

'Not particularly.' TV coroners always seemed to have bodies lying about on tables, slit open from sternum to pelvic bone. In reality, Bryant found that their real-life counterparts kept death filed away under lock and key, to be drawn out only in the most pressing circumstances.

'Oh, very well.' Kershaw was disappointed at being denied a chance to poke about with his retractable antenna. 'He's an asthma sufferer, dodgy lungs, liver's a little enlarged, otherwise in good health. There were no unusual external marks on the body, so my first thought was alcohol poisoning.'

'That was Dan's prognosis.'

'Yes, I spoke to him. It seems the boy was alone in the Underground Station. There were no other tracks, except where you managed to walk all over the crime scene, of course. The obvious conclusion is that he went down there in a state of confusion, perhaps thinking he was heading towards the surface. That fits with alcohol poisoning, as the breath-rate drops and dizziness sets in. Hypoglycemia leads to seizures, stupor turns to coma, blue skin colour, irregular heartbeat. Victims choke on their own vomit or their hearts simply stop. Binge drinkers can ingest a fatal dose before the effects catch up with them. I wondered if that was the case here.'

'According to the girlfriend, he usually only texted her when he was too drunk to speak, so we can assume he'd been hammering the booze that night.'

'I was thinking perhaps he had knocked back a bottle and thrown it aside somewhere in the station, but Dan didn't turn up anything. Still, the thought was planted, you know? So I made a list of other kinds of poisons that could have had the same effect.'

'I can't wait to hear how I fit into this,' muttered Bryant.

'Simple. I could smell something else on the boy apart from alcohol, and remembered your horrible old pipe. Tobacco. *Nicotiana tabacum.* Simple, but incredibly effective. He has all the signs: excess saliva, muscular paralysis, diaphoresis—'

'What's that?' asked May.

'Excessive sweating. His shirt was creased across his back as if it had been ironed into place.'

'Only one thing wrong with your diagnosis. Hillingdon wasn't a smoker.'

'He didn't need to be. The stuff used to be readily available as an insecticide until its lethal properties were recognized. It's easy to make a tea out of rolling tobacco. There are plenty of recipes for it on the internet because dope growers use it to kill mites on marijuana plants. He'd have suffered dizzy spells, confusion, tachycardia, low blood pressure, with worsening symptoms, leading to coma and death. The stuff's all over his face and the collar of his shirt. I think it's possible that somebody sprayed him with it. You could empty out a perfume sampler, like the ones they give you in department stores, and fill it up.'

'Gloria Taylor sprayed perfume samples on customers at Selfridges.'

'Then I'd say you might have found your link.'

'Are you definite about the cause of death?'

'One hundred per cent.'

'Well, you reached a solution without having to show me the inside of his colon, for which I thank you,' said Bryant. 'Although I'm not sure this brings us any closer to finding a culprit. How easy is it to transfer?'

'Liquid tobacco? Pretty easy, but it also washes off. The smell's harder to get rid of. Do you have any suspects in mind?'

'That's the trouble,' said Bryant glumly. 'We have half a dozen of 'em. Nikos Nicolau is apparently studying biochemistry, but he also suffers from claustrophobia. Every suspect also has a reason not to be one. I think this time I might need to employ modern crime-detection techniques.'

'A victory for the scientific community,' laughed Kershaw. 'John, you should be pleased.'

'I'm relieved,' May replied. 'I've banned Arthur from trying to wrap up the investigation by esoteric means.'

'Did you mean that?' asked Bryant after they had thanked Kershaw and taken their leave. 'You really want me to play it by the book this time?'

'Yes, I do,' said May with determination. 'And I don't mean the book of witchcraft, or the ancient myths of England, I mean *The Police Operational Handbook*, 784 pages of sound, solid common sense. You want us to survive, don't you? Well, that's how we'll do it.'

It was time to return to the house in Mecklenburgh Square, where they could break the news of Matthew Hillingdon's death and commence the property search. That was when Banbury's call came in.

'The partial from the sticker,' he said, 'we've got a match. It's Toby Brooke.'

'No.'

'Don't tell me no. I've got the results on the screen in front of me. As I said, it's a partial, but enough to bring him in.'

All the housemates were advised of their rights, and were ordered to be present on the premises. If they hadn't taken the detectives seriously before, they would have to now.

Bryant was thinking about the tobacco in the ashtray, and Ruby Cates admitting that she was the only smoker.

'You know those old Agatha Christie whodunnits where you get the butler, the chorus girl, the aunt and the Lord into the library, then Poirot goes through their motives before accusing one of them?' he said to May as they walked. 'I feel like him, except for one small detail. I'm sure it's not Toby.'

'You just don't want to believe it's him because you feel a kinship with working-class kids,' said May.

'It probably is his thumbprint, I just don't think he's the type to commit murder. He seems scared of his own shadow. If the sticker was on one of the bags or had been picked up from the bar and left lying about the house, any of the others could have touched it. The trouble is, I haven't the faintest idea how they could have killed Hillingdon. Out of the five, only Theo Fontvieille has an alibi that checks out. Meera found at least eight witnesses who saw him at the Buddha Bar, and at the end of the evening his car was still outside the club with the keys stuck inside it. Of course, Ruby Cates has her leg in a cast, which pretty much rules her out. There's no way she could have fled from the scene of a crime. Have you seen how long it takes her to get up a flight of stairs?'

'What about the others?'

'Renfield tracked down the callers who spoke to Nikos Nicolau via video link, and they're willing to swear that it looked as if he was calling from his bedroom. They could see his furniture and posters in the background. Plus, we have the log showing the exact time he made the calls. The waitress at Wagamama doesn't remember serving Rajan Sangeeta, so his movements remain unsubstantiated, and Toby Brooke's account of his whereabouts is particularly dubious, but that sort of rules in his favour. He's a bright lad, I'm sure he could come up with a decent alibi if he wanted to.'

'Why shouldn't it be a woman?' May wondered. 'Neither of the deaths required any strength or dexterity – just a push and a spray. Besides, we know that Ruby is strong.'

'I was thinking less about dexterity than visibility. Someone would have recalled a pretty girl with her leg in a cast.'

'Perhaps it's time to add Cassie Field to our list of suspects.'

'Why? Good heavens, we've enough already.'

'It turns out that Ms Field has a history of secret anarchy. She's the girl who threw yellow paint over the Minister for Agriculture last year. Janice received a call from Leslie Faraday at the Home Office. He knows we interviewed her. She's got a very impressive arrest file. That's why she came up with the anarchists' symbol for the bar. She used to meet there with her urban warrior pals.'

'But you're forgetting – she has an alibi. She was seen at the Buddha Bar, then half an hour later she arrived at the Karma Bar and spent the rest of the evening there, with the exception of a ten minute break a little after midnight when she went out for a cigarette. The station's not far from the bar, but to get there and back she'd have to be a marathon runner.'

'Then we have to bring in Toby Brooke.'

'Do we? I'd rather keep an eye on him for a while. Can we do that?'

'If he makes a run for it we'll be blamed.'

'I'll make sure he stays put,' Bryant promised.

'I spoke to Renfield a few minutes ago. He blew his cover and was forced to have a very strange conversation with Brooke. It seems the lad started to admit his guilt about something, then ran off.'

'Sounds like he's close to confessing.'

'Perhaps, but I want to do this the traditional way, with a formal interview. Go into Brooke's background and wear him down by sheer persistence. We have to interview them all again anyway, so we'll make it part of that process. The others shouldn't know what we have on him. Meanwhile we take the house apart, try and establish a link between Taylor and Hillingdon.'

'I'm going to leave this to you, then,' said Bryant. 'You've always said I have no understanding of the young. I remember interviewing those horrible schoolchildren who saw the Highwayman committing murder and I still get chills down my spine when I think of them. There's something wrong with today's youth; they have faces as blank as Victorian dolls and the morals of Balkan gangsters.'

They had reached the house. May rang the ground-floor bell. A lopsided thumping sounded in the hall, and Ruby Cates opened the door. *It must be tiring for her, getting about with that leg*, thought Bryant.

'Both of you at the same time?' she inquired, raising an eyebrow. 'This must be serious. You'd better come in.'

As Bryant had joked, the group were gathered around the edges of the sitting room, although they failed to resemble any of Miss Christie's characters. Most affected boredom, a pose adopted to mask apprehension.

May decided to seize the bull by the horns. 'I must inform you that Matthew Hillingdon has been found dead in a disused tunnel beneath King's Cross,' he began. 'His next of kin have been notified, and—' But suddenly everyone was talking at once. Only Toby raised his hand.

'How did he die?'

'We're not at liberty to discuss the details of the case, but I can tell you we believe he was murdered. Furthermore, you'll appreciate that as you were among the last to see him alive, we need to conduct certain examinations that may shed light on—'

'You suspect us!' said Rajan Sangeeta, genuinely outraged for once.

'We have to explore every avenue of inquiry, and that starts with searching your rooms.'

'You can't do that without a warrant.'

'Actually, we can if we suspect that there's evidence on the premises. I'd prefer your permission to act, but it's not a legal requirement. I'm afraid that's just the start. I'll need to impound all electronic communication devices, including mobile phones, laptops, PCs and so on, so I'll need all your passwords.'

'We need them for our work,' said Ruby. She sounded numb.

'I appreciate that, so we'll be supplying you with alternative computer access, and I can confirm you'll be able to request specific study documents, which we'll copy on to a separate hard drive exclusively for your use.'

'That's a bit over the top,' said Theo. 'It could throw my studies off-track.'

'Christ, Matt's dead and all you can think about is your bloody schedules,' Toby complained.

'It's all right for you, poor boy, you're going to fail anyway,' Theo barked back. He turned to the detectives. 'What can we do to get through this as quickly and painlessly as possible?'

'Our forensic team will be arriving in a few minutes to begin conducting searches of your rooms,' said May. 'You can take what you need, provided it's under supervision from a member of the unit. We'll detail all property removed from the site, and make sure it's returned to you as soon as we can. If anyone has any concerns or objections—'

'I don't want you searching my room,' Nikos blurted. Everyone turned to look at him.

'I'm afraid you have no choice in the matter,' said May. 'If you have nothing to hide, you have nothing to worry about. There are a few further things I want to bring up. Our assistant, Detective Sergeant Longbright, will need to update her statements from you all concerning your whereabouts on Tuesday night, with names and addresses of everyone who can confirm your whereabouts.'

'Why should we help you?' asked Theo. 'I mean, if you already have the powers you need?'

'A fair question, but I'd like to think you would want to do it for Matthew, to help us for his sake. We have no motive for his death. We need to find out who he was with that night. I'm sure I don't need to warn you about obstructing the due process of what is now an official investigation. Miss Cates, I understand you and Mr Fontvieille had a falling out – '

'Have you been following us? Who the hell do you think you are?'

'We're a specialist department under the control of the Home Office, and you are civilians. Trust me, you don't want to fall into the hands of the Metropolitan Police. What did the two of you argue about?'

'We need to borrow some money to pay the rent and electricity,' said Ruby. 'I asked Theo to cover the bills and he refused. I just thought he should agree to help us through a rough patch.'

'It's a matter of principle,' said Fontvieille. 'If we can't manage our bills now, how can we be expected to construct and run entire social environments which might one day involve millions of pounds? Think it through, Ruby.'

'Anyway, I borrowed the money from Toby,' Ruby replied.

'Ah yes, you're quite well off at the moment, is that right?' May checked his notes.

'An aunt died and left me some money,' Toby muttered. The lie was so blatant that it hung in the air, a balloon of falsehood waiting to be punctured.

'Well, you can give our Detective Sergeant all the details on that. Mr Fontvieille, I understand you used to date Cassie Field, the manager of the Karma Bar, is that true?'

'It's common knowledge,' said Theo airily.

'Not to me, it's not,' Ruby snapped back.

'What does it matter? It was, like, a whole eight months ago.'

The temperature in the room was rising fast, but in this case May knew that a confrontational atmosphere could pay off; the housemates were becoming upset and dropping their guard.

'We see that two of you have had trouble with the police in the past,' May continued. 'Mr Fontvieille, assault; Mr Nicolau, sexual harassment, was it?'

'I got into a fight outside a nightclub in Richmond,' said Fontvieille. 'Fairly normal behaviour for a Thames Valley boy, wouldn't you say?'

'And you, Mr Nicolau?'

'He was caught upskirting,' said Sangeeta.

'A load of us were doing it at the time,' Nicolau admitted. 'Kind of embarrassing to think about now.'

'Is this a youngsters' term I'm not familiar with?' asked Bryant, confused.

'It's the rather grubby little practice of holding a camera under a girl's skirt in public places – when she's on a Tube escalator, for instance – then posting the shot on the internet,' May explained.

'Oh, charming.' Bryant grimaced. 'Is there nowhere a lady is safe these days?'

'Where did they find you two?' asked Theo. 'You're like something out of a display case at the Victoria & Albert

Museum. Incredible. If this is going to take ages, do you mind if we order in pizzas?'

'You're not taking this very seriously, are you?' There was a thread of danger in Bryant's voice. 'You don't seem to appreciate that all five of you are under suspicion of conspiracy to murder. That is, an agreement between two or more persons to commit an illegal, wrongful act by sinister design, to use a rather archaic definition.'

The overheated room exploded into fits of bad feeling and sour temper, like a series of slightly disappointing fireworks going off. There were indignant complaints and toothless threats, declarations of rights and talk of lawsuits. It was the perfect time for Longbright, Banbury and Renfield to arrive.

Soon all doors had been flung open, all drawers emptied, wardrobes cleared, computers unplugged, belongings tagged and bagged, and the fight had gone out of the five students who watched forlornly as their lives were dissected before them. It seemed the quintet had finally realized that this was no longer a mere inconvenience, but something much darker and more devastating in its consequences.

36

EMPTY-HANDED

Law-abiding citizens are hard to trace. Albert Thomas Edward Ketch existed, of that there was no doubt, but he was unknown to the police. The DVLA had a clean driving licence on record, the borough of Islington listed a name on their electoral register, Barclays Bank had a closed account, and a former address in a St Pancras council block yielded nothing but statistical proof that Mr Fox's father had once been alive.

Longbright needed to put a face to the name. If Mr Fox's father remained intangible, at least Camden registry office had a marriage licence on file, which presented her with a partner. Ketch had wedded one Patricia Catherine Burton, who provided the registrar with an address in Wembley. She had moved the same year, presumably to live with her new husband, because the marriage certificate was posted to a different North London address. Her son had been delivered less than six months later at Hampstead's Royal Free Hospital, and had received health checks for the first four years of his life at clinics in the area. After that, the trail went cold.

'I'm running out of ideas,' she told Renfield as they finished filling in evidence forms for the Mecklenburgh Square house. 'I've got a little on the parents but nothing on the boy.'

'See if he was registered as a Young Offender under the name of Ketch,' Renfield suggested. 'A tenth of all the kids in London commit a serious offence at least once. If something happened to Mr Fox in his childhood, he might have gone AWOL and turned up on Islington's books, or Camden's.'

'Thanks, Jack. I should have thought of that. I'm tired. I haven't been sleeping well.'

'Hardly surprising. I'm going to grab a bite. Want me to pick you up something?'

'No, I'm fine. I want to get this lot sorted out.'

'You can't go off your grub and get all moody on me. Tell me you don't fancy a sausage sandwich smothered in brown sauce.'

'Strangely enough, I don't.'

Renfield headed off to the shops. She watched from the window as he strutted along the wet street with nothing more than food on his mind. *I should learn to be more like Jack*, she thought, returning to her paperwork.

'Ah, there you are,' said Bryant, ambling into the room. 'I was going to stroll back with you from Mecklenburgh Square but you'd vaporized. Those students may dress like a Gap advertisement but you should have seen the state of their fridge. Oswald Finch used to keep his cadaver drawers in a better state. Having said that, I did once leave a beetroot salad in with one his corpses, and he mistook it for—'

'Arthur, I'm not in the mood,' said Longbright. 'I'm sorry.'

'No, I'm the one who should be sorry.' He removed his hat and dropped into the battered armchair Longbright had installed for his visits. 'In my usual clumsy way I was just trying to cheer you up. Unfortunately, most of my conversation involves death, ancient history or mad people. No wonder I've never been very popular with the ladies. What did you think of our students?'

Longbright rose and blew a newly dyed blonde curl from her eye. 'A pretty ordinary bunch: a health freak, a geek, a jock, a wide boy and a nerd.'

'I love the way you categorize, it's all so simple for you. Think they're hiding any secrets from us?'

'Of course. They wouldn't be human if they didn't. I just think they'll turn out to be pretty mundane.'

'What do you mean?'

'Oh, crushes, alliances, jealousies, money worries.'

'Hatreds?'

'Strong word. Dislikes, perhaps. Toby Brooke isn't too keen on Theo Fontvieille.'

'Theo needles him about his background. According to John, the rich boy dated the girl from the Karma Bar, then dumped her, but he's so thick-skinned that he takes other girls to her establishment without realizing that he's upsetting her. Dear Lord, I'm sounding like a gossip columnist.'

The idea made Longbright smile. 'That's OK, they're just like any dysfunctional alternative family.'

'I don't believe it's a conspiracy. They wouldn't be able to organize a tea party without getting on each other's nerves, let alone kill someone and hide the evidence. If this was something they'd planned, they would never have left Matthew Hillingdon's travel card in the house, where it could be found.'

'Right now that and the partial print are the only pieces of incriminating evidence we have,' said Longbright.

'I'm convinced that the murderer is operating alone, without the knowledge of the others. That damned sticker links Taylor to the Karma Bar and Toby Brooke. I wonder how John's getting on with him.' Bryant watched Longbright wince as she lifted a box from the desk. 'How's your shoulder?'

'Not so bad. It didn't even need a stitch.'

'Let Colin take over from you when he gets back. He and Dan are going to go through the impounded evidence.'

'I'm fine,' Longbright promised. 'I'm much happier working.'

'OK, then you can carry on following the Indian chap all over town, if you wouldn't mind. I don't like the cut of his jib. I want all five housemates tailed over the weekend. We shouldn't let any of them out of our sight. I'm counting down the hours until the unit is pulled from service. I can't see us making an arrest in time, but let's keep watching them.' Bryant tapped his fingers beneath his beady eyes. 'All five, all weekend, everywhere they go.'

Bimsley and Banbury arrived back at the warehouse, and spent the next three hours searching the hard drives of the five housemates' laptops. They turned up little of interest. Only Ruby Cates kept her financial details on record, along with an online diary that confirmed her obsession with 'The Rat', who was easily identified by his customized Porsche. Theo had a few dodgy gambling sites bookmarked, Sangeeta had too many photographs of Ruby in his photo library, Nikos had similar photos of Cassie in the bar and an awful lot of porn, Cates had posted some cryptic remarks on Facebook, and Toby had worked hard at erasing details of the sites he visited. Their computer tracks seemed unusually guarded and cautious. To Dan's suspicious mind it was proof that the students knew they were being watched, but Colin thought they were merely being security-conscious.

All five had extensive music libraries of bands that

had become popular over the last few years. All five had infringed copyright laws by file-sharing movies, but that seemed to be the extent of their illegal activities.

The iPhoto files from Matt Hillingdon's laptop yielded some odd photographs that looked like colourful knitted versions of radio interference, so Bimsley forwarded them to Bryant's mobile, hoping that he might be able to figure out what they were – once he had managed to open them.

At 6:00 p.m. John May returned to the unit with bad news. He and Meera had just finished interviewing Toby Brooke. Unprompted, the student had shown them a sheet of altered stickers that had been left lying about the house, and had admitted to handling them. Their evidence was compromised.

It was now Friday evening, and the case had once more stuttered to a halt. Bryant was forced to admit that it was by far the most infuriating investigation he had ever undertaken.

It was time, he decided, to take more drastic steps, starting with a visit to North London's resident white witch.

37

BAD AIR

'What more can I do?' asked Bryant. 'We're back to one piece of evidence and five less-than-ideal suspects. John has banned me from using any of my more *outré* routes of investigation. And I have this ragbag of notions in my head that don't seem to connect – a red dress, some strange patterns from Hillingdon's laptop, a missing mobile phone, the way people move on the Tube . . .' He paused to take a good look at his old friend Maggie Armitage. 'What happened to you?'

The Grade IV White Witch and leader of North London's Coven of St James the Elder was spattered in pink paint – not a nice pink either, but a shade that could best be described as Tired Marshmallow. 'I was preparing a philtre for Dierdre,' she explained, 'because her sex life has taken a turn for the worse again. She met a Polish bus driver with a habit of calling round at 3:00 a.m., but the trouble is he's on nights, so he'd park a bus full of passengers outside her house while he came in.'

'That must have been inconvenient.'

'Not really. His route goes past her house.'

'I meant for her.'

'Oh, yes, that was the problem. She'd wanted to meet a man with his own transport, but technically of course he doesn't.'

'Doesn't what?'

'Own it. So I needed fennel for the potion. And Cheese and Onion crisps.'

'You put crisps in a love potion?'

'No, I was just hungry. So I put some bacon into the eye-level grill and went to the shops.'

'Why did you do that?'

'Well, you layer crisps on either side of the bacon and it makes a wonderful sandwich.'

'No, I mean why did you leave the grill unattended?'

'You know how my concentration has been since I fell off my bike.'

'No, how?'

'It wasn't a question. Well, when I came back the kitchen was on fire. Luckily I'd left a plastic washing-up bowl full of water on the rack above the grill, and when it melted it put out the flames.'

'That *was* a piece of luck,' said Bryant with heavy sarcasm. 'Just think, things could have turned out quite badly.' He surveyed the dripping, blackened remains of the kitchen.

'Well, they did,' said Maggie. 'He went back to his wife. And some of his passengers tried to sue him.'

'I don't think you should make any more love potions.'

'Oh, it wasn't a love potion. It was something to make him sleep so he'd go back on days. Unfortunately, it worked too well. He fell asleep at the wheel and went through the window of a lapdancing club in Liverpool Street. Which is why I'm painting the room pink. Because I can't get the bacon smoke off.' She raised the chain of her spectacles and squinted at him through polka-dot lenses.

Talking to Maggie was like using some kind of malfunctioning space communicator. Bryant decided to get to the point and keep it simple. 'I know you've got a memory like a sieve, but I did ask you on the phone whether you knew anything about odd happenings in Underground stations. I can be more specific now. Magnetism.'

Maggie peered over the top of her paint-spattered spectacles and frowned at him. 'Oh, you know about that, do you?'

'No. That's why I'm asking you.'

'No, I asked Yu.'

'Me?'

'No, Mrs Yu. I asked her to pop round. She's in the garden.'

Maggie's garden was a makeshift pet cemetery with a few desperate bluebells thrusting out of cracked paving stones. The goldfish had shuffled off its mortal coil in an earth-filled chimney pot, and the budgie had gone towards the light in a coal scuttle. Bryant looked out of the kitchen window and got a fright. For a moment he thought the moon had come out. Mrs Yu had a perfectly round white face and was peering in. She looked frozen.

'Sorry, love, I didn't realize I'd locked you out,' said Maggie, opening the door.

'It's bloody perishing in your yard,' said Mrs Yu. Although she was very Chinese in appearance, she had a strong cockney accent. 'I was chatting to your dog.'

'Her dog's dead,' said Bryant.

'Yes, he's buried under the fishpond. Bolivar says he's very happy, but he's not so happy about being so near Happy.'

'I'm sorry?' said Bryant. Things were becoming confused again.

'Happy was my cat,' Maggie explained. 'She's buried near the dog. Mrs Yu knows a lot about atmospheric disturbances, so I invited her over. Plus, I wanted her to return my wok.'

Mrs Yu laughed a lot. She tittered at the end of every utterance. When she wasn't laughing she was at least chuckling, and even when the chuckles faded she was still smiling. She plumped her big round frame down in the widest, most comfortable chair and elucidated. 'So you want to know about magnetism. There was a story going around a few years ago about the Tube. The guards started saying that the addition of extra metal flood gates throughout the system created some kind of supercharged atmospheric whirlpool. It was only supposed to happen when trains passed through the tunnels with great frequency, during the rush hour. See, before that, electrical particles ionized the atmosphere and escaped upwards on the air currents. But the iron flood doors slowly became magnetized, creating differences in pressure that made passengers feel sick and dizzy.'

'I'm not sure I put much store in that,' said Maggie. 'I mean, electrical whirlpools, it sounds a bit like those adverts for shower gel with ginseng extract to wake you up. You know, pseudo-science.'

'That's good, coming from a woman who believes you can find water under the ground just by wandering about with a stick.'

'Dowsing is scientifically proven,' Maggie insisted. 'I can always find water.'

'Of course you can,' said Bryant. 'You're a Londoner, it's impossible to get away from the bloody stuff. So, no likelihood of someone becoming disoriented and passing out in the Underground due to magnetic forces, then? Because I've heard there are powerful ley lines passing through King's Cross.'

'That's true,' said Mrs Yu, 'but there are other hidden powers at work under London. Wherever all four elements interact, you create conflict. King's Cross is one of the very worst sites . . .'

'What are you talking about?'

'The electric trains and power cables – fire. The underground rivers and pipelines – water. London clay – earth. The winds in the subway system – air. There are storms down there that disrupt the psychic atmosphere.'

'Meaning what exactly? You get headaches? You catch the wrong train? You start seeing dead people?'

Mrs Yu happily wagged a finger at him. 'Ill humours are not such a crazy concept. The Victorians believed germs were transported through miasma – the air itself. That's why they built Victoria Park in Mile End, as a barrier to protect the city's rich property owners from working-class diseases. They thought the germs would float across to them on the breeze.'

'Yes, but they were wrong, weren't they? John Snow discovered that cholera was water-borne. You think there's such a thing as bad air?'

'Well, we know that electromagnetic disruption can actually make people ill, and the jury's still out on radio masts, isn't it? There's still no air conditioning in the London Underground system. Back when the trains were pulled by steam engines, the engineers tried everything to clear the air. They built ventilation shafts that came up behind fake house-fronts in Bayswater. Later, when the Victoria Line was built, a structure called the Tower of the Winds was constructed in a garden square up in Islington. It was meant to introduce cool breezes into the tunnels, but wasn't much more successful.'

'I was just reading about plans to chill the subway system during heatwaves by using water from the lost rivers,' Bryant interjected.

'Nothing ever works,' sighed Mrs Yu. 'The air beneath King's Cross remains old and stagnant. It's polluted with all kinds of toxins, and its composition changes all the time.'

'Well, here's my problem.' Bryant seated himself wearily and helped himself to a ginger biscuit. 'My problem is – dear Lord, it sounds so absurd. How can I explain this? Some of our most successful prosecutions have been built around a tiny shred of evidence: a piece of broken glass, a bootprint, an overheard phrase. This investigation hangs on a sticker, a travel card, a few odds and sods, and a bad feeling, nothing more. They'll hang me out to dry if I get it wrong this time.'

'Then let me see if I can help,' said Mrs Yu.

Bryant set out his case. 'A student died of tobacco poisoning in the Underground. But even though – as you say – the air in the Tube is bad, there's been no smoking down there for years. My coroner says someone sprayed him with the stuff. According to his medical records, he suffered from asthmatic attacks. We didn't find an inhaler on him, so I'm thinking that the killer substituted his inhaler for one containing poison, then took it away. But I also have to look into the possibility of accidental death. You don't suppose certain toxins – heavier than airborne ones – could have sunk to the bottom of the system and poisoned him, do you? Through these whirlpool things? We tested the air and found nothing.'

'That's hardly surprising,' said Mrs Yu. 'Every time a train rushes past it displaces the air and transfers it to another magnetic collection point.'

'Surely it would be easier to accept your coroner's theory about the spray?' asked Maggie. 'I don't know why you're making life difficult for yourself.'

'It's what I do,' said Bryant glumly. 'If his death was an accident, then Gloria Taylor was also an accident, and suddenly there's no case. Which would be wonderful, because it would mean no one else is in danger. The alternative is to look for a clever, calculating killer who murders randomly, without remorse, and who leaves no trace.'

'Well, it seems to me that you're caught between two worlds, Arthur, the one that lies beneath London, and the hidden world in which this person you seek moves and connects. For once, you must try to think like a civilian and not like a policeman. I think the investigation is testing your powers in new ways. The Tube network isn't the only ghost system in operation – there's an entire world of invisible connections we never normally get to see. It's just a matter of finding the key. Let's consult the cards.'

She pulled a key from her crimson coiffure, unlocked a drawer in her kitchen table and brought out a packet of tarot cards. 'These are my special "Black Ace" Russian Tarots. I keep them locked up because they're dangerous in the wrong hands.' Maggie shuffled and Mrs Yu snickered.

'I hope they're more accurate than your attempt to read teabags,' said Bryant.

'Take a card.' She offered him the pack.

Bryant withdrew one and looked at it. 'Oh for God's sake, that's the nine of clubs,' he exclaimed in annoyance. 'I can never find it in a normal deck.'

'Oh, that shouldn't be there.' Maggie snatched back the card. 'Deirdre and I were playing poker last night. Choose five more and turn them over.'

He set down the five lurid pictures: a man being struck by lightning, a baby being bitten on the face by a cobra, a pair of Siamese twins being sawn in half, some lepers burying a screaming man alive and a skeleton on a drip. 'Oh, charming,' said Bryant. 'I take it my future wellbeing is under question.'

'You mustn't take them literally,' said Maggie. 'They're filled with codes and symbols. I'll tell you what I see. Six suspects, three deaths, and a desperate flight through tunnels of darkness. Do you want a piece of cake?'

'No,' snapped Bryant, 'give me a brandy. Listen, there's something I wanted to show you, but I can't get it to work.' He emptied the contents of his overcoat pocket on to the kitchen table, pulled a Liquorice Allsort off his mobile and handed the phone to Mrs Yu. 'Can you get it to the section with photos in?'

Mrs Yu flicked open the photo file with practised ease and examined the contents. Maggie peered over her shoulder. The screen showed a series of brightly coloured patterns, mostly diamonds and zigzags, like the backs of playing cards. Mrs Yu shrugged and snickered. 'You want to know what these are?'

'Yes, one of our detective constables forwarded them to me from the dead man's laptop. What are they?'

'You should know, you see them all the time.'

'Well?' It irritated Bryant when others took pleasure in knowing more than he did.

'They're Tube train seats,' said Mrs Yu, chortling away. 'Different livery patterns in different colour combinations. Thirteen pictures for the different London lines.'

Bryant grimaced in annoyance. 'Why would anyone want to take pictures of those?'

'You're the detective,' said Mrs Yu, as her giggles erupted into bubbling laughter.

38

ON THE LINE

It was now 11:15 p.m. on Friday night, and the surveillance teams were still working across London, hoping to break the case.

To keep things fresh, they had swapped their subjects. Longbright had followed Nikos Nicolau to the Prince Charles cinema, where he sat through a double bill of lesbian vampire movies before returning home. Banbury kept tabs on Rajan Sangeeta, but lost him in between two nightclubs in Greenwich. Bimsley was close by Toby Brooke, who was now drinking alone in a crowded bar on Brick Lane. Mangeshkar took Theo Fontvieille because she could pace him on her motorcycle, and he had now pulled up in Mecklenburgh Square. Renfield was covering Ruby Cates, first at the college, then at the Karma Bar and finally back to the house. For the most part, the PCU staff had managed to stick to their targets like shadows.

But there was a flaw in the plan. Nobody was running surveillance on Cassie Field. And Cassie was alone, on a deserted, rainswept railway station in South London.

*   *   *

'I just don't bloody believe it!' Theo shouted, hammering up the stairs of the house. 'Look out of the window.'

'What's the matter?' Ruby swung her grey cast to one side and rose from the table, where she was making notes on the rubbishy laptop that had been supplied by Dan Banbury.

'Take a look, dammit. Down there in the street.'

Ruby thumped her way to the front window and opened the curtains. 'What's the matter? I don't see anything.'

'Exactly. Someone's stolen my bloody car! I only left it a minute ago.'

'All right, calm down. Could it have been towed away?'

'What, at eleven o'clock at night? I'm outside restriction hours, and anyway, I have a parking permit.'

'You know how Camden traffic wardens are.'

'No, it's been stolen. I knew it. You can't keep anything nice in this city without some dickhead resenting you. I'm going to kill someone.' He stormed up and down the room in a rage.

'OK, the first thing to do is to ring the Jamestown Road car pound, just to make sure it hasn't been towed.'

Theo was pulled up short. 'How do you know where the car pound is?'

'I can drive, I just can't afford a car at the moment. Then call the police, or better still, get over to the station and fill in the necessary forms. If it has been stolen, you won't be able to claim on your insurance without a case number. You didn't leave the keys in the ignition again, did you?'

'No of course not, I only—' He patted his pockets. 'Oh no. I don't understand. Someone must have been watching the house and waiting for me to return, standing there in the bloody rain – I only just got out of the bloody thing.'

'And you did it again. You should never have had the

car customized. Come on then.' She stuck her hands on her hips defiantly. 'Do something about it, instead of just standing there feeling sorry for yourself.'

Bimsley had lost him. A couple of minutes ago, he had watched Toby Brooke heading back to the packed Brick Lane bar, where he had ordered himself a Kingfisher, but the student had vanished. Bimsley tried the toilet, but it was empty. The dive had been constructed on the ground floor of an old carpet warehouse, and, he now discovered, had a rear exit along a corridor on the far side of the building. Brooke had given him the slip. Furious with himself for having made such a fundamental error, he called Longbright and explained what had happened.

'I'll tell the others,' said Longbright. 'We need to know that the rest are all accounted for.'

'I'm sorry, Janice. It was my own stupid fault.'

'Don't beat yourself up. You could try the Tube station.'

'No good. We're halfway between Aldgate East and Liverpool Street.'

'Then you've got a fifty-fifty chance of finding him. Put in a call to the house and see if he's gone back there.'

Banbury was having similar trouble keeping tabs on Rajan Sangeeta.

A few minutes ago the Indian student had received a call on his mobile, and had immediately conducted a search of the bar where he was drinking. Someone had clearly tipped him off that the housemates were being followed. If a call had gone out, it meant that the others were attempting to slip off the radar too. Sangeeta waited until the bar had become severely congested, then pushed away through the crowd, leaving Banbury trailing far behind. Only two members of the PCU – Longbright and the late Liberty DuCaine – had received surveillance training, so when the student made his move Banbury found himself in trouble. Longbright had told him to fix the height of his target in his mind, but the room was being strafed with rotating rainbow lights, and Sangeeta had already slipped out through the throng.

Banbury was furious at being tricked. He called Longbright. 'Has anyone else made a run for it?'

'Toby Brooke's done a bunk, the others all seem to be accounted for,' the DS replied. 'There aren't enough of us to go around the clock. Go home, Dan. Get some kip. Nothing's going to change tonight. I'll see you in the morning.'

Banbury took one last walk around the pulsating bar and wearily abandoned his search.

Cassie Field was waiting for her train on Westcombe Park Station. She shivered and stared at the truculent downpour as it sluiced and slopped from the roof, and told herself once more that she had thrown away the evening. She had sought advice from an old schoolfriend, but had arrived at Sophie's Greenwich apartment to find her drunk and weepy. Sophie had been dumped by her creepy estate-agent boyfriend and was consoling herself with her second bottle of bad Burgundy. Cassie had been hoping for some prudent advice about her own love life, but instead had spent the evening listening to Sophie's increasingly slurred complaints about men, before having to hold her head over the sink. Feeling alone and friendless, she headed back to the station and just missed a Charing Cross-bound train.

Cassie retied her acid-pink jacket and watched the yellow carriage lights recede into the distance, as the train swayed and sparked towards the city. There was nothing to hear now but the sound of falling rain.

She wanted to talk to someone, but most of her friends regularly visited the Karma Bar, and there was a good chance that her confessions would reach the residents of Mecklenburgh Square. Her best bet was to try Sophie again, once she had sobered up and cleared her hangover. What a mess. Cassie's jacket was stained with rain and red wine, and the high heels she had chosen to wear had blistered her feet. The station platform was deserted; the overland line was used less frequently now that the Underground reached down into South London.

There was a grey shadow behind the steamed-up, grafittied glass of the waiting room. She couldn't see who it was, but the figure's body language was vaguely familiar. She wondered if she should go and look, but the pinging of the rails told her that there was a train approaching.

She walked to the edge of the rain-soaked platform and wondered how long it would take to get back indoors, where it was warm and dry. There was a sound behind her as the waiting-room door opened. She glanced back, but there was nobody there now.

She looked for the train, and saw that it was coming in fast. Typically, she had chosen to wait at the wrong end of the platform. Beyond the tracks, the ice-blue lights of the city glimmered in melancholy relief. She had never felt so alone and in need of a friend.

Cassie was still wondering if there was anyone else in whom she could confide when a pair of boots slammed into her shoulder-blades, barrelling her forward on to the tracks, right in front of the arriving train.

39

FLYING

By the time Dan Banbury and Giles Kershaw arrived, Greenwich police had cordoned off the platform and covered the body with a yellow plastic tent. 'Ghastly mess,' said Kershaw, checking under the tent flap. 'Her name's Cassie Field. She had John May's card in her wallet, so I take it she's involved with the case. Massive head injuries, so at least it was quick. What did the driver see?'

'He just caught a glimpse of her flying through the air, doesn't really know what happened,' said Banbury. 'He's in the waiting room. He's pretty shaken up.'

'The officer over there told me she jumped.'

'He only got here a few minutes ago, he's going by what the guard told him.'

'Where was the guard?'

'On the opposite platform, texting his girlfriend on his mobile, useless plonker. I'll try and get some more lights rigged up. They need some decent overheads on this platform. What a miserable bloody place to die.'

'She reeks of wine, and there are red-wine stains on her shirt. Very high heels. I know it's the fashion, but they can't be easy to wear. She could have been drunk and wandered too close to the edge. The platform's somewhat on the narrow side.'

'The driver said she was "flying". Ask him yourself. Like a trapeze artiste, he reckons, as in she either jumped or was pushed. He certainly doesn't think she slipped.'

'A couple of fresh bruises on her back,' said Kershaw, carefully turning the body over and raising her jacket. 'Are you getting this?' Banbury was operating the unit's camcorder, from which he would later pull stills. 'Neat little crescents. They look like heel marks, but they can't be. Too high up her back, as if she was kicked on to the line. Mind you, if they were we might get a boot match from them.'

'Flying,' repeated Banbury. He climbed back up on to the platform and looked around, thinking.

'Sorry Dan, what did you say?'

'I said *flying*. As in propelled. Like Gloria Taylor.' Banbury headed for the waiting room, where he stopped to examine the doorway. 'Giles, come and take a look at this.'

Kershaw left the police team and clambered back up, joining the coroner. Banbury was standing on tiptoe, running a penlight along the top edge of the waiting-room doorway. The room was a freestanding box constructed of steel struts and scratched plexiglass. The CSM pointed upward. 'Eight little channels in the dirt up there, four and four, a couple of feet apart. Any ideas?'

'I might have,' said Kershaw cagily. 'Have you?'

'Yes.'

'Go on then, you first.'

'Fingers. The killer climbed up on to that row of seats, stood on their backs, swung on the metal lintel to get momentum, then just let go. She wouldn't have seen or heard a thing, with the train approaching. The boots smacked hard into her back, the killer dropped down and ran off. How mad is that?'

'It'd take some nerve.' Giles flicked wet blond hair out of his eyes. 'Can you get prints from them?'

'I'll try, but it looks like the dust got pulled off in the process, leaving smears. The whole thing probably only took three or four seconds. No cameras at this spot to pick up her final moments. No one else on the platform. They're going to hold a couple of the passengers for witness statements, but my guess is that the windows of the train would have obscured their vision – it's been chucking it down for the last couple of hours, and the platform's shockingly underlit. If the killer was wearing something dark to blend in, no one would have even seen them.'

'Two deaths from the same household. Your old man's going to go crazy.'

'He's not my old man,' said Banbury with a grim laugh. 'You're still seconded to the unit, matey. Don't worry, though, from what I hear we've got the whole of tomorrow to work out what happened before we're kicked back out on the streets. At least you've got somewhere to go. I'll be down the Job Centre again.'

For the next half-hour they worked quietly beside each other in the falling rain, while the local police had loud arguments with each other about infringement of jurisdiction.

'Always the same with the Met,' Banbury muttered, searching the wet ground for evidence. 'They're more worried about who gets the case than that poor girl on the tracks. Hang on a minute.' He took his Maglite to the waiting room, crouched down and carefully picked up something he had seen on the floor, bagging it. 'What does that look like to you?' he asked Kershaw. Raising the bag into the light, he displayed an inch-long sliver of curved grey plastic.

'No idea. There's a fragment of raised lettering on the inside, very small,' said the coroner. 'Let me see.' He took out Bryant's old magnifying glass and read: *rty UC*.

'Pretty clear to me,' he decided. 'Property of University College Hospital. Standard NHS typeface. Looks like a piece from a plastic leg cast. Keep looking around.'

Banbury climbed over the platform fence and conducted a search of the gorse bushes behind the waiting room. A few minutes later he re-emerged covered in mud and brambles, carrying a dark bundle. 'You're going to love this,' he told Kershaw. 'I think the overcoat got discarded before the killer carried out that little trapeze stunt.'

'Can you identify it?'

Banbury unfurled the rainbow-striped material. 'It looks like the one Matthew Hillingdon was wearing the night he was killed.'

'You're telling me Miss Field was pushed under a train by a girl with a broken leg and a dead man?' said Kershaw. 'Bryant's going to love this.'

40

CONFLICTING EVIDENCE

The warehouse on the Caledonian Road was a good venue for a wake, which was just as well, as the PCU's Saturday-morning debriefing session had virtually turned into one.

It was 7:30 a.m., and the team looked beaten. No one had had more than three hours' sleep. The thought that Cassie Field's death should have been prevented nagged at them all. Arthur Bryant had another worry. Each death brought a new level of confusion to the investigation. Especially as it seemed that the manager of the Karma Bar had been kicked under a train by Ruby Cates.

'As soon as this meeting is over, you're going back to the house in Mecklenburgh Square to make an arrest,' Raymond Land warned. 'I want that woman brought in and held here until we can make the charge stick.'

'We have to be sure first,' said Renfield, speaking for everyone. 'I saw her go into the house just after 10:00 p.m., and she didn't come back out.'

'She could have left through the back door and climbed over the garden fence into the street behind,' said Land. 'She's an athlete, isn't she?'

'Yes, and her broken leg is in a cast.'

'Did you look to see if it was really broken when you matched up the fragment?'

'No, I didn't have to take it off. I could see the piece fitted perfectly.'

'That's not the point.'

'I've warned her not to leave the house until we return.'

'I'm going to let you chair this, John.' Land rubbed his tired face. 'I don't know where we're going any more.'

May rose to his feet. 'OK, let's go through alibis and evidence, taking into account what happened last night. We're not here to lay blame or assess performance. We need to put everything else aside and advance this very quickly.'

He and Longbright read the statements from the Mecklenburgh Square housemates and the Greenwich witnesses, ploughing through the pathology reports together and reconstructing what they knew about the deaths. Timelines were drawn across three whiteboards at the rear of the room. The low murmur of discussion sporadically burst into heated argument. The pipes ticked as the boiler struggled to warm the building. Meagre items of evidence were laid out and discussed, but after an hour they were no further on. Somewhere out in the surrounding streets, a killer watched and waited.

'What I see is that you're building a case against Toby Brooke here,' said Meera hotly. 'He has no proper alibi for the night Hillingdon was murdered. He went missing again last night at the time Field died. But just look at him – common sense should tell you he wouldn't hurt a fly. And what if it's not someone from the house at all? All you've got is a travel card swiped through at Liverpool Street Station on the night Hillingdon died. He might not even have used it himself.'

'They all deny returning it to his bedroom, but they swear no one else has been in the house,' May remarked.

'Well of course they'd deny touching it,' said Bryant, 'because that would implicate whoever claimed to have returned the damned thing. Dan, where are we on physical evidence?'

Banbury consulted his notes. 'The CCTV footage on Gloria Taylor and Matthew Hillingdon – completely unhelpful in Taylor's case, but I'm trying some new frame-enhancement software on Hillingdon's footage. There might be something before the end of the day on that. Nothing else new except the bootprints on Field's back and the piece of plastic found in the waiting room, which we now know matches Cates's leg cast. Giles and I carried out a re-enactment, and we're pretty certain how her bruises got there. No prints on the travel card or the rest of the stickers, but the initials on the card are definitely in Hillingdon's handwriting. Mr Bryant and I knocked up a rudimentary tobacco spray. It was ridiculously easy to make.'

'What about their technology?'

'OK, no surprises on any of the laptops, except that Toby Brooke has been buying a lot of expensive stuff on the internet lately. We checked all the call registers on the mobiles nothing untoward there. For all we know they might have had a few pay-as-you-go handsets knocking about. We know there was a spare house mobile for use in emergencies, but no one can find it now. Theo Fontvieille remembers seeing a couple of others at the house, one with a Hello Kitty doll attached to it. Nobody will back him up on that.'

'Anything else?'

'Yeah, the books about haunted Underground stations might have had Cates's name inside, but she swears it's not her handwriting, and it turns out they were taken out from UCL's reference library by Toby Brooke. A set of twelve photographs from Hillingdon's laptop appear to be close-ups of the seats of different Tube trains. Oh, and somebody stole Theo Fontvieille's Porsche last night.'

'Mr Fox,' murmured Banbury. The others looked at him. 'Oh, it's just that he had a photograph of a Tube station bench on his wall, then it was gone.'

'I thought we'd decided that the two cases weren't linked,' said May.

'We had,' Bryant reassured him. 'Don't worry. Let's go on.'

'Can we go back to the motives?' asked Longbright. 'According to the interviews, Gloria Taylor's workmates insist she had no enemies. But maybe she had something on her mind, because she forgot to take home her daughter's birthday present on the night she died. Hillingdon had no dodgy connections either. He was dating Ruby Cates, although it now appears she's been having casual sex with Fontvieille for a while.'

'Wait, how do you know that?' Renfield demanded.

'Simple, Jack. I asked her. We still don't know who Hillingdon drank with on Tuesday night, because most of the Spitalfields bars were rammed to the gills, and none of the staff recall seeing him. Plus, there are about a hundred of them. Cassie Field was positively adored. Nobody has a bad word to say about her.'

'I hate to raise this again,' said Renfield, 'but what if the deaths were random?' Everyone groaned. 'No, listen to me. Suppose one of the housemates has psychotic episodes and just – lashes out? So, a stranger on the Tube is attacked, and Field is literally kicked under a train.'

'Doesn't work,' said May. 'Hillingdon's death was premeditated, and if you're assuming it was a housemate, following Field to Westcombe Park Station in order to kill her means someone was waiting for an opportunity to get her alone.'

'Can I just bring in Tony McCarthy?' asked Bryant, as another groan went around the room. 'If you remember, the junkie is the only one who can identify Mr Fox. UCH is releasing him at noon today because they need the bed. I want to make sure it's common knowledge that he's back on the streets. There's a strong likelihood that Mr Fox will try to take him out again, and given your spotty track record on surveillance I reckon he's got a pretty slender chance of survival.'

'Why don't you just shake the details of Fox's ID out of McCarthy?' asked Renfield. 'I can put the fear of God up him without leaving any marks. Leave me alone in a room with him. He'll fall apart in minutes.'

'Thank you, Jack, we're a Home Office unit, not the Stasi. I'll let you know if we need the electrodes.'

'Just offering, that's all.'

'Whoever killed Hillingdon took his overcoat and wore it to kill Cassie Field at the station,' said Longbright. 'That doesn't make sense. Dan, did you get anything off it yet?'

'There were no hairs, a few skin flakes, a couple of small oily patches around the collar. I'm expecting the analysis back shortly.'

'So,' said Bryant, 'any questions?'

'Yeah, plenty.' Meera folded her arms defiantly. 'But are there any answers? I mean, do you think this is over now? That whoever's been doing this has achieved his – or her – aim and finished?'

'Have you actually been in the same room as us for the last hour?' Bryant snapped. 'I've told you, these acts are premeditated, but we don't know to what end. Until we understand the killer's psychology, we won't be able to tell if it's over. We have to assume it isn't, and find a way of protecting all the potential victims.'

'Can I remind you that we've less than ten hours to wrap everything up?' Meera retorted. '*Everything* – your Mr bloody Fox, this subway vampire, the lot. I've already been out of a job once this year, I don't want to be back in the same situation again.'

'Then come up with something useful,' Bimsley suggested.

'We break in,' said Renfield.

'What?' It was Bryant's turn to stare.

'We break into the house in the square. Just smash a window and storm the place. Put the fear of God up them. We've got legal entitlement. You reckon somebody there is arrogant enough to think they've got away with it – they won't be expecting a surprise visit.'

'Apart from the fact that Dan already took the house apart looking for evidence, ransacking the students' rooms while they're still asleep is not an option I want to consider. First you suggest torture, now burglary. Why don't we just go out and shoot them all?'

'You come up with a better idea,' muttered Renfield.

'Mr Bryant, you're sure it's one of the housemates?' Bimsley asked.

'I know it is.' Bryant smoothed his hand across his desk, which was still littered with playing cards. 'The proof is shapeshifting right here in front of me. I can see it – I just can't identify it.'

'Then we stick to them like napalm for the rest of the morning, until one of them makes a mistake.' He looked to the others for confirmation. 'What difference is it going to make? We can't do any more here, and it's our last day. There's nothing else left to do.'

'Can I just say that in the entire history of the unit, this has been the most disastrous investigation you lot have ever attempted.' Raymond Land spoke up finally, adding his opinion in the most unhelpful way possible. 'It's like something out of *The Muppet Show*. I've seen better organized water-balloon fights. Well, it's over now. We're no further on than when we started. We're dead. Finished. Washed up. We might just as well all go home and do some gardening. On Monday morning we're going to wake up with no jobs to go to, and this dump will be turned into a Starbucks. It's the end of my career. Well, thanks a bunch.'

Everyone booed and threw paper cups at him.

41

THE TRENCH EFFECT

DS Longbright was taken by surprise when Georgia Conroy called; she had not been expecting to hear from Pentonville Prison's former history teacher again. 'You told me to call if I remembered anything else,' Conroy explained. 'It's only a little thing.'

'That's fine,' replied Longbright, searching for a pen. 'Right now I'll be grateful for anything.'

'Well, you know I said Lloyd Lutine wanted me to go with him to visit Abney Park Cemetery?'

'Yes.'

'I thought it was odd at the time, because he'd given me the impression that he'd hated his father. He asked me to accompany him because he'd just discovered where he was buried.'

'How did he find out?'

'I don't know. Maybe he checked the Council records. As I said, I turned him down because it seemed a bit creepy. Then he mentioned something odd. That his father wasn't supposed to have been buried there. It wasn't allowed, there had been a mistake, something like that. I'm sorry, it's not much . . .'

'No, I'm glad you called.'

Longbright thought it through. If Mr Fox's father had also been raised in King's Cross, Abney Park would not have been his local cemetery. But people could be buried more or less wherever they wanted, so why should it not have been allowed? Thanking Georgia Conroy, she rang off and took her notes into Arthur Bryant's office.

'I know we're supposed to be concentrating on the Mecklenburgh Square case, but can you spare a minute?' she asked.

Arthur peered up at her over the tops of his bifocals. 'Is it urgent?'

'You're doing a jigsaw, Arthur.'

'It helps me to think.' He gave up trying to fit a piece and sat back, turning it over in his fingers. 'Queen Victoria's funeral procession. Two thousand pieces. I wonder how many mourners in the crowd travelled by Tube that day to watch it pass? Dan Banbury thinks someone chose to murder Gloria Taylor in the Underground system because of the sheer volume of people passing through it. He says it's difficult to solve a crime in a public place because the site always gets contaminated.'

'He's got a point.'

'I thought the killer might be re-enacting some kind of historical event connected with the tunnels – after all, they've been there for a century and a half. All three deaths are connected to the railway. Even Tony McCarthy was attacked underground. Despite my insistence that everything has been premeditated, John has a theory that we're looking for someone who's acting out of sheer panic. I can't see the sense in that myself. Meera thinks it's a man who hates women, and Matthew Hillingdon just got in the way. Bimsley and Renfield think we should be looking for an escaped lunatic. Raymond's right, in all my days with this unit, I've never had such a disagreeably confused investigation on my hands – and yet I know there's an absurdly simple answer we've all overlooked. It tantalizes and terrifies me to think that someone else may die because I can't see something that's right in front of me.' He threw the jigsaw piece down in annoyance. 'What's your opinion?'

'I need to talk to you about Mr Fox.' She told him about Georgia Conroy's phone call.

'Perhaps it wasn't about the location of the cemetery, but the grave itself,' said Bryant, rolling up the jigsaw and sliding it into his desk drawer.

'What do you mean?'

'The only people who aren't allowed to be buried on Christian sites are those of different faiths, and suicides. Could he have been a suicide, do you think, accidentally buried in a Christian spot?'

'I suppose it's possible.'

'Suicides happen all the time in the Underground system. Mr Fox had a photograph of a London Underground bench on the wall of his bedroom.'

'Some kind of sentimental memory?'

'One way to find out. Give Anjam Dutta a call at North One Watch.'

Longbright eventually got through to the King's Cross security headquarters. 'Can you do me a favour?' she asked. 'I need a list of all the one-unders you've had at King's Cross, going back as far as records allow.'

'That would be about thirty years,' Dutta told her. 'We never transferred anything older than that to the new data system.'

'How difficult would it be to get me those?'

'Not difficult at all. They've all been logged in. Give me a few minutes.'

While they waited for the email, Longbright and Bryant followed the thought. 'Mr Fox asked a virtual stranger to accompany him to his father's grave, and he still visits the site,' said Janice.

'So the death of his father could have been the turning point in his life.'

Bryant's laptop pinged. Longbright didn't have the patience to wait for Bryant to fiddle about trying to open his emails, so she leaned across him and launched the document, quickly running down the list of names. Most of the suicides were marked with ancillary files containing brief police statements. It didn't take her long to find what she was looking for.

'There you go.' She tapped the screen with a glossy crimson nail. 'Albert Thomas Edward Ketch went under a train on November the eighteenth at 4:00 p.m., on the Piccadilly Line platform of King's Cross Station, the third suicide that year. Hang on, there's a witness statement.' She clicked through to the attached page. 'Witness told attending police she had spoken to a boy she thinks was named Jonas. She insisted he had been sitting with Albert Ketch, waiting for a train, but the child was never traced.'

'No child traced,' mused Bryant. 'A key witness. It shouldn't have been that difficult.'

'It looks like they didn't even try to find him.'

'No. No, they didn't.'

'Why not?'

'They didn't have time to look.' Bryant clambered to his feet and searched the stacks of books balanced on crates around the edges of his desk. 'They couldn't conduct a proper search, because later that day—' He pulled out a volume on the history of the London Underground and threw it open. 'You see what I'm getting at?'

'Oh no,' said Longbright softly.

Bryant stabbed a finger at the page. 'November the eighteenth, 1987 was the date of the King's Cross fire.'

'The boy's name was Jonas Ketch. The bench—'

'The place where he last sat and talked to his father. I asked Dan to run out the shots of Mr Fox's room. What did I do with them?' Bryant found the sheaf of photographs and laid them out. 'There it is.'

The photograph showed the missing picture of the red metal bench. 'It looks like the boy saw his old man commit suicide right in front of him. Just an ordinary metal Tube station bench, but the background of tiles – that has to be King's Cross before it was redecorated.'

'So he took the boy there,' said Longbright, 'sat him down and talked to him. Then he rose, walked to the edge of the platform and dropped under the wheels of the incoming train.'

'Jonas Ketch's father died just three and a half hours before the King's Cross fire. Hang on.'

Bryant turned the page of his reference book, glanced at it and said, 'No one was ever able to discover exactly how the fire began, but they think someone dropped a lit match down the side of the escalator. It was one of the old wooden ones, and was covered in grease embedded with bits of paper and human hair that caught alight. Thirty-one people died, and another sixty were seriously injured. There had been a number of small fires at the site before, but this one spread in a completely new way. The escalator had steel sides and the flames rose at an angle that created the perfect conditions for something called the Trench Effect. An intense blast of flame that turned the ticket hall into an incinerator.'

'You think it was the boy?' Longbright was appalled.

'After seeing his father killed, he burned the station down in an act of fury.'

'My God.'

'It fits with everything we know, and would explain why death means so little to him.' Bryant returned to the laptop. 'Show me how to do this.'

'Don't touch it, let me. What are you after?'

'The names of all the fire victims.'

The list of those who died that day was public knowledge, and it took no time to locate a memorial site. 'That's why he wants to silence Tony McCarthy,' said Bryant, sitting back. 'It has nothing to do with the time they spent together at Pentonville. There's a Jim McCarthy listed as one of the victims of the King's Cross fire. Tony McCarthy's prison file records his parents as James and Sharon McCarthy. Suppose when they first met, Mr Fox—'

'Real name, Jonas Ketch.'

'Ketch accidentally revealed a little too much of himself. Suppose Mac realized that as a boy Ketch had committed an act of arson.'

'Killing McCarthy's father in the process.'

'It puts the case on an entirely different footing. You'd better make sure Renfield's there when Tony McCarthy comes out of UCH, and stays by him wherever he goes.'

'This is my case, Arthur,' Longbright pleaded. 'Let me do it, for Liberty's sake.'

'No, it's too dangerous. I want you to switch with Renfield and take one of the students.'

'That's not fair, and you know it. You owe me this.'

'Janice, your mother died in similar circumstances, trying to lure a criminal out into the open. Do you honestly think I'm going to let you risk your life as well? Put Renfield on it. I want you to stay right here, where I can keep an eye on you.'

Longbright stormed out of the detectives' room. Back in the corridor, she walked past Jack Renfield's office, stopping only to grab her jacket.

42

SLEIGHT OF HAND

'Hillingdon's overcoat,' said Bryant, wandering into the Crime Scene Manager's room, 'the oily patches are tobacco spray.' He looked very pleased with himself.

'How did you know?' Banbury asked. 'The results only just came back. I was about to come and see you.'

'The killer didn't forget the coat, he planted it.'

'What do you mean?'

'Someone in that house has been a bit too clever for their own good. The principles of magic: if you see the impossible happen, it isn't impossible. You've been tricked.'

'Sorry, Mr Bryant, I don't have the faintest idea what you're talking about.'

'In other words, you can only disappear from a moving train carriage if you were never on it in the first place.'

'Do you want me to get John before I go?' He made it sound as if he was offering to fetch a nurse for a rambling patient.

'No, go and keep an eye on – who did you draw this time?'

'The girl – Ruby Cates. Giles is covering for me until I

get there. I'm going to make her take that cast off.'

'Go on, relieve him.' Bryant waited for the door to shut and turned back to Professor Hoffman's book of card tricks. Holding it open with his left hand, he attempted to shuffle a fresh pack with his right, and sprayed cards all over the floor.

Outside in the corridor, John May saw a ghost. The sight brought him up short and chilled his blood. Fearfully, he slowly backed away.

Liberty DuCaine was sitting on an orange plastic chair in the hall, reading a copy of *Hard News*. But that was impossible; Liberty's bodily remains had been poured into a City of London Crematorium urn on Monday morning.

May looked at DuCaine, and DuCaine gave him a friendly smile. 'I'm here to see Janice Longbright,' he said cheerfully.

'Is she . . . expecting you?' asked May.

'Yeah, I'm Fraternity – Liberty's brother?'

Now May saw the differences between the pair. Fraternity's eyes were a little more deep-set and thoughtful. He was bulkier, with a dense neck and arms like heavy copper pipes. The black gym shirt under his tracksuit said 'Full Contact Fighter'.

'Sorry, I'm a little late. Some kind of problem with the Northern Line.' When he rose, he stood a full head above May.

'Don't worry. I'll take you to her office.' May wondered why Henley had turned him down, if DuCaine had achieved good grades. Despite the guidelines set by the Equal Opportunities Commission, physically imposing males were always useful on the street.

May pushed open the door to Longbright's office and found it empty, her coat gone. 'It looks like she's nipped out,' he said. 'Do you mind waiting?'

'No problem.' Fraternity walked around the room,

taking it in. 'She said she had some information about my case. I appreciate the help.'

'I'll have to leave you here until she gets back. We're having a very difficult day.' May headed to his own office, and found Bryant on his hands and knees, picking up playing cards.

'I see you're hard at work on the investigation, then,' he said.

'I am, actually. I know how Matthew Hillingdon was able to vanish from a moving train. Obviously, I had a rough idea fairly early on in the investigation, but it only became crystal clear to me a few minutes ago. Would you like to hear?'

May waited at his desk while Bryant picked up the cards and clumsily attempted to shuffle them. 'On Tuesday night, Hillingdon boarded a train at Liverpool Street Station, went west on the Circle Line to King's Cross and was supposed to catch the last southbound Piccadilly Line train. It arrived on time in King's Cross at 12:24 a.m., yes? He texted Ruby Cates from the King's Cross interchange at 12:20 a.m., telling her he was heading for Russell Square Tube, a two-minute journey. The CCTV showed him getting on to the train. The next shot we've got is of the train pulling out. But there was another event.'

'What?'

'Hillingdon shut his coat in the door, so they had to re-open the carriage doors. We don't know how soon after this the driver shut them again. Suppose Hillingdon ducked and ran down the carriage, getting off at the other end before the train left?'

'To go where? The cameras would have picked him up.'

'If you remember, there was one more train that night, leaving from the Northern Line platform three minutes later. The tunnel connecting the two lines was being retiled, and that camera wasn't working – Dutta told us that. So he hops on to the train, deliberately shuts his coat in the door, waits until the doors re-open, hops back off through the next set of doors, beyond sight of the working camera, and catches the northbound train.'

'Matthew Hillingdon's body was found in King's Cross, not at the far end of the Northern Line.'

'I didn't say it was Matthew who caught the other train, did I? Hillingdon was sprayed with tobacco somewhere in the station and left to die. The killer switched clothes with him. He put on Hillingdon's woolly hat and his ridiculous candy-striped overcoat, and ran for the train. The cameras picked up the hat and the coat. I mean, they could hardly miss, could they?'

'I know we only saw the figure from the back, but it looked like Hillingdon.'

'No, it *moved* like Hillingdon. Not a very hard motion to imitate, typical drunken student pimp-roll, feet at ten to two and arms swinging. And he was running, so the frames were blurred.'

'Then what happened to Hillingdon? If he'd been anywhere in the station, we would have seen him – oh my God.'

'Precisely. We *did* see him. He was caught by the cameras, and in the process became his own urban myth.'

'The Night Crawler.'

'Exactly. Not the ghost of a dead man, not a giant walking bat, and not a homeless person either. A dying student in a long black leather coat several sizes too large for him. He was pouring with sweat, so his long black hair was plastered around his head, and he was dying – crawling along the floor in the only direction he could manage – downwards. Disoriented and confused, barely able to breathe, he falls from the unused platform and hides in the cool darkness – but he manages to get the coat off and loosen his shirt collar before losing consciousness.'

'You think even that part was planned? That the black leather coat was chosen—'

'—by the killer to hide the victim. Probably, but what if it was somebody who actually knew about the myth of the Night Crawler?'

'That's something only the guards talked about,' said May. 'Isn't it?'

'No.' Bryant offered his partner a card. 'It's in a book called *Mind the Ghosts*. You brought back the paperback from the house in Mecklenburgh Square. It either belonged to Ruby Cates or Toby Brooke.'

'Or both of them. No, it can't be her. She's in a plastic cast. She's got a broken leg.'

'Except that Renfield didn't check to see if it was really broken. Tell me which card you picked.'

May turned over the card and studied it.

'It's the nine of clubs, yes?' said Bryant triumphantly.

'No. Mrs Bun the Baker's Wife.'

'Bugger,' said Bryant, 'I've mixed up the decks again.'

43

THE LURE

DS Janice Longbright arrived at University College Hospital just as Tony McCarthy was emerging, limping through the swing doors. He waved her away as soon as he spotted her. 'I just want to be left alone, OK? Don't come near me. I don't want no cops following me around all the time.'

'You'd rather have Mr Fox find you again?' asked Longbright, falling into step with him. 'Next time he's going to push that skewer through the soft underside of your jaw and up into your brain, assuming you have one. Is that what you want?'

'I can handle it.'

'How? Going to grow a moustache and dye your hair? Or have you got a gun at home? You'll need it, because he'll come after you again if you hang around his manor. Got somewhere else to go?'

'I can take care of myself.'

'You couldn't take care of a spider-plant, Mac. Don't you think the medical services are strained enough without them having to look after you?' She placed a strong hand on his skinny arm. 'I think you and I had better go for a little talk.'

'I've got nothing to say to you.'

'You already admitted you know Mr Fox's real identity.'

'No, I never.'

Longbright looked into his bloodshot eyes. 'Oh, you don't remember, do you? Did they give you a bronchoscopy?'

McCarthy looked blankly at her.

'Did they stick a bloody great tube down your throat?'

'Yeah.'

She knew they had; she had seen the equipment being prepared on the day she visited the hospital. 'It means you were dosed with a retro-amnesiac drug. You don't remember anything, do you? You were whacked out on meds, Mac, that's why you don't recall shooting your mouth off about Mr Fox. Or should we call him Jonas Ketch? Thought you were being clever, did you, giving us a few clues about a prison teacher, when all the time you knew who he really was?'

That brought McCarthy to a halt. 'You're doing my head in, I don't remember . . .' he pleaded.

'I think you should be asking yourself why I'd even bother to save the life of a grubby little junkie like you.'

'I'm not using any more.'

'Pull the other one, Pinocchio. The worst part about being you must be waking up every morning and remembering who you are. Not that you'll be waking up for much longer, with Ketch waiting to stick you.'

'What the hell do you want from me?' asked McCarthy, exasperated.

'Help me catch him and I'll save your miserable, wasted little life,' said Longbright.

*　　*　　*

It was 2:14 p.m. on Saturday afternoon, a relatively busy time at the King's Cross intersection, but today the Northern Line was seriously overloaded with passengers. Anjam Dutta set down his coffee and shifted his attention from screen to screen.

'We'll have to shut Staircase C ahead of the rush hour,' he instructed. 'And re-route the incoming Blacks across to Navy.' The safety and security team referred to the Tube lines by their colours when they were working at speed. 'What's happening out there today?'

He studied the two cameras trained on the main ticket hall. 'We've accounted for the Arsenal charity match and the Trafalgar Square rally – remind me what that's for?'

'Something to do with global warming,' said Sandwich. 'There's an anti-fur demo in Oxford Street, but West End Central's advice is that it'll be pretty small.'

'The traffic's still way up for a Saturday. You haven't picked up anything on the Net? Anyone running RSS feeds?'

'Local news, Sky, BBC, London Talk Radio, nothing unusual I can see,' said Marianne, 'but you're right, there's definitely something going on.'

'Keep your eyes open. If it gets any worse, we'll have to partially shut the station. This is really weird.' Dutta mopped his forehead and watched as a fresh surge of passengers descended the staircase to the ticket hall.

Janice Longbright wanted to get McCarthy off the street, so she dragged him into the New Delhi Indian Restaurant on Drummond Street, behind Euston Station, chucked him into the chair opposite and ordered spicy Thalis for both of them.

'I like this place because it's fast,' she explained. 'In fifteen minutes, when you get up from this table, you'll have told me everything you know about Jonas Ketch, or

I'm going to take you into the kitchen and shove your face into the tandoori oven, d'you understand?'

'I don't know why you're so aggressive,' McCarthy whined, going for sympathy.

'It's your choice, mate. Talk, or this'll be the worst Ruby Murray you've ever had.'

'I'll give you what I know about him, all right? I could tell he was bang out of order, soon as I met him.' McCarthy fidgeted around on his chair like a child at Sunday school. 'All sensible talk and that, but crazy behind the eyes. Damage, see. You can't trust damaged people.'

Longbright figured it took one to know one. 'How did you meet him?' she asked.

'I was doing eighteen months for receiving stolen goods, he came in to teach English. A lot of the inmates ain't got English as a first language. I got volunteered to help him. He never said much, but there was this one day, he was showing the class how to write a CV for a job using some prepared examples. When the lesson ended he got off sharpish and left some stuff behind, just papers in a plastic folder an' that. I was going to put our answer sheets back inside and leave it on the table, honest.'

'But you had a look through.'

'Well I had to, didn't I? And I saw this letter he was writing to his old man. About a dozen different versions of the same thing, all slightly different, written months apart from each other, like he kept starting it and changing his mind about what he was going to say. So I nicked one, I figured he wouldn't notice. When I got back to my cell, I read it. So get this: it's a kind of history of his life, all the stuff that made him angry. His parents was always trying to kill each other. Finally his old man, this bloke Al Ketch, took the kid out of the house one morning after some big bust-up with his missus, and dragged him down the Tube at King's Cross, saying they was going away on holiday.'

'Keep going.'

'Jonas hated his mother, right, so he reckoned the old man was taking him off somewhere where he'd never have to see the old cow again. He was all excited about going away with his dad. So he sits down with his dad on a platform bench and they're talking about their plans, how they're going to go to Spain and get a fresh start, how it's going to be great for both of them. Then his old man gets all excited, striding about, ranting, and when he's finished, he calms down and tells the boy he's leaving. Not *they*'re leaving, *he*'s leaving. He's had enough of them both, and he's dumping the kid. And Jonas worships his old man, right, he can't do no wrong in the boy's eyes. He thought his dad was taking them off some place where they'd be happy, and it turns out the bastard is abandoning him. And while the kid is watching, the old man turns away, goes to the edge of the platform and walks – just walks – under the train that's coming in. The kid is halfway there, heading towards his father just as he goes under, and he gets covered in his old man's blood. So he runs off in a right state, and when he gets home, he finds his mum has killed herself. She's taken an overdose of sleeping tablets and choked to death on her own vomit. How messed up is that?'

'And then you ran into Ketch again at St Pancras Station?'

'That's right, and he didn't even recognize me, 'cause it was two years later and I'd lost a lot of weight, being off prison food and on the smack, and he gave me a couple of jobs to do, just pocket-money stuff, and I couldn't tell him that I'd still got the letter, and that night I went home and read it again. And it freaked me out.'

'Why did it freak you out?' Longbright asked as their food arrived.

'Because by this time I'd worked out the date, hadn't I? I mean, I'm not likely to forget it, ever. His father died on the day of the King's Cross fire, just like my old man, only my dad was in the station and burned to death, and his died under a train in the morning. And that's when I knew, see. That's when I knew who started the fire. He didn't have to say nothing, I just knew. I could see it in his eyes. Kind of horrified he'd done it, and kind of arrogant as well. Trapped by something caused by his anger, something so terrible he'd never be able to leave the area until he'd come to terms with it. But that's not possible, is it? I mean, something on that scale. I watched on the news as they carried the bodies out. Even the survivors were completely black. The effect those scenes had on me – I guess that's when I started playing up, you know?'

He started to cry, and the trickle of a tear became a flood, so that he was forced to blow his nose on his napkin and turn away from her, nuzzling the heel of his hand against his forehead. The gaudy red Indian restaurant had become a confessional. Longbright suddenly felt sorry for him.

'Here's what we're going to do,' she said, drawing his eyes to hers. 'He'll know you're out of hospital now. He's around here somewhere. He'll follow you home and try to finish the job. But you have a chance of staying alive. I'll stay close by you, and keep my team on alert. When he shows his hand and moves in, we'll get him.'

'Is that it? You really think I'm going to survive that?' McCarthy was rubbing his red eyes, a frightened child. 'He'll stick me, and he'll give you lot the slip again.'

'You want to end this, don't you?'

'I know what you're up to. You just want to get the arrest, you don't care about me.'

'I'll bring him in, Tony, I swear. And I won't let you die. We need to get him somewhere that's enclosed, with escape routes we can monitor. Somewhere that's always being watched.'

'Where?'

'The station. You're going to perform that stupid wide-boy walk of yours, shout at the guards and passengers, generally make a bloody great nuisance of yourself, and draw him back to the spot where it all began.'

'People could get hurt. You're crazy.'

'You have no idea how crazy,' warned Longbright.

44

REMOTE CONTROL

Arthur Bryant found Sergeant Jack Renfield in the filthy junk-filled ante-room that passed for the unit's reception area. 'What are you still doing here?' he asked in obvious irritation.

'Dan's been trying out his new radios,' said Renfield. 'But don't worry, I'm on it.'

'What radios?'

'We're short-handed,' Renfield explained, 'so he's been developing these close-range radio mikes.' He held up something that looked like a pen refill, curved at one end. 'He's been dying to try them out. They're like the security headsets bouncers use, but they've got a better range. During surveillance we can stay in contact with each other, and we can track everyone's movements on the laptops.' He turned his screen around and pointed to a number of red dots pulsing on a Google map of London.

'Do they work underground?'

'I don't know,' Renfield admitted.

'We're after a killer who operates in the Tube network, you flybrain. This is not the right time to start testing out Dan's toys. I asked Janice to get you to cover Tony McCarthy as he came out of hospital. Didn't she come and talk to you?'

'No. I saw her go out a while back. She didn't say where she was going.'

'Stubborn bloody woman! Has she got one of those things?'

'Yeah.'

'Then see if you can raise her. And get after whoever it is you're supposed to be following.'

'Nikos Nicolau. He's been sitting on his fat arse in an internet café in Tottenham Court Road for the past two hours.'

'And what if he suddenly disappears? Where have the others gone?'

'Dan's gone after the stroppy Indian fella, Sangeeta; Colin's got Toby Brooke; Meera's got the rich one, Fontvieille; John's covering Ruby Cates. Raymond's in his room having a massive row with someone from the Home Office.'

'And I know exactly what Janice is up to,' added Bryant. 'Find someone to cover Nicolau – use Raymond if you have to, he'll kick up a fuss but we need everyone we can lay our hands on. Find out where Janice is, and bloody go after her. If it turns out that Mr Fox is following them, she'll need all the back-up she can get. This has the potential to blow up in our faces. We're close now, so I don't want anything to go wrong.'

'We're close?' Renfield was surprised. 'That's news to me. Hang on, I've got Dan on the line.' He talked with the CSM for a moment, then covered the phone. 'He just spoke to Janice. She's on the Euston Road with McCarthy in tow, heading east.'

'I know what she's up to. She's taking him back to the Tube station, where it all began. Your bug won't be any use there if they go down on to the platforms. Get to her first. Stay as close as you can, and keep in contact.'

'How can I if she goes underground?'

'I don't know, run up the stairs and call me as soon as you get a signal. You'll have to figure it out. I'll stay here. Someone has to keep an eye on you all.'

'You know me,' said Renfield, 'I'll have a go at anyone, but we could do with some more back-up than this.'

Just then, Fraternity DuCaine appeared in the doorway.

'Good God, you're not dead,' said Bryant, clutching theatrically at his heart.

'Yeah, I get that a lot. I'm his brother,' said Fraternity. 'Sorry, I didn't mean to make you jump. You don't know how long the DS will be, do you?'

'You could give us a hand while you're waiting,' said Bryant.

DuCaine shrugged amiably. 'Sure, no problem.'

'Good.' Bryant unleashed a gruesome smile. 'What do you know about card tricks?'

Anjam Dutta badly wanted a cigarette. He couldn't drink any more coffee. His nerves were on fire. Something very big and very bad was happening at his station. He had called his bosses, but all they could suggest was closing the entire interchange down. Dutta's eyes flicked from screen to screen, trying to make sense of what he was seeing. 'We've got a camera out on the Circle, Sandwich. Did you call maintenance?'

'Twenty minutes ago,' Sandwich told him. 'They're having trouble getting to their equipment.'

'I'm not surprised.' Dutta could see the problem: a knot of passengers blocking the path to one of the supply stores. Usually he could register travel patterns just by glancing at the screens. Football days were the easiest because supporters were helpfully dressed in their team colours. Other groups offered subtler clues. Rush-hour commuters knew their way around the system, and rarely strayed from their routes. They didn't queue for windows because they all had travel cards. Tourists stood in line for tickets and grouped around the two main maps. Schoolchildren, students, hen-night parties, clubbers aiming to arrive in time for cheap admissions, concert-goers – they were all easy enough to spot.

But this one had him puzzled. There was no pattern – just a massive increase in traffic, right across the station. Passengers of all types and ages were pouring in from every entrance, despite the fact that access had already been restricted. He checked the arrival times of the Eurostar trains and found no correlation there. The wall clock read 14:34 p.m. It was as if the rush hour had decided to start three hours early.

'What the hell is going on? I think we'll have to shut the East Gate completely.'

'We've never done that before,' said Sandwich. 'The BTP will be pissed off if you back passengers up on to the street.'

'The British Transport Police should be telling us about this, not the other way around. The Northern Line southbound platform is overloaded. They're virtually falling on to the rails.'

The system worked so long as the law of averages operated normally and only a fraction of those who held travel cards decided to travel at the same time. Today, though, it seemed as if the law of averages was on hold.

'So long as the trains keep coming in on time we should be all right, but if one of them gets a signal delay, we're screwed. Where are they all going? You'd better get everyone in here.'

*   *   *

Nikos Nicolau sat by the window in Costa Coffee, monitoring the messages on his laptop. They were climbing fast now. A few minutes ago they had stuck at 3,700, but suddenly they were hitting 7,000 and rising. There was a gullibility factor in people that you had to target by appealing to their vanity, he decided, as he posted another instruction. He figured the unit had probably sent one of their drones to keep an eye on him, but what would they see? An overweight geek sitting alone at his laptop in a coffee shop. He played on the cliché, because he knew it would blind them to his real nature.

Time for another post. He typed 'Thirty-two minutes to reach King's Cross'. Skipping through the messages, he felt like a chef adding flavours to a stew. *It needs something more*, he thought. *A fresh ingredient.* Looking at the original post, he had a brainwave. He re-coloured the words in day-glo greens, blues and yellows, then changed the font setting to 'Balloony', a script kids loved. Next, he dropped the message on to RadLife, a new social networking site targeted at tweens. *Damn*, he thought, *this is going to be so cool.*

He wanted to be there, but it was smarter and safer to handle the event remotely. This way he could keep it going right up until the last minute. Nikos wiped a patch of condensation from the window and peered out into the afternoon rain. *Watch me and learn, you losers*, he thought, hitting Send.

45

KILL PROXIMITY

Ruby Cates had unclipped the plastic cast on her leg and dropped it off at the University College Hospital out-patients' department. She emerged from the entrance a few hundred yards behind Tony McCarthy.

Now she was heading along the rain-battered pavements of Euston Road towards King's Cross Station. Her mind was racing. The police were suspicious. She had seen various members of the PCU lurking about outside the house, and for all she knew one could be following her right now. *That could work in my favour,* she thought, hopping between stalled taxis. *Things are getting seriously out of control.*

In the past week, it seemed as if the world had turned upside-down. Matt gone, Cassie dead. Everything that had seemed exciting a week ago had been wrecked or tainted. The true horror of what she had done was only now starting to sink in. *Get to King's Cross,* she told herself. *Put an end to it and get the hell out.*

*   *   *

Toby Brooke could see the man with no neck watching him in the reflection of the furniture-store window. He was wearing a black padded jacket and jeans, but couldn't help looking like a copper. He thumped miserably from one boot to the other and wiped the rain from his shaved head, but seemed fairly content, just standing there in the downpour like a dumb animal.

Brooke wanted to get away, but was running out of options. Everything had gone wrong, and he had a bad feeling about the way it would end. He thought about slipping into the store and leaving through the rear door, but knew it would not be so easy to shake off the man who was following him. The sight of a taxi with its 'For Hire' light glimmering through the sheeting rain forced his hand, and he hailed it, jumping inside before his shadow was able to react.

'King's Cross,' he told the driver, and sat back, turning to see if the policeman was managing to follow.

Meera Mangeshkar was five metres behind Theo Fontvieille, who was looking very unhappy indeed. *Rich kid*, she thought, *he's more upset about having his car nicked than he is about his so-called mate being killed. But where's he going?* Fontvieille had cut up from the house in Bloomsbury and was heading toward King's Cross Station. Tucked beneath his elegant Smith & Son umbrella, he was immaculately attired in a handmade suit and matching black overcoat. *Must be a bit of a shock for him, having to board public transport*, she thought. *Probably going to visit Mummy and Daddy's country pile.* Meera frowned, looking again. Ruby Cates had appeared behind him, near the overcrowded entrance to the Tube station.

The top of her spine tingled in alarm. Something was not right – all these people – what were they doing here in the afternoon? Crowds of them milling around, waiting to get through the station entrances. It just looked – dangerous. Cates was closing in behind Fontvieille, but had they even seen each other? From here it was hard to tell. Meera tried to get nearer, but the crowds pressed in.

Dan Banbury sat watching Rajan Sangeeta eat a salad in the UCL cafeteria. The student was idly twirling an alfalfa sprout between his forefinger and thumb as he scanned a paperback copy of Herman Hesse's *Steppenwolf*. *I've really drawn the short straw here*, thought Banbury. *This one's far too boring and studenty to be involved in anything dubious.* He sat back on the uncomfortable plastic banquette and waited for something interesting to happen.

'Keep going,' said Longbright, giving Mac a shove in the back. 'What's the matter?'

'This is his territory.' Mac was frightened now. They had stopped by the clogged Underground entrance and were quickly hemmed in by new arrivals.

'If you try to give me the slip, I'll leave you somewhere he can get at you and withdraw police presence, do you understand?'

'He knows I'm here. He always knows when I'm in the station.'

'He can't be everywhere at once, Mac.'

'This is his home.'

The crowd was still moving. After waiting a minute, they slowly descended the staircase into the ticket hall. So many people were milling around that the makeshift queue barriers for the ticket office had all been pushed back. They weren't descending to the platforms or using the tunnels, they were just standing there, as if waiting to be told what to do next. A cluster of BTP officers stood off at one side of the crowd near the security control centre, but they seemed uncertain how to act.

'Now what?' asked Mac, panicked. 'He could be anywhere, I don't know where to look. He could be creeping up beside us right now.'

'You're going to start making me nervous if you don't shut up,' Longbright warned. 'I want you somewhere with maximum visibility.' She pointed to the guards waiting to feed passengers through the unused ticket barriers. 'Go over there and start an argument with one of them. Tell him your travel card doesn't work and you want a refund. Tell him he looks like a warthog, tell him anything. Make it loud and be bloody minded – I'm sure that'll come naturally. Wait.' Her earpiece crackled into life. She listened to Renfield and nodded. 'Go.'

There were at least three other members of PCU staff in the station, but things had a habit of going wrong where Mr Fox was involved. Watching Mac thread his way towards the guards, the memory of Liberty DuCaine suddenly filled Longbright's head, and she turned around in alarm, half expecting to find a killer standing behind her.

46

JOKER IN THE PACK

According to the reports reaching John May, three of the five housemates were making their way separately to King's Cross Station, along with Longbright, Renfield and Tony McCarthy. Only Sangeeta and Nicolau were away from the site. Did that remove them from suspicion, or implicate them further? And why were the others all heading to the one place where the PCU was most likely to catch Mr Fox? *You're being paranoid,* thought May as he tacked through the stalled traffic. *Arthur's done it to you again, forever trying to join the dots where no links exist. It's a massive terminus, it's the weekend, and students are more likely to use public transport, that's all.*

The rain pockmarked the pooled tarmac. May darted under the station awning and queued to enter the station, several rows back from Ruby Cates, who was no longer sporting her cast.

What am I doing here? he asked himself angrily. *I swear, this really is the most chaotic investigation of my career. When I look at our methodology through the eyes of Home Office officials, I can honestly see why they're so keen to retire us. The unit's working methods confuse its own staff, so God knows what they do to outsiders. Arthur put his faith in me to close this quickly, but I'm damned if I can see how to do it. There's something missing that I'm simply not equipped to spot. And now he's back at the unit with his jigsaws and his playing cards, letting me slowly hang myself. It's as if he no longer cares what happens to the unit or to any of us.*

He angrily pushed his way down the steps into the ticket hall, where he was spotted by Longbright. She shook her head at him. *No sign of Mr Fox.* But there was McCarthy, having some kind of arm-waving argument with a baffled barrier guard.

Looks like everyone's decided to travel today, thought May. He checked his watch; 3:39 p.m. *Not a very satisfying end to our careers – a dead officer and two unresolved cases.*

The problem with the students of Mecklenburgh Square was not one of culpability but motive. Without that, the investigation could never be resolved. It seemed to May that the suspects, the victims and the investigators had created a perfect deadlock. As the minutes ticked away, May patted the rain from his jacket, stuck his hands in his pockets and leaned against the tiled wall, watching and waiting as the human whirlpool swirled aimlessly around its vortex. There was nothing else he could do.

Arthur Bryant's office had started to resemble a magician's display room. Apart from the books of magic, there was now a working model guillotine and a full set of Chinese linking rings on his desk. Several packs of cards were strewn over the floor, along with random items of evidence, including a number of volumes on the London Underground, the paperback edition of *Mind the Ghosts*, the students' opened laptops, Hillingdon's rainbow raincoat and a series of enlarged frame grabs of Tube train seats from a mobile phone.

At times like this, Bryant found it helpful to break confidence and discuss the case with a complete outsider, although he took the risk that Fraternity DuCaine might simply think him unhinged.

'You see, I keep coming back to the cards,' he said, spreading a pack across his desk. 'I can't explain my thinking to you, because I can't entirely explain it to myself.'

'Let me get this right,' said Fraternity. 'You see a connection between the playing cards and the death of a woman on a staircase?'

'Believe me, I know how that sounds. But the colours and shapes keep repeating themselves in my head.'

Fraternity looked more confused than ever. 'No, I'm still not getting it,' he said.

'Let me see if I can explain.' Bryant opened Professor Hoffman's manual of card conjuring. 'I've been trying to learn the system of finding marked cards that's recommended in this book, but I don't have a mathematical mind. One way of doing it is to locate imaginary points on the backs of the cards. Hoffman teaches you to superimpose patterns over seemingly random choices. If you're careful, you can divide the back of a card up into thirty different points. I look from the diamonds and hearts on the faces to thirteen photos taken of the Tube station seat covers, and every illogical cell in my brain starts to vibrate. But what exactly am I looking at?'

'I have no idea,' Fraternity admitted. 'We didn't do anything like this at Henley.'

'What happened to you there? Do you have any idea why you failed?'

'It couldn't have been anything that occurred during the training period. My coursework was good and I got on just great with everyone.'

'Then it must have been somewhere else. Where did they put you out in the field?'

'I did two weeks at Albany Street station. That seemed to go OK.'

'Just OK?'

'Well, until the end, at least. I'd been placed under some uptight dude who seemed like he'd skipped a few stages of his diversity training.'

'He had a race problem?'

'No, not that. The inner-city boroughs would collapse without a heavy proportion of ethnic staff. Besides, I got the feeling that if you really have issues you can get posted to an area where you only have to deal with your white brothers.'

'So what was it?'

'I was supposed to go for a drink with the team at the end of my last day, and my ex-partner came by unannounced. I was kind of embarrassed about that.'

'Why?'

'At the time, he was one of the principal dancers in Matthew Bourne's production of *Swan Lake*.'

'Ah. Yes. I can see how that would do it.'

'Look, he was between performances and wanted to wish me well. You wouldn't know—'

'You don't need to explain. Officers always know. Your mentor had championed you to the others and suddenly felt he'd lost face.'

'I guess that's a possibility.'

'And he was in charge of your field report. Why didn't you say something?'

'It would only have made matters worse. I didn't feel comfortable talking about it. And I had no real proof.'

'I can look into this for you. Do you remember the name of your senior officer?'

'Sure. He was a sergeant. A guy called Jack Renfield. I

tried to get in touch with him one time, but they told me he'd moved on. They wouldn't say where.'

'I won't be able to retroactively change your report,' said Bryant, 'but if we survive beyond the end of the afternoon, I may be able to recommend you for a position here.'

Fraternity's smile was sunlight after rain. 'You really think that's a possibility?'

'It would mean confronting Renfield. He's at the unit, you see. Albany Street was angry about losing him to us, that's why they refused to tell you where he went. You think the two of you could discuss the matter civilly, without any bloodshed?'

'Could I hit him once, maybe?'

'All right, but first help me with the cards. What am I missing here?'

'OK.' Fraternity narrowed his eyes at the card backs, then glanced across at Professor Hoffman's manual. 'You're learning how to mentally mark cards so you can track them through the pack, right?'

'Right.'

'And you got these seat patterns. Why would anyone take pictures of those?'

'To track something – somebody – from line to line.'

'That's what I see. There are twelve underground lines, right?'

'Yes.'

'But you've got thirteen shots. This one isn't a line. OK, it's a bit out of focus but it looks like red polka dots to me.'

Bryant mentally slapped himself. 'That's a close-up of the dress Gloria Taylor was wearing when she died.'

'Man, that's a hell of a dress. She must have been the most noticeable woman on the Tube that day.'

'Of course – it made her easy to follow. She got on at

Bond Street and changed at Oxford Circus. Maybe the killer was with her all the way. It's like tracking a playing card through the deck. He chose her because of the dress.'

'A sexual obsessive?' Fraternity suggested.

'Then why not simply touch her or try to strike up a conversation? Why push her down the stairs?' Bryant realized he could answer his own question. 'She almost left the station, then turned around and went back. She'd forgotten her daughter's birthday present. And then she was pushed because someone was angry with her. Angry that she didn't go through the barrier and leave. You track the card through the pack. But the card lets you down, and you lose your temper and knock the cards over. Everything else that has happened is because of that one moment.'

'It's a game,' said Fraternity, looking at the fallen cards. 'And someone didn't like to lose.'

'What kind of game has stakes so high that you'd actually shove a stranger in the back?' He looked back at the pack of cards, and the upturned nine of clubs. 'I marked that one so I could trace it through the pack.'

'Sorry, Mr Bryant, not with you.'

'You don't mark a card the second before you turn it over. You mark it right at the beginning, so you can keep an eye on it through the shuffle. The killer didn't put the sticker on Gloria Taylor's back just before he killed her. He did it so that he could prove that she was the marked card. She wasn't hard to keep track of in the Tube crowds, because of the way she was dressed. But he had to show someone else that she was the victim. Matt Hillingdon's mobile was missing because it revealed the marked card.'

'I'm still not getting a clear signal from you, Mr Bryant,' said Fraternity. Getting used to Bryant's way of thinking sometimes took decades.

'I need to run the security-camera footage from Monday evening at Bond Street Tube.' Bryant indicated that Fraternity DuCaine should grab the nearest phone. 'Then I'll know who killed Gloria Taylor.'

47

ROLL

Here we go, thought Nikos Nicolau, counting down the seconds in the corner of his screen. *This is going to be so damned cool. From team player to team leader at the touch of a button.* The screen counter had stopped at 11,353, but if even a fraction of that number turned up he'd have proved his point. The bait-and-switch site had worked like a dream, setting up a Flash Mob that would last for four minutes, the duration of the song.

He waited until exactly 3:00 p.m. then hit Play. A video of the band appeared onscreen, and the first power chord sounded. The band was called Snap Monkey (feat. Aisho DC Crew) and the song 'Perfect People' had become a club anthem two years earlier, because the band members had taught the movements of their supremely vacuous song to the inmates of a South Korean prison. Since then it had replaced Michael Jackson's 'Thriller' as the most imitated dance song ever to hit the Web. Even tiny kids in nursery schools knew the steps, which were a damned sight cooler than anything Michael Jackson ever recorded. And the best part was that he could get them to

RickRoll* in the station without ever noticing the irony in the song's lyrics.

Nobody can be controlled.
Nobody can be patrolled.
What we do is what we love.
Nobody orders from above.
Where we are is where we stand.
The hottest lovers in the land.

And here he would be, controlling them through a broadcast to 11,353 iPods, BlackBerrys and assorted PDAs, beamed into the grand concourse of St Pancras International Station. He remembered the KissRoll staged there a couple of years back, two hundred lovers smooching beneath the disproportionately vast, tacky statue called 'The Kiss' that dominated the station atrium. But this was on a different scale entirely.

More importantly, it would bring an end to the argument he'd been having with Rajan and the others about pedestrian flow in public areas. Rajan had argued that the public could be persuaded to walk in non-instinctive directions if properly directed. Groups generally moved in broad clockwise circles, Nikos had told him, because the country drove on the left and people were used to driving clockwise around roundabouts. Customers entering shops usually headed left, circling the store and exiting from the right; it was the natural thing to do. But in countries where they drove on the other side of the road, the system was reversed.

The webcam feeds sent back by his viewers a few minutes earlier showed that the group in the station

*Named after the singer Rick Astley, whose fans turned up at stations to perform his greatest hit.

was automatically following a clockwise route. Social engineering only worked if the instructions didn't contravene human instinct. Certain rules held true whatever the circumstances; build a block of flats with lifts opening on to the street, Nikos had argued, and they'd be avoided by residents because the lift-space became the property of the street rather than the tenants. Design a public lavatory where the urinals could be seen from the pavement, and the British would be reluctant to use them. Deep-rooted beliefs in what constituted public and private spaces were hard-wired into the human psyche.

But something was wrong. The café's broadband speed was pitifully slow, but as he checked the incoming feeds he could see that no one was dancing. The song was already past its first verse. What had gone awry? The chorus was coming up.

> *Gonna live like perfect people.*
> *Gonna love like perfect people.*
> *Live and love like perfect people.*
> *Live and love like perfect people.*

It wasn't exactly Rimbaud, but it felt about right for the duped drones down on the concourse. He studied the feeds again. Nothing. They weren't dancing. Why wasn't anything happening? The video was playing perfectly. He could see it on the site. He opened the site's admin page and checked the stats. He ran through the set-up and hit log, but found nothing unusual.

Then he saw it.

Although the destination was correct in the body of the site instructions, the Flash box he had created to run as a site banner was wrong. Where he had typed in the location of the event, a pre-logged template had set the destination to King's Cross Station instead of St Pancras.

He had forgotten that although the two stations shared the same complex, they were entirely separate termini. He had lost concentration for a moment and clicked through to the wrong place.

Breaking into a sweat, he toggled back to one of the video feeds and zoomed out to take in the whole scene. Instead of the great vaulted ceiling of the Eurostar terminal, he found himself looking at a cramped, tiled hall. He had sent his Flash Mob to the wrong station.

Christ. The concourse at King's Cross Underground was minuscule compared to the one at St Pancras. A sinking sickness invaded Nikos's stomach. He had instructed 11,353 people to meet there. Maybe some of them had figured it out and had made their way to the right meeting point, but what if the rest were trying to cram themselves into the small Underground ticket hall beneath the main station? The result could be a massacre, like the ones which occurred at Mecca or the Heysel football stadium; people could be crushed to death in the ensuing chaos.

Sweating violently now, he killed the video and wiped his trail, removing the online instructions, shutting down the website, clearing the computer's history. He was using his backup laptop, the one he had stored in his UCH locker, the one the police didn't know existed. If there was any comeback, at least he had bought himself some time – until someone ran a trace from the host.

He knew that he would have to go and see for himself. It would be like rubbernecking at a traffic accident, but he had to make sure that his conscience was clear. Slipping the laptop into his rucksack, he zipped up his jacket and ran out into the rain.

48

MAELSTROM

The scene in the station was becoming nightmarish. The crowd had started dancing but there was no space to move, and their synchronized movements had quickly fallen apart. A party of schoolchildren was disgorging from the Victoria Line escalator, but the hall was so crowded that they could not pass through the barriers, and had become trapped halfway. Children were screaming and crying. The staircases were ranked with passengers unable to move in any direction. A sense of barely controlled hysteria was breaking out in the claustrophobic hell of the ticket hall.

John May could do nothing but watch. Longbright and McCarthy were nearest the barriers, and he could still see Ruby Gates fighting her way towards the Tube escalators. Had she seen Theo Fontvieille nearby? And had either of them identified Meera or Colin? *We're all in trouble here if anything bad happens,* he realized. He called Bimsley.

'There's no way of getting anyone out, Colin, so they'll have to force people down on to the platforms and get them to board outbound trains. Try and connect with the

others. I want you all on this floor. If you go to a lower
level I'll lose radio contact with you.'

'OK boss.'

Arthur Bryant and Fraternity DuCaine made their
entrance into the station via a staff elevator that delivered
them into the ticket office. Anjam Dutta was there to meet
them. The security officer looked stressed but in control.

'We've got crowds backed around the exterior of
the station,' he explained, ushering them through an
unmarked door and walking them to the surveillance
room. 'I'm trying to clear the exits but I can't close them,
because I need to get people up first. We've never had
a situation like this before. Usually only a tenth of the
population should be travelling at a time. But we think
we've found the source.'

'What is it?'

'Somebody arranged the staging of a Flash Mob in the
station, but the induction site was pulled a few minutes
ago.' He got a sweetly blank look from Bryant. 'It was
a passing fad a while back. People click on a site that re-
routes them to a different destination, and that destination
sends instructions to laptops, mobiles and PDAs, telling
them to meet in a certain public place and dance to music
played out on MP3s. The craze died out after companies
copied it to use as sales tools We've got all our staff and
the LTP trying to move the crowd. In general, people have
lived through enough terrorist alerts not to panic, but
they're getting pretty close to the edge right now.'

'We have PCU members out there tracking suspects,'
Bryant explained. 'Our leads may be connected with the
situation you've got on your hands here.'

'You're telling me there's a murderer crowded in there
with the general public? You're supposed to be helping us,
Mr Bryant, not making matters worse.'

Bryant looked up at the staff roster of security guards.

Photographs of Anjam, Rasheed, Sandwich, Marianne, Bitter and Stone were arranged in a row on corkboard, their weekly duty roster marked beneath them in black felt-tip pen. 'They're all out on the floor right now?'

'Yeah, you can see Marianne near the Circle Line tunnel, and there's Sandwich, by the lift. Stone's over at the barrier.'

Bryant glanced back at the ID of the man the others had nicknamed Stone. He found himself looking at an earlier incarnation of Mr Fox. 'When was that taken?'

'Two weeks ago.'

Bryant checked the fine print beneath the photobooth shot. *Jack Ketch.* 'He sat in on my briefing session with the security staff,' said Bryant. 'Inattentional blindness. You have got to be kidding. He's been here under our noses all the time?'

'And now he's out there,' said May. 'Come on.'

The detectives pushed themselves into the crushing chaos of the crowd. 'Janice,' May called on his radio, 'brown leather jacket and glasses, to your right. Mr Fox is less than three metres away from McCarthy. You have to move the boy out of there.'

'I can't, John, we're stuck here.'

'Then we'll come to you.'

The Flash Mob song had come to a rowdy, ragged end, and the disappointed crowd was looking lost, not yet ready to disperse. Tannoy announcements were proving ineffectual in easing the constrictions.

Anjam Dutta could see the pressure points reaching maximum density. His mobile showed an incoming call from John May.

'We have to clear the hall fast,' said May. 'Can you open all the ticket barriers and leave them up?'

'There's an electronic override, but it'll lose the network a fortune. I have to have authority—'

'Someone could get killed if you don't. Just do it, Anjam. I'll take full responsibility.'

Dutta released the safety guards and punched in the code that released all of the barriers simultaneously. The crowd surged forward and poured through to the Victoria, Piccadilly and Northern Line escalators. The pressure in the ticket hall began to ease at once.

Longbright saw Mr Fox standing on the other side of Tony McCarthy, pushing his way between tightly packed bodies. 'Mac,' she called, 'he's right behind you. Run.'

McCarthy panicked, and instead of going up to street level, fled down in the direction of the escalators. Mr Fox broke his cover and set off after him.

Ruby Cates reached the barriers just as they opened. She was swept through with the crowd, but managed to pull free and head towards the southbound Victoria Line platform.

'Hey, Ruby.' Theo was on the step below her. He turned and grinned. 'I thought I saw you in the ticket hall. What was that all about?'

'Someone's idea of a joke. I'm surprised no one was squashed flat. Where are you going?'

'Oxford Circus. I want to buy some trainers. How about you?'

'Victoria. I'm going to Brighton.'

'Who you got down there?'

'Just some friends.'

'How long are you going for?'

'Probably just for the weekend. I need a break.'

'You didn't say you were going.'

'I decided when I heard about Cassie. There's so much awful stuff going on, the police are hanging around the house, everyone's on edge. I haven't been able to concentrate on anything.'

They stepped off the escalator together. 'I can't believe

you didn't tell me you were getting out. I thought you were serious about us.'

Ruby looked uncomfortable. She turned the ring on her finger, studying it too intently. 'I've been thinking, I'm not so sure I want to be with anyone just now. I need some space to think. I'll call you from Brighton, OK?'

'What happened to spending more time together? Listen, I could come down with you, just for tonight. I don't have to go into town. I don't really need another pair of trainers.'

'No, that wouldn't be workable. I'm staying with these people I know.'

'Well, it seems like you're running away. Are you meeting someone down there?'

'No, of course not.'

'Then why is it I don't believe a word you're saying?'

The platform had become overcrowded. The guards were warning everyone to stand back from the platform edge as there was a train approaching.

'Tell you what. As a token of trust, give me that back.' He pointed to the diamond ring on the third finger of her right hand.

Ruby gave an awkward laugh. 'Actually I was going to leave it on your bedside table this morning but I couldn't get the damned thing off. It's a little too small for me. This is my train.'

'Give me the ring, Ruby.' There was menace in his voice now.

She gave him a strange look. 'I told you, I can't get it off.'

When he grabbed her arm she was so surprised that she momentarily lost her balance, and was almost pulled under the arriving train.

Longbright could see Mac bobbing and shoving ahead towards the red and silver train that was just opening its doors. Mr Fox – she could only think of him in the identity he had used to kill – was closing in fast behind him.

Further ahead, Mr Fox was feeling a strange, cold serenity descending over him, a feeling that always seized him in the moments before he killed. He saw everything at a distance; among all those scurrying little people was the pathetic junkie Mac, desperate to escape, searching a way out like a Tube rat sensing a coming inferno. Sweat was leaking from his hairline down his sallow, diseased cheeks. He looked badly in need of a fix.

Perhaps that was the answer; perhaps the entire interchange needed to burn again, to sear itself clean in a rising tide of flame. But no, that wouldn't work now. Steel had replaced wood, smoke sensors and cameras lined the walls. And what would another conflagration resolve? The horror of the past could not be erased with a second atrocity. The memory of that terrible day could never be burned away.

Mr Fox allowed the silver skewer to slide down into his palm. He felt its cool heft in his hand, demanding to be used. Killing could calm him.

But now the doors of the Victoria Line train stood open, and Mac was free to board. If he did, Mr Fox knew he would lose the opportunity presented by the crush of the anonymous crowd. He stamped hard on a woman's foot and shoved her aside, moving in to commit the act that would provide him with a temporary respite from the ever-present pain of remembering.

Just as he reached towards Mac, a tall young man stumbled into his path. The man was grabbing at his girlfriend's hand, trying to twist a ring from her finger, and the girlfriend had turned to slap him in the face. The crowd – mostly made up of old ladies, it seemed – pushed back with force, and suddenly they seemed to have linked arms, forming a solid barrier across his path. It was absurd, but he could not pass between them to reach his target. He watched, stalled, as Mac jumped to safety, moving nimbly between the closing doors of the carriage.

Now the young man was twisting the girl's hand and Mr Fox heard the snap of her finger, saw her scream, knew that some other drama was unfolding before him, but all he could see was Mac escaping, getting away to some place where he could talk to the police; and then he knew he had lost, lost it all, because of the old ladies and this damned man and his stupid lovers' tiff, and the needle-sharp point of the skewer had risen in his hand as if moving of its own accord.

He slammed it down into the young man's arm and pushed, shoved it through the artery above his wrist until the point emerged from the other side. But he couldn't get the skewer back out, no matter how hard he pulled.

The student released the girl and collapsed with a roar of pain. The pensioners before him were suddenly replaced with familiar faces, and he saw that he was surrounded by members of the Peculiar Crimes Unit.

The centre of the group slowly opened to reveal the crumpled face of Arthur Bryant, closely followed by John May. The most humiliating moment came when a woman, the big blonde detective sergeant they called Longbright, twisted the silver skewer from his grip and removed it from the victim, confiscating his beloved weapon.

From the day he watched the burning match tumble down the side of the escalator, a part of him had always prayed for this moment to arrive. With delicious anticipation, he waited to hear the words that would finally seal his fate.

Instead he saw Arthur Bryant look past him and announce, 'Theodore Samuel Fontvieille, I am arresting you for the murders of Gloria Taylor, Matthew Hillingdon and Cassandra Field.'

49

CHARISMATIC

'Two arrests before six o'clock,' Raymond Land was excitedly telling Leslie Faraday over the phone. 'They've done it! No, I've no idea how. Nobody ever tells me anything. Oh, really? Oh, I thought you'd be pleased.' Land found himself looking into the receiver, a dead line burring in his ear.

This time, Mr Fox found himself locked in a cell at Albany Street police headquarters, and there was no way for him to escape – not that he wanted to. On the contrary, he seemed almost relieved to be behind bars, as if somehow the memory of those painful years between his destruction of the Tube station and his return to killing had finally been laid to rest.

He refused to speak to anyone, and flinched when his features were recorded, fearful that his true face might be placed on display for all to gawp at. And gawp they would, for even as he lay in the corner of his cell, his jacket thrown over his eyes to shield them from the overhead lights that were never dimmed, the Home Office was leaking the story to the press.

Having been so protective of his true identity, Jack Ketch, alias Lloyd Lutine, alias Mr Fox and a dozen other names, would now face his greatest fear – exposure of his most horrific, shameful secret. Thinking back to the moment when he ran crying up the escalator with the burning match in his hand, he buried his face ever more deeply into the cloth of his jacket, savouring these last few moments of darkness, knowing that the blaze of publicity would soon obliterate him, as the braying clamour of morons began.

The PCU had dragged all the members of the Mecklenburgh Square household back to the unit's headquarters for a final showdown, and this time batteries of police recorders and cameras were there to cover the event. Theo Fontvieille had been stitched and bandaged, and was seated with plastic ties securing his wrists. The others found chairs or spaces on the floor where they could sit. The two Daves had been sent away, despite their protestations that they hadn't had time to repair the hole in Bryant's floor, but everyone else was in attendance, and it was Arthur Bryant, of course, who chose to take the centre stage.

'Well, it's been quite a week for all of us,' he said, looking around, his blue eyes shining, 'but tougher for some than others. Now that we're all together, I think we should dispense with formalities for a while and talk about what happened.'

'We should be taking separate statements from each of them, sir,' said Renfield, 'to prevent corroboration.'

'No, I think the only way to put this together is to hear everyone out,' Bryant contradicted. 'They're not in the mood to provide alibis for each other any more.' He turned to the students. 'So, let's imagine we're playing a game. I'll be the Bank. Although strictly speaking, Mr Nicolau, you should be the Bank, shouldn't you?'

Nikos looked awkwardly at the others, wondering how much he should say.

'Come, come, Mr Nicolau, this is no time to be shy. I imagine you were very excited when you came up with the idea for the game, weren't you? All those nights spent online could finally be put to some use.'

Nikos cleared his throat and edged forward in his seat, conscious of the police cameras recording him. 'Yeah, it was me who came up with it, but it was never meant to end up like this. I don't know what Theo's been up to because I had no part—'

'Let's just stick to the facts for now. We'll have plenty of time later to ascertain everyone's level of involvement. Why did you come up with the game? When did you first think of it?'

'It began in the Karma Bar,' he mumbled. 'A bunch of us were sitting around, and we were all complaining that we were broke.'

'We were talking about our student loans, and the rent and all the bills,' said Ruby. 'I was always having to lend the others—'

'Please, let's stick to the point,' warned Bryant. 'We'll get to you in due course. Go on, Mr Nicolau.'

'I said I thought we should try to make some money with online gambling. I knew a lot about statistics and had a few ideas for beating the odds. What I didn't know was that *he* –' here Nikos pointed angrily at Theo, ' – had been gambling online for quite a long time. I explained to the others that the main problem was the number of players. You're more likely to die in a plane crash than win most lotteries, because there are too many punters participating. I said if we could just keep the number of players limited, we stood a chance of making some real money. So we tried out the game for a few weeks, just accumulating small sums. Matt – Matthew Hillingdon

– was the overall winner. But we realized that in order to make any decent amount of cash, everyone would have to put a lot more in the pot.'

'Who came in on the game?' asked May.

'There were the six of us at first, but Cassie dropped out because she didn't want anything more to do with Theo. He had started sleeping with Ruby.'

'That's not why she dropped out,' said Theo quietly. 'She couldn't raise her share of the stake.'

'So there were five players,' Bryant prompted.

'Yeah. We each put five grand in, but it still didn't seem like enough if we were going for one winner.'

'You were all broke, yet you managed to raise five thousand apiece,' said May. 'Obviously the definition of "broke" has changed a little since my day.'

'My dad's brother owns a chain of Greek restaurants,' said Nikos. 'He's a complete idiot. On the same day of every month he takes a suitcase containing around £65,000 to his bank in Paris, all cash. He goes on the Eurostar. So on Monday morning I set up a Flash Mob in St Pancras Station to create a diversion, and while that was happening Theo robbed him.'

'It was like taking sweets from a very stupid child,' said Theo. 'He kept the bag attached to his wrist with plastic binders.' He held up his own wrists. 'I just cut them with kitchen scissors while he was standing there watching everyone dance.' He sniggered, looking to the others for approval.

'So then we had a decent stake to work with,' said Nicolau. 'Ninety grand in all. I wanted to find two more players to make it an even hundred, but Theo wouldn't let me. He really wanted to keep his odds of winning high.'

'Yes, this image you perpetuate of the bored rich kid isn't quite accurate, is it?' said Bryant. 'You'd clocked up some serious gambling debts, your last business venture

– property, wasn't it? – had failed spectacularly, your car was repossessed – not stolen – and your family had cut you off without a penny.'

'You have no idea,' said Theo. 'I'd surrendered my savings, I sold my watch, my pen, everything I owned, and replaced them with fakes. You have to keep up appearances, after all. Some guys in Shoreditch were going to come round and break my arms if I didn't pay them by the end of the week.'

'Tell us what happened next.'

'Well, now that we'd raised a decent stake, we started playing in earnest,' said Nicolau. 'Toby had been the previous week's winner – five players, five days of the week we drew straws to see who would get which day.'

'And it was my turn to play again on Monday,' said Theo.

'How long had you been playing?'

'This was week three. It's an elimination game. We decided that each player should have three lives. If you were knocked out three times, you'd lose your stake and be out of the game. And I had two strikes against me. The winner of each week got what we called living expenses, until the final overall winner was decided.'

'Of course, Toby had to flash his cash about,' Sangeeta complained.

'I think at this point you should tell us what the game involved,' said Bryant, striding about with his thumbs in his waistcoat like an old-time prosecutor. The image would have been more appealing if the waistcoat had not been held together with safety pins.

'We wanted to come up with something that wasn't just based on luck,' said Nicolau. 'We thought it should require some skill, bravado even. I was talking to a guy who worked for London Underground, and he told me about a game he'd heard of, a gambling dare you could play on the Tube. You pick a stranger, text the amount of your placed bet, then follow the stranger on their journey, and whatever they do scores you points.' Nicolau was warming to his subject, forgetful of the fact that the game had ended in a series of brutal murders.

'I laid down the ground rules. First, you send a photograph of the line you're going to play on – we'd taken shots of the seat livery in all the different carriages – then you photograph your mark – the person you've picked to bet on. To make sure there's no switching, you also put a sticker on their back to tag them in your pictures. Then you film the different things they do, like reading a book or listening to an iPod – all of the activities score points – and you send the results to the next player's mobile to verify them. Then you score more points for how many stops they travel, and if they get off at the station you've pre-designated, you win that day's pot.'

'We weren't allowed to talk to outsiders about the game,' said Toby, his head in his hands. 'I had to borrow the stake money from my uncle. I don't know why I got involved.'

'And with the aid of the robbery, you were able to up the ante,' said Bryant.

'It wasn't a robbery.' Theo was utterly dismissive of the idea. 'It was taking money away from a total creep who would have only spent the profits from his shitty little restaurants on gold bath taps and plasma screens for his stupid villa in Cyprus. And it was my turn to play. I went to Bond Street Tube and saw this woman in a bright-red polka dot dress, and knew at once that I'd be able to track her through the system without losing her, because she looked different to everyone else. Man, it was a total winning streak – everything I suggested she would do, she did. I sent the photos and texts to Matt's phone – he was going to be the next player – and told him that I staked her destination as King's Cross. I'm good at reading people. I was sure she would get off there, and she did. I followed her up the escalator to the ticket barrier, and just as she got to it, the bitch turned around and went back down.

'Well, in that one second I lost everything. Three strikes, I crashed out of the game, all because she wouldn't take another two paces through the barrier. I don't know what happened – I think I just nudged her in anger, I couldn't control myself – and I was amazed to see her fall down the stairs. She was wearing these really high heels. So I just carried on past as if I hadn't seen, as if it was nothing to do with me, and caught the first train that came in. I was in a suit and tie. Nobody looked twice at me.'

'Jesus, Theo.' Rajan and Toby were staring at him in horror. Ruby, nursing her broken finger in the corner, remained sullen and silent.

'You don't understand how frustrating it was,' Theo told them. 'It was kind of an accident.'

'Not if you pushed her!'

'Yeah, but I didn't mean her to die.'

'Let's move on,' coaxed Bryant. 'What happened after that?'

'I thought no one would find out, but when I got home I realized I'd sent all my photos to Matt. That woman was all over his phone. I had some time, though, because the story didn't get picked up and none of the others knew what had happened. I saw a way that I could still come out on top. Matt came upstairs and told me he had seen the pictures on his phone, so he knew I had been eliminated from the game. I made light of it, bluffed it out – I'm a very good poker player.'

'Yeah, he only lies when he opens his mouth,' muttered Ruby.

'On Tuesday night, I took Matt out for a drink with the intention of getting him hammered, although he was already half-cut when he turned up. We hit a bar in Spitalfields – there are so many around there and they're all so crowded that I knew no one would remember seeing us. I'd taken his asthma spray and switched it with one filled with tobacco tea. Then I gave him the spray and waited for him to get sick, but it took longer than I'd expected. Earlier that day I went around the Tube station and checked the cameras, and I could see that a couple were out, but I figured it would be more luck than judgement if I got away with it, because I wouldn't know exactly where he'd collapse. The most useful thing was that Matt trusted me.'

My God, thought May, looking into Fontvieille's dead eyes, *he really sees nothing morally wrong with what he's done.*

Theo was anxious to explain, and appeared to be enjoying himself. 'It was all pretty simple stuff. I switched coats with him, then he started to pass out behind one of those great big caged fans they've placed in the tunnel entrance. I was pretty sure it was a blind spot and the cameras couldn't pick him up. And I'd been careful to keep my distance from him ever since we'd left Liverpool Street. I even sat on the escalators while he stood, so I wouldn't be seen. I heard the train approaching, so I left Matt and ran for it. I'm only an inch taller, and in Matt's hat and rainbow coat I figured I'd look like him from behind. I jumped on to the train but shut the coat in the door – I hadn't realized how long it was – but when the doors opened I had a better idea. I went to the other end of the carriage, got off and headed for the last Northern Line train.'

'You'd prepared a lot more than that, though, hadn't you?' Bryant suggested.

'Yeah, I'd taken Matt's travel card – we used regular tickets 'cause they can't be traced – and I left it in Toby's room. And I wrote Ruby's name in his library books, just to confuse things further. But the best part went wrong. Before I met up with Matt, I drove to the Buddha Bar with Cassie and made a big deal about leaving the Porsche outside. Everyone remembers that car because of the personalized numberplate. I wore my red scarf and made sure they all noticed me. I figured I'd go out, meet up with Matt and come back at the end of the evening, and everyone would be so wasted they'd tell anyone who asked that I'd been there all night. Only as I got out of the car, I locked my bloody keys inside it.

'Then I remembered an old trick. If you lock your keys in your car and you've got spare keys at home, all you have to do is call someone on their mobile from your mobile. You hold your phone about a foot from your car door and have the other person press the 'unlock' button on the spare keys, and it opens your door. So I called the house and Ruby answered the phone. I was kind of in a panic and I think she sensed that. Didn't you, Ruby?'

'Don't involve me, you scumbag,' she warned. 'Everything you said, everything you ever told me was a lie.'

'Hey, it's what I do.' Theo grinned at her. Incredibly, it seemed he was comfortable making jokes.

'Go on,' said May.

'I asked Ruby to help me unlock the car, and knew I'd compromised my alibi. So I thought to hell with it, and I asked her to say she saw me come home earlier than I did. I knew she was nuts about me, so I was kind of in the clear. I got to the bar to meet Matt – he'd already had a massive head-start drinking with some old mates from Nottingham, but he still wasn't drunk when we left. I had to wait a few minutes for the booze to kick in. I got him out of breath at King's Cross and persuaded him to use the spray, went back to collect the car and then headed home. I had the evidence from Matt's mobile, and no one would ever suspect a thing. Plus, it looked like the money would default to me, because the game was to be stopped if the next player couldn't take their turn. In this case, the next player had died – or at least, gone missing – I hadn't expected him to crawl off like that. There were two small problems I needed to deal with, though, because you guys were starting to sniff around the house.

'First, Nikos was still holding the cash, and I knew it would be found if the house was searched. So he came up with a good idea – he went to some jeweller's in Hatton Garden and used the money to buy a ring. You know what Jews are like, they see wads of money and don't ask questions.' He smiled ingratiatingly at everyone, making Longbright's skin crawl. 'And to keep Ruby sweet, I told her she could wear it – to prove how sincere I was, you know?

'Everything had fallen back into place. I mean, obviously we couldn't play on with you watching us, so the game was declared over. The others were angry, but like I said, we'd put a clause in the rulebook saying that in the event of a *force majeure* the last high score would take the pot. I could claim the ring and pay off my debts.'

'But they had no proof that you were the winner,' said May.

'Yeah they did, because I had the photos on my phone. I just said I didn't know where Matt had gone. I kind of implied he'd found out about me and Ruby, and had stormed off. But Ruby didn't believe me. And then Cassie figured it out.' Theo shook his head, irritated by the thought. 'Because you went to see her about the damned stickers. She knew one had been placed on the back of a woman who'd died on the Tube – you told her. And she told me she knew I was involved. That girl – it was one of the reasons we broke up – she could always see right through me. I asked her what she was going to do about it, and she said she didn't know. She wanted to talk to an old friend of hers, a lawyer. I knew then that she had to be removed. I followed her to Greenwich – I was still wearing Matt's coat because I'd put my black leather Marc Jacobs original on him and I didn't want to get my clothes dirty – but I didn't find a chance to get her alone. I kept trying to think of a way to kill her, but it was really difficult coming up with something good, you know?'

'You managed it, though.'

'Oh, yeah. I stayed outside the flat, watching as the pair of them got drunk, but I couldn't tell whether Cassie had told her about me. I couldn't see properly from outside. I wasn't about to kill the friend as well – I mean, where would it have stopped? But then Cassie went back to Westcombe Park Station, and there was nobody on the platform. It was too good an opportunity to waste. By this time, I could tell that your investigation was falling apart, because it was so easy to provide a vague alibi.'

'So you pushed her on to the line.'

'Well, I'd managed to kill a complete stranger just by nudging her, so I figured it should work again. I couldn't think how to guarantee that she'd fall, but then I saw the steel frame of the waiting-room door, and it was just like going to the gym.'

'And you implicated Miss Cates by leaving behind a piece of her plastic cast.'

'I thought that was a nice touch, yeah? I came up with lots of cool little touches like that, but I don't suppose anyone even noticed. I had to deflect attention away from myself, obviously. The last thing I had to do was get the diamond ring back from Ruby – it had seemed like a good idea to have her look after it. But then the little bitch did a runner and pretended she couldn't get it off her finger.'

'Who told you about the game?' Bryant asked Nikos.

'I was talking to some guard at King's Cross,' said Nicolau, 'and he told me about it.'

Bryant shot his partner a meaningful look, as if to say *I suspected as much.*

As the students started arguing with Fontvieille, John May turned to his partner. 'All right, I give up. How did you get to him? What made you sure it was Theo?'

Bryant looked over at Fraternity DuCaine and grinned. 'Once we realized it was a game, the rest was easy. You see, it was a cheat.'

'What do you mean?'

'Fraternity and I looked at the players, then took a guess at the type of game they were playing. We saw at once that if it was something that required social skills, then the game was rigged. I mean, look at them. Ruby hobbling about with a plaster cast. Toby, a borderline stalker and a hopeless closet case, which was why he spotted Jack Renfield following him—'

'You mean he thought I was trying to pick him up?' said Renfield, utterly horrified.

'That's why he was so cagey about where he went at night,' said Bryant. 'So, Ruby was incapacitated, Toby was crippled with shyness, Rajan was downright unpleasant – forgive me, Mr Sangeeta, but you do lack social skills – and Nikos was simply unprepossessing. There was only one person in the group who strangers would truly be comfortable next to.'

'Are you telling me that was all you had to go on?'

'It made sense. Mr Fontvieille here kept on about his wealth, but it didn't ring true. Look at him – he looks like he hasn't slept for a month. So I ran a check on his car and found it had been repossessed, not stolen. We called his parents and heard about his history of getting into debt. And we checked the security footage at Bond Street Tube. Lo and behold, here was Theo, following Gloria

Taylor down into the station. Once we had the basic idea, it only took minutes to sort out what had happened. We followed the joker in the pack. Then, when we saw the station besieged by fans of Mr Nicolau's website, I enlisted Dan's help.'

'What do you mean?' asked May, puzzled.

'Well, I needed to protect our staff, didn't I? We had two murderers both on the move in a tight, crowded space, so I asked if he could use the same technology to help us.'

'I downloaded one of Mr Bryant's databases and sent an urgent text to everyone on it. We thought they'd be in the area,' said Banbury.

'What was it?'

'Friends of the British Library. They're running a series of events just down the road.'

'Textiles and tapestries of the Middle Ages,' added Bryant.

'You mean Mr Fox was stopped by ladies from a *knitting club*?' said Renfield.

'They're tough old birds,' said Bryant, patting his pockets. 'I wouldn't want to mess with them. Well, I think it's time for a pipe. Can I leave you to finish up here? If anyone needs me, I shall be out on my verandah, contemplating the evils of the world.'

'All right, you lot,' shouted Raymond Land, holding up his hands. 'Let's have some peace and quiet. You might want to start thinking about your statements.' He wagged his finger at Fontvieille, who appeared suddenly exhausted. 'You're not so clever now, are you, sonny? You obviously reckoned without the sheer professionalism of a crack investigation unit.'

Land took a step back and vanished down the hole in the floor.

50

THE WAY AHEAD

The detectives were standing in the only magic shop actually situated in the London Underground system. Davenport's Magic emporium had existed for decades opposite the British Museum, but had now moved to one of the dead-end tunnels beneath Charing Cross Station. Few commuters knew of its existence – why would they? – but its crimson curtains hid a world of misdirection, deception and amazement.

Realizing that card tricks were not his forte, Arthur Bryant was shopping for something bigger.

'What are you looking for?' asked May.

'I'm not sure,' Bryant replied, looking around. 'Perhaps I could saw a girl in half, produce doves from unfeasible places or explode my landlady.' Alma was hosting a charity lunch for the women from her church, and he was keen to provide her with a magic act, whether she wanted one or not.

Daphne, formerly Radiant Lotus Blossom, assistant to the Immortal Mysterioso (available for weddings, bar mitzvahs and children's parties) came over to demonstrate an illusion. 'How are you with rabbits, Mr Bryant?' she asked. 'I had to give up the old act because I put on a bit of weight and got stuck in the cabinet of swords a few times,' she confided, dropping a French Chinchilla into a glittery tube and running a sabre through it. 'You can do this with a small child, providing they're not easily moved to tears.'

'I don't think he should practise on anything living,' said May. 'They might not stay living for long.'

'And then of course the Immortal Mysterioso turned out not to be immortal after all. Bowel cancer. So I put away my spangly tights and came to work here.' Daphne held up the gold canister to prove that nothing had actually penetrated the rabbit. 'It works on cats, too. Especially if you don't like them. Could I interest you in X-ray goggles?' She pulled out what appeared to be a diving helmet with rotating spirals over the eye-holes. 'Very popular for mind-reading acts.'

'You always accuse me of being a bad judge of character,' said Bryant, poking May in the ribs, 'but Theo Fontvieille bothered me from the moment I met him. He was too gaunt, too energetic. He made light of everything, acting as if nothing in the world ever touched him, but behind the banter there was a terrified child, screaming in the dark.'

'That's true. The first time I laid eyes on him he left me feeling uneasy,' May agreed. 'But he kept his nerve, bluffed his way through and almost got away with it.'

Bryant shook his head sadly. 'I thought I'd finished my learning, but apparently not. Human nature is like an iceberg, mostly hidden from view. Imagine the terror of waking up every morning and remembering who you are, wondering how on earth you're going to get through the day.'

'You could say that of Mr Fox,' added May. 'Or even of Mac. All of them were haunted.'

'Well, those two were damaged by irreversible childhood traumas, but Theo – he's the most interesting. I honestly think he suffers more than any of them. Every time he wakes, he realizes afresh that he has no soul, nothing inside that really cares for anyone or anything. You meet people like him all the time, the desperate players trying to cut one final deal that will make them rich and allow them to keep their kids in private schools.'

'Perhaps I could just intervene?' said Daphne, trying to break up what sounded to her like a very depressing conversation. 'We've got something new in involving a blowlamp and half a dozen squirrels that will make your eyes stand out like chapel hat-pegs.' She ran its instructions seductively up her arm.

'Self-preservation is a very strong instinct,' said May. 'He was quite happy to murder his friends if it meant he would survive. It's almost as if he thought they wouldn't mind giving up their lives for his.'

'That's just arrogance,' Bryant replied. 'He honestly thinks he's worth more than the others. But at night the truth must surely rise to the surface and terrify him.'

'Put your finger in here,' urged Daphne with a faint air of desperation. It had been a slow morning. Bryant did so distractedly, and she slammed down the guillotine on two carrots and the detective's digit.

'I'm not so sure Theo has quite that level of self-awareness. He's the kind of man who'll go to jail and write endless newspaper articles about the experience afterwards. I wonder if that's better – choosing never to wake from the dream.'

'Life is all a dream,' said Bryant, smiling gently. 'A wonderful, wonderful dream. The object is to make everyone else who shares it with you as happy as possible.'

'An admirable sentiment,' May agreed, smiling back at his old friend. 'Come on, the weather's supposed to clear up this afternoon. Let's get out into the sunshine while we can.' He turned back to the disappointed magic assistant. 'Thanks for the demonstration, Daphne. I think my colleague is going to try a different act. Perhaps he'll take up tap dancing.'

They left the magic shop arm in arm, laughing.

The Watercolourist

Beatrice Masini

The Watercolourist

MANTLE

First published 2016 by Mantle
an imprint of Pan Macmillan
20 New Wharf Road, London N1 9RR
Associated companies throughout the world
www.panmacmillan.com

ISBN 978-1-4472-5770-7

Copyright © Beatrice Masini 2013
Translation copyright © Clarissa Ghelli and Oonagh Stransky 2016

Originally published in Italian 2013 as *Tentativi di botanica degli affetti* by Bompiani, Milan, Italy

The right of Beatrice Masini to be identified as the
author of this work has been asserted by her in accordance
with the Copyright, Designs and Patents Act 1988.

1 3 5 7 9 8 6 4 2

A CIP catalogue record for this book is available from the British Library.

Printed and bound by CPI Group (UK) Ltd, Croydon, CR0 4YY

The Watercolourist

She doesn't know. She doesn't know if this is love, this rubbing of fabric against fabric, this warm and rugged fumbling. Fingers. Fingers everywhere. Hands touching places no stranger's hand has ever been. A strained gasp. To want and not to want. Here, this, where, what, why. And now the pain: piercing, tearing, leaving her breathless; unceasing, insistent, like pain without compassion, a rasping of flesh inside flesh. *No, not like that, no.* But words are useless. Nothing changes.

Her other self, silent and composed, watches from afar. Her eyes are pools of pity. *Why pity? What if this is actually what it is like? What if it is supposed to be like this?* She doesn't know any more.

She continues to listen to the agony stampeding inside her, nailing her to the wall, snatching from her very throat a sound that doesn't belong to her. It isn't her voice; it is neither laughter nor lament. It is a horrible sound, the sound of a wild beast suffering, nothing more. *How long will it go on? Will it ever stop?*

And later, when it is finally over, the question lingers: is this love?

Six years later

There is a queue in front of Santa Caterina. She arrives in a rush and out of breath, tripping over her own feet, now and then turning around to look behind her. She stops and hides behind a pillar. She is not alone.

In front of her, a short, thickset fellow takes a quiet and unmoving bundle out from under his cloak and, without hesitating, places it inside the wooden pass-through in one smooth and careful movement. As if he has done it before. He doesn't linger but turns around and walks away, the hem of his cloak flapping at his back. Like smoke vanishing into the darkness.

Next is a woman who wears no bonnet. The dim light of the street lamp is bright enough to illuminate her face as she places her tiny, shaking, angry bundle in the sliding drawer. It is not a cry that emerges; it is a wail, a bleating. The woman hesitates, leans forward towards the infant and is herself almost swallowed up by the drawer. Her shoulders shake. She straightens up, turns around and walks off, bareheaded, poor, in tears. She is likely a seamstress, mending hems. She is very young, almost a girl. Not a maid, though. It must have been her first time but it probably won't be her last.

It is her turn now. She herself has nothing to entrust to the city's custody, nothing from which to free herself with anger, relief or sorrow. She knocks on the wooden door and waits. The door swings open and a large, ample woman comes out, wiping her hands on her apron. As it closes behind her, she leans against the doorway.

'You got the money?' she asks, without preamble.

The girl nods. She holds out a pouch, trying in vain to meet the woman's gaze.

'So, is she all right?'

'She's fine, fine.'

The woman snatches the pouch, her eyes downcast, and slips it into her open, damp blouse, her large breasts drooping like the ears of a dog. She spits on the ground like a man.

'She's healthy. She's fine. The supervisor went to see her last month. It's just that the woman died.'

'Oh.' The girl holds her breath. 'Now what?'

'Now nothing. She's been moved to another family. But don't worry, she's fine.'

'Is she big? Is she well behaved?'

She knows it is silly to ask such questions. This spitting, milk-oozing woman doesn't know a thing. She won't know if her little girl's skin has been ravaged by smallpox or if she has escaped the outbreaks entirely; if she has started drawing her first letters or if there is no one there to teach them to her. It is a miracle in itself that the woman is able to tell her that her daughter is still alive. And she knows that this, too, could be a lie.

The fat woman grows impatient.

'I have to go. I got seven new ones last night. Plus the ones from today. Three have died already. It's better that way, though, because I've got almost no milk left. I would have had to start feeding them cow's milk, and they would have died anyway. Cow's milk isn't good for little ones.'

The girl pretends not to hear the woman.

'I'll come again when I can. How is your child?' she adds politely.

'Ha! I've sent mine off to the countryside. Just like yours.' The fat woman laughs a horrible laugh, turns, opens the door and disappears back inside.

Alone now, the girl looks up at the moon without seeing it. Lowering her gaze, she sighs, adjusts her bonnet, and leaves. She doesn't cry. She stopped crying long ago. But her grief and doubt are an obsession and the woman's few words have done nothing to soothe them.

Part One

꧁ ꧂

Inside the carriage there is the overwhelming smell of sweet vinegar, perspiration and possibility. Bianca looks out of the dirty window and sees the sprawl of Bergamo: its trees, walls and towers, red mixed with green, green mixed with red. Then a new scent, an earthy one. Probably from those low trees with slender trunks, thick foliage and supple thorns that claw at the sides of the carriage as they pass by. Springtime. The best season for travelling, except when rain transforms the roads into swamps. Bianca is lucky, though: hers isn't a very long journey. One night at an inn isn't enough to call it an adventure. She knows where she is going. There is no mystery involved.

All that brilliant green seems to force itself in through the window. The old woman travelling alongside her, enveloped in a cloud of camphor, starts muttering.

'What is there to see? It's just the countryside. Personally, I don't like the countryside. I prefer the city.'

The fragrance of camphor, mixed with the lady's bodily odours, which are intensified by the unseasonable heaviness of her black garments, grows stronger with every gesture and suffocates the smells of nature, ruining them. Bianca opens the window in search of fresh air and breathes in only dust. She coughs.

The old woman ties the ribbon of her hat under her chin. She keeps mumbling to herself, but Bianca has learned not to pay her any attention. She wishes she could push her out of the carriage door and leave her there, on the ground, enveloped by

7

her own vile odour, in the middle of the fields that she so detests. That way Bianca could continue the trip alone and enjoy the silence that is not quite silence: the rhythmic pounding of hooves, the creaking of the carriage, the calling voices of peasants outside, the fleeting sound of women singing, a concerto of birds. As she travels, she becomes someone else, not the person she has always been. Not even the one *they* are expecting. She is in limbo. She always felt this way when she and her father journeyed together, too. Only their bond defined who they were. But now everything is different.

She looks down and picks a leaf off the sleeve of her turtle-dove-coloured dress. Bianca's path has been decided. A powerful magnet pulls the carriage towards the halfway mark of their journey. Some call it destiny, others duty. And even though she knows that dresses for travelling ought to be dark in order to hide the dirt, she has chosen a light one so that every trace of change will be evident. This is her last adventure. Once she arrives at her final destination, she will be who they want her to be, or who they *expect* her to be.

Maybe.

❧ ❧

The master, Don Titta, isn't there when she arrives at Brusuglio in the evening. He isn't in the living room with the rest of them, in any case. His three daughters sit on the sofa, all dressed in white, their dresses flouncing, their tiny black feet hanging down like musical notes. Donna Clara, the older lady of the house, is dressed in black from head to toe and, with her marble eyes, looks like a large insect in her shiny satin. Her beauty hangs stubbornly from her cheekbones. The younger lady of the house, Donna Julie, Don Titta's wife, is dressed in white. She smiles kindly, though somewhat vaguely, on account of her guest. Lastly, there are two almost identical boys who come and go endlessly.

The living room is pale green and filled with the light of dusk. It seems cool to Bianca after her long, sticky journey. She feels dirty, dusty and out of place. And so she simply gives a slight bow, which to some may appear rude, but the younger lady understands.

'I will have Armida attend to you at once,' she says with a hint of a French accent. 'Go upstairs now. You must be exhausted. We will have time together tomorrow.'

Bianca climbs the stairs and goes down a long tiled and carpeted corridor. She is shown to her bedroom. It isn't very spacious but it is charming, with a white and gold sleigh bed. There is even an unexpected luxury: a bathroom entirely for herself. Armida, a giant of a woman with a solemn but gentle face, has already run her bath.

Bianca tests the water with her fingers. She hasn't even taken off her bonnet and is already imagining herself submerged.

'Is it too cold? I'll bring you a pot of boiling water.'

The woman is halfway down the hall when Bianca stops her.

'No, thank you. It will be fine.'

Armida comes back with the quick step of an experienced domestic servant.

'Then let me help you.'

Bianca draws back, embarrassed.

'I can manage on my own.'

Armida smiles, bows deeply, and then walks back towards the staircase.

Finally Bianca is alone. She frees herself of her travelling dress. She kicks off her undergarments, now grey with dust.

She takes a million bobby pins out of her hair, steps into the bath and crouches down, her knees to her chest, enjoying the sweet feeling of her breasts against her bones. Then she relaxes and settles back. Water seeps into her ears, cancelling out all noises except for the deep, low sound hidden inside seashells. Bianca has only ever seen the sea at night: twice – once coming in and once going out. It was a yawning nothingness, ferocious, black, cloaked in fog and frightening. But she still likes water more than anything.

She resurfaces and leans out, dripping wet, for a vase of peach-rose bath salts. She sniffs the pungent scent of artificial flowers and then hears the children playing outside. The boys are running, kicking up gravel, and arguing over something precious. Their accent is almost foreign: soft and harsh at the same time. She doesn't like it.

She emerges from the bath, enjoying the shivers that run down her clean body. She takes a dry linen towel, wraps it around herself, and goes back into her bedroom. A tray has been positioned on a little table with crooked legs. There is some milk, two white rolls, a cold chicken wing and three plums. She sits on the soft carpet and dines, clean and half naked, like a goddess, the wind billowing the curtains as if they are the sails of a ship at sea.

❧ ❧

She meets Don Titta for the first time two days after she has arrived, in the afternoon. Before this, she has been uncertain what to do with her time.

'For that, you need to speak to him. He's the one who summoned you here, isn't he?' Donna Clara remarked drily, giving Bianca the impression that she disapproved of the entire project.

So Bianca takes walks in the park, intent on measuring the extent of its wilderness and discovering where it turns into moorland, which she has heard can be somewhat dangerous.

'There are wild dogs out there,' the housemaid warned as she brushed, or rather pulled at, her hair.

Bianca, fighting the urge to cry out in pain, imagined the moorland filled with extraordinary creatures like shaggy, ferocious bears. In reality, the only creatures that cannot be ignored are birds. Thrushes, skylarks, blackcaps and thousands of other tiny unidentified creatures fill the sky with their baroque songs.

As she bends down to examine an unknown flower, focusing on the pale green-veined striations on the white petals, she doesn't notice him approaching. At the sound of snapping branches she turns around sharply and freezes. She doesn't know what to do next.

To say that they have met then, though, is an exaggeration: she has simply seen him. He doesn't even notice her. He continues striding on, at a rapid pace. He looks like a giant: tall, thin, bony – sickly even. His head is bare, he wears no frock coat; he looks more like a villain than a gentleman. His shirt is not even fully tucked into his trousers. His clothes cling to his body with the same sweat that drenches his hair, making it appear darker than it probably is. He walks briskly, his arms swinging wide and his hands spread. He mumbles to himself. A poem, Bianca thinks. Perhaps this is how he composes them: he wanders through the woods and allows himself to become transfixed by divinity. Maybe it's even in Latin.

'So you saw him?' Armida asks the next day, in the matter-of-fact way of the domestic help, who see and know everything, as she brushes her hair, pulling a little less this time. 'He roams around like a vagabond, talking to himself. He calls out plant names. Blah blah blah here and blah blah blah there. He does it for hours on end. Gentlemen are truly strange.'

He isn't present for lunch.

'My son has gone to Milan to attend to urgent business,' explains Donna Clara, before starting her soup. 'Be sure to make yourself available when he's ready to speak to you.'

Bianca would have enjoyed chatting with Donna Julie, but after just two spoonfuls of soup, the younger lady pushes herself away from the table and rises.

'I have to attend to little Enrico,' she says apologetically. 'He's got a fever again.'

And just like that she disappears up the staircase, followed by a maid carrying a tray of treats for the ill child. The little girls come in from the nursery in single file in search of their mother, awaiting their after-lunch ritual: a sweet and a kiss. But she is gone. So they stand there like lost ducklings. Their governess hurries them away, paying no attention to the youngest one's shrill screech.

Bianca still confuses the girls' names. Even though there are only three of them, they all look alike. Pietro, on the other hand, sits at the table with the adults. His eyelids are heavy; he has prominent dark brown eyes. They are almost black, opaque and unreadable.

'Does the little red pony belong to you?' Bianca asks now, trying to make conversation with him. 'What's his name?'

But he just looks down at his plate in silence.

Bianca spends the rest of the day reorganizing her clothes, going back and forth to the laundry, and freshening the items that need to be aired out, which is pretty much all of them.

When she comes down that evening, the only person at the dinner table is Donna Clara. She gives no explanation for the absence of the others and limits herself to glaring at Bianca impatiently. The cook serves stewed quail. Donna Clara throws herself at the frail little bodies rapaciously, sucking on the bones and drawing out the tender, dark meat. Bianca hates game. It is meat that was once so alive and is now sentenced to rot. She eats two slices of white bread then peaches with lemon juice for dessert.

'You're a delicate little thing,' observes the elderly lady, licking her lips.

※ ※

The next day, Bianca sees the master of the house approaching from afar and gives a hint of a curtsey. She is worried that she is wasting both her time and his being here. With her standing there, in his way, he has no choice this time but to look at her, the pale thing that she is. But instead of stopping, he walks on. He isn't any more composed than on the first day she saw him. Again, he is mumbling his strange botanical rosary. She watches him grab hold of a large buzzing insect with a swift movement of his right hand and hears as he squashes it between his index finger and thumb. And then he is gone, his mumbling and rustling footsteps gradually receding. She imagines the bug's cartilage cracking and squirting its thick and greasy fluid onto his fingers as if they are her own.

※ ※

Enrico recovers and goes back to bickering with Pietro. The two boys are very similar, with Enrico being the more timid. He always has a sullen look, as though expecting defeat. Instinctively, Bianca prefers him. She watches him chase after

Pietro, who has taken possession of the pony and cart and is now flogging the animal mercilessly. The pony runs and runs, as though fleeing from the pain, kicking up wings of gravel down the driveway. When Enrico realizes that he is never going to be able to catch Pietro or the pony, he throws himself down on the grass in frustration. Bianca walks over to him, pretending to have seen nothing.

'What's the pony's name?' she asks.

'My brother says you're a foreigner and we don't like foreigners,' he replies defiantly.

'Listen to me. Do you hear what I am saying? I'm not a foreigner.'

'I'm not going to listen to you. You're a spy. You'll spy on me and then tell Mamma everything, even if it isn't true.'

'What could I possibly tell her? That I saw a little boy chewing on a blade of grass?'

'My brother is horrible,' Enrico continues bitterly. 'He always wins because he's bigger. When I get big . . . do you think I will grow up to be bigger than him?'

He finally looks up at her. In the light of day she sees that his eyes are greenish-grey.

'I think so, yes,' answers Bianca, looking him up and down. 'You may be smaller now, but if you eat lots and exercise, you'll end up taller than him, I'm sure.'

It could happen: Pietro has a fairly solid build with robust, sculpted legs but Enrico has the long, delicate bone structure of a foal.

'Then one day I'll beat him and get the pony back, since it belongs to both of us. That's what Papa said. But Pietro always keeps it to himself.'

'Do you want to tell me his name?'

'Furbo. I named him. Do you like it?'

'It's nice. It suits him.'

'Well, I'm leaving,' says the little boy, standing up and smoothing out the wrinkles in his trousers. He wanders off without saying goodbye. But after a few steps he turns around. 'I guess you might not be a spy.'

※ ※

Five days after her arrival and she has still yet to formally meet him. She doesn't know what to do any more. His mother keeps saying he is in Milan, but now and then he emerges from the woods and startles her, only to quickly disappear again. And so, Bianca decides simply to start working.

The little girls, all dressed in white cotton, are playing Ring-a-Ring o' Roses on the great lawn, their brown hair gleaming in the sunlight. She sets up her easel near the poplar tree, places a pad upon it, and opens the mahogany box that holds her pencils on one side and her charcoal sticks on the other. The sight has reminded her of a Romney painting she saw in England, on one of the stops along her reverse Grand Tour.

In that painting, three little girls and a boy, dressed in summer sandals and tunics, dance like tiny deities while an older sister plays on the drums, an annoyed look across her face. The older child is clearly from another marriage, while the four dancers are siblings. And undoubtedly this bothers the older girl tremendously.

'Lady Anne looks as though she'd rather be somewhere else,' Bianca said to her father, as they stood contemplating the painting in one of the sitting rooms of the estate, which was located in some idyllic corner of the English countryside that was itself a work of art.

'You are right,' he agreed, without lifting his eyes from the painting. 'One can only hope that she eventually married well.'

'What on earth do you mean?' Bianca cried.

'I'm only teasing,' her father said firmly. 'I only said it to see if you were listening. Although really, do you think that she had any other option?'

That memory is fading fast. She is here now, and the colours of this reality are different and fiercer than any painting. The whiteness of the little girls is almost too painful to look at against the full greens of the forest and meadow.

Donna Clara comes up behind her quietly, announcing her arrival by clearing her throat. Bianca is always startled by how thin she is. Once it might have been considered a virtue but now her figure seems almost comical. Bianca gives a slight curtsey without interrupting her pencil strokes.

When you are working, her father said, *never stop what you're doing just because someone tells you it's teatime.*

This echo lasts only a second; short but penetrating. And when she comes back to her senses, as if emerging from a trance, she readies herself to respond to a circumstantial comment with a circumstantial smile. Instead, Donna Clara just coughs.

'You're quite talented. My son has chosen well. He and his eccentricities . . .'

Bianca wipes her hands on a rag, pleased with the unexpected compliment.

Meanwhile, the girls have finished playing and come over to the easel, their tiny hands behind their backs. They look at the picture, curious but confused. Their governess apologizes quickly.

'They wanted to see your drawing, but . . .'

Of course they are disappointed. They expected to see clear representations of themselves. They shift their gaze from her to the piece of paper and back again, perplexed, waiting for an explanation or perhaps some kind of magic. They expect her to take a brush, dip it into her watercolours and fix everything.

'Those marks,' Donna Clara explains patiently to the girls, leaning forward a little, 'are the lines of your bodies. Miss Bianca has caught you in the moment. This is Giulietta, lifting her foot in the air. This is you, Matilde, and here is Frances-china, skipping. Your faces will come later. You aren't running away, but the moment is. Isn't that right?'

Bianca nods.

'All paintings start out like this – a sketch, a jumble of marks,' Bianca explains. 'Some stay sketches, others turn into finished paintings. Do you girls draw?'

'I can draw daisies,' says Giulietta, the eldest.

'One day we can try and draw together if you'd like,' Bianca hears herself say.

Donna Clara breaks up the group as if they are a brood of chicks.

'Shoo, shoo, leave Miss Bianca alone now and go back to your games. Oh, what good children,' she adds to Bianca as they run off. 'Angels from heaven, here to bless our lives.'

Bianca is surprised to hear such simple, affectionate words when just a moment earlier, in speaking to the children, she had used such a different tone. With newfound respect, Bianca watches as the elderly lady leaves.

※ ※

The following evening he joins them at dinner. At last. He looks elegant, dressed in a light grey waistcoat. His face, in the candlelight, is no longer ghostlike. Actually, he looks like a truly healthy man who spends much of his time outdoors. He extends his hand to her in a modern half-bow. The children sit very still, delighted by their father's presence, and keep shooting him reverential glances. Donna Clara stares at her son feverishly, as if to keep him from disappearing again, turning away only to oversee the servants. Even Donna Julie seems more serene than usual and for once she stays at the table from the beginning to the end of the meal, without running off to take care of someone. Her charges are all present. She has fair skin, a braided bun of thick brown hair, and a long, delicate neck. Every so often she rests her elbow on the tablecloth in a childish, coy manner, before resuming her composed posture again as if it were a bad habit.

They have potato and leek soup, cold chicken in aspic, and a medley of shredded carrots and courgettes, all of which are truly pleasing to the eye. The meal ends with a blancmange with wild strawberry sauce. It is a meal for convalescents. Or for kings. Or for convalescent kings.

'The children picked the strawberries. They got incredibly dirty but it made them happy doing it,' says the young mother, rolling her Rs in the French way with charm.

He eats voraciously in a silence that is more intimate than solemn. He stares straight ahead, absorbed in his own thoughts.

'I have been toying with the idea of letting the children have a small vegetable garden,' he says finally. 'Beyond the shed, by the well, so that it's easy for watering. It is important that the children have a garden.'

'But the season is almost over. What could you plant? And really, Titta, next to the well? I think it's dangerous.' Donna Clara speaks assertively, pressing her napkin to her lips. 'I think I'll have another helping of dessert,' she adds. Her empty plate disappears and a new portion of blancmange arrives instantly.

'Your mother is right,' says Donna Julie. 'The girls barely know how to swim yet. And they're so fragile.'

'I hope you're not worried that they might get too much sun.

At least they would look a little healthier. They're as pale as linen,' the master of the house says. 'And you, signorina, do you have freckles? I imagine you were raised in the English manner.'

Bianca, addressed for the first time, wipes her mouth delicately on her napkin while thinking of her reply.

'In the English manner? I wouldn't know. I'd say I was raised rather rigorously. My father always had clear opinions when it came to children. I learned to swim when I was three years old. Everyone knew how to swim at the lake. My brothers and I spent all our time outside, in every season. During the winter they would dress me like a boy in leggings and trousers, to keep me warm and comfortable.'

Donna Clara raises her eyebrows while swallowing her last pink and white spoonful of blancmange. She licks her lips as a cat would its whiskers.

'My mother didn't entirely agree with his approach,' Bianca adds, looking at the older lady. 'But then she gave up arguing.'

'Is your mother English as well?' Donna Clara asks, her plump hands resting at either side of her plate.

'No, she was Italian,' answers Bianca.

'Oh, I'm sorry.'

'We had an English tutor,' Bianca offers, to fill the silence.

Donna Clara glows with approval.

'Just like our own Innes! He's away now, taking the waters in the Venetian countryside. He took a break from us, so to speak.'

'Did your tutor take an interest in plants?' Don Titta asks her. 'Or did you start to botanize on your own?'

His eyes are animated and observant. His tone soft and worldly. It occurs to Bianca that the forest ghost she has previously encountered could have been his crazy twin brother. Their physical appearance is the only trait that connects them.

She pauses for a moment before answering, weighing that verb in her mind – *to botanize*. She likes it tremendously.

'I started out on my own, when and where I could,' she explains. 'I would ask the names of flowers and trees, and then compare the leaves with images in books, and learn the scientific nomenclature. I used to own a herbal encyclopaedia. I did the kinds of things that all children do. And then, a dear family friend helped me learn a great deal more.'

She lapses momentarily into silence, distracted by the recollection of afternoons spent at Conte Rizzardi's home, with that smell of dust, old paper and tanned leather, a smell that would forever remind her of her fondness for study. The large estate and its domesticated wonders lay outside; theory was separated from practice by just a pane of glass. There were countless volumes of books – she used to call them the diaries of flowers – and they were ready to spill their knowledge and complex terminology.

'The flowers are not shown in the manner in which they truly exist,' the count had explained. 'It is only a representation. There is always a slight margin of difference between the way the eye sees and the hand draws.'

She recalls the old man's patience, the way he'd take her by the hand out to the vegetable and flower garden to see the originals.

Don Titta's voice brings her back to reality.

'If you could come by my study tomorrow morning after ten, we can discuss the tasks I would like to entrust to you.'

He then pushes his chair aside and stands.

'Would you please excuse me,' he says, and leaves the room.

The two boys wait for him to disappear down the corridor before imitating him and running off in the opposite direction, towards the French window, which opens onto the darkness.

The girls and the women remain seated. The younger lady is surprisingly animated, her cheeks flushed.

Donna Clara observes, 'Julie, my dear, you look quite rosy this evening. Have you started to follow my very own wine treatment? A nice glass of Marsala after a meal will have you wanting more, to be sure. You should try it too, Miss Bianca,' she says, turning to Bianca. 'It won't do you any harm. I'll call for some.'

The maid appears with a tray, decanter and tiny glasses. The liquid looks like aged gold in the crystal. As it touches Bianca's lips, it releases a burst of sun and almonds. It is heavy, full-bodied.

Donna Julie raises her glass to look at it through the light.

'What a lovely colour. Like an ancient coin,' she says, but puts it down. 'I apologize, Mother, but I just can't tonight. I don't need it. I am so pleased that he's doing better that I don't need it to feel well.'

Donna Clara flashes a piercing glare in her direction, as if to quiet her. Then she looks down and, without waiting for the maid to do so, pours herself some more wine.

※ ※

Donna Clara advises that Minna will serve as Bianca's personal maid.

'She's too delicate for heavy labour and needs to learn a trade,' she says, holding the girl's arm and forcing her to bow clumsily in front of her, intimating that Minna can learn her trade at Bianca's expense as Bianca herself is young and probably doesn't know any better. And with that she leaves the room.

Minna is just a young girl. She has pink cheeks and dark brown hair, which she wears in a bun with a few loose curls.

Her mouth is sealed shut with shyness. Bianca tries to meet the child's gaze, but it is as if a dark force keeps her chin glued to her chest. Bianca pretends not to notice. She continues to organize her clothes, something she hates doing because it reminds her of their inadequacy. Minna approaches her timidly, aware of her duties as maid, and begins to help put away her freshly laundered undergarments. Someone knocks at the door. Minna hurries forward to open it.

'Oh, it's you!' she says, glowing with happiness.

'May I come in?'

The person at the door is another young girl whom Bianca has noticed before, out walking with the governess. She is older, taller, but must be twelve or thirteen at the most, with lively grey-green eyes and freckles on her cheeks.

'I'm Pia, signorina, here to serve you,' she says.

There is nothing really for her to do. However, Bianca soon realizes that she has only come up out of curiosity. Pia looks around the room, peeking into the half-closed wardrobe as if hoping to uncover a mystery. Then she looks over at Minna, who has shrunk into a corner.

'You're a lucky one, aren't you?' she says with unabashed envy, running over to hug her tightly. Minna lets herself be hugged without moving her arms or altering her expression. 'You deserve kisses! That's what you deserve.' Pia plants one on her cheek. 'There, there, what good are kisses if we don't give them?'

The little one continues to stare at the floor, without smiling. Pia, satisfied, curtseys, offers her respects, and then leaves.

What a strange household, Bianca thinks to herself, *where maids have such independence*, but the scene has cheered her up.

Minna, meanwhile, comes back to her senses, stands up straight, and gives a deep curtsey, holding up each side of her skirt as the little girls have been taught to do by their governess.

'I am Minna, my lady, here to serve you. What would you like me to do? Shall I brush your hair? Shall I organize your clothes? Shall I put your hairbrushes in order?'

Bianca smiles.

'For now, nothing. You're free to go. I need to get my things ready and I like doing that myself. I will expect you tomorrow morning at seven, at the door to the garden.'

Minna looks at her, disappointed.

'But . . .'

'Go downstairs now. I'm sure they will have something for you to do in the kitchen.'

Minna mumbles something then turns and walks away, no further bows or farewells – insulted.

🦋 🦋

Bianca's meeting couldn't have gone any better. He ushered her into his study; a room of modest size, lined with books. There was no pale green, antique-rose or peacock-blue wallpaper here, as in the rest of the house. Instead, there were several ox-blood leather straight-backed chairs. A sombre pattern of brown rhombuses lined the walls and a black crucifix hung above the empty fireplace. He sat behind a large desk. She took a seat in front of him. They talked. They talked about botany, classifications, colours and chemistry. Bianca noticed right away that he was knowledgeable, passionate and precise. He only spoke of things of which he was certain. She could tell he was progressive on account of his ideas and the way he spoke about implementing them.

'Some people here think I'm crazy. I'm the stereotype of a

city gentleman obsessed with foreign ideas and with domesticating nature. But we mustn't ever stop. We mustn't rest. The countryside hasn't changed for centuries, and yet progress affects it just as much as it affects all of us. And it is precisely for this reason that I feel it is my duty to experiment.' Then, as though he had been too solemn, he added with a furtive smile, 'It's also a lot of fun. It helps keep my mind on something. Otherwise, things get too stirred up in here.' He motioned towards his temple before brushing back a strand of hair from his forehead. His hands were elegant, she noticed: he had long fingers, delicate wrists, and manicured nails. 'I'm no theoretician, don't be fooled,' he said, trying to read Bianca's stare. 'But I know what soap and water are for, I know it is proper to wash and be clean.'

They shared a brief laugh, and then, somewhat more seriously, they passed on to more concrete topics of discussion: numbers, deadlines and her fee. They discussed everything that had been previously written out in black ink on white paper. There were still some wrinkles that needed smoothing out. He addressed each clause of their agreement carefully, as if he was worried he might offend her. She thought it might be disagreeable for him to discuss such topics with a woman. But she proceeded calmly and agreed a deal which, at least in premise, would be profitable for both parties. Except for one, rather important, detail.

'Sir, it's almost summer. This year the season is extraordinarily hot and it seems that the heat will last. You have called me here now yet you are hiring me for a task that will only be completed next spring. This means that I will need to be here for an entire year and possibly longer. Am I correct in my understanding?'

He gave a quick smile.

'Everything has been taken into consideration. The winter will offer you the perfect time to reflect and draw. When the family returns to Milan you can enjoy a bit of the city with us, if you like, as I hope you will, while we wait for the pleasant weather to return. I am keen for you to be able to experience these subjects in all their states: life, dying, death and resurrection. It's quite crucial to really understand what you will be portraying. Time is secondary. Don't you agree?'

'I see,' she said, nodding. She had never before been so far from the house she had grown up in for such a long period of time. But the place she had once called home no longer belonged to her.

He jotted down a sum on a piece of paper and handed it to her. The figure was so incredibly high that she could not refuse it. A year it would be.

And so she stood up and shook his hand. It was the right moment, before either of them was at a loss for words, before the silence between the two strangers became as deep as a well. Bianca didn't want to find herself in any complicated situations. All she wanted was to be at ease in the house. If she encountered Don Titta in the garden again, with his long beard and dirty shirt, she would once more pretend not to see him. She would imagine it was his restless twin, a harmless creature, a village madman. This estate was almost a village, was it not? She would ignore him, like everyone else did, either out of respect or because he was the lord of the house and a poet. And, Bianca thought as she left his study, everyone knows that poets are unlike ordinary men.

☙ ❧

'It's a simple task. You're smart and you'll do it well. Of course, there's the chance that you might get bored with the environment and the people. It's a test of patience for you. A form of discipline. It will do you good. Accept the offer.'

Bianca is thinking back to her final conversation with her father, many months prior, after she received the letter. It was a long yet concise missive; the penmanship was pointed and oblique, the paper ruled and heavy. There was a wax seal on the verso of the envelope, which she kept touching with the tip of her finger.

'Why me, Father?' she asked him.

'Because there's no one like you. Not here. Because you're unique, darling.'

'But to be so far away for so long . . .'

'It was bound to happen sooner or later. It's what you've chosen to do. You didn't think you'd be here your whole life, did you? I didn't raise you that way. You are perfectly able to take care of yourself. You have seen some of the world. My only concern is that you might bury yourself in the countryside. Personally, I would prefer that you went to the city. But on the other hand, you need to be where your subjects are. Follow them. This is an important commission. It could mark the beginning of a career . . .'

She did as he bade. She was already buried in the countryside after all; the difference would be the company.

The letter proposed a commissioned project in a tone that Bianca couldn't define. It was both serious and vague. Or perhaps it was just the unfamiliar nature of the idea itself and what it implied that confused her. The sender of the letter had seen and appreciated some of her watercolours of landscapes and botanical subjects, it seemed – the ones she had sold on the insistence of her neighbour and long-time friend Count Rizzardi to an illustrious guest.

The intended project was to depict every flower and plant on a specific estate in Lombardy.

'I would like to bequeath to posterity not only my compositions in verse and prose, as is my craft, but also my flowers and my plants, which are no less significant to me. I am inclined to spend much of my time with them and desire to capture their perfection in order to have them forever with me, even in winter, even if they might never flower or bloom again. A large part of my culture is experiment, chance, failed attempts. As an amateur, the pleasure is as great as the risk.'

He's a gambler, Bianca thought. She liked the idea. She wrote back herself. Perhaps the sender was expecting a letter from her father; at the time she was no more than eighteen years old. But the letter was addressed to her, was it not? Don Titta was clearly a man of liberal ideals with a modern point of view. He was widely seen as a worldly man too. But it was also known that he had chosen a sober and secluded existence for himself.

'You will live within our family,' he specified in the letter. 'Ours is a simple life, far from everyday distractions.'

'Sounds like an interesting fellow,' her father added. 'It seems as though he understands what he needs and despite his profession has managed to free himself from the lures of fame. It's admirable, I'd say. See it as a great adventure, Bianca. And I will be here, waiting for you, if you don't take a different path along the way. Though, of course, I will be happy either way.'

'What other paths?' she protested. 'The only right path is the one that will bring me back here.'

'Anything can happen,' he said solemnly.

And like that, they made up their minds.

※ ※

Anything can happen.

His disease arrived swiftly. They had been out on one of their favourite walks, at La Rocca. As always, the lake looked different from so high up. She wished she could fly over it and see their little white house, the details of their garden, and the winding, rocky path that disappeared into the shadows of the parkland.

'Look at the lake, Papa,' she had said. 'It looks like it's made of turquoise.'

She turned back and saw him bent over, speechless with pain, deathly pale. Bianca knelt down beside him, overcome with fear. And yet, amazingly, she managed to contain it. They waited together for the pain to subside a little and then set out homewards. He leaned on her out of caution. She was his walking stick in flesh and blood.

'It's nothing,' he said reassuringly at the dinner table that night, still quite pale but stronger now. 'It's just a sign that I'm growing old, Bianca. I'm not made for La Rocca any more.'

'Then we will simply have to take our walks at the Cavalla,' she answered, relieved. 'There's a nest of baby geese near Villa Canossa. I will show it to you tomorrow. The goslings are about to hatch.'

Instead, she went alone. He chose to stay at home and rest. The baby geese had just been born and were grey, damp and snug. The mother's beak was red, ready to cut into something. Bianca kept her distance and sketched them on the pad she always carried with her. On her return trip, she saw the doctor's carriage from a distance. Her father died two days later, seized by another attack, this time fatal.

Everything had been decided far in advance: the property was entrusted to Bartolomeo, some of the money went to Zeno to finance his military career, and some went to Bianca, who was granted lifetime occupancy of her own little quarter of the household. Thank heavens Bianca still had somewhere of her own. Bartolomeo, who had filled out after his successful nuptials, and his pregnant wife quickly started eyeing the home and the garden with the cynicism of new proprietors. To watch them wander about the beloved rooms talking about carpets and decorations made her unbearably sad. They had agreed that Bianca's rooms would remain locked and intact until her return, but it was still torture for her to say goodbye to her collection of silhouettes and miniatures, her small rosewood desk, and her balcony that looked out onto the lake. It had been torture but also a relief, because it was evident that the spirit of the home had departed with their father. Her leaving had come at the right moment.

Her neighbour Count Rizzardi was, as ever, a gentleman.

'Remember,' he said, 'there will always be a room for you in my home.'

But all of a sudden he had seemed so old to her, as if her father's death had forced him, too, closer to that threshold.

Zeno had his own opinion about work and women.

'You're a girl, for heaven's sake.'

'So what?'

'So it isn't right that you go prancing off alone, waving that letter around. It's a passport to trouble, I'm telling you.'

'What should I do then, according to you?'

'You could get married. Girls tend to do that, you know.'

'Not all of us.'

'But you're pretty.'

'And I have no dowry. My only asset is this,' she said, waving her fingers in his face. He took hold of her hand, pretended to bite it, and then hugged her tightly.

'You're going to get yourself into a sticky situation, Bianca.

You could always live with me, you know. You could be my manservant.'

'Oh, sure,' laughed Bianca. 'I could cut my hair, wear boy's clothing and sleep on a cot outside your room.'

'When you were younger you could easily have passed for a boy. And you bossed us both around.'

They smiled in recollection.

Bartolomeo, on the other hand, seemed relieved at the prospect of her departure. Until then, he had been living in discomfort in his wife's home and waiting for his inheritance. It was evident that he now wanted to enjoy his new circumstances to the full, without any obstacles.

'Come home whenever you want,' he said, because he had to, because a brother should say that. She pursed her lips into a smile, trying to remember the boy with stars in his eyes, the boy he was, before becoming the rotund dandy now standing in front of her.

❧ ❧

'There's something I'd like to show you, if you'll follow me?'

Bianca wipes her hands on a rag. Donna Clara leads the way. She uses a highly varnished black cane, but is incredibly quick for a woman of her small stature. She crosses the lawn, goes into the house, up the stairs, and down a hall that Bianca has not yet explored. As she moves, Donna Clara's starched clothes crackle and whine. Bianca wonders whether she still wears a whalebone corset, as was the vogue in her youth, and if so, who tightens it for her each morning.

She stops in front of a small painting, near a row of nymph statuettes. It is a portrait of a mother and child. Positioned right in front of a window, it soaks up all the natural light. Bianca studies the work with the eye of a professional. The dark background allows the two heads to float out of time and space. One has curly brown hair, while the other's is straight and blond. The mother has a frivolous, somewhat disquieting look, perhaps due to her curls or the glow in her eyes. Bianca notices a resemblance between the little boy and the girls who play outside: the same curve in the cheek, round eyes and colouring. She understands.

'I was pretty, wasn't I?' says Donna Clara, leaning on the pomegranate-shaped handle of her walking stick. 'That's my boy . . . he was five years old there. Then I sent him to boarding school and left for Paris with my Carlo, and I didn't see him for a long time. An eternity, it seemed. But when Titta grew older, our paths crossed again. He came to Paris when he was twenty and we've never been apart since.'

And then, as though fearing she has revealed too much, she wraps her shawl around her, turns around and walks away, leaving Bianca to contemplate the painting on her own. She notices other details now: the boy's gaze seems restrained and distracted, as if there is a dog somewhere beyond the picture frame, barking and inviting him to play. She notices his mother's sharp expression, like that of a fox, with her slight, coy smile. The pair are positioned closely within the frame, but it is clear that each one anxiously wants to be elsewhere.

※ ※

Bianca starts her work. Following the generous instructions of her master – it makes her smile to think of him as her master, and yet that is his role – she takes all the time she needs. Each morning she carries out her box and easel and a large, somewhat frayed, straw hat. Soon, hampered by all the trappings, she decides to leave the more bulky props behind. Feeling light and reckless, she goes off to where domesticated nature ends and wild nature begins. Wild is perhaps an exaggeration, for in fact, she and Minna – who follows her like a shadow – are never entirely alone. There is always some gardener snipping, pruning, collecting and carrying away dry branches. The men don't look up from their work, nor do they speak to the ladies. Bianca constantly gets the feeling that she is being watched. But each time she turns around, the man nearby will be looking elsewhere and seems interested only in his pruning tool, his axe, or the clutch of weeds he holds in his clenched fist, raising them to examine the naked roots. It feels like wandering in a forest full of Indians: eyes and blades everywhere. But this is the only fear that the women allow themselves. Though, in fact, Minna is also afraid of insects, which is strange for a girl who has grown up in the countryside. She runs away from bumblebees, horseflies and praying mantises.

'They won't harm you,' Bianca says, picking up an insect in the palm of her hand to examine its big eyes before placing it back on a leaf, which it grips like a castaway at sea. But the girl keeps far away, and stares in admiration at Miss, who isn't afraid of anything. Maybe it is because she is English. *The English are strange*, Minna thinks.

Insects, children, flowers: how limited Bianca's new world is and yet, at the same time, how incredibly full of potential ideas. Insects and children: Pietro has the malicious insistence of a hornet. Enrico, on the other hand, has the feeble blandness of a caterpillar that knows only its own mouth. The girls are like grasshoppers, green, lilac, baby blue, all eyes, never at a standstill. Minna looks like a young beetle: the tiny, iridescent kind that never knows where to perch, and is capable only of short flights.

Bianca sketches and captures specific moments, sensations, gestures and movements. She speaks the plants' names out loud. She is drawn to the plants and flowers whose names she doesn't know. The estate at Brusuglio offers an unlimited variety of new species. There is the *Liquidambar*, rooted into the earth, and pointing to the sky as if it is an arrow. There is the little green cloud, a *Sophora*. There is *Sassafras albidum* with leaves that look like gloved hands. There is the *Catalpa* tree, known as 'the hippopotamus' because it is so large. And then there are the shrubs: the *Genista*, the *Coronilla*, the *Hamamelis*, with its dishevelled and fading flowers, and the *Mahonia*, which smells like honey. And then the plants with modern names like *Benthamia* or *Phlomis*, names which often sound too lofty in comparison to their humble appearance.

It doesn't feel like work. It isn't that different from her ardent childhood and adolescent pastime, except for the absence of the person dearest to her. A gracious but inadequate group of strangers has taken his place. As a unit, they only make her long for her own family even more.

❦ ❦

Everyone in the household is very devout. A small parish church has been built near the estate by Carlo, Donna Clara's deceased lover and the previous master of the house. The pungent smell of its recent construction blends with the overpowering scent of incense. The priest, a burly old man with a kind face, entrusts the censer to a young altar boy. Bianca lets herself become distracted by the trails of light blue smoke. She contemplates the Good Shepherd, who gazes out at everyone, one by one, from beside the apse. She feels surrounded by lambs. The children sit in the second row with their governess. Pietro takes something out of his pocket and shows it to Enrico, covering it with his other hand like a shield, so his sisters cannot glimpse it. Of course, they stretch out their necks to see and, in so doing, miss echoing the psalm. Their grandmother turns around from the front row with a threatening scowl. The girls fall back into line and the object disappears into Pietro's pocket once more. Enrico sighs. The children's mother and father are two composed backs of solid mass.

Bianca's gaze wanders. Several old women sit in another row. Not many country folk could allow themselves the luxury of attending two services a day, morning and evening. Since Bianca is not a believer, she wonders how she would cope with these rituals.

It is Don Dionisio, the elderly priest, who surprises her. She is wandering in the park one day when he approaches with a timid bow. He holds out his arms towards hers.

'Come with me,' he says, opening his hands to her and taking a few steps backwards. She raises her arms and makes to move forward. He stops and drops his hands by his side, as if he has asked too much of her too soon; hers are left hanging in air. She doesn't really know how to behave with Catholic priests, or with priests in general, but she senses that obedience is appreciated so she hurries to catch up to him. They walk on, both lifting their skirts from the ground in strange unison. He stops in front of a small door to the side of the church, which has, it seems, been built for a dwarf. 'Here we are.' He pushes it open, bends forward, blocks the passageway for a moment, and then disappears inside. She follows him in, head bowed. She finds herself inside a simple, bare vestry, where a crucifix hangs between two tall, narrow windows of light brown glass, which create an amber light. 'That door is always open,' he says. 'Prayer doesn't always happen on a schedule. It's not a postal carriage. God comes to us when we least expect him. And you can do the same.'

From that moment on, Bianca doesn't enter the realm of the

kingdom of God on a twice-daily schedule. She doesn't have to explain herself to anyone and no one asks her a thing about it. Donna Clara seems perplexed but not altogether amazed.

The governess whispers to her in confidence and with a hint of envy, 'Innes doesn't come to service either, you know.'

But prayer occurs within the home, too, and without any forewarning. Donna Clara keeps a jet rosary on her at all times, wrapped around her wrist like a bracelet, a Christ figurine dangling from it like a strange sort of charm. Whenever the conversation turns into an appeal to the saints and Mary, she slips it off and clings to those beads that reconcile the heavens and earth. Donna Julie follows her example. The children mumble their Hail Marys in a distracted singsong. Don Titta, on the other hand, doesn't pray. When he is present, he simply lowers his head and folds his hands together, as if prayer is just another opportunity to leave this world and get lost in another. Bianca takes advantage of those moments to study them all. She is the only one to keep her eyes open.

☙ ❧

Innes, the English tutor who doesn't attend Mass, returns from his salubrious holiday. The little girls, who have been anxiously awaiting his arrival since morning, dash towards him as soon as he descends from the carriage, screaming with glee. The boys look up silently from their game – a complex construction made up of small pieces of wood – but only when their governess tells them to, do they stand to greet their tutor, taking their time to brush away the sawdust from their trousers. Innes sweeps Giulietta up while the other girls hug him tightly around his knees. He is very tall, Bianca thinks, enormous, even for an Englishman. She is sitting in the shade of the portico with a book in her lap. Innes laughs and stumbles forward, the little girls still clinging to him. When Donna Clara comes out, everything resumes its order. The sisters let go and line up. The boys join the group so that the family formation is complete. Bianca stands with the others while the servants, Berto and Barba, unload a worn suitcase and an incongruous carpet bag embroidered with purple flowers. When the carriage departs, the governess runs to shut the gates, too excited to leave it to the valet, before taking her place at the end of the line and staring intently at the new arrival.

'Dear, dear, dear Innes!' Donna Clara exclaims, opening her arms to him and clutching him briefly. Her face only reaches to his chest. 'I trust you are well rested and fortified. You must tell me everything about the Paduan spas. I, too, would like to take the waters there one day . . . when I find time to leave the family!'

As always, Donna Clara has placed herself in the precise middle of the circle that is her whole world. Her gaze is its radius and it is as though everything that happens has to be connected to her in some way, to make her shine – if only from reflected light. Such is her arrogance, and it is supported by rank and habit. Innes doesn't pay it the least attention, or per-haps he is just used to it.

'Donna Clara, you have no use for miracle waters. Here at Brusuglio lies the fountain of youth. I am certain it's some-where here on the estate and you're keeping it secret while I wander high and low to find it!'

Innes speaks Italian with no trace of an English accent. Bianca finds out later that his mother is Italian, too. He switches immediately to his paternal language when talking to the children and when Donna Clara introduces Bianca to him.

'And here is Miss Bianca, with whom you will have a lot in common, I'm sure. But you must speak our language together from time to time. We don't want any conspirators in the house!'

And with this, the children take hold of him and drag him away to see a brood of ducklings. They are halfway down the path when the master of the house leans out the top-floor window.

'Innes! Finally!'

The Englishman turns around with a smile, unable to free himself from the grasp of the little ones.

'My friend, I've just returned and already I'm being held captive!'

'I can see that,' replies Don Titta. 'As soon as you manage to escape from that tribe of savages, you will find me in my study.'

Innes smiles in agreement before letting himself be dragged off once more.

❦ ❦

His full name is Stuart Aaron James Innes. He studied at Oxford before the collapse of his family business – shipping and trade in the Indies – forced him into another, truer, profession. His natural passion for travel and a strong desire to avoid ridicule from his peers led him to leave England. This is his third appointment as tutor. He has already been to Paris and the Savoy region before being stranded – his words – in the Milanese countryside. He tells her all this in their common language, standing together beneath the portico, waiting for dinner to be announced. Darkness falls sluggishly, little by little, first swallowing up the forest in the distance and then the confines of the great lawn. His hair is curly and somewhat long. He constantly brushes it away from his face in an unintentional, almost feminine, gesture. His eyes are of a piercing blue, strong yet distant. He wears a thin, precise moustache and has a hint of a beard that gives him a medieval air. His elegance is sober and neat. His frock coat, though on its last legs, is impeccably pressed and beautifully cut. After telling her his story Innes is quiet for a long moment, taking in the view of the estate, which is so beautiful in this, its bluest hour.

'I am pleased that you are here,' he says. 'I feel like your presence will make my exile more tolerable.'

Bianca thinks this comment rather dramatic and somewhat forward, and hides herself behind a silence that he interprets as shyness. And perhaps this is for the best.

At the dinner table that evening, he and Don Titta are the only ones to talk. They speak of another poet, an Englishman and old acquaintance of Innes's, who lives somewhere between Venice and the countryside. The man in question keeps his horses at the Lido so that he can ride along the beach, where sea meets sky. They speak, too, of a mutual friend, Jacopo, who died in uncertain and mysterious circumstances.

At one point, Donna Clara throws her napkin down on the table in irritation.

'Can't we talk about something that is of interest to us, too?'

Her son glances over at her with calculated slowness.

'I am surprised you do not find any of this interesting. It concerns all of us.'

Bianca would like to know what he means and struggles to find the way to phrase her question, but stops when Donna Julie places a delicate hand on her husband's arm.

'Your absence has been a burden to your mother. Don't be surprised if she seeks your full attention at one of the rare times you are at dinner with us.'

There is an exchange of glances between Titta and Innes that reveals a certain tacit understanding.

'I apologize, Mother dear,' he says. 'Sometimes I forget that time passes differently for me than it does for you.'

Satisfied, Donna Clara replies, 'It's because we're women and without you men we're nothing and we know nothing.'

'Only if you want it to be so,' he retorts.

She lets the matter drop and changes the subject, moving on to a discussion of silkworms and the experiments Ruffini is conducting in Magenta.

'Perhaps, we can go and visit. What do you think?'

❧ ❧

And just like that, the whole family is back together, and life in the villa regains its pleasant routines. The poet joins them more frequently for dinner since Innes has returned; it is clear that he appreciates regular male company. Unlike the governess (whom Bianca starts calling Nanny, quickly followed by everyone else), who is encouraged to disappear after meals with the children, both Innes and Bianca remain seated at the table. Their opinions, it seems, are both desired and appreciated. They speak about everything, from the astronomical cost of seeds from Holland to the washerwoman's marriage and the secret societies of illuminati in Milan.

Innes, who goes to the city twice a week to attend gatherings of a group of fellow countrymen living abroad, always returns with news that excites something more than a polite curiosity in the poet. And just like that, the two of them will begin a discussion that often uses the word 'fatherland'. The term explodes like a firecracker in the centre of the table. Mother and daughter-in-law will look at each other worriedly. Donna Clara will abruptly interrupt with some mindless topic of discussion: Enrico's latest stomach ache, the umpteenth doctor's visit on account of Giulietta's fever, or the pestilence of rabbits. Bianca, who has seen and heard more than would generally have been allowed for a woman of her age and status, and who has also learned a great deal from her father, is still not quite the free and complete creature that she desires to be. So she remains silent, hushed by good sense, and yet impatient and eager to say something bold and intelligent that will make these two men look at her in admiration and realize that women have minds too. But no, she says nothing. She doesn't have a legacy of ideas; her best tutor left her too soon. Bianca is like a half-finished marionette, a prisoner carved out of wood. But she may not fully know it. *If you could see me now, Father,* she thinks, *how I take in every new word, every modern sentence in an attempt to understand how the world is changing, just as you wanted me to* . . . If he could see her, he would surely be troubled.

❧ ❧

She overhears voices while walking past an open French window.

'She's beautiful but glacial too. Her name suits her. White is a frigid colour. She's like snow and ice and wind and storm. And hail.'

Someone chuckles.

'She doesn't show off, she keeps to herself. You can't expect her to mingle with us servants. She's an artist, she is.'

'Sure, an artist,' another voice speaks sarcastically. 'She's a servant, but one that gets a nice big bag of coins. All we get is soup, these rags on our back, a cot up in the attic and a kick in the arse!'

This brings laughter all round.

She wants to walk away but stays there, needing to hear more. She tries to shrug the comments off, but finds she can't. She just feels angry and upset. What irritates her most though is their accent, how they stretch out their 'e' sounds, as if they are made of rubber. And at the same time, behind her back, the servants laugh at the way she pronounces her own 'e' – quick and closed – and at her clenched double consonants. Deep down she knows they aren't malicious, though. They are just suspicious of anything new, like all country folk.

On another day a further snippet of conversation comes from another window, painting another portrait of Bianca.

'She's not talkative, and as far as conversation goes, she's as bristly as a porcupine, but she does draw like an angel. Or a devil! Anyway, it's the same difference,' Donna Clara says to a mysterious listener. And then she presses a finger to her lips and shushes herself, snickering slightly.

Bianca cannot see the gestures that soften the maliciousness of the words, though. She can only hear the pair's laughter. She walks away, vexed. She wanted to find out what they thought of her and now she knows.

❧ ❧

Since the return of Innes, evenings unfurl predictably. The men talk among themselves. The women sit in silent disapproval, eyeing them, and desperately seeking to change the subject. Bianca listens, watching Innes's demeanour and her master's fervour.

'Do you really think that things can go back to the way they were? I'm sorry, Don Titta, but I think you're dreaming. The memory of that Italian officer being killed by the mob just because he wore an Austrian uniform is still fresh in their minds.'

'It was not as if we wanted to kill him! It was an accident. You know how these mobs can be.'

'Of course. I can't imagine you, of all people, stabbing a poor disarmed man with an umbrella. But other people have other predilections. Need I remind you of the chef who was roasted at the Tuileries? Or Simon the executioner with blood up to his ankles? Listen to me, thanks to the death of that poor devil, the Austrians will have an easy time slamming their iron fist down on the table. There will be no lenience, not even towards you patricians.'

'It's too late to go back to tyranny. The people are tired. Populations are no longer indistinct masses; they want to claim their own identity. And we – we who know, we who understand – must try to act as new men or at least attempt to renew ourselves. Even if this means risking our world.'

'You should hear yourself, using words like "too late" and "no longer". You are so absolute, so excessive, my friend. When people have bread for dipping into their soup, calm will return. And we shall stick to fighting our princely battles in the safety of our salons.'

'What you say is terrible, Innes. Offensive, even. You make me feel guilty for how things are being played out. Though I suppose you are right. If I stay here, I am hiding behind a screen.'

Donna Clara looks up from her embroidery and interrupts the conversation with measured amusement.

'Ah, the new one *is* charming, isn't it? The chinoiserie is exquisite. Donna Crivelli saw it and ordered the exact same one . . .'

It is strange to hear the men speak so openly in front of the women. Usually their more serious discussions – complete with whispers and sudden outbursts – are reserved for the other drawing room and paired with cigars and alcoholic beverages. Bianca follows this exchange attentively but achieves only a vague understanding of it. She knows there is unease in Milan following recent violent acts. Even her journey here, to Bru-suglio, risked being postponed. But the waters calmed and she took her uncomfortable carriage ride.

The last time she heard about world events directly was from her father. She no longer has anyone who will explain things to her. Zeno, in his letters, writes only about parties, hunting scores, or young ladies named after flowers.

Now Don Titta frowns at his mother as if he is surprised to see her sitting there, like she is a fly on a glazed cream puff.

'You know, the Oriental screen, the one we put in the bou-doir up in the gallery,' Donna Clara insists.

'Indeed, it's incredibly useful,' her son observes drily. 'You never know when a gust of wind will blow in and hurl you across the room like a balloon.'

'Speaking of that, you know, I read in the *Gazzetta* that you can take a day trip by hot-air balloon from Morimondo now. You just need to book in advance.'

'It's not for me,' Donna Julie chimes in. 'I'm not going all the way up there. I'm too scared. If man were born to fly, our Lord would have designed us with wings like birds.'

'And a beak to peck with,' little Pietro interjects. Out of place and largely ignored, he chuckles to himself.

'To fly . . . what a dream,' Innes adds. 'We have no idea what feats man is capable of. This is the mystery and the miracle of science, is it not?'

'I prefer poetry,' observes Donna Clara. 'And not just because it provides us with food on our plates and a roof over our head. I've always admired it.' Placing a hand on her heart, she starts to recite:

> *Je serai sous la terre, et, fantôme sans os,*
> *Par les ombres myrteux je prendrai mon repos.*

'How lovely, Mother dear,' Don Titta says with a sigh, tossing his napkin onto the table in an act of surrender. 'Balls, screens and musty rhymes . . . I can't take this any longer.'

'Well, taste is taste. Poetry doesn't have to make us laugh, now, does it?' objects Donna Clara.

'Ask our Tommaso what he thinks of poetry when he arrives.'

Donna Clara can't resist the urge to get in the last word.

'Wonderful idea, my dear son. I will ask our Tommaso. That boy needs to have his head examined. You know, you are setting a terrible example for young people who aspire to an artistic life. *You* were good enough to succeed, but art is not meant for all. Let's just say that not all buns come out perfect.'

'Interesting. First I am told I am an artist and now I'm a pastry chef.'

'Well, what difference does it make? You knead with words, you knead with flour. People are as greedy for verses as they are for cream puffs. Luckily!'

Titta and Innes laugh heartily. Donna Clara looks around proudly, to see the impact of her witty remark. Donna Julie and Bianca only smile weakly. To Bianca, the thought of poetry being bought and sold like pastries – verses on a platter to be picked up with two fingers and eaten – disturbs her profoundly. It seems out of place and hateful, and she wonders why Don Titta is laughing.

❧ ❧

'Our Tommaso' arrives to stay. Tommaso Reda is also a poet. His family wanted him to read law, but he was against the idea and felt summoned to a higher calling. Somewhat of a dreamer, he had even been locked up in prison for several nights on account of his erratic behaviour. Finally, Don Titta offered the boy help – and shelter too – something which angered Tommaso's father. Donna Clara explains all of this to Bianca without hiding her disapproval.

'It's not like his poems are as good as my son's. In my opinion, he doesn't even have a voice,' she says, stressing her words. 'He's just a figurine, a *gros garçon* used to having anything and everything. And Titta, God bless him, took him in like a stray cat only because he pities him. But this isn't a hotel. Not at all.'

Why the younger poet evokes such compassion in the master escapes Bianca. He is a young man of medium height, elegant and intense, with a worried look in his deep, dark eyes that contrasts with a cockiness stemming from the privileged status into which he has been born. He wanders indifferently about the home in which he is a guest. He has been coming here ever since he was a child, knows the estate inside and out, and everyone knows him. He eats little and drinks a great deal. He sleeps until late and his candle is the last to go out at night. This moderately excessive lifestyle blesses him with a feverish air and a pallor suited to the role he has chosen for himself. Bianca cannot decide if she likes him or not.

'Nature really does provide us with the most delicious things,' comments Donna Clara at the table one day. Her son nods in agreement as he enjoys the last glossy grains of rice from his plate.

'And the most beautiful,' adds Bianca impulsively.

'You are absolutely right,' Donna Julie agrees, looking over at her children all seated in a row.

But Bianca meant something else. She looks out of the French window again and admires the imperfect contours of the poplar trees, their tips like brushes painting the deep blue sky.

Don Titta leans forward.

'Yes,' he says, 'and art is the attempt to imitate the inimitable. There's something frustrating about that, isn't there? I obviously speak for myself, Miss Bianca. Perhaps it comes easily to you?'

'Oh, I don't know,' she answers, her mind returning to the table. 'My aim is more one of interpretation.'

'Which inevitably means transformation,' he remarks.

Bianca purses her lips into a smile.

'Perhaps. But that doesn't worry me. Mine is purely an attempt.'

"The advantage is that no poppy or anemone will complain about their portrait not looking like them. Or rather, I should say that *I've* never heard them complain,' Tommaso intervenes, smiling coyly. Bianca ignores him. 'But, who knows? Maybe they do complain,' he says, pursuing the fantasy.

'What? You think flowers can speak?' intervenes Giulietta, the only child to have followed the conversation, with all the attention possessed of a nine-year-old.

Enrico and Pietro chuckle.

'And you can hear them,' Enrico says, making a circular gesture with his index finger near his temple.

'I'm not crazy,' retorts Giulietta, offended, 'but I do listen!'

'And you're right to do so. Of course flowers can speak,' intervenes Bianca. 'But they have such tiny, soft voices that all the other noises drown them out. They are born, they live, and they die; why shouldn't they be able to speak?'

'This conversation is nonsense,' says Donna Clara, who has a fondness for eccentricities but only those she champions. 'Have you ever considered painting children's portraits rather than likenesses of flowers? There's a business in that.'

'Yes, indeed,' intervenes Tommaso, 'given that everyone is convinced that their child is the most beautiful in the world.

Surely you would find clients in Milan. Rich men who marry beautiful women in order to breed well. Men who don't always get it right the first time, but try and try again . . .'

'We can help you, if you'd like,' Donna Clara adds, not picking up the irony of Tommaso's comment. 'We know people, I mean.'

'No, that is not my profession,' Bianca says firmly.

'But you are so talented,' Donna Julie adds.

'And, anyway, Miss Bianca,' says Donna Clara with a laugh, 'if, in the end, you find that painting a convincing, realistic portrait of a child is impossible, you can always create one of your own instead.'

Her son and daughter-in-law laugh. Bianca blushes. She hates being the centre of attention but smiles nonetheless. Sly old lady. She certainly knows how to lead a conversation. It is an art that Bianca still has not mastered, and perhaps never will. It is easy to imagine Donna Clara perfectly at ease in a Paris salon, surrounded by beautiful minds, an elegant and respectable man at her side listening to her playful quips complacently. What sort of man was Conte Carlo, her lover? Why is there not even one portrait of him in the entire home? After all, the house was originally his. The older woman inherited it when he died. Perhaps they are hidden away like relics in the secrecy of her private chambers, or inside the locket around her neck, shut away like prisoners within her bosom . . .

'Miss Bianca? Miss Bianca? Where did you disappear to?' It is Innes. 'Our little dreamer,' he jokes.

'I wasn't dreaming. I was just thinking. Is it not allowed?' she answers, thrown by his intimate manner.

'If it takes you away from us, then no, my dear, it isn't. You must remain here. Propriety imposes this on us.'

Bianca looks at Innes in confusion. It's something Donna

Clara would say. She wonders whether Innes is mocking the mistress.

Don Titta intervenes.

'Personally, I don't mind. You are free to go where your heart and mind take you, on the condition that you will come back and join us here on earth occasionally. I understand.'

'Of course you do! You love to visit that secret place that Miss Bianca disappears to, isn't that right?' laughs Donna Julie. 'Far away from here, from us, from our incessant voices, the buzzing disturbance that we are.'

'But I love my crazy bees, too, and you know it,' he says, smiling. 'And love has the right to disturb me whenever it feels like it.'

≈ ≈

He said, 'Whenever *it* feels like it.' He should have said, 'Whenever *I* feel like it.' If she hadn't heard him with her own ears and seen how pleasant and serene he is, Bianca would never have identified this as the man who walks indifferently past his children while they call out for his attention, eager to show him their recently finished drawings. At other times, he shuts himself in his studio for days, refusing trays of food placed at the door. He won't even open the window of his study. Donna Clara paces beneath it, looking up, waiting for a nod, for some sign of life. Sometimes the poet has nightmares and calls out during his sleep. She has heard him. It isn't a dog or a local drunk, Minna tells her. It is him.

'He does that sometimes when he is writing,' she says.

Bianca begins to understand why the children are always so insecure in front of him. They are stuck between shyness and the urge to reclaim his other, kinder side, the side that sends the gardener to plough the grounds at the confines of the estate into five parcels so that each child can have their own garden. Each area is labelled with a wooden tag and the children have their own set of miniature hoes and spades and tiny bags of seeds to plant. Don Titta is a complicated man, this much is certain. One moment he is there and the next he is gone. He isolates himself for weeks so that he can pursue, capture and tame his muses. And then, all of a sudden, he resurfaces: a pale and serene convalescent. He becomes that other self then, the man who joyfully goes out on a limb for everyone. The man who kneels down next to Pietro and Enrico, fascinated, as they watch a watermill churn over the brook. Who admires the girls as they dance to the rhythm of Pia's drum, smiling so sweetly he looks almost foolish.

If their father is either fully present or fully absent, their mother, delicate and devout Donna Julie, is a constant source of love. It bubbles up from deep inside her. Precisely because of her uninterrupted presence, though, she runs the risk of going unnoticed. It is her daily devotion that watches over the children's health and their metamorphoses, providing woolly sweaters, poultices, decoctions or mush as needed. She offers them all the nurturing that they require. But the children, observes Bianca, are no longer so young that they need such doting attention. They are at a point when they desire something else: games, friendships, stories and laughter. Kisses and hugs are excessive. They reciprocate with swift pecks on the cheek and then wriggle free, the same way they do from unwanted scarves and sweaters. Although when Donna Clara offers herself to them, they greedily take everything they can get their hands on. They adore Innes too, like little puppies. He is the only one who can get respect from the two boys, and the girls love him unconditionally – maybe because he is as tall as their father but not as distant; maybe because he swings them around him as if on a wonderful carousel ride.

శ్రీ శ్రీ

One day, through an open window, Bianca hears Nanny complaining.

'Oh, that Miss Bianca . . . she's going to take him from me. I know it. And she doesn't even speak French!'

Bianca is astounded: Nanny is revealing her feelings to a maid! And probably a smart one like Pia. She wonders what would happen if she were to make a dramatic entrance, draw back the curtains, as in a Goldoni comedy, and say, 'You're wrong, mademoiselle. Innes is all yours. I'm looking elsewhere.' The foolish girl would be at peace but it might also kindle the fires of her hope, which is a mere illusion. She ought to realize on her own that Innes is unattainable. Maybe she wants to delude herself. Maybe it makes this house, her prison, more tolerable. But the children will grow up, Nanny will have to find another home, and by then Innes will surely be far away. He doesn't strike Bianca as the type to stay fixed in one spot for very long. Not here, anyway. He is a dreamer. And the dreams will ultimately carry him away.

She stands very still, thinking and listening. Pia, surprisingly, comes to Bianca's defence.

'What are you talking about? Miss Bianca isn't a bad person . . .'

Bianca wishes that she could transform herself into a beautiful statuette. No one would notice her; she would simply be an ornament, an ornament preferable to the one she feels she already is. Words would simply slide off her smooth skin. She recalls a French story her father used to tell, the one about an ancient statue, a Venus in a garden somewhere, that fell in love with a young man. Every night the statue would visit him, leaving mysterious traces of dirt in the hallways of the villa. To prevent him from marrying his flesh-and-blood fiancée, she held him so tightly that she killed him. Even statues have a soul. The advantage is that no one knows it, and they can conceal or reveal them as they please.

As she turns the corner of the house, Innes comes towards her, as though he has been waiting for her behind the bushes.

'And where are you off to, Miss Bianca? To explore the wild moors?'

Bianca turns to look behind her. If she has seen this exchange, Nanny will have fainted, her suspicions all but confirmed.

'I was just going to walk down to the fields, where it is a bit less wild,' she says with a smile.

They start walking together. He has to slow down and she has to quicken her pace. Once their initial differences are dealt with and the doses of irony are measured out and understood, Bianca realizes that not only does she enjoy Innes's company, but she also doesn't care what Nanny thinks.

'Were you referring earlier, perhaps, to our employer's wild habits?' he says. They exchange a smile of understanding, but he then becomes serious. 'He is a great man, you know. I feel fortunate to work for him. And so should you. The bourgeoisie of the Po Valley, the landed gentry, the aristocrats who inhabit these spaces that exist somewhere between land and sky, are rarely so enlightened. More often than not they are simply satisfied with conforming to the landscape.' And then Innes changes both the subject and his expression. 'I have something for you. It has just come from London, where it seems to be a great hit. It's a romance novel and I am sure you will appreciate it.'

'Don't you want to read it first?' Bianca asks, trying to suppress her curiosity.

'I've already read it. My nights are inhabited by books. It's the only benefit of having insomnia: one has more time to dedicate to passions. I also sleep a little during the day, when it's nap time for the children.'

She notices his paleness. His eyes are more deeply set than usual. In the vivid daylight, barely screened by the leafy tree-tops, she notices, too, a vertical line that runs from the corner of his eye down his cheek. It looks like a scar from a duel but is merely a crease of age, perhaps a distinctive sign, a message saying this is the spirit at work. Bianca has begun to suspect – and in this she is correct – that Innes is a revolutionary. Merely thinking of this word sends chills running down her spine. It evokes torture, chains, prisons, heads rolling in pools of blood. His frequent visits to the city surely serve a duplicitous purpose. And the role of tutor in a noble and respectable family is a wonderful cover.

Bianca senses that even the master of the house is involved. Their partnership in these matters explains many things: Don Titta's secrecy and his frequent trips to the city residence (which she imagines as being dusty and decaying, in ruins, given the fact that none of the women ever want to go) with the excuse of researching the novel he has been writing for the past ten years. The risk of course is even greater for Don Titta than for Innes. He is the poet, loved and pampered by all for the person he appears to be: an elegant, charming seeker of words. Bianca, who is familiar with his work, finds his poems pleasing but wan. She doesn't see great passion in his verses but rather delicate sentiment, idylls, still-life depictions of an illuminated life, a life which does not truly exist.

Perhaps at heart he is a collector – that would explain why he is driven to commission portraits of his flowers and plants as though they are people. But what if, under that Arcimboldo of petals, strange herbs, exotic fruits and foliage, there is a different man, a man filled with strong ideas, waiting for the right moment to reveal his true identity to the rest of the world?

His novel. The revolution. Perhaps he is writing a novel *about* the revolution. Bianca feels only a detached curiosity about these matters. She is aware that they are important, that it is an issue of rights being denied, and that the insurgents operate through contempt, secrecy and violence. Apparently, there is no other way to protest and change the direction of things. There will be blood. It is inevitable.

Bianca, though, feels engaged in her own transformation. It has turned her world upside down and set her apart from everyone else. She tries to imagine the new and daring map of the world to come. She feels like a seamstress working on a corner of an enormous tablecloth: she has her portion to bring to completion and she simply fills it with stitches and then unstitches them, little understanding how that same motif will multiply and echo across the cloth.

The book that Innes lends her takes her breath away. It keeps her awake at night; it steals away her common sense, and creates a confused knot of sensations inside her. It is entitled *Ponden Kirk* and focuses on a desperate and impossible love story, on injustice, and on ghosts that inhabit a desolate moor near the sea. She can imagine Tamsin's small hand, white against the black of night, scratching at the windowpane. Or perhaps it is only a branch. That hand, the description of those curls and amber eyes, eyes that are common here but rare in the north, takes hold of Bianca's heart. She feels the darkness that surrounds the beloved character of Aidan and feels for him with her innermost soul. It is completely different from *Udolpho*; Emily is a silly goose in comparison and not worthy of holding Tamsin's umbrella. Tamsin would hate umbrellas, anyway. Bianca is certain of this. If she ever did own one, she would have snapped it in two in a burst of rage or forgotten it under a hedge, torn it with carelessness or allowed it to be swept away by the wind. All of a sudden, everything Bianca has read that year is discarded in favour of this novel.

Innes smiles and tries to answer Bianca's insistent questions about the writer.

'The author's name is D. Lyly, with a "y". That's all I know.'

'No first name?'

'No first name. I think it must be a pseudonym. It has to be a woman.'

'Another Ann Radcliffe?'

'Why not, my dear?'

'I tremble for her.'

'You tremble?'

'Out of repressed envy.'

D. Lyly, Delilah, Dalila: a woman of deceit. Deceit in order to exist. To write. In comparison, Bianca's pencils, charcoals, all the accoutrements of her drawing, seem as bland as the oatmeal that her mother served her at breakfast while her brothers enjoyed pumpernickel bread and sausages. Her flowers are mawkish in their light green and gold frames. The leaves in her sketches have been dead for an age. Everything she does is so graciously finished – and so useless. Life looks so much better alive than when it is drawn on paper. When it is written about, on the other hand, life becomes stronger, colourful, more vital. And what is more, writing comes to life each time you read it. A leaf drawn on a piece of paper does not. When a leaf dies, you have to wait for spring to be able to see it again, and it will never be the same leaf it once was.

Bianca is curious. She wants to find out more about this mysterious Lyly, who is very possibly a woman. Who knows what depths and peaks of passion she has experienced in order to be able to render them so miraculously well on paper? Maybe she is like her character Tamsin, both impulsive and obstinate, reaching out for everything she wants against all obstacles. She is never defeated, only by death. But no, not even that can stop her . . .

'The author is most likely a middle-aged man with gout,' observes Innes playfully. 'He spends every day at the club and has never travelled further than Hampstead.'

'You like teasing me,' Bianca protests.

'You should write, if you think you might enjoy it,' says Innes, both indulgently and in all seriousness. They are walking together in the rain as if they are in England. They cross paths with servants and peasants who look at them askance. It is one thing to *have* to get wet, but another to do it on purpose, dragging one's skirt through the high grass in a strange pique. 'Write. Try it out. No one is stopping you. I know that your true talent is drawing, but it needs to find its right course. Don't tell me you're only interested in herbals. That's just the surface.'

And so, with that challenge, Bianca gives writing a go. On a stormy night, illuminated by candlelight, she starts a fictitious diary. It doesn't come easily to her. She gives herself a false name, rolling it around in her mouth as though it is a strange sweet, unsure whether to keep sucking on it or spit it out. She writes out the false name three, five, ten times, tilting her flourishes here and there. Finally, she recounts her experience travelling from Calais to Dover. She leaves out the more distressing details, the jumbling of innards, and favours a more romantic sketch: two mysterious characters in wind-swept capes, the moon peeking out from behind the clouds . . . She rereads it. It has all been said before. She gives it another go, adding the innards and their by-products. The effect makes her shiver. There is action and atmosphere, but it all feels shallow. She cannot find the right words. She ends up with blackened fingers and torn-up pages. It is better to read than to write, she thinks. And what's more, it's easier.

She gets into bed to read the novel, and is immediately reunited with Aidan; she locks that silly Tamsin in the storeroom, ignores her small fists pounding on the door, steals her cape and effortlessly clambers up on a horse behind her hero. Together they ride off bareback, the beast trembling beneath her thighs, her arms gripping his waist tightly. He, too, trembles with the fury of the gallop. It is pouring with rain, and the moon is shining . . .

The moon is always present, she reflects as she closes the book, thunder sounding far off in the distance. She looks out at her own moon through the distorting glass pane of her window, and thinks it looks like a fried egg. *It is always with us,* she thinks, *even when we don't see it. And we need it like we need the sun. It's the other side of the coin, the splinter of darkness we carry with us, wedged into our hearts.* She sighs and picks up a pencil and begins to draw. She draws the fried egg in the sky, the profile of a sycamore, a star like a tiny kiss of light. This much she can do. And this she will continue to do.

❧ ❧

The feast day of San Giovanni is a small but important tradition in the household. Friends from the city visit on the way to their own summer retreats in the countryside in a kind of farewell until October. It is an opportunity to show off the estate and prove that some things never change. Bianca learns about the feast only during the commotion of the preparations, from the servants' incomprehensible, fractured sentences; from the contrasting expressions of Don Titta and his mother, who is reassured by the agitation and shouts orders left and right like a captain from the bridge. Don Titta confirms his own place by retreating into his chambers. When his opinion is needed about the menu, the flowers or the music, he raises his eyes to the sky and purses his lips as though to hold back any impertinence.

St John's Wort is in bloom during the period of the feast. Bianca has an idea, voices it, and it is approved. Her role is to prepare dozens of *boutonnières*: a cluster of the little yellow flowers bound in ivy shoots. She sends out troops of children to search for the smallest ivy – *only the ends of the branches, about this long, no more than that, be careful not to cut yourselves, don't run with scissors in your hand,* and so on. Despite Nanny's worrying and the devastating pruning job, the mission is completed. When the ladies and gentlemen arrive, the children present them with these *boutonnières*, sprayed with water to appear fresh, from two trays in the foyer. The guests, of course, remark on the children's growth before pinning the gifts to their chests.

'Oh, how big you've got, Giulietta. You look like a young lady.'

'And is this Enrico? He looks like his grandmother. What a beautiful boy.'

Nanny watches the children from behind a pillar, ready to sweep up her prey as soon as the last guests make their entrance. The gates close, keeping out the local peasants, who are travelling to their own festival in the village piazza, and who stop to watch the arrivals. They hang onto the gate and spy for a while on the gentlefolk and their painted carriages, neatly assembled along the gravel drive like a collection of exotic insects.

'See that one? That means Berlingieri is here, too. That light blue and black carriage is from Poma. Can you see the family crest on its door?'

Bianca watches the townspeople and listens to their voices, the rise and fall of their strange dialect, so difficult to understand. Once the soirée here is over, Pia and Minna will head to the festival in town. They have been talking about it for days. They will let their hair down and dance like lunatics, they say. Whether it is her wild streak or simply her impetuousness, Bianca knows that eventually her feet will lead her there too. The urge is irresistible. But not yet. The evening is about to commence. She greets the guests and leads them towards the refreshments, illuminated by a fringe of lanterns.

᪥᪥ ᪥᪥

La Farfalla is Don Titta's most recent and well-known literary work. It is so popular that even Bianca has heard of it. The master of the house recites some appropriate verses, even as moths flit about them rather than the butterfly of the title. When he concludes, he bows and basks in the applause.

'You've given us all a little flutter of excitement, Titta!' says a beautiful lady in pale rose, causing her friends to laugh.

'You must have swallowed a Lepidoptera,' he answers back.

'Oh, how horrid! You're a Lepidoptera.' More laughter follows.

'Unfortunately, dear Adele, the butterfly is a female.'

'Well, next time write about dogs then,' says Young Count Bernocchi, strutting like a peacock to the front of the room.

The women in the kitchen, poets by association, have put Bianca on her guard when it comes to the young count, with a memorable verse:

> *An occhio [eye] of regard to Bernocchio,*
> *his pockets are full of pidocchio [lice],*
> *he has a very long occhio and even longer hands.*

With this introduction preceding him, Bianca is instinctively cautious. Young Count Bernocchi is definitely not handsome. He is short with an enormous belly. He wears a horrible, outdated white wig that makes his forehead look excessively broad. And the socially inexpert Bianca suddenly finds herself standing next to him. As the guests begin to move off in different directions, he corners her in the room, with the intention of keeping her there for some time.

'So, Miss Bianca, have you grown accustomed to the wilderness? You're surely used to big cities: London, Paris . . .'

'Yes, I have been there,' Bianca replies curtly and almost impolitely. Her short response doesn't offer him anything to build on. She isn't trying to be rude, though, she simply lacks confidence. They have just been introduced to each other but he already seems to know a lot about her. Of course, the opposite is also true, but at least Bianca has sense enough not to show it. The diminutive that precedes his name is a joke: despite his advanced age, he still has not inherited his father's position as count. This father, the servants have told her, clings to dear life with his teeth. So even though he is past forty, Young Count Bernocchi seems frozen in eternal adolescence.

He inspects her through an eyeglass that is so out of fashion it is deeply comical. It surely isn't often that someone cuts him short. He furrows his brow and continues, as though nothing has happened.

'Vienna, Turin, Rome . . . In my opinion, the Grand Tour is nothing more than a grandiose invention. It allows for European *fainéants* to continue to practise the activities they enjoy most. It prevents them from getting involved in the fields of humanities and economics, which they should leave to people summoned to that duty – and the true engine of the world – and it gives them the opportunity to dissolve a giant portion of their assets into travel, hotels, rent and thoughtless purchases of mediocre works of art . . . Actually, this healthy circulation of money does quite a bit of good.'

'Didn't you travel, too, in your youth?' Tommaso suddenly appears at her side.

Bianca senses a slight tension in his tone, held in check by politeness. The phrase 'your youth' is actually a slight. Clearly Bernocchi cares a great deal about his appearance, but his excessive regard for it only highlights the defects of his age. His over-enjoyment of food and wine has led to puffy features and skin coloured by a reddish network of veins.

'But of course,' he answers calmly. 'And, rightly so; I include myself in the category of drones of which I speak. Let's just say that I have always had the good sense not to consider myself destined for great accomplishments and have been deaf to the callings of the Muses, who can do great harm if summoned forth by the wrong person.'

If this offhand comment is intended for Tommaso, he doesn't seem to notice. Instead, he offers Bianca his arm and they move off. Disgruntled, Bernocchi follows the couple to the centre of the sitting room. There everyone is seated, attentive, and ready to resume the show. Donna Julie seems lost in one of her daydreams. Innes's long fingers fiddle impatiently with the hems of his trousers. He provides silent company to the old priest, who appears either intimidated or profusely bored, or maybe a bit of both, thinks Bianca. His big white head droops forward over his threadbare tunic as though he is inspecting a strange landscape.

When Pia enters the room with a tray of refreshments, the old priest is shaken out of his stupor. A beautiful smile, affectionate and warm, spreads across his worn face. A grandfatherly expression, Bianca thinks. Pia is silent. After depositing her tray on a small table, she takes a step back to make room for Minna, then responds to the priest's gaze with a kind smile. At times she seems to go back to being a child, the way she likely was before her work aroused an endless guile within her. Right now she looks like an infant who wants to take her old guardian's hand and let herself be guided. But of course she cannot. The moment passes. Pia bows, turns around and disappears. A smile lingers for a few more seconds on the old man's face until a glass is forced into his hand and he comes back to his senses.

Bianca is not the only one to have noticed the exchange. Donna Clara, for whom Innes has given up his seat, turns to the pious man.

'Did you see how grown up your student has become?'

'Yes,' Don Dionisio says, sipping his drink.

'There's not a holy dove story there, is there, Father?' Young Count Bernocchi asks, stifling a yawn. 'Charity is best when we practise it on ourselves, Donna Clara. At least that way we don't risk delusions.'

Donna Julie shoots him a glance.

'Do you know that Pia reads stories to the girls? She plays with them and cares for them too. She's so precious to us, our Pia.'

'Do you mean to say that she even knows how to read? How is this possible?' Bernocchi asks, raising an eyebrow.

'And why not?' Don Dionisio says, putting his glass down on the tray excitedly and with a dangerous rattle. 'Pia is a girl just like any other. And she's quick to learn.'

'Don't tell me she knows Greek and Latin, too,' Bernocchi says with a smile.

'A bit, actually,' retorts Don Dionisio, before withdrawing into a hostile silence.

'Ah, how generous and enlightened contemporary Milan is!

Not only does it take in, raise and feed orphaned children, it also follows them step by step down the road of life, providing them with a higher education which will certainly come in handy when they are milking cows, raking hay and waxing the floors! Even the great Rousseau entrusted his bastard children to public care. And who better than he, with his illustrious work to prove it, to know the best way to raise a child?'

'Oh, you . . . you speak nonsense. And anyway, Rousseau was wrong.' Donna Julie speaks quickly, animatedly, as if a flame of thought has been lit from deep inside. She casts a feverish look at Bernocchi. She is no longer the poised, invisible creature she usually is. 'Rousseau was a monster to force poor Thérèse to give up her children. They ought to remain with their parents. They ought to live with them, enjoy their affection, receive kisses and spankings alike . . . only in this way will they learn to love: by example. Isn't this true, my dear husband?'

Don Titta bows his head in agreement. Bianca watches Donna Julie attentively as she recomposes herself, the colour in her cheeks fading. Never has she spoken with such vehemence.

'I know you have your ideas, Donna Julie,' Bernocchi retorts. 'You even nursed your children yourself, isn't that true? Or at least, that's what people said. I must say that I never saw you do it, but I would have liked to . . . you, the most spiritual of women, engaged in such an animalistic act. What a strange spectacle that must have been.'

'It wasn't for the public,' says Don Titta, frowning.

'Come, come,' Donna Clara interrupts, throwing her hands in the air. 'We don't want to start a fight on account of that boring man, Rousseau.'

She laughs her full-bodied laugh, throaty and frivolous.

'Donna Clara, you will never change,' Bernocchi speaks gallantly. 'You always were the queen of the salon.' As soon as he says this, though, he bites his lip, aware of the involuntary offence that does not go unnoticed.

'Oh, yes, dear Bernocchi. Those were good times. Now vanished forever.' She sighs and puffs out her taffeta chest, and with another gesture – her hands are never still – she shoos away a thought. 'But we are all much simpler and happier now. A little wild, but happy. Isn't that right, Julie? Isn't that right, my son?'

'Really, you are very special,' says Annina Maffei, a dark-haired lady in an intricate dress. 'You've created your own entourage. You pride yourself on being simple and rustic, but deep down you are very unique. You have a governess for the children, whom you refer to as Nanny even though she's French. You have dear Stuart for English, which, if you don't mind my saying, is an incomprehensible and violent language, worse than German. You even have a domestic painter and a poet in residence. Everyone in Milan gossips about you. And here you all are, hiding out. What I would do to bring you to a show at La Scala!'

Donna Clara seizes on this comment.

'Have you seen the most recent performance by Signorina Galli? How is she?'

'Signorina Brignani is far better, in my modest opinion,' replies Bernocchi. 'Signorina Galli is always the same. Exquisite and angelic, a little too much so. Signorina Brignani is small, exotic and spicy . . . if you know what I mean,' he adds, looking for signs of understanding from the men. 'But anything's better than the sylph-like doldrums of Signorina Pallarini.'

Tommaso nods with an all-too brief smile. Innes contemplates a corolla of tulips in a vase on a table behind him. Don

Titta assumes that distanced stare which is his usual defence against the world. Don Dionisio, the old priest, is immersed in his own private meditations, which look dangerously similar to sleep. And Bernocchi is vexed: he hates it when his quips fall flat. So he stares at Bianca, cocking his head slightly to one side and wetting his lips lasciviously. Despite herself, she blushes. A second later, his gaze drifts over to Pia, who ought to have been dismissed by now but who stands staring at Contessa Maffei's too ornate but nonetheless extremely enchanting gown. Pia neither notices Bernocchi nor feels his gaze on her, which even from a distance lingers a little too long.

※ ※

Bianca dismisses herself with a curtsey, which always works for a person of her status – somewhere between hired help and guest. But when she realizes that she has left her mother's ivory fan downstairs, rather than wait until the next day to retrieve it and risk finding it broken, she returns. Shrewdly, she stops at the threshold. Young Count Bernocchi is talking about her.

'It seems as though that awful Albion has given us the gift of an authentic gem. A coarse gem, of course, as brusque as she is pleasant. She needs only to be cleaned and polished with patience. Do you really think she will stay and draw all your flowers? You, my friend, are an eccentric man. It is you that everyone talks about in the city. Our poet peasant.'

'It's a shame she has freckles. She looks like a quail's egg,' Donna Annina says.

'And what about a man? Will you find her a husband? Or is she one of those modern girls who want to be "independent"?'

※ ※

64

'We must marry her off.'

This had been declared at every dinner with both insistence and some menace. Bartolo used to announce it to their father without even looking at her, as if she were merely one of the furnishings.

'By all means, we must not,' her father would reply, steadfast and unwavering. 'Bianca doesn't need to be married. We have given her the independence she needs to choose what she wants, even a husband if she so desires. But only if she desires.'

'But, Father, really. She is in her prime. Who will want her in five years? She will end up being an independent old maid with ink on her fingers and too much pride.' Bartolo spoke with sarcasm.

'Bartolomeo, I don't want to discuss this any further. Your sister will do what she pleases.'

Bartolo's face would redden and Zeno would slump down in his chair, raise his glass towards his brother and gulp down its contents mockingly. She would have given anything to disappear when she was at the centre of an argument or the cause of one. Her father would look at her with a kind smile but really she didn't know *what* to do with all her freedom. She wished she could have chosen to stay in that dining room with its walls of fading colours forever.

⊱ ⊰

She has heard enough. Bianca walks into the room with neither a smile nor a greeting, picks up her fan and leaves again, annoyed. She ignores their surprised gazes. Even Donna Annina blushes.

She looks at her reflection in the candlelit mirrors in the hallway and sees a delicate face with light freckles and high cheekbones. Wisps of hair fall out of her chignon. *Perhaps I am odd but so what?* she thinks. *I am me. J'ai quelquechose que les autres n'ont point*, she tells herself snobbishly. Too bad that the mirror in her room, aged by the modest white candle in its holder, shows only a blurry image of a half-formed woman.

Why should she stay in the house on her own? The night is young and there is another celebration going on, not too far away. All she needs to do is go down the servants' stairs, sneak through the small gate, and venture down the dark road with its strange shadows created by strange houses.

The street lamps are illuminated and cast a yellow glare on things, softening their contours. She follows the pounding of a drum and soon finds herself in the piazza, in front of the old church. A stage has been built and people are jumping about in a kind of dance, offering an enthusiastic, disorderly accompaniment to the violin. Giant torches at the corners of the stage shed light on the dancers. The musician, who stands on his own platform, has a large nose that looks even larger in the shadows. He has a slender face and wears dirty leggings that lend him an air of scruffy elegance. He is talented in his own right, even if his instrument screeches savagely. Bianca leans up against a wall in the darkness and watches. The torches reflect the people's red, straining faces. It is a revel of witches and wizards, united by the beating of the drum to celebrate Walpurgis Night. It is innocuous but not innocent. Bianca watches a girl jump down from the stage, laugh, and run, only to be followed by a young man who catches up with her, grabs her, turns her around, and kisses her on the neck and mouth with violent rapture. The girl tries to wriggle free but that only incites her partner further. He presses her up against the wall with kisses. A tug on Bianca's sleeve distracts her from the show.

'Miss Bianca! You sneaked out too?' Pia laughs excitedly and looks at her in complicit understanding. She follows

Bianca's gaze to the couple and shrugs. 'Our Luciana, she never can get enough.' She laughs again and takes Bianca by the arm. 'Come with me. Want to dance? Let's dance.'

She drags Bianca onto the stage, where the dense crowd shifts to make room for them. Bianca knows nothing about this kind of movement. It is some sort of noisy square dancing where couples shift from side to side, hooked by the arm. Pia guides her expertly, though, and it only takes a few seconds for her to understand the configuration of steps. There is the smell of camphor, leather, warm bodies and dust; of best outfits and shawls taken out of trunks; of jerkins tarred with sweat and pulled with twisting gestures. The smells mix with the sweet aroma of hay and flowers and the warm night. Pia laughs. Bianca laughs too, and they dance until they are tired. Pia leads Bianca to a stand resting on two barrels where Ruggiero and Tonio are busy filling mugs with red wine, young and tart. It doesn't quench their thirst and it leaves a tinny aftertaste. Pia gulps hers down and slams her mug back on the wood with wilful, masculine violence.

'We are all equal on the night of San Giovanni,' she says. Bianca doesn't understand what she means by this: men and women? Noblemen and country folk? Pia and Bianca? She doesn't ask because it isn't important. Pia takes her by the hand and then leads her down an alley. They turn a corner and continue along the side of a house. Bianca is silent, bewitched by the young girl's initiative. She has the feeling that they are being followed but when she turns around there is no one.

They continue on, through the wild undergrowth, where it becomes increasingly dark. Bianca calculates that this path must lead towards the fields. And precisely where the shrubbery ends and the great stretch of cultivated land opens up, a wonder lies waiting for them. Fireflies. There are hundreds, thousands, millions of them, suspended between sky and land, busily flying to and fro. They are dancing, too, guided by the instinct to draw circles, arcs, vaults and volutes in a breathtaking spectacle. It doesn't matter if there is no music here. The delicate singing of the crickets is all they need, the perfect accompaniment for the procession of tiny floating candles.

The shadow, if it is a shadow, leans upon a tree trunk and sighs.

☙ ❧

The following day, in the kitchen, all the talk is about Saint Peter's ship. The ship sits in a bottle, slightly chipped at the top. It has, as every year, been set up on the high windowsill so that people can parade beneath it. It has sails made of egg whites, and inside the bottle are thousands of bubbles. It is a ghost ship that has been caught in the fury of the northern seas, and has survived thanks to a miracle. Tradition has it that the family and staff consign their wishes to this small boat before it ferries the wishes off somewhere secret where they will be kept safe.

It is always this way and in the morning everything is as it should be; the servants have cleared away the remains of the party but something still lingers, something unfinished, which the fresh morning air cannot dissipate. Life goes on. Real life, not shiny or flashy, but a life that nonetheless emits its own pale radiance. It is like a replica of a precious jewel worn by a lady who keeps the original locked up in a safe for special occasions.

'I wish I could travel,' whispers Minna, contemplating the egg-white ship on the windowsill.

'You're not supposed to say what you wish for, silly, otherwise it won't come true,' Pia says, berating her with the wisdom of a thirteen-year-old.

'It won't come true, anyway,' Minna mumbles, before heading down to the laundry and the mountain of tablecloths that need washing.

'I don't care. *I'm* not going to say my wish out loud anyway,' Pia insists, looking for Bianca's approval.

But Bianca only smiles. What can she say to these girls? They have essentially been born prisoners. How can she console them when their future is already laid out? It is written in the stars. It cannot be any other way.

Bianca hovers there for a bit and considers. *Each and every one of us makes our own destiny. But this is only really true for men. Am I different?* she thinks. It is a pity that the great equality they experienced the night before disappears with the light of day. It is a pity it isn't contagious, that it cannot be gifted, a little bit at a time, like a mother yeast that is passed from home to home, making different doughs rise in the same way. Whoever has the power to transform things, or to transform themselves, doesn't share it. *Come dawn, we were all Cinderellas,* Bianca says to herself. *We had to slip back into our grey rags, pick up our brooms, and clean up the shards of our dreams before we stepped on them and wounded ourselves.*

The thought makes her furious. She storms outside, forgetting a hat, swooping the rest of her things up along the way. The gardeners mumble veiled greetings and then watch her lewdly. She notices nothing, just keeps on walking, up and down the hills and then beyond the ditches. Despite the water and mud, it isn't hard to find what she is looking for: those strange, small, wild orchids – the sweet peas. They crawl up and around the big bushes of lavender and across the elastic slouch of lespedeza, which in its current flowerless state looks mute but is still beautiful. The jasmine, likely not happy with the fact that the sweet peas have bloomed, proposes its own new reddish shoots like fumbling hands moving towards new adventures. She stops and sighs.

On closer inspection, she discovers new details. The garden is so big and variable that the poet's experiments overlap and get confused. Even those left unfinished – and there are many of them – reveal their own kind of harsh and rebellious grace, the secret charm of possibility. Bianca begins to draw and soon everything is restored to its place, at least for now.

❧ ❧

Some days are simply not long enough for all the life that runs through them; the climate is perfect, shifting miraculously from cool to warm, from shade to sunshine and back again to the shade. For the days are not always clear – at times the clouds pass rapidly overhead and stain the ground below. On those days, every natural thing seems to have just been born and at the same time seems to be a hundred years old, every natural thing looks back at you in challenge: you inconsequential crumb, you miserable, minuscule mortal. You understand that everything of significance has already happened and will continue to happen long after you're gone. And instead of feeling frustrated, you feel a profound happiness because you realize that this is how it is supposed to be, it's the course of non-human life, things that need to be contemplated but not understood, for this kind of comprehension is simply too vast for brains the size of a fist. Whatever you do on those days, you come away feeling both satisfied and incomplete: nothing will ever compare with so much glory and yet you have wasted all this time on banalities. You should have just sat still and reflected on what was happening: both everything and nothing. That would have been better. And instead you busied yourself like an ant, filling your hours with mindless tasks:

eating, sleeping, talking. And when the day disappears into the velvet blue there's nothing left to do but pray that tomorrow will be identical, but it won't be, because perfect days are always different, one from the next; no one can ever recall two being alike.

⁂

Some days begin badly for Bianca but get better as the dissatisfaction, anger and capriciousness that force her to hate everyone – first and foremost herself – melt like frost in the sunlight. It takes so little, sometimes just an excuse, to laugh or even smile. Since she cannot fly as she might wish, she chooses to walk very slowly, thankful for her two feet.

She thinks of the time she went to the kitchen to ask for some clean rags and found Donna Clara seated there on a high altar, like a gargantuan queen, intent on teaching the cook something new. She read recipes out loud from Agnoletti's *Nuova cucina economica*, some in perfect Italian and other parts translated into dialect, naming ingredients, directions and measurements. The cook wanted to know what was wrong with her gnocchi, and why they weren't good enough any more.

'Listen,' Donna Clara said. 'Here it says to add two eggs to the mixture to make it more compact, do you understand? Do you usually do that? No? Well then, don't complain if your gnocchi are too soft.'

They are a strange family: at times snobbish and then practical and down to earth. Sometimes they mix with the peasants and moments later they give off airs of superiority. First they laugh and then they are serious. Even Donna Clara's ailments have something comical about them.

'I've got an awful headache. It's as if a beast with large hands were squeezing the back of my head . . .'; 'Today I have a stomach ache. It's as if a beast with large hands were taking hold of my intestines and shaking them . . .'; 'If you only knew what a backache I have today. It's as if a beast with large hands were punching me here, here and over here . . .'

Old Pina, maid and Cerberus to Donna Clara, is the only one who pays any attention to her complaints. She cocks her white head to the side like a perplexed chicken and spews out suggestions of herbal remedies in no particular order: aniseed for the belly; bittersweet to rid her of phlegm; fava plants, but just a little, for her headache. The other maids listen, containing their smiles with bowed heads. And when Donna Clara drags herself to the living room awaiting the treatment most suited to this day's ailment, the giggling begins.

'Be careful the beast doesn't put his big hands up your skirt! Because that'll definitely make you feel better.'

'But how big is he?' snickers another maid.

'This big!'

Bianca doesn't engage with them but can easily imagine the vulgar gestures that accompany the exchange. She pictures a mythological animal, some sort of Minotaur, slipping into bed with Donna Clara and massaging her white shoulders with his giant hands in a prelude to providing her with the kinds of pleasures that are now only memories for the lady of the house. Bianca wonders about those memories. She herself does not yet possess any.

❧ ❧

'What kind of name is Minna?' Bianca asks. It sounds almost Nordic to her but she cannot imagine how the girl's parents – two peasants with red, rugged faces – came to choose that name from the Litany of the Saints or a list of relatives.

Minna, who has been folding shirts, drops what she is

doing, sits down on a stool, crosses her legs, rests her elbows on her knees, and looks Bianca up and down.

'It's a long story.'

'I'm listening,' Bianca says, brushing her hair.

Minna begins to tell her story. It is clear from the start that it is one she enjoys recounting.

'Minna is the name that they copied by mistake from the document that the parish issued. They already had a Mirta, Carlo, Battista and Luigina. There was no room for me in the house, and since I was born at harvest, in May, and Mamma had to go and work in the fields and couldn't even breastfeed me, they left me at the group home in Milan.'

'What do you mean?' Bianca says, putting down the brush and facing the girl. It seems the story will indeed be long and complicated.

'The group home was where they brought us abandoned babies,' Minna explains.

'An orphanage,' says Bianca, convinced now of having understood.

'Oh, no, Miss Bianca,' Minna laughs, covering her mouth with her hand. 'I had a mamma and a papa, I told you. I still have them. Not only orphans get abandoned, you know. Poor children are abandoned too. Sometimes just temporarily. They came back for me when I was five.'

'And until then you lived in the institution?'

Minna raises her eyebrows. 'Institution?'

'Yes, the place where they keep abandoned children – the home, as you call it.' She has seen one in Paris. It was a big building, white and elegant. Her father told her about this custom of entrusting newborns to the public institution so that they could grow strong and educated, as was their right.

'Oh, no, Miss Bianca, you don't understand,' Minna says. 'In this place in Milan, there's a kind of big wooden drawer that slides in and out of the front door. Babies are placed in it and they are pushed through into the building. But the babies don't stay there. They only remain when they're newborns. They are taken in, inspected to make sure that they're healthy, and then given to a wet nurse in some village. The real parents provide clothes, a blanket and some money now and then if they can. The new families are either farmers, they herd geese or they work in the fields. They take good care of the babies. Every so often someone goes to check on them. If a baby dies, the money stops coming and it's all over. When the mothers and fathers – the real ones – want their babies back, they go and get them. If they want them. If and when they can afford them. They came to get me when I was five,' she says again, proudly. 'But my name was wrong. My document said Erminia but either the priest was old and deaf, or the man who copied the name into the book wrote it wrong, or the priest read my name wrong to the people of Cusago who took me in, because he said Arminna, or something that wasn't even a Christian name, so they had to give me the name of a normal saint. Anyway, they changed Arminna to Minna. When I finally came home, the name stuck. Now I'm used to it. It's like dogs and cats: if you start calling them something else, they don't understand.'

So that is Minna's story, Bianca thinks. Not at all Nordic. Bianca wonders if Minna has any memories from those five years she spent with strangers; if they cared for her well; if they treated her like their own child or like a servant. Maybe she won't be able to answer. Probably she has forgotten everything; or perhaps she doesn't want to talk about it. Bianca looks at her with newfound respect. That little girl with the face of a kitten has dealt with her own trials and tribulations, and yet, here she is, alive and whole. That is not insignificant. That is the stolid force of one who takes life as it is, because nothing can be done about it.

Bianca turns to the mirror and looks at Minna's face in the reflection behind her. 'Would you like to finish my hair?' She sees the child smile from ear to ear. Minna is finally being considered more than just a maid – a lady in waiting. Bianca doesn't mind if Minna pulls her hair; it is only because she is excited. It is all right if she doesn't fix the tiny bone pins tightly enough in her bun, even if it means she can hardly move her head throughout dinner. Later Bianca sees Minna's reflection again in the mirror in the dining room, when she peeks in to check on the public effect of her hairdressing.

No one notices her hair except Tommaso, who hurries to sit next to Bianca after dinner.

'You have the neck of a nymph,' he whispers while others are chatting amongst themselves.

Bianca frowns. She doesn't know how to take compliments. She has never learned, never having had the time or the occasion to do so. Instead of blushing or looking down, as is customary, she stares at him fiercely. *What nerve.* Her neck flares with anger. She feels it transforming into a scarlet map of an archipelago, and she places her hand to her throat and coughs.

'Have you caught a cold, Miss Bianca? You ought to take care of yourself and wear a scarf,' Donna Clara says, unwittingly dissipating all embarrassment with her prickly thoughtfulness.

Tommaso turns away, resting his elbow on the table and leaning his chin in his hand. He changes the topic.

'Titta,' he says, 'if it's no burden, I'd like to talk with you about something that is dear to my heart . . .'

The two men get up, bow and take their leave. Bianca's flush of colour slowly fades under Innes's severe gaze.

೫ ೫

Perhaps encouraged by a new sense of trust – and not quite ready to accept that what has occurred between them is a one-off – Minna never leaves Bianca's side even though she doesn't need an assistant and has already told her so. But Donna Clara thinks a domestic painter should have an assistant and Bianca fears that by turning Minna down she will offend the older lady. So, in addition to letting her care for her hair, Bianca allows Minna to carry her paintbox and easel. And when the drawing session is over, she lets the girl clean her brushes, but always under close observation for those little hands can also be rough. Minna follows her wherever she goes, as loyal as a puppy, curious to the point of appearing insolent. She is a domestic servant who has barely been domesticated herself. Initially, Bianca suspects that Minna follows her so that she can watch her paint and tell the others about it later. But then she understands the loyalty of servitude.

'I don't tell people about our conversations. I swear to you, may I die as a spy,' Minna tells her, crossing her fingers in an X and kissing them.

'Cross my heart, hope to die,' Bianca says, in English.

'What?' Minna asks.

Bianca explains the rhyme and has Minna repeat it. Later Minna goes to the girls in the courtyard and tells them that she knows English. And she does know a little: several rhymes, deformed and mumbled, *yessir, yesmadam*, things that she has picked up in Innes's lessons. Bianca enjoys correcting the child's pronunciation and has her repeat Mother Goose rhymes like 'Mary had a little lamb'. She chooses rhymes about animals so it is easier for Minna to separate the words from the rhythm and connect them to the inhabitants of their own courtyard: the geese, the baby lamb, the cats, dogs and ducks. Each time she learns a new word, Minna's face brightens, amazed by these tiny discoveries. It occurs to Bianca that because the pleasure of learning isn't being imposed on Minna, but rather gleaned with the eagerness of someone who is not privy to it, she absorbs everything. The other children, meanwhile, sit at their desks in the nursery and repeats dull phrases in French that echo all the way down into the garden. The maids in the kitchen giggle and repeat their own lessons: *mossieu a un shevall, madame a un paraplooie, bonshoo, bonswa, addieww.*

Pia joins Minna and Bianca as often as she can. Her presence has a strange effect on Minna. At first the younger girl seems annoyed, but then she calms down and almost seems relieved not to have to take on assignments that are too complicated for her. With Pia around, Minna plays happily on the sidelines. She will take a little dolly out of her apron, give Pia her seat, and still manage to keep herself under control. As Bianca retreats into her world of drawing, Pia also disappears into a secret world. She doesn't carry toys or dollies in her apron. She has a book. The first time Bianca realizes this, her surprise is evident.

'I'm allowed, you know,' Pia says defensively. 'The books come from the library – I don't steal them! Don Titta said I could borrow them. All I have to do is show him which book I want so he can see if it's right for me.'

From then on, Bianca looks with amusement at the books the maid chooses. She sees *Breve storia della rosa, Il Castello di Otranto* and *I fioretti di San Francesco.* She understands now why Pia's vocabulary is a mix of popular dialect and more polished words.

The three girls keep each other company, each in their own silent world.

Pia too, though, is only a child. And sometimes she is over-come with excitement. Once they reach their selected location, she will set down Bianca's box of colours which she happily carries for Minna, and run off, like a little horse, until she reaches the limits of the woodlands. Then she'll come back laughing, worn out but calmer, breathlessly justifying herself.

'That feels good!'

Once, upon her return from a galloping excursion, her bonnet slips off and reveals light blue satin ribbons braided through her glossy brown hair.

'The ribbons come from the young misses,' Pia explains quickly. 'But they're mine now. They were a bit spoilt, and they weren't wearing them any more, and so they gave them to me. This too, look.' She lifts up her dark red skirt to show off a white lacy underskirt. 'Even my knickers,' she says, laughing and twirling. 'But they belonged to Donna Julie.' She looks at Bianca for signs of understanding. 'I'm more comfort-able in these.' She pulls up the skirt to reveal a pair of white knickers with bows at the ankles. Donna Julie is very petite and not much bigger than the girl. It occurs to Bianca that this passing down of used clothing must raise some dissent in the kitchen.

In fact, Minna is staring at her friend as if she wants to hit her, but then she bursts into a smile that is too genuine to be false. Pia understands.

'The maids don't want me around. They say I'm the misses' darling. But I am always alone with the cook and with Minna, or with the girls, so it's all right. And now,' she adds, with sin-cere glee, 'you're here too.'

Sometimes Pia sings.

'Sing the one about the fire,' Minna says, clapping her hands. And so she begins.

> *Brusuu, brusà*
> *Chissà chi l'è staa?*
> *Sarà staa quei de Bress*
> *Che i fa tutt a roess;*
> *Sarà staa quei de Cusan*
> *Che i è svelti de la man.*
> *Brusuu, brusà*
> *Chissà chi l'è staa?*

> Burn, burn
> Who made it burn?
> Maybe it was the folk from Bress
> Just like they do all the rest;
> Maybe it was the folk from Cusan
> Who are fast with their hands.
> Burn, burn
> Who made it burn?

Bianca doesn't like this song. It is shapeless, like a sweater that has lost its form following too many washings. Her favourite is far softer, sweeter.

> *Ninna delle oche*
> *Tante, medie o poche*
> *Bianche con le piume*
> *Ninna delle brume*
> *Che vengono drumeumee*
> *Che vengono e vanno*
> *Sommesse, senza danno*
> *Che celano nel manto*
> *Un cavallino bianco*

Cavallo e cavaliere
Li voglio rivedere
Mi porteranno via
Lontano a casa mia
Ma casa mia dov'è
È dove sono re
Son re e son regina
Ninna della bambina.

Lullaby of the geese
Many, some, or just a few
White feathers
And foggy song
They come in autumn
They come and go
Soft and no trouble
In their capes
Hides a white horse
Horse and rider
I want to see them
They'll carry me away
Back to my home
But where's my home
It's where I am king
I am king and I am queen
Lullaby of the little girl.

'That's pretty,' Bianca says the first time she hears it. 'Sing it again.'

And Pia, in her strong, clear voice, obeys.

'Don Titta wrote it for his daughters,' she offers, without anyone asking her. 'I wonder what it's like to have a father like him. Sometimes he plays with them, too. I've never seen a father like that on this earth.'

'Well, they don't get to see him very often. He's very busy and often travels to the city . . .' Bianca stops herself mid-sentence.

'Yes, but it's better than nothing, isn't it?' Pia pushes away one thought with another. 'Antonia, my friend from the piazza, gets beaten by her father every night. He drinks too much and then strikes her and her mother. Sometimes her arms are black and blue; they look like plums from the garden. And Minna's father doesn't even look at her.'

She says it without malice and Minna nods, never taking her eyes off her faceless dolly.

Pia laughs bitterly. 'I wonder what my own father was like.'

'Maybe he's still alive,' says Bianca.

'No,' Pia says. 'He died for sure. Otherwise he would have come back to get me. But let's pretend that he didn't die. We're allowed to dream. Yes, let's pretend he went to the other side of the world in search of his fortune and that one day he will come back for me and he will be a lord and I will become a lady and he will be happy that I studied and am not ignorant like the others. I know how to behave in society; I even know English, and we would go to live in a palace. First, though, we would visit my mother's grave. He knows where it is. I'm sure he does.'

Quiet falls over the little group. Bianca doesn't know what to say. Finally Pia breaks the silence and continues.

'She's dead, you know. She passed away giving life to me. She flew into the arms of the Lord, up there, where it's more comfortable. Don Dionisio told me, so it must be true.'

❧ ❧

Ribbons, second-hand knickers, books on loan. There are other manifestations of Donna Clara's favouritism for Pia too, and sometimes it seems excessive to Bianca. Pia is just a maid after all and Donna Clara is the lady of the house. Sometimes, in the evenings, Donna Clara makes Pia get up on a stool and recite poetry for whoever is there. A circle of tired but curious listeners will form and Pia always has a handful of new verses ready. She'll blush slightly, close her eyes for inspiration and begin, her hands folded in front of her to prevent herself from fidgeting.

> *Pensoso, inconsolabile, l'accorta ninfa*
> *Il ritiene e con soavi e molli*
> *Parolette, carezzalo se mai*
> *Potesse Itaca sua trargli dal petto;*
> *Ma ei non brama che veder dai tetti*
> *Sbalzar della sua dolce Itaca il fumo,*
> *E poi chiuder per sempre al giorno i lumi.*
> *Nè commuovere, Olimpio, il cuor ti senti?*

> Distressed and inconsolable, the clever nymph
> Held him and with soft and gentle
> Words, caressed and tried
> To remove beloved Ithaca from his chest;
> If only he could see the smoke rise above his sweet Ithaca
> And then forever close his eyes to the light of day.
> Does this move you, Olympian, can you feel your heart?

The maids comment on her performance.
'I didn't understand one word of it, but she's good.'
'Those little words sound just like caresses.'
'She follows her lessons well.'
Judging from the comments, it sounds like Pia really is

everyone's daughter. She bows, hops off the stool, picks it up, and nods to Nanny, who then pushes the two boys forward, dressed up in sheets. Enrico is Telemachus and Pietro is all of the suitors. They recite their parts timidly, their eyes fixed on Tommaso, who has taken it upon himself to teach them the verse and who whispers along with them, sending nods of encouragement. They conclude with a happy brawl with small wooden swords, round shields and leather armbands made by Ruggiero. No one can stop them. The duel goes on – it lasts an age; the verses of Homer are forgotten and all that is left is brotherly rancour mixed with joy, jab after jab.

☙ ❧

'Pia trusts you. She sees you as a mentor. I have never seen her so content. And I am pleased with the way you treat her,' Donna Clara says one day to Bianca, taking her aside in an imperious yet intimate manner.

'I can tell that she is very dear to you,' observes Bianca, trying to appear nonchalant but taking advantage of Donna Clara's conversational mood.

'Yes, you're right. It's not just our Christian duty that pushes us to treat her favourably. Pia is truly a special girl. She's so alive. My granddaughters are such delicate daisies; they take entirely after their mother, poor dears. Even my darling Giulietta: she cries over nothing and is always ill. I love them because they are my flesh and blood, and it's the law of nature. But it is nice to let oneself, every so often, choose whom to love. And Pia is my choice. When she is older, I will be sure to give her a real dowry, not like the Ospedale Maggiore, with their horse blankets and two cents. We will help her find a good husband who will respect her – a shopkeeper, a merchant, or a small property owner.'

Bianca falls silent, irked by this compunction. *You treat her as if she were your doll,* she thinks. *You grant her certain privileges that other servants only dream of. It's all fine now, while she's young, but when she's grown up she will have to fend off jealousy. You are using her.* Bianca would like to voice some of these things but the words stay bottled up inside. She has no right to speak her mind to Donna Clara. She has the feeling too that there are other things at work in the background, blurring the focus of this painting whose only distinguishable feature is Pia's face. She has been told that the girl's father has disappeared and her mother is dead. But if Pia truly is a foundling, how do they know all these things? Who told them? And what if her story is the same one told to many lost girls, the details sewn together like a quilt? Do they simply feed the girls' fantasies?

Pia will end up heartbroken, Bianca says to herself. The thought pains her and she silently promises to watch out for the girl as long as she can.

☙ ❧

Bianca needs to focus on her work. She decides that she will make all the preliminary sketches in the summer and then, during the winter, when her subjects are temporarily away, she will begin painting. Without the liveliness of colour before her, though, it will be difficult. She therefore compiles a selection of different colour swatches. She takes large pieces of paper and draws rows and rows of the same-sized rectangles, and fills them with the colours she knows she will need: innumerable shades of green and brown; creamy whites; whites with hints of pink, orange or yellow; the powerful vermilion of the upside-down fuchsias and the fresh bougainvillea from Brazil; the lilac blues of plumbago and rosemary. She positions the mixtures in front of their originals to verify their intensity, force and sweetness. What she discovers is a palette of harmonious colours, shading from the palest to the most intense. It is beautiful to see. Pia is fascinated by the chart; she devours it with her eyes and speaks the names of the colours out loud, savouring them as though they are flavours. Burnt sienna. Scarlet. Viridian. Lapis lazuli. Carmine.

Bianca's work does not end there. Next, along the border of each rectangle, she jots down in pencil the proportions of pigment that she has used in each mixture, hoping to catch the exact hue. How much is science and how much is enthusiasm, she doesn't know. Painting, though not a science, takes precision. It requires methodology and application, two predispositions that are not natural to Bianca, but which she has nonetheless mastered, as one does an exacting yet healthy sport that reinforces both muscles and posture.

She also has lovely calligraphy. One day Don Titta calls her to his study to ask her to copy out, in alphabetical order, all the names of the flowers, plants, shrubs and vegetables that grow in Brusuglio, or at least the ones that grow within the confines of the walled garden.

'It's part of a bigger task that I need your help with,' he explains, showing her the ledgers he has prepared precisely for this purpose. One lined column takes up a third of the page and the rest is filled with small squares. It is for accounting. He plans to fill it with the dates of the plants' arrival, their costs, the origin of the grafts, and comments on their outcome: if they wither in two months, resist, die, are struck by scale insects or powdery mildew, and so on.

'I need to catalogue. In these kinds of things I am consistent,' he says. 'I would like to do it myself, but I would have to dedicate all my time and mental energy to it. And now my mind is possessed by other thoughts . . .' He draws a small vortex in mid-air with his index finger. 'I'm like a coil: infinite. One thought attached to another attached to another . . .'

Bianca wonders if that's how poetry comes into being. Does it start with a chain of thoughts, and then – either suddenly or with premeditation – a flow of words fills out the chain the way a hand fills out a glove? She doesn't dare ask. She has not reached that level of confidence with him yet. She fears that he might be thrown by the question and she understands that for the general well-being of the family it is best for him to be calm. When he is absent, cooped up in his study for days on end, or out on his long walks, he does not talk about his plants, the harvest or the possibility of a drought. It is as if the persona of poet is too fastidious and demanding to be able to live with that other self, the one that drags him literally back to earth – towards the land, flowers, plants, vines and grain. But it is also evident that Don Titta feels nostalgia for the part of him that he has to neglect at times.

'If only one could keep ledgers of sentiments as well,' Bianca blurts out. She brings a hand to her mouth in shock. What has she said? Why did she say it? The master looks at her in surprise and then smiles.

'Even a man as highly unrealistic as myself could tell you that this would be useless. So, when will you begin the task?'

Tomorrow. There is always a tomorrow for postponing things. The days are long and slow and she is already busy. But despite the large undertaking, she decides to add a miniature drawing to each of the entries, as well as copying out the names. It will make the ledger even more precise and complete, with its old papers, documents, accompanying letters, receipts in French and English, and accounts of seeds purchased from afar.

From these master books, Bianca discovers more about the grand ambitions of the garden project than by visiting the greenhouses and fields in person. She learns how atypical shoots are planted and if the climate is conducive to them. She gets a sense of which seeds prosper and which wither. Every so often, though, she has to get away from her desk and get more precise information from Leopoldo Maderna, the head gardener.

At first Maderna looks into Bianca's eyes and answers every one of her questions in an irritated tone, as if he disapproves strongly and does not understand the hasty need for results from such a project. But then he contradicts himself, becoming excited.

'The black locust trees are rooting well. Actually, the roots are propagating and are shooting up from the ground in places you'd least expect them. It's exhausting to rip them out because they're formed like an upside down T, like this.' He holds out his left palm horizontally, the middle finger pointing up, to explain the shape. 'To pull them out you need to get really deep down. There they are – over there, and there.' And he points all around, along the horizon, at some green splotches. 'They're tall now. And they make up a wonderful dividing hedge, a flexible wall, but they prick worse than brambles.'

Bianca thinks about the green tangle that surrounded the home of Sleeping Beauty. Was it planted with *Robinia pseudo-acacia*, with those small, seemingly innocent, bright green, oval leaves that never seemed to age?

There are trees everywhere: *Acer negundo* and *platanoides*, a grove of *Salix babylonica*, and the *Liriodendron*, with its aspiration for height and yellow flowers as big as fists. There is *Ailanthus*, as beautiful as it is fetid; *Gleditsia*, a thorny locust even crueller than the black variety. And there is *Inermis*, constrained to a sapling. Leopoldo tells her too about *Andromeda arborea* with its beautiful star name, which looks like a blazing fire in autumn. And the *Clematis* from Lake Como, which

Bianca has always found overly dramatic, but she doesn't say so because Como is Maderna's home town and she doesn't want him to stop talking now that he has started. Anyway, it is no use, he says, the *Clematis* won't take. He points to these plants, struggling to climb the taut lines along a south-facing wall that ought to supply them with the necessary shade and instead puts them to shame. Maybe they prefer the north. There are the *armandii* and the *cirrhosa* varieties, with their three, pointy, garnet-coloured flowers. They are lovely, yes, but too sparse to make an impression. The *intricata* is all leaves and might remain as such, and the *pagoda*, with its exquisite name, hints at sophisticated chinoiserie. Passing from the delightful to the useful, there are vines from Burgundy and Bordeaux, but they aren't faring too well.

'The issue here is the land; it's only good for *Bersamino*, that fussy grape that comes from young Don Tommaso's parts. To find really beautiful vines, one needs to take the Via Francesca, or go beyond the Po River to the foothills of the mountains,' Leopoldo explains, as he guides her through the estate. 'These are grown in the French manner, as dwarves.' Together they skirt the neat bush-trained vines from which hang miniature bunches of acid-green grapes. 'You'll see how good these grapes are, but a few is all that Don Titta's table needs. Let's hope that powdery mildew doesn't take hold of them first.'

After conversations like these, Bianca goes back to the study, rereads her notes, compares them with the organized shopping lists written by Don Titta, verifies the spelling and checks them against guides and dictionaries. She discovers that out there, though she does not know where exactly, there really is everything: cherry, apple, pear, apricot and plum trees, in millions of varieties. If the world were to end, everyone in town could live for weeks off these fruits.

Bianca finds she doesn't want to know a thing about the repugnant art of silkworms. The mulberry trees, on which they feed, are numerous.

'You mustn't plant them too close together,' Leopoldo tells her. 'In the first year you breed only three branches, and keep them clean cut. We planted eight hundred and then another eight hundred. If we have too many leaves, we can always sell them.'

In fact, she has seen many young boys coming and going with baskets full of fresh leaves to give to the silkworms that live in the peasants' homes. They take care of them day and night like guests of honour. If you get close enough, you can hear the incessant gnashing of their jaws.

'They are a Japanese green breed,' Leopoldo explains with pride. Bianca, who does not want to see them, not even from afar, imagines them as being fat, bound in tiny flowered pieces of fabric, and wrapped in silk string. She knows they work hard, but she doesn't want to even try to appreciate them. Leopoldo, who clearly feels more comfortable with her now, takes a dark pleasure in inviting Bianca to see where they blanch the worms.

She saves the best for last, like a child before a plate of sweets. The flowers. Obviously, she focuses on the ones with which she is less familiar. She knows a fair amount from her studies, from her books and from visits to the most import-ant botanical gardens in Europe. She has already come across hydrangeas and their exaggerated richness in Kew Gardens, but she learns that they are almost unknown in Italy. To get there, they come from France by sea and then wagon, like enslaved princesses. Bianca fantasizes about the shrubs in their jute sacks and the young mahogany-coloured servants who bring them fresh water every day, water that the servants want to drink themselves but cannot. She pictures the ship sailing on and on. What if there was a storm and the boat was wrecked – where would those plants end up? At the bottom of the sea? Would they breed with algae and decorate the hair of mermaids? Or would they drift along the surface, helped by the current, until reaching some desert beach, forming a grove in a new corner of the earth that has previously been known only to monkeys? No, the hydrangeas that Leopoldo Maderna is so proud of are merely the outposts of a whimsical invasion commanded by a French friend of Don Titta's, named Dupont. In the ledger, Dupont is nicknamed 'the flower correspondent'. He has sent plants from Paris at regular intervals with several folio sheets from the *Almanach du bon jardinier*. Plants also come from the offices of Longone Constantino da Dugnano, a great cello of a man, big-boned and rather slow, who carries his last name proudly and who has the tendency to blush every time he sees a woman. He brings shoots that need to be transplanted in a hurry.

Almost all the flowers are Parisian by birth. This explains, perhaps, their reluctance to take root in these rustic lands. The *Lathyrus*, for example, is something of a failure in all its forms. The *Bignonia* fare better, and actually are so invasive that their orange flowers are overwhelming. The *Digitalis*, with its poisonous qualities, has been planted in the far reaches of the gardens, where no child would think of feeding their dolls with those colourful tube-like flowers. The light blue and lilac *Lobelia* create colourful stains along the border of the great valley, light and dark hues depending on the tyranny of shade and soil. The *Achillea, Aquilegia canadensis* and *Rudbeckia*, with their ordinary gay colours, grow semi-wild and are planted at the far ends of the garden. Pink sachets of *Silene*, as light as silk, stand shivering along the confines of the field. This is neither an Italian nor a French country garden; it is different from everything, a bastard child, whose mother is beauty and father is experimentation. It lacks the charm of the English garden, where rare flowers look like dishevelled weeds, where roses rest against tree trunks like weary girls, and where emerald-green grasses are compact and lovely with moisture. It is a garden of contradictions, like its owner. It is high and low at the same time, plebeian and haughty.

To learn the names of things makes Bianca feel somewhat omnipotent. To learn the history of a seed, its timing, and its ways gives her a strange sense of self-possession. Copying down all that information in the correct order – and adding her personal touch of a tiny ink drawing of a leaf, flower or fruit in the column she has created herself – is Bianca's own way of making sense of the world. She expects to receive compliments from the entire family once her work is finished: the poet's sincere gratitude, an evening of oohs and aahs, the little girls being allowed to turn the pages so they can recognize the flowers and fruits they have seen thousands of times, and learn to spell out their Latin and common names. They will ask if they can copy the drawings, and Bianca, with enthusiasm, will promise them a colouring book with the best drawings on a larger scale for their small hands. She will enjoy a small triumph and ignore envious glances or sly comments – the honey on the rim of the cup that holds a bitter drink.

᪥ ᪥

One day, Bianca walks into the library in search of *Traité des arbres fruitiers*. She saw it in the hands of the master a few days ago. It is a beautiful edition with hand-coloured tables. Don Titta purchased it in Paris, he told her once at dinner, when he decided to dedicate himself – 'ignorant as a newborn' – to the land. Instead of taking the book and leaving, however, Bianca cannot resist the urge to leaf through it immediately. She stares at the drawings of the dappled skin of a pear, and then at the rust-coloured network of some strange apple, its name sweeter than its actual flavour. Behind her, Don Titta approaches in silence.

'Are you interested in apples, Miss Bianca?'

She jumps, then, regaining her composure, turns around and takes a step back. He is so close to her she can smell his clothes: a scent of verbena, somewhat feminine.

'I was curious to see how Monceau managed with fruits,' she says. 'In the drawings from a century ago they always look so small. Not to mention the branches – so spindly they're frightening.'

'A little, but that is their natural structure – they look like the hands of old men. But as far as the fruits themselves go, it is because you have ours in mind. Brusuglio is a rediscovered paradise, or better, an Eden where we have been happily forgotten.' He speaks without a hint of irony. 'Our apples, do not fear, do not bring damnation. There are no prohibited fruits here or sick ones. You can bite them to your heart's content. You know the unwritten rule: nothing halfway. We have magnificent plants, or nothing,' he finishes with a smile.

Bianca returns the gesture. She knows about Don Titta's attempts to plant white cotton and the Nanking cherry. The former caught on at first, for in one of the ledgers there is a triumphant message detailing a bountiful crop: five kilos of raw cotton transformed into eighty aune of precious percale through octane spinning. But it was only a one-time miracle. The cold, frost, rain and hail brought it to a bitter end. Too many enemies for a small plant that wants only heat.

Even now they are going through a strange season. It rains

like there will never be sun again. The children, confined to the house, are bursting with suppressed energy. A faint green mist presses against the trees, concealing the edges of the world.

'Shall we send out a dove?' Innes suggests. Both Donna Clara and Donna Julie look at him with disapproving glances. 'Or a dog?' he corrects himself. Bianca lets out a little chuckle.

'Dogs don't like to go out in the rain,' Pietro replies. 'That's why they end up pooing in the house and stinking it up.'

Shocked laughter follows from the little girls and from Enrico.

'Stinky poo, stinky poo,' Enrico sings.

'Children!' Their mother tries to call them back to order. Nanny covers her mouth in shock. Innes, master of deflection, distracts them.

'Do you know how many days the Great Flood lasted? Seven? Five? One hundred? Twenty?'

Satisfied looks come from both mother and grandmother. It is always a good time to review the sacred scriptures.

❧ ❧

In the space of only two days, all three girls fall ill. Hiding her own cough, Donna Julie shuttles back and forth between nursery and ground floor, carrying either insipid food or smelly herbal concoctions. The poet, as always in such family crises, shuts himself in his study. Tommaso, afraid of being left alone with the boys, does the same. Donna Clara spends her time worrying. Innes is left to entertain the boys, turning down Nanny's offer of help. Bianca passes the days in the extremely humid greenhouse, watching drips of water run down the panes of glass from her place on the iron bench, identical to the kind she sat on in the Condorcet gardens. Bianca feels good in the rain, and in water, generally. It has always been that way. It is her element – if not by nature, then by choice. Being there, surrounded by it, she daydreams the way she did while swimming in her slow, precise manner across the dark lake at her home. It is as though she is in a light green bubble. The aromas of the greenhouse, accentuated by the prevailing moisture, daze her. Memories take her away from this world, which clutches her like a tight corset even though it has all the elements of comfort – freedom, independence, and a certain amount of fun. She doesn't know quite what to make of this nostalgia. It isn't a feeling that she enjoys. She thinks it useless, a wasted exercise, to want things that are no longer attainable. She doesn't really miss the lake because she knows it is still there. Its quiet, mineral existence carries on without her. She knows she can get to it in two days by carriage. When you know something is there, when you can reach out and touch it, it exists. It's there, even if you *don't* touch it. Really, the sole person she misses terribly is inside her, ready to answer when she calls, present the way that spirits are always present, their company perceived only when you listen hard enough. And yet, Bianca feels, something is missing.

༅ ༅

'Who was it?' Don Titta storms into the nursery, dripping with rain, his frock coat steaming before the fire. He looks like a ghost, a slight mist blurring his contours. His hair, long and darker on account of the water, sticks to his pale cheeks, and his eyes flash. The little girls whisper, then Franceschina runs to seek shelter in Nanny's arms. Even the boys huddle together instinctively.

'Who was it?' he repeats, holding out the *Traité* before him, its cover blackened and soaking wet.

Bianca feels a pain shoot through her. Without speaking,

she comes closer, takes the book from his hands and places it on the rug in front of the fire. Kneeling down before the book, she opens the pages carefully, separating those that are already buckling together.

'You know my books mustn't leave the library,' Don Titta says sternly. 'You children used it to copy out the fruits, isn't that right?' No one answers. 'Isn't that right?' he repeats more loudly.

Five silent heads nod yes.

'But we stayed inside. We didn't take it out there,' Enrico objects, as if the book is a rare animal to be kept in a cage.

'I would like to know who brought it up to the rotunda, and above all, who left it there.'

Silence.

'I saw Miss Bianca carrying it under her arm. She was going that way with a box of coloured pencils.'

It is Pietro.

'It's true,' says Bianca. 'I took it with me. But I also brought it back, of course, before it started to rain.'

'Well, I'm only saying that I saw her with the book,' Pietro repeats, staring at his feet. Bianca does not lower herself to reply. *Imagine that*, she thinks, *being accused by a child*.

Don Titta walks out, leaving them alone.

'This is serious,' Bianca says, looking at them all, one by one. 'You all know that this is a precious book and that your father is very fond of it.'

Pietro is silent.

'It wasn't Miss Bianca,' Francesca says to Pietro. 'I saw her coming back.'

'What if we hang it up to dry?' Giulietta proposes and the others laugh a little too loudly, needing to release some of the tension in the room.

'That's not a bad idea,' Bianca says. 'But not now. First let's finish what we were doing.'

Their game, however, has lost its momentum. Dinnertime is slow in arriving. Later, Bianca unstitches the book's binding and hangs up the pages, a quarto at a time, in the room where they hang the bed sheets to dry. Pia helps her, pronouncing the Latin names of trees as they pin the pages to the lines with wooden clips. As the forest of paper grows denser, shaming the masses of socks, underwear and leggings, Bianca almost forgets her anger towards Pietro, his lie, and the prank that she is almost certain hides behind it all.

❧ ❧

'Signorina, Miss Bianca! Signorina!'

Bianca is sewing the dried and ironed pages back into their binding and sighs in resignation. The job takes the kind of patience that she doesn't have: her thimble is too big and her finger keeps falling out of it, causing her to prick herself repeatedly. In the end she just gives in. The *Traité* will be decorated with a patchwork of pinpricks of blood, the silent witness to a sinister pact. Who would ever need the image of a Saint-Germain pear? A fruit vendor, perhaps? And what does Tommaso want from her now? Bianca puts down the needle and thread in irritation and reluctantly lifts her head.

'Yes?'

'I'm sorry about the book. I told Titta that I saw you bring it back to the library.'

'Were you spying on me, perchance?'

Tommaso's face reddens. 'I would never, Miss Bianca. I was only in the right place at the right time, as they say.'

'Thank you, but I don't need a lawyer in training to defend me from the accusations of a spoiled and deceitful child. Or are you practising for when you get your life back together?' Bianca isn't sure where all this malice has come from but she doesn't feel like holding back. Her index finger burns with piercings. She puts the tip in her mouth and sucks on it.

'Oh, wonderful. Now you, too. You're like my sister: a portrait of wisdom. In reality she's so hideous that no one wants her.'

'If my brother said that about me, I'd spear him with a paintbrush.'

'I see you also know how to tease . . . No, but seriously, you should know how important it is for me to be here. I live in Don Titta's shadow. He is my mentor, master and model.' Tommaso speaks with fervour.

Bianca wonders why he is telling her all this. What is going on? A second earlier they were teasing each other.

'I will never become as important as him,' he continues. 'I've decided to have my plebeian muse speak in the manner most appropriate to her. In dialect. Would you like to hear something? I need to reveal her to the public, my simple muse, to see what kind of effect she has on people.'

Bianca does not know whether she should be annoyed or pleased by Tommaso's attempt at winning her trust. She hasn't asked for it. The language of the town bothers her too; it is different from the rugged singsong dialect that she heard as a little girl. But she realizes that it is just a matter of familiarity, that each one of us finds beauty in that which we are most familiar with.

Tommaso falls silent, waiting for encouragement. He smiles, blushes, rakes his hand through his hair, and all of a sudden the pale-faced dandy is taken over by a young boy with dishevelled wisps of hair across his forehead and a vein of cheerfulness. Bianca understands only about half of the words he recites: a confused story about nuns in love, it seems. She smiles despite herself, so great is the passion which ignites him. One strange verse catches her attention:

> *Mì t'hoo semper denanz de la mia vista,*
> *Mì non pensi mai olter che de tì,*
> *In di sogn no te perdi mai de pista,*
> *Appena me dessedi, te see lì,*
> *Mi gh'hoo semper in bocca el mè Battista,*
> *Semper Battista tutt el santo dì . . .*

> You are always before my eyes,
> I can't think of anything but you,
> In my dreams I never lose sight of you,
> As soon as I lie down you are there,
> The name of Battista is always on my lips,
> Always Battista, all the blessed day . . .

The performance ends.

'Miss Bianca?'

'Yes?' Bianca comes back to earth and applauds, as deserved. 'Bravo.'

Tommaso composes himself. 'Really, you liked it?'

'Well, I must admit that it wasn't all very clear to me . . . maybe I liked it because I didn't know what you were saying. But it has a melody to it. Isn't that important in poetry? That it has a melody?'

'Oh yes, as long as it's a tune and not a toot!'

He has gone back to his wisecracks. This improper side of Tommaso is much more fun. Bianca looks at him in fake shock and they both burst out laughing.

༺ ༻

'I've noticed that you're becoming more intimate with our junior poet,' observes Innes coldly, a few days later.

'Are you jealous?' Bianca asks, a hint of a smile on her lips.

Innes ignores the insinuation.

'Tommaso definitely has some artistic feeling inside him but he's just wasting his time,' he tells her.

'At least he's not a drone, like Bernocchi.'

'Don't be so quick to judge, Bianca. Drones are not bad insects.'

'If you like Tommaso so much, why does it bother you that I talk to him?'

'I didn't say I liked him. I said that I see something in him, but I can't stand watching him waste his energy. I think that for his own good he should leave. Everything that is holding him back, including certain gracious maidens who are willing to indulge him, harms him. As long as he lingers in the shade of the oak tree, he will remain as fragile as an offshoot.'

'You're accusing me of exerting too much influence over him, Innes. He's here because of his master, mentor and model. But wait,' Bianca says with a little shrug, 'maybe that's not the right order.'

'Right. But now that the cuckoo has made his nest here in Brusuglio, it's going to be difficult to get him to leave.'

'I think a nest is exactly what he needs.'

'Don't deceive yourself, Bianca. He's your age: neither a babe nor an orphan. He's a man. This "nest", as you call it, allows him to prolong his boyhood at the expense of others, avoiding confrontation with hardship. If he truly wishes to live as a poet, he should tend to his own matters, make his own decisions and sever ties.'

'But he won't get a penny from his family if he gives up, the poor thing.'

'Poor thing? He could be a handyman by day and write at night, if he really cared so much about it. He could rent a room at an inn and sort out his thoughts. But here he finds warmth or a breeze depending on the season. He drinks and dines well. He is cared for. Sooner or later his clothes will wear out and I don't think Don Titta will want to buy him a new wardrobe.'

'You are quite vicious. You sound like me.'

'Perhaps I do only feel envy, Miss Bianca. He is so young; everything is still possible for him and it irks me to see him throwing away such an opportunity by fooling around with the ideas he has of himself.'

'And what are you, old? Come on. At thirty, a woman is old and a man is in his prime. Soon, I will surpass you in this gloomy race. I will be in mourning for my withered years of youth while you will still be a promising shoot.'

'That's what disturbs me.' Innes grows solemn and melancholy. He becomes reflective, as though Bianca isn't there. And she, who has failed in her attempts to amuse him, is annoyed with herself.

ॐ ॐ

'The ghost is back!' Pietro lunges into the room, bringing a gust of cool air with him that remains even after Nanny has shut the French window. He removes the cap that his grandmother and mother force him to wear even during the summer, on account of his earaches, and drops it on the floor. Nanny retrieves it swiftly. The boy's colouring is vivid and his hair dishevelled, making him more attractive than usual, livelier. He stomps his feet in excitement: 'I saw it! She was on top of the rotunda, and when I got near, she disappeared inside! She's in the rotunda!'

The girls cover their mouths and hold their breath. Donna Julie sighs and looks away, as if to erase the sight of her son looking so wild. She detests these sorts of displays.

'You could have taken me with you!' Enrico whines.

'I like doing things on my own.'

Donna Clara takes Pietro's hands in hers and warms them while speaking to him both reassuringly and with reproach, a combination she often uses when talking to the boys, as though forcing them to reason is a vain effort.

'Oh my, you're so cold! Now you're bound to get sick and drive your poor mother crazy. You know you're not allowed to go out at night-time. You know nobody likes this story about a ghost. And you mustn't tell lies – we have told you thousands of times. What were you doing outside at this hour anyway?'

She casts a surly glance at Nanny.

'I was busy with the girls, signora,' Nanny says in her own defence.

Pietro, triumphant – and happy to take both blame and merit – realizes that for once they are one and the same, and clarifies his story.

'Nanny has nothing to do with it. She was in the nursery and I was very quiet. I slipped out. You can't expect to keep us prisoners like girls or workers.'

Donna Julie ignores the offensive juxtaposition and tightly presses her hands together in prayer, imploring the saint who is supposed to protect children from the evils of the world, even when they are good.

'But Pietro—'

'She wore a veil,' the boy continues, throwing his cape back over his shoulders. 'She was walking above the ground. She was frightening, but she didn't scare *me*. I got so close, I almost grabbed her, but then . . . well, she ran off. It was dark up there, so I decided to come back. To tell all of you,' he concludes, transforming his cowardice into bravery.

Enrico watches him with clenched fists and repressed anger. The girls take sides. Matilde and Franceschina stare at him, spellbound, while Giulietta remains sceptical. Bianca sides with Giulietta: Pietro does not have the makings of a hero. And most likely he has made up half of what he has said. However, this particular ghost is clearly nothing new.

Donna Julie lowers her head.

'Ghosts do not exist,' Donna Clara insists.

'I'm telling you, it was a ghost,' retorts Pietro. 'It was the same one, Nonna, the black one with the veil in front of its face, the one you saw in the fields that time, the one that terrified you.'

'I was only spooked,' Donna Clara replies. 'But since ghosts do not exist, they don't really spook anyone. Now go upstairs and get changed. And don't bother coming down for dinner: liars are not welcome at our table.'

Donna Julie is clearly tempted to intervene but refrains with difficulty. She has a hard time challenging authority. Bianca thinks it unfair that Donna Clara exerts control whenever she wants. Pietro isn't her son. But on the other hand, the child isn't being pleasant either and to see his embarrassment brings Bianca a brief but sharp sense of joy, which goes hand in hand with Enrico's sour glare. Pietro shifts his weight from one foot to the other in anticipation of a reprieve, until he realizes that his mother's indulgence won't cancel his grand-mother's punishment. And so he goes up the stairs, his eyes downcast.

Donna Clara inhales as deeply as her silk corset permits and then shakes her head.

'Too much imagination. They listen to too many stories, these children. I'm always telling you that, Julie.'

'Actually, I saw the ghost once, too,' Matilde says, surprising everyone. Matilde, who never speaks unless spoken to, has bright red cheeks. Her sisters stare at her, flabbergasted.

'Enough of this chat,' her grandmother says. The child hushes.

Soon it is dinnertime. Enrico shoots a suspicious glace at his brother's empty seat, uncertain whether to envy him or to appreciate that his absence allows him for once to be the only boy. As he lays eyes on the meal, he explodes with joy: stuffed veal sweetbreads are one of his favourites and now he can have twice as much. It is as if not being found guilty of anything this time makes him innocent forever. Bianca watches with poorly concealed horror as the child devours his plate of offal. She will never eat, nor has she ever eaten, anything of the sort. It feels like savagery to put something so holy and at the same time so intimate in one's mouth, stripped from the body of a once-living being. Enrico passes his days with animals – dogs, cats, rabbits and lambs – doling out snuggles and violence in equal amounts. He obeys all his impulses and he follows his cravings. Bianca looks down at her own plate of pale lettuce and then over at Donna Clara. She relishes her food with the same joyful ardour as her grandson.

'If I am not being indiscreet, can you tell me more about the ghost?' Bianca says.

Donna Clara looks up from her meal, her fork in mid-air, and then waves her free hand as if to shoo away a pesky fly, gesturing at the boy, and shaking her head quickly. Bianca gives up; she will keep her curiosity to herself. But at dessert, after the children have said goodnight and followed Nanny upstairs, Donna Clara continues.

'In the presence of the little one I wanted to avoid talking about it,' she says. 'Children are so impressionable.'

Bianca wants to counter the comment but keeps her thoughts to herself. This isn't the time to interrupt or distract her. Soon, mollified by *une petite crème*, the older lady gives in.

'You, of all people, should know that any ancient dwelling, or even merely an old one, has phantoms. We have the Pink Lady. I don't know whether you have ventured out north of the fields, but there is a dilapidated turret out there. It is said that those are the ruins of what was once the castle of the Pink Lady, who lost her soon-to-be husband in battle just before being married. Romantic stuff, you know.' She shakes her head slowly back and forth in an expression of disapproval. 'Like those novels that are in vogue now. Anyway, the widow-to-be closed herself in the castle and never came out, dead or alive. It's a story that everyone around here knows. And you understand how children can be: they listen and they repeat. They invent. They must have overheard it from the help. Some fool in an apron shrieks and sees what they want to see.'

'That's too bad. I would have liked to paint its portrait. The phantom's, I mean,' jokes Bianca.

Donna Clara smoothly changes the course of the conversation.

'This Chantilly *crème* is excellent. It seems as though the cook has finally learned that in order to make it you need to have a delicate touch.'

'I made it,' Donna Julie says with a smile.

'Oh no!' Donna Clara exclaims. 'You mustn't tire yourself out, you know that.'

'Tire myself over whipped eggs and cream?' laughs Donna Julie.

'What will they think when they see the lady of the house

amidst the pots and pans,' objects Donna Clara, forgetting about the time she herself spends in the kitchen. Although in truth she never lays a finger on a pot.

'I like it. It's fun for me,' insists Donna Julie. 'You never let me do anything.'

'Oh well, if you want to get sick again . . .' Donna Clara says, scraping her bowl with a spoon. Bianca eats in silence, savouring the cream's airy texture, its softness and the contrasting tartness of the fruit.

'My mother taught me how to make cakes,' Bianca says. 'Would you like the recipe?'

Donna Julie lights up.

'I'd love to try it but only if you help me.'

'Of course! With all the children,' Bianca says, smiling.

Donna Clara scowls and asks for another helping.

'I don't understand you two. The idea of getting your hands dirty with dough, bringing the children into the kitchen . . . it will only confuse the help and people will lose their sense of place.'

'The children are always sneaking into the kitchen, anyway, and I don't see anything wrong with it. Perhaps they will enjoy themselves more than they do with Nanny. They will certainly learn more. And with my hands, I can't be a lady. Look,' Donna Julie says calmly, holding out her small white hands marked by imperfections; they are swollen, rugged, even, to look at.

'I always say you work too much. It isn't proper. You should wear gloves.'

'I'm tired of doing what I should.'

'You're making a mistake.' Donna Clara speaks without even looking at her.

'You, of all people . . .'

The sentence hovers over the table in mid-air, powerful

enough to cause the old signora to finally look up from her plate and into the eyes of her daughter-in-law.

'I what?' Donna Clara replies disdainfully.

'You . . . you, at least, have lived,' mumbles Donna Julie. And then it is as if a sudden gust of wind extinguishes her tiny flame. She lowers her head and is silent.

⁂

Later, while she is unbraiding Bianca's hair, Minna, who as usual has heard every word, cannot resist the urge to speak her mind.

'Don't listen to Donna Clara. She doesn't want to talk about it because she says it distracts us. The Pink Lady is an old story and is over. No one believes it. The ghost, however, does exist. She's real. She comes to evening vespers every Monday.'

'If she's always so punctual, she must be English,' Bianca jokes. 'With a pocket watch hanging from a long chain.'

'Oh, that I cannot say. What I do know is that she appears out of nowhere and disappears into thin air.'

Minna stares at her in the mirror.

'Seriously, Miss Bianca. Open your eyes and you will see.'

Bianca knows that in order for ghosts to exist, someone has to believe in them. She lets herself be lured into imagining the phantasmagorical creature as though she is a gullible child.

⁂

The rains end, the ground dries out, the sun returns and summer makes its way back – one last time before the winter decline. It is hot and the world, invigorated by the hydration, is green with life, blooming, exultant. On Monday, when the church bells chime for evening Mass and a handful of old ladies hobble towards prayer, Bianca makes her way towards the northern gate. She takes a basket, her gardening gloves and a pair of shears. Her apparent goal is to find some unusual roses that grow in the beds farthest from the house. There she kneels among the bushes that flower far from anyone's sight. Roses have an air about them that is too uncertain for her taste, and yet they are beautiful. Their heads hang close together and their smell is faint. Bianca slips on her gloves and chooses several stems, but not the longest ones. She wants to use a specific crystal vase that she has spotted in the bottom of a cupboard. When she looks up from her basket, she is startled by what she has really come to see. Far off in the distance stands not a phantom, but a woman. She is dressed in dark clothes and wears a veil that drapes down beyond her shoulders like a short cape, giving her a monastic look. This trend hasn't yet arrived in these parts but Bianca recognizes it from certain foreign magazines. Maybe the woman is a traveller. Maybe Bianca is jumping to conclusions; perhaps she simply chooses that apparel because she does not want to reveal anything about herself. Even without a veil, though, the uncertain light of early dusk will hide her facial features. Because of the tall grass, she looks like a silhouette on a theatrical stage.

In the time it takes Bianca to gather her skirts and quicken her step towards the gate, the veiled woman has disappeared. Bianca tries to see where she went but the gate is closed, and she cannot follow the shadow any further.

❦ ❦

'What nice roses,' Donna Clara says to her later, as she arranges the trimmed flowers in the glass vase. 'Your hunt was successful, I see.'

Bianca is silent. Her real prey has escaped her. At least she will have her portraits of the roses, which will last far longer than the flowers themselves. She imagines everyone admiring the dark tangle of thorny stems beneath the surface of the water.

❧ ❧

A good hunter is dedicated. He returns time and again to the place where he first catches sight of his prey. In order to make the hunt his own, the hunter must be patient and methodical. The following day Bianca seeks out a point in the garden where she remembers the wall is slightly lower. She climbs over it without too much difficulty in an old grey pinstriped skirt that has seen some wear and tear, and retraces the woman's steps across the flattened grass, searching for clues. She isn't sure what she is looking for. If there are traces, she will never be able to find them. She isn't a dog that can follow its sense of smell. But she is lucky. Right there on the ground where the path gives way to the tall grass, she finds something. Bianca kneels down and picks up the strange object. It is a small pillow of striped pink and green velvet, sewn in a delicate golden whipstitch. In the middle, on a pink background, is an embroidered lamb with a real bell hanging from its neck. Bianca shakes the pillow and the bell jingles softly. It looks like it has been made for a tiny bed in a doll's house or like an elaborate sachet to be placed among one's linens. Bianca brings it to her nose: it has no scent.

❧ ❧

The following Monday brings steady rain. But on Tuesday the sun shines once more. Bianca climbs over the wall again and into the fields. She doesn't come across any surprising finds this time but does meet someone, just not the person she was hoping for.

'Well, look who's here: our painter! Out and about, and

disguised as a servant, no less. A delectable Colombina. What are you doing, Miss Bianca? Are you dressed up for charades? Or are you simply strolling incognito in search of new and original subject matter? Are you a fan of the people, dedicated to marrying their filthy cause? Listen to me, forget about them: flowers like you thrive in closed gardens. Or come with me to the city and I will show you how beautiful life can be . . .'

It is Bernocchi. He is dressed in a light blue spencer designed for another kind of figure. His trousers and white socks amplify his more than robust thighs and calves. He removes his hat and plunges into a deep bow, showing off a florid and sweaty neck. It is a most unpleasant spectacle and encounter for Bianca, who would give anything not to be subjected to the prying gaze of this man. She tries to defend herself with indifference.

'Conte Bernocchi . . . well, this is the last place I'd imagine to find you.'

'Indeed. I arrived early and asked to be let out right here. I wanted to take a stroll in the open country . . . like you. I hoped to find out if here, among the tall grasses, lay the font of your inspiration. But of course, the fields are filled with interesting little creatures like yourself. Ah,' he says, looking off into the distance with a malicious air. 'Now I understand . . .'

Innes is crossing the field towards them, approaching from the house with long strides. When he arrives, he rests his hands on the wall from within.

'Who is luckier, the people inside or the people outside?' Innes says with a smile. Bianca's sombre expression does not escape him, nor does her plain outfit. He reaches across the barrier wall. 'I beg of you, come back to us. We simply will not let you run off,' he speaks light-heartedly, as he helps her climb back over the obstacle. Count Bernocchi peers at her naked calves, made visible by her movement, looking away only when Innes glares at him.

'Do not expect me to do the same,' he jokes. 'I am not a born gymnast like you English folk. I'm taking the long way round. A healthy stroll will do me good. Please tell them to prepare refreshments, as I will certainly need them upon my arrival. And let them know that I will bring an armful of roses with me, like a damsel. Like our Miss Bianca.'

Bernocchi walks off down the path, swinging his walking stick.

'Then be not coy . . .' mumbles Innes quietly in English, but Bernocchi either does not hear him or fails to understand because he doesn't turn around.

Innes and Bianca share a laugh. There are moments, and this is one of them, when it is right to suspend the rules of the salon: forget the plaster mouldings, ignore the delicate crystal and china, and walk past the family portraits. This is the joy of conspiracy. How nice to discover that Innes doesn't care for Bernocchi either.

Half an hour later they see him on the great lawn, stretched out on a chaise longue, his belly in full view, admiring the girls as they play with Pia. Each time Pia runs off to catch the ball, the count's head follows her.

> *Nella pozza c'è un lombrico*
> *Molle interrogativo*
> *S'inanella sotto l'acqua*
> *Non sai dir se è morto o vivo.*
> *Rosagrigio grigiorosa*
> *Dentro il fango cerca sposa.*
> *Se nessuno troverà*
> *con se stesso a nozze andrà.*

In the puddle there is a worm
A wet question
Twisting under water
You can't tell if he's alive or dead.
Pinkish grey, greyish pink
He seeks a bride in the mud.
And if he finds no one to bed
He will have himself to wed.

'Hurray, Papa!'

The children clap their hands and laugh, especially Pietro and Enrico, who has a particular fondness for worms. Over the years they have chopped up thousands for play soups or just for fun, watching them writhe in silent pain.

'How do you do that?' Giulietta asks. 'I want to write poems like you.'

Don Titta caresses the little girl's cheek and she snuggles up to him as if she is a kitten. Enrico crushes the sweetness of the moment.

'I know where to find lots of caterpillar moths! We can make homes for them!'

The children run off, even the little ones, followed by Nanny and her pleas.

'Don't touch them, they're dirty!'

The adults remain seated, awaiting their coffee.

'All children are poets by nature,' Don Titta declares. 'It's in the way they look at things.'

'Yes, but really, Titta, to speak of worms like that when we've just finished eating.'

The reproach comes from Donna Clara while the others have all smiled indulgently.

Bianca looks around at them, trying to understand them.

Beatrice Masini

Innes exudes a certain detachment but a minuscule contraction of his mouth reveals a smirk held back with difficulty. Everyone else ignores the exchange, inclined in the name of peace to accept the vagaries of their host. Donna Julie nods and picks up on the bit of the conversation that interests her.

'They are our angels,' she says.

Bernocchi looks up at the sky and then down at his pudding, driving a spoonful into his mouth.

Children as poets and angels? Children are complicated, difficult, often sick, a source of anxiety, frequently whiny, and usually incomprehensible. At least *these* children are. They have been confused by rules that have often been contradicted with exceptions and turned into new rules. They are different from others and aware of the privilege that is bestowed upon them as their grandmother's pets, their mother's stars, and their father's arrows of hope. They are never simply children. Innes is the only person who approaches them from a different angle: he teases without humiliating; he reignites dormant interests; he knows how to engage and challenge them. He is a natural-born father. Maybe it's easier to educate other people's children than it is your own, Bianca thinks to herself, in the same way that it is easy for her to play with children, too. Playing is one thing she can do with ease.

One time Bianca lures them into the kitchen, taking advantage of Donna Clara's absence, to make a batch of fairy cakes.

'Sweets for fairies? Really?' Matilde asks, her face revealing incredulous conviction.

'They're called that because they are tiny and delicious and because they are the same ones that fairies have with their tea.'

'But fairies don't really exist . . .'

'You bet they exist; they are this tall' – Bianca makes a C

112

shape in mid-air with her thumb and index finger – 'and they have wings.'

'And they drink tea every day like the English,' Pietro intervenes drily.

'Every day,' Bianca repeats solemnly. 'But now, enough chit-chat. If you used your tongue to mix your dough, it would be perfect.'

'My tongue? Yuck!'

'Yes, exactly. Hush and get to work.'

The twenty minutes in the oven feel like an eternity. While waiting, the children listen to her story about how a fairy is born each time a child laughs.

'So if we laugh they will come?'

'They will come and will never want to leave.'

'Never ever ever?'

'I don't believe it,' Pietro says. 'It's all horse feathers.'

'If you don't believe in fairies, you won't see them.'

'That's right, Matilde! That's exactly how things work.'

The scent of the sweet dough rising makes the girls clap their hands. Finally, there they are: the fairy cakes, perfectly golden on top.

'They're too beautiful to be eaten,' Matilde says.

'Now I understand why fairies love them so,' Giulietta adds.

'What are you talking about?' Pietro says greedily. 'I am going to have mine now.' He snatches two and runs away, followed by his brother, who grabs two in each hand. The girls look at Bianca, who, in turn, smiles at them.

'And now we will get the tea ready.'

She offers a cup to Innes when he peers in from the threshold, while the girls, who have been patiently waiting and couldn't care less about the drink, savour the strange cakes with their eyes closed. They have made these treats with their own hands, and as such they have to be exquisite.

'They are the best cakes in the whole world,' Francesca says with her mouth full, every so often peering at the window to check for the fairies. Bianca reminds her that they need to save a few for them. Innes smiles and raises his teacup in a toast. Bianca does the same. A cup of tea really is the best thing in the whole world. It is the taste of certainty in the face of uncertainty; it's like coming home.

'You're a rotten liar,' Innes says later on, as they walk together through the open countryside.

'Me? Why?'

'You've always said you don't like children.'

'I don't. Not all children. But these interest me.'

'If only mothers and fathers thought the way you do, they would make their children quite content. But I have another theory.'

'Let's hear it, Signor Know-it-all.'

'Perhaps you're not lying. But it could very well be true, so let's take it as the truth: you do not like children. The fact is,' and Innes pauses to look her in the eye, forcing her to reciprocate, 'that you, too, are still a child. And that is why they like to be in your presence.'

'I see. And what should I do now? Pretend to be offended? Slap you?'

'Do what you see fit, as long as you don't act like a prim young lady. There must be some benefit to the candour of the wilderness. Can't you see? It invites us to resemble it. It asks us to be what we truly are. What harm is there if every so often you allow yourself to be young?'

Right, what harm is there? Bianca gets up on the tips of her toes and snatches Innes's hat from his head. She then hurls it like a disk, sending it flying through the trees before it lands in the middle of a small clearing. Innes smiles and walks off slowly to retrieve it, watched by two surprised gardeners.

☙ ❧

At some point, Minna falls ill with a cough that won't go away. Perhaps it is due to the changing weather or from wearing clogs with no socks. She is not allowed to go outside. Even housemaids have the right to not be well. Consequently, the duties of assisting Bianca are passed on to Pia, who is pleased to do it. She gossips, she organizes, and if Bianca asked her, the girl would crush stones and boil tinctures like a true studio apprentice. Bianca watches her eager and precise hands at work, amused and inspired. She is not at all like Minna, who is clumsy in her youth and inexperience, and who only does things to follow orders, because it is expected of her. Minna completes tasks for Bianca in the same distracted way that she plucks a duck in the kitchen or washes clothes at the well. When Bianca later asks to keep Pia as her maid, she doesn't realize the storm that will be unleashed. In all good faith, she has imagined that for Minna one task is the same as another, a notion that, once she is better, the servant girl hastens to clarify. At first she doesn't say anything; her silence is downright hostile. She brushes Bianca's hair jerkily, and pulls at it like she did when she first arrived. She is so ill at ease that one clumsy gesture sends a porcelain vase of dried flowers crashing to the floor.

'Pardon me, I'm so very sorry. I didn't mean to.'

She bends down to pick up the shards but then drops everything again in a rage.

'It's all her fault I'm so worked up. It's her fault if I break things,' she says, crouched to the floor, her tiny face looking up.

'Whose fault?' Bianca asks, knowing the answer.

'That witch. Mamma says that she tricks everyone, even ladies like you. That . . . Pia.' She spits out her name as if it is a cuss word.

'Oh, come now, Minna, what an awful thing to say. I thought you two were friends.'

'Friends? I turn my back for a second and she steals my place.' Minna is silent for a moment. She forces herself to take command of her insolence, bites her lip, takes a deep breath, but still can't hold back. 'She always gets what she wants. Who does she think she is? She's no one's daughter; she was placed in the home just like I was, but no one came back for her. She should just be quiet, that's what my mamma says. She's lucky she ended up in a respectable house like ours, instead of having to keep the bed warm for some bum up in Brianza.' The venom seeps out, unstoppable. At this point Bianca is too curious to change the course of conversation. 'Oh no, but we aren't good enough for her. She always has to be different. Hasn't she told you about her "lamb" and the rest of it?' She pronounces the word 'lamb' with a grimace and in a strange voice, imitating her new enemy. Bianca is lost now. Minna sees that she has confused her listener. 'Do you not know about the "lamb"?'

And from that point forward Bianca becomes truly perplexed. Minna incoherently blurts out details, complicating the picture she has already tried to paint before: the world of children given up as newborns so that parents can save money, children who are sometimes taken back and restored to their regretful parents, but not always. The story has become so contorted and complicated with technical details now that Bianca has difficulty understanding.

'She says that when they left her at the orphanage she was wearing beautiful swaddling clothes. That's what she says. And when Don Dionisio went to get her with his sister, who weaned her so that she would be able to serve in his household and be like a daughter to her, she who had no children, he said that there was a tiny piece of paper pinned to her that said she was the daughter of a woman who had died in childbirth. He said that she was dressed in the clothes of a wealthy little girl, and that inside her bassinet she had a pledge token with a lamb on it that was embroidered in gold and silver. Of course, she couldn't have been a poor girl like the rest of us. She had to be a princess in the orphanage, too.'

'Wait a second. You're going too fast, I can't follow you. This lamb—'

'Me, I didn't see my pledge token, and even if I had seen it, I was too little – three days old – and I wouldn't have remembered it. But anyway I didn't have one. And I didn't say I had one either. My parents were poor folk, and the poor folk don't give pledges to children who would lose them, of course. They keep the pledges there, at the orphanage,' Minna continues with an air of impatience. 'They keep them safe alongside all the belongings of the other abandoned children from Milan. Pia's pledge is a little square, about this big,' and Minna draws an imaginary square with her tiny thumbs and index fingers. 'The mothers put the pledges in the swaddling when they know they will come back for their children one day. Then, when they do come back, say after three years or so, they can tell the people at the orphanage: I left my baby here on such and such a day and she had a pledge that looked like this or that, and the people at the orphanage look in their books to check so that they don't give the parents the wrong child, and if it's all true they go and find the child, who in the meantime has gone to live in the countryside with some farmers – the fake parents, I mean. And if the child is still alive they give him back to his real parents and together they live happily ever after. Pia had a pledge with a lamb on it, but poor parents leave half a playing card, half a San Rocco devotional card, half a medallion, something that poor people have. And they hold onto the other half so that when you unite the two parts, it makes up the whole, and that means you get the right baby. Your baby. Do you understand?' Minna is silent now. She is out of breath and her face is flushed. She stands up, the shards of the porcelain vase crackling under her clogs, but she doesn't notice. 'Anyway, the truth is, no one wanted her back, so it's about time that she stopped showing off and learned her place, and that's that. And with that, I pay my respects and wish you a good night.' Minna stomps off with tiny, angry steps, leaving behind a cloud of confusion.

Bianca feels disconcerted. What is all this nonsense about abandonment and recovery, beautiful swaddling lambs and pledges? Aren't two abandoned girls under one roof too many? Or is it normal around here to just dispose of your burdensome children? What does Don Dionisio have to do with anything? Perhaps Minna is just stringing together bits of gossip she has overheard in the kitchen, embellishing them with spite and fantasy. It is surely just childish confusion, a joke born of jealousy, something that happens downstairs in every large household. Minna is a good girl really. She will get over it. She'll probably even feel sorry about what she's said. But Bianca also realizes that Minna knows how to find the right words, even complicated ones, despite being red with rage. She has been under the impression that the girl is accustomed to getting distracted and lost in thought, but not this time. The little girl has spoken and heard this speech many times and it clearly always leaves a bad taste in her mouth.

❧ ❧

Bianca tries to think about other things but in vain. She feels irritated with herself for not being able to soothe Minna's spite. She replays the girl's monologue inside her head, trying to make sense of all that scattered information. And then, all of a sudden, she remembers the little pillow she found. She opens the drawer of her nightstand and, pulling out that odd square she'd found on her walk in the woods, she thinks back to Minna's words.

Pia's pledge is a little square, about this big . . . The mothers put the pledges in the swaddling when they know they will come back for their children one day.

Bianca isn't sure if this is a pledge because she has never seen one. Neither has Minna really, so she can't ask her. But if it is, what was it doing lying in the grass without a child? Or maybe – could it be that somebody has abandoned a newborn in the woods and left the token behind? No, it cannot be. She would have heard rumours about it, and the child most likely would have been torn to pieces by wolves. *Don't be foolish, Bianca* tells herself, trying to repress the absurd thoughts that crowd her head. And yet she continues to rack her brain, unsettled and intrigued. This is better than a novel. This is real. That odd pillow embroidered with so much care actually exists – and it has to mean something. Bianca decides she will take it upon herself to discover what that meaning is.

※ ※

The rivalry continues. Pia and Minna don't talk to each other. The little one is steadfast, obstinate, and convinced that she has been subjected to an unforgivable wrong. Pia shrugs and calls the other girl crazy, but Bianca can see how sorry she is, how she torments herself to make the situation right again. Bianca, who feels guilty for having unleashed the dispute, finally finds a remedy after explaining the situation to Donna Clara.

'A conflict, you say? Why on earth, when we treat them so well?'

Yes, Bianca thinks to herself, *like little animals in a cage.*

'You know how young people are: they have their tantrums, their little fights.'

She thinks minimizing the situation is the best way to achieve her goal. She makes an offer. At first Donna Clara seems a little uneasy and looks at her with suspicion: is Bianca, a stranger, trying to lay down the law in her own home? Who cares about the housemaids' bickering? And yet, it is clear that she feels a special kind of love for those girls and wants justice and harmony on her land. Bianca understands all of this.

'Very well. Just keep me informed. What little scoundrels they are! We give them everything: clothes and shoes, warmth and food.'

Bianca cannot help but comment.

'I suppose you're right. Once man's primary needs are met, other aspirations are awakened. It is inevitable.'

Donna Clara looks at her with a scowl. She won't let herself be taken for a fool.

'You are a true intellectual, Miss Bianca. Ah, women with brains . . .'

And with that, the rotating shifts begin. One day it is Minna's turn, the next Pia's. Sometimes both of them divide the tasks: the one who brushes Bianca's hair doesn't accompany her, and vice versa. When Bianca tells them of her new plan, they listen to her in silence. Minna is stubborn, retaining her identity as the violated one. Pia, on the other hand, is pleased. And it is she who holds her hand out to the other.

'Can we make peace?'

Minna glances at Pia with her outstretched hand, and stares at a point in the sky in front of her. Then she giggles, shrugs her shoulders, and lets herself be hugged. Bianca gazes from one girl to the other, amazed at how different they are despite being raised under the same roof. The little one is contentious and a trickster, with a sharp tongue and a sly mind. The older one is generous, willing to give up some ground for the love of peace. It is useless for Bianca to play favourites. But perhaps Minna will change, if guided appropriately. She hopes that Pia, on the other hand, will never change: she is beautiful and sincere, somewhat vulnerable perhaps, but only inasmuch as the other is armed, and nonetheless strong in her simplicity, keeping her one step ahead of the game.

❧ ❧

The following Monday it rains again but this time Bianca can no longer resist. She takes down a rain cloak from the coat rack outside the kitchen and walks out. It takes only three steps for her to regret making the decision: all kinds of smells linger on the oilcloth fabric – dog, gravy from a roast, ash. An overall film of dirt that has come to life, thanks to the humidity in the air. It isn't very pleasant being enveloped by such intense smells; they suffocate the wonderful scents of the wet park. But it is too late to go back now and besides, Ruggiero's cloak does the job: the drops of rain roll right off it.

Her sixth sense has been right. The ghost is there. But this time she has pinned her veil up to her hat. She moves forward through the tall grass slowly, holding her skirt with both her hands. She stares into the distance. Even from far away, Bianca can see her large eyes and pale skin. Her pace is long and elegant. Bianca is ready to approach her. She isn't far. She will find out for certain who she is. But then she freezes suddenly, overcome by a wave of dread as well as respect. The lady stops, lowers her head, and stands as still as a statue. A sudden gust of wind blows the veil over her face. Now she is frightening, and truly ghoulish. Bianca turns around and darts back to the gate, which she has left ajar. She closes it behind her, turns the key in the lock, and takes it. And then runs as fast as she can.

She sketches her vision that same night so as not to forget any details. That veil, embroidered with small droplets, is like a bride's, fit for a fairy-tale princess. The woman's eyes are large and deep, even behind the grey material. She has a generous mouth, a determined nose and an imperious chin. Bianca is certain that she will be back.

❧ ❧

But, in fact, she never returns. She isn't there at the vespers hour the following Monday, Tuesday or Thursday. Her absence does not go unnoticed. Even the help gossip about it.

'She's not coming back.'

'Her soul must have finally found peace, poor thing.'

'Maybe she died of the flu.'

When Bianca asks around for more information, the women hush, look at one another, and change the topic. Apparently, since she has stopped coming, she no longer exists. Soon there will be another curiosity to serve as the topic of discussion while plucking quails. Like old Angelina's son, for example, who won't stop growing: he is twenty and looks and eats like an ogre. Or the button seller, who has the eyes of a gypsy: they say he robs virgins of their souls, or something easier to come by.

Bianca is bothered by the chatter and anxious about the disappearance of the ghost, who has shown her art by vanishing. But she is done with thinking about it. She feels silly pondering such a futile curiosity. And in any case, there are other things that need to be done: in the kitchen, the nursery and the study. The children wail, the guests wine and dine, the help swear and complain, the owners give orders, and then they all sit down to tea. Flowers blossom and wither. She needs to pick them while she can.

> *Manina béla, con to soréla,*
> *'ndo sito sta'?*
> *Dalla mama, dal papà.*
> *Cossa t'hai dato?*
> *Pane, late,*
> *Gategategategate . . .*

> Little hand,
> With your sister,
> Where did you go?
> To Mama and to Papa.
> What did they give you?
> Bread and milk and
> Tickle tickle tickle . . .

'Me too, me too.'

'Do it to me, too.'

The children stretch out their arms so she can tickle their palms. The house seems full of them, a centipede of little hands. All the children are desperate to be distracted from the boring rain.

'What does it mean though, Miss Bianca? We don't understand.'

She speaks in rhymes from her 'recent childhood', as Innes calls it.

'Will you do it to me, too?'

Silly Tommaso, he always makes his way into the nursery

hoping for an escape. He gets down on his knees, and then onto all fours like an animal, making the children laugh. Bianca giggles but then shoos him away.

'We are busy learning,' she says.

'I don't see Nanny. Did you lock her inside a trunk?' he asks.

It is a tempting hypothesis and brings titters all round. Tommaso, still on all fours, moves backwards out of the room, swinging his head like a loyal dog.

'Now we're going to play dressing up,' she says.

'That's for girls,' the boys complain.

'Fine. You may be excused. Should I ask Tommaso to accompany you?'

'Nooo, we'll stay.'

'Miss Bianca, Miss Bianca, what should we do? Who should we be?'

Bianca considers.

'You should dress up as the person you most want to be.'

They all have good ideas and run off to prepare. Pietro and Enrico grab two old capes – whether they are uniforms or costumes it is hard to say – and twirl them around themselves like toreadors. The girls laugh.

'I'm ready!' Pia announces from her hiding place. Minna incites her to come out by clapping her hands and cheering her on. Bianca looks at Pia's creation. She cannot believe that the girl can have made it herself. She wears a headdress of dress swords that looks almost dangerous. She is like a peasant girl from another era, ready for a country wedding.

'What do you mean, another era?' mumbles Minna when Bianca says this. 'What peasant girl? She's a spinner, can't you tell? That's a party outfit that the ladies who work with silk wear. My mother comes from those parts. I took it out of my hope chest, but don't tell anyone. And be careful it doesn't get ruined, Pia – I'm going to wear it on my wedding day.'

'If anyone ever wants you,' Pia says, teasing.

Minna frowns seriously. Then she bursts out laughing and everyone laughs with her. Meanwhile Pia, dressed as the bride, looks down and smiles to herself. This is a performance and she is every bit the young actress.

Minna disappears behind the Chinese screen while the smaller girls fumble through a chest of hats, scarves, vests and old corsets. In between oohs and aahs and a couple of sneezes, they transform into other characters, and run to look at themselves in the mirror. They laugh with the complicit goodness of sisters when they get along.

'Have you really never played this game?' Bianca asks in surprise. 'We used to play dressing up all the time.'

She was the first one to explore the attic, probing the wide, damp space, with its tall, narrow windows that open out onto the world like eyes. She went back there a second time, with more ease. In the dresser she chose, among other things, this armful of clothes. When she asked permission to use them, Donna Clara only shrugged. 'I know nothing. I have never been up there. You're free to take whatever you want.'

Her accomplices, Minna and Pia, help her choose the strangest and most attractive items; they beat the dust out of them with broomsticks, lay them out in the sun, then hide them from the little girls to ensure they are a surprise. The scheme has worked.

Minna keeps chatting in that little voice she uses when she is excited.

'And who will the groom be, Pia? Shall we hand you over to Pietro or to Enrico? Or would you prefer Luigi, the bell ringer?'

This is followed by much laughter. Luigi is a scrawny teenage boy who gets pulled upwards every time he rings the church bell. Pia pointed him out to Bianca once, as she was guiding her to an alcove inside the sacristy.

Finally, Minna appears from behind the screen, standing with her arms crossed and a smug expression across her face. The breeches and lace shirt transform her into a charming young man.

'It is I who want you to be my wife, my damsel! Will you accept my offer?'

She falls to her knees at the feet of the bride, who clenches her shawl tightly around her, feigning reluctance. Everyone begins to laugh, and then suddenly the laughter fades and the bride falls silent. Pia stares at the doorway.

'What happened?' Minna asks.

When Pia doesn't answer, they turn around one by one. The girl looks down. Bianca first sees his reflection in the mirror, the rest of his dark clothes blending into the gloom of the hallway behind him. She turns to face him, ready to defend the children.

'We were only playing,' she says but her tone comes out more apologetic than she would like. They aren't doing anything wrong; this is the playroom, and it is raining outside.

Don Titta doesn't say a thing. It is as though he is hypnotized by Pia. The girl looks at her master with a serenity that could be mistaken for arrogance. Bianca wants to interrupt the exchange. She is afraid Pia will be punished for her impudence. But the master continues to stare at her, his head tipped to the side like a painter studying his model, thoughtful and detached.

Matilde interrupts the silence and hugs her father.

'You see how pretty I am?'

Don Titta finally snaps out of his daze and holds out his arms to pick up the little one, who pushes her curls back with both her hands to make herself more attractive.

'I'm dressed as a valet, can you tell?' She wiggles her feet in their blue silk slippers. 'I also have a feathered cap . . .'

She pulls away from his grasp to go and get her hat. In all the playing, it has rolled under the sofa.

Still, Don Titta is silent. Bianca doesn't know what to say. She wants him to leave and take the awkwardness with him. And finally that is what he does, without even a goodbye.

Liberated from his presence, the playroom seems more spacious, almost luminous. It looks like the sky beyond the glass window is finally lifting too. Minna holds out her hands to the other girls.

'Let's play Ring-a-Ring o' Roses.'

And whilst they sing the song, a little out of tune, Bianca remembers how they played on that first day, when she had just arrived, before Pia had entered the picture and everything had seemed so innocent, so pure. It's not Pia's fault, of course. She sings loudly in ignorant bliss, her cheeks as pink as a bride's. Then she leans towards Francesca, and then to Matilde, and whispers something in their ears, obtaining muffled laughter in return. She frees her hands from her playmates' and places them on her hips. And in an instant, she returns to a country girl, her feet moving in a complicated dance. She is talented. Everyone slows and then stops to watch her in awe. The swords in her hair tremble with every jump, capturing the soft light of the candles. She dances as though she has no memories, as if she is alone under the dark summer sky, listening only to the music inside her head, happy and free.

ॐ ॐ

'Will you also include their meanings?'

Bianca hates being watched while she is working. She could shoo away the children or Nanny but not Donna Clara. So she pretends not to hear, hoping that the lady will change the topic or wander off. But she remains.

'You should. A yellow rose for jealousy, a red rose for passion, a white rose for innocence, a lilac rose for excitement. I'm quite good, aren't I? Like mother, like son.'

The children laugh with their grandmother without fully understanding the conversation, giggling only because she does. Enrico reaches for a piece of charcoal, Giulietta smacks his fingers, he growls like a dog, and Nanny clucks her tongue in disapproval. Bianca ignores them and keeps on drawing. Donna Clara continues.

'The secret messages in colours. What was it? Mallow for understanding, tuberose for delight, myrtle for infidelity?'

'What about daisies?' Matilde asks, holding out a bunch of wilted daisies in her clenched fist.

'Innocence, little one. It's your very own flower.'

Bianca puts the finishing touches on the fuchsia (for frugality) and then gives up, letting go of her pastel somewhat brusquely. It rolls to the edge of the table, wavers a little, and stops. Francesca holds out her hand but there is nothing to rescue.

'No, I don't believe those things,' Bianca says. 'I can't. Flowers, the poor creatures, are faithful because they depend on our care. But they are also traitors, because so little is needed to take them away from us: frost, wind, a worm. They do not have a brain. They only have their costume. It is we who must learn to be better: constant, patient and helpful. We mustn't expect anything in return, only the gift of their beauty when it comes.'

A shadow appears in the doorway of the greenhouse.

'Well said, Miss Bianca.'

The voice of Don Titta makes her jump. The children turn to swarm around him. Bianca makes an effort to clean her fingers with a rag. The poet crosses his arms and leans against the door. Innes stands just a couple of steps behind.

'At ease,' he continues. He studies her. 'Look at what an interesting colouring this work gives you: sky blue and crimson hands, as if you have been catching butterflies. Something I advise against doing, Pietro, or,' he adds, 'I will get very angry. Do you understand?'

Although Pietro hasn't considered the idea beforehand, he is now smirking, and runs off to prepare for the cruelty to come. Bianca wipes an indigo stain from her palm; it doesn't want to go away, she will need to use soap. Donna Clara interrupts.

'Surely the lists of plants are much lovelier now, in any case? Before they were only black, or black with red ink for the French grafts. They reminded me of police rosters.' She frowns. Her son ignores her and continues speaking to Bianca.

'You are right to do as you do. He who soils his hands is the true gardener; anyone else is just a hobbyist.' Bianca hides her fingers behind her back, aware of the dirt under her fingernails from where she sunk her fingers into the earth at the foot of the path in order to feel how warm and grainy and alive it was. Innes notices and smiles. Don Titta continues. 'I will never be at your level. I am only a mere horticulturalist, a theoretician who ponders questions from behind a desk. We are in need of a modern-day Linnaeus to decide the names for all things green, so that they can be fixed forever, for everyone. I could seriously dedicate myself to that cause. What do you think, Innes? I suppose it, too, could be considered a form of unification.'

'Well, if you ask me,' Donna Clara interrupts, 'when they're on my plate and well cooked they're one and the same. It's the flavour that counts; do your treatises speak about this?'

Innes rolls his eyes a little at Bianca, who would laugh but coughs instead.

'Are you perhaps allergic to the leaves? That would be too bad, given your vocation. In any case, we have pickled snow peas for dinner tonight, not green beans. We have already finished those,' Donna Clara concludes and begins to leave the greenhouse with the children.

'Are you coming too, Papa?' Francesca tugs on her father's hand and he surrenders willingly, closing in on the procession with the little girl by his side, who is just happy to have him to herself.

Bianca is left feeling unsettled. She wouldn't mind continuing what she had set out to do but now she is distracted. Innes steps forward, leafs through the nearly complete master copy and nods.

'This is a small masterpiece, Bianca. You truly are the lady of the flowers. You know them like you own them.'

'I'd say the opposite is true: that they own me. Beginning with the fact that they take up all my time, all my enjoyment and, essentially, everything else. But let's not talk about me. It's boring. What about you? What are you master of? Tell me.'

Innes sits on the elegant and uncomfortable chaise. He looks out of place; he is far more comfortable in a worn leather armchair, book in hand.

'I don't know, Bianca. I don't know. I want what is not for me.'

'Even philanthropists deserve to be happy,' she jokes.

'Oh, come now, don't be naive,' he says seriously. 'One

doesn't deserve happiness; one takes hold of it when it comes along, if it comes along, out of pure luck. One takes a bite out of it like an unexpected fruit, knowing that it will never fill us up.' His voice softens. 'Don't pay attention to me, please. Life will explain itself to you in due time, provided that you listen.'

'I don't like you when you're serious.'

'In the end,' Innes continues, as if he hasn't heard her, 'no one said that happiness was the way out. I, for example, am happy with a far less resplendent gift – generosity.'

'Giving or receiving?'

'Bianca, Bianca, this is your biggest flaw. You couldn't be light-hearted if you tried. Or maybe it's a virtue. Your question is an important one but I am not going to give you an answer. Not now. It's a beautiful afternoon. Will you come with me?'

'What will that answer?' Bianca asks, confused.

'Your question, obviously.'

They laugh together. She stands and they walk out, arm in arm, from the warm shelter to the perfect briskness of early evening.

Bianca walks in the garden. She marvels over the shapes and colours of the vegetables poking out like jewels among the shrubs: the horns of the late courgette flowers, the red-faced cheeks of the tomatoes, the cardinal-vested aubergines. Without even thinking, she picks some of these fruits of the earth and puts them in the pocket of her apron. As she walks back towards Innes, she inhales the holy aroma of the rosemary that grows along the path and caresses it with her free hand.

It is the scent, more than the gesture itself, that reawakens a vivid memory. She remembers strolling with her father in the Botanical Garden of Padua. They gave a few *scudi* to a monk so they could wander about, but he stood nearby and kept an eye on them.

'I could walk away with a cutting in my parasol,' joked Bianca.

Her father, using his body as a guard, picked a little rosemary branch from a bush and placed it in the parasol's folds, making her giggle.

'Who is simpler, the herbs or the people who grow them?' she asked in all seriousness. She was only fifteen and they had just begun their trip. She had never had her father's full attention before. It was a privilege that never tired her, and in exchange she offered her unconditional attention, like a student in the presence of a revered tutor, overflowing with love.

'A good question,' he replied. 'I believe the two things go together: if you aren't pure at heart, you will contaminate the plants that you care for. If you aren't simple, you cannot possibly be pure at heart. Simple herbs are those that cure ailments and restore health. The monk is surely a simple person or else he wouldn't be standing there in his sandals. He would be in a hall full of frescos, in a crimson robe, or on his way to Rome. But I am certain that he is a happy man even without all of those other colours.' He added, 'Your name is Bianca because we wanted you to be simple, essential and pure. Because we wanted you to choose your own colours.'

The gravel crunched underfoot. Gusts of wind made purple petals rain down from a tree, like a child throwing confetti into the air.

'Do you want me to become a painter?' Bianca asked, pausing and turning to face her father. 'What if I am not capable?'

'Don't be so literal, Bianca. I mean you should be something different, something greater.'

She blushed and felt simple-minded, but then understood.

'You mean like choosing the colours of a flag or a banner?'

'Precisely. Warriors of certain tribes in North America paint their faces before going into combat to show everyone the colours of their courage. There's no need to paint your cheeks with your own colours. The important thing is to recognize that you have them.'

On that same visit she saw a sycamore tree. When she asked the monk about it, he bragged as if it was his very own baby.

'It's over one hundred and thirty years old.'

Bianca wondered how he could possibly know this. Maybe someone in the seventeenth century had taken it upon himself to record the date in the register. '*Planted a shoot of* Platanus orientalis L. *It looks promising; we will make it the Methuselah of our domestic forest.*'

The monk kept on speaking in a pedantic tone.

'As you can see, the trunk is hollow. This is due to a bolt of lightning that struck the tree when it was a hundred years old, but did not kill it. Indeed, it still bears leaves and fruits and seeds every year.'

'So it's a plant without a soul?' Bianca asked her father, wanting to make the monk feel uncomfortable. He did, in fact, blush and tried to come up with an explanation.

'The spirit is in the leaves, flowers and fruits. The spirit is not the heart of the tree, I mean. The tree has no heart.'

Returning to her studio with vegetables inside her apron after her walk with Innes, Bianca reflects that she still doesn't really know her own true colours. She places the vegetables in a basket, but it looks too much like a Baschenis still life. Resting in an almost random fashion on the rough table, however, they are perfect. She draws them and then colours them in. She is not sure who would find this little bit of garden pleasing, but it is beautiful. It is life. When she finishes, she picks up a tomato with her hands, which are still dirtied with colours, and bites into it. She eats it greedily, sucking down both the juices and the colour. Red is also a taste.

୫ ୫

At times, Bianca thinks, children – and especially boys – really are unbearable. Pietro needs total attention. He is greedy and manipulative. He always wants to be right, and as the firstborn he enjoys certain privileges that the other children are denied. These defects accentuate his propensity towards tyranny. Enrico follows him around and imitates his every move, as best as he can, since he is more fragile and inclined to cry. Taken together, the boys are pernicious. One day, Bianca finds Pietro throwing a spider into another spider's web. From a distance she can't understand what he is doing. She sees him lying on the ground next to his brother, tossing something and then looking into a void. She walks up to them, curious, just in time to see the spider envelop the stranger in an excited frenzy. The victim is moving and then it stops. Pietro glances up at Bianca. She has stood in his light. He looks her up and down with daring eyes, his lips pursed in a smile.

'You're cruel,' Bianca says.

'Even Papa does it,' he replies. He looks around for another little insect and finds an ant to condemn. Bianca turns and walks away without saying a word. She never knows quite what to say to Pietro.

The next day he comes up to her with his younger brother as if by chance while she is strolling in the gardens. He has his hands behind his back as if he is a miniature adult. He stands in her way, like a bandit.

'I have written a poem, like Papa. Would you like to hear it?'

Bianca nods, without letting herself be deceived by his innocent tone. He takes the piece of paper that he has been hiding
in his hand, unravels it like a messenger, and reads aloud:

> *I ossi dei morti*
> *son lunghi, son corti*
> *son bianchi, son morti*
> *Ti fanno stremir.*
> *Sta' attento alle spalle*
> *se vengono piano*
> *se hai tanta paura*
> *ti fanno stecchir.*

> The bones of the dead
> Are long, short,
> White and dead
> They worry you
> Watch your back,
> They sneak up on you slowly
> If you're too scared
> They will even kill you.

'Did you like it?' he asks, waiting for the usual overindulgent
praise.

'There's a missing rhyme and a word that's not in Italian that
I do not understand. Also, "ossi" are animals' bones, you should
use "ossa" for human bones. That's another mistake. Principally,
though, poems about bones are no longer the fashion.'

'Maybe they're not popular any more, but they certainly are
spooky. If you saw bones, you'd scream so loud you'd shatter
glass. Be careful, because this place is full of bones. Aren't I
right, Enrico? They grow like your dear little flowers.'

Enrico, playing the part of a good sidekick, nods. Pietro walks away with his hands behind his back, gripping the piece of paper like an offended dignitary. Enrico follows him.

శౖ ఇ

'Minna, what's this story about bones in the garden?'

'Who told you about the bones, Miss Bianca?' Minna says, eyes open wide in alarm.

'I overheard the boys talking . . .'

'Oh, those two troublemakers. It's an ugly story. Do you really want to hear it?'

'Go on.'

'Well, they say the bones belong to Don Carlo.' She sniffles a bit, and then tells the story rather too quickly, as if she feels guilty. She looks off into space, frowning as she speaks. 'Don Carlo owned this house. My grandfather says that he was a good man, for a count. When he died, he left everything to Donna Clara, and then everyone else came, like grasshoppers. And the bones, well . . . at first the old lady did everything she could to make Don Carlo's tomb beautiful. Masons came, even a master mason from Bergamo. And then, well, they moved the tomb. There was a party . . . well, not really a party, more like a second funeral, with a priest and everything. Even Frenchmen came from France and they gave speeches about how great a man he was. I never saw him myself. I was tiny, but they told me. They sealed the coffin in the tomb. At first Donna Clara went there every day, praying and making daisy crowns, as though she was a saint. Then I suppose she got tired of it. Or maybe her son wanted her to stop when he moved in. Anyway, they tore down the tomb. It took two days. I remember because by then I was older. And they used the stones to build the rotunda up there on the hill. The coffin disappeared. They say that the bones are still here, that they wander around. It makes me frightened to think of dead people's bones.'

'Who are *they*?' Bianca dares to ask, trying to make sense of the girl's words.

'People. Everyone,' Minna concludes, wringing her hands beneath her apron. 'Why do you want to hear these ugly stories, Miss Bianca? You wouldn't want the ghost of Don Carlo to get angry and come and tug on your feet at night, would you?'

Bianca laughs.

'Ghosts don't exist, Minna,'

Not until we conjure them. That's when they begin to take shape, when we imagine them. Once we summon them forth, for whatever reason, there's the chance that they will never want to leave. They become so tightly wrapped up in us that they blind us with regret, guilt, and the sting of renewed grief.

※ ※

There are moments when Bianca thinks of Pia as a friend. She is not *really* her friend but she wishes she could be. Theirs is a relationship that needs no words but feeds only on glances, gestures and trust. It is an understanding that concentrates on things of small importance, transforming what little they have into things infinitely more precious. Pia gives Bianca gifts of flowers that she picks and arranges herself with an innate tenderness, mixing the high with the low – wild snapdragons, buttercups, a nosegay of miniature roses – as if she has always been doing it. She will put them in a teacup – with black and gold decorations – and suddenly the flowers are fit for the gods. Bianca gives Pia ribbons – not old, used ones but new and crisp – a lace collar, and three handkerchiefs with decorated borders.

'Do you ever daydream, Pia?' Bianca once asks her impulsively.

They are lying on the grass, looking at the sky, hands behind their heads, feet close together.

'Yes, I like the ones I have where I am in charge,' Pia answers coolly. 'I like to invent a life as it will never be.'

'But you don't know what your future will bring.'

'Oh, yes – if I've already imagined it, then it cannot be. For this reason I invent things that are impossible. That way I can have fun and not waste my time.'

Hers is a practical economy of self-satisfaction.

'So what do you daydream of, then?'

'I cannot tell you, Miss Bianca. You'd laugh at me.'

'Me? Never.'

'What about you? What do you daydream of, Miss Bianca?'

'I only dream at night. And I never remember anything afterwards, except for the fact that it happened. No . . . once my father came to visit me. He was dressed in a long white shirt, like the Christ of the lambs, and he wanted to hug me but he was too far away.'

'What about your mother?'

'She never laughed. And then she died,' Bianca says, grateful that they are not facing each other.

'Maybe she knew. That she was going to die, I mean. But even Donna Julie . . . she only laughs rarely.'

What about your mother? Bianca wants to ask. *The pretty swaddling and all the rest?* But she holds back. She doesn't want to risk losing what they have. They can say anything to each other and know that there won't be any consequences; neither will either repeat what the other has said, and they don't need to be ashamed of anything.

'Do you think Tommaso is good-looking?'

'Oh, come on, Pia. He's only a boy.'

'I know. But his hair is as smooth as silk. I'd like to run my fingers through it, mess it up a little.'

'It's messy already!'

Laughter, and then silence.

'Anyway, *I* think he's good-looking,' Pia continues. 'Even Luigi will turn out to be good-looking. His father wants to send him to become a servant at Crippa of Lampugnano. We will never see each other again.'

'It isn't that far away. He can always come back to visit.'

'A maid is like a prisoner. And anyway, I only like to look at him. I don't want to marry him or anything. It's better to be alone. I'm used to it.'

'But one day it will happen.' Bianca turns onto her side, propping herself up on her elbow. The child is still on her back with her eyes closed.

'Do you feel the same way, Miss Bianca?'

Sometimes silence is the best answer.

❧ ❧

'So, you finally decided to paint portraits. I told you it was more worthwhile.'

Bianca is startled to discover Donna Clara standing behind her, and this time in the space she has carved out in the study. She has no place just for herself downstairs, and so when she does work there, these interruptions happen often. Even so, she needs to get out of her room. Donna Clara pulls out the portrait of the mysterious woman that Bianca has composed quickly and then never touched again. She fixes her lorgnette on her nose in a nest of flesh and wrinkles.

'Beautiful. It reminds me of someone . . . Was it done from memory?'

'No, actually it wasn't. It's a woman I met.'

'Tell me, who? I know, I know . . . but no, it can't be. There's no way you could know her. My mind is deceiving me, my age, my imagination, and all the rest of it.' Donna Clara strides around the room as she speaks, bobbing her head from side to side like a bird. And then she discards the idea. 'Anyway, it's a good job. Very good. My compliments.'

Bianca is silent: what can she possibly say in return? The old woman puts the composition back down on the desk.

'When will you do my portrait? Although, thinking about it, I don't really want a painting of myself. My mirror is good enough. It's a sad day, my dear, when you don't recognize the person in the reflection and she's staring you straight in the eye. You'd like to make her disappear with a wave of the hand – shoo, you ugly beast! – and instead see the person you once were. But that other woman is gone. She's lost, never coming back. Time is no gentleman, not one bit. So unless you can be kinder than the mirror . . . but I know you. You are fixated on the truth and you'd make me into a monster, into the monster I am.'

She chuckles, turns around, and walks away.

There is nothing to laugh about later, however, when Bianca comes across her sketch of the mysterious woman torn in half, and deliberately placed on top of a pile of her other drawings. Just two days have passed; she hasn't shown it to anyone else, nor has she reworked it. She has only put it aside, as one does with ideas when they are still unclear. Whoever wished to slight her clearly looked for that specific drawing.

Bianca lifts the two pieces of torn paper and fits them together, her hands trembling. The woman stares out at her, her eyes slightly off-kilter and her mouth folding into a smile. She is beautiful, achingly beautiful, aching *but* beautiful. And she no longer exists.

The sabotage is unexpected and fills her with anger.

The children's mother and grandmother are not around; they have gone to the city to run some errands. Although it is late summer, it is still incredibly hot, as hot as July. Even Donna Clara admitted yesterday, after three lemon sorbets failed to restore her energy, 'It's as hot as hell here in Brusuglio. Summer is scorching. And then in winter we freeze. No matter how you look at it, we lose. Although, the sky is so beautiful when it's clear, it's heavenly. I always tell my son, not even in my beloved Paris did I see such skies.'

Bianca is shocked that someone would actually tear her drawing. She decides that she will have to deal with it in her own way, and in the meantime do something that makes *her* happy, for once. Nanny is taking her nap now and she sleeps heavily. The boys have gone with Ruggiero to see the foals in the Bassona stables and won't be back until nightfall. The cool water of the brook is inviting and far enough away that no one will hear them splashing about. Minna is Bianca's accomplice.

'I'll help you, Miss Bianca. But will the girls be quiet?'

Bianca doesn't know and doesn't care. She wants to have some fun. If someone finds out, she can always count on the master's support. Hasn't he applauded the English form of education some time ago at dinner? And so, off they go, one after the other, Minna leading the procession with a basket of delicious snacks hanging from one arm.

The girls are perplexed.

'Where are we going?' Giulietta speaks for everyone. She understands that this isn't going to be just like any other picnic.

Usually they go up to the clearing or to the meadows with the birches, but no further than that.

'It's a secret,' Bianca tells them, as she guides the girls along the trail that brings them to the far reaches of the estate, where the brook divides the cultivated land from the wilderness.

'Are we allowed to do this?' whispers Francesca, intelligent enough to realize that secrets can also often be trouble.

'Yes, we are,' Bianca reassures her. 'Just because you have never done it, doesn't mean it's not allowed.'

They are all pleasantly surprised to find Pia already there, sitting on the ground and leaning against a tree trunk, braiding a garland of different kinds of white wildflowers.

'What are you doing here?'

'I overheard you speaking to Minna, Miss Bianca. But I know how to keep secrets. May I stay?'

There is an absolute calm to her manner. She already knows that Bianca's answer will be yes. Actually, Bianca almost feels bad for not having asked her earlier or sending someone to seek her out. But Pia is already standing, joyful and incapable of bitterness.

'And now what?' Francesca asks. She still does not understand exactly what they are doing there.

'Now we will take a dip,' Bianca explains.

'In the brook?' Giulietta asks with a smile.

'In the brook,' Bianca echoes. 'It's cool and clean. You'll see how nice it feels.'

Being obedient, the girls don't react, but it is clear that they would prefer to be somewhere else, even in the nursery, although it is the hottest room in the house, with their dolls, the tired wooden pony, and the wooden blocks. They stand there, transfixed, arms hanging by their sides, staring at the water. It has never looked so frightening. Pia begins to undress

Francesca, Minna helps Giulietta, and Bianca takes care of Matilde. It is she, the youngest one, who screams first.

'I'm not taking off my clothes! It's embarrassing!'

Bianca picks the child up and carries her behind a tree that is wide enough to hide her.

'No one will see you here,' she says, continuing to undress her with a calm firmness. Matilde's little body is round and pale and her tummy juts out. Bianca would love to draw her now. The other girls, undergoing the same treatment, don't say a word. And then finally Giulietta shrieks, her voice suffused with excitement.

'Can we learn how to swim like Pietro and Enrico?'

'Better than Pietro and Enrico!' answers Bianca, coming out from behind the tree holding Matilde by the hand.

Bianca quickly steps out of her own clothes and stands in her undershirt and slip. If she was alone, she would also remove those items but she suspects that none of the girls have ever seen an adult fully undressed. She is sure that Pia and Minna wouldn't mind, but the other three might.

Giulietta looks at Bianca closely.

'Miss Bianca, you have freckles on your arms, too!'

Bianca smiles. 'I've always had them. What can I do, erase them?'

Giulietta laughs at the idea, and then gets distracted by Pia, who looks so different without her bonnet. Pia slips down the smooth bank of tall grass and splashes into the water, laughing.

'Is it cold?' Giulietta asks.

'It's delightful,' answers Pia, moving through the water like a dog.

'Look, she's floating!' Francesca says.

'Everyone can float. All you need to do is move around a bit,' explains Bianca, entering the water slowly. The water in the brook is not deep. It comes up to her waist, and is stingingly fresh. She feels sand and grass beneath her feet. The ground is firm.

'So who's coming in first?' she says, holding her arms up high, ready to embrace the most fearless one. Surprisingly, Matilde makes her way forward. She only needs to be in someone's arms. When her tiny feet touch the water, she lets out a little shriek but doesn't cry. Bianca holds her tightly as the water swirls around her undershirt.

Francesca is more courageous. She takes a seat on the grassy bank and lets herself slide into the brook as Pia has done. In an instant she is standing with the water up to her chest and laughing in excitement.

Minna and Giulietta hold hands and enter the water together cautiously, shrieking when the stream takes hold of them. Everyone is finally in. Pia has swum off and now turns back towards them, creating ripples in the water. They all hold hands and make a sort of ring, Bianca with Matilde in her arms. The game ends when Minna does some sort of dive, throwing herself forward, disappearing and then reappearing again, her hair dripping in front of her face. They all laugh. Minna raises her arms victoriously.

'It feels so good.'

'Can I go underwater too?' Giulietta asks.

'Yes, but remember to blow your air out, otherwise you might drown,' Pia explains and shows her how, by going underwater herself and emitting a whirlpool of bubbles.

'What should I do with my eyes?'

'Do as you please. Keep them open and you'll see green. Keep them closed, and you won't see a thing.'

Giulietta goes down and then comes right back up, coughing and rubbing her eyelids.

'I have water in my nose!' she complains.

'Pinch it closed,' Pia says and again shows her how.

The little girl makes another attempt, this time with her nose pinched. When she resurfaces she is smiling.

'I saw green, I saw green!'

Matilde, still in Bianca's arms, moves her tiny feet back and forth in excitement, splashing rhythmically.

Francesca copies her older sister.

'I saw a fish!' she exclaims as she resurfaces.

Everyone laughs. Above them, the sun toys with the leaves. Splashes of light pass through the branches, rest on the surface of the brook, and then disappear. There is no noise, only the humming of cicadas and the slow swishing of water. They enjoy the moment silently. Bianca looks at all her companions' faces, one by one, and their differing expressions of pleasure. Giulietta wears a concentrated smile, trying hard not to forget a thing. Francesca, though, smiles widely and holds tightly to Minna's hand. Minna gazes up at the sky, now a light blue above the leaves. Matilde looks serious, her eyes large, dilated by wonder.

And then, just like that, the quiet moment ends. Pia, who Bianca now notices is actually quite curvaceous and not so little, pulls herself up the bank, takes the garland she has left there, and crowns herself with it. She laughs and goes under the water again, kicking her feet and splashing the other girls, who shield themselves with their hands.

Pia stands up in the brook, combing back her hair with her fingers, pulling it away from her face in an elegant motion. The little ones copy her. It is then that Bianca notices the resemblance. It is in the shape of her head and her facial structure, and it is shockingly apparent.

The perplexity on Bianca's face must be evident.

'What's wrong, Miss Bianca? You've gone all white,' Pia says, then giggles. She laughs cheerfully, and so do the others, and then suddenly none of them can stop.

After their outing, the only trace of the crime is a few white shirts and knickers hung out to dry on the clothes line behind the kitchens, bottoms up, like ghosts dangling from the trees. Nanny, who has no idea what has happened, is surprised by the girls' fatigue, and she comes down to chat to Bianca after having put them to bed.

'They were dead tired and went to sleep immediately. If only they were always so cooperative. Ah, I see Ilide did some laundry? But, it's not laundry day today . . .'

Bianca and Minna look at each other conspiratorially. Pia is not there. She must have gone on one of her walks. The evening is mild and quiet. The half-moon hangs in the air, as bright as a lantern.

❧ ❧

The afternoon dip hasn't been enough to satisfy Bianca. And so she retraces her steps back down the path that she, the girls and the maids took, but this time alone. The leaves shield the moonlight now and make it hard to see, but she knows the way. It is as if the smell of the water guides her – a green, pleasant, familiar and natural scent. Like her very own, within the folds of her sheets.

This time, given that she is alone and darkness hides her, she removes all her clothes the way she used to do at home in the small swimming hole near the manor, which belonged to a *conte* who only left the house to go to church. It is dark and deserted. The water feels more daring, though, and it caresses every bit of her body, even the most hidden parts.

The moon is high and the trees along the bank form a straight corridor, fringed only by some light branches. The moonlight casts parallel shapes on the black water. Bianca leans back, her feet anchored to the soft muddy ground, and looks up but doesn't let herself go. It is as if she doesn't want to lose control, abandon herself. She breathes in the perfume of the wet country night mixed with the velvet smell of the water. She feels good.

Her hand brushes up against something. Tangled in a branch is Pia's crown of flowers, still intact. Bianca frees the wreath and lets it float off. She follows it, moving her arms and legs gently, only enough to keep afloat. She allows herself to think about what she hasn't had time to before, but which presses on her mind like a migraine. Is it conceivable? How can it be? But . . . the shape of her face. It certainly is possible. Everything about Pia's history leads Bianca to believe that it is possible. It is strange, though, that the girl lives there, so close to him. Maybe it is chance. Or maybe it is a bolder way of challenging fate, displaying the fruit of the crime right under everyone's noses. But whose fault is it, after all? Certainly not Don Titta's. It is never a man's fault. It must be the mother's fault. But who is the mother? Is she still around, somewhere, or has she been forgotten like a minor historical figure? And when did it all happen? *He came to Paris when he was twenty,* Donna Clara said. Something must have happened at some point between the era of the curious child in the portrait and the twenty-year-old man going to meet his mother in Paris.

No, it cannot be. It is too much like a romance novel, Bianca tries to reason. But . . . the likeness. If the others notice it, if they know . . . She has to make sure that Pia never removes her bonnet. No one can find out, no one can suspect a thing.

Or maybe – the thought shoots across her brain in all

clarity – everyone knows already. *Yes, that's it*, Bianca thinks. It explains Donna Clara's inexplicable surges of affection towards Pia, Minna's hangdog gaze and cruel tongue, and the women's gossip in the kitchen. What about the ghost, though? And the priest? Is he an accomplice, too? Is it possible?

No, it cannot be. Perhaps she alone sees a resemblance because she has an outsider's eye and is able to identify the invisible ties that connect different people, like a spider's web. The others may never have noticed.

Or maybe Bianca is imagining it all. It is just the excitement, the intense heat. It is her eagerness to put order into all the coincidences and mishaps she comes across, to frame them on the same canvas. As if classifying and understanding are one and the same.

There is the sound of twigs snapping and then footsteps on leaves.

'Who's there?' whispers Bianca. In the silence her voice is as loud as a scream.

Nothing. It is a hare, or maybe one of those ferocious wild animals that besiege Minna's dreams. Bianca lets herself go then, falling backwards, water filling her ears. She hears nothing more except for the far-away rumble of a much greater and deeper body of water, like the echo of the ocean. Even her body remembers her own lake. It is a different kind of memory from all others and it is reawakened by her every movement in the brook. The green water is cold against her skin. Algae move around at the bottom like the hair of the dead. She feels that good sort of melancholy that takes hold of her every time she remembers her home.

There is another rustle, this time louder and closer. But Bianca doesn't hear it. She floats on the water and stares at the moon. She doesn't notice the shadow crouching among the bushes, watching her drift in the current. His gaze takes in her small breasts, the way her hair swirls around her head like a cloud, and her knees and feet poking out of the water.

Part Two

And then comes winter. Or rather, autumn arrives but it feels like winter. After a mild and colourful October, the skies become tinted with grey and vary only slightly in hue: pewter, stormy with a streak of blue, deep blue with leaden edges, steel, silver, iron and platinum. The temperature plunges. One morning, on waking, Bianca sees that the great lawn has turned completely white. It reflects the pale sky and promises only cold, not the joyful feeling of snow. Chilblains appear on Minna's delicate fingers. Bianca takes it upon herself to cure them with a white paste she brought with her in a ceramic jar that has the consistency of artists' *gesso*.

'This is Serafina's magic paste. Trust me, they will go away. You just need to be patient enough for your skin to absorb it.'

Minna, at first suspicious, soon realizes her luck. She can think of nothing nicer than sitting in one of the pink pinstriped armchairs in the nursery and waving her hands in the air while the cream dries, without having to do a thing more. She doesn't even have to bring the girls tea. Actually, the girls take it upon themselves to serve *her* tea, with all the clamour and ceremony and dangerous clinking of porcelain cups at risk.

Minna's miraculous healing from her chilblains and the teatime ritual are amongst the final events of their serene country life that year. The ladies decide, in a flash, that the change of seasons, though inevitable, is entirely unwelcome, and in response they want to close up the house and move back to the city. The poet seems unhappy with the decision and for some time he resists. Eventually, though, he surrenders to the fact that it is expensive to warm the entire household, worn down by the endless complaining of how they will be better off in the city, with the good fireplaces, fewer windows, and so on. Don Titta stays on a little longer after their departure with his faithful Tommaso, with the excuse of having to finish a commissioned ode that will pay many of the bills. He lets the caravan of women, children and luggage set off without him. Bianca suspects that the Big Bear only wants a bit of solitude; no one will deny him that. She has started calling him this in her head recently and in the fragmented letters she mentally writes to her father, a habit she hasn't quite lost. Only common sense prevents her from taking up a quill and transforming everything into a real missive:

> *Imagine a bear after hibernation, dearest Father, one of those bears you showed me when I was a little girl in that book of Russian fables, with dirty and rugged fur, a thin body, pinched muzzle, and drooping shoulders. This is the master of the house. He looks uncomfortable in his clothes, which seem to be cut for a man of another size. He will never become a bear of formidable stature and will always remain the thin being he became after his long sleep. He is always in search of something, with a great disquiet about him, so much so that it almost inspires compassion. You can see him wandering through the woods in search of honeycombs and fruit, and if he turns around, you will see the beast in those deep, dark eyes. You will be afraid of him, and fear and respect will linger on even when you see him play with his cubs on a sunny summer day. But it's never really summer for him; it is always the beginning of spring. He has just awoken and he doesn't understand or remember what sense there is in*

the world around him. Even when he is full, his eyes are hungry.

Whatever reasons he has to stay on, the Big Bear proves shrewd in sparing himself the total chaos of their arrival in Milan. Although the domestic staff have been on alert for several days – the personal maids have gone on ahead to prepare – it feels as though they have reached a lodging that has not been lived in for a long time. The trip has been short, but it is next to impossible to gaze out at the road along the way because the children are so rowdy. They do nothing but scream and bicker, and Nanny soon gives up scolding them, leaving Bianca the duty of entertaining them with new games. It is foggy and there is little to see in the wide stretches of cold, open countryside. The streets of the city soon make themselves heard, though, through the sounds of hooves on cobblestones, bells, and the calling of tradesmen. The facade of their town house is dark and closed. It looks out onto a cobbled piazza and is surrounded by other homes in a similar style.

The bleakness Bianca feels when she first sets eyes on the house is briefly interrupted by the grandness of the foyer and its red-carpeted staircase. But that soon fades as they make their way to the bedrooms, which are melancholy and look uninhabited. It is all so sadly chaste. Only the living room, with its frescos in pastel colours, has the guise of magnificence. The other ceilings are all dark, with solemn miniature decorations lost in the shadows. Not even the children's cries of joy when they come across forgotten old toys and the shadows of their younger selves enliven the bleak atmosphere. The bedrooms that have been closed off for some time feel cold, as cold as the living rooms in the villa in Brusuglio, pierced by its numerous windows.

And then, slowly but surely, things get better. The light becomes denser, enveloping the house. There is a milky glow on grey mornings and an uncertain light on clear ones. The rooms surrender and begin to welcome the intruders, to the point of finally allowing them to be lived in. The house is much smaller than the family's country home and feels less mysterious. An opaque glass skylight situated above the staircase promises – and yet shuts off – the sky above. It makes the sky look small and square, especially when there isn't a cloud in sight. The garden is lush and quite remarkable: palms, banana trees and oriental sweet-gum trees create an exotic backdrop. Two struggling grapevines recall the countryside, and a pair of very young magnolias, situated closer to the house, stand tall. Donna Clara's bedroom is the most beautiful. It is on the second floor and looks out onto the garden, which, seen from above, winds between the other houses like an escape route towards nature. Her walls are adorned with a delicate motif of pink and pale scarlet rhombi and the furniture is exquisite. She cannot resist pulling Bianca in and dragging her over to a very small picture which might otherwise go unnoticed. It is of a *putto*, a child embroidered in *petit point* and protected by a glass cover.

'Queen Marie Antoinette made that in prison, before they chopped her head off, poor thing,' Donna Clara explains. 'She gave it to one of her guardians as a gift and she in turn sold it to a friend of mine in Paris, who then gave it to me. Doesn't it just give you the chills?'

Yes, it is somewhat eerie to think of a gloomy jail cell where time can never move slowly enough, counting down to death. What a bizarre gift to give to a friend. Who knows what it means. There are no other macabre relics in that bedroom, only graceful watercolours depicting non-existent landscapes, crystal bottles on the older woman's bureau, and the vague scent from open drawers.

The servants' quarters are at the narrow top of the house. It is as if that section of the building has nothing to do with the frilly bedrooms and elegant salons below. Bianca happens to walk into one of the rooms while she is exploring but leaves hastily, disturbed by the low ceilings, iron beds, rough wooden floors and damp. Her own bedroom is downstairs, near the others. It is a small beige room that has the bland feeling of a guest room. Tommaso and Innes sleep at the end of the dark corridor, far from the clamour of the others. Nanny has her own bedroom near the nursery that is furnished with salvaged furniture, but she doesn't complain. She never complains.

The room that attracts Bianca the most is Don Titta's study. And even though it is completely out of bounds at all times, one day she sees the poet passing through the French window of his study into the garden, and decides to linger. It is dark inside, despite being morning. Rows of books line every surface. The bookshelves are protected by doors of mesh that absorb the meagre light. There is a sharp smell of old paper. The chimney is both dark and damp; a cylindrical heater of recent manufacture allows for modern heating, but in the absence of a legitimate inhabitant even this looks cumbersome and gloomy. On the desk of peeling Moroccan leather there are large ink spills, creating geographical maps of imaginary countries, and a pile of dark blue notebooks that Bianca recognizes from Brusuglio. On a tray rests a row of quills, ready for use. The inkpot is full. Instinctively she leans forward to smell its bitter aroma, which she has always liked. She looks for other clues about the poet, but the fragment of free wall space bears no paintings or images, just a crucifix engulfed by shadows and grief. Footsteps on the parquet floor in the hallway outside force her to leave quickly, and she pauses only when she arrives at the square of grass in the courtyard, which is still green but for the areas where dead leaves have now fallen.

æ æ

There are no large windows from which to throw all domestic tensions, but there is a great deal of coming and going, and doors opening onto other doors. It takes Bianca some time to realize how this concentric house works. It is a maze, a puzzle. Soon she finds her way, though, and is able to move around lightly and silently, making the most of the play of doorways and using them to her advantage. She listens and overhears, and absolves herself by telling herself that although these exchanges aren't meant for her ears, only chance has led her there.

'Everyone knows that she was a whore when she was young.'

'But she is so sanctimonious now. All she does is talk about her grandchildren, as if they were the stars in her sky.'

'Well, anyone can feel regret. The beauty of religion is that there's always a shortcut to forgiveness, even in the most extreme cases. She has carried herself forward, and has done things right. It's not as if she waited for her deathbed to bury her past. She even had to take in that burden of a son. Luckily, her daughter-in-law brought in a dowry of sanctity and money in equal parts . . . I imagine the old lady will end up in Purgatory because she sure as hell won't be singing psalms with the angels.'

'And what makes you think you'll end up in heaven to hear the singing?'

'Me? I wasn't talking about me. I wouldn't mind a little atonement, actually: virtue is so boring . . .'

In the city, the family receive more guests, and in addition to the usual ones there is a whole host of new characters. Tommaso, surrounded by these people, retreats into his shell like an irritated hermit crab, although he remains kind to Bianca, to the point of irritation. Once, he stopped to admire a drawing she had done of the girls – the one she started on her first day in Brusuglio, and which she then finished upon Donna Clara's insistence.

'You have style and personality, Miss Bianca. But be careful not to lose yourself in fashion.'

Bianca actually wishes she could spend some of her money on clothes, but she is set on increasing her savings, which are growing ever so slowly, month after month. Soon she comes to the realization, though, that it is one thing to be in the country, where her somewhat outdated but nonetheless refined outfits give a decent impression, and another to be in the city where ladies are elegant and proud. *We are avant-garde. We might look to Paris, but Paris looks to us, too,* their clothes seem to say.

Even Donna Clara and Donna Julie, who are so at ease in the country in their uniforms of ordinance – black for one and a lighter colour for the other – are more worried about their appearance in Milan. They correct – or perhaps pollute – their usual sobriety with certain bold touches that make them stick out. All they need to do is put on a turban wrapped in a complicated way or wear a waterfall of frills on their sleeves to set the children off in giggles. They stare at the two women, puzzled, and then make their inevitable remarks.

'Where's the rest of the bird?' Enrico asks when his grandmother comes down to dinner in a feathered headdress.

All the credit goes to Gandini, the seamstress, who has been summoned to the confused household and put to work. Bianca is unable to hide her dismay when the ladies appear wearing the craftswoman's most recent creations. It seems as though elephant sleeves are the latest trend, puffy at the top and narrow at the wrist, like a trunk, in the Kalmuk style. On the delicate arms of Donna Julie the styles derived from the Russian steppes look graciously frivolous, but on Donna Clara they look comical, though no one smiles when they see her. And in fact, her guests' compliments are futile. It is clear that neither of the two ladies are emblems of avant-garde fashion. They let themselves be convinced by the skill of the seamstress and are only vaguely aware that her adaptations of French fashion aren't perhaps all that successful.

When Carola Visconti makes an entrance into the living room one day wearing a light green spencer with egg-yellow braided decorations, a long, fitted, dark green dress, and a nocked bow and heron on her head, Donna Clara suddenly looks like grey wattle. And Donna Julie, wearing a fichu over the square neckline of an old emperor-style dress, appears no more than a provincial girl who has just left the convent in her dead mother's clothes.

❧ ❧

Bianca discovers with a mix of delight and chagrin that the city is full of things to buy. Many of the generous guests to the house offer her gifts with a joy that appears authentic. She receives a small crystal phial containing the essence of fraghe by Giuseppe Hagy – three drops to be sprinkled inside the folds of one's handkerchief, like the three distilled droplets of the queen's blood. She accepts many *boutonnières* of greenhouse violets too to decorate her jackets. She enjoys the desserts of the Galli – dates sliced vertically and filled with bits of pink and green marzipan, and pralines from Marchesi wrapped in brown paper and entirely delectable. And finally, she receives four brand-new outfits sewn by Signora Gandini. These come as a complete surprise. They are carried into the house for a fitting and then taken in accordingly. Bianca's face lights up when she sees them arrive.

When the time comes for the fitting, the smell of the new fabric is intoxicating and their rustling sounds are music to her ears. As she looks at her reflection, she discovers details about herself that she didn't even know existed. Her *décolletage* and her tiny waist are prominent in the two evening gowns. The seamstress has to fold and take in the fabric.

'You know, my dear, that your hourglass figure is most esteemed,' she says.

She also has a round and svelte *derrière*. It is strange how the French language can make any word sound pretty. A charcoal-blue outfit in 'a colour made for you' wraps around her waist and draws attention to her curves, thanks to a short blazer that ends just above her lower back. Naturally, Donna Clara and Donna Julie are privy to the entire fitting – front-row audience members – muttering comments under their breath that Bianca chooses to ignore.

A few days later, in addition to the new outfits, she also finds three complete sets of undergarments from Ghidoli, everything from long underwear *à l'anglaise*, which combines modesty and elegance, to exquisite lace undershirts. Bianca puts her pride aside and is overcome by vanity and pure joy. She thanks the ladies with her heart, her eyes, and with words, too.

'Go and get changed. Seeing you well dressed will be the greatest thanks of all,' Donna Clara says.

That evening, she comes down to dinner in her favourite outfit: a pinstriped dress of white and light green silk that reminds her of daffodil stems and makes her feel just as delicate. In the large and somewhat cavernous living room it feels cold, despite the lit fireplace, and Donna Julie runs upstairs to fetch her a white cashmere shawl. At times, the house still feels like an invaded fortress, leading Bianca to think that it was happier before they arrived – sealed, empty, and alone.

Bianca's room has a floor made from irregular red tiles. She often trips over them, and it feels as if the whole floor is waiting for her to fall. The pale wallpaper with a pattern of rhombi does nothing to brighten the room, and even with the tall window, the light that seeps in is always greyish and dirty. Pigeons coo on the windowsill, which Bianca does not like. They look like rats with wings, stolid and insistent. They are everywhere here, she soon finds out.

The city is revealing itself to her little by little, like a bashful and discreet lady batting her eyelashes and playing coyly with her fan. At first she finds it hostile. It is too silent or too noisy or just strange. She doesn't know many other large cities. Verona, compared to this, is a village, with its semicircle of coloured *palazzi* surrounding the arena. London, as seen from numerous carriages, is large and grey, white or red. There is nothing mysterious about it, nothing scary or miraculous. Not like this place, which reveals itself slowly, like the closed hand of a child holding a secret, being pried open finger by finger.

When she applies herself, Bianca sees things she has never imagined. Everything is bigger here. The markets are more market-like. In Verziere, the green stalls are set up at the feet of the statue of the tortured Christ. Apparently it is also the place where witches have been burned at the stake. When Bianca takes walks there, she observes the vendors as they hawk their goods with full-blown obscenities, trying to detect traces of evil on their dishevelled faces. The streets are more street-like, with cracks engraved in the manure and the incessant traffic of public and private carriages. They rumble by like a stormy sea, so loud they bring on headaches. Even the churches are more church-like. Guided more by instinct than piety, she discovers that there is an infinite variety of them. The Duomo, with its lacy facade, reminds her of the evanescent play of sand when it seeps through her fingers. Santa Maria delle Grazie, with its firm, erect cupola and mystical silence, relays the cold numbness of the monks – God's dogs, as her father used to call them. She watches the monks there walking on the flagstones under which other monks sleep in eternal rest, smiling remotely, their hands hidden under their elegant black-and-cream-coloured tunics. In the cloisters, bronze frogs spit streams of water onto the emerald stone of the fountain. San Lorenzo, with its indoor and outdoor columns, reminds her of a peeling set design. It is like the travel writer, Lady Morgan, said: Milan is a city of bricks transformed into a city of marble. And yet the cement and mud reappear so rapidly, just by turning a corner or crossing a piazza. It makes her think that the city's transformation has been hasty, or interrupted.

Bianca wanders alone, relying on her shrewd independence where she can, knowing full well that her behaviour is at the limits of respectability and delighting in the thrill this gives her. She keeps several coins inside the small green velvet purse that came with her new clothes and relies on these to get her out of sticky situations, such as when she gets lost and needs a carriage. She'll hail one, stare straight back at the suspicious driver and show him the coins in her palm. Bianca gets lost often because she daydreams as she walks. She looks at things without really seeing them, and when she shakes off her daydreams, she no longer has a reference point, no street corner, palazzo or bell tower that she can refer back to. She is like Theseus without his string, reawakened from a nap. She likes it that way. It reminds her of the adventures she had with her father, on foot in London, and the thrill of wandering into neighbourhoods like Soho or Bethnal Green, knowing that, with her arm in his, she could go anywhere. Although now things are different; there is the thrill, but there is awareness too. The open road tempts her with the ambiguous lure of adventure.

❧ ❧

In the beginning, the family encourage her to go out for strolls, but when she starts venturing out more frequently, they begin to get suspicious.

'Where has she gone to this time?'

'To look for trouble, that's what I say.'

This is the gossip from the kitchen. Donna Clara limits herself to open curiosity.

'What wonderful things have you seen today, Miss Bianca?'

And when Bianca answers vaguely or simply describes a facade or street corner in her own approximate, particular and distracted way, the older lady just shakes her head and sighs.

'My dear girl, are you sure? I don't think I've ever encountered anything like that.'

Of course you haven't, Bianca wants to answer, *because you only travel in coaches*. Milan has surely changed a lot in the previous ten, twenty, even thirty years too, and Donna Clara no doubt knows Paris better. It was the city of her second youth and the home of her most recent love, and it has a way of always insinuating itself into her conversations. Her tired litany includes references to Carlo, Claude, Sophie, the *maisonnette*, and then Carlo once more, although any mention of them is quickly brushed away.

Bianca feels that she is on a mission. She wants to fully understand the city on foot, as a woman of the people. This goes hand in hand with her approach to drawing, as it has evolved over time in the countryside and at the end of the autumn. The mission is made possible by their move to the city. She doesn't speak of it to anyone, not even Innes, who in any case seems to be preoccupied with his own activities.

'Is he writing a novel as well?' Donna Clara teases on many occasions, making Donna Julie giggle.

'What are you saying, Mother? His novel is his life. He's not writing it, he's living it.'

The thought of Innes competing against the poet makes even Bianca smile. She has noticed a tacit understanding between the two men that she cannot quite fathom. Is it a simple masculine alliance or some other serious passion that they hide under their waistcoats and living-room banter? She never dares ask, even if Innes does treat her with the sort of gentle familiarity that makes him feel like her accomplice in the household that welcomes them with open arms. Arms that grip a little too tightly at times.

While Bianca is slowly learning about the city, several other fundamental insights come to her, thanks to the family itself. One night, the three ladies, accompanied by Innes, go to see a performance by La Sallé at La Scala. Bianca is not as impressed by the gold and velvet decor as Donna Clara expects her to be. Actually Bianca watches the audience more than the dancers themselves, observing their expressions and reactions. She has already been to La Fenice, Covent Garden and the Opéra, and has told them so, trying not to sound presumptuous. This theatre definitely has a particular charm, but she enjoys spying on people, trying to understand their intentions and conversations – about couples, love and other scandals. Bianca wears her new light blue velvet dress and the diamond necklace that her father gave her mother, which became hers after the inheritance was divided, despite predatory glances from her sister-in-law.

A splendid snowflake rests in the hollow of her neck and pulses with her every breath.

'You look delightful,' Innes whispers into the camellias in her hair. The show begins before her embarrassment can set in. Since the women are seated in a box facing the stage, Innes chooses to stand in order to see clearly. She feels his gaze on her neck and shoulders, delicate and constant. What is there to contemplate, aside from the performance? Certainly not the armoured back of Donna Clara, traversed vertically by a row of tiny buttons, ready to burst off like lethal bullets. Nor the white wool and silk that covers Donna Julie's own petite form. Distracted a bit by her own self-conscious vanity, Bianca nonetheless enjoys the performance to the very end. She doesn't know much about dancing, but she has always watched and appreciated opera. The new fashion of wearing ballet slippers that La Sallé seems to have invented gives the star a lightness in her step and allows her to flutter above everything else. Her veils don't entirely conceal her slim and handsome arms, but it is a happy kind of indecency that makes one question why arms cannot be revealed in all their glory. Her long tutu, as it swirls around her, intensifies her inconsistent character. The dancer is not just a sharply dressed woman gifted with acrobatic talent; she is something else, too. She is an image, a yearning, and a desire for a life where sylphs truly exist – spirits without a body. During the intermission, Donna Clara comments on the character.

'Everybody wants a lover like that. Maybe because she's attractive. But beauty doesn't last; it's a moment and then it's over.'

Bianca imagines the older woman is thinking of herself, and thinks it unfair to assume that ballerinas need to be as light in their everyday existence as they are onstage.

Innes offers all the women rose-flavoured sweets, small crystals filled with faint colours. Donna Julie consumes them with a childlike delight but Donna Clara refuses, asking for the more mundane pumpkin seeds, toasted and lightly salted.

Bianca peers out at the theatre's other boxes in search of the beauties that are so often talked about: Signorina Bongi, Signorina Barbesino, Signorina Carrara Stampa. She wonders if there is a Milanese form of beauty and thinks she identifies it in ladies with light olive-coloured skin, dark eyebrows, large eyes, and rosebud mouths that are full of promise. She wants to sketch these ladies, one beside the next like a bouquet of flowers in season. But then she thinks of the boredom, the complaining, the empty silence of interminable poses, and realizes she is happy to have more docile and yielding subjects.

At the end of the performance they linger for a while in the foyer, so that all their lady friends can welcome back Clara and Julie 'from the wild'. Their friends have white curls and surprisingly slim frames, notwithstanding their age. They wear dark grey, almost black, velvet dresses.

'And this is your Miss Bianca, is it not? Why, how precious . . . she doesn't even look foreign.'

Bianca doesn't like being talked about in the third person, but she hides her impatience under a slight smile, which pleases Donna Julie.

'You did well, Bianca,' she tells her later. 'Those monkeys can really wear you down.'

'Come now, Julie,' Donna Clara intervenes. 'We shouldn't speak of our friends like that.'

'Your friends, maybe,' Julie whispers snidely as they climb into the carriage.

Again, Bianca is amazed by Julie's sharpness. If only she would unsheathe it more often. With her sense of irony, she would make an exceptional rival to Donna Clara during their living-room skirmishes. But she never engages in them. Perhaps her role of model mother is a front to avoid the boredom of society.

'Now that you've been to La Scala, it is safe to say that you're an official Milanese lady,' jokes Donna Clara the following day during lunch, which is actually their breakfast, since they've all slept late. Bianca smiles patiently. She doesn't want to be Milanese any more than she wishes to be Turkish or barbarian. She belongs to her own world and doesn't need to borrow someone else's. But she has learned to keep her mouth shut, remembering with a smirk that silence is one of the virtues that best suits young ladies. Her tendency to speak her mind, which at first was considered a curiosity, is now the target of reproach. As adventurous as Donna Clara's previous life might have been, she is – in public and at home – tremendously conventional. Bianca has learned it is worth adjusting to this situation, even if it means keeping her mouth shut.

Sometimes Bianca wonders whether all this repressed behaviour, hesitation, and silence actually hides a duality that is far from noble. When, in the name of decency, is one supposed to stop being sincere? To what extent are silence and consent a form of courtesy and not grim opportunism? Bianca thinks about these things over and over. The more she considers, the more her thoughts darken. She has no one to confess them to and so they get tangled up inside her.

❧ ❧

Everyone rejoices when Pia finally joins them in Milan from Brusuglio. She has travelled alone in a carriage. When it arrives in the courtyard and the valet opens the door, Pia holds out her hand like a lady, but her eyes are full of laughter. The children, who have been waiting for her since morning, run towards her like marbles strewn across the floor. They hang from her arms and neck, all of them, even the boys. Pia looks charming in her austere jacket, which surely came from someone else's closet. She is composed and behaves like a proper young lady. She emanates a sweet haughtiness that she may have picked up from the ladies who visit the villa, serious but not without a trace of affectation. Bianca waits her turn to embrace the girl, and in so doing discovers that Pia had grown so much that their eyes almost meet at the same level now. Pia reveals her brown-heeled shoes, the tips of which are slightly scuffed and which fasten with a velvet bow.

'From the young lady,' she whispers.

During Pia's absence Bianca has thought a lot about the different pieces of her puzzle. She has moved them here and there until an image became clear. Of course, there are still many dark areas: things unsaid and unknown. But there are too many coincidences to ignore it entirely. There are also many fragments. Bianca has the eagerness and spirit of an amateur; she feels an immense, inexhaustible pleasure in classifying others' inclinations and passions. It is hard to say if this comes from her habit of considering the genealogical life of plants, which provides reassurance with its familial divisions and sub-divisions and makes everything understandable to the eye, or whether it is a passing fancy of her age, an affectation of a young lady who thinks she knows everything there is to know about the world, but who cannot truly recognize herself in the mirror. The truth is that the botany of affections is an inexact science, but it is the dearest thing to her at this time. One day it will pass. One day she will be overcome by her own first-hand passions. But for now, it gives her days both rhythm and meaning. She could have worried about consequences, but Bianca does not understand herself well enough to worry.

Now Bianca smiles complacently, folds up her imagined composition and puts it away, pleased. She could try to reconstruct it for someone to see how much of it is clear. But whom? Everybody is already too caught up in the web. Bianca fears, rightly, that her taciturn nature might tangle the threads even further. There is always a third option: delve deeper, continue her investigation outside of the family, alone. To what end? Just to know. To be certain. Then she will be able to decide what to do. What will it take, really? The courage to ask a couple of questions and trust the answers. The guests that come to the house are interesting, intelligent and honest people – they will surely be pleased to satisfy the curiosity of such a pleasant and alert young lady. All she needs to do is guide her conversations with the lawyer, the official, or the full-breasted benefactress in the right direction. Bianca applies herself to this puzzle with the zeal of a young scholar who wants to achieve excellent marks. She makes witty remarks here and there. She prepares her terrain. If she hesitates, it is only because the timing has to be just right. She knows how to do it and she enjoys the wait. Also because, whether she likes it or not, she has to roll up her sleeves and work.

※ ※

Away from the envious eyes of Minna and the silly kitchen maids, Pia blossoms and prospers. It is as if, all of a sudden, she has taken a step forward, detached herself from the shadows of domestic help and reclaimed her place at the front of the stage in a key role. No one scolds her if she reads or lounges about because that's what everyone does during that endless winter. And she doesn't really lounge about that often. She spends most of her time with the children. She is more joyful than Nanny and more creative at inventing games for them to play, keeping them happily distracted. The children don't venture out in the city. Both mother and grandmother are against it. There are vapours from the sewers, they say. There is the danger of whooping cough. And there are the other kinds of children, hordes of them, ready to attack.

'But they would have such fun. They could ice skate on the frozen lake,' Bianca insists, but in vain.

And so the tiny prisoners are kept within their confines. They don't suffer that much because they don't realize what they are missing and therefore don't even desire it. And Pia does everything she can to make their captivity more enjoyable. Christmas comes. There is the scent of honey from the forced hyacinths that grow along the windowsill and colourful wooden toys from Germany. There is the medicinal scent of tangerines that lingers so long in the air it becomes bothersome.

A new year comes but nothing changes: the city is still frozen, closed under skies that appear to have forgotten they too once possessed a colour. Everyone remains happily at home. The chimneys and the fireplaces burn at full force, but Donna Clara doesn't complain about the bills from the wood and coal suppliers, even if they deliver enough fuel to power a steamboat.

Bianca works hard, like a madwoman, she thinks to herself. It is a happy damnation, because it makes her feel at one with the world, worthy of her place, which belongs to no one but her. Her work brings her money, too, cash in velvet and damask pouches.

To think that only a couple of months earlier, when winter descended on them all of a sudden, she suffered and thought she wouldn't make it. She became obsessed with flowers during the one season that denied her them. For several long weeks she did nothing but colour in corollas, like a child. *Here, do this, good, fill in the empty spots, don't go over the lines.* Without the true colours in front of her, though, and because her ruled blocks of paper now seemed pathetic, she got frustrated. What would she do until spring returned? And what if it never returned, as the lugubrious, short, grey days suggested?

'If winter comes, can spring be far behind?' Innes quoted to her, in an attempt to console her as she traced the streaks of rain on the window with her finger.

'Nice. What's that?'

'A verse by a friend.'

'No. Spring, what's that?' she replied, depressed, without even looking at him.

A slow, thick melancholy had settled inside her, a profound dullness that could not be dissipated even by the vivacity of the children. *You should go out*, she told herself, as she ripped out pages from her sketchbook – more images of dead leaves. But where would she go? With her empty pockets and four outfits? The thought only made her angrier, and it was followed by bitterness and unease. *My dear father, what am I to do now? If I cannot even do this, what place shall I have in this world?* She would have preferred to have an entire army of human models, male or female, chubby boys or bored ladies, to draw. It would be better than her vain efforts.

One morning though, Pia brought her a vase full of bare branches. Not one leaf on them. Empty and yet full at the same time.

'What . . . ?' Bianca stuttered. Then she was silent and looked more closely. She looked harder still and then that was enough. She saw. The tall white vase was simple and lacked adornment, not even a touch of gold; it had probably been fished out from under some staircase. The branches, in all their bony grace, pushed upwards, reaching out arthritically towards something – towards the idea of leaves, the leaves that betrayed them, left without warning (as is their habit), at the beginning of autumn.

And just like that, Bianca made up her mind: *I will draw you, poor dead hands. And we shall see where it takes us.*

Surprisingly, she produced one of her better works. Actually, it was more than better. It marked the beginning of a new era, a fresh way of looking at the world that excluded colours and instead opened her eyes to new shapes. Flicking through some of her old sketchbooks, Bianca smiled. It took her but a moment to reject an entire army of colourful corollas made with complicated patinas and to embrace this new direction, composed of straight, curvy and broken lines, light and dark silhouettes. Leaves and flowers were reduced – no, elevated – to their essence. The intricate bare branches had been collected from the Milanese garden. They turned out to be an ideal subject for her new artistic calling. Her marks were clean and neat. The branches were bones of black ink, freed of one meaning and prepared to take on another.

Her audience was uncertain when they saw the new work.

'Miss Bianca, did you run out of colours? I can lend you mine, if you'd like,' Giulietta offered, perplexed.

'I liked your roses better,' added Matilde, nodding her little head to stress her statement.

'These are so . . . strange,' Donna Clara said.

'It's true. I have never seen such modern botanical drawings,' Donna Julie interrupted, surprising all of them.

And her husband, so frugal with displays of affection, took Donna Julie's hand and kissed it.

'Well done, dear wife. You have caught the essence of her work, just as our Bianca has done with her neo-botany.'

Donna Julie blushed but did not pull back her hand, delighting in both her husband's tenderness and Donna Clara's uncomprehending gaze.

Even Innes complimented her work.

'Brave is she who sails unknown waters,' he said, winking at her to soften his words.

And so, released from other obligations, and indeed encouraged, Bianca closed her box of watercolours and expanded her collection of pencils and charcoals. She spent an entire morning in Brera at the dimly lit Barba Conti shop. It was an odorous cavern where paints and powders were crowded together on high shelves, and filled with gleeful and impoverished students from the Accademia. While she waited her turn, she took her time to explore the place.

That afternoon a shop boy in a dark apron delivered a package of four reams of fresh, heavy paper and an entire set of charcoals. Against all logic, the much despised and feared winter became her season of renewal, a spring of experimentation and new endeavours. Oh, what pleasure she found getting her fingers dirty and extending her thought process down to the charcoal stick itself, her dowsing rod, foreseeing and extracting life from dead things. It was pure joy not to think and just to act, to trust in instinct. Technique gave her confidence, but it was the spontaneous movement of her hand that made invention possible. But there really was nothing to invent. Leaves and flowers existed already. They weren't the little faces of false young mistresses, trapped inside senseless poses within miniature ovals. Nor were they landscapes depicting orderly ruins and roaming shepherd boys and musicians. Leaves and flowers had their own unmistakable traits. It was the way one presented these – overlooking colours in favour of texture, getting to the basics – which continued to transform the working habits of this young artist. Because that was what she was. An artist. She had finally found her calling.

Dear Father, if you could see me now you would approve. You always appreciated the new over the old. You would be the first to receive a collection of my very own alive/dead leaves, or dead/alive, if you prefer. Truthfully they are more alive than ever, first when they flow from my fingers, and then when they are framed under glass . . . they are my natural preserves, delectable to the eye. I feel a deep pleasure in distilling them: it's my own way of removing them from the corruption of the world. Just as Daphne transformed herself into branches and fronds in order to escape Apollo's grasp, I, too, seem to be able to transform into that which I draw. I feel those veins and the sap that runs through them mixing with my blood . . . I know what I am fleeing: triviality frightens me most of all.

Like any artist, Bianca knew that she had to confront her public. Friends and family were called upon to express their opinion. Her first series of four branches in black and white had been carefully framed by Signor Grassi and hung above an antique table in the house's main entrance. The opinion was divided.

'She's got an odd little noggin,' Bernocchi exclaimed, looking more and more like a large frog in his dark coat. 'I'd be curious to know what goes on inside it . . .'

The women were unpredictably enthusiastic. There was a moment of suspense as they awaited the decisive opinion of Signorina Caravatti. Then, after a long pause of intent silence, the lady tipped her bountiful white head of hair to the side.

'I could never imagine a branch and a few leaves to be so *expressive*. I want my own series. Of course, if and when your time permits,' she added, alluding politely to the binding contract which tied Bianca to the family, of which no one spoke explicitly because, after all, Bianca wasn't a servant. What was she? It was hard to say. A dependant? In order to survive she was dependent on the commissions of others. But truthfully, she was also the owner of her own time and her own hands.

'I am certain my husband will have nothing against it,' Donna Julie said immediately.

Bianca felt like she was floating. To work for others as well as for the family would allow her to boost her savings. This was her first true step towards independence. Only now could she fully understand her past occupation: she had been, essentially, a masked governess. But no longer. Now she had a profession. She started to fantasize as the other women, following Signorina Caravatti's comments, devoted themselves to paying compliments and giving her comical directions.

'Perhaps a bouquet of roses, you know, the ummm . . . what are they called again? Well, you certainly know better than I.'

'Or the modest jasmine.'

'I do love jonquils so . . .'

Please, let them be, Bianca was about to say, but refrained. She recalled the enchantment of the English fields in springtime, the bicoloured daffodils blowing in the wind and the clouds chasing the sun. She remained silent. After all, she was a businesswoman now and the flowers belonged to those who bought them.

She thus welcomes the silent joy of habit into her day. Her desire to feel a struggle is once again renewed. She wants to carry through: to prepare, work hard and bask in the result. All of this in order, with order. Bianca's ambitions thrive on planning her personal black-and-white garden. Her funds grow inside her armoire and she counts and recounts the money with a passion that borders on greed. If it weren't for her sense of irony, she would be like a greedy princess from an eastern fable.

As her secondary obligations to the external world increase, she reminds herself that she needs to maintain her primary ones. She can dedicate herself to the art of commerce only in her free time and still has to take part in the family's mundane events, obligatory visits, and the occasional, unavoidable Mass.

Being a perfectionist, Bianca devotes herself entirely to her activities, disdaining any shortcuts of repetition. Each and every drawing has to be unique, or at least quite different from the others. Once she has exhausted the possibilities of the household garden, which has given her twisted branches of every shape and size, she starts to look elsewhere. Donna Clara, her accomplice, is able to secure for her an off-season visit to the botanical gardens. The numb, vegetal architecture of late winter there serves as inspiration for one of her more happy works: the sleeping hawthorn.

She finds inspiration everywhere. One day, a piece of a leaf slips out from the pages of her red morocco leather-bound Bible. It is as fragile as a relic, the colour of tired hay, only barely more than dust. It brings back memories.

Dear Father, how bizarre was your ability to find four-leaved clovers in any corner of wild grass. You used to say that all you needed to do was read the anomaly in a repeated schema of threes, and the four would appear out of nowhere. It was obvious to you. I remember how, when we were out for a walk, you would suddenly kneel down with an air of understanding.

I knew in that moment that you would stand up with a four-leaf clover in your hand, for me.

Remember the time we stayed out all afternoon when I was only a little girl, and you were able to come across an entire bouquet of them? You tied them together with a strand of grass and gave them to Mother as a gift. She looked at you with delight and clapped her hands as if you had offered her a precious stone. Remember? Remember?

She doesn't know if he can remember from where he is now or even if she remembers correctly herself. And yet, it is precisely this random recollection that inspires one of her more successful series. She draws long and wide meadows of clovers in which is hidden one single, isolated, four-leafed clover. Everyone wants one; it is a game: they scrutinize the picture with their naked eye or with a magnifying glass, and have the utmost fun. And that's when it stops being pleasurable for her, and when she begins to understand Tommaso's advice about art that is also fashion – which this has definitely become.

⁂

'I can never thank you enough, Pia.'

'For what, Miss Bianca?'

'For your idea. For . . .'

Bianca points to the objects scattered on the table: leaves, her English pencils, charcoals, sketches, and the branches in their vases.

'For everything.'

'It was just a moment's whim, Miss Bianca. Nothing more.'

'But in order to be inspired one needs to have both a heart and a brain.'

'I don't know about that but I definitely do things better when the heart is involved.'

Pia is clumsy. This awkward speech, which comes out hesitatingly, is not her style. Bianca's eyes mist over.

'I'd like so much to . . .'

But she is unable to complete her sentence because Pia curtseys quickly, turns and leaves the room, avoiding the embarrassment of gratitude. Bianca shakes her head, amazed once again at the young maid's mild manners. *It doesn't matter; there will be all the time in the world for me to repay you*, she thinks to herself. *And you'll see . . . you'll see what a surprise is in store for you.*

※ ※

The market offers its own marvellous displays of cut flowers and bouquets. They arrive twice a week on trucks from the Ligurian coast and are as colourful as they are odourless, as if somewhere along the journey a toll collector has demanded their perfume as tax. It doesn't matter to Bianca, though. She only needs their shapes, lines, positives and negatives. She becomes friendly with one vendor, a small, heavy man with piercing grey eyes whose name is Berto. He saves her his choice cuts of the first blooms from the greenhouse: carnations with ruffled heads, noble and pale calla lilies, and a certain kind of rose that climbs incredibly high and that seems cold despite its warm colour. Bianca has many preferences but only one aversion. She detests gladioli, with their off-tone colours, the primitiveness of their green fleshy stalks, their swollen tongue-like buds, and their flaccid bells. She pushes them away as though just the sight of them is painful. Berto doesn't even try with these any more. Instead, being a polite and astute businessman, he offers her the best of a small private creation:

miniature narcissus flowers with white bells that seem to capture the purity of snow, clusters of tiny white muscari firmly connected to their bulbs, their home and source of food. Bianca takes the trays and keeps them far from the fire and close to the windows so that they can at least taste the cold air through the cracks and live longer. After they have bloomed, she places the wrinkled, potato-like bulbs back into their jute sacks as she has been instructed to do, confident that they will bloom again, although she barely has the patience to wait an entire year.

Her heart, though, belongs to hellebores. Until now she has only known the kind that grow in English gardens, clouded with frost, candid and simple, with a few striations of green and pink. The ones that Berto brings her have double and triple blossoms; they are opulent, of an intense violet and blue, and in stark contrast with the cream-coloured stamens. Sometimes they are fringed with purple, reminding her of the veils of frivolous widows. Often they are green, almost an acid shade, and veined with crimson. There are some that are speckled like wild beasts, dotted with lavender on pale pink.

'They are strong but delicate. Just like you,' Berto tells her after they have been working together for some time. 'They must be planted in the ground. They will die in pots.'

They agree that he will bring her several of these plants when they are ready to return to the country. She is sure the poet will be happy to add them to his list of experiments. Meanwhile she is content to place pots of them on the balcony on the first floor of the great hall. As far as shade is concerned, the garden, though barren, provides enough because it is walled in. Hellebores love darkness and it is winter after all. She waits until their blooms reach their peak and then despondently cuts back the stems, hurrying to wash her hands afterwards because the flowers are full of poison. She places the cuttings in a tall, narrow vase, their heads tilting as if they are looking around perplexed at their new arrangement. And then she begins to draw them. She uses an infinite range of hues for the pinks, violets and crimsons; the minuteness of the pistils, which vary from kind to kind, like small eyes; the webbed veins on the petals, rosy-cheeked children who have played too long out-doors.

The drawings are a great success. All the ladies want to have one of Bianca's hellebores, maybe even two or three, to hang above their nightstands or in their studies, to look at while they write love letters.

'And to think that in nature they seem so very modest, almost invisible,' one of them says when she comes to retrieve her very own portrait of the flower.

'There never was a flower more suited to you, Signorina,' Bernocchi says to the guest. She turns, smiles lightly, and walks away, convinced that this is a coded compliment.

'Do you know, Bianca,' he continues, winking, 'what helle-bore means in the language of flowers? It means scandal.'

Innes frowns and tries to catch Bianca's eye, but she is not in the mood and simply sighs. Bernocchi has become a coat rack, a tea cosy, an embroidered fireguard; he is a household object of communal use, ready to come alive when one least expects it. Fortunately, no one pays any attention to him. Unfortunately, he is always around.

※ ※

If only she could just let go of those thoughts about Pia. If only she could let herself enjoy the present. Every so often doubts like these brush through her. She knows she is doing the right thing by acting on Pia's behalf, though, so she stops question-ing, and focuses on confirming her suspicions. Pia will gain her fair advantage, her rights will be restored, and she will have a future. But what about Bianca? She'll have to be content with the shadows.

Now that she is, in one form or another, a young and successful portraitist, Bianca can interrupt her work temporarily and pursue her hunt. She devises a plan as she is drawing, her hand moving spontaneously across the paper, and it seems perfect in its simplicity. Naturally, if she could confide in someone she would feel more certain, but she has her own certainties to rely on. She doesn't worry that the picture is missing either details or precision. She owes this to Pia, her young benefactress who has inspired the path of black and white. At first she has simply been curious, but now her courage is kindled by gratitude. And anyway, what will it take? She has only to make a visit, knock on a front door, ask some questions. The worst thing that could happen will be that the front door will be locked, or there will be no answer. She needs to prepare.

She chooses to wear a grey dress with silk trimming, which conveniently ages her, and a flimsy hat that ties with a big bow under her chin. She slips on her grey kid gloves and fastens their rows of tiny buttons. She places the precious token she discovered and a couple of coins in her green purse. She leaves the house, careful not to run into anyone so she won't have to lie about where she is going, and hails a coach on the street by the gardens. She reasons that a lady being chauffeured is more credible than a lady on foot, even if the journey isn't very far.

She descends from the carriage in front of Santa Caterina alla Ruota, the driver not hiding his vague disapproval at the choice of destination. From a distance she sees the pass-through wooden drawer in the church's door that Minna has told her about. Her curiosity becomes mixed with a feeling of unease. Up close it doesn't look so strange, though. It is a kind of rough wooden cradle. She has imagined it differently, more like an object of torture. She knocks on the door and waits. Behind the grated peephole an old woman's face appears. She wears a kerchief on her head like a peasant.

'What do you want?' the woman asks.

'I am here because I need some information about a girl,' Bianca replies.

'We can't give out information to just anyone. Are you family?'

'No, but I have her pledge token.' She opens her purse and shows a corner of the small pillow.

The peephole closes and the door opens with a clamour of locks and bolts. The old woman lets her in, closes the door, and walks away without saying a word. Bianca hesitates for a moment and then follows her down a long hallway illuminated by tall, barred windows. Seen from up close, her guide isn't all that old, and her manners reveal a certain genteelness. Her outdated black dress contains a trace of elegance in the tubular sleeves, and her kerchief is neatly folded and tied behind her head, not under her chin like the townsfolk. Walking swiftly, she pauses and turns around for a moment to inspect Bianca, who clutches her own fashionable hat with an intent expression. Bianca hopes that she doesn't seem too frivolous and that she has chosen the right dress for the occasion. Instinctively, she lowers her head and folds her hands together as if she were in church.

They walk together through an area of the cloisters that is sleepy with cold. The woman appears both clumsy and cautious in her movements, like someone with bone problems, but her feet move rapidly and silently. Bianca glances to her side and sees a wall of headstones, the graves of men and women, with phrases engraved into the stone in Latin. Her guide stops in front of a small, low doorway. She ducks into it. Bianca goes to follow, but is stopped halfway.

'You wait here.'

The small door shuts firmly. Bianca looks around. She stamps her feet to keep warm. The chill grows more intense. Maybe the humidity of past centuries held within these thick walls is designed to mercilessly ward off intruders. There are no voices, though, no crying. The door creaks and the woman reappears.

'The Signora will see you now,' she says, holding the door open for Bianca, then closing it behind her after she's passed through.

The room is small with a high ceiling and a remote window – part cell, part study. There, a heavy woman dressed in black sits at a monk's table. Her hair is a shiny white. It neatly frames her severe, though almost youthful face. The contrast between her white hair and smooth skin is surprising.

The woman does not stand. She inspects Bianca and then points to the straight-backed chair in front of her.

'Biagina informed me of your request. Can I ask who you are, why you are here, and what is your intention, if I may be so bold?' She speaks in an authoritative tone. 'And how did you come to be in possession of the pledge token?'

Bianca bears the scrutiny of those serene brown eyes and, as clearly as possible, explains the whole story. Her version of it, at least. She pieces the tale together, relying on gossip, real events and conjecture. Saying it out loud makes it feel even more concrete. If it isn't really the truth, she is close at least. An abandoned child was entrusted to an elderly couple. The wife was the sister of the town priest. The married couple lived with the priest. The little girl brought sunlight into the home of the elderly couple. She was bright and alert. Unlike her peers, who were condemned to forced labour by families who earned from them, this girl was raised with all possible comforts, given her situation. She had pretty clothes, good food, toys and affection. The priest, her uncle, taught her how to read and write. Her adopted parents passed away when the girl was too young to take care of the priest but old enough for it to cause rumour and gossip if she did. So she was sent to work in the household of the local lord, enjoying a privilege or two above the rest of the maids due to her vivacious intelligence and the priest's protection. Bianca mentions that all of this should appear in legal documents.

The old woman takes notes, scratching away at a piece of paper. At the end of Bianca's speech, she puts down her quill and sighs.

'Convincing, indeed,' she comments. 'But this could be the story of tens of hundreds of abandoned girls over the last two centuries. You certainly have not gone out of your way to come here and tell me a fairy tale, though. You must have good reasons. Let's be frank, young lady.' And here it seems to Bianca as though the woman is stressing the words *'young* lady'. 'Are you the mother?'

'Oh, no. No, no, no,' Bianca replies hastily. She hasn't considered the possibility of being so grossly misinterpreted. 'I am . . . too young. I'm just a friend.'

'Whose friend?'

'A friend of the child. Of the girl. Of the daughter, I mean.' Bianca catches her breath. 'And to confirm everything that I have so far said, I have brought this.'

This is her *coup de théâtre*. She puts her hand inside her purse and pulls out the small velvet pillow, which she has wrapped in a white cloth. She uncovers it and places it on the table, between herself and the woman, who takes it, turns it over in her fingers, lightly palpates it, and then smells it. She returns it to the table and looks at Bianca.

'It was found on the border of the property where the girl lives,' Bianca explains. It isn't a lie. It is the truth, only somewhat modified. 'I have reason to believe that a woman left this with you, a woman who every so often makes an appearance there. Someone who deserves, more than any other woman, the right to know the fate of this girl. I believe that this woman is her mother.'

Bianca lets the sentence fade out. They both sit in silence. The older lady picks up her quill and then puts it down again.

'We shall see,' she says. She excuses herself and stands, leaving Bianca alone in the room. She is definitely a lady. One can tell from the shape of her hands, from the way she walks, by the elegant cut of her dress. It is difficult to know what she is doing here, why she is here and not outside, riding through the city in a carriage. Perhaps she is freshly widowed. This, more than her position, would explain the black dress. Perhaps she is one of those generous souls who, unsatisfied with living their own life, take up the causes of others. Donna Clara would know, but Bianca cannot ask her. And nor does Bianca know how she can drop Donna Clara's name into the conversation without putting the whole endeavour at risk.

The woman re-enters the room through a side door, holding in both hands a large green book stuffed with papers and objects.

'It ought to be in here.'

She places the book on the desk, opens it and traces her finger down the pages. Bianca tries to read upside down but in vain: the handwriting is too small, oblique and somewhat faded; a damp stain extends across one page, eating away at many of the sentences.

'Here.'

The woman takes the token again, turning it over in her hand.

'The description matches. "A pink and green pledge with the image of a lamb embroidered in gold and silver thread. A thin linen shirt with the initials cut out. Fine linen swaddling with initials cut out. The baby girl, in good health, one month old, was received and given to the custody of Berenice A. on such and such a date. The child was passed on to the care of family M. in such and such year, with the following belongings, etc., etc."'

She turns the page. This time the *coup de théâtre* is all hers. There is the pledge. It is the twin of the one that Bianca has brought, only less aged. It has the same pink and green embroidery and small embroidered roses. Bianca reaches out a hand but the woman shuts the book quickly. The volume is full of irregular lumps. It surely contains more of those awkward and strange relics.

'And so?' asks Bianca, after a brief moment of silence.

'And so what?' The gaze of the woman is precise and penetrating.

'The two tokens are identical. This proves that my story is true.' Bianca ends her sentence by placing both hands on the table, one next to the other.

'It only proves that there are two identical tokens in existence,' objects the woman. 'The story which you so compassionately shared with me could be true just as it could be false. Try to understand: I have no reason to doubt your good nature. You seem like an honest young lady, prompted by the desire to help and perhaps driven too by a certain, natural curiosity – which in itself is not bad, but could lead to harm. I do not know what secrets people have told you to make you come here today. But in any case, there are rules to this game. The fact that you have the token does not give you any more rights than if you had come here empty-handed.'

The woman glares at Bianca pointedly, as though trying to convey a warning. Bianca decides to ignore the insinuation nestled within the speech – that somebody has sent her. She isn't there to buy the truth, and the idea that it could be for sale hasn't even crossed her mind.

'You cannot tell me anything else?' she says instead. 'My young friend has reached an age where she would like to know more about herself, about where she comes from . . . And I am here of my own free will.'

'Ah, my dear, you will have time to discover that free will is a strange beast.' The woman seems to want to continue but stops, biting her lip, as if she has already ventured too much. 'Your young friend,' she continues, 'has no right to know anything about her past. These are the rules. Weren't you aware of them?'

'Actually, no, I wasn't,' Bianca says, straightening up in anger. Why is there such reticence here, such resistance?

'Legitimate parents or legal guardians have full liberty to reconnect with the children they have entrusted to this precious institution, as is the case with your friend about whom I have already generously shared information. But the children have no right to find out who their parents are, if the parents don't explicitly ask. Just think of the harm it could bring. We need to remember that there must have been a good reason for these parents to separate themselves from their children. Even if,' she says, lowering her voice and adding in a whisper, 'often the reasons are simply not good enough. In any case, whether it was destitution or fear of scandal, whether our children came from high-profile families or from the most wretched ones, for us they are all equal once they arrive here. We cannot allow ourselves to make distinctions. Please understand,' she added. 'I am not required to tell you this but I will: from the swaddling and the token, your girl seems to have been born into a good family, which complicates things. Perhaps the mother bore this child out of wedlock. Or she was married but produced this child with a man who wasn't her legitimate husband.'

The woman ticks off both hypotheses on her fingers.

You forgot one, Bianca thinks to herself. *A young man might have run away.*

'It is risky for us to dig further,' the lady continues. 'We might crack open a hornets' nest. This is all I can share with you, young lady. If you are guided by good intentions, as I believe you are, the best you can do for your girl is assist her in her physical and spiritual growth and make sure that she is good and devout. When the time comes, if you have the authority to do so, help her marry in the most opportune way.'

'But . . .' Bianca's objection lingers in mid-air. The woman has already stood up and motions for Bianca to do the same.

'I will walk you out.'

Bianca picks up the token, places it back inside her bag and follows the lady from the room. They walk back down the hallway, more slowly this time. Bianca wants to find an excuse to ask more, to think of another way to seem more convincing, the way a generous protectress occupied with a legitimate investigation should be. Instead she is shown the door.

'May God be with you and with your protected one,' the lady says in farewell. The woman who guards the door stands up to open it. 'Entrust yourself to the lamb, which rids the world of sin, or at least, in immense clemency, ignores it,' she concludes.

Bianca can do nothing but curtsey and exit, pushed out by that calm, heavy gaze. The door closes firmly behind her.

Outside on the street the jumble of coaches, carriages, and shouting tradesmen is deafening and in stark contrast to the silence of the place she has just left. Bianca feels defeated. But resolutely she straightens herself up and heads back towards the house, as Donna Julie has taught her.

In the city you must always look like you are going somewhere.

She is so lost in her thoughts – replaying the last scenes in her head, the details, seeing again the large water stain on the paper, the piercing gaze of the woman – that she doesn't notice someone blocking her way. She has to stop suddenly to avoid bumping into the figure. Her eyes take in a pair of scuffed shoes, then two legs splattered with mud, followed by a layer of coats, a dirty neck, and a splotch of fresh mud on a boy's cheek. A flimsy, faded cap completes the portrait of a young street urchin.

'Go away,' Bianca says nervously as she attempts to walk around him. But he steps in front of her again and flashes a hint of a smile.

'Miss, do you need help?'

'Of course not,' answers Bianca.

'But yes, you do. Didn't you just come from the orphanage? And didn't you want to know certain things that they didn't tell you?'

Of course, she thinks. The coming and going of people like herself who seek buried information is certainly not new around here. There is bound to be someone who will try to profit from it. The young boy – he must be thirteen or fourteen – continues walking beside her.

'I have a friend who works in there. She can find out what you're looking for.'

'They already told me everything,' Bianca says, slowing down reluctantly. The boy continues in a confident tone.

'Oh, no. There's the public registry and there's the secret registry, which they don't show to outsiders. In the secret one they write other things, like names. The real names. And when someone comes to ask about a child, and who that person was, the when and why . . . well, my friend is good at finding out these things. Trust me,' he says with a wink. 'Only two *scudi*. One for me, one for her.'

Bianca hesitates. How embarrassing it would be to buy secrets. Then, on impulse, she decides that she likes this boy, that two *scudi* isn't that much and anyway, she would have spent them sooner or later.

'Can you read?' she asks.

'No, Miss, I can't, but my friend can. And anyway my memory is good. I keep everything up here,' the boy taps his temple.

The transaction is quickly concluded. She gives her name, they set a date to meet again and she pays half of the compensation. She will pay the other half once the information is retrieved, in precisely two weeks, in the same place, at noon.

What do I have to lose but money? Bianca asks herself, placing the coin on the child's curiously clean palm. If only Pia's happiness could cost so little.

'What is your name?' she asks.

'Girolamo,' he says, taking off his hat. 'Here to serve you, Miss.'

He runs off before Bianca has the chance to question him further. Instead she follows him with her eyes and watches him disappear down a dark alley that swallows him up as if he was made of the same matter. She leaves reluctantly then, feeling the weight of things unfinished.

Her feet move her forward while her mind retraces the encounter. She lingers on a phrase, embroiders a detail, and doesn't notice where she is going. As if waking from a trance, she finds herself seated on a stone bench by a big brick church. She has no idea how she has got there. She regains her senses, feels the cold seeping in under her clothes, and around her the heavy stares of men. No, these aren't men; they are dirty delivery boys bringing rolls of hides to the leather artisans in the area. The air is swampy; she is near the canal, and it gives off a diabolical stench.

I need to get out of here, Bianca thinks. She stands up with resolve, ties her hat ribbons under her chin, jumps over some puddles of dark liquid, and then looks up and around for the golden Madonna statue, a beacon for people navigating the streets of the city.

Miss Bianca, where on earth did you ruin your skirt like that? In the Naviglio? one of the maids will probably ask her later. Carlina, Titina, Annina . . . they lead their lives in the shadows, give themselves up to some dolt, and then become forgettable like all the others. She won't answer their questions if they ask. And she doesn't answer the question that she suddenly hears behind her, making her jump.

'Miss Bianca! You aren't lost, are you? Miss Bianca?'

She is just about to turn around but he is faster and steps in front of her. It is Tommaso. He greets her, taking off his hat and offering her his cheek. How different he is outside; no longer a shy extra, so much surer of himself. Bianca hesitates.

'I understand the cloudy allure of our shadows,' he continues. 'And I understand what drives you here: boredom is stronger than a machine.'

Bianca is silent but then regains control of herself.

'Ah, but I am never bored. Maybe you were bored – is that why you ran away? Or did your muse allow you to leave?'

She finds that this is the right sort of tone for him, the affectionate banter of siblings.

'My muse, my muse,' he replies, guiding her quickly across a wide field beyond which stands a row of luminous Greek-style columns. 'My muse is a tyrant, that's for sure. But my muse is also my only faithful partner. I can't be with her, and I can't be without her. I won't ask what you were doing in that sewer in full daylight,' he adds, meaning the opposite.

Bianca decides to take him at face value and remains silent.

'You are indeed mysterious, Miss Bianca.'

'Me? I'm like a piece of white paper,' she replies teasingly.

'An appropriate comparison. Anything can sprout from it. Perhaps it was already written but in the ink of conspirators, revealing itself only to the astute eye . . .'

'Oh, be quiet. Don't we have enough conspirators around the house already?'

A skilful move: Tommaso's attention is diverted.

'Don't be like Donna Clara, I beg you. She sees shadows everywhere,' he says.

'That's because she is afraid for all of you,' replies Bianca immediately.

'And for herself. She couldn't bear to lose what she has built with such tenacity. Her little citadel of ease and respectability would topple down if her most intimate guests and her very own son insisted on playing politics.'

'And isn't she right to worry? She's a woman: she defends what she has. Her horizon is the house and the garden.'

'Exactly. And she can't see beyond the front door. But the day will come when women will stand by our sides instead of lagging one step behind.'

'Like in a dance?' Bianca tries to joke.

'Certainly. At the great ball of the new world.'

Without realizing it, Tommaso has quickened his pace, and Bianca is forced to almost run to keep up.

'Slow down,' she protests.

'I apologize but these discussions touch me deeply,' he says, amending his gait.

'More than poetry?'

'Much more. We should all have the courage to hang our harps from the willow tree; the heart cannot sing if it isn't free.'

Bianca is silent. She is touched. This Tommaso is completely different from the one she knows. He is so intense and alive.

As they walk silently towards the house, a house that belongs to neither of them but which they have both made their own, united in their search for a calling, she almost forgets what happened earlier.

෯ ෯

'If you suspected something, Innes . . . something good, that could do a person dear to you some good, that could change her life, what would you do?'

'If it was only a suspicion? Nothing, my dear. I would keep it to myself, and I'd try to make it a certainty.' Precisely. Even Innes would do as she has done. So why not confide in him? Could he be her ally, her accomplice? He is so capable and in control. 'But to change someone's life is presumptuous, Bianca. If I were you, I'd take care.' He is also so inflexible. As straight as a cypress tree. A man of only logic. 'I know you, Bianca. You are plotting something. I can see it, and I don't like it.'

They are alone in the living room, waiting to be called to lunch. The long, dull moments in a large household.

'Oh, come now, don't be so serious. I was just wondering.'
She thinks it best to be light-hearted to distract him. She will
only tell him when it is necessary. Only when every bit of evidence is clear. In the meantime she defends herself. 'You are
always plotting, too. You and Don Titta. I see you. Sometimes
I can even hear you. No, don't worry, I can hear but I don't
listen. But I do sense something even from behind closed doors.'

'What you do not know will not harm you, Bianca.'

He is so serious he is almost frightening. And yet he is, too,
a man to whom gravity is becoming, perhaps because he is then
especially handsome when laughing or smiling. Like now: his
whole face is lit up with a smile, distracting her.

'I'm happy to be a source of laughter for you,' Bianca says
condescendingly.

But she is just teasing and he knows it. In fact, he takes her
arm and grips it firmly before letting it go.

'I, too, would like to be entertaining to you but I fear that
I don't have such an amusing personality.'

'If I wanted to be entertained, I'd go to the theatre, where
everything is pretend, even passion. It's real passion that interests me. Your passion,' she says.

He misunderstands, perhaps on purpose.

'Mine? There's little passion here. Horses, maybe, but I
cannot afford my own. Literature, yes, because it costs less. Life,
with all that it sets aside: surprises and trapdoors, twists and
turns.'

'In one word, revolution.' Bianca indulges herself but he
doesn't react.

'I like *you* because you never give up, Bianca.'

Since when does he know her so well? The idea that he
thinks he knows her deeply makes her wonder. Or is it something else, this strange and growing intimacy? Bianca isn't sure,

so she keeps quiet. The pair exchange glances. Bianca feels confused, light-headed and naive. Their exchange has been far from innocent.

⁊⁊ ⁊⁊

'It's not right, Titta. It's not right at all.' It is evident that Donna Clara is in a bad mood as soon as she starts complaining about the wrinkles in the tablecloth. There is only one, Bianca notes, and it is almost imperceptible and for the most part covered by the pewter centrepiece overflowing with tulips. Then Donna Clara complains about the tepid and flavourless consommé. And the soft bread. When the food is not to her liking, there is usually something else she isn't happy about. It doesn't take long before she explains. 'They say that the Austrian gendarmes visited the Viganò family and it wasn't as a simple courtesy.'

'Yes, I heard about it, too,' Don Titta says calmly.

'They say that Count Eugenio had quite a shock. They say,' she continues, lifting up a letter that has been resting on her lap, 'that they might come by here. I am going to put my foot down and say no, Titta. These indulgences have got to stop. They say' – her tone goes up a notch as she waves the letter about – 'that you refused to write an ode for the new general whose name I can't even pronounce. They asked you to write it but you said no, so they asked Monti, and he agreed and got a hefty compensation, as well as praise from the governor. Is this true?'

'Yes, Mother, it's true. How can you doubt your informers?'

'Don't play with me, Titta. You didn't say anything.' In the frenzy of this discussion, her son is reduced to a rebellious child. 'May I remind you that money is necessary to survive? May I also remind you that in order to live there must be peace? And peace must be cultivated.'

'That which you call peace, Mother, I call collusion. Complicity.'

'Ah, I see. I wonder why we never attribute the same meaning to some words. But fine, let's pretend to be a gang of rebels. We'll all end up with our heads chopped off, like the queen.'

'Mother, let's not get ahead of ourselves. Aren't the Austrians notorious for being intelligent governors?'

Donna Clara misses the irony or perhaps chooses to ignore it.

'What do you think – that the era of Theresa is over? They're not standing there just for fun. But anyway, I don't want to have a *political* discussion.' She pronounces the word with a grimace. 'I just want to say that your rekindling of patriotic love might take the bread away from the mouths of your children.'

Donna Clara looks around the room to see the effect of her words on the others. Bianca stares at Tommaso, who in turn stares at the pale turnips on the dinner table. He has no intention of intervening. Innes watches a blackbird hopping on the windowsill. Outside it is drizzling.

'I would rather starve than eat from a foreigner's hand,' Don Titta says calmly. 'My children won't die of hunger: we always have the countryside and its fruits.'

'Right, and what about the creditors lined up outside our door?'

'Can we please stop discussing these things in front of everyone?' Donna Julie interrupts, blushing, a sour note in her voice.

'Everyone?' Donna Clara blurts out, making Bianca feel like a decorative object. 'It's not like we're going to get through this by hiding facts behind good manners. I have nothing left to give you, nothing. I've sold my most precious joys . . .'

Bianca looks at Donna Clara's hands, heavy as ever with diamond rings and other valuable stones. Clearly, she thinks to herself, those are less precious joys.

'No one asked you for a thing, Mother dear,' Don Titta says. 'You've given us a home and your affection, and this is the greatest gift. Don't worry. We will manage. The novel—'

'The novel, the novel! You've been working on it for ten years. Ten! And what about those beautiful poems that brought you bread and fame at the same time? I don't mean the ones for the Austrians – God no, let us not soil our hands if we really want to play at being heroes. But at least the others. The innocent ones. What went wrong?'

'They were useless, Mother. Useless word games for useless people who sit in their living rooms drinking rose-water and concealing their laughter. I'm tired of creating useless things. Just have faith, and you'll see.'

'I do have faith, but in the dear Lord, not in your soiled paper . . .'

'Signora, may I serve you some soufflé?'

In his many years of service, Ruggiero has learned how to clear the air over the dining-room table. And, as suddenly as it arrives, the storm dissipates. Bianca, who would have voluntarily collapsed onto the floor a moment before to create a distraction, now exchanges furtive glances with Innes and sinks her fork into the golden mound on her plate. Donna Julie's face is pale. She has deep, crocus-coloured shadows beneath her eyes. It is another small, pathetic family brawl, no more important just because it is about money and pride. Incriminations are launched without tactic and accusations swell out of proportion. These aren't battles. They are just card games in which everyone is bluffing. At least the soufflé holds up. And, thankfully, lunch ends soon after.

Later, in the living room, Bianca opens the French window to feel the cold air outside. The winter garden appears to have shrunk. Those trees, which will never be part of a forest but which try so hard to grow nonetheless, give her a sense of refuge and relief. City life is complicated. It is onerous to be so intimate with a family that is not one's own, and to be part of the burden. The simplicity of nature would restore her, she thinks, even if she were a prisoner.

She slips into the darkness, breathing in the dank smell of dead leaves and wrapping her shawl tightly around her. The cold clears her mind. Who is right – the women of the house with their small concerns, or the poet? He is brave, yes, but perhaps he is also thoughtless. Is it more important to protect the nest and defend it from turbulence and change or journey untethered towards the unknown? *What manly questions,* she tells herself with a hint of irony. She is proud of having thought of them, even though she doesn't know the answers. She has no connections to tie her down, no big ideas to carry her away. She only has some intelligence, talent and a spark of imagination that is enough to nurture both.

'Noisy as always, no?'

It is Innes.

'You scared me,' she says.

'I don't believe you. You didn't even blink before Donna Clara's wrath.'

'Because they weren't talking to me. But I felt oppressed nonetheless. No, rather, I felt like a bird in a cage being clawed at by a cat.'

'I understand. You will get used to it. As you know, Italians are always a bit theatrical. But it's a tempest in a teapot. He always does what he pleases.'

'You admire him.'

'At times. I care about him, and therefore I forgive him some things.'

Bianca finds it difficult to decipher Innes's facial expression in the darkness.

'And I care about you too, don't get me wrong. But everything passes, even words as heavy as stone. Only art is destined to last. Only that counts.'

※ ※

She receives a package. It is wrapped in damask printed with tiny flowers on a pale background. It is heavy in her palm and tied with a bright green silk ribbon. Bianca sits on her bed and pulls the ribbon impatiently. The fabric falls away and a smooth, round, white rock appears. It is almost too smooth to be natural. She turns it over in her hands and notices a pale vein where the stone is slightly hollow. Only time could have done that. There is a note that says in small capital letters, *NIVEA LAPIS*. White stone. Her name set in stone. Bianca Pietra smiles. She weighs the stone in her hand again and caresses it with the tip of her index finger, testing its dense yet porous consistency. She wonders who sent it, but puts the thought aside. It won't get her anywhere. Oh, to be a stone once in a while, impenetrable, impermeable.

Her father once gave her a coat of arms with the motto *Semper Firma* underneath it. The insignia was of a white stone resting on a horse-chestnut leaf on a blue background. The mysterious gift-giver must know about her father's present. But no, she thinks, that is impossible; no-one knows about this, it happened years ago, and the coat of arms disappeared long ago too. Could it be that someone simply had the same thought as her father? She asks herself if this is a gift or a warning. But it is somehow nice not to know. The stone is not an egg. It can never be cracked open. It will forever hold its mystery and this makes it both dangerous and beautiful.

ॐ ॐ

One night Bianca cannot sleep. Having finished all her books, she leaves her bedroom, intent on choosing one or two new ones from the library, which Bianca is sure will be empty at this hour – the men have gone out. From the staircase where she is standing, the house appears murky grey. A sliver of moon, visible through the skylight, lights her path. But after two or three steps, Bianca realizes she is not alone. Tall twin shadows are standing in the entrance. And although they are dressed in heavy overcoats, she recognizes them and is instantly curious. Should she go back to her room, pretend not to have seen anything? No. She goes down the stairs. She isn't doing anything wrong. The pair look at her briefly, and nod. Innes speaks first.

'Would you like to come with us?'

'Where?'

He puts a finger to his lips.

'Come.'

Don Titta walks back and forth impatiently. His cape dances around him, falling and swishing with his movement. Innes disappears into the closet and comes back with a third cape. He holds it out for her. It feels like a yoke on her shoulders. He responds to her quizzical look with a flash in his eyes that she has never seen before and which makes her even more curious. Her hesitation lasts only a second. She will not say no. Innes hooks the cape under her throat, the way a father would, and takes her by the hand. The intimacy of the gesture makes her flinch.

There is a sound at the door – the signal. They go outside. The cold February night air is as clean as glass. The cobblestones in the piazza are covered with a thin film of ice that shines under the street lamps. She has just enough time to hop into the carriage before it starts on its way. She smells the damp fabric inside and sees small clouds of her breath in the momentary light. Don Titta looks out at the shadowy city. It is deserted. Innes, seated next to her, tries to speak to her with his eyes. But what is he trying to say?

Bianca feels agitation building up inside her. Something she hasn't felt before. She isn't dressed appropriately; her cape isn't heavy enough; she is wearing the wrong shoes, no gloves, no vest. It is winter after all. Where are they going, on a winter's night, all dressed in black, two men and a woman, and no chaperone? She imagines them talking about her later: *No, Miss Bianca stayed home tonight. Actually, she followed them for a bit until they pushed her out of the carriage and then they left her on the pavement. She was not needed. No one wanted her there. Adieu, go home, go back to bed with your books; can't you see we're busy living?* The other Bianca, the one who *is* invited to come along on the adventure, sits up straight.

He is sitting so close to her. To touch him, all she needs to do is reach out her arm. What an idea! Why should she touch him? Why indeed. Innes's warmth emanates from under his clothing. Bianca no longer feels cold, maybe she has a fever. It has to be a fever, this kind of fire inside her, a little below her heart.

The carriage slows down and then comes to a full stop. They have arrived. Don Titta steps out without offering to help her. Innes does, though. But he doesn't lower the stairs. He just picks her up by the waist and lifts her down. She smells tobacco and spices, and then the frigid cold takes her breath away. The street is empty. Via a small stone bridge, they pass over the canal. There, two churches stand side by side like old friends.

The silence is interrupted by the sound of footsteps. Another caped figure arrives, this one with messy curls and the flash of a familiar smile. It is Tommaso.

'So you've come, too,' Innes says, with some disapproval.

'How could I miss out on this madness?' His grin, growing wider, turns into a smirk. 'What about her?'

Her? Me? What am I, a parcel, an object? Bianca thinks, taking a step forward to stand her ground.

'Why not?' Innes says. 'Come on, there's no time to waste.'

The driver has already lowered a trunk, placed it on the ground and opened it up.

'The light?'

'Here it is.'

Sparks fly, the fuse catches, and light is cast on Ruggiero's round face. Bianca sees now that he bites his lip and looks around furtively. What sort of game is this?

The cold has all but disappeared. Innes and Don Titta take turns fishing out fragile wooden and canvas objects from the trunk. Lanterns. They light them, stuff them with small scrolls of paper and toss them up in the air, giving an extra push to the more fickle ones, which fall back down. Once she gets a clear picture of what is going on, Bianca helps, passing the lanterns – which are fragile in her hands – to the person who is ready to light them. Over and over. Several drift down towards the water and go out with a brief sizzle. But a small horde swarms into the sky above, their light reflecting off the black waters. A few catch fire – a brief flame and then nothing. Many endure and take flight.

There are more pieces of paper than lanterns, so once she has finished assisting, Bianca takes one out and unravels it.

'People of Milan, friends, and strangers: now, when we have most to fear, is the time for us to be courageous . . .'

Tommaso reads out loud over her shoulder, almost too close to her, painfully present.

'Well put, Titta. Now it's my turn. I have my own system and it might be more efficient than yours.'

Innes shakes his head while Tommaso takes a handful of papers, goes down to the canal, pulls out a few small boats made of waxed canvas from his sack, and launches them into the water.

'I should have used bottles, like the castaways that we are.'

Don Titta, who has been silently contemplating his flying messages, leans out over the bridge and mutters some words, indistinctly at first, as if weighing them, then more loudly.

> *Giochi dolceamaro, bimbo mio:*
> *affidi le tue barche alla corrente*
> *ignaro e sorridente*
> *pago del loro navigar di stella*
> *nel piccolo mare dei tuoi occhi . . .*

> *Bittersweet games, my child:*
> *Entrust your boats to the current unknowing*
> *And smiling, repaid for their*
> *Journey under the stars*
> *In the small sea of your eyes . . .*

'Titta, Titta, our private wandering minstrel,' Tommaso teases from below. 'You have a rhyme for every occasion. As usual, I'm envious.'

The cold is even more acute now, the flickering lights growing distant in the night sky and on the water; the trunk is empty, the wick has died out, and Ruggiero is back at his place in the driver's seat of the carriage.

'Are you going home?' Innes asks Tommaso in an effort to be polite.

'You know I have no place to live. There's a party at the Crivellis'. I might stop by. He has invited some French girls.' He smacks his lips.

Innes frowns.

'Don Titta's right. Everything is just a big game for you.'

'And what's wrong with that, my friend? It is night-time; we have engaged in a most civil and noble folly – a nice, reckless gesture that will not amount to anything. I tell you, we could just as well have risked more.'

He bows mockingly to Bianca and blows her a kiss. Then he turns around, raises his arm in a goodbye, and walks back along the shoreline to join his friends.

Don Titta doesn't say a word. He still contemplates the vanishing lights.

'He's right. Our message will only end up educating the washerwomen. We weren't daring enough, Innes. It's the heart of this city that needs to be reawakened. The higher the risk, the greater the reward.'

'This is only the start, Titta. Our first time. We are mere beginners, schoolchildren. We will learn to do better. There's the lake, the sea, and as much sky as we'd like. Now let's head back.'

Bianca is startled for a moment when Innes says 'lake'. A fleet of wooden ships on her lake? Please, no rebellion, only poetry. Now the tutor turns to face her, making her visible again, real.

'Come on, it's late for you.'

He takes her gently by the elbow and leads her towards the carriage. She trips, her legs frozen with cold. He swiftly picks her up, as though they are dancing, and places her inside the carriage. He then clambers in himself, followed by Don Titta. Ruggiero flicks the reins and the horses set out for home.

❧ ❧

Everything looks much smaller from the carriage on the return trip. Don Titta slumps back against the seat, his long legs in their tight-fitting trousers stretched out before him, his hand resting palm up on top of his knee, as if asking for something. She dreams of putting her hand in his, a kind of silent gift. Surprise, an awkward press of skin against skin, a reverse handshake. Innes, seated close to his friend, cannot take his eyes off her. Three is plainly one too many.

They arrive home and shuffle up the stairs, each to his own room. No 'goodnights' are exchanged; the night will not be a good one, it will only bring wide-eyed reflection.

The next morning, her shoes look like papier mâché. The soles have peeled off and the upper part is damp and hard. She ends up hiding them at the bottom of the cloakroom, so that no one will find them, not even the maids, who always have something to say. But Alcina finds them anyway and dangles them in front of the others in the kitchen.

'If Miss Bianca wants to go out and run free at night, she should at least wear her overshoes or a nice pair of boots. Am I right?'

'Yes, you are. But you know that young ladies have their heart in their feet. They're head over heels, I tell you!'

'As long as someone doesn't come knocking . . . and knock her up!' Raucous laughter ensues. Bianca walks in, snatches the shoes from Alcina and walks away. Fortunately, because of their strange dialect, she hasn't understood a thing.

❧ ❧

The long, harsh winter seems never to end. Perhaps it is the ailments that afflict the children, but a grey patina shrouds the windows of the house on Via Morone. No one goes out, for fear of infection. And they don't receive any guests for the same reason. It is the horrible boredom of February. Everywhere it is the same. What is the point of going to visit friends only to hear them talk about mucus and phlegm?

It has even happened in the famous salon of Signora Trivulzio. What an odd place that is, Bianca thinks. It is as if the salon exists in a bubble: its four rooms of yellow damask, those candles laid out on great big trays of silver instead of in the usual candelabras, the waiters in yellow, blending in with the tapestry. Bianca imagines it as if it were a theatre set – a house without kitchens, bedrooms or closets. She thinks of a stage, and behind the curtain, the props: Signora Trivulzio's costumes hanging on a rack, her shoes lined up on a strip of carpet, and an elegant toilette replete with little bottles ready for her *maquillage*.

Bianca wishes she could share these thoughts with someone. Innes has gone to Magenta to discuss some new academic theories with Pellico, his oft-mentioned but never-seen colleague. Maybe, like Signora Trivulzio's house, Pellico doesn't really exist either.

Don Titta has authorized Innes's leave and actually encourages him to go; he plans on joining them and his own friend, the host, Count Porro Lambertenghi. Bianca tries to imagine the four of them together, the ranks mixed in the way these liberal patricians enjoy and Donna Clara does not. But in her present situation, the older lady cannot oppose resistance.

Donna Clara is tired and grey, like everything around her. For the first time she looks weak. She is curiously compliant and more considerate with others, a behaviour that only a short while ago she abhorred. With her son gone and her daughter-in-law banished to her own quarters due to a bout of her secret illness that everyone knows about and nobody speaks of, she does nothing. Bianca is reluctantly made witness to the sad display of this weak and vulnerable Donna Clara.

'Things change, the world changes. And when you don't like it any more, they say you simply no longer understand it. That you're ageing. I don't understand all these polemics based on good government and the rest of it. Who are we to say that one man is good and another is not? Kings, believe me, are all the same. And the people without a king is like a chicken with its head cut off.'

'But you aren't the people. *We* are the people,' Bianca ventures.

They are sitting in the boudoir next to Donna Clara's bedroom, a small room, usually well lit but gloomy now, like the rest of the house. They are having coffee, a speciality blend purchased from 'the Turk', who isn't really Turkish, but who has a shop at the end of Corsia dei Servi. Neither the aroma nor the heat of the beverage, sweetened with pillows of whipped cream, is able to lift the old woman's spirits.

'No, we aren't the people. We are women. We float somewhere between here and there, tied down by ropes, like great balloons.'

Bianca holds back a smile as she imagines a fleet of women floating ten feet above ground, tied down by the ankles, bobbing lightly in the breeze.

'It's as if they've created a limbo just for us,' Donna Clara continues. 'When we are useful – for love, children, looking after the house – they pull us down. Otherwise they just leave us there, in the air, so we don't cause too much disturbance, with the excuse that we are light and can't possibly understand.

Thirty years ago it was the same thing. Nothing has changed. Heads still roll, blood is spilled, everything seems as though it's about to change, but then we are right back where we started. A woman's only power is her beauty, and then it fades. If I had a choice, I'd be the girl who could still fit into that corset over there.' She motions towards a half-dressed mannequin covered in a delicate architecture of sticks, lace and silk. 'I used to laugh, drink champagne and chat with the most refined intellectuals in the world, in Paris. Look at me now; look at what I've turned into. I can't even glance at myself in the mirror for fear of seeing the other me. I've turned into a peasant woman, sanctimoniously sent to the country for eight months of the year and the rest of the time a prisoner of this city, surrounded by the blood and urine of children.'

Bianca shudders, as she always does when Donna Clara shifts from formal to personal with her. She never knows whether to consider it a concession of intimacy or a gesture of slight disdain. The old woman keeps talking. Bianca realizes it makes no difference how she responds.

'She won't last, that one,' Donna Clara continues in dialect.

'What, beauty?' Bianca asks, trying to understand.

'No, no,' Donna Clara replies. 'My daughter-in-law, she's too delicate for this world. She's like this piece of china.'

She holds up a cup. It is almost transparent in its delicacy. With the flames from the fireplace flickering behind it, it really does look like a shell. She puts it down.

'When she dies, what will we do?'

Bianca feels obliged to alleviate such pessimism.

'What are you talking about? It's just the winter. It's been hard on us all. When the nice weather comes, signora will regain her strength, you'll see.'

Bianca doesn't really believe her own words. Why is the

poet away with other men discussing things that are only important to him instead of being here, alongside the woman he has married, who is suffering? How can he not know that any day could be her last? Is he a monster? Has he simply given up? Or does he know something that no one else does? Bianca has seen Donna Julie run to her room, racked with coughing. The children have thrown all sorts of tantrums to hide their fear. Anxiety is everywhere: in the eyes of the help, in the presence of the doctor's coach in the courtyard, and in the red-splotched handkerchiefs that the washerwoman sluice again and again, trying to restore them to their original whiteness. Too many children, too much life.

In spite of this, Donna Julie always appears so serene, wrapped in a peacefulness that softens the effects of grief and transforms them into a sweet, deaf, anticipatory nostalgia. It is as if she has already gone far away and will return only for brief visits. The world is too much for her. Her absence is felt more than that of her husband; the children ask about her unrelentingly and are allowed only brief visits, one at a time. They sit in line outside her door. Bianca sees them waiting patiently and silently, their feet dangling from the sofa, their eyes fixed on the door handle, eager to see it open. If the old woman is right, there won't be much time before they will be left only with the bitter tears of loss.

🐟 🐟

Two weeks pass. Bianca finishes a new series of drawings, divides them into their separate folders, and gives orders for them to be picked up. She feels liberated. Instead of putting on her smock after her morning tea, she pulls on her gloves, hat and redingote.

'I'm going out,' she announces to no one in particular, and

runs downstairs with the frenzy of a child who has been freed from her tutor.

'She's as mad as a horse, but I suppose that's why we like her,' Donna Clara says before devouring her *oeuf au vin*, which she has requested for additional sustenance at breakfast. She, too, is trying to combat the recent weakness she has been feeling. She has said it must be due to the change in the weather.

Donna Julie's health has, in the meantime, improved. A miraculous recovery brings her back to the centre of her world – her home and children. The unsettled climate of the past few days is suddenly replaced by mannerist optimism.

Bianca doesn't hear Donna Clara's comment as she leaves and it wouldn't have mattered to her anyway. She is already in the courtyard, admiring the intense blue rectangle of sky above their house. She smiles at Rossetti, the doorman, and gives him her final instructions: the folders should not get bent and the servant who picks them up should treat them with great care.

Via Morone is as bleak and grey as always but that turquoise strip of sky hangs like a path that needs to be followed. She heads towards the open spaces of the Corsia del Giardino, with its coming and going of carriages. On her left she sees La Scala poking out into the piazza like the great chair of a giant. Bianca crosses the street and heads towards the arches where it is said that a maiden with an unforgiving name died of a forbidden love. She passes under them as if they are the entrance to a new world, and walks on through the gardens of Acqualunga, watching the ducks and thinking of her own lake at her father's house. She isn't concerned with botany today so doesn't even notice the young fan-like leaves of the ginkgo tree, which blow in the wind like small flags. She has a destination.

She walks around the pond, passing well-behaved children and their governesses who are busily launching wooden boats that have waited all winter to come out. Girls jump skipping ropes and play with hoops. Two men on horseback look over the scene benevolently. A young lady in light blue stands in an arc of sunlight. It is a perfect *tableau vivant* for this first day of sunshine. It is not yet spring but it feels like it.

Bianca suddenly notices that an old woman in rags has approached the young lady in blue. She speaks to her, gestures, and holds out her hand. The lady in blue takes a step back, freezes, then turns around, fumbling for something in her bag and handing it to the woman. Then she leaves in a hurry. The tableau is ruined, but the occurrence is interesting. What had the old woman wanted? And why was she so insistent? Maybe she had a secret to sell, a secret like the one Bianca is about to buy herself.

The sunlight disappears into a cloud of haze, as if it has been siphoned out of the picture. It is now only a sour, cold March morning. The chill makes Bianca quicken her step. As she walks she looks at her reflection in the windows and likes what she sees. A young, independent woman taking great strides in the world, on her own. It had been easy. No, that wasn't true. But it hadn't been all that hard either. Mainly, it just happened. Could it have taken place any other way? Was there another way to be content and at ease in the world? Bianca sighs and then smiles to answer her own question. A gentleman, passing her, tips his hat, as if to return her greeting. Bianca smiles again at the misunderstanding, and then turns back. The gentleman slows and turns, too, flashing her a grin. Bianca hastens her step. He was a stranger – how embarrassing! Part of her, though, almost wishes that he *would* follow her. After a while she turns back again, but he is now far away.

Now there is nothing to smile about. The city grows darker and uglier with every step. The boulevards narrow into alleyways and houses lean against each other carelessly as if drunk. A beastly stench comes from a dark rivulet that passes through the middle of the street. *What am I doing here?* She reminds herself: *I'm seeking the solution to a mystery.* This neighbourhood is like an entirely different city; gone is the airy vastness of the great tree-lined boulevards; there are no piazzas with ornate churches here. Are secrets always so crooked? Perhaps it is their nature, she tells herself, trying to ignore a woman in rags squatting on the steps in a doorway, surrounded by barefoot, naked children playing in the mud. A rusty sign for an inn squeaks in the breeze, the only music around.

She isn't scared. She has no fear. Dozens of heroines before her have ventured to even darker depths, with only their courage and sincerity to shield them. Many have revealed lies in order to see the true and just triumph. She is not frightened, but she is cold. The returning sun shines crookedly down these alleys, and only meagrely at this time of day. Foul, fetid smells emanate from the cracks in the walls. Cellar windows leak frigid bursts of air that snake around her ankles. She wouldn't be surprised to see claws emerging from a grate. She walks faster; the alleyway is long and she has to travel its full length. Finally, the houses separate, the sky becomes visible again in all its vastness, and a young boy stands waiting, leaning against a fountain, his arms crossed, clogs mired in dirt. He has a smirk on his face – no, it is more of a smile.

☙ ❧

Afterwards, Bianca looks around and notices the hackberry trees. Their roots are so strong that they crack open rocks. Their Italian name, *bagolari*, is too plain for a tree that is so true, so beautiful, vertical, sensitive and strong. They have the arms of day labourers with veins and muscles, and a delicate grey bark filled with sap. The air is filled with pollen that makes her eyes red and itchy, and it is hard to breathe. Springtime cannot be rubbed away; it is an assertive and capricious child that likes to step on people's feet. The skies have never been this way – and yet memory tells her that they always were. Springtime always brings first times. She suddenly senses the countryside beneath the paved roads. She feels the streets ready to be freed of their winter coats. Daisies poke out of cracks between the cobble-stones. Life is coming back, blessed and expected. Men's eyes are flirtatious, insolent and possessive. She needs to laugh – laughter is good, and it makes her feel safe. The air is like a cool wine that burns and freezes simultaneously. You could drink it from your skin, from your hair, from everything.

The expedition has been a success and the day is splendid. Bianca returns on foot, the road made shorter with so much to think about. She has her drawings, her projects, and what's more, this magnificent season that pulsates inside and out. Now that she knows, everything is possible.

☙ ❧

'Come, my little one. Let me look at you. May I hug you?'

'May I call you Mother?'

Bianca imagines that beautiful word falling silently from Pia's lips, erasing all hesitation and boundaries, confusing everything into an embrace. It will be so simple, and each of them will reclaim their rightful place in the order of things. Pia will step forward uncertainly, her head bare, her hair as shiny as chestnuts. It will be wonderful to see her self-assuredly show herself the way she truly is, tender and pure. Pale, almost translucent. She will be reduced – or rather elevated – to the essence of herself in this most precious of moments. And the woman – the mother, who will now have the right to call herself this – will be made youthful again through her repressed joy. Shadows under her eyes still speak of countless nights of torment but the light that will radiate forth will smooth out all wrinkles. Her lips will utter that serious and perfect word 'daughter'. Hands will seek hands, hands will reach for arms, the pair will embrace, and this hug will dissolve all doubt.

At that point in time, in her imagination, Bianca will leave them. It is hard for her to see more than this. She is certain it will happen. Perhaps it won't happen in that exact way, but it will happen.

It will be so lovely to see them together.

🙞 🙜

She has to make it happen. But how? Who could act as her accomplice, if not Innes? The moment has come for her to speak to him without reticence or deception. It is simple, really. She practises her speech in her head:

I understand everything now. It's all clear. You knew all along, didn't you? You could have told me. But no, of course not, I understand. Loyalty, your sense of honour, duty, et cetera. Save yourself the sermon. Now that I know, and now that you know that I know, I need your help. We must do something. That poor girl has the right . . . what right, you say? You, of all people? Of course, in front of the poet you bow down to all noble principles. Or is there something else I should know? You need time?

I solved the puzzle myself. What, it's not a puzzle? Well, you are correct. There is no mystery. It's the same old story. No, I can't, I won't ignore the situation. It is for her own good, you understand? Don't you want to give her even the smallest glimmer of hope? She's been nailed to a fate that she didn't ask or wish for. She could have so many possibilities in life; she needs so little, and could reclaim everything. What's that? Like me? You flatter me, really, you do.

But I am a poor role model. Trust me. I have had everything all along, and I did nothing to deserve that which she has been denied. Talent, you say? You really believe that my talent makes a difference? It doesn't count a whit more than fortune, or fate, or whatever you call it. And how do you know that she doesn't possess unspoken talents? She is still only a child . . .

Bianca's imagined Innes is complacent in his silence, the best confidant for the situation. If only she had the courage. But she is scared. She doesn't know how to give herself courage. She is also frightened that he might stop her for any number of excellent reasons. So she contradicts him in her head. But it is only a matter of time and patience. A fourteen-year-old secret can wait another couple of weeks. So she waits, convinced that eventually she will be able to move the chess pieces across the table. She doesn't understand that the game is not hers to play, and that she has no power really, not even over the poorest pawn.

꩜ ꩜

Bianca's drawing needs full outlines before she can fill in the shadows, and several details are still missing. She needs to imagine the poet before he became a poet, back when he was just a reckless boy, a city boy with a long name and an empty brain, before the muses kidnapped him, before the desire for domestic piety pushed him to seek his perfect bride. She needs to find out more by teasing it out of Donna Clara.

Bianca is like a cat with a ball of yarn. She almost feels bad about having to trick Donna Clara, but she has to find out.

It is a pity that the poet's mother is so cautious. She ignores the inappropriate parts of the story and sheds light only on her preferred ones, the parts that illustrate her in all the glory of filial love. The rest of it might not have even occurred. Don

Titta was born when he decided it was the right time, which is to say when he was twenty years old. But Bianca keeps her ears open for clues as the story progresses.

'I remember it well. He arrived in Paris on the tenth of April. Before that, you know, the season wasn't right and the road not safe, so he waited for the first safe journey. He waited because he knew I would be worried about him crossing the Alps, up there in the snow among the wolves and avalanches.' Bianca smiles sympathetically as Donna Clara takes advantage of the occasion to bask in her memories. 'They got along from the very start, my Carlo and my Titta. Father and son in spirit, I used to say. Ah, I recall those first strolls in Parc Monceau, our garden of delights . . . We needed to get to know each other again, he and I. We recognized ourselves in each other, you know? Between mother and child there can be no other way.' Bianca nods but has stopped listening. She subtly counts on her fingers. Pia was born in the December of the same year the poet arrived in Paris. Therefore, it is plausible and possible. All she needs is proof, some kind of confirmation.

Donna Clara cannot stop talking. 'It was the most beautiful time. Today everyone is fixated on their children. But I sent my boy to a boarding school with the priests because that was the right thing to do and his father wanted it. And then, when things unravelled as they did, and his father left us for the Lord, I went to Paris with my Carlo, and the boy stayed here in order to finish school. The good Lord wanted us to be reunited, but as adults, as equals. I don't know if children really need their mothers when they are young. They don't know a thing; they barely even know they are alive, and, as I see it, the more a mother worries, the more a child is spoiled. And then we forget . . .'

It is almost as if she is trying to justify herself. By comparing her own behaviour with that of her daughter-in-law, she wants to come to some absolute conclusion, prove she hasn't made a mistake, that she has done the right thing. It is true that the times have changed. But it is also a fact that conventions make life comfortable and easy. They help us to avoid confronting complicated and risky sentiments.

Bianca thinks of her friend Fanny, who lost her heart to Zeno, only to be informed by her family that she would instead be married to Cavalier Gazzoli, a man twenty years older who owned an immense property near the rice fields of La Bassa and whom she had never met. She cried for two weeks. She cried even harder when she met her husband-to-be: pudgy, wearing a wig, his nose a network of veins. Then she visited his home, Villa Salamandra, and came back amazed by the number of rooms. 'You could play hide-and-seek there,' she said. 'And the vast gardens!' Her tears dried up. Everything became quite lovely, mosquitos included. Which was all well and good as Zeno, with his good looks, never even looked at Fanny.

'I was everything for my Carlo,' the older lady continues. 'I was his confidante, a sister, a mother, a true-life companion. And I knew I was lucky that I had found my soulmate. Then when Titta came back to me, I had the both of them.'

As Donna Clara lists the glories and joys of her life, it occurs to Bianca that she truly has been fortunate. She's had everything, and what she didn't have, she acquired. First a solid husband. Then a rich, intellectual lover. Then, once her youth faded, she had her son, a fashionable poet whose fame reflected back onto her. Bianca doesn't need to exert herself to piece together the joyful past of the proprietress. Everyone knows that Carlo, whom she followed to Paris when her husband was still warm in his coffin, was her lover long before her marriage. Everyone also knows that Titta and Carlo (who could well have been his father although this was never officially stated) never got along. It is known too, that when Carlo died, Donna Clara was somewhat relieved. She was tired of being a mediator between the two men, ready to bring her French romance to a conclusion, eager to continue her life of comfort with her lover's money in his countryside villa that she'd inherited, and happy to indulge Titta's desire to leave Paris. And yet she insists that she would have gladly stayed on in the city and become the next queen of a new salon; that she'd go back tomorrow if she could.

Donna Clara is astute and accustomed to worldly things; she knows that her story has unfolded in the most elegant way, far more than the predictable, banal debaucheries of Parisian life could ever have permitted. As her beauty fades, familial piety becomes more important. In other words, it is all for the best. It is a shame, though, that she can only talk about Carlo when Titta is not around. All traces of that other man and his rural domain – his drawings, writings, collections – are in the attic of the country house, inside a long row of chests covered by old rugs that a maid has once shown to Bianca.

At this point, having obtained the information she wants and from a primary source no less, she takes her leave with the excuse of having a drawing to finish, while the old woman continues to recite her litany to herself.

The drawing isn't an excuse, actually. Outside the viburnums have flowered and Bianca wants to draw their white flowers before they fade. Viburnum: the word rolls off her tongue like a plump berry. She picks up a pencil and asks herself which is more beautiful, the word or the flower. Perhaps poetry *is* a superior art, she thinks. It summons things with a sound and on paper with a symbol, while her art is mute and rallies only one of the senses, never producing echoes. She wishes she could share her complex thoughts with someone to see if they are absurd or actually make sense. She might surprise them.

Should she have run away from Donna Clara? There is nobody else in the house to keep the lady company. No, she is better off being quiet and drawing, she thinks. It's what she knows how to do best.

Be quiet and draw, be quiet and take a walk, but most importantly, be quiet. The house is a cocoon of enforced peace. The three men disappear once again, this time to discover more about silkworms, it seems. When Bianca raises an eyebrow at Innes, he shrugs without even trying to answer her silent question. Traitor.

Donna Julie gets her much-needed rest. She is always resting these days, with Donna Clara watching over her, dealing with a silence that must be unbearable for her. The children have been instructed to behave. Pia is absorbed and pensive; she minds her own business, as if she feels something stirring in the air, the distant arrival of a storm. Bianca leaves her alone.

Sometimes Bianca gets the feeling that her own voice no longer works, she uses it so seldom. It is fine only for 'good morning,' 'goodnight' and 'a little more soup, thank you, but no dessert'. Bianca's interior monologues remind her of the watery spirals of bindweed, which she tries to draw. By evening, though, she can no longer stand the peace and runs out to the garden.

Thanks to the insistent rains and mild weather, the city garden has reached its most luxuriant state and has become a neglected realm of delight. She enjoys this weather. She likes to watch the earthworms, how they contort their bodies to smell the air with their nose, only to return underground, ready to eat up the world. And then there is the moving loyalty of the bulbs. They are the ever-faithful dogs of the flower world, ready to bloom in the same place, year after year. But in that small swatch of green between the high walls of the buildings, their generous little hands close too quickly. No one takes the time to look at them, and then suddenly, they are gone.

What a waste, Bianca thinks as she caresses the tips of the palmetto leaves and the corners of the banana plant, burning with green. *What a waste*, she thinks again, the thought itself like a sharp splinter of glass that one picks up so that someone else does not step on it and bleed. *When does spring end? Is summer really more beautiful, when everything has happened, when everything has already been decided, when imagination is useless?* For the first time, Bianca has the feeling that what was will not always be; that any kind of flowering is merely a delicate deceit. There is no grand design. There is no room for the unexpected. It is all anticipated, predictable, and therefore as if it has already happened. *Where will I be when this tree is laden with fruits? What will I be like? Will something have changed, or will I still be here, leafing through pages?* Bianca delights in these thoughts. She lets herself be transported by a melancholy that makes her feel both serious and adult. She doesn't realize, however, that she had spoken out loud.

'I've never heard someone summon forth autumn with such grace.'

The man's voice catches her by surprise and makes her jump.

'Is that you?' she asks the shadow with some discomfort, although she is unsure why.

'I've returned alone. Silkworms aren't for me. They require too much patience. I was scared when I saw the house so dark and silent. The servants are too quiet. It's as if they have a secret. Is something happening that I don't know about?'

'Only the same old dramas.'

Bianca tries to sound light-hearted, but the phrase comes across as brazen, or perhaps just overly sincere. In any case, it is true. What is more normal than Donna Julie's perpetual discomfort? Tommaso completes her thought.

'If it had been severe, we would have received word and, in any case, I am certain that tomorrow morning at breakfast I will be given an abundance of details. I can wait. But you, so alone in this damp garden . . . you'll catch cold. Or are you demanding your share of attention?'

Bianca is stupefied. What did she say or do, now or even prior to that, for him to know her so well? Has he guessed? Or is this just another innocent skirmish? Tommaso often says things only for the sake of saying them. He conquers boredom through provocation. How long has he been spying on her, listening to her strange rant? She isn't quick enough to answer so he presses on.

'Don't be afraid. If you are so eager to taste the fruit, inevitably it will be attracted to you.'

There is so much intimacy in that sentence. It is the sort of intimacy that is not permitted but is often stolen without consideration. Bianca wraps herself up tightly in her shawl, trying to avoid those burning eyes, which, even in darkness, see her clearly.

'Come on, Miss Bianca,' he jokes. 'It's almost dark and we're alone. It's not right for a well-mannered lady like you. But what do we care about conventions? And do you really want to be afraid of me? Look at me: I am only a half-poet bound to a great oak tree that ignores me, an insignificant lichen stuck to the bark on which it feeds. And you, on the other hand, are so intrepid, free, a working woman . . .'

Bianca collects her thoughts and pride. She doesn't like the carelessness in Tommaso's concealed, offhand manner. She finds it offensive.

'You know nothing about me.'

'You're right. And that seems only fair after all the effort you have put into hiding your cards. From me, at least. Anyway, we know nothing of anyone, especially when one has the arrogance to believe he knows everything. Perhaps you are mistaken about me, too though.'

'How could I be, when you define yourself with such precision? I abide by your own self-portrait. And anyway, I'm not judging you. I don't have the impulse or the desire to do so.'

Tommaso is silent. He sighs.

'I've erred again. Miss Bianca, you have the power to confuse me. Please use it sparingly; be generous and kind. My poor heart cannot bear such torment.'

'Now you're teasing me.'

'Me? Never. I, I . . .'

'It's getting chilly. Goodnight.'

And with that, Bianca leaves the garden, passing through the open French window without waiting for a reply. Well played, she thinks. She has left him speechless. But she is left exasperated and tired and moreover she doesn't quite know what their exchange has signified.

She feels too the burning sensation of wasted opportunity. They have been in the garden. It is night. She could have spoken out.

I don't like him, I don't like him, she repeats to herself as she climbs the stairs. She goes into her bedroom, but her half-closed window summons her. She cannot help but lean out on such a beautiful night and ask the darkness for confirmation. Tommaso is still down there. She sees the embers of his lit cigar. It looks as though he is coughing. *No, he's laughing. Or crying.* Is he crying? Bianca has the feeling that he knows she is watching him, so she stands up but lingers at the curtain still. Is he crying?

⚜ ⚜

Bianca isn't stupid. She is rash, impulsive, equipped with a ferocious imagination, tumultuous and passionate. She is also timid, contemptuous and arrogant in convenient doses. But she is anything but stupid.

So why, now that everything is clear with Pia, is she still protecting Don Titta? He is guilty and will soon be charged with a crime that is terrible in its very banality.

Maybe he doesn't know about it, she thinks. Or more likely, maybe he didn't know at the time. Maybe he found out later and is still coming to terms with it. She thinks back to his bewilderment that afternoon in the nursery, when, perhaps for the first time, the truth had become apparent to him. Why should he have known? He has been away from Milan for so long. It is one of those things and life moves on. Maybe the woman has kept quiet; her family, if they even knew, remain silent and act as if nothing has happened, as one does in this world of scandals. Only others know.

As sly as a detective, she realizes she needs a perfect stranger with a clear-headed gaze to help her put events in the right perspective. How happy the poet will be when he realizes the precious role that Bianca has played in unveiling the mystery. A spirit as righteous as his will surely be content to fix his mistakes. How grateful he will be to her for having finally created an opportunity for sincerity. Bianca likes to imagine it this way. She does not understand that certain truths are not meant to be paraded around like banners, but need to remain carefully folded up in the bottom of trunks. This ignorance of hers is forgivable. It stems from her youth, naivety, and tendency to see and draw the world only in black in white.

✥ ✥

But things do not happen quite the way she had planned.

'Titta, Titta . . .'

Donna Clara mumbles her son's name and looks around the crowded room for him. Donna Julie stands next to Bianca and smiles with great effort. Her eyes are glassy and she wears two splotches of artificial pink on her cheekbones as a kind of mask. It takes her a long time to become aware of Bianca's presence, and when she does, she turns to look at her as if to explain.

'This is one of the most luxurious salons in Milan, you know. Things happen here.'

Bianca follows the gaze of her companion until it rests on Don Titta, surrounded by a cluster of people. He is facing away from them. Bernocchi hangs off him as if he is a beggar. Even from far away, she can tell that the count is speaking quickly and animatedly. Then she sees him go silent and stare at Titta, as though listening to his reply. Bernocchi takes his hands off the poet's arm and makes to walk away, but Titta detains him by placing a hand on his shoulder. Their positions change: they face one another directly. The discussion continues. Don Titta glances away and then back at Bernocchi without stopping the conversation. He looks away again, but this time slowly and deliberately. Bianca follows the direction of his gaze: it is focused on the entrance. The lady of the house is welcoming someone now, her shoulders largely concealing the guest. Bianca catches sight of a long, shiny, smoky grey skirt. Donna Clara and Donna Julie look in that direction too, the expression on their faces darkening. Donna Clara seems excited, while Donna Julie's face simply clouds over. Another couple stand behind the woman who has just arrived. Bianca turns back to Don Titta and Bernocchi; they seem stunned, as if hypnotized. Their eyes are fixed not on the hostess but on this newly arrived guest. Bianca looks at the woman again. She is dumbfounded. It is *her*: the ghost, more real now than ever. As the woman moves into the room, she looks around in search of a cluster of people to join. She freezes for a second and her forced smile cracks. Then she continues forward towards two elderly ladies dressed in black.

Don Titta and Bernocchi say goodbye by gripping each other's forearms, like a move in a wrestling match. Bianca cannot see their faces any more, just that strange gesture uniting them. Who is about to leave? And where is he going? Who is stopping whom? And why? Donna Clara, who has been mute until now, chirps to interrupt the silence.

'Isn't there anything to drink here?'

Her voice comes out hoarse. She coughs to clear her throat.

'I'll get something for you,' Donna Julie replies and walks away in a rustle of clothing.

As soon as she is gone, the lady of the house takes Bianca's arm and directs her firmly towards a group of women who want to meet her. They speak of flowers, naturally. Of flowers and commissions. Bianca has to concentrate and act complacently, receive compliments, make promises, and book appointments. Viola Visconti follows the conversation with a triumphant smile, as though Bianca has been her creation. Bianca smiles back generously in return.

When she is finally set free, she sees Don Titta cornered by his mother and wife in a screen of flesh and fabric. Bernocchi has vanished. The ghost, too. But that comes as no surprise. Perhaps Bianca has only imagined her. Or it could merely have been someone who looks like her. She walks towards the back room where she has been told there is a Luini painting of rare beauty. But she never gets there. The back of a figure in grey, with tiny buttons dotting her spine, blocks her way. The lady is leaning out over a balcony railing and looking down at the dark street below, from which comes the sound of a departing carriage. As the sound retreats, the lady straightens. She turns around, shocked to see Bianca standing in front of her. Bianca feels herself blush but doesn't know why. She has nothing to be ashamed of.

The two women fall silent and study each other for as long as they can, without conversing. With one penetrating look, Bianca takes note of the woman's amber skin – it is beginning to slacken along her jawline. Her chestnut-brown locks of hair are so dark they look, and perhaps are, artificial. She wears too much colour on her cheeks and a large, oval brooch speckled with small seed-like pearls at the centre of her neckline. Bianca stares at her in silence, unabashed.

The other woman responds with an uneasy smile and then flutters her fan aimlessly.

'Nice evening, isn't it?'

'Yes, it is a nice evening indeed,' replies Bianca, who has no desire to speak about the weather.

'Do . . . we know each other?' the woman asks.

'No. But that's just because no one has introduced us yet.'

'Yes, of course. Let's not pretend. What good would that do?'

'Exactly. It would be useless.'

If Bianca could see herself from a distance, she would say that the two of them face each other like insects at battle. One advances and the other recedes in barely perceptible movements; it could be an exchange of pleasantries or the defence of one's territory. But beneath the surface there is so much more. Both of them are accustomed enough to the rules of society to know better than to go for the eyes.

'Shall we see each other tomorrow, at the fountain in the gardens? We will be able to talk there,' Bianca says, beginning to feel nauseous from this stealthy game. 'Goodnight.' Then, without even waiting for a response, she walks away. Her heart is racing. Her improvised rashness has given her a sense of vertigo. She isn't at all certain that the other woman will agree to the meeting.

Donna Clara walks up to her now, brandishing a tiny glass.

'I see you made a friend. What do you think of her?'

She looks Bianca up and down slowly.

'Are you talking about the woman in grey? I thought she was someone else. Salons aren't the best place to get to know new people,' Bianca observes, trying to sound offhand.

'Oh, and why not? In places like these, witticisms shine. When there *is* wit, of course,' Donna Clara says drily.

'Of course,' echoes Bianca indifferently, following the older woman's piercing gaze back to the woman in grey. Their trajectory is diverted by Donna Julie.

She is panting, rosy-cheeked and speaks in a rush.

'Here you are. Nice evening, isn't it? I can't remember the last time I had such a lovely time. Signora Visconti really knows how to throw a party. And you? Are you having a good time too, Miss Bianca?'

She is confused and excited, when she is usually so quiet and calm. Her eyes burn feverishly, flickering here and there as if she wants to stop everything and take it all in. Then Donna Julie freezes and her face goes pale. Bianca looks over to see what she is looking at: Don Titta is speaking with the ghost.

The pair are wan and unsuitably serious. They look intently at one another, staring in silence. At this distance it is impossible to comprehend the meaning of their exchange. But Bianca has her proof now. She has received her confirmation.

৯ ৯

The report from her young informant, Girolamo, was extremely clear. Bianca was not expecting much, just a couple of confusing words hissed into her ear. Instead the boy has maintained his promise and given her a name and a history, written in dark penmanship on a piece of heavy paper smudged with dirt.

> *Costanza A., unemployed, moneyed, single, twenty years of age, entrusts her daughter to the care of the hospital and the services of Alberta Tonolli, midwife. Her daughter, one month in age and in good health, still needs nursing. The child has been baptized in the name of Luce but will receive the new name of Devota Colombo. The child does not cry. She is clothed in a batiste white camisole stitched with ringlets, she is swaddled in plain white cotton, she wears white leather shoes tied with a pink lace ribbon, and a bonnet with the same ringlet embroidery as her camisole. She is resting in a French-style carriage cushioned with strips of fine linen and has three other camisoles and three less precious bonnets. She is wrapped in a white woollen blanket with bunting. Her pledge token is a pink and green velvet pillow embroidered with a golden lamb with a silver bell. The mother has declared that she is intent on reclaiming her child as soon as circumstances allow her to do so.*

The child who was given up is vividly described, Bianca thinks as she rereads the note, piecing together the details, making the fragments fit with care, like trying to mend a broken teacup. That dry farewell must have agonized the mother. Bianca sees in her mind the authority figure that interrogated and the other figure that surely wept. She tries to imagine the scepticism of the official in charge. Perhaps they let women handle these things because they are gentler and can feel that unspeakable grief across the table. *The child does not cry.* But somebody else did. Fourteen years ago, a baby girl by the name of Luce, then renamed Devota, was brought to Santa Caterina alla Ruota and abandoned there. The age corresponds. The rest is evident. Devota's Christian name is changed to Pia: the same name in a simplified form, an ugly orphan name so that she will never forget her poor beginnings. The identifying token of the lamb pillow is unique, though, an unclassifiable luxury in that cold hospital.

Everything is so clear, so obvious. *Costanza A., unemployed* . . . If she was twenty then, she'd be thirty-four now. How could Bianca ever have searched all of Milan and its surroundings, all of its 150,000 inhabitants, for a thirty-four-year-old woman who is well-off enough to have entrusted her child with an exquisite set of goods, but so alone that she had to give up her newborn to public charity? A woman who wanted to return for the child when in fact the girl was adopted by a country priest? Bianca never dreamed that she would meet the target of her own investigation at a social event. It is clear that the woman is discomfited, but she is not grieving. Bianca wonders whether time really does heal all wounds, as people say when they want to appear wise. But if that woman really is Pia's mother, and has been so rash as to go out searching for her daughter, why has she stopped behind the gates? What has kept her from tearing down all the obstacles in her way? And if everyone knows about it, as it is beginning to seem to Bianca, then why hasn't anyone

taken a step forward? Why perform that strange dance of confrontation and retreat? Questions, so many.

෴ ෴

Bianca doesn't really expect Costanza A. to show up at their
rendezvous. She disguises the sortie so that she will not feel too
silly when she is disappointed. The season is so mild that the
children are able to brush aside the hesitations of both mother
and grandmother and go outside. Of course, they are over-
dressed, bundled up in their stuffed jackets. But Nanny has the
good judgement, for once, to allow them to remove some of their
clothing as soon as they turn the corner. She quickly becomes a
porter, lagging behind with her bundles. Bianca leads the group
and holds the two smallest girls by the hand. The other three
children follow, Enrico and Giulietta arm in arm, Pietro with
his hands in his pockets and his cap to one side, like a ruffian.
The route isn't long but they travel slowly. There are so many
things to stop and look at: an old woman selling bunches of wild
flowers, three identical boys dressed in light blue who are playing with hoops, and a stray dog with a thin snout like a ferret
who runs off after some delicious smell. And then there are the
palazzi, carriages, and small shops. This is a game of discovering
a city that has, until then, been a mystery to them.

They finally reach the green swells of the park and the wild
smell of grass that makes them want to run freely. There are
other children sailing boats in the big pond, and some mallard
ducks floating there too.

'Why is one colourful and one not?'

'The one without colour is female. The male is dressed as
if he were a soldier at a grand ball. But she looks as though
she had to rush out of the house and didn't have much time to
prepare.'

231

The children laugh.

'That's because we men are better,' says Enrico, stealing a glance at Pietro in search of approval. For once the older brother disagrees.

'I don't like soldiers. Papa says they are persecutors.'

Nanny smirks but Bianca ignores them. She looks around, pretending to focus on the landscape. She feels sure the lady in grey will not come.

But there she is. Bianca recognizes her from her bearing. She wears grey again, a spent grey this time, almost penitential. Bianca whispers something to Nanny above the heads of the children, who are busy watching the launch of cutter ships, and wanders off. In a sign of understanding, the woman in grey follows her. They stand beneath a row of linden trees pruned into boxes and planted so close to one another that the foliage meshes together in a geometric tunnel. If someone were to observe them, they would see only shadows.

'I decided to come,' the woman says, as if she herself is unable to believe it.

'Indeed.'

Bianca sighs and hesitates for a moment. Then she recites the speech that she has so often rehearsed at her window, to the fire, to the mirror, to no one. The words slip out of her easily and in a long and weighty chain. Words connect, affronted and accusing. Instinctively, the woman takes a step back, as if Bianca might strike her. She fumbles with her hands and blushes, red splotches surfacing on her neck and cheeks: the ugly signs of shame. When Bianca finishes, the lady in grey looks down at the ground.

Almost to herself, she says, 'It's all true. But it's all in the past now. I do not want to think about it any more.'

'But not even a year ago you were playing the part of ghost for all of Brusuglio! Do you remember?' Bianca asks, convinced that the woman must be mad, and that maybe it is for the best.

'Yes, I do remember. And I am sorry.' The woman speaks in a low whisper. 'But you see, things have changed. I . . . I am about to be married. You will laugh at me,' she says, but it is she who laughs a dry, low, bitter laugh. 'I'm a withered old maid, but I might have found an arrangement. My parents did everything for me. I did not ask them to. I do not have the right to ask for anything. Who am I to say no?'

She seeks Bianca's eyes and then looks down again and shakes her head.

'What do you want to know? You are young and beautiful and independent. Your name is on everyone's lips here in Milan. You're the rising star of illustrated botany.' She recites the words as if she is reading the headlines of a newspaper. 'You have everything. You can manage on your own. I have always done what others expected of me. Always. Up until . . . after I gave the child away. I spent my days berating myself for my mistakes. I didn't know any better.'

Bianca feels neither compassion nor pity.

'The child, as you called her, is a girl now. Or did you perhaps forget that, too? I don't understand you.' Bianca tries to keep her calm, but disdain has got the better of her and her words become sharper. 'How could you possibly deny her like this? You bury the past, and that's that? It seems as though she is dear to you. You look like you are desperate to see her. And now I can help you.'

Bianca adds this impulsively, without really meaning to say it. It isn't entirely true. She will help Pia for Pia's sake, not for the sake of this woman who has abandoned and avoided her child. But ultimately, won't it have the same outcome?

The woman looks at Bianca as though she hasn't heard a word. She continues her train of thought.

'People are right: what good is there in rummaging in the past? It's like turning over a stone and watching the insects and worms wriggle in the sunlight. I could only do her harm at this point.'

Haven't you done enough harm already? Bianca thinks to herself. *You and your stupid apparitions, the artfully abandoned token, and all the rest of it?*

'I didn't know better,' the woman says and gazes off into the distance.

If she could, Bianca would hit her, right there and then. But what is stopping her? Nothing. So she slaps her, just once, and only the kind of slap a small hand can give, but it's piercing. It leaves her palm burning. The woman brings her fingers to her cheek, perplexed, and as Bianca takes her hand away, she looks at it in horror, as if she is expecting to see it stained with blood. Despite their position, a little girl playing with a hoop nearby has witnessed it all. She freezes in place and lets go of her toy, which keeps on rolling and then, finally, falls into the grass. Bianca turns to stare at the child until she runs off. What is a tiny slap compared to the kicks, punches and torn-out hair that this woman really deserves in order to bring some justice to the world? But what sort of justice would that be?

The mistake is made, though, and the outcome is immense. In front of Bianca now stands a contrite little lady, a poor woman searching for another chance, a woman who has turned her back on the past. She is ashamed. And Bianca is ashamed, seeing her own reflection in this lady, seeing her own silly passions laid bare before the dark conspiracies, mysteries, plot twists, and imagined happy endings. She feels foolish. Her actions are like those in a cheap novella printed on inferior paper, paper that is good only for wrapping vegetables. Costanza A. will marry a rich old man. Maybe she will be blessed with a child at a late age to replace the shadow of her little girl. Or perhaps she will lead an isolated, second-hand life. The only thing real in all of this is Bianca's illusion that Pia's life will change. The mistake lies in having nurtured this illusion as if it is something precious. It is living one kind of life whilst reasoning that one is entitled to another.

Bianca cannot think straight. She stands face to face with the ghost that she has been chasing, who is nothing more than a pale woman with three red stripes along her cheek and great, hollow eyes. Eyes that now avoid her own. She is a woman who probably dislikes herself but who has learned to absolve herself; a woman who cannot wait to leave and to forget. Bianca only comes to her senses after Costanza A. has turned around and walked away without a goodbye. There is nothing left to say.

Bianca looks for a bench. There, she sits down and reflects. She tries to calm her heartbeat. Enough is enough. She throws her head back and looks up at the light blue sky above, in all its obtuse honesty. The little girl comes back to reclaim her hoop, regards her warily, and runs off again. It is time to leave.

Bianca can hear the other children, her children. She follows their voices and finds them in the middle of a big field doing cartwheels and tumbling about, their clothes horribly soiled with green striations, evidence that will be impossible to conceal and which will raise loud complaints in the laundry room. But it has been worth it. They wanted to play horseback, to roll in the carpet of grass, and smell its sweet murkiness. Bianca claps her hands and organizes an impromptu game of horsemen and princesses. She plays the part of a horseman.

Nanny, as usual, does nothing. The rest of them laugh, trip, gallop and fall about. By the evening, Giulietta has a fever.

ॐ ॐ

Once she has calmed down, Bianca thinks things over. She has been a presumptuous fool. She is a more provincial, faded copy of Emma Woodhouse, far less witty and with fewer accomplishments, who has tried to organize a mixed-up world and then recompose it to fit her own design. She doesn't possess a vision of a final version; really she is sustained by nothing at all. She can only busy herself with flowers, examine them through a lens up close. It is right for her to limit herself to this.

What had the ghost said in the park? *Your name is on everyone's lips.* Thank heavens her name isn't on everybody's lips for her demented attempt to repair the lives of others. No one – or almost no one – is aware of her theories; only a handful of strangers who have no interest in sharing them, people who have been paid to talk only once and who will therefore now remain silent. The comfort of knowing this, though, does not make her feel any less embarrassed. She has learned her lesson. Or at least, that's what she believes. She doesn't realize that she still has many lessons to learn, things that cannot be taught, things that one only picks up a little at a time, through living. How can she know? Her life has been lived in a glass box, like the ones she keeps her most precious subjects in, sealed and yet still vulnerable. She has viewed the world only from inside this glass, as though waiting for a storm to break it open. There is no defending herself, no escaping. She can only hope that the clouds will rain down somewhere else. But that is a lame hope: it will be better to stop and run for shelter, or dash out into the open and feel the cold rain on her body. She will risk it to feel alive. She wants to feel alive.

It doesn't take much to console a young woman who doesn't like herself. Bianca only needs to know that someone else likes her. And, after the white stone, Bianca soon receives other gifts. She finds them in unusual places: at the door to her bedroom, under her breakfast teacup, resting impudently on her empty desk. A green and white shawl made of lightweight cashmere, and as warm as an embrace, has been wrapped in a piece of flowered fabric. A few lines of writing, perhaps the beginning of an unfinished poem, or maybe the end of one – *It is here that my heart rests* – have been folded around a small silver box full of seeds and other symbolic items. A false pomegranate that looks incredibly real, its peel speckled with brown flecks. It is evident that someone is courting her in a discreet and ingenious manner. Someone who knows her well but doesn't want to scare her. Someone who wants to remain in the shadows, at least for now, and so sends her messages from there. Whoever it is knows that it will be pointless to give her flowers and so focuses on objects instead. Bianca loves the fact that she doesn't know who the sender is. It doesn't force her to make decisions or to react. At this point in time, choosing a witty remark or expressing a common courtesy would be difficult for her.

That is how she is: resolute to the point of being reckless where it concerns other people, and as uncertain as a child when her own feelings are tangled and confused. It is easy for her to recognize these sentiments in others and classify them with the detachment of an academic. But she doesn't even try to decipher herself. Perhaps her admirer has understood this and is taking advantage of it in his own elegant and malicious way. This option shouldn't be excluded. But Bianca doesn't even dig that deep. She is satisfied with the surface and with the portrait it gives her in return; she is a Narcissus who leans over to enjoy the best possible reflection.

She is tired of her own conjectures and imagined fantasies. They haven't led anywhere. She needs to work; she has many commissions, and she ought to bring them to a conclusion before returning to Brusuglio, where she will have to dedicate all her energies to her main project. Her contract lasts until autumn. Everything has to be completed and handed in by then. She is expecting intense months ahead and is prepared for them; work doesn't scare her. If there is something she fears, it is herself. The self that she doesn't know and that she doesn't understand. But she will never admit it, and in fact ignores it. She keeps her eyes on the ground and stumbles forward, as if she is playing blind man's buff. Be careful not to fall, Bianca.

৯৫ ৫৯

But still there are things that Bianca cannot let go of. She is like a dog tugging on a glove or shoe. She doesn't fully understand that the game is over. And because the dream of a happy ending – with its round of applause and smiles and gratitude – has dissipated, she feels spite. She feels anger at the poet and his indifference. Here is a man who has lived two lives with ease. First, the immoral life of a young libertine and then the inspired life of an artist. Now he is satisfied with his current family, with the compassion they inspire in him, and with their boring, comforting, shared rituals. She wants to stop him in the hallway, grab him by the shoulders, and shake the truth out of him.

How can you, Don Titta, you, the model of paternal love – strange in your ways and as bizarre as you please, but so damned good – how can you ignore your own daughter? She is an outcast who moves and breathes just one step away from those who have the privilege of bearing your name. She has nothing, only a licence stating she is an orphan and the future prospects of a maid. How can you be two people? Is it because of the customs of the era or because of your breeding? Or does the combination of the two, a topic so dear to you, foster this conflict? Are they really just words? Simple living-room banter?

If only she could speak these words, as honestly and as angrily as she feels like saying them. She wants to see his expression change, to see him laid bare, unarmed, stripped of his high rank, and suddenly sincere. In his sincerity, he will be humble, thankful and magnificent. She wants to be the one to tear the veil from the mirror and show him his true face. *Don Titta, one can always change*, she will say. *One can always make right that which went wrong.* He will be so committed to her afterwards for giving him the courage of truth. She wants to be the inspiration for his renewal. It is an arrogant thought, at first just fleeting, and then cultivated in a myriad of variations. She is just one step away from understanding what she truly feels – but it is the one step that she doesn't take. At the age of twenty it is difficult to be honest with oneself. And then her anger will cease. She will turn on her heels and make her way back to the house in the heat of scorn.

Her anger never lasts long though. It explodes like a storm and then dissipates into mitigating rivulets. She fumes and then is quiet in tumultuous succession. And she loves in silence, too, so secretly that even she isn't aware of it. Hers is a love like water, that takes the shape and colour of that which holds it.

❧ ❧

She loves, and because of this, she forgives. In the end, since she forgives herself, she can extend the privilege to whom-ever she desires. It happens quickly. All she needs is a spark of intuition, a notion that she can hang on to. She finds it on the balcony overlooking the garden: there Don Titta and Pia are standing under the shelter of the catalpa tree. She draws back but remains nearby, in the shadows of the corridor. Even if they turn around, they won't be able to see her. But they don't turn. They are too involved in their conversation. Bianca is a little far away to read the words on their lips.

She should feel her usual anger, the usual repertoire of venom: *You are her father but you act like her master.* But the sweetness of their exchange – hands moving in mid-air, nods of understanding, conversational gestures – everything about those two bodies reflects a closeness that isn't there merely by chance. They aren't speaking about that evening's dinner menu or about Enrico's tantrums or the umpteenth book on loan. Something else unites them, Bianca is certain of it. She leans back against the wall, relieved, and full of unexpected joy.

What if she can actually bring together these two people who have been so cruelly separated, and thereby obtain a semblance of justice? If all that is needed to fix things is desire, can't she just desire it for them and imagine it a million times over? Won't that bring about some tiny result, even if it is infinitesimal? It will still be the right and natural one that she has imagined. All won't be for naught, Bianca tells herself. Although, she suddenly thinks, if these two are speaking to each other like this already, something must have happened.

All of her rage, suspicion and acrimony suddenly vanish. How strange, Bianca thinks. There's so much grace and intimacy in their exchange. As she continues to watch from afar, she feels like a spy, even if it has happened by accident. She can't help staring at them. She can't avoid it. Perhaps Don Titta is actually doing what he can for the girl, given the circumstances. And perhaps he does this every day, lightening his conscience and eliminating his guilt. No, the evidence is always there in front of him, the vibrant memory of his mistake. Maybe he actually holds on to it, nurtures it, wants it close by. Bianca acquits him in a rapid verdict.

Now that she has her target centred, she can finally walk away from it. She smiles to herself and goes to her bedroom, leaving the pair to say whatever they need to say to each other, whatever their hearts tell them. They are alone in the world, like two lovers who have finally found the courage to be themselves.

❧ ❧

In the days following, nothing much happens; there are no announcements, revelations, or clarifications. There is only a quiet normality, as if each of them has returned to their ranks and is pleased to be where they are. Bianca grows agitated. She draws and scribbles, and then tosses everything away. She breaks her charcoal and gets her hands and arms dirty. She goes downstairs, intent on finishing her drawings, but is left speechless when the poet walks out of the room in a hurry, without even taking his hat. He casts a glance at Innes but the latter does not respond. She slips away from Tommaso, who has in the meantime handed her a tiny glass of cordial or rose-water, and goes back upstairs, opening the window and looking for answers in the treetops outside.

When she goes back downstairs she is intercepted by Donna Clara, who needs a confidante for some of her gossipy affairs. She spends half an hour nodding like a mindless doll. She ignores the little girls, who wave to her as she walks by. She ignores Nanny's look of silent reproach. She sends for Pia, but in front of her smiling innocence she falls silent. She cannot make up her mind about anything. In the end she asks only for a cup of tea.

જ ৡ

Love and war. Love is war. It's a careless occupation by a foreign territory within you – daytime, night-time, in everything you do. One is invaded, one resists, one surrenders. And surrender is productive. If one could measure the benefits by placing a piece of oneself on a scale and on the other side what is produced, lost, and what remains, the only certainty would be that something is consumed. If you fantasize about what you want, do you lose it? Or does it become ruined? There's always an abyss between the desired and the achieved; the abyss attracts and summons like a wall that needs to be climbed over or jumped from.

Should I come forward and take what's mine? Should I take what's not yet mine? Should I move towards what I want but do not know, or should I wait for it to be placed into my hands? To take or to give? To give in? Should one do this?

Should I sit on the sofa with my hands in my lap and a smile on my face? Should I peer out of the window into the night to see who is in the shadows?

We give some things and we want some things. In the end, what counts is what we can give. I can give something. But can I, a lone female in this world, only desire, hope, and then finally say yes? Can I also say no? Yes, the arrow points to the future. No, the stone drags you to the bottom with the algae, dazed as though dead. Father, how many things you neglected to teach me. You left me too soon. By your side, I could have learned how to distinguish and evaluate, how to listen to myself, how to understand. No, that's not true. I would only have been able to interpret your eager and curious signs. I would have carried myself towards an easy place and given up on thinking and deciding. I would have been happy that way. That, too, would have been a kind of love. But I don't know it now. Or perhaps you would have helped me understand myself. With infinite patience, you would have helped me to understand an unknown language. You had already decided to let me go before everything else happened, before this torment. And now I know nothing. I do not know myself.

❧ ❧

It happens. The living room is empty of unwanted presences. She stands in front of him. For just a moment she sweeps away all conventions: he is her equal. She has to do it; she can do it.

'I must speak with you.'

'I, too, need to speak with you. But it's so difficult to be alone in this house. Even talking is difficult.'

'I know. I wanted to tell you that I understand. You have a position . . . you choose to ignore the legitimate rights of someone less fortunate . . . I understand, but I do not accept it. A man like you, so open, so progressive. It can't be . . .'

Everything is said without hesitation. Followed by the just reply, the beautiful humility of an admitted fault. A shadow hides his face; he leans in towards her, their eyes lock, for once. A sigh.

'You are right. I take full responsibility for my mistakes. But the day will come when finally everything will be clear, everything will be able to be said in the light of day. Miss Bianca, this day is not far off. I imagine it in my darkest moments when I feel there isn't anything left to hope for, when oppressive fetters bind me to my role, as you point out. That's when everything will change. Only then will we be allowed to be ourselves.'

'So then . . . you . . .' She trembles, encouraged. Yes, yes. It is about to happen. Yes.

'I want to say that the moment is close, the moment when things will change forever, there will be no going back, and we will no longer hide. Do you understand?'

He takes her hands in his and squeezes them. Bianca doesn't know what she is supposed to understand. She is confused. Has she understood, or not? And then, as if in a farce, there is a distraction. A sound close by. They let go of each other's hands. It is Tommaso.

'Ah, here you are. I was looking for you, Titta. Our friend has arrived.'

Don Titta turns around sharply.

'Yes, certainly. I'm coming.'

A bow, and he is gone. Tommaso casts a bewildered look at Bianca before closing the study door, where apparently someone is waiting for them. Has he heard everything? Has he seen them holding each other's hands? No, the poet's back faced the door.

Bianca stands alone. Their conversation has been left hanging. In that other room, voices rise and fall in excitement; there is an invasion of arrogant strangers. Here, things have been said that cannot be undone, like a flood consuming everything in its path. He has said that he will no longer hide. He has said it. What else is there? Bianca, swept up by the current, floats on its dark waters, a blessed Ophelia in her innocent, though not harmless, folly.

❧ ❧

Later, Bianca shudders when Bernocchi's eyes seek her out in the sitting room. She calms a little when he lowers them back to the curled pages of his *London Review*, which he has clearly

brought with him to show off, and which he attempts to translate aloud from English into Italian as he reads.

'"She knows far too well that the man she loves can never
be hers unless extraordinary circumstances take place, a situation which she desires but which she doesn't dare hope for.
And yet she continues to love . . ." Let me say this, Innes. Your
friend, the writer, is the first and last of the romantics. What a
delightful portrait of female innocence he has put together.
To think of enjoying such pure love – and pure because it is
impossible. What an honour, what privilege, and what relief!
And listen to this here: "They hide their advanced age by speaking without hesitation of their youth . . . or they show off their
frenzy of virtue in manifesting a passionate indignation for the
same . . ."'

'Might I interest you in an English lesson or two?' Innes
interrupts, poking fun at Bernocchi. 'At a moderate price, of
course.'

'Why don't you read it, then?' Bernocchi says, irritated, and
hands him the paper. 'It is quite difficult to translate on the
spot. Go on, read, right there, the part that talks about love. It
will be instructive to all of us.'

Bianca feels averse to all of this but tries not to show it.
They are so mistaken. Everyone is wrong. Love is not *always*
impossible. But she mustn't and won't say anything. She looks
up, surprised to see Tommaso staring right at her gravely.

Innes leafs through the pile of papers. The Italian language
in his mouth sounds lovely and exotic, precise, though slightly
blurry.

'As you wish. "Love is no longer a cunning rascal, laughing
in his heart while he pretends to cry, nor is love a small curly-
haired boy . . . Today love bears the expression and the grave
posture of an old sage. Do not imagine him running around

naked like a cherub, as he once did. Today love is dressed from head to toe in the clothes of a lawyer."' Tommaso chuckles and stamps his feet on the ground. Innes continues. "'Love's quiver has turned into a blue postal bag, and his arrows into documents and contracts, his most powerful tools, for both men and women." Is that enough for you?'

'Oh, more than enough. For once, your Foscolo was right. "Listen to me; love no longer exists." How did he phrase it? Didn't he compare love to a child that had grown up and become a serious businessman? And thank goodness. Everything that can be bought can also be measured.'

'Indeed,' intervenes Donna Julie, who has been silent until now. Her boiling point is slow to reach, but once she achieves it, her lid bursts off. 'How rotten this world is when we make a business out of sentiments,' she exclaims, more desolate than disdainful.

Bianca shoots her a perplexed look.

'Ah, but I didn't say that. You misunderstand,' Bernocchi retorts. 'Sentiments, unfortunately, are utterly unreasonable and difficult to tame. All of us, sooner or later, will fall prey. The important thing is to know how much damage they can cause and to try, as reasonable beings, to control them.'

'I continue to abhor the world you describe,' Donna Julie insists.

'Or perhaps it is me whom you don't like very much? Poor, wretched me,' Bernocchi says.

Everyone's eyes are on the count, judging him, nailing him to the armchair from which he tries to rise, ready to flee. But the depth of the chair combines with his own feebleness and the weight of those stares keeps him fixed in his place.

⁂

'To hear Bernocchi speak of love is an outrage. What could he possibly know, that toad who I doubt has ever been kissed? How can he claim to lay down the law? And everyone just sat there listening to him, nodding their heads like asses. Don't you find it horrible?'

Bianca, enraged, looks at Innes leaning against the doorway, his hands behind his back. They are alone. The others have gone to get ready for dinner. The count has finally left.

'Bianca, Bianca, brazen and contemptuous Bianca. Come along, they were just words, thrown like harmless darts.'

'Harmless, perhaps, but not innocent.'

'You have the right not to like them, but also the right to ignore them.' He pauses, then says more seriously, 'Be wary.'

Bianca throws back her shoulders and faces him with an air of challenge. She paces up and down nervously, marking the carpet with her feet.

'What are you trying to say?' she says, finally.

'You're playing with fire,' he answers elusively. 'I wouldn't want to see you burn your feathers.'

'Is that how you see me: as a chicken? Or better, a wild goose with her feathers clipped? Rummaging in the yard among the rest of the fowl?'

'If you're fishing for compliments, then I actually see you more as a young heron with its claws stuck in the mud: elegant in flight, clumsy on the ground.'

'Of course. And soon they will pluck me for dinner. Is that what I should be careful of?'

'I'm telling you to watch out for yourself,' answers Innes solemnly.

He must have understood. Yes, of course, he has known all along. But what Bianca wants is a friendly shoulder to lean on, not an authoritative guardian. She cannot accept seeing everything reduced to dry accounting, to hear someone tell her not to run risks.

Donna Julie was right in her argument but then suddenly she had fizzled out. She is too inconsistent, barely worth considering, at least not until she made that comment. Consequently, Bianca has simply propped Donna Julie and her counter-argument up against the wall and forgotten about her as though she is transparent. It embarrasses Bianca to think of taking away from Donna Julie something that is legitimately hers. It is like pricking blood from a vein. She of all people, who is so innocent; she'll hold her wrist out for a phlebotomy with a smile on her face, convinced it is for her own good . . . how embarrassing. What confusion. What folly.

'Are you all right, Bianca? You've changed colour.'

Innes is attentive. Suddenly he is next to her; he takes her hands and squeezes them. He seems sincerely worried. He bends over her, so close that Bianca can smell the Indian scent of his cologne, and just barely below that, the warm current of his skin. Bianca realizes that Innes is not just a friend. He is also a man.

He is too close. Bianca slips out of his grip, turns, and flees. Innes's gaze follows her as she runs up the staircase in a hurry, anxious to be alone with her thoughts.

❧ ❧

Dinner is torture. Innes seems angry and doesn't say a word to her or to anyone. The absence of his conversational grace, which usually fills the pauses and dissipates the conflicts, weighs over the entire table. Bianca cannot even look at Donna Julie. Don Titta is distracted. Tommaso hasn't come down, apparently unwell. Donna Clara begins a soliloquy based on the preaching of Don Dionisio, the only merit of which is that it fills the silence, interrupted on occasion by the clink of china and crystal. It is sad to eat in divided company.

⁂

They disband in a hurry after dinner. Before disappearing upstairs, Innes looks at her in pained anger. She ignores him and immediately forgets it. The women disappear to the sitting room. Bianca starts to follow them but then returns to the library to recover her personal copy of Shakespeare that she has left on a side table. Don Titta is there, leafing through one of his magazines. She takes the book and holds it tightly, as if it carries her salvation. This is where she wants to be. She needs to try again, to be clearer this time. She has feared and desired a situation like this for so long. Instead of leaving, she looks over at him. He, provoked by the power of her eyes, puts down the newspaper and returns her stare. It isn't the right time for words to muddle the situation. How different this silence feels compared to the one in the dining room. How much purer and more profound; it is a kind of water that provokes thirst, then appeases and renews her. Bianca stands there for a long time, hanging onto that gaze that tells her everything she needs to understand, perhaps even more.

But in a large house one is never alone. There are shutters that need closing and curtains to draw, and almost invisible beings appear to complete these duties. The order of each day depends on them. They enter rooms, ignoring the glances that extend like taut strings between the other people, the people who have a place in the world. The beings tread over these strings or skirt around them, but don't trip on them since they don't really see them. Their duties break the tension.

More than a minute has passed – a long, yet fleeting minute – and then it is over. Bianca walks away without saying a word.

She is sure that she has said in silence everything that she has wanted to verbalize. She is sure she has received the correct answer too, the only possible and acceptable one. It is the misunderstanding of silence.

She climbs the stairs in a hurry, clutching her book like a buoy. Once in her room she leans against the wall and lets herself drop down to the floor. The book slips out of her hands and falls open. Bianca picks it up. In the dim candlelight that one of those invisible beings has lit, she searches for a message in the words on the page. *Tolle et lege.* If only, if only there is a little note, a letter, something.

Nothing. The open page merely says things that she isn't willing to understand:

> Now is the winter of our discontent
> Made glorious summer by this son of York;
> And all the clouds that low'r'd upon our house
> In the deep bosom of the ocean buried.

No, wait, something *is* there. A piece of paper pokes out like a bookmark. Cautiously, Bianca picks it out with two fingers. It is what she least expected to find: a portrait of her mother at the age of twenty. Beautiful and remote, this is how she needs to be remembered. Her father used to use these commemorative portraits on sepia-coloured paper as bookmarks; he took notes on their backs, and caressed them secretly with the tips of his fingers. It isn't surprising to find one inside this book. *Would you, Mother, whom I did not know well enough, would you understand? If you were still here, perhaps I wouldn't be searching for other people's mothers. Would you judge me harshly? Are you judging me now, your paper eyes piercing me from afar? Are you condemning my passion because it is insulting, illegitimate, and useless? Or perhaps you're just holding me in your arms without saying a thing?*

The face stares back at her, unperturbed. Bianca remembers her mother just like that, as a woman who didn't smile. Or was that a mask? She closes the book on her mother's face. *Enough. You're a stranger. You have no right to scold me like that. You aren't here.* And meanwhile the moment has been ruined. The night of discontent will be a long one.

❧ ❧

The days pass and nothing happens. The steady stream of secret gifts ends. Don Titta leaves again and takes Innes with him. The house full of children and women feels like a prison. Bianca forces herself to catch up on her work and make up for the time she has spent fantasizing. Work is good for her. It numbs her and rids her of thoughts; it leaves her feeling exhausted and empty, while her folders fill up and the money rolls in. *Will I end up like this: rich and unhappy?* She fastens her purse strings without even counting her money. She is far from being either rich or happy – what she feels is physical exhaustion.

'It is springtime and we need something to invigorate us,' Donna Clara announces, convinced that there is no bodily or spiritual discomfort that does not have a chemical solution. She sends one of her most trusted maids to the herbalist for an infallible recipe. Bianca and Donna Julie, both under her care, are forced to surrender. In the end, it is just a concoction of boiled herbs to be drunk once a day. The table is set with nutritious food and Donna Clara makes sure that the two young girls, as she calls them, eat everything on their plates, the same way that Nanny oversees the children. There is something comforting in feeling looked after. Bianca gives in to the concoction, feeling just a tiny bit of residual guilt towards her companion, who is far more feeble and sick than she. But she puts her guilt aside. In the end, she hasn't acted on things, she has only *imagined* them, and dreams never harm anyone except those who invent, cultivate and nurture them.

One thing still bothers her, though, and after it is resolved, she promises herself that she will behave. She will fold her wishes up like a handkerchief and put them away in her pocket, and that will be the end of it all. She has to clear the air with Pia. She feels the need to tell her. It all began by trying to do what was best for her. She needs to talk to her, to explain herself. She needs to find the right time and just do it, get it over with. She has to absolve herself sincerely. Bianca has not confronted Pia because it is the simplest thing to do; she does it now because she knows she won't be able to escape the trap of the young maid's gentle lamb-like eyes. She has failed with everyone else but with Pia she cannot afford to.

※ ※

Pia stares at her for a long time and seems not to understand. For once, she has taken a seat on the sofa and she fumbles with her hands on her lap and kicks her feet, as if she cannot wait to get up and leave. She looks so dazed that Bianca feels like shaking her. *On the other hand*, she thinks, *what was I expecting from a person who all of a sudden has found out who her real mother and father are?* It is as if she has been struck by lightning. Bianca smiles encouragingly and gives the girl a gentle pat on the shoulder, waiting.

'And when you finally understand the situation, we will decide what to do,' she hears herself say, not knowing how exactly she can help.

The moment couldn't be more perfect. A cool evening breeze flutters in from the open window in a pale blue wash of light. Pia, bewildered, her lips pursed into an adorable smile, has the inanimate grace of a Flemish portrait. Bianca observes her promising beauty like an indulgent older sister, with a vague air of consolation. When she finally looks up, Pia does not cry, her voice does not tremble; she is submissive and serene.

'You . . . you are confusing me,' she starts to say, her hands fluttering from her lap into the air, in a childlike gesture.

How strange the words sound to Bianca, as though they have been stolen from one of the books Pia reads in secret, as if the character is speaking to someone she is fond of. But the maid continues in a different tone.

'You speak of things that I am owed. You tell me that you are thinking of my well-being. But I do not understand. I am happy like this. What do you expect, Miss Bianca? This is my destiny. Don Dionisio says that it is the duty of a good Christian to accept what the heavens have laid out for them, and that I should thank heaven for what I have. I look around and see so many people who have a lot less than I do: young girls, beaten, ignorant and alone. I not only have a bellyful of food, clothes on my back and a roof under which to sleep, but a lot of other things, too.'

Pia brings her hands down to her lap again and secures one in the other, as if to keep them from flying away.

Bianca is speechless. Is the child ungrateful, after she has spent so much pity on her? The correct answer comes to her slowly. Pia hasn't asked her to do this. No one has. She has done it all on her own. And then come waves of anger, a river of fury, because the young girl, as stupid as she sounds at that moment, really and truly does deserve better.

'Pia, Pia, Pia,' mutters Bianca finally, unable to contain herself. 'Are you telling me you don't care to know?'

Pia doesn't speak. She just presses her lips shut, raises her eyebrows, and then looks down in apology. But she doesn't say sorry.

'Really,' Bianca insists, 'are you satisfied with hand-me-down skirts and ribbons and with having to ask for permission to put a book in your pocket now and then? Are you satisfied with so little in order to be happy?'

'I don't know any other kind of happiness apart from the happiness I feel now,' replies Pia simply. She shrugs, opens her hands in a gesture of surrender, and repeats herself. 'I am happy just the way I am.' She crosses her arms in front of her and stares back at Bianca. It is as if her look is saying, *You're the one who doesn't have what you want; you don't know what you want. You're the orphan. Don't unleash your anxieties onto me.* 'May I be excused, Miss Bianca?'

Pia doesn't wait for a reply. She gets up and leaves, without even turning around. Bianca lowers her head and bites her lip. Pia's look has said so much, and it hurts Bianca to admit that the girl has been right.

Part Three

The joy of returning to Brusuglio in nice weather cancels out her last memory of the estate in autumn, when an oppressive sky and a thick layer of fog had smothered everything. She is now able to substitute that memory with the colours and well-defined margins of everything in bloom; she recognizes the place first through her body, nose and skin, and only later with her head.

An entire year has gone by since Bianca's arrival. At twenty years old, it seems like a lifetime. It has taken her this long to call this place, populated by strangers, home. That other house, the one at the lake, is far away. This house, with its wide-open windows, seems to want to embrace her.

Minna leaps on her when she sees her, and then steps back, lowering her chin to her chest in embarrassment. She has grown an entire foot, as children and plants often do between seasons, and her face has taken on certain features that have not been present before.

'Shall I put your clothes away, Miss Bianca?' she whispers, eager to get back to her place.

Bianca takes her by the hand and twirls her around.

'First let me look at you. Go on, stand up straight. Look me in the eyes. Do you know that you truly are a good-looking girl?'

Beautiful, too, are the round faces of the kitchen maids, suddenly illuminated by gleeful curiosity. They greet her with due reverence and then run off.

'Miss Bianca, how elegant you are.'

'You look like a lady, Miss Bianca.'

To Bianca it is as if they are saying, *How could this be? Weren't you merely one of us? Or just slightly more?*

Then, as soon as Pia descends from the second coach, Minna jumps into her arms. Pia lifts her up and laughs.

'You're as heavy as lead, doll face. You didn't get fat now, did you?'

'What a beautiful dress! What a lovely hat!'

'I'll let you try it on later.'

There is laughter of relief and rediscovered complicity. Now everything can go back to normal.

But there is little time for pleasantries. Donna Clara has arrived and descended from her personal stagecoach. Giulietta, who's had the privilege of travelling with her, throws herself out of the carriage in a frenzy, almost knocking her grandmother down.

'Giulietta! Is that how a young lady behaves? I want to see all of the domestic help immediately, in the east courtyard. Call Ruggiero for me . . . Ah, here you are, I didn't see you there, as skinny as you are. My goodness, the hedges. Why has no one pruned them? And what about the lawn? What are those yellow splotches? Does everything stop when I am not here? And move that cart – it's offensive.'

As always, nothing is right, and will be fixed only when she asks for it to be done.

Donna Julie passes into the house delicately and unobserved. It seems as though she is better, but she is still pale. She smiles at everyone, almost gratefully, and everyone smiles back at her. The children run off, Nanny chasing after them. She needn't have bothered, as they will certainly not let themselves be caught, but she doesn't know where else to go. The men will arrive later, in time for dinner, and the wave their arrival will cause will be cushioned by habit. It will be an intimate dinner, serene, *en famille*, before the holiday rituals attract neighbours and friends to them like flies to honey. People will flock to them, summoned by the serenity that radiates from their small world, hoping to catch this infectiousness as if it is a desirable illness.

※ ※

Pia seems to have forgotten the encounter that was supposed to have amounted to glory, but which is instead now buried under the sand. Bianca watches how the young maid focuses on reclaiming her place in that world. Bianca wishes she could have her to herself but she feels she needs to let her go. And yet, it occurs to Bianca that she must have planted some seed of doubt because shortly thereafter she sees Pia immersed in conversation with Don Dionisio. They keep being interrupted by every kind of disturbance   the voice of Donna Clara, a servant who walks too close by – but they always take up again where they left off, whether it is an hour later or the following day. It is as if they never get tired of telling each other things. Perhaps Pia seeks approval from her protector. Perhaps she expects to learn more from him. Perhaps truth has to be brooded over like an egg, before it will hatch in all its awkward beauty. Perhaps – and this hypothesis feels like an oncoming headache and Bianca does not want to admit it – not all truths deserve to be revealed. She wishes she could listen to those exchanges, though. She wishes she could *understand*. For someone who thinks that she has understood everything, not knowing is complete torture.

※ ※

She is not tired and cannot sleep. It is warm and the novelty of her surroundings keeps her awake, even when an unnatural yet perfect peace has settled over the house, broken only by the song of the cicadas that rises over the gentle sound of crickets. She imagines everyone sleeping: the maids in their quarters upstairs, stretched out on the wooden floor close to the tiny windows; the poet in his loose nightshirt, the sheets kicked to the end of the bed; Donna Julie, pale as the pillow on which she rests her head, the sheets tucked under her chin; Donna Clara, freed from her corset, her mouth slightly open, breathing with difficulty; the little girls, their hair sticking to their foreheads with sweat, their eyelids threaded with pink and blue veins. A house asleep. She imagines Minna and Pia awake, though, their eyes bright and vigilant, the spell finally broken, intent on telling each other stories in whispered voices.

She doesn't feel like reading. Instead, she gets up to take in the beautiful stillness of the garden. It is a beauty made up of blacks and greys; the only white the marble contour of the fountain and the gravel splashed with moonlight. A nocturnal bird cackles mockingly. Silence.

There is the rustle of shifting pebbles and light, careful footsteps. And then, two small, quick shadows come out from behind the corner of the villa and cross the path cautiously. Once on the great lawn, which swallows up the sound of their feet, they run to its centre, where a new sycamore tree has just been introduced to replace the one struck by lightning. Enrico is ahead and runs faster; Pietro follows behind with a bundle under his arms.

Bianca smiles and remembers when she used to play with her own brother Zeno and his friends Berto, Tiziano and Tilio. Once, at night, they even climbed to the top of La Rocca. It was an easy trek during the day along a path shadowed by oak trees, but scary and dangerous at night. They couldn't see where to step, the stones were slippery with moss, and there was a heavy curtain of leaves above their heads that shut out the moonlight. But in the end, holding each other's hands, they made it and were able to look down at the lake from above, sitting together on the stone throne built for an ancient queen.

The two boys are happy to be out on the lawn. Pietro puts down the bundle and gives it a kick. It is a white ball and looks like it is made from strips of silk. When they kick it, it gives off a thudding sound, which seems odd. Is it leather? Bianca, now curious, goes downstairs and walks outside. She won't scare them. She'll promise to be silent. And maybe they will let her play with them.

When they see her approaching, the two children stop running and freeze in their places. Bianca is unable to read their expressions. She tries reassuring them and promising complicity.

'But . . .' Her words fade into nothing.

The thing has rolled towards her. It is not a ball. It is not made of fabric or leather. It is a skull. A human skull. It smiles at her impassively before rolling over to display its white nape.

The moment feels like an eternity. Bianca brings a hand to her mouth to stop herself from screaming.

Pietro comes to her side. He is breathing heavily. He flips his hair with an almost effeminate gesture. When he speaks his voice is coarse, breathy, and yet authoritative.

'You'll be sorry if you say anything. You'll be sorry if you tell on us. You'd better keep quiet. Otherwise I will tell on you and then you'll be in big trouble.' He smiles a frightening, adult sneer.

Bianca turns and walks away without saying a word. She is ashamed to have something to be ashamed of.

珍 珍

Another night, after dinner, Tommaso takes her by the hand and pulls her up off the sofa, possessive and insistent.

'Let's go for a walk. It's warm, and the moon is out.'

She refuses. She isn't in the mood.

'Oh, yes, you must go. You kids should have fun, not sit around with us old folks, listening to us say the same old things.'

Bianca hears Donna Clara's bass line of malice, that old strain of envy. Innes excuses himself. As he leaves the room, it is useless to try to make eye contact with him. When he is like that, Bianca has learned, it is better just to let him be, and wait for the clouds to clear.

Once they get outside, Tommaso is silent, as if he is a wanderer of the moor. The silence makes her feel uncomfortable so she starts a conversation.

'I would have thought that you preferred literature to nature at night.'

'He rejects me. He has something else on his mind, and it's not his devoted puppy. Dogs have a basic defect: they die of loyalty. I think I've decided that I'd rather live.'

Instinctively, Bianca moves further away from him, as much as she can while remaining polite; he must feel her coldness because he adds: 'You shouldn't believe everything I say, my dear Bianca. And don't worry, you aren't a substitute. If literature is everything, nature is even better.'

His expression is impossible to read. Every so often he turns and looks back at the house, as if he wants to flee from its gaze. They walk for about a mile down the gravel path and then turn up a little hill. The dark grows darker. She sees steps: sheets of stone, as white as dragon's teeth. She is about to rest her foot on the first step, and tries to loosen her arm from his, but he doesn't let her go. He actually pulls her towards him and pushes her up the stairs.

'I want to show you something,' he says. It is the ice chamber. 'Have you ever been in there?'

'No, and I don't think I ever will,' Bianca says.

'Ah, but it's worth it,' Tommaso replies, turning the key in the lock. 'Another of the amazing secrets of Brusuglio to discover.'

Inside, he rummages about with a flint and a lantern that seems to have been placed randomly on the floor. But there is nothing random about it, she realizes; he has wanted to bring her here. Her heart skips a beat. Is she scared? Scared of Tommaso? The door is still ajar, she can still escape. But curiosity gets the better of her.

The dim light reveals a low brick vault. It is surrounded by alcoves and inside there are blocks of ice wrapped in clean cloths. She can see the squares of paralysed deep green water; they are opaque and have the same colour as the lake. The place feels like a Roman catacomb. She shivers not only on account of the cool air, which makes the room as cold as a cellar, but for what lives within. It smells strange. It reminds her of the mix of dust and bones she had inhaled during archaeological visits, when not even a handkerchief in front of her face had been sufficient to suppress the musty air. Here, the cool air enters her nostrils and rises to her head. It is the coolness of the abyss.

Bianca blinks. She feels like she did when she needed to rise from the depths of the lake's dark waters that she remembers with love. She is almost amazed to see Tommaso still by her side. He lifts the lantern and shines the light all the way around.

'Nice, huh? In its own way, of course. This place is full of surprises. You should come to see my home, one day. Up in the attic . . .' Then he stops and suddenly becomes serious, almost bitter. 'I can't even go there any more. They treat me worse than a mouse. Do you know why I have brought you here?'

Let him speak, Bianca tells herself. And he does.

'Of course you know why I brought you here. I am sure of it. A young, bright woman such as yourself. Sharp and cold as a blade. You are the ice queen. Why are you so cold, Bianca, why?' He places the lantern carefully in one of the alcoves and kneels down before her. He takes her by the hand and gazes at her with the expression of a transfixed martyr. How ridiculous he looks. The dim light gives him the appearance of a wax statue. 'I kneel here before you as humble as an ancient cavalier, ready to serve you, prepared to dedicate myself to you.'

Bianca takes her hand out of his with a small laugh.

'Go on, laugh at me,' he continues. 'But I am serious. Do you understand me? Serious! Is it possible that only other people's seriousness attracts you? Mine is not an insurmountable wall or a deep trench that separates. It is the opposite: it is a solid link, a bridge of souls, an arch in the sky that begins at your feet.'

What is he talking about? What does he mean? Does he have a fever? Without thinking, Bianca feels his forehead with her fingers, as she would a child. He looks at her with a calm smile.

'There. You see how easy it is to take pity on me? And how little it takes to make me happy? I can do the same: I can make *you* happy, today, here, on this earth. If you let me. Let go of fantasy, forget about them, and choose me. For some time now, I have worshipped you from the shadows.'

Bianca is dumbfounded. She hears the alarm of danger, a voice in her head. It is freezing in here. She wraps herself tightly in her shawl and takes a step back as he goes on.

'Ah, I see the shawl I gave you. May you always be enveloped in my passion. Did you realize it was me?'

Heavens, no, she thinks. She was convinced that the gift came from somebody else. What about the other things? Instinctively, she jerks the fabric off her shoulders. It is the shirt of Nessus, poisonous when it is recognized as such. He watches her and mutters.

'You torture me. Does it bring you pleasure? What pleasure could there be in other people's grief?'

Bianca is tired of this. It is cold. She turns around and walks out. Tommaso stands and follows her. She begins to run. She hears him close the iron door behind her and turn the key, as if to close in his prey, though it has already fled. Or has it?

❧ ❧

The following day, in the sunlight, all that cold air seems never to have existed. It feels only like a vague aversion, a mosquito bite that has almost healed, but then reawakens, the venom still pulsating under the skin. An irresistible bother.

Nothing has happened.

And yet it feels like everyone knows. Donna Clara sings an old love song; Nanny smiles faintly; Innes reads his newspapers in silence and doesn't pass her tea. What do they know? Bianca thinks, growing annoyed. There really is nothing to know.

But every time she runs into Tommaso, she blushes. And it seems like he bumps into her on purpose: in the living room, the greenhouse, the garden. Always with no witnesses around. Even when there are witnesses, it doesn't matter. He keeps at his game. He will kneel down, put his hand on his heart, over the lightweight batiste shirt that he wears unbuttoned at the top, like a true romantic, as if posing for a portrait. As quickly as he appears, he'll then disappear, swallowed by the folds of a curtain, a door, or a hole in the ground. Bianca feels like there might be an entire army of Tommasos, ready to jump out in front of her, disrupt her train of thought and make her blood boil. Why? For what? In the end he is just fooling around. No one ever takes him seriously and she will not be the one to start. But her irritation begins to mix with something else too: for truthfully she likes it. She likes it a great deal.

He hasn't tried to kiss her. Bianca doesn't realize it then, but this is how he wins. Now all he has to do is wait.

He hasn't pronounced the word 'love', either. Not even once. Bianca doesn't pay any attention to that. She doesn't even think about it. She doesn't think about the gifts or about the gift-giver. She understands the shawl, but the rest of them? They are too elevated to be the fruit of the intelligence of this boy. He hasn't claimed them, even if he could have. And so Bianca keeps on deceiving herself, and keeps nurturing a small certainty, which is good for her.

❧ ❧

And then the heat comes: the white heat of summer, impossible to escape from, except in the early hours of the morning. It lasts all day and deep into the night and it isn't even summer yet. Everyone is irritable, the children most of all. They are tired of the same old nursery games and forbidden from going outdoors during the peak hours. After only a few minutes outside, they are drenched in sweat and covered with dust. Soon they have violet circles under their eyes, as if they have been persecuted by insomnia. Their cheeks are as pale as winter.

Bianca doesn't have time for them. She feels sorry for this, but she has to finish a series of hydrangeas before they lose their freshness. She knows that in August the plants will be faded and although she prefers them that way, rather than as they are now, with their big, tousled pink and green heads, her portraits are meant to capture subjects across their lifespan, not only during one interesting state of decay. If it had been up to her, she would have willingly set aside the assignment in favour of a brief holiday. She can think of many ways of entertaining the little ones far better than Nanny is doing.

Bianca smiles to herself as she prepares her colours. She remembers how easy it had been to say goodbye to a governess once she had been used up, and how exciting it had been to wait for a new one to arrive, descending from the sky, equipped with a flowery carpet bag of new tricks and distractions. It is time for Nanny, the poor thing, to change her lifestyle and get married. But how will she find a husband? She should forget about Innes. Tarcisio is the one. Tarcisio would be perfect for her. He is a peasant, yes, but a landowner. He is independent, not shy and clumsy like the others, and he has a certain rugged handsomeness thanks to his impossibly blue eyes. What magnificent children they would have with Nanny's copper-coloured hair, the only remarkable thing that she possesses. Bianca shakes her head, scolding herself. But then she starts in again. The game is irresistible. The pair could live in that little house beyond the town walls. It is small but fair. All it needs is a fresh coat of paint, maybe a nice pink, like the shade they use for homes at the lake. She wonders how pink will look against that landscape. Surely Nanny could afford to buy a new outfit too, perhaps in a light grey, a skirt with a fitted jacket that accentuates her waist and plumps up her flat chest. Bianca begins to draw the outfit she envisions: the skirt fluttering at the bottom, a braided row in front, on her head a simple hat held in place

by a knot under her chin, and a small bouquet of three blos-
soming peonies surrounded by magnolia leaves.

If I ever grow tired of flowers, Bianca thinks, *I can devote my
time to fashion.*

The problem with Bianca's work is that when she finishes
the flowers, she has too much time left over for thinking. And
desiring. She wonders what the watermill is like at this time of
year, if the water is still green and translucent like the fountain
of Melusina. She has no time to go there though, no time at all.
The hydrangeas call out to her.

Sometimes, at dusk, a small procession of carriages come
from the city, friends in search of cool air, who pass the evenings fanning themselves and watching the ice gems from the ice
chamber melt in their glasses. Even their conversations seem
limp and tired. By the end of the season, all the gossip has dried
up. Not even Bernocchi is able to scrape a scandal together.
Don Dionisio gets older and sicker. He has to stop every three
steps to catch his breath. Pia is always nearby, ready to offer
him a cool beverage.

Essentially, nothing really happens. If Bianca was a little
older, she would know that this is how a storm announces itself.
A bubble of still air pushes forward, a river of emptiness is
created, and then things fall apart. Attention is lax and omens
fade. Later, she will say that it has all been predictable, and
therefore avoidable. Later still, she will tell herself that no good
comes of thinking that way. It has happened and nothing can
be made right again.

🙞 🙜

It is an accident. These things happen in a household full of
children. A ball made of Florentine leather – this time a real
one – flies through the open French window and crashes into

the glass bell jar that sits on the mantelpiece above the French fireplace. The objects under the bell jar are also French. Donna Clara has told their stories countless times; they are relics from a life that seems to belong to someone else, far off in the distant past. They are neither beautiful nor ugly, and of value only to the person who owns them. They are small, motionless things of questionable taste. There is a stuffed dove, its marble eyes fixed on nothing. There are some gesso flowers and fruit created by Garnier Valletti of Turin, based on certain garden fruits of the Hesperides. And finally, there is a miniature tree, which in reality is merely a small branch shaped like a tree trunk. From it hang three small, straw-like garlands in pale, almost unnatural colours: one blonde, one nearly grey, and one almost white. They are three locks of Carlo's hair that have been cut at different times of his life. The last lock of hair was cut shortly before his death.

The ball crashes into the room and sends these grim relics and shards of broken crystal flying across the floor. The little dove is bent out of shape but continues to clutch at its branch with an odd arrogance. The strands are scattered, and the fruit chipped. Donna Clara, attracted by the clamour like a fly to honey, stands immobile in the doorway. She covers her ears with her hands, as if she does not want to hear any explanations. The maids come running and then disperse to find brooms and dust pans. Bianca, who has been arranging flowers in the foyer, finds Donna Clara on the floor like a bent black tulip. In trying to retrieve the hairs, she has scratched her finger and her blood drips on the white strands, resealing an ancient pact.

The cause was a naughty child. Though it was not done deliberately, Pietro is sent to his room without dinner, even if it is only three in the afternoon and dinner still an eternity away. He stays in the nursery until the following day. When he emerges, he is not at all penitent. It was just an old decoration, wasn't it?

Giulietta asks for the white dove before it is thrown away, and it is given to her. From that day forward, she carries it in the pocket of her smock or between her fingers. She doesn't want it to fly off, as birds have a habit of doing.

❧ ❧

The weather changes. A heavy nocturnal downpour brings forth the summertime in its full force but the following morning the park is in ruins. Broken branches, flower heads, and torn leaves sprinkle the great lawn. Matilde comes running.

'Look what I found,' she says, proudly dangling a small dead country mouse by the tail. Nanny draws back – *quelle horreur* – but she is the only one to do so. Everyone else is spellbound by the creature's perfect little body, its damp fuzz, the delicate pink fringe around its closed eyes, and its miniature paws.

'Should we give him a funeral?'

Enrico manages to obtain a gold-bordered chasuble from the church sexton. He runs back to them wearing it, holding up the long tunic with one hand so as not to trip. He stops, lets go of the folds, and recomposes himself, opening his arms and broadcasting pagan blessings for the deceased.

'Can I say a prayer?' Francesca asks. 'Dear Mouse, I hope that you are happier in Paradise than you were here. You died young and you didn't know very much. I hope a piece of cheese waits for you in heaven. Amen.'

'Amen,' everyone replies and they bury the little mouse in a box beneath a bush of *Olea fragrans*, where he will not be forgotten.

Besides this small loss, the world cannot be better aligned.

In the time it takes the gardeners to tidy up after the storm's damage, the sun has dried the garden. The rain leaves everything green and crisp, as if it is springtime. Nature is restored to a glistening state and the timing cannot have been better: they have to prepare for the estate's annual reopening festivities. Truthfully, the ladies would choose not to have a party, but their friends are expecting one.

'It has to take place,' the poet says in his strict manner. 'And I have a reason for it. It is a secret reason. Be patient, and you will find out.'

Everyone does their part to help. Donna Clara, pleased to be in charge once again, declares that the house, although it has been properly cleaned after their arrival, needs to be scrubbed again from top to bottom, eliminating every hint of dust and spider's web.

Donna Julie is still tired. The heat has taken its toll on her and the thunderstorm hasn't been enough to restore her strength. In any case, taking charge is not something she is good at. Instead, she relaxes in the shade of the sycamore tree, resting beneath its sweeping, low branches on a new chaise-longue made of braided straw and light-coloured wood   a homecoming gift from her husband. Bianca has sought refuge in that spot many times herself before the arrival of the chair. The location makes it easy to forget about the surrounding world.

The children run off in all directions to rediscover the estate, which still appears surprisingly new to them, though a tad smaller. In the back of the house, through half-open windows, Donna Clara can be heard commanding her troops through organized chaos.

Bianca seeks out her own hiding space. The greenhouse has suffered damage from the hail and many of the windowpanes have been shattered. She sweeps up the pieces of glass and moves the plants around, which leaves her a luminous, ventilated and sheltered space. It is one of those rare instances where a loss becomes an advantage, at least until the windowpanes are replaced and the greenhouse will go back to serving its intended purpose as a warm, damp, stifling place. At that point Bianca will have to find another refuge. Meanwhile, she stays there and works. She feels somewhat lazy, which is unusual for her and which she blames on the tantrums of the weather, just like everyone else.

She is in the greenhouse when she receives a letter. The big celebration is only two days away and the letter announces that she too will have a visitor. Bianca reads it, looks around, rereads it, and puts it away. She fixes her hair as if to organize her thoughts, picks up the missive, and goes to search for the mistress of the house.

❧ ❧

'He will be our guest of honour,' is Donna Clara's dutiful answer to Bianca. But there is also a vein of sincere curiosity. 'Are you saying that he will bring his military attaché with him? Interesting. Just so you know, I have always preferred Minerva to Mars. As far as my son is concerned, I am sure you know how he feels . . . and one of these days he's going to get all of us into trouble with his crazy ideas. But of course, your brother will be welcome in our household, whatever his uniform may be. Did you say that you look alike? No? That's too bad. Attilia, two more bedrooms need to be prepared in the west wing. Now, if you'll excuse me . . .'

Bianca listens as Donna Clara gives more orders.

'You have plates to dust and silverware to polish. Be careful of the Chinese vases! Have the floors been waxed? And what about the quails' eggs? Can someone please tell me if the quails' eggs have been delivered?'

ஃ ஃ

Zeno looks so handsome in his uniform. He had brought it with him in his trunk, neatly folded away, so he could secretly show it off to his sister. The red jacket accentuates his blond hair and the blue of his childlike eyes. *Or perhaps*, thinks Bianca, pushing him back so she can get a better look at him, *I will always see him as a child*. Tassels and ribbons on his cap create a crown of almost feminine complexity that borders on the ridiculous and must surely be uncomfortable. But perhaps one actually goes to battle in rags, half naked like savages, leaving those lofty hats behind.

'You seem happy,' she says and he takes her by the waist and spins her around.

'I am, dear sister. This is what I wanted. You, on the other hand, seem as light as a fairy. Don't these barbarians feed you?'

She places a hand on his mouth to silence him and together they laugh. She hasn't felt so happy in centuries, it seems. So much at home, and at ease. But there isn't much time for intimacies. He and his friend, Paolo Nittis, a tall and slender soldier with a coiffed moustache and shiny hair and who cannot take his dark eyes off her, have arrived in the middle of the afternoon and at the height of the preparations.

'Have you a nice room for me, my trusted valet?' Zeno asks with a smile as she accompanies them to their quarters.

Because of the heat, she has left all the flower arrangements until last. The cut flowers wait for her in a washtub full of water and ice. She dips her hands in fearlessly, allowing the cold to move up her wrists through her body, like a long shiver, until it reaches her head. *I will do the flowers,* she thinks, *then go upstairs, get changed, come back down and celebrate.*

❧ ❧

It is the beginning of summer, the night of San Giovanni, the night damsels wait for a sign from the heavens to tell them their lot in love. A year ago she felt out of place and ran away from that celebration to follow the calling of another. Now she will do differently. She is more at home in this small world. She can allow herself to have some fun, can't she?

Once she is back in her bedroom, she peels a small pear that she has stolen from a triumphant display in the house's entrance, throws the peel over her shoulder, turns around, and attempts to decipher the letter that the peel forms. Is it a P, B or D? She would appreciate some help in understanding. Then: *What of it?* she thinks. *My little brother is here and we will laugh and dance. It doesn't matter if there are no other cavaliers for me. We will talk together on the great lawn in the torchlight; we will drink sparkling wine, and in silence we will promise each other things, as lovers do. And it will be all right if the promises are not kept.*

Before leaving the city, Bianca made time to visit Signora Gandini's shop to order two summer dresses. She has paid for them with her hard-earned cash and because of this they seem like the most beautiful dresses in the entire world. It is difficult for her to decide now which one to wear. She almost misses the days when she owned only one elegant gown, the one she wore for her eighteenth birthday. Perhaps she should wear it: the white muslin double-skirted dress of plumetis. Although it is starting to become a bit tight across her chest. No, no, she will wear one of her new gowns. Should she wear the antique rose or the jade green? She knows that the pink one makes her features softer – even the milliner has said so. She has unstitched some of the roses that the seamstress placed at the neckline because she finds them too girly. The other dress accentuates the colour of her eyes, though, and she is almost certain that no one else will be wearing that style.

'Very few girls can wear this sort of dress. It makes most of them look like fish, or ghosts. But not you. You were born to wear green.'

And so she opts for the jade. It has a high waist in the Paolina fashion, which seems destined to last forever, and a thin, triple-braided ribbon that falls down her side for almost the whole length of the dress, becoming untied at the very end.

'You are the perfect model for this dress,' Signora Gandini had said. The neckline is square, generous, almost daring. 'Only girls with a little bosom can wear this.'

Et voilà, a defect has been transformed into a virtue by way of fashion. She's had three minuscule flowers for her chignon made from tightly rolled-up pieces of the same fabric. She needs Minna or Pia to help her with them. But where are they?

Bianca draws closer to the window, still barefoot and impatient. She is just in time to see Count Bernocchi descending from his coach, making it rock dangerously from side to side. He looks up towards the facade, sees her, smiles, and gives a quick bow. Bianca draws back, hoping he might mistake her for a curtain. Perhaps he hasn't recognized her and only wishes he had seen her. She feels her cheeks burn. Bernocchi has become so insistent of late. He calls her a 'beautiful little flower'. He even sent her a complete garden of sugared almonds, replete with petals and leaves, which had aroused admiration from them all, especially from certain hungry family members who had wolfed them down. He tries to make time with her alone, and Bianca avoids him as much as possible. She flees from his ambushes in the corridors. And when they are in the presence of others, which is almost always, he stares at her with big, rheumy eyes that make her almost miss his sardonic look. Even Donna Julie notices his strange silences.

'Did the cat get your tongue?' she asked once.

Now Bianca turns her attention back to the pear skin lying on the floor. B for Bernocchi, with a big belly, she thinks. But P for Paolo, Zeno's tall friend. Solemn and composed, the soldier's gaze burned straight through her. He had one of those dark stares that are hard to read.

'Did you know, my dear sister,' her brother said, 'that all Sardinians are dwarfs except this one? Where do you come from, my friend, the land of Snow White?'

Paolo's answer was a blinding smile.

P is also for poet. But the poet only stares at her in silence. Behind his impenetrable eyes is an entire world, a world in which there is no dancing, only fighting for causes worth fighting for. His weapons are words sharpened in anger.

There is a letter for everyone's name and yet not one is right. Bianca's heart sings the easy song of youth, of blood coursing through her veins, of a new dress and beautiful new jade-green shoes. She wears a bracelet of tiny white roses which she has made herself, and which she, without the help of Minna or Pia, has to tie around her left wrist. *No one will have jewels like this; I am the lady of the flowers.* And she wears one more thing: her mother's earrings, tiny pearls like droplets falling from two golden knots. 'Knots of true love,' her father said when he handed her that gift, 'the love of which you are a sign.'

That night, Bianca skips down the stairs as if she is flying. She slows down as she reaches the foyer with its hundreds of candles and takes one step at a time, as though the dancing has already commenced. Outside, the dusk creates puddles of near darkness where the trees are low and thick. Happy swallows scribble across the still light-blue sky above the sycamore tree.

Bernocchi, thankfully, is out of sight. Zeno and Paolo look up and watch her descend the stairs, as one does for a young woman. And when she reaches the last step they bow to her and take her by the arms, one on each side, two glowing escorts in white and blue.

'You are truly enchanting,' whispers Paolo, his eyes fixed on her.

'That's enough, you. She's just a girl,' Zeno says, his voice rising. It is the first time he has ever protected her. He is the younger of the two, after all.

'Shh.' She silences both of them, feeling superior and exquisite.

Bianca frees herself and walks in front of them to the dining room, where, by Donna Clara's instruction, a modern buffet has been prepared. She has done well in choosing her green dress, she thinks with a hint of frivolity, because the room, which is two or three tones darker, is an ideal background for her. She has to stop thinking like this. It isn't her party. It is an occasion to celebrate the beginning of summer, the reopening of the house, and the secret announcement – which is no secret at all – regarding the upcoming publication of Don Titta's novel.

Indeed, it is really a party for the poet-turned-writer and for his wife, who has patiently stood at his side through turbulent times, almost dying while doing so. But that's what a writer's wife has to do, is it not? Or perhaps that is the role of any wife.

Donna Julie looks ravishing in an ivory silk gown that contrasts sharply with her dark hair, which she wears down for once, straightened with care in two *bandeaux* with only a couple of rebellious curls. Fixed to her hair is a small bunch of tiny flowers (so that's where Minna and Pia have been). The whole effect makes her look like a delicate bird. Hanging from her long, white neck – devoid of the usual foulard that protects her from the cold – is a cross of diamonds, her only adornment.

Donna Clara, on the other hand, parades all of her rings and pendants, including a long *chevalière* that hangs over the generous shelf of her chest before falling into nothing.

'Are those the keys to the heavenly kingdom?' Bernocchi asks, covering his venomous mouth with one hand, his eyes enraptured by the perpetual movement of her golden key pendants. He is far enough away for Donna Clara not to hear him, but the others do.

Bianca feigns indifference but secretly she smirks. Everyone knows that they are in fact the keys to the now-silent harpsichord and to the crystal box in which Donna Clara keeps her most precious relics. Or so they say. Who knows if she has now added the dead man's hair to that pile, Bianca asks herself with a shiver of horror.

And then she stops thinking. She laughs, dances, drinks, dances again, drinks again, laughs, drinks some more, runs, blushes, pales, and dances. She travels from one cluster of guests to another, tirelessly. She talks, answers and quips, as lively as ever. During the formation dancing, Zeno whispers to her.

'Is this really you, sis? I didn't think you were so worldly.'

'I'm not, in fact.'

'I thought you had come here to work, not to learn new dances or how to become a coquette ... Who is that man pouting over there? He's been staring at you all night.'

Tommaso's face floats over the large knot of his white tie. He stands to the wall as if nailed.

'The dances aren't new. And I'm not a coquette!'

'But you are new indeed.'

'Hush, hush.'

And yet, perhaps Zeno is right. It was one of those moments that make her feel as though something has just changed, or has to change. She gallops forward in dance.

Am I really altered? she asks herself in a moment of rest, fiddling with a lock of hair that has fallen out of her chignon, standing in front of one of the tall nebulous mirrors at the entrance. Perhaps it is the stain of time on the glass, or the light from the chandelier, but she really does look different. She looks back at herself impudently, without ceasing to fix her hair. This Bianca is less *bianca* and more lively and green, like one of her rare hellebores. She is a winter flower: she has survived the frost, and has lifted her nonchalant head from the cold to look around, deciding she likes the world the way it is and that she will stay a while.

All this takes place in a moment. Suddenly, a tall shape appears in the reflection behind her. A man wrapped in shadow or perhaps a cloak. No, it isn't a cloak. This isn't the season for cloaks. Who is it? The shadowy figure disappears but not before giving her an indiscreet look, a look that disturbs her greatly, even if her shoulders are covered, her neckline is conservative, and her ankles are not visible. For a moment, Bianca feels stripped bare. She blushes to the roots of her hair and waits for the flush to subside before rejoining the guests.

Her embarrassment lasts only a moment, though, and she soon feels the pleasurable warmth that rises when one has danced much, drunk a great deal and been admired by many. Thanks to her slight intoxication, Bianca jokes with self-confidence. She flees artfully from Signora Villoresi with a polite curtsey. The lady wants to commission a set of dead leaves – that's exactly how she says it, a set, as if she is dealing with a service of dessert forks. No work tonight. But Bianca forgets that the reason she is there, and not dressed as a Nanny or a tutor, is thanks to those dead leaves. Foolish Bianca, for whom one glass of sweet wine and a sugared compliment are enough for her to forget who she is. But who is she really? She is a girl on her own who feels like having fun. Who can blame her? Donna Clara and Donna Julie would warn her if they could read her heart. With the wisdom gleaned from the experience of the one and the calm erudition of the other, they would tell her that too much light is deadly for nocturnal butterflies. But she wouldn't listen. She would nod her head, yes, but close off her heart. Her ears hear the music summoning her again. She contemplates the couples whirling across the large stage of smooth wood, positioned at the foot of the stairs.

'Care for another dance, Miss Bianca?'

It is too late to avoid Bernocchi without being rude. She shouldn't be, it wouldn't be proper. And she has to admit, he does know how to dance. He focuses so hard on it that he doesn't have time to chat, which is helpful. Bianca eyes his chubby ankles, his shoes of yellow damask that look as though they have been cut from the coat of a reptile, and feels his perspiring hand tight on her back, even through the shield of her clothes. Now it is time to change partners. Her new partner places his hand on her waist – light and airy this time. He doesn't dance as well, but he is handsome and tall. It is Paolo Nittis from Sassari, which has to be a city full of snakes and stones, with all those S sounds to its name. She wonders if all Sardinians have eyes the colour of spilled ink. Since he is the first she has ever encountered, which feels a little like seeing an exotic bird in an enclosure, she asks him. He blinks, as though he hasn't understood, and then smiles, revealing his white teeth.

'Come see for yourself with your own eyes,' he laughs. 'My land is wild and untamed.'

'And you?'

He seems to find her question amusing.

'I'd say I have been domesticated, by now. My uniform has helped a great deal.'

'Oh, what a pity. I have enough domesticated puppies around here to keep me company.'

Nittis casts a quick glance around the room at the men dressed in the latest style of frock coats, their hair combed back. Everyone looks the same, a pack of hounds.

'Woof!' laughs Bianca. She feels Nittis's hand release her and suddenly she is in someone else's more familiar grasp. She has never danced with Innes, but it is as if she has always done so.

'Tonight I like you more than usual, Miss Bianca. You are bold.'

They share that same sublime, dry precision of the language.

Bianca looks up towards the facade of the house, certain that Nanny is peering out of one of the windows, protected by the darkness. Governesses, poor creatures, are only invited to parties in novels. They wear new dresses and flowers in their hair, and stay seated all night long. They lose their gloves and stain themselves with lemonade. *I am not a poor thing. I am not a governess. I am a free woman, I know how to read, how to write, how to do arithmetic, how to draw, how to uncover mysteries and solve riddles . . .*

'What are you thinking about?'

The question seems banal, but Bianca has had enough practice in navigating salons to know that banal and silly questions do not really exist. Only banal answers.

'I am thinking about how fortunate I am,' she answers, looking up at Innes both because the difference in height requires her to do so and because she wants to see his reaction.

'I think so too,' he says. 'But fortune is cultivated in the greenhouse, you know. It is a rare flower that doesn't last.'

'Please do not speak of flowers. Not tonight, I beg you.'

'Is our gardener on her way out? Has she hung up her gloves and apron?'

Together they smile. It is lovely to be made fun of without needing to take offence. How different that same phrase would be if Bernocchi had spoken it. But Innes can say anything to her. Why is this so?

'What are we, you and I?'

He understands her immediately and grows serious.

'Brothers. Neighbours of the house and of the spirit. Accomplices.'

'Friends?'

'That's different.'

She bites her lip and then curtseys, as required by the dance. If she could, she would hug him. *Perhaps this is the first time, in all my life, that I feel at home,* she thinks. *Does that mean this is the right place for me? Is this my place in the world?* Thoughts scatter, like frightened birds. A moment, and then all that is left is a lingering intuition and the disappointment of not having seized it.

Suddenly, the master of the house bows before her briefly and formally, as is his manner.

'May I have this dance?'

What an absurd question, Bianca thinks, letting herself be guided towards the centre of the stage. She would accept even if she were exhausted, even if all the guests had left and the house were empty, even if there was no more music. Sometimes, one doesn't have the right to say no. And anyway, a dancing poet?

'It's almost an oxymoron,' she thinks out loud. He looks at her without understanding. Thank goodness a good deal of the phrase had been lost to the orchestra.

He is, in fact, a decent dancer with a natural ability that can only have come from intense practice and habit at some point in his life. It is as if he ceased to dance only yesterday and is now ready to take it up again, although Bianca knows very well that this isn't the case.

She looks around her and everyone's faces appear the same: dilated smiles on dolls' heads. She sees Donna Clara's acute and questioning eyebrows, Donna Julie's innocent smile, Bernocchi's smirk, Don Dionisio's mild indifference, Tommaso's paleness, and all the others – perplexed, curious, ironic.

'What about your wife?' Bianca asks suddenly, worried about conventions. He still hasn't asked Donna Julie to dance. He started off the evening by accompanying his mother.

'She never learned to dance,' he replies.

She thinks about Donna Julie: her modest ways, her sober clothes, her lowered gaze, prayers and fasts. Bianca has heard the story many times in the maids' quarters. His mother chose this wife for him, a fresh young girl ready to marry; she was young and rich, from a good and pious family, ready to move from one cloister to another. He loves her, though. It is evident. He looks for her now, they exchange a spark of understanding, and he keeps on dancing.

Earlier, when he made his announcement, it was the same. Donna Julie did not stand by his side. She placed herself in a part of the salon that allowed her to survey everyone and everything. Invisible, yet always present. He gave her a look before signalling to the musicians to fade out the polka. The guests interrupted their dancing and gathered around the French window. He made his way forward, creating an empty space at the centre of the hall.

'Friends,' he said, 'you are here because it is the beginning of summer, because we have returned to our much-loved Brusuglio and because we want to share with you the joys of the season before they turn to suffering – the light kind of suffering that nature inflicts on us. In fact, I am pleased to say that we were able to eliminate all the mosquitoes for tonight's celebration.' People laughed and he continued.

'We have also been able to summon a light breeze to comfort the warm bodies of those who love dancing. We know that it won't last. There will be heatwaves and crops to think about. But those are my concerns. You know that I am a country poet – and perhaps more country than poet – that's up to you to decide.' More laughter.

'But there's another reason I have invited you here. Many of you know that for years now I have been working on a project that has absorbed my days and nights. Some people called me mad, and perhaps they are right. But my feat is finally over, and I will now begin the second part of my adventure. In September, my historical novel will be published.'

Applause.

'And then I hope that someone will read it.'

Laughter.

'Actually, no, I hope that people will purchase it – either out of curiosity or simply to see what has gone through this madman's head. Ultimately, I only want people to buy it. I don't even care if they read it!'

More laughter.

'I know that many of you appreciate me as a poet. Recently, the poet in me has become a sort of youthful brother to consider with the kind of indulgence we tend to reserve for young people. Let us bid him farewell. Let us say that he's leaving for a journey abroad, from which he will return changed, unrecognizable. Or perhaps he won't come back at all. I invite you now to discover the writer, the older brother, raised by the severe schooling of life and certain to have at least one story to tell.'

'And you – where are you in all this?' someone called out, bringing more laughter.

'Oh, at the moment I am in Brusuglio, where the land and my family summon me and ask me to be both of the soil and father of family.'

Applause followed and trays of drinks were passed so that they could toast.

'To our friend Titta, who always knows how to amaze us.'

'To the poet we won't forget.'

'To the novelist we want to get to know.'

Other whispered sentences were hidden behind sips of white wine, phrases uttered in a tone that showed more concern than criticism.

'Is he sure about what he's doing?'

'How much will it cost him? To self publish, what an idea! It will be his ruin, trust me.'

'And his family? How will he maintain them while he waits for his glory to arrive?'

'With what it costs to keep up this house . . .'

The comments she heard expressed mild unease but were not malicious. The poet truly has many friends, Bianca thinks as they dance. She wishes she could ask him, as one friend to another, if he really is serene. She wants to know if he thinks he has done the right thing. She wants to ask what the novel is actually about. She wants to tell him that Enrico, more than any of his other children, needs him as a guide and a companion; that he is being spoiled by his mother and grandmother and turning into a whiny brat. She wants to tell him that the girls shouldn't be mollycoddled and should have more independence. They are fun and intelligent. They deserve more attention and more ample horizons than the ones framed by the windows of their nursery. But it isn't the right moment to do so. If he is really going to dedicate himself to the countryside with vigour, there will be other opportunities. Everything is possible and even more so now. She should be happy to have him close by. He ends the dance with a bow and a farewell, but holds onto her fingers for a moment longer than necessary.

'Thank you. Really,' he whispers.

What is he thanking her for? Bianca will never know.

❧ ❧

He takes her by the hand without saying a word, imperiously, like someone with the right to do so. She says nothing. He leads her quietly up the stairs, careful in his movements so as not to bump into columns or the decorative objects on top of them. He opens the door to a room that is bound to be empty at this hour and then closes it behind them. Windows of moonlight illuminate the pavement. Someone has forgotten to draw the curtains, which is not new for this room. The shadows in the darkness are phosphorescent, luminous. The lightness of his first kiss melts her lips like a snowflake in a child's palm. The fabric roses in her hair get caught in a cuff. They are ready to come undone and surrender, one petal at a time. *Where should I put my nose? Here.* That is good. His mouth is good too. She imagines the secret obscurity inside, the flash of her tongue on his teeth; she can taste traces of tobacco and alcohol – an aroma light enough to be pleasing. *Do I taste good?* She thinks back to when she was little and how she would bite flower petals to see whether they tasted the same way they smelled. They all tasted like green. *I'd like to taste like a flower. It would be logical.*

Should I stop and defend myself? Should I? I still can. I should shield myself with armour. Armour – what a metallic-sounding word. She imagines a flimsy sword. She pictures herself brandishing a flower for protection. From what? From a kiss? No, he isn't dangerous. *It* isn't dangerous. It isn't. When one kisses one ceases to think. And that's all.

But this isn't love. This is something that resembles it, a copy, a surrogate. Love, the real thing, has to be something else. It *is* something else, something impossible; it belongs to that other man, the man that belongs to another woman, the master of the house, unattainable. *That which we cannot have is perfect, intact and incorrupt.* For now, she will take what comes her way, what she is offered, because this is youth, it is frightening, and it makes her feel good. Because: yes.

What follows is not what she expected or even wanted. She wants to say no at that point, to leave, deny everything, and return to the coy games, glances, or even just to the kissing. By the time this occurs to her, it is too late.

No, this isn't love, this rubbing of fabric against fabric, this warm and rugged fumbling. Fingers, fingers everywhere. Hands touching places where no stranger's hand has ever been. A strained gasp. To want and not to want. Here, this, where, what, why. And then the pain: piercing, tearing, leaving her breathless, unceasing, insistent, like pain without compassion, a rasping of flesh inside flesh. *No, not like that, no.* But words are useless. Nothing changes.

Her other self, silent and composed, watches from afar. Her eyes are pools of pity. *Why pity? What if this is actually what it is like? What if it is supposed to be like this?* She doesn't know any more.

She continues to listen to the agony stampeding inside her, nailing her to the wall, snatching from her very throat a sound that doesn't belong to her. It isn't her voice; it is neither laughter nor lament. It is a horrible sound, the sound of a wild beast suffering, nothing more. *How long will it go on for? Will it ever stop?*

And later, when it is finally over and the folds of her dress cover her wound, the question lingers: is this love?

Of course not. It is what it is.

He rests a hand on her cheek almost out of pity. She would feel anger for that if only anger could make its way forward through the thick confusion. And then he leaves, shutting the door behind him soundlessly. She is alone in the semi-darkness, somewhere between the doll's house and the window's luminous rectangle. She slides down the wall to the floor and slumps over like a wilted flower. And then she cries.

❦ ❦

Everyone has left. The house sleeps a satisfied sleep charged with success. But here and there is work to be done. The musicians drink mulled wine outside the kitchen. Bianca can smell its sharp wintry scent from the dark hallway.

'It's June but it doesn't feel like it,' one of them says. 'We shouldn't have played outdoors. My violin has rheumatism and so does my shoulder.'

'True, but in rich people's houses it is always summer,' comments another musician.

'Only us poor folk know about seasons.'

A female voice speaks, low and rugged, from inside the kitchen. 'You really think of what you do as work?'

'It depends on one's point of view,' says the first violinist in a tired tone. 'May we have some more wine? And a warm pie, one of the leftover ones? Or have you eaten them all up? You cook for an army at these parties. It's as if they never ate. Thank you, you're a good woman, and an excellent chef. Don't you, perchance, desire a husband who can play?'

'I have one already, but I am the one who plays the instrument, when needs be.'

Laughter and then silence.

Bianca slips into the darkness. She would like some mulled wine. Or maybe not. No more wine. Never again. She opens the French window and walks down the steps. At this hour, the forest has not yet made up its mind about what it will become. It has the purity of a print scored with ferocious black shadows. Not even the forest can promise or guarantee peace. Is there peace on this earth?

No.

Bianca turns around, thrown by a presence behind her. It is Nanny. She is evidently very worked up as she has forgotten to put her robe over her flannel nightgown. Nanny, who always feels cold, now stands barefoot. Bianca notes all the details, including the two fleshy shells that poke out of her braided hair: Nanny has big ears. Bonnets, however silly they seem, serve their miserable purpose.

Nanny claws at Bianca's arm and shakes her.

'Have you seen her?'

She cannot imagine which of the three girls is missing.

'Francesca has disappeared,' Nanny adds coarsely. 'I heard a noise; I got up and went to look in their bedroom . . . She's nowhere to be found.'

* * *

They find her body in the brook. She has been carried downstream by the current for more than two miles. Unable to drag her any further, the water has left her there, like a broken doll, her head bumping against the wooden dyke, her nightgown sticking to her skin. Her eyes are open, her tiny face serene. It is not yet dawn.

❧ ❧

Later, Giulietta tries to explain.

'We went down to the brook together yesterday afternoon. Alone. There was so much confusion and no one was looking after us.'

Everyone glances at Nanny but it isn't her fault. They recruited her in the kitchen and she couldn't be in two places at once.

'She wanted to learn how to swim like me so that she could show everyone and prove that she was a big girl. She had almost learned. She almost didn't sink under the water any more.'

And then? The questioning continues as if adding more details will help clarify, correct and soften.

'And then we got tired. Matilde didn't want to walk any more and I had to carry her. She even fell asleep. We changed our clothes. Nanny came and fed us dinner early and then we went down to greet the guests.'

The girls wore identical mauve dresses tied at the waist with violet ribbons. They left their hair down, which was unusual for them, and wore headbands. Francesca's band kept slipping down onto her face like a pirate's bandana. Her hair was very fine and had recently been washed by the fresh water of the brook.

'Mamma let us have one dessert each. I chose the pastry with the raspberries and she chose a *petit four* with a pistachio on top. She got her whole face messy with cream but no one scolded her.'

Children get lost in the details. Adults are indulgent when they have something else on their minds. *Oh, Franceschina, what a messy girl you are! You look like a clown. You're so funny. Isn't that right? Isn't she funny? Our little star. Now up you go. It's bedtime, girls.*

'And then Nanny came down to get us,' she continues.

Bianca remembers how Nanny came out of the shadows in her ugly, dark silk dress, not at all fit for a party.

'And she brought us to bed. I fell asleep right away. I was so tired. Matilde, too.'

There is a pause. She looks at their tense faces, searching desperately for approval.

'Then the dark man came in. It must have been him.'

If only there had been a dark man. If only one of the statues had awoken and descended from its pedestal to vindicate some ancient wrongdoing. If only there had been a faceless monster that could be held responsible for all of this.

Bianca has no difficulty imagining what happened. The little girl was restless and couldn't fall asleep because of the sounds from the party: the music, the chatter, the laughter. She got up and went to the playroom window, the one protected by bars – a prudent yet useless measure – and sat on her knees and watched. She looked down on the great lawn from above; a splotch of darkness delineated by stains of light. There was beautiful Mamma, and Miss Bianca in green (a play on words like the ones she always enjoyed). There was Papa, at the centre of the crowd. Everyone looked as tall and dark as he did, as they laughed, drank and talked. *Sometimes, my papa makes other people laugh,* she must have thought. *If I learn to swim, he will be happy. Miss Bianca will be happy too. Everyone will be happy because it's something only big boys do. I could go and practise and stay up all night trying. No one will see me. I will learn how and then tomorrow I will show everyone. I will say: I have a surprise for you. Come, come and watch me, and everyone will follow me like the children of the Pied Piper, and then I'll jump in and everyone will tell me how good I am, and that I was brave to learn all by myself. I can do it. The others are sleeping but I'm not scared. It's a bit dark but I'm not scared. The moon is bright enough for me.*

෮ ෮

It rains for a full two days. It is as if the sky is crying. If the sun dared come out, someone would extinguish it or shut it down, such is the sentiment in the air.

On the afternoon of the second day, Bianca finds herself in the nursery playroom without realizing how she has got there. It is empty. Donna Julie and Donna Clara don't want to leave the children. Bianca, though, doesn't think that being with two crying women will be good for them. If adults cry, there are no more rules; the world is upside down. Innocence is gone from the nursery. No one feels safe anywhere. Nothing is sacred; nothing can remain untouched, not even childhood. Bianca straightens an overturned chair. She closes the doll's house by shutting one of its facades onto the bewildered faces of its inhabitants. She goes over to the window with bars on it. There are fingerprints on the glass, a small hand, a palm print and five little fingers, open wide. There is no need to measure it to know that it is Franceschina's. She is the one who, on the night of the big storm, found the courage to look out at the world. Her sisters covered their ears with their hands, trying to shut out the sounds of thunder. Bianca tried to calm them down.

'It's just angels moving furniture. Even they get tired of the sky and like to change things around sometimes.'

Francesca was the only one who listened to her.

'What is their furniture like? Is it made of clouds? And if it is made of clouds, why do they make so much noise?'

She pushed the chair forward to test its own sound, until it bumped into an uneven brick and tipped over.

Farewell, Franceschina. You died young. You didn't have time to learn much. If you ever feel like moving a bedside table or chair, we will listen for the soft, distant thunder, not the frightening kind, and know that it is you.

For a moment Bianca thinks of calling in the child's mother and grandmother to show them that last trace of her, but then decides against it. There are already so many signs to erase: her doll, Teresa, with her dishevelled head of hair; her clothes in the wardrobe; her little shoes under the bed. Traces of her that need to disappear. They lead nowhere; there is no mystery to solve. They only speak loudly and boldly of the little girl's absence.

Bianca returns to her senses. As if awakening from a difficult sleep, she feels a moment of confusion. She senses that something is not right. There is something else, she remembers, and she feels embarrassed. She feels like a monster. That death, ugly and unjust to the umpteenth degree, is, in that instant, merely a painful distraction. It is like a terrible headache, the kind that makes her eyes hurt, that forces her to press her index fingers into her lids in order to feel more pain, hoping that one grief will cancel out the other.

By thinking about Franceschina, she does not think of herself. And, of course, there *is* no comparison. Franceschina is gone. There will never be another Franceschina. She, on the other hand, is alive. Thank God. Alive. Everything is still possible – forgetting and forgiving. Although these both seem so remote, she thinks of them as old accomplices that support and encourage one another. *Certain wounds heal,* she thinks.

And some do not. Downstairs is a woman with a wound that will never heal.

⁂ ⁂

Guilt hits her again like a backhanded slap, a kick in the stomach, a hand clenched around a heart. These feelings come to her cruelly and regularly. When it seems as though her cheek has lost its sting, her eye burns in its socket. When the depth of the punch has tapered off, her stomach is seized by anxiety. Although no one has ever accused her, she cannot forget that single playful swim that took place almost a year ago. Once she thinks she sees a slight look of disapproval in Pia's eyes. Although perhaps it is just fatigue. The meeting of two exhausted beings. Her eyes burn constantly. As soon as she finishes crying she is ready to start up again, to spill tears that can never wash away the grief, tears that fall like alcohol onto an open wound; that burn like fire in her flesh.

⁂ ⁂

'What does the death of a child really mean? When they're little, they're all the same: all children are promises. Whether the promises will be maintained, no one can know for certain. And how many did Donna Julie lose already? Two? Three? That didn't prevent her from bringing more life into this world. Isn't this a woman's trade? Everyone, ultimately, is capable of being a mother. So come now, all of us, let us remember that life awaits us.'

Fortunately, very few people actually hear Bernocchi's grim funeral oration. He mumbles it in a low voice from a pew at the back of the church. A few do hear, though, and no one wants to add anything.

Francesca was unique, as we all are. She had the right to

become her own person, as we all do. Bianca casts a glance at Bernocchi, who looks as empty as the void she feels inside. She then goes back to staring at the backs of the people in the front row, their shoulders hunched over, locked in their grief. Visitors have come from the city in a melancholic procession similar to the one of two nights earlier, wearing crêpe instead of muslin, black instead of white and pink. They come with puffy eyes, burning eyelids, and irritated skin due both to their suffering and to the cruel light of morning. But they will leave their grief there, with the flowers, the too-many flowers, all of them white and destined to wither under the too-brilliant sun. Once the guests return to their homes, they will feel discomfort mixed with relief; they will throw themselves with new vigour into everyday tasks because Death has passed them by. Father, mother and grandmother speak to no one after the ceremony. They walk slowly to the cemetery behind the coffin, which has been hoisted onto the shoulders of four peasant men but which is so small that one of them alone could carry it under his arm. Don Dionisio shields the family and shakes his head.

'I beg of you, please. The family wishes to be alone.'

Some guests climb back into their carriages immediately, a touch disappointed by the lack of show. Others linger in the church piazza, engaging in brief circumstantial conversations – they can't even remember which one Franceschina was. As Bernocchi has said, she was only a little girl.

'Shall we go to the tavern to drink something and refresh ourselves?' Signor Bignamini proposes.

Attilio is pleased to receive so many clients at such an odd hour. He hasn't even opened, but he quickly pulls the chairs down, pours some wine, and slices up some bread.

Bianca stands to the side with Innes and Minna. Pia whispers something into the elderly priest's ear. He nods and they hug farewell. He goes then to the cemetery while she stays behind.

'He says we should pray for acceptance,' she says. 'That the Lord sometimes does things that we can't understand. Things that not even he understands.'

The four of them quietly make their way back towards the villa. What is there left to say? Afterwards, the pall-bearers are given a glass of wine in the kitchen. They recount the devastating story of the cemetery. The tomb, which already houses the children Bernocchi spoke of that Donna Julie has lost – Battista, Andreina, and Vittorio: which makes three, not two as Bernocchi had suggested – had been opened to make room for the small coffin. Donna Clara gasping with tears and Donna Julie and Don Titta's frightening silence. The good-hearted maids cry when they hear this. The image of the little one, her habits and her fixations, is all too clear in their minds.

'She loved my almond pudding so much,' sighs the cook. 'She could have lived off it. She ate barely anything else, poor babe.'

'Do you remember when she didn't want us to break the chicken's neck? Remember how she tied a bow around it and looked after it as if it were a puppy?'

'And what about when she asked me if I would make a dress for her dolly that was identical to hers?'

Children's fancies are different, and yet all the same. Bianca walks out then and sits on the steps, her elbows on her knees, and looks at the garden and its unresponsive beauty. A small cloud hovers alone above the sycamore tree.

'What are we going to do?' she asks Innes, who in the meantime has sat down next to her.

'I don't know. We will keep on, I suppose. He has his novel, and thank goodness for that. A big world to fill his mind. She will become all the more apprehensive, poor thing. And Donna Clara . . . well, she will reclaim her post at the rudder. It will come easily to her. It's a big estate – there is so much to watch over and debts to oversee. She will put on her accounting gloves and her owl eyeglasses. That will be her distraction.'

Bianca wishes she could smile. She tries to but she feels as though her lips would crack. So she stops.

'And what about you?' she asks.

'Let's talk about you. Are you all right?' he says, changing the subject. Bianca feels him staring at her. She knows his gaze well. Without waiting for an answer, he continues. 'Sometimes the best way to confront grief is to stand still and wait for it to subside. To agitate oneself, to flee, is not worth it; it doesn't get rid of grief. It is better to give oneself time. Often, time can cure a wound that reason can't bring back to health. Seneca said that, not me,' he concludes and then looks straight ahead.

What if it really was that way? What if we could go back to our previous lives, to our habits, and to the natural rhythm of things, and let the tears slowly dry? In that very moment, Bianca wants only for nothing else to change. She wants her world to freeze, to be held still under a sheet of glass, like her leaves and flowers. The two of them look at each other. Perhaps he understands. Maybe not. He must be thinking back to her first question.

'I think that it would be a bad idea if I left now. But that doesn't necessarily mean that it is a bad idea in itself.'

Ah, here we go. Bianca knew it.

'You will be the first to know my decision, if this is indeed the case,' he concludes. 'We are fortunate: we can leave when we like, if we want to. This isn't our life. Turning our backs on all of this will be painful. But possible.'

He takes her hand and squeezes it. She does not pull away. She loves this tall, long-limbed man with his tumultuous thoughts and distracted gaze. She loves him and she trusts him more than any other man in this world.

Zeno, her adorable little brother with eyes as bright as the buttons on his uniform, left the night of the party, avoiding the tragedy. Nittis, with eyes like spilled ink, promising and elusive, left with him. Perhaps soldiers are all like that: they grab what they can find, take it with them, and run away. They are forgivable thieves, aware that sooner or later a bullet could catch them. We have to let them go. Innes, too, is a soldier, only he is in a dress shirt. He won't flee though; he is heading towards something that he desires, that still does not exist but which is possible. That is the difference. And Don Titta, so carefully drawn to his own standards, can go nowhere.

Bianca recalls a fragment of a conversation that took place one spring afternoon in the living room when all the windows were open.

'A writer or a poet possesses words, and for this reason he also possesses the things his words define,' Tommaso said, pressing the fingertips of his hands together in concentration.

'Correct,' Don Titta replied. 'If to possess is to know, then we who work with words understand and possess the world, or at least we make this ambition our daily goal. But to give things a name, my friend, makes us neither wise nor happy. If anything, it only makes us more aware.'

'You don't really think that we are put on this earth to be happy?' Tommaso asked almost scornfully.

'Every so often,' Don Titta replied, staring at his children as they ran on the gravel path. 'Every so often I like to deceive myself that it is so.'

'But if your happiness depends on others,' Tommaso countered, following his gaze, 'then you have little chance of preserving it.'

'What are you suggesting? That's it's sufficient for a stylite on top of a column to be happy? Or a monk in his hermitage? I want to be happy in the world,' Don Titta said.

'I, on the other hand, am content with the small world that is my study,' Tommaso replied.

'And here,' concluded Don Titta, 'our thoughts diverge. Believe me, we are nothing without love. And I speak of pure love, not the love that asks or deceives, but the love that gives and commits. We end up depending on it, it's true. And it depends on us. It creates connections. And connections are complications. But I want to be complicated, and of this world.'

He then stood up, opened the French window, and called out to Giulietta, who stopped what she was doing and ran into her father's arms.

In 'this world' Don Titta is the master of words, but in love he isn't any more a master of himself. He cannot go anywhere. Maybe he would like to, but his world is calling him, holding him back – it needs him. And now that world is inhabited by one small shadow more.

⁂

Bianca leafs through her folders, prepares her charcoals, ties on her apron, and sits down at the table inside the greenhouse. Nobody has repaired the damage to the glass yet and therefore it is still miraculously cool with currents of fresh air. But what is the point of portraying the lightness of the honeysuckle now? There are other things out there: the stain of lichens on the stone cheek of a *putto*; the sick symmetry of mushrooms that crawl like insects on a severed trunk; the vibrations of a spider's web, magnified and yet endangered by droplets of rain. A dirty, fragile, poisonous kind of grace. She wished that nothing would change; instead everything has been transformed.

Maybe it is her perspective, but suddenly she sees other, darker things where before there was only the pure, mild grace of a garden, cultivated with love. Beauty does nothing but take risks.

❧ ❧

It is strange how time ungoverned dilates and expands indifferently, stretching out and emptying the hours. Whereas before it was so important to fill time with rituals and rhythms that are just and necessary, now nothing matters. There is no work, there are no errands to run. They wait.

It is too early for people to force themselves to forget; the grief is so fresh that one can only relive it, amazed by its everlasting energy. Days and weeks go by. Not one event can disturb the surface of this void. What matters lies beneath and within, and it grows incessantly.

❧ ❧

Then, one evening, something happens.

There is the sound of confusion at the front door but no one pays it any attention. Everyone has taken a seat: one here, one there. It is an empty shell of an evening, just like the others, but Donna Clara has insisted and so they arrange themselves as directed. Only Donna Julie is missing, rightly excused from all obligations and formalities. Bianca looks towards the doorway. She thinks she is the only one who sees Ruggiero peek in, but no. Innes jumps to his feet and approaches the butler, who delivers a message to him in a whisper.

'We have visitors,' Innes announces. He looks at Don Titta, who raises his head sluggishly, as if it is unbearably heavy, and then lowers it again in silence. 'We need to get ready.'

Tommaso rises, walks towards the closed window, and

300

gently moves the curtain back. Donna Clara, hostile, watches him, as if it is his fault.

'Visitors? We were very clear when we stated—'

'I'm afraid these men won't listen to your requests,' Tommaso says, glancing back at the others. He is strangely vigilant, almost excited. He stands tall, with his hands in his pockets. The door to the sitting room opens.

'Lieutenant Colonel Steiner, of the Royal Imperial Army,' Ruggiero announces, stepping aside to present a blond, fairly young official with blue eyes and a neat appearance.

The master of the house rises slowly. Instead of walking towards the visitor, he turns to Tommaso, who stands looking out the window still, his back to the scene.

'May I help you?' Donna Clara spits from her place on the sofa, looking the official up and down.

'Good evening,' he says. His accent is heavy. He articulates every word. It takes a long time to put together a full sentence. 'In the name of his Majesty . . . information . . . search . . . documents . . .'

Bianca hears the man's speech emerge fragmented, with little meaning. She cannot tell if she is distracted or if the Colonel's Italian is truly pitiful. She looks at Innes and then at Tommaso; they both appear calm. Don Titta keeps his back turned, as if none of this concerns him. The moment feels long and drawn out, suspended in the air. Nothing happens. And then two soldiers appear behind the official, awaiting their instructions. From the clinking noise in the foyer, it is clear that there are others, too. They will spread out through the house, open drawers, throw books and flip over tables. It happened at the Maffei home, at the Confalonieris', the Galleranis', and even at Bernocchi's country house. It is a vicious game of dominos:

search, discover, and condemn. It is both expected and unavoidable. Bianca feels herself grow cold. The slow chill wraps around her, starting at her legs and fixing her to the sofa.

And then, just before the soldiers start to move in, a figure dressed all in white and ignited by pure willpower appears among the soldiers. It is Donna Julie. She ignores the strangers and walks straight past them, a tiny creature amid robust, meaty men.

'Titta,' she says. 'The children need you.'

It is as if he doesn't hear her.

'Titta,' she repeats, slightly louder this time. He finally turns and slowly walks towards his wife, puts an arm around her shoulder, and leads her away. The official stares at the couple, speechless. Who do they think they are, ignoring him like that?

'Perhaps I wasn't clear enough,' he says, then repeats his message. This time any hint of kindness has vanished from his voice. It is an error. It is Donna Clara's turn now to speak.

'This family,' says the old woman as she struggles to get up from her seat, clutching the armrest with both hands, 'has recently been struck with a loss. Look at us.' And with her hand she makes a wide gesture across the living room: dark clothing and despair. The official has a brief doubt: if this is a farce, it is well played. But what if it isn't? 'How could you have the gall to come here at a time like this?' Donna Clara continues. 'I will be sure to let the governor know. The Milanese nobility still counts for something in this tortured, upside-down world that doesn't even honour death. Leave us in peace. Leave, now. Immediately. Go.'

Lieutenant Colonel Steiner doesn't know how to respond. His informers are trusted sources; the spying took place weeks ago and in the meantime they have undergone all the necessary checks in order to avoid diplomatic incidents, in case the accusations turn out to be unfounded. Although they clearly aren't unfounded. And so Steiner has decided to act. Perhaps, if Donna Clara cried and wrung her hands, he wouldn't have pity on them. But their stone-like faces, the heavy dignity of grief that has brought the household to a standstill, their eyes – including those of the domestic help, who stare straight back at him instead of looking down in fear – cracks his self-confidence and zeal.

'I didn't know,' he says finally. 'I apologize.'

Much later, troubled by the thought of having made a mistake and thereby wasting an opportunity, he wonders whether it has all been staged. These Italians, he thinks, with their tendency to dramatize everything, you can never fully trust them. But he only needs to leaf through the newspapers to learn it has all been true and that he has behaved as a wretched slave of duty. But justice will take its course. How much time will he allow them to grieve? Not long. He needs to pound down his iron fist on these discontented traitors. They have everything and they have risked it all. It is too bad for them. They don't know what they are about to lose. If only they stayed in their living rooms and protected their young, there would be less trouble for everyone.

Meanwhile, at the house, the message has been received, loud and clear. The inevitable has arrived. Things will have to change, and not in the definitive and brilliant manner that they have worked towards in the darkness. Governments aren't toppling and declarations won't be made. No, this is not the time for a compromise. This is the time to perfect the art of the getaway. Only in this manner can order be restored, at least temporarily, at least for those who can get away. How much time do they have? No more than a week.

Many things happen in that week.

⚜ ⚜

'Young Tommaso left like a thief in the night.'

'He must have got scared.'

'He must have gone home to his mamma.'

'But they don't even talk to each other! He told me as much when he brought me his shirts. Rich people are strange, I tell you. I think that boy cared more for this family than for his own mother.'

'Well, why did he go back to his family in the end, then?'

'You know how it is: families unite in times of difficulty.'

'Oh, don't be a know-it-all. Tommaso was just a coward. In this house, rebels sip tea in the living room. In Tommaso Reda's house, they kiss the Austrian flag, so soldiers don't go there at night to knock things about and make a mess.'

'You're right. And guess who would have to clean up the mess?'

Voices bounce off one another, intersecting, insinuating, supposing, sentencing. The farmer speaks elegantly, the cook always knows the details, and the others, the extras, become animated only when no one else is looking at them. There is an indistinct hubbub of gestures and sounds. Bianca tries to soothe her headache by staying in bed, but in order not to hear them all she would have to close the window, and the fresh morning air feels good.

So, he has left. At night, like a thief. In this, the help's verdict is painfully correct. He has taken what he wanted. Thief. Bianca buries her head in her pillow and cries tears that the fabric quickly absorbs. Thoughts run through her like clouds rushing past, high in the sky. *I should have known. I could have held back. I should have trusted myself. What a monster. I hate him, I liked him, I wanted him, I didn't want him . . . well, not like that, or maybe . . . yes, it was my fault, his fault, mine, his, mine, mine, his. Mine.* She is certain of only one thing: no one can ever find out.

꽃 ꕯ

There hasn't been a day in my life when I haven't expected this kind of grief.

On one of those days, which pass like all the others, when he neither eats nor sleeps, Don Titta writes three short pages. It is Innes, Bianca later discovers, who takes the ink-stained papers out of his master's hand. He is the first to read them. He is the one who waves them gently in the air and says, 'Titta, we must publish this.'

Don Titta doesn't want to, but he is too spent to resist, and in any case, he no longer cares about anything.

'I know you wrote this for yourself, Titta, to flush out your soul, but this is precisely what the people need. Clean words, clear words, words that show the world who you really are.'

'I am nothing,' Don Titta replies, resting his forehead against the windowpane. 'I am nothing, and I care about nothing.'

'You are a grieving father who is not afraid to show his suffering. That's all.'

'They will think that I'm taking advantage of the situation.'

'So it isn't true that you don't care. And anyway, they will think the same thing that they think about your poetry: that it is good for the heart because it says what no one can put into words. This is why you are here, you poets and writers. To find the right words, the words that everyone would like to be voiced and that no one else can. I am going to see Marchionni. I'm sure he will agree.'

And Marchionni, who is a publisher as well as a loving father of three small children and an experienced business-man, understands very well. Soon the city newspaper stands and bookshops are inundated with the inexpensive light blue pamphlet. Actually, it cannot even be described as a pamphlet, more of a broadside. No one will get rich from it, but it certainly helps Don Titta's fame. The title, *On the Death of My Child, My Daughter,* repulses and attracts at the same time. People stand in queues to get it; there are discussions in the cafes; they print a second run. It is so popular that it arouses the suspicion of the imperial authorities. They are convinced that it is actually a coded message, a subversive leaflet cunningly edited by one of the most dangerous and deceitful conspirators, known for his connection to the inglorious cause for independ-ence; and who has, up until now, escaped from the claws of investigation. It is said that the police even use decoders to read between the lines for something that is not there. Instead, that miniature diary of enormous loss leaves them teary-eyed and with a lump in their throats.

Perhaps Innes is right: everything in this family has ended. Only art still counts for something. And if the vocation of a writer is to extract art from life, then Don Titta does what he can with what he has. Maybe there will never be a novel pub-lished now. Maybe the poet's lucky star has burned out just as he is preparing to become a great writer. But these pages exist. These pages are memorable because they are courageous and alive, because they pulsate with a suffering that everyone can recognize – those who have known it and those who fear it. Sorrow makes people feel. This unnameable beast is always lying in wait, far away and yet nearby, too. It never leaves anyone in peace. Don Titta's writing also captures something else, something that Donna Julie supports and that an anonymous critic of *Rivista delle lettere* notices: a new way of being a parent, a way that erases the mechanical indifference of continuity of the species in favour of choice. *Everything that we choose*, the anonymous critic writes in conclusion, *is moral responsibility first and social responsibility second.*

᪣ ᪣

What about the things that we don't choose? What about the things that are imposed on us through force? Bianca broods over this as if it is an illness, as if she has caught some kind of repulsive infection by chance or by mistake, because she hasn't known how to defend herself, or because she is weak. What would Tommaso say about these things? Nothing. His silence is heavy. And he passes on to Bianca the nauseating feeling of an unasked-for presence. The idea of him taking responsibility would make her laugh if she had the desire and strength to do so. She would gladly choke that critic. He thinks he knows everything, but he will never have to carry a child in his womb, whether he wants one or not. He is only good for creating one and then leaving, paying off his lover with a satchel of coins and ignoring the child's existence. He might be asked to pay for its education in some squalid, provincial boarding school. He might legitimatize the child or disown it. He might even love it, if he so desires, if he is inspired to, if the fashion of the times dictate it. He will do what the nobles and the rich always do: whatever he pleases. But some people cannot do as they please and must only do what they can.

Nothing can go back to the way it was. This new, unknown and unwanted person makes its way forward, leaving only signs. Bianca has a sour flavour in her mouth; deathly exhaustion catches her by surprise; gone is her desire to do anything; she sleeps at all hours of the day; and her breasts swell painfully. These are the symptoms of the thing she fears. Bianca is sharp enough to recognize them. She will have to do everything on her own. But what can she do?

I didn't know any better, the ghost, Pia's mother, had said. That crazy woman had been humiliated by life itself. It all comes back to Bianca now. For the first time, instead of anger, she feels pity for the woman, which in turn becomes pity for herself. *It was easy to think I knew everything. I felt like I was on top of the world. And then the bubble burst. It wasn't the world; it was merely a soapy illusion full of beautiful, false colours.* She has fallen. Bianca is a fallen woman. Suddenly the phrase takes on an entirely new meaning, so literal she can see it. It is easy to stay fallen, to cake yourself with mud and hope that no one will recognize you, especially if nobody holds out their hand to help you get back up on your feet. Bianca remembers herself on the night of the party, descending the staircase and being greeted by Zeno and Paolo. It is all too vivid, almost false in its gaiety. A couple of weeks earlier, which now feels like a century ago, she didn't need their hands, she knew how to walk on her own. Bianca doesn't want anyone to know about what has happened, but now everyone will.

If only she could make a switch and exchange the life of this child, whom no one has asked for, with the life of Franceschina, who was called forth from the honest love of matrimony, who had a place, who knew how to be loved. But these kinds of bargains don't exist. They aren't conceivable. There's no logic in the drawing of one's destiny, just scribbles in the margins, ink spilling from a quill, clumsily, incompetently, by mistake or by chance. Then the mark left on the paper is clear, while the quill returns to a lake of blackness.

As if Bianca's own story – the story of her flesh, the narrative that weighs under her skin and in her heart like a stone – isn't enough, there is that other story, the one that has already been played out. It only adds to her grief. Of all the places she could go, the church seems to be the most suitable refuge: no one is ever there. It will be silent. It is there that Bianca learns that she needs silence to speak to the departed, and that they need it too, to be able to speak to the void inside her. All her beloved and departed come to her now. No one is missing: her mother, with her heavy gaze of reproach; her father, his hand pressed against his heart as if to stifle the sorrow; Franceschina, her little feet running, in an echo of her brief race through the world. She hears Don Dionisio arriving, his breath raspy. He doesn't know. But he can keep a secret. What difference will another mistaken child make? In this world children are almost all the results of mistakes. Bianca is startled when the old man places a hand on her shoulder. He slips onto his knees beside her and starts to pray. She does the same, but without believing for a moment that somewhere, someone is listening.

What if the baby is Franceschina's ghost and she has returned to avenge herself or just to get a second chance at life? What if the baby is Bianca's punishment or a ransom? Maybe she needs to accept this second-hand being, raise her and let her destroy her life in order to reclaim her own. In so doing, might she settle the score? Bianca's grim fantasies allow for every possible hypothesis, with the cruellest one being the simplest. She needs to die and, in so doing, kill it. She needs to finish them both off at once, without making a show of it. Parsley concoctions, rusty irons, a pool of blood and it will all be over. Who will care? She no longer has a father who, like Don Titta, will cry at the absurdity of his own survival. Her brothers have their lives to live; she is merely a childhood memory to them, a gracious figurine frozen on that distant moor. And no one ever cries for long about the death of hired help. Bianca feels alone in the world and therefore is. She sees herself float away in a boat made for one, with a trunk full of colours, drifting away over pewter waters towards a steely sky. She watches herself from above; she feels pity; she cries. She is cold. Nothing can ever warm her now, now that shame moves inside her. Shame, and life too.

⁂

She and Innes sit in a stagecoach, alone. They are taking a quick trip to the city to retrieve forgotten and indispensable things for Don Titta and Donna Julie; it is a way of getting away from the house's heavy, oppressive grief. Bianca feels these parents need to open the doors of their emotions and let them out, allow them to evaporate, but the voices of the children on the gravel are almost unbearable.

The carriage moves beyond the confines of the estate and the odd statue of seven nymphs dancing in a semicircle that has always made the guests and Bianca smile. But not now. The orderly fields of modulated greens speak of the sober beauty of hard work and good land. But there is no one there to listen to their words.

'I'm leaving,' Innes says suddenly.

'But . . .' Bianca mumbles. *What about those things you said? How will I manage without you?* These unspoken thoughts press at Bianca's lips but don't surface, held back by the remains of dignity.

'I'm going back to London. I have some friends there. A small family of exiles is building up around them. Apparently, they have this incredible tendency to love failures.' Innes smiles weakly. 'For me, the land here is starting to burn.' He speaks distantly. It is as though he can see himself from the outside and finds himself to be hopelessly lacking.

'What if I came with you?' Bianca says.

It just pops out, without thought. But it feels right. It is the only possible decision. Innes looks at her, somewhat worried.

'All of Nanny's darkest fears would come true,' he says with a smile.

'Yes, you're right,' says Bianca, returning the gesture weakly. She sighs wearily and continues. 'I'm expecting a child.'

She cannot read Innes's expression in the half-light, but she can imagine it: lips pursed together, frowning. The questions, the conjectures. She is about to offer an explanation, but is defeated by her humiliation. This is the time for honesty. She waits. He is quiet. The sound of the horses' hooves grows excessively loud and then distant, as if she is underwater. She will have to say something, explain things, explain herself. Answer questions. Shame herself. But she is better off holding her breath. His voice brings her back to the surface.

'Then we shall get married.'

Bianca struggles. She no longer knows where she is. She wants to go under again. She tries to but cannot. It is as if her body is telling her to stay afloat, life grasping life.

'Do not fear,' Innes continues. 'I shall only ask you to be my friend. And I will be your friend. It will be our pact. You will like London. I realize that you know it a little, but the London I am thinking of is a completely different city. We'll have to settle down, grow accustomed to the fog, and forget the sun and this blessed land. And we'll have to work. Seriously, I fear that we've been spoiled here. It won't be easy in the beginning. But we'll make it. We know how to do things and there are two of us. And soon there will be three.' He takes her hand, opens it, and gives her palm a quick, dry kiss, after which he clasps it gently and places it back on her lap. 'And perhaps, over time, there might be more.'

Bianca does not dare look at him. She allows herself to be jostled by the rhythm of the coach. That small kiss burns her skin. She would like to rub it out but she cannot. She doesn't want him to misunderstand. She doesn't know if it is burning from torment or because it feels confusingly joyful. Is it the poor elation of relief or is it something else? Enough questions. Whatever the answer, at this point it doesn't matter.

≈§ ?≈

When it comes time to pack their cases, Bianca agonizes. She feels caught between being gone and having not yet arrived. She doesn't know what to do with her time. Her gloves don't match and her things are in disorder. She thinks about how messy her hair will be during the journey. This is not a holiday; she should feel contrite and oppressed. But amid the feelings of guilt, fear and melancholia, she also feels the flutter of a bird taking flight. Somewhere inside; not in her heart, though. Her heart is unfeeling, petrified, or perhaps just absent. It has been crushed and has disappeared into her veins through a flow of blood.

She thinks back to the sycamore tree she saw with her father in Padua. She pictures the great tree clearly – the black fissure at its centre, and yet the branches laden with leaves that were shady, fresh, alive. In the same way, she feels alive and yet heartless. But it is her head that is fogged up with worry. This is what guides her through her final hours as she collects her things. She takes the essentials, the items that make us who we are, or who we'd like to think we are. Things she cannot leave behind: a box of coloured pencils, her brushes, a stack of sketches. She takes her precious keepsakes: her mother's earrings, her letters, miniatures, a diary. She takes the money, hard earned and in satchels, so that the wheels of their coach will slide across tracks of gold. She doesn't take the gifts: the white stone egg, the shawl, the pomegranate, the box of seeds. She leaves them on her vacant desk to be dispersed among people to whom they mean nothing.

ᕽᔥ ᕽᔥ

'I'm coming with you,' Pia says calmly.

Bianca notices a bundle at the girl's feet: a raggedy, red blanket that likely contains her few things.

'But Pia, you have a home here. A family,' Bianca says.

'He . . .' She bites her lip in silence. 'He is sick, he is going to die soon, he told me. And then I will have no one. The others, they don't need me. But you do. And when the baby is born . . .'

The baby. Pia knows. Without realizing it, Bianca glances down at her stomach. It is the same as it has always been, the fabric of her dress covers it and holds it in. So how did Pia find out? Maybe everyone knows. It is better not to ask. It is better to believe that the young girl who looks at her so patiently and assuredly from top to bottom possesses the intimate gaze of a Cassandra. The baby. Bianca can no longer hold her stare. She buries her head in her hands and hates herself because she cannot think of anything else to do. *How much do I detest him?*

As if reading her mind, Pia takes a step forward and places her hand on Bianca's arm. 'The child will need to be loved. He isn't the one to blame. Children should never carry the blame.'

You, of all people, know this, Bianca thinks. She is overcome by a wave of tenderness that allows her to forget herself. *You, of all people.* Bianca rests her hand on Pia's arm. It is all set.

ᕽᔥ ᕽᔥ

The last trunk is shut. She glances around the room at its orderly emptiness. There is the sound of rapid footsteps on the gravel. The window is half open. It is very early. There are voices: subdued but crystal clear.

'Take it. It's the least I can do.'

'About time.'

'Oh, come now, don't judge me. I can do that on my own. I cannot change my life; I've never been capable of it. Allow me at least to contribute to changing the life of another.'

'Your quasi-divine omnipotence is too much.'

'Do I appear arrogant? I apologize. For once, I assure you, it isn't arrogance that moves me to act this way. Enough, stop being difficult, you cannot afford to. You know very well that you will need it, all of you. Don't worry. It's nothing personal. You won't have to think of my august profile each time you spend some of it. And when you settle down, send me your address.'

'What if I direct her towards an improper profession and use your money for myself? For gambling or opiates or any other form of degradation available to us?'

'Come now! I know and trust you, Innes. In any case, this money is also for the cause. I cannot say it is "our" cause, for I give it no honour. I deny it every day with what I am and my inability to act. But this way, from afar, in silence . . . I can make a contribution.'

'So, basically, I have to leave with a burden – a debt to you. That's not light luggage, you know.' Innes's voice is sarcastic but his tone is serious.

'Not even all my money can make good what I am contracting with you today.'

'So handle your fortune with caution, because we will need it. Goodbye . . . and thank you.'

She hears footsteps on the stairs. Outside there is silence. And then she hears Young Count Bernocchi walk back down the gravel path, slowly and heavily. Not young any more.

⁂

It is a torment to say goodbye. Things go unsaid, the grief is challenging, blessings and smiles and questions are uttered and hinted at. Don Titta embraces Innes tightly and gasps with emotion. Donna Clara's eyes are glassy and almost frightening. Nanny, with tears in her own eyes, whispers, 'In the end you managed to take him from me.' Minna stands shyly behind everyone. She holds a silk kerchief with a handful of coins in it under her apron. The others are awkwardly absent. They won't have understood. What will they choose to believe? Bianca no longer cares.

Soon after they have said their goodbyes and just before departing she turns to Innes, won over by a crumb of her old curiosity, which lifts her spirits.

'What did Bernocchi want from you?'

'He wanted to commend me his soul. Not his own, of course. And anyway, since I am no priest, I suggested that he look elsewhere.'

'And what about the money? He did offer you money, didn't he?'

'Bianca, you are incorrigible. Let's say that it was his modest contribution towards the creation of a better world. It was just a start. The rest of it will come a little at a time, once we settle down. No, he hasn't converted to our cause; he likes his world the way it is. It was an act of contrition, late but well timed. I doubt that he could ever consciously be generous: he would find it too banal. He feels only slight regret.'

Bianca stares at him without understanding.

'Enough with the secrets,' Innes says clearly. 'The money is for Pia.'

A spark flares in Bianca's mind. Is it possible? Is young Pia pregnant, too? That's why Pia had understood. If only she had been more vigilant, wiser, more careful. Bianca's expression must reveal her thoughts, because Innes is staring at her, perplexed. He shakes his head.

'No, Bianca. No, no. What on earth did you think? Pia is Bernocchi's daughter.'

So she is *his* daughter. The truth hangs like an empty nest in the bare branches of a tree in winter. It has been there all along, well hidden, but there. *You didn't see it*, she thinks. *That possibility didn't even exist to you.* But when finally it comes forth in its naked simplicity, she recognizes it, nods, and accepts it. It is no less true because she hasn't thought of it. She leaves the fact suspended there, austere and pure. And everything goes back to its place. *Pomo pero, dime'l vero. Dime la santa verità.* (Apple-pear, tell me the truth. Tell me the blessed truth.)

'You really didn't know?'

It is all so simple in the end. All she needed to do was look at things with the right perspective, without letting herself be blinded by the light of misunderstanding. Don Titta could never have been an unknowing father, or even worse, a knowing accomplice. Don Titta is a man who honours his children, although perhaps a little more in death than in life.

Innes looks at her indulgently and with mild surprise. She hopes he cannot read her mind. She has been so silly. She has been stupid. She has no defences now and carries the burden of nobody's child.

'For what it's worth . . .' Innes says, and then turning around, he asks, 'You are in agreement, aren't you, Pia?'

She comes towards them from the kitchen with two heavy

baskets of provisions for the first leg of their trip: fruit, biscuits, cordial. Without knowing what they have been discussing, the girl smiles at them. Innes takes her burden and she curtseys her thanks.

Of course Pia is in agreement. All that has happened before means nothing, even if it has led to her being there now. She might never have been born. She might have been sent back to where she came from when she was still an infant. She could have remained entangled with her destiny as a servant. She'd be lining up with the rest of her peers for that sad and indifferent goodbye, and then she'd have to hurry back to her poorhouse duties. Instead Pia now stands on the right side of the wall. She climbs in, situates herself in the corner, fixes the folds of her skirt, and waves her hand out the window even before leaning out to show her face to whoever wishes to remember it. It is as if she has rehearsed this act of liberation thousands of times. She is going out into the world and the world is ready to unfurl before her. This is only the first act. Pia is going to London. She, who has never been anywhere, is going to London. So everything truly is possible after all.

❧ ❧

Everything *is* possible, including dying in an ice storm in the Alps, the coach tipping over on one side, like a ship on a wave, the wind whistling by them, the wheels barely making it through the two feet of snow, the cold scratching deep into the dark cabin. Snow in summertime is far worse than in winter because it is unexpected.

They could be caught by a band of French highwaymen in their capes and cone-shaped hats, grim characters who come down from the mountains with their rifles to impose a harsh sentence in the name of black hunger. They could be chased and finally captured by the Austrian forces, the kind that shows no compassion, and sent to Spielberg.

Everything is possible. But nothing happens. These three beings have already been part of a storm; they have already confronted and defeated their own bandits, let themselves be manipulated by suspicion, ill will, and hearsay. The trip is as smooth as the crossing of multiple borders can be, with exhausting interactions at customs, exchanges of documents and money; with the lice in the cold inns, the greasy food and greasy bowls; with drunkards' songs that sound the same in all dialects. The late-summer rain diligently beats its meek song down on the rooftop of their carriage; they see the occasional comrade whose eyes are sharp and who wants to peer in. Outside, postcard images roll by, postcards no one cares to write. There are damp rice plains, solid mountains and pure blue skies. There is France, with its damp haystacks and fairy-tale castles surrounded by woods of marzipan.

Bianca has been sleeping through a great deal of the journey. She blames it on travelling sickness, but is seized by a strange sort of lethargy. Her body has advised her to rest because she knows that later on the creature will steal her sleep away. Therefore, in the final scenes of this story – or of this episode at least – we shan't look at the world as we would normally, over her shoulder, trying to make sense of things through her eyes. No, Bianca's eyes shall remain shut in an imitation of rest that absolves her from the effort of paying attention. Ultimately, it is better that she does not look outside. Otherwise her memory might tease her into remembering that she has seen these lands before with an unnameable, now-departed companion, and she would feel sadness, great sadness. In recompense, she now has a different companion inside her, an unknown parasite who has turned her life upside down. She doesn't know where she is going. Or rather, she knows but doesn't want to imagine it. She will have all the time in the world soon, and more. Is it any wonder that she avoids looking out at the landscape? This journey isn't one of pleasure. It is necessary. Let's leave her to rest, or pretend to sleep, and let's move quietly away so that we can obtain that tiny bit of perspective that changes everything.

At last, the moment arrives. As if in a dirty dream, the dusty profile of a thousand rooftops and a million chimneys appears outside the sweat-glazed windows of their final coach ride.

'Is this London?' Pia asks, with a dazed look.

'This is London,' Innes replies without even looking out of the window.

It feels to him like the trip has been far too short. He will never go back. He can't. It is only a small consolation to know that he is now safe. He didn't even go to Rome. He would have liked to die in Rome. Not deliriously lost, like Keats. He's had his fill of poets. No, he wishes he had become the head of a group of intrepid, uniformless men, out waving a flag that has yet to be imagined. It is still early days, though; he needs to be satisfied with being alive and elsewhere.

'Where are we going now?' asks Pia.

'Home,' Innes says.

Pia draws closer to the window.

He thinks back to what he has left: a locked door, a few things, things he can't have and can't be, now or ever. He looks over at Bianca, who is as pale and parched as a flower that has been without water for too long. She is alive, though. Alive for herself and for the unnamed creature. Pia's not even pretending to be tired. Her eyes shine with the future. A young woman, a girl, and an unborn baby – for the first time Innes feels old. The three of them need him. And he, a new kind of man, will always be there for them.

A Note from the Author

The Watercolourist was inspired by voices and places, by the voices that places own. Places are characters. First of all, the garden at Villa Manzoni in Brusuglio, near Milan. As the plaque at the front gate indicates, this was the summer residence of Alessandro Manzoni: writer, poet and statesman. The novelist of Italian literature. The villa was a place of leisurely activities and bucolic interests, where the writer grew cotton, planted rare grape cultivars that he ordered from afar, attempted to make wine, took an interest in silkworms, tended to exotic plants, and christened his favourite catalpa tree 'Hippopotamus', due to its enormous size. It is a fascinating place for children, who have always wished to trespass, to climb the wall and enter that charming park, as vast and as obscure as a jungle.

The Watercolourist was also inspired by a town house: Casa Manzoni, on Via Morone in Milan, the winter home of Alessandro Manzoni. Here, people skilled in the art of conversation gathered to discuss the future: whether it was the Great Novel that Manzoni was working on, or the Republic of Italy, a daring idea which was taking shape at that time.

A third inspiration came from the city of Milan, and in particular those neighbourhoods where so little has changed that it is easy to imagine what life was like two hundred years ago. A city of brick that was transformed into a city of marble; a 'city of contradictions', as the keen traveller Lady Sydney Morgan once described it.

Fifteen years ago, while working on a children's book project about foster parents, I had the chance to visit the historical archives of the Brefotrofio, the former orphanage of Milan. There, inside those large sliding shelves, surrounded by the smell of metal, moisture and dust, rest the traces of many lives, summarized in the dry language of bureaucracy. Everything had its origin there: the church documents that attest to a state of poverty, which in turn justified the need to resort to institutions; the requests and promises of parents ('that she may be named Luigia', 'we are giving her up out of poverty; I beg your kindness; we will come back and get her'); and especially the tokens and keepsakes – medals and medallions, little images cut in half, embroidered pillows, crucifixes, anything that would allow the parents to deposit and reclaim their children in months or years, and always under the mask of anonymity. Sometimes, when the parents were finally ready, it was too late. The children might have died as infants of smallpox or infection, or from an epidemic or ailment in the distant homes of those who raised them. The antique pages of those ledgers are misshapen and deformed by the objects they contain; they press at the pages as if struggling to tell their own stories.

It was a place where one didn't want to be alone. Both Pia and Minna's stories started there.

It took me about ten years to pull the stories together, to let them breathe, to find a way to cut, paste and sew them, and to understand how they could become a work of fiction. Everything finally clicked in place thanks to Bianca Pietra. Twenty years old at the beginning of the nineteenth century, Bianca is the true creator of the story, which takes shape in her hands; literally, as she is the watercolourist.

A woman of flowers, Bianca is devoted to her ephemeral subjects, but she is neither ephemeral nor frivolous. She is deeply committed to her work, and to the occupation we all share: the building of self-awareness. Finding one's place in the world. Discovering one's purpose. She is not a solitary soul lost on the moors, nor a porcelain doll nodding and smiling in a drawing room while waiting to be whisked away by a decent husband. Half English by blood, she is Italian, *Italianissima*: passionate, chaotic and dynamic. A truly romantic girl for a romantic novel.

I must say I took some liberties in weaving all these stories together. It is not likely (though not impossible) that a lady of the Milanese bourgeoisie of the early 1800s would have personally taken her illegitimate child to a centre for public assistance. She would probably have used a go-between such as a midwife, trusted servant or priest. It is even more likely that she would have had the child raised by other family members or individuals close to the family, and would have supervised the child's development from a distance. But Pia needed to be a girl of non-humble origins who had been entrusted to public care. This led to some slight stretching of the customary habits regarding abandonment at the Ospedale Maggiore, a sad but powerful institution that alleviated many family hardships in the Milan of the past. Minna's story is more typical: she was first entrusted to a wet nurse and then sent to a family in the country to be raised until her own family had the means to retrieve her.

I admit I made some deliberate 'mistakes'. The names of the ballerinas at La Scala who affected Bernocchi so deeply are all invented. Some types of flowers and plants I mention were not yet known in that period of history, at least not in the form described, and derive from later grafts and cultivations. The regular flower trade along the coast of Liguria only began in the middle of the nineteenth century.

And finally, the kidnappings. 'What good are kisses if they are not given?' is a line from a poem by Vivian Lamarque. Other citations are more or less obvious: Homer, Ronsard, Shelley, Prévert, Grossi, Foscolo, Mallarmé, Auden, Tagore, Neruda, Barrie, Meneghello. Don Titta's poems are entirely his own creation.

Ten years is a long time, but it flew by, as time tends to do. Writers of historical fiction need to take breaks for research, need to deviate from the path now and then. And I enjoyed my detours so much. Writing-time is different from clock-time, anyway. When we write, it is as if time becomes a place. It is that house in the country where you wish you could live but cannot; each time you return there, you have to open the windows to air out the rooms; it is an orderly, empty space you would like to complicate with your dearest clutter. Then, once you are settled, you never want to leave. It's where you want to be. When you're there, filled with the lives of others, you wouldn't want to be anywhere else in the world. Nor you could.

January 2016, Milan